Measurement, Judgment, and Decision Making

Handbook of Perception and Cognition
2nd Edition

Series Editors
Edward C. Carterette
and Morton P. Friedman

Measurement, Judgment, and Decision Making

Edited by
Michael H. Birnbaum
Department of Psychology
California State University, Fullerton
Fullerton, California

Academic Press

San Diego   London   Boston
New York   Sydney   Tokyo   Toronto

Copyright © 1998 by ACADEMIC PRESS

Academic Press
a division of Harcourt Brace & Company
525 B Street, Suite 1900, San Diego, California 92101-4495, USA
http://www.apnet.com

Academic Press Limited
24-28 Oval Road, London NW1 7DX, UK
http://www.hbuk.co.uk/ap/

Library of Congress Card Catalog Number: 97-80319

International Standard Book Number: 0-12-099975-7

PRINTED IN THE UNITED STATES OF AMERICA
97   98   99   00   01   02   QW   9   8   7   6   5   4   3   2   1

Contents

1   The Representational Measurement Approach to Psychophysical and Judgmental Problems

Geoffrey Iverson and R. Duncan Luce

2 *Psychophysical Scaling*

Lawrence E. Marks and Daniel Algom

3   *Multidimensional Scaling*

J. Douglas Carroll and Phipps Arabie

4   *Stimulus Categorization*

F. Gregory Ashby and W. Todd Maddox

5   *Behavioral Decision Research: An Overview*

John W. Payne, James R. Bettman, and Mary Frances Luce

Contributors

Numbers in parentheses indicate the pages on which the authors' contributions begin.

Daniel Algom (81)
Tel Aviv University
Ramat-Aviv
Israel

Phipps Arabie (179)
Faculty of Management
Rutgers University
Newark, New Jersey 07102

F. Gregory Ashby (251)
Department of Psychology
University of California
Santa Barbara, California 93106

James R. Bettman (303)
Fuqua School of Business
Duke University
Durham, North Carolina 27706

J. Douglas Carroll (179)
Faculty of Management
Rutgers University
Newark, New Jersey 07102

Geoffrey Iverson (1)
Institute for Mathematical Behavioral
    Sciences
University of California
Irvine, California 92697

Mary Frances Luce (303)
Wharton School
University of Pennsylvania
Philadelphia, Pennsylvania 19104

R. Duncan Luce (1)
Institute for Mathematical Behavioral
    Sciences
University of California
Irvine, California 92697

W. Todd Maddox[1] (251)
Department of Psychology
Arizona State University
Tempe, Arizona 85281

[1]Present address: Department of Psychology, University of Texas, Austin, Texas 78712

Lawrence E. Marks (81)
John B. Pierce Laboratory
  and Yale University
New Haven, Connecticut 06519

John W. Payne (303)
Fuqua School of Business
Duke University
Durham, North Carolina 27706

Foreword

The problem of perception and cognition is in understanding how the organism transforms, organizes, stores, and uses information arising from the world in sense data or memory. With this definition of perception and cognition in mind, this handbook is designed to bring together the essential aspects of this very large, diverse, and scattered literature and to give a précis of the state of knowledge in every area of perception and cognition. The work is aimed at the psychologist and the cognitive scientist in particular, and at the natural scientist in general. Topics are covered in comprehensive surveys in which fundamental facts and concepts are presented, and important leads to journals and monographs of the specialized literature are provided. Perception and cognition are considered in the widest sense. Therefore, the work will treat a wide range of experimental and theoretical work.

The *Handbook of Perception and Cognition* should serve as a basic source and reference work for those in the arts or sciences, indeed for all who are interested in human perception, action, and cognition.

Edward C. Carterette and Morton P. Friedman

Preface

The chapters in this volume examine the most basic issues of the science of psychology, for measurement is the key to science. The science of psychology is the study of alternative explanations of behavior. The study of measurement is the study of the representation of empirical relationships by mathematical structures. Can we assign numbers to represent the psychological values of stimuli so that relations among the numbers predict corresponding relations of behavior?

All the chapters in this volume build on a base of psychological measurement. In Chapter 1, Iverson and R. D. Luce present the foundations of measurement theory. They give a thorough introduction to the representational measurement approach, and they contrast this approach with others proposed to explain human behavior. Their chapter includes many examples of applications in psychophysics, decision making, and judgment.

Judgment is the field of psychology in which the behavior of interest is the assignment of categorical responses to stimuli. These categories might be numerical judgments of the psychological magnitudes of sensations produced by stimuli, or they might be more abstract categories such as whether an item is edible.

When the stimuli have well-defined physical measures, and the experimenter intends to study the relationships between physical and psychological values, the research domain is called *psychophysics*. For example, one can examine the relationship between judgments of the heaviness of objects and their physical weights. In Chapter 2, Marks and Algom give a careful survey of this field, considering both historical issues of psychophysics and modern controversies.

There are many judgments in which the physical dimensions are not well understood, such as the judgment of beauty. Other judgments rely on physical measures that are difficult to define, such as the likableness of a character described in a novel. A judgment researcher might ask people to estimate the utility of receiving various prizes, to evaluate how well a student has mastered the material in a university course, to rate how much one would like a person who is "phony," or to judge how much fault or blame should be assigned to victims of various crimes. Judgment tasks usually require the assignment of numbers to represent the judge's introspected psychological values. To what extent are these numbers meaningful measures of the psychological value they purport to represent?

The study of judgment cuts across the usual disciplines in psychology. Social psychologists might ask people to rate others' attitudes toward minority groups, the perceived willingness of others to help someone in need, or the likelihood that a person would conform to society's norms in a given situation. Personality psychologists often ask people to rate their own feelings and behaviors. For example, people might rate their agreement with statements such as "I feel nervous and shy when meeting new people" or "one should always obey the law." In clinical psychology, the clinician may assign clients into diagnostic categories of mental illness or judge the degree of improvement of clients' behavior in therapy. In marketing, the analyst may be interested in how consumers' judgments of the value of a product depend on its component features.

Although applications occur in many disciplines of psychology, the term *judgment* applies when the investigation involves basic principles assumed to apply across content domains. The term *scaling* refers to studies in which the chief interest is in establishing a table of numbers to represent the attributes of stimuli.

The term *unidimensional scaling* describes studies in which stimuli may have many physical dimensions but there is only one psychological dimension of interest. For example, how does the psychological loudness of sinusoidal tones vary as a function of their physical wavelengths and amplitudes? The tones differ in the psychological dimensions of pitch, loudness, and timbre, but the experimenter has chosen to study the effects of two physical dimensions on one psychological dimension, loudness, so the study would be classified as unidimensional. Similarly, one might study the judged beauty of people in a contest or the quality of different varieties of corn. The beauty of the contestants and the quality of corn depend on many physical dimensions, and they also may be composed of many psychological features or dimensions; however, the term *unidimensional* is applied when the investigator has restricted the problem to study one psychological dimension. The first two chapters present many examples of unidimensional research.

The term *multidimensional scaling* refers to investigations in which stimuli are represented by psychological values on more than one dimension or attribute. For example, beauty contestants may differ not only in beauty but also in congeniality, intelligence, and sincerity. Beauty itself may be composed of dimensions of perhaps face and figure, each of which might be further analyzed into psychological components, which might be features or dimensions. Sometimes, a single physical dimension appears to produce two or more psychological dimensions. For example, variation in the physical wavelength of light appears to produce two psychological dimensions of color (red-green and blue-yellow), on which individuals may judge similarities of colors differently according to their degrees of color blindness on the dimensions. Investigators use multidimensional scaling to analyze judgment data, such as judgments of similarity, and also to analyze other behavioral data.

In Chapter 3, Carroll and Arabie introduce not only traditional, geometric multidimensional scaling but also theories of individual differences and more general models, of which feature and geometric models are special cases. In geometric models, stimuli are represented as points in a multidimensional space; similarity between two stimuli in these models is a function of how close the stimuli are in the space. In feature models, stimuli are represented as lists of features, which may be organized in a tree structure. Similarity in feature models depends on the features that the stimuli have in common and those on which they differ. Carroll and Arabie discuss relationships between these models and empirical investigations of them.

Judgment, multidimensional scaling, and decision making are all fundamental in the study of categorization. How is it that people can recognize an item as a chair, even though they have never previously seen it? Even a 3-year-old child can identify a distorted cartoon as a cat, despite never having seen the drawing before. Knowing when two stimuli are the same or different constitutes the twin problems of *stimulus generalization* and *discrimination*. These topics are important to the history of psychology and were the subject of much research in psychophysics using human participants and also using animals, whose life experiences could be controlled.

In Chapter 4, Ashby and Maddox summarize research on categorization, conducted with humans. In addition to the problems of stimulus representation and category selection, the study of categorization tries to explain how the dimensions or features of a stimulus are combined to determine in what category the stimulus belongs. Ashby and Maddox present classical and current models of categorization and discuss experimental investigations of these models.

Decision making is such a general idea that it provides an approach to all of psychology. Whereas a personality psychologist may study how behavior depends on an individual's traits and a social psychologist may study behavior as a function of conformity to society's expectations for a situation, theorists in decision making analyze behavior as the consequence of a decisional process of what to do next.

Decision making is broad enough to include all judgment studies, for one can consider any judgment experiment as a decision problem in which the judge decides what response to assign to each stimulus. However, the term *decision making* is often employed when the subject's task is to choose between two or more stimulus situations rather than to select one of a set of categorical responses.

In a decision-making task, a person might be asked to choose a car based on price, safety, economy of operation, and aesthetics. How does a person combine these factors and compare the available cars to make such a choice? Decisions under risk and uncertainty have also been explored in the behavioral decision-making literature. In risk, outcomes of varying utility occur with specified probabilities. A judge might be asked, "Would you prefer \$40 for sure or \$100 if you correctly predict the outcome of a coin to be tossed and \$0 if you fail?" This is a risky decision, because the probability of correctly predicting the coin toss is presumed to be $\frac{1}{2}$.

In decision making under uncertainty, probabilities are unknown. "Would you prefer \$100 for sure or \$800 only if you can successfully predict (to the nearest dollar) the price that a given stock, now worth \$9 per share, will have when the market closes one week from now?" Because stock prices are uncertain, it is difficult to know how to use the past to predict the future. People may have subjective probabilities concerning the likelihoods of future events, and it is a topic of great importance to understand how people use such subjective probabilities to form and revise beliefs and to make decisions. In Chapter 5, Payne, Bettman, and M. F. Luce summarize the literature of behavioral decision making that attempts to address these issues. Iverson and R. D. Luce also consider decision-making topics from the measurement perspective, and Marks and Algom discuss influences of decision making on psychophysics.

The authors of these chapters have provided excellent introductions to active research programs on the most basic problems of psychology. These chapters not only consider the major ideas in their fields but also relate the history of ideas and draw connections with topics in other chapters. Each chapter unlocks the door for a scholar who desires entry to that field. Any psychologist who manipulates an independent variable that is supposed to affect a psychological construct or who uses a numerical dependent variable presumed to measure a psychological construct will want to open these doors. And the key is measurement.

Michael H. Birnbaum

The Representational Measurement Approach to Psychophysical and Judgmental Problems

Geoffrey Iverson
R. Duncan Luce

I. INTRODUCTION

This chapter outlines some of the main applications to psychophysical and judgmental modeling of the research called the representational theory of measurement. Broadly, two general classes of models have been proposed in studying psychophysical and other similar judgmental processes: information processing models and phenomonological models. The former, currently perhaps the most popular type in cognitive psychology, attempt to describe in more or less detail the mental stages of information flow and processing; usually these descriptions are accompanied by flow diagrams as well as mathematical postulates. The latter, more phenomenological models attempt to summarize aspects of observable behavior in a reasonably compact fashion and to investigate properties that follow from the behavioral properties. Representational measurement theory is of the latter genre. We are, of course, identifying the end points of what is really a continuum of model types, and although we will stay mainly at the phenomenological end of the spectrum, some models we discuss certainly contain an element of information processing.

Two features of the behavior of people (and other mammals) need to be taken into account: (1) responses are variable in the sense that when a subject is confronted several times with exactly the same stimulus situation, he or

Measurement, Judgment, and Decision Making

she may not respond consistently, and (2) stimuli typically have somewhat complex internal structures that influence behavior. Indeed, stimuli often vary along several factors that the experimenter can manipulate independently. Thus, behavioral and social scientists almost always must study responses to complex stimuli in the presence of randomness. Although somewhat overstated, the following is close to true: We can model response variability when the stimuli are only ordered and we can model "average" responses to stimuli having some degree of internal structure, but we really cannot model both aspects simultaneously in a fully satisfactory way. In practice we proceed either by minimizing the problems of structure and focusing on the randomness—as is common in statistics—or by ignoring the randomness and focusing on structure—as is done in the representational theory of measurement. Each is a facet of a common problem whose complete modeling seems well beyond our current understanding.

This chapter necessarily reflects this intellectual hiatus. Section II reports probabilistic modeling with stimuli that vary on only one dimension. Section III extends these probabilistic ideas to more complex stimuli, but the focus on structure remains a secondary concern. Sections IV through VII report results on measurement models of structure with, when possible, connections and parallels drawn to aspects of the probability models.

The domain of psychophysical modeling is familiar to psychologists, and its methods include both choice and judgment paradigms. Although not often acknowledged, studies of preferences among uncertain and risky alternatives—utility theories—are quite similar to psychophysical research in both experimental methods and modeling types. Both areas concern human judgments about subjective attributes of stimuli that can be varied almost continuously. Both use choices—usually among small sets of alternatives—as well as judgment procedures in which stimuli are evaluated against some other continuous variable (e.g., the evaluation of loudness in terms of numerals, as in magnitude estimation, and the evaluation of gambles in terms of monetary certainty equivalents).

Our coverage is limited in two ways. First, we do not attempt to describe the large statistical literature called psychometrics or, sometimes, psychological measurement or scaling. Both the types of data analyzed and models used in psychometrics are rather different from what we examine here. Second, there is another, small but important, area of psychological literature that focuses on how organisms allocate their time among several available alternatives (for fairly recent summaries, see Davison & McCarthy, 1988; Lowenstein & Elster, 1992). Typically these experiments have the experimenter-imposed property that the more time the subject attends to one alternative, the less is its objective rate of payoff. This is not a case of diminishing marginal utility on the part of the subject but of diminishing replenishment of resources. It is far more realistic for many situations than is the kind of discrete choice/utility modeling we examine here. Space limitations and our hope that these models and experiments are covered elsewhere in this book have led us to omit them.

II. PROBABILISTIC MODELS FOR AN ORDERED ATTRIBUTE

Most experimental procedures used to investigate the ability of an observer to discriminate the members of a set of stimuli are variants of the following two:

1. Choice Paradigm. Here the observer is asked to choose, from an offered set of n stimuli, the one that is most preferred or the one that possesses the most of some perceived attribute shared by the stimuli.

2. Identification Paradigm. Here the observer is required to identify which of the n stimuli is presented.

The simplest case of each paradigm occurs when $n = 2$. The choice paradigm requires an observer to *discriminate* stimuli offered in pairs, whereas the identification paradigm forms the basis of yes–no *detection*. We focus on discrimination and detection in this section; see section III for the general case of each paradigm.

In this section we are concerned primarily with psychophysical applications in which stimuli are ordered along a single physical dimension such as line length, frequency, intensity, and so on. Accordingly we use positive real numbers x, y, s, n, and so on to label stimuli.

For a discrimination task to be nontrivial, the members of an offered pair x, y of stimuli must be close in magnitude. An observer's ability to decide that x is longer, or louder, or of higher pitch, and so on than y is then difficult, and over repeated presentations of x and y, judgments show inconsistency. The basic discrimination data are thus response probabilities $P_{x,y}$, the probability that x is judged to possess more of the given attribute than y. For a fixed standard y, a plot of $P_{x,y}$ against x produces a classical psychometric function. A typical psychometric function, estimated empirically, is shown in Figure 1. The data were collected by the method of constant stimuli: subjects were presented a standard line of length 63 mm together with one of five comparison lines that varied in length from 62 to 65 mm. Note that, in these data, the point of subjective equality is different from (here it is smaller than) the 63 mm standard length—not an uncommon feature of this psychophysical method.

The family of psychometric functions generated by varying the standard affords one way to study the response probabilities $P_{x,y}$. It is often more revealing, however, to study $P_{x,y}$ as a family of isoclines, that is, curves on which $P_{x,y}$ is constant. Fixing the response probability at some value π and trading off x and y so as to maintain this fixed response probability generates

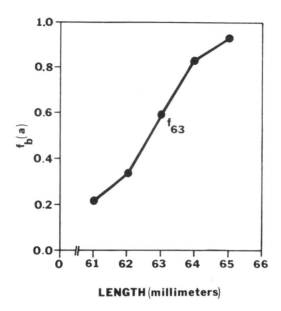

LENGTH (millimeters)

FIGURE 1   A typical psychometric function. The proportion of "larger" judgments is plotted as a function of a physical measure of the comparison stimulus. In this case the standard was a 63 cm length. From Figure 6.2 of *Elements of Psychophysical Theory*, by J.-C. Falmagne, New York: Oxford University Press, 1985, p. 151; redrawn from the original source, Figure 2.5 of "Psychophysics: Discrimination and Detection," by T. Egen, which appeared as chapter 2 of *Experimental Psychology*, by J. W. Kling and L. A. Riggs, New York: Holt, Rinehart and Winston, 1971. Reprinted with permission.

a sensitivity function ξ_π: $P_{x,y} = \pi$ if and only if $\xi_\pi(y) = x$. Writing $\xi_\pi(x) = x + \Delta_\pi(x)$ defines the *Weber function,* or π-*jnd* of classical psychophysics. For instance, the symbol $\Delta_{.75}(x)$ denotes the increment added to a stimulus x so as to render the sum detectable from x 75% of the time; in classical psychophysics the arbitrary choice $\pi = 0.75$ served to define the just-noticeable difference.

Trade-off functions offer a convenient way to organize and study a wide range of psychophysical data. Equal loudness contours, intensity-duration trading relations, speed-accuracy trade-offs are but three of many examples that could be mentioned. For the detection task, the fundamental trade-off involves two kinds of error: one, an error of omission, arises when an observer fails to recognize the presence of a signal as such; the other, an error of commission, arises when an observer incorrectly reports the presence of the signal. The trade-off between these two sorts of error underlies the *receiver operating characteristic* (*ROC*), the basic object of study in yes-no detection.

In this section we provide an overview of models describing families of psychometric functions, sensitivity functions, ROCs, and other trade-offs such as speed–accuracy. Link (1992) is a modern text that covers much of the same material in detail, albeit from a diferent point of view.

A. Discrimination

1. Fechner's Problem

The simplest class of models for response probabilities involves an idea proposed by Fechner (1860/1966); namely, that a comparison of stimuli x, y is based on the difference $u(x) - u(y)$ of internal "sensations" evoked by x and y. Here the numerical scale u is assumed to be a strictly increasing function of the physical variable. Confusion between x, y arises because the difference $u(x) - u(y)$ is subject to random error (which Fechner took to be normally distributed[1]). In other words,

$$P_{x,y} = \text{Prob}[u(x) - u(y) + \text{random error} \geq 0].$$

In terms of the distribution function F of the error, this amounts to

$$P_{x,y} = F[u(x) - u(y)], \tag{1}$$

where each of the functions F and u is strictly increasing on its respective domain. The form for the response probabilities given in Eq. (1) is called a *Fechner representation* for those probabilities. Fechner's problem (Falmagne, 1985) is to decide, for a given system of response probabilities, if a Fechner representation is appropriate and, if so, to determine how unique the representation is.

These and other related matters have received much attention in the theoretical literature (Falmagne, 1985; Krantz, Luce, Suppes, & Tversky, 1971; Levine, 1971, 1972; Suppes, Krantz, Luce, & Tversky, 1989). A key observable property enjoyed by all systems of response probabilities conforming to the Fechnerian form of Eq. (1) is known as the *quadruple condition* (Marschak, 1960): for all x, y, x', y',

$$\text{if } P_{x,y} \geq P_{x',y'}, \text{ then } P_{x,x'} \geq P_{y,y'}. \tag{2}$$

This property is easily seen to be necessary for a Fechner representation. In terms of scale differences, the left-hand inequality of Eq. (2) asserts that $u(x) - u(y) \geq u(x') - u(y')$, which rearranges to read $u(x) - u(x') \geq u(y) - u(y')$ and in turn that inequality implies the right-hand inequality of Eq. (2). It is a far more remarkable fact that the quadruple condition is, in the presence of natural side conditions, also sufficient for a Fechner representation; see Falmagne (1985) for a precise statement and proof of this fact.

The uniqueness part of Fechner's problem is readily resolved: the scale u is unique up to positive linear transformations, that is, u is an *interval* scale (see section IVB.3). This is not surprising in view of the fact that positive scale differences behave like lengths and can be added:

---

[1] Also called Gaussian distributed.

$$[u(x) - u(y)] + [u(y) - u(z)] = u(x) - u(z).$$

See section IV.C.6 for an account of the theory of measurement of length and other extensive attributes.

Although the quadruple condition presents an elegant solution to Fechner's problem, it is not easily tested on fallible data; for a general approach to testing order restrictions on empirical frequencies, see Iverson and Falmagne (1985).

2. Weber Functions

Another approach to Fechner's problem is afforded by the study of the sensitivity functions ξ_π (or equivalently the Weber functions Δ_π). To assume the validity of the representation Eq. (1) is equivalent to assuming the following representation for sensitivity functions:

$$\xi_\pi(x) = u^{-1}[u(x) + g(\pi)]; \tag{3}$$

where $g = F^{-1}$. In these terms an alternative formulation of Fechner's problem can be framed as follows: What properties of sensitivity functions guarantee a representation of the form Eq. (3) for these functions? A condition that is clearly necessary is that two distinct sensitivity functions cannot intersect—sensitivity functions are ordered by the index π. Moreover, sensitivity functions of the desired form can be concatenated by the ordinary composition of functions, and this concatenation is commutative (i.e., the order of the composition makes no difference):

$$\xi_\pi[\xi_{\pi'}(x)] = u^{-1}[u(x) + g(\pi) + g(\pi')] = \xi_{\pi'}[\xi_\pi(x)].$$

These two properties allow the collection of sensitivity functions to be recognized as an ordered abelian group,[2] and the machinery of extensive measurement applies (see section IV.C). For a detailed discussion, see Krantz et al. (1971), Suppes et al. (1989), Levine (1971, 1972), and Falmagne (1985). Kuczma (1968) discussed the problem from the viewpoint of iterative functional equations.

The previous remarks reflect modern ideas and technology. Fechner studied the functional equation

$$u[(x + \Delta(x)] - u(x) = 1,$$

[2] A mathematical group G is a set of objects (here functions) together with a binary operation $*$ (here composition of functions), which is associative: for all objects x, y, z in G, $x*(y*z) = (x*y)*z$. There is an identity element e (here the identity function) and each element x in G possesses an inverse x^{-1} such that $x * x^{-1} = x^{-1} * x = e$. The group is abelian when $*$ is commutative, i.e., $x*y = y*x$.

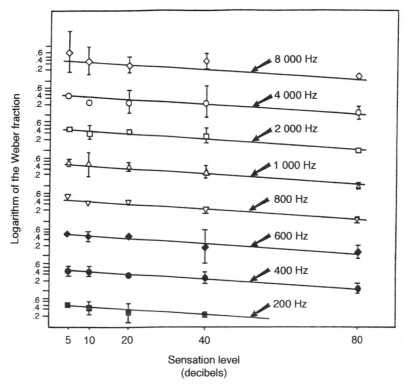

FIGURE 2   Weber functions for loudness of pure tones in which the logarithm of the Weber fraction is plotted against the sound pressure level in decibels above threshold for eight frequencies from 200 to 8000 Hz. In such a plot, Weber's law would appear as a horizontal line. From Figure 1 of "Intensity Discrimination as a Function of Frequency and Sensation Level," by W. Jesteadt, C. C. Wier, and D. M. Green, 1977, *Journal of the Acoustical Society of America, 61,* p. 171. Reprinted with permission.

called Abel's equation, and incorrectly reasoned that it could be replaced by a differential equation (Luce & Edwards, 1958). He did, however, correctly perceive that *Weber's law*—namely, the assertion that $\Delta_\pi(x)$ is proportional to x for any value of π—provides a rapid solution to Fechner's problem. In our notation Weber's law is equivalent to the assertion

$$P_{cx,cy} = P_{x,y}$$

for any positive real number c and all x, y. It follows at once that $P_{x,y}$ depends only on the ratio x/y of physical measures and that the scale $u(x)$ is logarithmic in form. Although Weber's law remains a source of useful intuition in psychophysics, it provides at best an approximation to the empirical data. For example, in psychoacoustics, pure tone intensity discrimination exhibits the "near-miss" to Weber's law (Figure 2). On the other hand, Weber's law holds up remarkably well for intensity discrimination

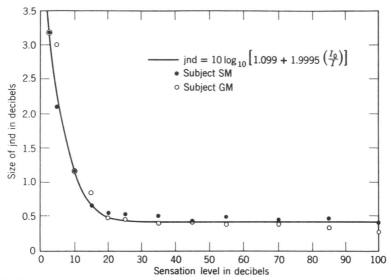

FIGURE 3   Weber function for loudness of white noise in which the Weber fraction is presented in decibel terms versus the sound pressure level in decibels relative to threshold. Again, in such a plot, Weber's law would appear as a horizontal line, which is true for most (recall, this is a logarithmic scale) of the stimulus range. From Figure 5 of "Discrimination," by R. D. Luce and E. Galanter, in R. D. Luce, R. R. Bush, and E. Galanter, *Handbook of Mathematical Psychology* (Vol. 1), New York: John Wiley & Sons, 1963, p. 203. Reprinted with permission.

of broadband noise (Figure 3). For further remarks on Weber's law and the near-miss, see section VII.B.1.

3. Random Variable Models[3]

Suppose that a stimulus x elicits an internal representation as a random variable $\mathbf{U}_x$. In these terms, the response probabilities can be written

$$P_{x,y} = \text{Prob}(\mathbf{U}_x \geq \mathbf{U}_y). \tag{4}$$

Such a representation was first proposed and studied in the literature on individual choice, where the term *random utility model* has become standard (Block & Marschak, 1960; Luce & Suppes, 1965; Marschak, 1960). Although this representation does impose constraints on the response probabilities, for example, the *triangle condition* $P_{x,y} + P_{y,z} + P_{z,x} \geq 1$, it is not well understood (see Marley, 1990, for a review) and is clearly very weak. For these reasons it is useful to explore the consequences of specific distributional assumptions on the random variables involved in Eq. (4).

[3] We follow the convention of using uppercase bold letters such as **X**, **Y**, and **Z** to denote random variables. We shall write vectors as bold lowercase letters such as **x**, **y**, and **z**. A vector-valued random variable is not distinguished notationally but rather by context.

In a trio of seminal papers, Thurstone (1927a, b, c) made the assumption that $\mathbf{U}_x$, $\mathbf{U}_y$ are jointly normal. Doing so gives rise to a relation known as Thurstone's *law of comparative judgment;* see Eq. (5) for a special, but important case. In many circumstances it is reasonable to suppose that $\mathbf{U}_x$ and $\mathbf{U}_y$ are not only normal but independent. The *stability* of the normal family—the fact that the sum (or difference) of two independent normally distributed random variables remains normally distributed—allows Eq. (4) to be developed in terms of the means $\mu(x)$, $\mu(y)$ and variances $\sigma^2(x)$, $\sigma^2(y)$ of $\mathbf{U}_x$ and $\mathbf{U}_y$:

$$P_{x,y} = \Phi([\mu(x) - \mu(y)]/\sqrt{\sigma^2(x) + \sigma^2(y)}), \tag{5}$$

where Φ is the distribution function of the unit normal (mean zero, variance unity). This representation is *Case III* in Thurstone's classification.

When $\sigma(x)$ is constant across stimuli, one obtains the simple *Case V* representation:

$$P_{x,y} = \Phi[u(x) - u(y)], \tag{6}$$

where $u(x) = \mu(x)/\sqrt{2}\sigma$. This model is a special case of a Fechnerian representation; compare it with Eq. (1).

Thurstone offered little to justify the assumption of normality; indeed, he admitted it might well be wrong. However, in many stochastic process models, information about a stimulus arises as a sum of numerous independent contributions. Such sums are subject to the central limit theorem, which asserts that their limiting distribution is normal; an explicit example of this sort of model is discussed in section II.C.

Other authors, for example, Thompson and Singh (1967) and Pelli (1985), have proposed models in which discriminative information is packaged not as a sum but as an extreme value statistic. Invoking a well-known limit law for maxima (Galambos, 1978/1987) leads to a model in which the random variables $\mathbf{U}_x$ and $\mathbf{U}_y$ of Eq. (4) are independent, double-exponential variates with means $\mu(x)$, $\mu(y)$. The following expression for the response probabilities results:

$$P_{x,y} = 1/[1 + \exp(\mu(y) - \mu(x))] = v(x)/[v(x) + v(y)], \tag{7}$$

where $v(x) = \exp[\mu(x)]$. The expression given in Eq. (7) is often called a Bradley-Terry-Luce representation for the response probabilities.

The expression in Eq. (7) also arises in choice theory (section III.A.2), but is based on quite different considerations (Luce, 1959a). The following product rule is a binary property that derives from the more general choice theory: for any choice objects a, b, c,

$$\frac{P_{a,b}}{P_{b,a}} \cdot \frac{P_{b,c}}{P_{c,b}} \cdot \frac{P_{c,a}}{P_{a,c}} = 1. \tag{8}$$

The product rule in Eq. (8) is equivalent to the representation in Eq. (7).

B. Detection

1. Receiver Operating Characteristics

The basic detection task requires an observer to detect the presence or absence of a signal embedded in noise. On some trials the signal accompanies the noise; on other trials noise alone is presented. On each trial the observer makes one of two responses: signal present, "yes," or signal not present, "no." Two kinds of error can be made in this task. One, called a *miss* occurs when a no response is made on a signal trial; the other, called a *false alarm* occurs when a yes response is made on a noise-alone trial. Corresponding correct responses are called *hits* (yes responses on signal trials) and *correct rejections* (no responses on noise trials).

Because hits and misses are complementary events, as are correct rejections and false alarms, the yes–no task involves only two independent response rates and it is conventional to study the pair of conditional probabilities P_H = Prob(yes|signal) and P_{FA} = Prob(yes|noise). The two probabilities move together as a function of an observer's tendency to respond yes. Such biases can be brought under experimental control by employing an explicit payoff schedule: punishing false alarms depresses the frequency of yes responses, and P_H and P_{FA} each decrease; rewarding hits has the opposite effect. By varying the payoff structure, the pair (P_H, P_{FA}) traces out a monotonically increasing curve from $(0, 0)$ to $(1, 1)$ in the unit square. Such a curve is called a *receiver operating characteristic,* abbreviated *ROC*. An alternative method of generating an ROC involves varying the probability of a signal trial. Figure 4 shows typical ROCs generated by both methods.

A single ROC is characterized by fixed signal and noise parameters; only an observer's bias changes along the curve. By varying signal strength, a family of ROCs is obtained, as in Figure 5. For a wealth of information on detection tasks and the data they provide consult Green and Swets (1966/1974/1988) and Macmillan and Creelman (1991).

2. Psychometric Functions

In classical psychophysics, it was common practice to study the psychometric function obtained by measuring the hit rate P_H as signal intensity was varied. Instructions were intended to practically forbid the occurrence of false alarms. This strategy is fraught with difficulties of estimation: P_H must be estimated on the most rapidly rising part of an ROC, so that small errors in P_{FA} become magnified in the determination of P_H.

3. Statistical Decision Making

Detection can be modeled as a problem of statistical decision making. In this view, evidence for the signal is represented as a random variable whose

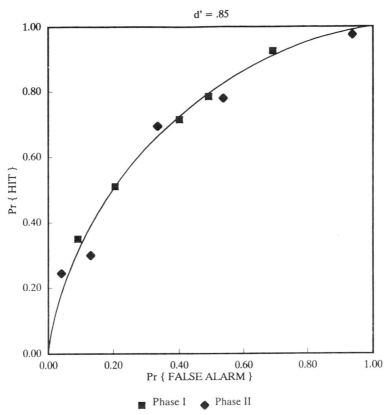

FIGURE 4   A typical receiver operating characteristic (ROC) in which the probability of a hit is plotted against the probability of a false alarm. The stimulus was a tone burst in a background of white noise. The data were generated by varying signal probability (solid square symbols) and payoffs (solid diamonds). From Figure 7.6 of *The Wave Theory of Difference and Similarity*, by S. W. Link, Hillsdale, NJ: Erlbaum, 1992, p. 121. Redrawn from *Signal Detection Theory and Psychophysics* (Figure 4-1 and 4-2, pp. 88–89) by D. M. Green and J. A. Swets, Huntington, NY: Robert E. Krieger, 1974. Reprinted with permission.

values are distributed on a one-dimensional "evidence" axis. On signal trials, the evidence for the signal is a value of a random variable U_s; on noise trials, evidence is a value of a random variable U_n. Large values of evidence arise more frequently on signal trials and thus favor the presence of the signal. An observer selects a criterion value β on the evidence axis, which is sensitive to payoff structure and signal probability, such that whenever the evidence sampled on a trial exceeds β, the observer responds yes, indicating a belief that the signal was presented.

Of the various candidates for the evidence axis, one deserves special mention. According to the Neyman-Pearson lemma of statistical decision

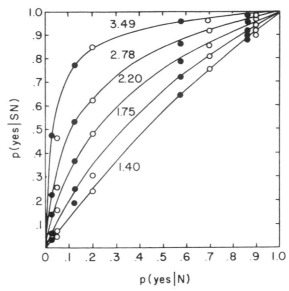

FIGURE 5   ROCs obtained using a five-point rating scale and varying signal strength over seven levels (the weakest and strongest levels are omitted in the plot). The stimuli were 60 Hz vibrations to the fingertip; the curves are identified by the amplitude of the stimulus in microns. The procedure involved two conditions, represented by the open and closed symbols. In each, the probability of no signal was 0.33 and a signal, 0.67. In the case of the open symbols, the three weaker signals were more likely than the four stronger ones (signal probabilities of 0.158 and 0.066, respectively), whereas for the closed symbols the three stronger signals were more likely than the four weaker ones (again, 0.158 and 0.066). Thus, there was a single false alarm estimate for all seven intensities corresponding to each of rating levels. From Figure 3.24 of *Psychophysics: Methods and Theory,* by G. A. Gescheider, Hillsdale, NJ: Erlbaum, 1976, p. 79. Redrawn from the original source "Detection of Vibrotactile Signals Differing in Probability of Occurance," G. A. Gescheider, J. H. Wright, and J. W. Polak, 1971, *The Journal of Psychology, 78,* Figure 3, p. 259. Reprinted with permission.

theory, the optimal way to package evidence concerning the signal is to use the likelihood ratio—the ratio of the density of sensory data assuming a signal trial to the density of the same data assuming a noise-alone trial. Large values of the likelihood ratio favor the presence of the signal.

However there remains considerable flexibility in the choice of a decision statistic: any strictly increasing function of the likelihood ratio produces an equivalent decision rule and leads to identical detection performance. A common choice of such a transformation is the logarithm, so that evidence can take on any real value. It is worthy of note that ROCs that are concave (as are those of Figures 4 and 5) are compatible with the use of the likelihood-ratio as a decision statistic (cf. Falmagne, 1985).

On the other hand, there is little reason to suppose human observers can behave as ideal observers, except in the simplest of circumstances (see Green & Swets, 1966/1974/1988, for further discussion). More likely than not, human observers use simple, easy-to-compute decision statistics that will not, in general, be monotonically related to the likelihood ratio (see, e.g., section II.C).

4. Distributional Assumptions and d'

It should be noted that the representation of an ROC in terms of decision variables $\mathbf{U}_s$, $\mathbf{U}_n$, namely,

$$P_\text{H} = \text{Prob}(\mathbf{U}_s > \beta), \quad P_\text{FA} = \text{Prob}(\mathbf{U}_n > \beta) \qquad (9)$$

is not at all constraining, despite the rather heavy background imposed by statistical decision theory. If one chooses $\mathbf{U}_n$ to possess a strictly increasing, but otherwise arbitrary distribution function, it is always possible to find a random variable $\mathbf{U}_s$ such that a given ROC is represented in the form of Eq. (9) (cf. Iverson & Sheu, 1992).

On the other hand, empirical families of ROCs obtained by varying some aspect of the signal (such as intensity or duration) often take on a simple, visually compelling form. The ROCs given in Figure 5 are, above all, clearly ordered by varying stimulus amplitude. This suggests, at least in such examples, that ROCs are isoclines of some function monotonically related to signal strength;[4] moreover, because these isoclines do not intersect, a Fechnerian representation may hold (recall the discussion in Section II.A):

$$\text{Stimulus strength} = F[u(P_\text{H}) - u(P_\text{FA})].$$

In other words, there exists the possibility of transforming an ROC into a line of unit slope by adopting $u(P_\text{H})$, $u(P_\text{FA})$ as new coordinates.

It is not difficult to show that this possibility does occur if $\mathbf{U}_s$, $\mathbf{U}_n$ are members of a location family of random variables, differing only in their mean values. Based on explicit examples and, above all else, on simplicity, it is commonly assumed that $\mathbf{U}_s$, $\mathbf{U}_n$ are normally distributed, with a common variance. This assumption is responsible for the custom of plotting ROCs on double-probability paper (with inverse normals along the axes). If the normal assumption is correct, ROCs plot as parallel lines of unit slope, with intercepts

$$d' = z_\text{H} - z_\text{FA} = [\mu(s) - \mu(n)]/\sigma, \qquad (10)$$

[4] Suppose the value of a real function F of two real variable is fixed: $F(x,y) =$ constant. Then such pairs (x,y) trace out a curve called an isocline or level curve of F. Different isoclines correspond to different values of the function F.

where $z = \Phi^{-1}$ (probability) and Φ is the distribution function of the unit normal. The measure d' depends only on stimulus parameters and is thus a measure of detectability uncontaminated by subjective biases.

The remarkable fact is that when empirical ROCs are plotted in this way, they do more or less fall on straight lines, though often their slopes are different from unity. This empirical fact can be accommodated by retaining the normality assumption but dropping the constant variance assumption. Using the coordinate transformation $z = \Phi^{-1}$ (probability)—recall Φ is the distribution function of the unit normal—the following prediction emerges:

$$\sigma(s)z_H - \sigma(n)\, z_{FA} = \mu(s) - \mu(n), \tag{11}$$

which is the equation of a line of slope $\sigma(n)/\sigma(s)$ and intercept $[\mu(s) - \mu(n)]/\sigma(s)$. Unlike the case discussed earlier for which $\sigma(s) = \sigma(n)$, that is, Eq. (10), there is now some freedom in defining an index of detectability, and different authors emphasize different measures. Those most commonly employed are the following three: $[\mu(s) - \mu(n)]/\sigma(n)$, $[\mu(s) - \mu(n)]/\sigma(s)$, and $\dfrac{\mu(s) - \mu(n)}{\sqrt{\sigma^2(s) + \sigma^2(n)}}$.

Note that the latter index, the perpendicular distance to the line (Eq.11) from the origin, is closely related to performance in a discrimination (two alternative/interval forced-choice) paradigm using the same signal and noise sources as employed in the detection task. Formally, the prediction for the forced-choice paradigm is given by Eq. (5) with s,n replacing x,y, respectively. One obtains

$$z_c = \Phi^{-1}([\mu(s) - \mu(n)]/\sqrt{\sigma^2(s) + \sigma^2(n)}), \tag{12}$$

where z_c is the transformed probability of a correct response in the two alternative tasks. The ability to tie together the results of different experimental procedures is an important feature of signal detection theory, one that has been exploited in many empirical studies. For additional results of this type, see Noreen (1981) and Macmillan and Creelman (1991), who confine their developments to the constant variance assumption, and Iverson and Sheu (1992), who do not. In section II.C we sketch a theory that unites detection performance and speed-accuracy trade-off behavior under a single umbrella.

5. Sources of Variability

A question first raised by Durlach and Braida (1969), Gravetter and Lockhead (1973), and Wickelgren (1968) concerns the locus of variability in this class of signal detection models. Eq. (9) is written as if all of the variability lies in the representation of the stimuli, and the response criterion β is treated as a deterministic numerical variable. For the case of location families of random variables, the data would be fit equally well if all the variability were attributed to β and none to the stimuli. Indeed, because variances of independent random variables add, any partition between stimulus variability and criterion variability is consistent with both yes-no and forced-choice data. The problem, then, is to design a method that can be used to estimate the partition that actually exists.

Perhaps Nosofsky (1983) provided the cleanest answer. His idea was to repeat the stimulus presentation N times with independent samples of noise and have the subject respond to the entire ensemble. If subjects average the N independent observations, the mean is unaffected but the variance decreases as $\sigma^2(s)/N$. On the other hand, there is no reason why the criterion variance $\sigma^2(\beta)$ should vary with N. Substituting into Eq. (10), we obtain

$$\frac{1}{d_N^2} = \frac{\sigma^2(\beta) + \sigma^2(s)/N}{\mu(s) - \mu(n)} , \tag{13}$$

which represents a linear trade-off between the variables $1/(d'_N{}^2)$ and $1/N$.

Nosofsky carried out an auditory intensity experiment in which four signals were to be identified. The two middle signals were always at the same separation, but the end signals were differently spaced leading to a wide and a narrow condition. The quantity d'_N was computed for the pair of middle stimuli of fixed separation. Figure 6 shows $1/(d'_N)^2$ versus $1/N$ for both the wide and narrow conditions. The predicted linearity was confirmed. The value (slope/intercept)$^{1/2}$, which estimates $\sigma(s)/\sigma(\beta)$, is 3.96 and 3.14 in the wide and narrow conditions, respectively; the ratio $\sigma(s,$ wide$)/\sigma(s,$ narrow$)$ is 7.86, and that of $\sigma(\beta,$ wide$)/\sigma(\beta,$ narrow$)$ is 6.23. Thus it appears that the standard deviations for stimulus and criterion partition about 3 or 4 to 1. Nosofsky also reanalyzed data of Ulehla, Halpern, and Cerf (1968) in which subjects identified two tilt positions of a line; again the model fit well. The latter authors varied signal duration and that manipulation yielded estimates of $\sigma(s)/\sigma(\beta)$ of 14.22 in the shorter duration and 4.57 in the longer one. The criterion variance was little changed across the two conditions.

6. COSS Analysis

A far-reaching generalization of Nosofsky's ideas was recently proposed by Berg (1989) under the name of COSS analysis (*conditional on a single stimulus*). Rather than assume an observer gives equal weight to all sources of information relevant to detecting a signal, Berg's theory calls for a system of differential weights. COSS analysis provides an algorithm for estimating these weights in empirical data. There is a growing body of evidence that

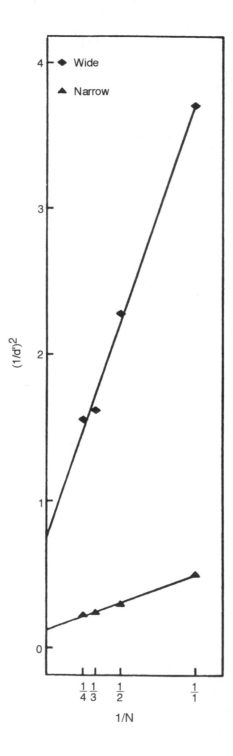

observer's do not usually employ equal weights, even when, as in Nosofsky's paradigm, they should; rather, the pattern of weights takes on a variety of shapes depending on the structure of stimuli and the demands of a particular task. Berg (1989), Berg (1990), and Berg and Green (1990) discuss tasks that produce rather different weight patterns.

Since its inception about eight years ago, COSS analysis has had a major impact in psychoacoustics, where it was first applied. However, the technique is very flexible and one can expect it will find application to any task calling for the detection of complex stimuli that vary on many dimensions.

C. Stochastic Process Models

The models we have considered thus far are largely phenomenological. They allow for useful interpretations of data, but they do not attempt to capture the complexity of stimulus encoding as revealed by physiological studies. Yet efforts to create more realistic models of information transmission, however crude and incomplete, seem to be of considerable merit. We now sketch the results of one such enterprise.

Physiological studies conducted in the 1960s and 1970s (summarized in Luce, 1986, 1993) of the temporal coding of simple tones by individual fibers of the eighth nerve revealed that histograms of interpulse times were roughly exponential in their gross shape. (This rough exponential shape ignores fine structure: There is refractoriness, and the actual distribution is spiky, with successive peaks displaced at intervals of $1/T$, T being the period of the input tone.) Assuming independence of times between successive pulses, such exponential histograms suggest that the encoding of simple auditory stimuli can be modeled as Poisson processes of neural pulses,[5] with rates determined by stimulus intensity (see Green & Luce, 1973); however, more recent work casts doubt on the independence of successive pulse durations (Lowen & Teich, 1992).

[5] A Poisson process can be thought of as a succession of points on a line, the intervals between any two consecutive points being distributed independently and exponentially. The reciprocal of the mean interval between successive events defines the rate parameter of the process.

←——————————————————————————————————————

FIGURE 6   Plot of estimated $1/d'^2$ versus $1/N$, where N is the number of independent repetitions of a pure tone that was to be absolutely identified from one of four possible intensities. The middle two stimuli had the same separation in both conditions, which were determined by the separation—wide or narrow—of the two end stimuli. d' was calculated for the two middle stimuli for each of eight subjects and then averaged; an average of 187.5 observations underlie each point of the wide condition and an average of 150 for the narrow one. The least-squares fits are shown. From Figure 2 of "Information Integration of the Identification of Stimulus Noise and Criteria Noise in Absolute Judgment," by R. M. Nosofsky, 1983, *Journal of Experimental Psychology: Human Perception and Performance, 9,* p. 305. Copyright 1983 by the American Psychological Association. Reprinted by permission.

A Poisson process allows two basic ways for estimating the rate parameter:

1. Count the number of events in a fixed time interval (the *counting strategy*).
2. Compute the reciprocal of the mean interarrival time between pulses (the *timing* strategy).

In a simple detection task involving pure tones in noise, Green and Luce (1973) argued that if an observer can use these two decision strategies, then it should be possible to induce the observer to switch from one to the other. An observer whose brain counts pulses over a fixed time interval may be expected to perform differently from one who whose brain calculates the (random) time required to achieve a fixed number of events. Indeed, the counting strategy predicts that ROCs will plot as (approximate) straight lines in Gaussian coordinates with slopes $\sigma(n)/\sigma(s)$ less than unity, whereas for the timing strategy the ROCs are again predicted to be (approximately) linear on double-probability paper but with slopes exceeding 1. Green and Luce found that observers could be induced to switch by imposing different deadline conditions on the basic detection task: when observers were faced with deadlines on both signal and noise trials, they manifested counting behavior (see Figure 7, top); when the deadline was imposed only on signal trials, observers switched to the timing strategy (see Figure 7, bottom).

The very nature of these tasks calls for the collection of response times. Green and Luce developed response time predictions for the two types of strategy. Predictions for the counting strategy are trivial because such observers initiate a motor response after the fixed counting period: mean latencies should thus show no dependence on stimulus or response, in agreement with observation. For the timing strategy, however, different speed–accuracy trade-offs are predicted on signal trials and on noise trials. Again, the data bore out these predictions (see Figure 11 of Green and Luce, 1973). The issue of averaging information versus extreme values was also studied in vision; see Wandell and Luce (1978).

III. CHOICE AND IDENTIFICATION

A. Random Utility Models

1. General Theory

A participant in a choice experiment is asked to select the most preferred alternative from an offered set of options. Such choice situations are commonly encountered in everyday life: selecting an automobile from the host of makes and models available, choosing a school or a house, and so on. To account for the uncertainties of the choice process, which translate into data

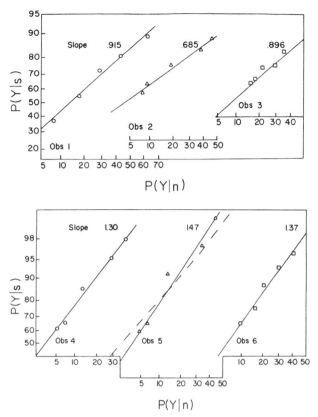

FIGURE 7   ROC curves (in z-score coordinates) with estimated slope shown. The upper panel shows the data when a time deadline of 600 ms was imposed on all trials. The lower panel shows the comparable data when the deadline was imposed only on signal trials. Adapted from Figures 4 and 9 of "Speed Accuracy Trade-off in Auditory Detection," by D. M. Green and R. D. Luce, in S. Kornblum (Ed.), *Attention and Performance* (Vol. IV), New York: Academic Press, 1973, pp. 557 and 562. Reprinted with permission.

inconsistencies, choice models are typically framed in terms of choice probabilities $P_{a,A}$, the probability of selecting an option a from Set A of alternatives.

A *random utility* model for the choice probabilities involves the assumption that each alternative a is associated with a random variable $\mathbf{U}_a$ that measures the (uncertain) value or utility of that alternative. In these terms it is natural to assume that

$$P_{a,A} = \text{Prob}(\mathbf{U}_a \geq \mathbf{U}_b, \text{ all } b \text{ in A}), \tag{14}$$

generalizing the binary choice situation discussed earlier in section II.A.3 [see Eq. (4)].

Without specific assumptions on the family of random variables $\{\mathbf{U}_a | a$ in A$\}$ appearing in a random utility representation—for example, that they are independent or that their joint distribution is known up to the values of parameters—it would appear that Eq. (14) does little to constrain observed choice probabilities. However, following Block and Marschak (1960), consider the following chain of expressions involving linear combinations of choice probabilities:

$$P_{a,A},$$
$$P_{A,A-\{b\}} - P_{a,A},$$
$$P_{a,A-\{b,c\}} - (P_{a,A-\{b\}} + P_{a,A-\{c\}}) + P_{a,A},$$
$$P_{a,A-\{b,c,d\}} - (P_{a,A-\{b,c\}} + P_{a,A-\{b,d\}} + P_{a,A-\{c,d\}})$$
$$+ (P_{a,A-\{b\}} + P_{a,A-\{c\}} + P_{a,A-\{d\}}) - P_{a,A},$$
$$\ldots, \text{ and so on} \tag{15}$$

where A $= \{a, b, c, d, \ldots\}$ and where the notation A $-$ B, B a subset of A, represents the set of members of A that are not also members of B.

It can be shown that Eq. (14) requires each of these so-called Block-Marschak functions to be nonnegative. In other words, the nonnegativity of Block-Marschak functions is a necessary condition for the existence of a random utility representation of choice probabilities. A remarkable result of Falmagne (1978) shows the *same* condition to be sufficient for a random utility representation.

A random utility representation of choice probabilities is far from unique: Any strictly increasing function applied to the random variables $\{\mathbf{U}_a | a$ in A$\}$ provides another, equivalent, random representation of the same choice probabilities [see Eq. (14)]. To address this lack of uniqueness, consider a variant of the choice paradigm in which the task is to rank order the alternatives from most preferred to least preferred. Define the random variable $\mathbf{U}_a^* = k$ if alternative a is assigned rank k, $k = 1, 2, \ldots$. Following the earlier work of Block and Marschak (1960), Falmagne established three results:

1. The random variables $\{\mathbf{U}_a^* \mid a$ in A$\}$ provide a random utility representation (whenever one exists).
2. All random utility representations for a given system of choice probabilities yield identical ranking variables $\mathbf{U}_a^*$.
3. The joint distribution of the ranking variables can be constructed from the choice probabilities.

For a detailed discussion of these facts, see Falmagne (1978).

Recently Regenwetter (1996) generalized the concept of a random utility representation to m-ary relations. The applications of his theory include a model of approval voting and an analysis of political ranking data.

Despite this impressive theoretical analysis of Eq. (14), very little in the way of empirical application has been attempted; Iverson and Bamber (1997) discuss the matter in the context of signal detection theory, where the random variables appearing in Eq. (14) can be assumed independent. Rather, the impact of specific distributional and other assumptions on Eq. (14) has dominated the field.

2. Luce's Choice Model

The assumption that the random variables $\mathbf{U}_a$ appearing in Eq. (14) are jointly normal (following Thurstone, see section II.A.3), does not lend itself to tractable analysis, except in special cases such as pair-comparison tasks. This circumstance arises from the fact that the maximum of two or more normal random variables is no longer normally distributed. Only three families of distributions are "closed" under the operation of taking maxima, and of these the double-exponential family is the most attractive. We mentioned in section II.A.3 that the assumption of double-exponentially distributed random variables mediating discrimination of two stimuli leads to the Bradley-Terry-Luce model for pair-comparison data [see Eq. (7)].

If one assumes that the random utilities in Eq. (14) are members of a location family, that is, of the form $u(a) + \mathbf{U}$, $u(b) + \mathbf{U}'$, $u(c) + \mathbf{U}''$, . . . where $\mathbf{U}, \mathbf{U}', \mathbf{U}''$ are independent with a common double-exponential distribution, namely,

$$\text{Prob}(\mathbf{U} \le t) = \exp[-e^{-t}]$$

for all real t, it follows from Eq. (14) that, for a Set A of alternatives a, b, c, . . . ,

$$P_{a,\mathrm{A}} = v(a) / \left[\sum_{b \in \mathrm{A}} v(b) \right]. \tag{16}$$

This expression also arises from Luce's (1959a) theory of choice.

Yellott (1977) has given an interesting characterization of the double-exponential distribution within the context of Eq. (14). He considered all choice models involving random utilities of an unspecified location family and he inquired as to the effect on choice probabilities of *uniformly expanding* the choice set by replicating each alternative some fixed but arbitrary number of times. Thus, for example, if a choice set comprises a glass of milk, a cup of tea, and a cup of coffee, a uniform expression of that set would contain k glasses of milk, k cups of tea, and k cups of coffee for some integer $k \ge 2$. Yellott showed that if choice probabilities satisfying Eq. (14) were unchanged by any uniform expansion of the choice set, then, given that the (independent) random utilities were all of the form $u(a) + \mathbf{U}$, the distribution of the random variable $\mathbf{U}$ is determined: It must be double-exponential.

3. Elimination Models

The choice model Eq. (16) has been the subject of various criticisms on the basis of which new theories have been proposed. Suppose, for example, that one is indifferent when it comes to choosing between a cup of tea and a cup of coffee. Intuitively, the addition of a further cup of tea should not affect the odds of choosing coffee. Yet the model Eq. (16) predicts that the probability of choosing coffee drops to one third unless, of course, equivalent alternatives are collapsed into a single equivalence class.

Tversky (1972a, b) offered a generalization of Luce's choice model that escapes this and other criticisms. In his theory of *choice by elimination,* each choice object is regarded as a set of features or *aspects* to which weights are attached. The choice of an alternative is determined by an elimination process in which an aspect is selected with a probability proportional to its weight. All alternatives not possessing the chosen aspect are eliminated from further consideration. The remaining alternatives are subject to the same elimination process until a single alternative remains. This theory reduces to Luce's choice model in the very special case in which alternatives do not share common aspects.

Practical implementation of the elimination-by-aspects model is made difficult by the large number of unknown parameters it involves. This difficulty is alleviated by imposing additional structure on the alternatives. Tversky and Sattath (1979) developed an elimination model in which the choice objects appear as the end nodes of a binary tree, whose interior branches are labeled by aspect weights. That model requires the tree structure to be known in advance, however. The additive tree model of Carroll and DeSoete (1990) allows the tree structure to be estimated from data, which are restricted to pairwise choices.

4. Spatial Models

The tree structures assumed by Tversky and Sattath (1979) are not the only means for coordinating choice objects geometrically. It is often sensible to represent choice alternatives as points $\mathbf{x}$ in an n-dimensional space. Pruzansky, Tversky, and Carroll (1982) surmised that perceptual stimuli are adequately represented by multidimensional spatial models, whereas conceptual stimuli are better represented in terms of more discrete structures such as trees.

Böckenholt (1992) and DeSoete and Carroll (1992) have given excellent reviews of probabilistic pair comparison models in which a spatial representation is fundamental. To give a flavor of such models we sketch the *wandering vector* model presented by DeSoete and Carroll (1986), which is based on earlier ideas suggested by Tucker (1960) and Slater (1960).

The wandering vector model represents choice objects in an n-dimensional Euclidean space, together with a random vector $\mathbf{V}$, which fluctuates from trial to trial in a pair comparison experiment and which constitutes an "ideal" direction in the sample space. The vector $\mathbf{V}$ is assumed to be distributed normally with mean vector μ and covariance matrix Σ. A comparison of options i and j is determined by three vectors: $\mathbf{x}_i$ and $\mathbf{x}_j$, the vector representatives of options i and j and $\mathbf{v}$, a realization of the "wandering" vector $\mathbf{V}$. Option i is preferred to option j whenever the "similarity" of i to j as measured by the orthogonal projection of $\mathbf{x}_i$ on $\mathbf{v}$ exceeds the corresponding projection of $\mathbf{x}_j$ on $\mathbf{v}$. The binary choice probabilities are thus given by

$$P_{ij} = \text{Prob}(\mathbf{x}_i \cdot \mathbf{V} > \mathbf{x}_j \cdot \mathbf{V}),$$

where for any vectors $\mathbf{x} = (x_1, x_2, \ldots x_n)$, $\mathbf{y} = (y_1, y_2, \ldots y_n)$, the inner product $\mathbf{x} \cdot \mathbf{y}$ is the number $x_1 y_1 + x_2 y_2 + \ldots + x_n y_n$. Using standard theory of the multivariate normal distribution (Ashby, 1992b), one obtains

$$\begin{aligned} P_{ij} &= \Phi[(\mathbf{x}_i - \mathbf{x}_j) \cdot \mu / \delta_{ij}] \\ &= \Phi[(u_i - u_j)/\delta_{ij}]. \end{aligned} \tag{17}$$

Here $u_i = \mathbf{x}_i \cdot \mu$ is a (constant) utility associated with option i, and $\delta_{ij}^2 = (\mathbf{x}_i - \mathbf{x}_j) \cdot [\Sigma(\mathbf{x}_i - \mathbf{x}_j)]$. Note that the form of Eq. (17) is identical to that of Thurstone's law of comparative judgment (see section II.A.3).

The quantity $\delta_{ij} = \delta_{ji}$ is a metric that can be interpreted to measure, at least partially, the dissimilarity of options i and j; Sjöberg (1980) has given some empirical support for this interpretation. On the other hand, there is a considerable body of evidence that empirical judgments of dissimilarity violate the properties required of a metric (Krumhansl, 1978; Tversky, 1977).

A multidimensional similarity model, which appears to address the various shortcomings of the choice models sketched here, is based on the general recognition theory presented by Ashby, Townsend, and Perrin (Ashby & Perrin, 1988; Ashby & Townsend, 1986; Perrin, 1986, 1992). We encounter that theory next in the context of identification.

B. Identification

1. Ordered Attributes

For stimuli ordered on a one-dimensional continuum, an observer can distinguish perfectly only about seven alternatives spaced equally across the full dynamic range (Miller, 1956). This fact, which is quite robust over different continua, is in sharp contrast to the results of local discrimination experiments of the sort discussed earlier in section II. For example, jnds measured in loudness discrimination experiments employing pure tones vary from a few decibels at low intensities to a fraction of a decibel at high intensities suggesting, quite contrary to the evidence, that an observer should be able to identify 40 or more tones of increasing loudness spaced evenly over an 80 dB range.

Such puzzling phenomena have prompted a number of authors to study the identification of one-dimensional stimuli as a function of stimulus range (Berliner, Durlach, & Braida, 1977; Braida & Durlach, 1972; Durlach & Braida, 1969; Luce, Green, & Weber, 1976; Luce, Nosofsky, Green, & Smith, 1982; Weber, Green, & Luce, 1977). The data from these studies are accompanied by pronounced sequential effects, first noted by Holland and Lockhead (1968) and Ward and Lockhead (1970, 1971), implicating shifts in response criteria over successive trials and, to a lesser extent, shifts in sensitivity as well (Lacoutre, & Marley, 1995; Luce & Nosofsky, 1984; Marley & Cooke, 1984; Marley, & Cooke, 1986; Nosofsky, 1983; Treisman, 1985; Treisman & Williams, 1984). Despite the difficulties of interpretation posed by these sequential effects, a robust feature of identification data is the presence of a prominent "edge" effect: Stimuli at the edges of an experimental range are much better identified than stimuli in the middle. As the stimulus range is allowed to increase so that successive stimuli grow farther apart, performance improves, but the edge effect remains. This finding, among others, illustrates that the hope of tying together the data from local psychophysics with those of more global tasks remains an unsettled matter.

2. Multidimensional Stimuli

The basic identification task generates data in the form of a confusion matrix, whose typical entry is the probability P_{ji} of responding stimulus j to the actual presentation of stimulus i. A model that has enjoyed considerable success in accounting for such data is the *biased choice model* (Luce, 1963):

$$P_{ji} = \frac{\beta_j \eta_{ij}}{\sum_j \beta_j \eta_{ij}} . \tag{18}$$

Here η_{ij} is a measure of the similarity of stimuli i and j, whereas β_j represents a bias toward responding stimulus j. Shepard (1957, 1987) has argued that $\eta_{ij} = \exp(-d_{ij})$, where d_{ij} is the distance between alternatives i and j regarded as points in a multidimensional vector space. We have already mentioned that some literature speaks against similarity judgments being constrained by the axioms of a metric (Keren & Baggen, 1981; Krumhansl, 1978; Tversky, 1977). Ashby and Perrin (1988), who favor the *general recognition theory* (which attempts to account for identification and similarity data within a common multidimensional statistical decision framework), provided additional evidence against the biased choice model.

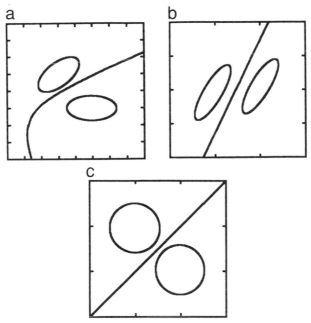

FIGURE 8   Examples of optimal decision boundaries for three types of stimuli. From Figure 1.5 of *Multidimensional Models of Perception and Cognition,* by F. G. Ashby, Hillsdale, NJ: Erlbaum, 1992, p. 29. Reprinted with permission.

General recognition theory (GRT) identifies each alternative in an identification experiment with a random vector that takes values in a fixed multidimensional vector space. This vector space is partitioned into disjoint regions, each of which is characteristic of a single response. For illustration, consider the simplest case involving a pair of two-dimensional stimuli, say, A and B, with densities $f_A(\mathbf{x})$ and $f_B(\mathbf{x})$ governing their respective perceptual effects. Statistical decision theory suggests partitioning the two-dimensional sample space on the basis of the likelihood ratio f_A/f_B. When the perceptual effects of A and B are jointly normal, curves of constant likelihood ratio are quadratic functions that simplify to lines when the covariance structure of A is the same as that of B (i.e., $\Sigma_A = \Sigma_B$).

Figure 8 generalizes to any number of stimuli varying on any number of dimensions. Figure 9 depicts hypothetical response boundaries for four two-dimensional stimuli labeled by their components: (A_1, B_1), (A_1, B_2), (A_2, B_1), (A_2, B_2). The response boundaries are chosen so as to maximize accuracy.

General recognition theory yields a conceptually simple expression (though one that is often analytically untractable) for the confusions P_{ji}. If R_j

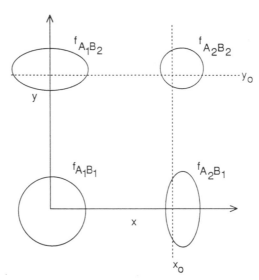

FIGURE 9   Contours of equal probability and decision boundaries for a four-stimulus recognition task. From Figure 6.2 of "Uniting Identification, Similarity, and Preference: General Recognition Theory," by N. A. Perrin, in F. G. Ashby (Ed.), *Multidimensional Models of Perception and Cognition,* Hillsdale, NJ: Erlbaum, 1992, p. 128. Reprinted with permission.

is the region of the sample space associated with response stimulus j and $f_i(\mathbf{x})$ is the density governing the perceptual effect of stimulus i, then

$$P_{ji} = \int_{R_j} f_i(\mathbf{x})\mathbf{dx}. \tag{19}$$

Numerical methods are normally needed to evaluate such expressions (Ashby, 1992b), in which $f_i(\mathbf{x})$ is multivariate normal.

A competitor to GRT is Nosofsky's *generalized context model (GCM)*, which is an outgrowth of an earlier model of classification proposed by Medin and Shaffer (1978). Unlike GRT, which has its roots in multidimensional statistical decision theory, GCM is based on the idea that people store exemplars in memory as points in a multidimensional space and classify stimuli by proximity in that space to the various exemplars. Nosofsky (1984, 1986) elaborates the model and its assumptions, and in a sequence of articles extends it to take into account phenomena bearing on selective attention (Nosofsky, 1987, 1989, 1991).

These two models, GRT and GCM, seem to account about equally well for a large class of identification and classification data. Because of the different ways each model interprets the same data, a certain amount of scientific controversy has arisen over these interpretations. However, despite their differences in detail, the two models retain much in common, and one hopes that this fact will promote a third class of models that retains the best features of both GRT and GCM, putting an end to the current disputes.

It has long been thought useful to maintain a distinction between "integral" stimuli—stimuli that are processed as whole entities—and "separable" stimuli—stimuli that are processed in terms of two or more dimensions (see, e.g., Garner, 1974; Lockhead, 1966). Taking such distinctions into account within the framework just presented provides additional and testable constraints on identification data. For a detailed discussion of this and related matters, see Ashby and Townsend (1986), Maddox (1992), and Kadlec and Townsend (1992).

IV. ADDITIVE MEASUREMENT FOR AN ORDERED ATTRIBUTE

In this and the following sections, we shift our focus from models designed to describe the variability of psychophysical data to models that explore more deeply the impact of stimulus structure on behavior. To do so, we idealize response behavior, treating it as if responses exhibit no variability. With few exceptions (e.g., section IV.D), current models do not attempt to combine significant features of both stimulus structure and variable response behavior. It has proved very difficult to combine both phenomena in a single approach due to, in our opinion, the lack of a qualitative theory of randomness.

A. Ranking and Order

Stimuli can be ordered in a variety of ways ranging from standard physical procedures—ordering masses by, say, an equal-arm pan balance or tones by physical intensity (e.g., decibels)—to subjective attributes—perceived weight, perceived loudness, preference among foods, and so on. In each case, the information that is presumed to exist or to be obtainable with some effort is the order between any two objects in the domain that is established by the attribute. Let A denote the domain of stimuli and let a and b be two elements of A, often written $a, b \in A$. Then we write $a \succsim b$ whenever a exhibits at least as much of the attribute as does b.

The order $\succsim$ can be established either by presenting pairs and asking a subject to order them by having the subject rank order the entire set of stimuli, by rating them in some fashion, or by indirect methods some of which we describe shortly.

Of course, as we observed in section II, for most psychological attributes such consistency is, at best, an idealization. If you ask a subject to order a and b more than once, the answer typically changes. Indeed, one assumes that, in general, a probability $P_{a,b}$ describes the propensity of a subject to order a and b as $a \gtrsim b$. There are ways to induce an order from such probabilities. One is simply to use the estimated propensity as the source of ordering, namely,

$$a \gtrsim b \text{ holds if and only if } P_{a,b} \geq \tfrac{1}{2}. \qquad (20)$$

If a Fechnerian model holds (Section II.A.1), this is the order established by the underlying subjective scale u. Another order, which often is of considerable importance, is not on the stimuli themselves, but on pairs of them:

$$(a, b) \gtrsim (a', b') \text{ whenever } P_{a,b} \geq P_{a',b'}. \qquad (21)$$

Still another way to establish a psychological order is by measuring the time it takes a subject to decide whether a has more of the attribute than b. If $L_{a,b}$ denotes the mean response time for that judgment, then replacing P in Eq. (21) with L yields a potentially new order that is well defined. In practice, these two orders are not wholly independent; witness the existence of speed-accuracy trade-offs. Some authors have conjectured that $L_{a,b}$ may be a decreasing function of $|P_{a,b} - \tfrac{1}{2}|$; however, nothing really simple seems to hold (Luce, 1986).

The purpose of this section and the subsequent two sections is to study some of the properties of orders on structures and certain numerical representations that can arise. This large and complex topic has been treated in considerable detail in several technical sources: Falmagne (1985); Krantz, Luce, Suppes, and Tversky (1971); Luce, Krantz, Suppes, and Tversky (1990); Narens (1985); Pfanzagl (1971); Roberts (1979); and Suppes, Krantz, Luce, and Tversky (1989); and Wakker (1989). For philosophically different approaches and commentary, see Decoene, Onghena, and Janssen (1995), Ellis (1966), Michell (1990, 1995), Niederée (1992, 1994), and Savage and Ehrlich (1992).

1. Transitivity and Connectedness

To the extent that an order reflects an attribute that can be said to exhibit "degree of" or "amount of," then we expect it to exhibit the following property known as *transitivity*: For all a, b, $c \in A$,

$$\text{if } a \gtrsim b \text{ and } b \gtrsim c, \text{ then } a \gtrsim c. \qquad (22)$$

Transitivity is a property of numbers: $12 \geq 8$ and $8 \geq 5$ certainly means that $12 \geq 5$. At various times we will focus on whether transitivity holds.

A second observation is that for very many attributes it is reasonable to assume the following property, which is known as *connectedness*: For all a and $b \in A$,

$$\text{either } a \gtrsim b \text{ or } b \gtrsim a \text{ or both.} \qquad (23)$$

The orders defined by Eqs. (20) and (21) obviously satisfy connectedness.

When both $a \gtrsim b$ and $b \gtrsim a$ hold, we write $a \sim b$ meaning that a and b are indifferent with respect to the attribute of the ordering. It does not usually correspond to equality; two objects can have the same weight without being identical. If $a \gtrsim b$ but not $a \sim b$, then we write $a > b$. Whatever the attribute corresponding to $\gtrsim$ is called, the attribute corresponding to $>$ receives the same name modified by the adjective *strict*. Equally, if $>$ has a name, $\gtrsim$ is prefixed by *weak*. So, for example, if $>$ denotes preference, $\gtrsim$ denotes weak preference.

Should one confront an attribute for which connectedness fails, so that for some a and b neither $a \gtrsim b$ nor $b \gtrsim a$, we usually speak of a and b as being *noncomparable* in the attribute and the order as being *partial*. For example, suppose one were ordering a population of people by the attribute "ancestor of." This is obviously transitive and equally obviously not connected. All of the attributes discussed in this chapter are assumed to be connected.

A connected and transitive order is called a *weak order*. When indifference, $\sim$, of a weak order is actually equality, that is, $a \sim b$ is equivalent to $a = b$, the order is called *simple* or *total*. The numerical relation $\geq$ is the most common example of a simple order, but very few orders of scientific interest are stronger than weak orders unless one treats classes of equivalent elements as single entities.

2. Ordinal Representations

One major feature of measurement in the physical sciences and, to a lesser degree, in the behavioral and social sciences is the convenience of representing the order information numerically. In particular, it is useful to know when an empirical order has an *order preserving* numerical representation, that is, when a function ϕ from A into the real numbers $\mathbb{R}$ (or the positive real numbers $\mathbb{R}_+$) exists such that for all $a, b \in A$,

$$a \gtrsim b \text{ is equivalent to } \phi(a) \geq \phi(b). \tag{24}$$

Because $\geq$ is a total order, it is not difficult to see that a necessary condition is that $\gtrsim$ be a weak order. When A is finite, being a weak order is also sufficient because one can simply take ϕ to be the numerical ranking: assign 1 to the least element, 2 to the next, and so on. For infinite structures, another necessary condition must be added to achieve sufficiency; it says, in effect, that $\langle A, \gtrsim \rangle$ must contain a subset that is analogous to the rational numbers in the reals, that is, a countable order-dense subset. The details, listed as the Cantor or Cantor-Birkhoff theorem, can be found in any book on the theory of measurement (e.g., Krantz et al., 1971, section 2.1, or Narens, 1985, p. 36).

One feature of Eq. (24) is that if f is any strictly increasing function[6] from $\mathbb{R}$ to $\mathbb{R}$,[6] then $f(\phi)$ is an equally good representation of $\langle A, \gtrsim \rangle$. When a

[6] If $x > y$, then $f(x) > f(y)$.

representation has this degree of nonuniqueness, it is said to be of *ordinal scale type*. One drawback of this nonuniqueness is that little of arithmetic or calculus can be used in a way that remains invariant under admissible scale changes. For example, if ϕ is defined on the positive real numbers, then $f(\phi) = \phi^2$ is an admissible transformation. If $\phi(a) = 5$, $\phi(b) = 4$, $\phi(c) = 6$, and $\phi(d) = 3$, then $\phi(a) + \phi(b) \geq \phi(c) + \phi(d)$, but ϕ^2 reverses the order of the inequality. Therefore great care must be taken in combining and compressing information that is represented ordinally (see section VI).

3. Nontransitivity of Indifference and Weber's Law

A very simple consequence of $\gtrsim$ being a weak order is that both the strict part, $>$, and the indifference part, $\sim$, must also be transitive. Although the transitivity of $>$ seems plausible for many attributes, such may not be the case for $\sim$, if for no other reason than our inability to discriminate very small differences. The measurement literature includes a fair amount of material on orderings for which $>$ is transitive and $\sim$ is not. Conditions relating them are known that lead to a representation in terms of two numerical functions ϕ and δ, where $\delta > 0$ is thought of as a threshold function:

$$a > b \text{ is equivalent to } \phi(a) \geq \phi(b) + \delta(b), \tag{25a}$$

$$a \sim b \text{ is equivalent to } \phi(a) - \delta(a) < \phi(b) < \phi(a) + \delta(a). \tag{25b}$$

Orders exhibiting such a threshold representation are known as *semiorders* and *interval orders,* the latter entailing different upper and lower threshold functions (Fishburn, 1985; Suppes et al., 1989, chap. 16).

One major question that has been studied is, when is it possible to choose ϕ in such a way that δ is a constant? This question is very closely related to the psychophysical question of when does Weber's law (just detectable differences are proportional to stimulus intensity) hold in discrimination. To be specific, in a context of probabilistic responses, suppose a probability criterion λ, $\frac{1}{2} < \lambda < 1$ (e.g., 0.75 is a common choice) is selected to partition the discriminable from the indiscriminable. This defines the algebraic relation $\gtrsim_\lambda$ in terms of the probabilities by

$$a >_\lambda b \text{ is equivalent to } P_{a,b} \geq \lambda \tag{26a}$$

$$a \sim_\lambda b \text{ is equivalent to } 1-\lambda < P_{a,b} < \lambda. \tag{26b}$$

It can be shown that for $\gtrsim_\lambda$ to have a threshold representation, Eq. (25), with a constant threshold, is equivalent to the Weber function of P satisfying Weber's law (see sections II.A.2 and VII.B.1).

B. Conjoint Structures with Additive Representations

Let us return to the simpler case of a weak order. The ordinal representation is rather unsatisfactory because of its high degree of nonuniqueness, so one is led to consider situations exhibiting further empirical information that is to be represented numerically. That consideration is the general topic of this subsection and section IV.C.

1. Conjoint Structures

The sciences, in particular psychology, are replete with attributes that are affected by several independent variables. For example, an animal's food preference is affected by the size and composition of the food pellet as well as by the animal's delay in receiving it; the aversiveness of an electric shock is affected by voltage, amperage, and duration; loudness depends on both physical intensity and frequency;[7] the mass of an object is affected by both its volume and the density of material from which it is made; and so forth.

Each of these examples illustrates the fact that we can and do study how independently manipulable variables *trade off* against one another in influencing the dependent attribute. Thus, it is always possible to plot those combinations of the variables that yield equal levels of the attribute. Economists call these *indifference curves,* and psychologists have a myriad of terms depending on context: *ROCs* for discrimination (section II.B.1), *equal-loudness contours,* and *curves of equal aversiveness,* among others.

The question is whether these trade-offs can be a source of measurement. Let us treat the simplest case of two independent variables; call their domains A and U. Thus a typical stimulus is a pair, denoted (a, u), consisting of an A element and a U element. The set of all such pairs is denoted $A \times U$. The attribute in question, $\succsim$, is an ordering of $A \times U$, and we suppose it is a weak order. One possibility for the numerical representation ϕ is that in addition to being order preserving, Eq. (24), it is *additive* over the factors A and U,[8] meaning that there is a numerical function ϕ_A on A and another one ϕ_U on X such that

$$\phi(a, u) = \phi_A(a) + \phi_U(u), \tag{27a}$$

that is, for $a, b \in A$ and $u, v \in U$,

$$(a, u) \succsim (b, v) \text{ is equivalent to}$$
$$\phi_A(a) + \phi_U(u) \geq \phi_A(b) + \phi_U(v). \tag{27b}$$

---

[7] Witness the shape of equal loudness contours at low intensity, which is the reason for loudness compensation as well as intensity controls on audio amplifiers.

[8] The terms *independent variable, factor,* and *component* are used interchangeably in this literature, except when component refers to the level of a factor.

Such additive representations are typically used in the behavioral and social sciences, whereas the physical sciences usually employ a multiplicative representation into the positive real numbers, $\mathbb{R}_+$. The multiplicative representation is obtained from Eq. (27) by applying an exponential transformation, thereby converting addition to multiplication: $e^{x+y} = e^x e^y$.

2. The Existence of an Additive Representation

Two questions arise: What must be true about $\succsim$ so that an additive representation, Eq. (27), exists; and if one does exist, how nonunique is it? Mathematically precise answers to these questions are known as *representation* and *uniqueness theorems*.[9] It is clear that for such a strong representation to exist, the qualitative ordering $\succsim$ must be severely constrained. Some constraints are easily derived. For example, if we set $u = v$ in Eq. (27b), we see that because $\phi_U(u)$ appears on both sides of the inequality it can be replaced by any other common value, for example, by $\phi_U(w)$. Thus, a necessary qualitative condition, known as *independence* in this literature,[10] is that for all a, b in A and u, v in U,

$$(a, u) \succsim (b, u) \text{ is equivalent to } (a, v) \succsim (b, v). \tag{28a}$$

Similarly, one can hold the first component fixed and let the second one vary:

$$(a, u) \succsim (a, v) \text{ is equivalent to } (b, u) \succsim (b, v). \tag{28b}$$

For a long time psychologists have been sensitive to the fact that Eq. (28) necessarily holds if the attribute has an additive representation, and in plots of indifference curves (often with just two values of the factors) the concern is whether or not the curves "cross." Crossing rejects the possibility of an additive representation; however, as examples will show, the mere fact of not crossing is insufficient to conclude that an additive representation exists. The reason is that other conditions are necessary beyond those that can be deduced from weak ordering and Eq. (28).

For example, suppose we have two inequalities holding with the property that they have a common A value in the right side of the first qualitative inequality and the left side of the second one and also a common U value in the left side of the first and the right side of the second qualitative inequalities; then when the corresponding numerical inequalities are added and the common values canceled from the two sides one concludes from Eq. (27) that

$$\text{if } (a, w) \succsim (g, v) \text{ and } (g, u) \succsim (b, w) \text{ then } (a, u) \succsim (b, v). \tag{29}$$

[9] The term *uniqueness* is used despite the fact that the thrust of the theorem is to tell just how nonunique the representation is.

[10] Mathematically, it might better be called *monotonicity*, but the term *independence* is widely used.

This property is known as *double cancellation* because, in effect, two values, w and g, are canceled. In recent years it has been recognized that at least both Eqs. (28) and (29) need to be checked when deciding if an additive representation is possible (see Michell, 1990).

It is not difficult to see that we can go to three antecedent inequalities with an appropriate pattern of common elements so that Eq. (27) leads to further, more complex conditions than Eq. (29). Do we need them all?

The answer (see Chap. 9 of Krantz et al., 1971) is yes if we are dealing with a finite domain $A \times U$. For infinite domains,[11] however, it turns out that the properties of weak order, independence, and double cancellation—that is, Eqs. (22), (23), (28), and (29)—are sufficient for those (important) classes of structures for which the independent variables can reasonably be modeled as continuous (often physical) variables. Such continuous models are typically assumed in both psychophysics and utility theory. The added conditions are a form of solvability of indifferences (see the next subsection) and a so-called *Archimedean property,* which we do not attempt to describe exactly here (see section IV.C and chap. 6 of Krantz et al., 1971). Suffice it to say that it amounts to postulating that no nonzero interval is infinitesimal relative to any other interval; all measurements are comparable.

3. The Uniqueness of Additive Representations

The second question is, how nonunique is the ϕ of Eq. (27)? It is easily verified that $\psi_A = r\phi_A + s$ and $\psi_U = r\phi_U + t$, where $r > 0$, s, and t are real constants, is another representation. Moreover, these are the only transformations that work. Representations unique up to such positive affine (linear) transformations are said to be of *interval scale type* (Stevens, 1946, 1951).

4. Psychological Applications

Levelt, Riemersma, and Bunt (1972) collected loudness judgments over the two ears and constructed an additive conjoint representation. Later Gigerenzer and Strube (1983), using an analysis outlined by Falmagne (1976) that is described in section IV.D, concluded that additivity of loudness fails, at least when one of the two monaural sounds is sufficiently louder than the other: the louder one dominates the judgments. To the extent that additivity fails, we need to understand nonadditive structures (section VI).

Numerous other examples can be found in both the psychological and marketing literatures. Michell (1990) gives examples with careful explanations.

---

[11] Of course, any experiment is necessarily finite. So one can never test all possible conditions, and it is a significant inductive leap from the confirmation of these equations in a finite data set to the assertion that the properties hold throughout the infinite domain. For finite domains one can, in principle, verify all of the possible cancellation properties.

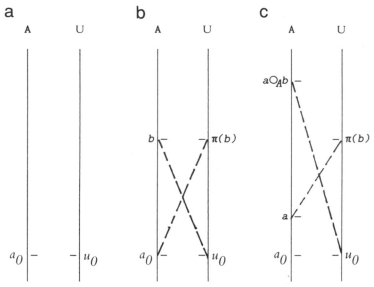

FIGURE 10 The construction used to create an operator $\bigcirc_A$ on one component of a conjoint structure that captures the trade-off of information. Pairs connected by dashed lines that intersect in the middle are equivalent. Panel (a) schematically represents the components as continua with distinguished points a_o and u_o. Panel (b) maps the interval $a_o b$ to the interval $u_o \pi(b)$. Panel (c) illustrates adding the latter interval to $a_o a$ to get the "sum" interval $a_o(a \bigcirc_A b)$.

C. Concatenation Structures with Additive Representations

1. Reducing the Conjoint Case to a Concatenation Operation

It turns out that the best way to study independent conjoint structures, whether additive or not (section VI.B.2), is to map all of the information contained in $\langle A \times U, \gtrsim \rangle$ into an operation and ordering on A. Consider the following definition:

$$a \gtrsim_A b \text{ is equivalent to } (a, u) \gtrsim (b, u). \tag{30}$$

Independence, Eq. (28), says that the order induced on A by Eq. (30) is unaffected by the choice of u on the second factor.

Inducing an operation on A is somewhat more complex. The general procedure is outlined in Figure 10 and details are given in Krantz et al. (1971, p. 258). It rests first on arbitrarily picking an element from each factor, say, a_o from A and u_o from U. Next, one maps what intuitively can be thought of as the "interval" $a_o b$ of the A component onto an equivalent "interval" of the U component, which we will call $u_o \pi(b)$. The formal definition is that $\pi(b)$ satisfies the equivalence:

$$(b, u_o) \sim (a_o, \pi(b)). \tag{31}$$

Clearly, one must make an explicit assumption that such a solution $\pi(b)$ can always be found. Such a solvability condition is somewhat plausible for continuous dimensions and far less so for discrete ones.

The third step is to "add" the interval $a_o b$ to the interval $a_o a$ by first mapping the interval $a_o b$ to $u_o \pi(b)$, Eq. (31), and then mapping that interval back onto the interval from a to a value called $a \bigcirc_A b$ that is defined as the solution to the indifference

$$(a \bigcirc_A b, u_o) \sim (a, \pi(b)). \tag{32}$$

The operation $\bigcirc_A$ is referred to as one of *concatenation* or "putting together." It turns out that studying the concatenation structure $\langle A, \succsim_A, \bigcirc_A, a_o \rangle$ is equivalent to studying $\langle A \times X, \succsim \rangle$, and because of its importance in physical measurement it is a well-studied mathematical object (see Krantz et al., 1971, chap. 3; Narens, 1985, chap. 2). For simplicity, let us drop the A subscripts and just write $\langle A, \succsim, \bigcirc, a_o \rangle$.

2. Properties of $\bigcirc$ and $\succsim$

It is clear that those concatenation structures arising from additive conjoint ones will involve some constraints on $\bigcirc$ and on how it and $\succsim$ are related. It is not terribly difficult to show that independence of the conjoint structure forces the following *monotonicity* property:

$$a \succsim a' \text{ is equivalent to } a \bigcirc b \succsim a' \bigcirc b \text{ and} \tag{33a}$$

$$b \succsim b' \text{ is equivalent to } a \bigcirc b \succsim a \bigcirc b'. \tag{33b}$$

Intuitively, these conditions are highly plausible: Increasing either factor of the operation increases the value. The double-cancellation property implies the following property of $\bigcirc$, which is called *associativity:*

$$a \bigcirc (b \bigcirc c) \sim (a \bigcirc b) \bigcirc c. \tag{34}$$

A third property is that a_o acts like a "zero" element:

$$a_o \bigcirc a \sim a \bigcirc a_o \sim a. \tag{35}$$

Solvability ensures for every $a, b \in A$ not only that $a \bigcirc b$ is defined, but that each element a has an inverse element a^{-1} with the property:

$$a \bigcirc a^{-1} \sim a^{-1} \bigcirc a \sim a_o. \tag{36}$$

Finally, we formulate the Archimedean property of such a structure. By repeated applications of Eq. (34), it does not matter which sequence of binary groupings is used in concatenating n elements. Let $a(n)$ denote n concatenations of a with itself. Suppose $a > a_o$. The Archimedean assumption says that for any $b \in A$ one can always find n sufficiently large so that $a(n) > b$. Intuitively, this means that a and b are commensurable.

3. Hölder's Theorem

In 1901 the German mathematician O. Hölder proved a version of the following very general result (Hölder, 1901/1996). Suppose a structure $\langle A, \succsim, \bigcirc, a_\circ \rangle$ satisfies the the following properties: $\succsim$ is a weak order, monotonicity, associativity, identity, inverses, and Archimedeaness, Eqs. (22), (23), and (33) through (36). Such structures are called Archimedean ordered groups, the term group encompassing the three properties of Eqs. (34) through (36) (see footnote 2). The result is that such a structure has a representation ϕ into the additive real numbers, which means that ϕ is order preserving, Eq. (24), and additive over $\bigcirc$:

$$\phi(a \bigcirc b) = \phi(a) + \phi(b). \tag{37}$$

From this fact, it is fairly easy to establish that a conjoint structure satisfying independence, Eq. (28), double cancellation, Eq. (29), solvability, and a suitable Archimedean condition has an additive representation.

4. Ratio Scale Uniqueness

The nonuniqueness of Hölder's additive representation is even more restricted than that for conjoint structures: ϕ and ψ are two additive representations if and only if for some constant $r > 0$, $\psi = r\phi$. The class of such representations is said to form a *ratio scale* (Stevens, 1946, 1951). A conjoint representation is interval rather than ratio because the choice of the "zero" element $a_\circ$ is completely arbitrary; however, in Hölder's additive structure the concatenation of the zero element with another element leaves the latter unchanged and so $\phi(a_\circ) = \bigcirc$ in all representations ϕ.

5. Counting Yields the Representation

The key to the construction of a representation is to fix some element $c > a_\circ$ and find the number of copies of c that are required to approximate any element a. This is done by considering m copies of a and using the Archimedean axiom to find the smallest n, which is a function of m, such that $c(n)$ just exceeds $a(m)$, that is, $c(n - 1) \precsim a(m) \precsim c(n)$. One shows that n/m approaches a limit as m approaches ∞ and defines $\phi(a)$ be that limit where, of course, $\phi(c) = 1$. Next one proves that such limits are additive over $\bigcirc$.

6. Extensive Structures

If one looks just at the positive part of A, that is, $A_+ = \{a: a \in A \text{ and } a > a_\circ\}$ with $\succsim$ and $\bigcirc$ restricted to that part, one has the added feature that for all a, $b \in A_+$, both $a \bigcirc b > a$ and $a \bigcirc b < b$, and $a > b$ implies $c > a_\circ$ such that $a \bigcirc c > b$ ($c = a \bigcirc b^{-1}$). Such a structure is called *extensive* (in contrast to the intensive structures discussed in section V). One can use Hölder's theorem to show that any extensive structure has a ratio scale representation into $\langle \mathbb{R}_+, \geq, + \rangle$, the ordered, additive, positive real numbers.

These structures were, in fact, the first to have been formalized as models of certain basic types of physical measurement. For example, if A denotes straight rods, with $\gtrsim$ the qualitative ordering of length obtained by direct comparison and $\bigcirc$ the operation of abutting rods along a straight line, then Eqs. (22), and (23), and (33) through (36) are all elementary physical laws. Mass, charge, and several other basic physical quantities can be measured in this fashion.

Aside from their indirect use in proving the existence of additive conjoint measurement representations, extensive structures have played only a limited descriptive role in the behavioral and social sciences, although they can serve as null hypotheses that are then disconfirmed. It is not that there is a dearth of operations but rather that one or more of Eqs. (33) through (36) usually fail, most often associativity, Eq. (34). For example, various forms of averaging, although involving $+$ in their representation, are not associative (see section V). Receiving two goods or uncertain alternatives is an operation of some importance in studying decision making, and it is unclear at present whether or not it is associative.

7. Combining Extensive and Conjoint Structures

Often the components of a conjoint structure $\langle A \times U, \gtrsim \rangle$ are themselves endowed with empirical operations $*_A$ and/or $*_U$ that form extensive structures on A and U, respectively. Many physical examples exist, for example, mass and velocity ordered by kinetic energy, as well as psychological ones such as sound intensities to the two ears. An important question is, how are the three structures interrelated?

One relation of great physical importance is the following *distribution law:* For all $a, b, c, d \in A$, $u, v \in U$,

$$\text{if } (a, u) \sim (c, v) \text{ and } (b, u) \sim (d, v), \text{ then } (a *_A b, u) \sim (c *_A d, v), \quad (38)$$

and a similar condition is true for the second component. It has been shown that if ϕ_A and ϕ_U are additive representations of the two extensive structures, then there is a constant β such that

$$\phi_A \phi_U^\beta \tag{39}$$

is a multiplicative representation of $\langle A \times U, \gtrsim \rangle$. (Luce et al., 1990, summarize the results and provide references to the original literature.) The exponent β characterizes the trade-off between the two extensive measures. For example, in the case of kinetic energy β is 2, which simply says a change in velocity by a factor k is equivalent to a change in mass by a factor k^2. Such trade-off connections as given by Eq. (39) are common in physical measurement, and their existence underlies the dimensional structure of classical physical measurement. Moreover, their existence, as embodied in Eqs. (38) and (39), is also the reason that physical units are always products of powers of several basic extensive measures, for example, the unit of energy, the erg, is $g \cdot cm^2 / s^2$. (For details see chap. 10 of Krantz et al., 1971, and chap. 22 of Luce et al., 1990.)

Luce (1977) also studied another possible relation between an additive conjoint structure whose components are also extensive. Let $a(j)$ denote j concatenations of a, and suppose there exist positive integers m and n such that for all positive integers i and $a, b \in A$ and $u, v \in U$,

$$(a, u) \sim (b, v) \Rightarrow (a(i^m), u(i^n)) \sim (b(i^m), v(i^n)). \tag{40}$$

Under some assumptions about the smoothness of the representations, it can be shown that the representation is of the form:

$$r_A \phi_A^{\beta/m} + r_U \phi_U^{\beta/n} + s, \tag{41}$$

where $r_A > 0$, $r_U > 0$, and s are real constants. For example, the Levelt et al. (1972) conjoint analysis of loudness judgments over the two ears supported not only additivity but the power functions of Eq. (41); however, see section IV.D. The power functions arising in both Eqs. (39) and (41) are psychologically interesting because, as is discussed in section VII.C, substantial empirical evidence exists for believing that many psychological attributes are approximately power functions of the corresponding physical measures of intensity. Of course, as noted earlier, later studies have cast doubt on the additivity of loudness between the ears.

D. Probabilistic Conjoint Measurement

The variability that accompanies psychophysical data rules out the possibility of direct empirical tests of algebraic measurement axioms. Probabilistic versions of both extensive measurement (Falmagne, 1980) and conjoint measurement (Falmagne, 1976) have been proposed, although as we shall see they often exhibit the difficulty alluded to in section I. We treat only the conjoint case here.

Consider the discrimination of pure tones (a, u) presented binaurally: a denotes the intensity of a pure tone presented to the left ear of an observer, and u is the intensity of the same frequency presented, in phase, to the right ear. The data are summarized in terms of the probability $P_{au,bv}$ that the binaural stimulus (a, u) is judged at least as loud as stimulus (b, v).

One class of general theories for such data that reflects the idea that the stimuli can be represented additively asserts that

$$P_{au,bv} = H[l(a) + r(u), l(b) + r(v)] \tag{42}$$

for some suitable functions l, r, and H with $H(u, u) = \frac{1}{2}$.

To generate a loudness match between two binaural tones, one fixes three of the monaural components, say, a, u, and v, and seeks b such that $P_{au,bv} = \frac{1}{2}$. Of course, this must be an estimate and is therefore subject to variability. This suggests replacing the deterministic, but empirically unattainable prediction from Eq. (42) that

$$l(a) + r(u) = l(b) + r(v) \tag{43}$$

by a more realistic one that substitutes a random variable $\mathbf{U}_{auv}$ for b:

$$l(\mathbf{U}_{auv}) = l(a) + r(u) - r(v) + \mathbf{E}_{auv}, \tag{44}$$

where $\mathbf{E}_{auv}$ is a random error.

This proposal illustrates the difficulty in simultaneously modeling structure and randomness. The assumption that the error is additive in the additively transformed data seems arbitrary and is, perhaps, unrealistic. Certainly, no justification has been provided. One would like to see Eq. (44) as the conclusion of a theorem, not as a postulate. Of course, writing equations like Eq. (44) is a widespread, if dubious, tradition in statistics.

If the random error $\mathbf{E}_{auv}$ is assumed to have *median* zero, then the random representation Eq. (44) simplifies to the deterministic Eq. (43) upon taking medians over the population. This suggests studying the properties of the function $m_{uv}(a) = \text{Median}(\mathbf{U}_{auv})$. Falmagne (1976) showed, in the context of natural side conditions, that if the medians satisfy the following property of *cancellation*,

$$m_{uv}[m_{vw}(a)] = m_{uw}(a), \tag{45}$$

then they can be represented in the additive form of Eq. (43): $l(a) + r(u) = l[m_{uv}(a)] + r(v)$. The linkage between the median functions and algebraic conjoint measurement is provided by a relation $\precsim$ over the factor pairs:

$$au \precsim bv \text{ is equivalent to } m_{uv}(a) \le b. \tag{46}$$

It is straightforward to show that $\precsim$ is a weak order and that cancellation, Eq. (45), implies the double cancellation condition, Eq. (29), of conjoint measurement.

Falmagne found the cancellation condition to be supported by empirical data, in agreement with earlier work of Levelt, Riemersma, and Bunt (1972). Later, however, Gigerenzer and Strube (1983) showed that cancellation breaks down when one of the monaural components sufficiently dominates the other.

Special cases of Eq. (42), namely,

$$P_{au,bv} = F[l(a) + r(u) - l(b) - r(v)] , \tag{47a}$$

$$P_{au,bv} = F\left(\frac{l(a) + r(u)}{l(b) + r(v)} \right) , \tag{47b}$$

$$P_{au,bv} = F[l(a)r(u) - l(b)r(v)] , \tag{47c}$$

were investigated by Falmagne, Iverson, and Marcovici (1979) and Falmagne and Iverson (1979). Of these, the second, Eq. (47b), was found to provide the best account of discrimination data. Note that this additive-ratio model suggests an alternative form to Eq. (44), namely,

$$l(a) + r(u) = [l(\mathbf{U}_{auv}) + r(v)]\mathbf{E}_{auv}. \tag{48}$$

Once again, it should be apparent that the theoretical representation of both structure and randomness seems to rest on arbitrary assumptions before the analysis can proceed.

E. Questions

The reader probably has some unresolved questions about the measurement structures we have examined. One likely question centers on the curious fact that these examples have included only three scale types: ordinal, interval, and ratio. The psychologist S. S. Stevens (1946, 1951) was the first to point out that only these scale types seemed to play a serious role in the physical sciences. Is there a reason for this? During the 1980s it was discovered that, indeed, there is a fairly deep reason, which we examine in section VI.

A second major question for psychologists is whether measurement is limited to additive conjoint and extensive structures. Additivity is clearly too restrictive for the behavioral and social sciences. Do we understand nonadditive structures well enough for them to be useful in science? The answer is yes, and the general theory is outlined partly in section V and more fully in section VI.

V. WEIGHTED-AVERAGE MEASUREMENT FOR AN ORDERED ATTRIBUTE

In addition to the attributes endowed with concatenation operations that have additive representations, other important attributes have averaging representations. To illustrate the scientific range we cite four examples:

- Numerical weighted averages, such as

$$\mu x + (1 - \mu)y, \tag{49}$$

where the weight $\mu \in (0, 1)$, abound in statistical data processing.
- When two physical objects at different temperatures are permitted to come into equilibrium with each other, their final temperature is a weighted average of the two initial temperatures with weights that depend on the compositions and volumes of the objects.

- Psychophysicists sometimes study subjective attributes, such as brightness or loudness, by having observers produce stimuli that lie a specified fraction along the subjective interval between two experimenter presented stimuli. When the fraction is $\frac{1}{2}$, the method is called *bisection*. We denote the bisection point of stimuli a, b either by function notation $F(a, b)$ or operator notation $a \bigcirc b$.
- In theories of decision making, *uncertain alternatives* (or *gambles*) are alternatives consisting of outcomes determined by chance events arising in some "experiment."[12] In the binary case, $a\bigcirc_E b$ denotes the uncertain alternative in which consequence a is received if event E occurs and b otherwise when the "experiment" is conducted. The simplest example is a lottery. An important class of theories for such binary gambles, known generically as *subjective expected utility* (*SEU*), takes the form of weighted average representations.

Clearly, understanding those structures leading to averaging representations is of broad scientific interest. This section describes some of what we know about these structure and their applications.

A. Binary Intensive Structures

1. Betweenness, Idempotence, and Bisymmetry

Consider again a structure $\mathcal{A} = \langle A, \succsim, \bigcirc \rangle$, where $\succsim$ is a binary relation and $\bigcirc$ a binary operation on A. Our first concern is to develop properties that $\mathcal{A}$ must exhibit in order to have a weighted average representation. As before, weak ordering, Eqs. (22) and (23), and monotonicity, Eq. (33), must be satisfied. But it is easy to see that other properties of extensive structures fail.

For example, when $\bigcirc$ has an averaging representation, $\bigcirc$ cannot be positive in the sense that both $a \bigcirc b > a$ and $a \bigcirc b > b$, but rather a *betweenness* property holds: For all a, b, $\in A$ with $a \succsim b$,

$$a \succsim a \bigcirc b \succsim b \text{ and } a \succsim b \bigcirc a \succsim b, \tag{50}$$

from which it follows immediately that for all $a \in A$,

$$a \bigcirc a \sim a, \tag{51}$$

which property is called *idempotence*.

Another property that fails is associativity, Eq. (34); it is replaced by a relationship among four, not three, elements. Using Eq. (49), consider the separate weighted averages of w, x and y, z. Then the weighted average of these two averages is easily seen to be

[12] The term *experiment* is used here in the special sense of statistics, not in the usual psychological sense.

$$\mu[\mu w + (1 - \mu)x] + (1 - \mu)[\mu y + (1 - \mu)z] = \mu^2 w$$
$$+ \mu(1 - \mu)(x + y) + (1 - \mu)^2 z.$$

Observe that because $x + y = y + x$, this is the same as averaging the pairs w, y and x, z and then averaging the results. Therefore, the qualitative analog is

$$(a \bigcirc b) \bigcirc (c \bigcirc d) \sim (a \bigcirc c) \bigcirc (b \bigcirc d), \tag{52}$$

a property known as *bisymmetry*.

2. The Representation and Reduction to Conjoint Measurement

A concatenation structure $\mathscr{A}$ that satisfies weak ordering, monotonicity, and betweenness is called *intensive*. One can show that an intensive structure that is bisymmetric, suitably solvable, and suitably Archimedean has a numerical representation ϕ and a constant $\mu \in (0, 1)$ such that for all $a, b \in A$

$$\phi(a \bigcirc b) = \mu\phi(a) + (1 - \mu)\phi(b). \tag{53}$$

One way to prove this is to define $\succsim'$ on $A \times A$ by:

$$(a, c) \succsim' (b, d) \text{ if and only if } a \bigcirc c \succsim b \bigcirc d. \tag{54}$$

One then shows that the assumed properties are sufficient to prove that the conjoint structure[13] $\langle A \times A, \succsim' \rangle$ satisfies the conditions of section IV.B, so it has an additive representation. Of course, there were two functions in that representation, see Eq. (27), but in this case, where $U = A$, they can be proved to be proportional.

As with conjoint measurement, the representation of Eq. (53) is of interval scale type.

From an empirical point of view, the upshot of this result is that idempotence and bisymmetry are the key properties distinguishing a structure having an averaging representation from an associative structure with an additive representation.

Probably the most extensive uses of averaging operations in psychology are found in three areas: statistics, individual decision making (section V.C), and applications of a method called functional measurement (section V.D). Although binary models are of some interest in these applications, the most interesting cases involve combining more than two entities at a time. We turn to those cases in the next section before taking up applications.

B. Generalized Averaging

One can continue to think of combining more than two things as an operation, but usually we use functional notation. Therefore the structure is $\langle A,$

---

[13] This is the special case of the earlier conjoint structures with $U = A$.

$\gtrsim, F\rangle$, where $F{:}A \times \ldots \times A \to A$ (just as $O{:}A \times A \to A$); so a typical result from the operation is written as $a = F(a_1, \ldots, a_n)$. It is not difficult to see that monotonicity generalizes to saying that for any component i,

$$a_i' \gtrsim a_i \text{ is equivalent to}$$
$$F(a_1, \ldots, a_i', \ldots, a_n) \gtrsim F(a_1, \ldots, a_i, \ldots, a_n).$$

Idempotence becomes

$$F(a, \ldots a, \ldots a) = a.$$

There is no obvious generalization of bisymmetry, but we do not really need one because it suffices to require that bisymmetry hold on any pair of components for any arbitrary, but fixed, choice for the remaining $n - 2$.

The resulting representation on assuming weak order, monotonicity, idempotence, and suitable solvability and Archimedean properties is the existence of $\phi{:}A \to \mathbb{R}$ and n numerical constants μ_i such that

$$\mu_i \geq 0, \ i = 1, \ldots, n, \quad \text{and} \quad \sum_{i=1}^{n} \mu_i = 1 \tag{55a}$$

$$\phi[F(a_1, \ldots, a_n)] = \sum_{i=1}^{n} \mu_i \phi(a_i). \tag{55b}$$

C. Utility of Uncertain Alternatives

1. Subjective Expected Utility (SEU)

For decision making, the model is somewhat more complex and developing proofs is considerably more difficult. But the representation arrived at is easy enough to state. A typical uncertain alternative g assigns consequences to events; that is, it is an assignment $g(E_i) = g_i, \ i = 1, \ldots, n$, where the E_i are disjoint events taken from a family of events and the g_i are consequences from a set of possible consequences (e.g., amounts of money). Lottery examples abound in which the events are often sets of ordered k-tuples of numbers, where k usually is between 3 and 10, to a few of which award amounts are assigned.[14] The SEU theories in their simplest form assert that for a sufficiently rich collection of events and uncertain alternatives there is a (subjective) probability measure S over the family of events,[15] and there is

[14] For example, in California the "Daily 3" requires that the player select a three-digit number; if it agrees with the random number chosen, the player receives a $500 payoff. Clearly there is 1 chance in 1000 of being correct and at $1 a ticket, the expected value is $.50.

[15] The term subjective arises from the fact that the probability S is inferred for each decision maker from his or her choices; it is not an objective probability.

an interval scale utility function U over uncertain alternatives,[16] including the consequences, such that the preference order over alternatives is preserved by

$$U(g) = \sum_{i=1}^{n} S(E_i) U(g_i).$$ (56)

This is the expectation of U of the consequences relative to the subjective probability measure S. The first fully complete axiomatization of such a representation was by Savage (1954). There have been many subsequent versions, some of which are summarized in Fishburn (1970, 1982, 1988) and Wakker (1989).

2. Who Knows the SEU Formula?

Note the order of information underlying the SEU formulation, Eq. (56): The patterns of preferences are the given empirical information; if they exhibit certain properties (formulated below), they determine the existence of the numerical representation of Eq. (56). It is not assumed that the representation drives the preferences. The representation is a creature of the theorist, and there is no imputation whatsoever that people know U and S and carry out, consciously or otherwise, the arithmetic computations involved in Eq. (56). These remarks are true in the same sense that the differential equation describing the flight path of a ballistic missile is a creation of the physicist, not of the missile.

The mechanisms underlying the observed process—decision or motion—simply are not dealt with in such a theory. Many cognitive psychologists are uncomfortable with such a purely phenomenological approach and feel a need to postulate hypothetical information processing mechanisms to account for what is going on. Busemeyer and Townsend (1993) illustrate such theorizing, and certainly, to the degree that psychology can be reduced to biology, such mechanisms will have to be discovered. At present there is a wide gulf between the mechanisms of cognitive psychologists and biologists.

It should be remarked that throughout the chapter the causal relation between behavior and representation is that the latter, which is for the convenience of the scientist, derives from the former and is not assumed to be a behavioral mechanism. We did not bring up this fact earlier mainly because there has not been much tendency to invert the causal order until one comes to decision theory.

---

[16] This use of the symbol U as a function is very different from its earlier use as the second component of a conjoint structure. To be consistent we should use ϕ, but it is fairly common practice to use U for utility functions.

3. Necessary Properties Underlying SEU

The most basic, and controversial, property underlying SEU and any other representation that says there is an order-preserving numerical representation is that $\succsim$ is a weak order. Although, many accept this as a basic tenet of rationality, others question it both conceptually and empirically. For a thorough summary of the issues and an extensive list of references, see van Acker (1990).

Aside from $\succsim$ being a weak order, the most important necessary properties leading to Eq. (56) are two forms of monotonicity, which can be described informally as follows. *Consequence monotonicity* means that if any g_i is replaced by a more preferred g_i', with all other consequences and the events fixed, the resulting g' is preferred to g. *Event monotonicity* means that if among the consequences of g, g_1 is the most preferred and g_n is the least and if E_1 is augmented at the expense of E_n, then the modified uncertain alternative will be preferred to the original one.

A third property arises from the linear nature of Eq. (56). It is most easily stated for the case in which the chance events are characterized in terms of given probabilities and the representation has the simplifying feature that $S(p_i) = p_i$. In this case we speak of the alternatives as *lotteries* and the representation obtained from Eq. (56) with $S(E_i)$ replaced by p_i as *expected utility (EU)*.

Suppose g and h are lotteries from which a new lottery $(g, p; h, 1 - p)$ is composed. The interpretation is that with probability p one gets to play lottery g, and with probability $1 - p$ one gets to play h. Then, chance picks one of g and h, which is then played independently of the preceding chance decision. When g is run, the consequence g_i occurs with probability p_i, $i = 1$, . . . , n, and when h is run, the consequence h_i occurs with probability q_i, $i = 1, . . . , m$. Assuming EU, we see that

$$U(g, p; h, 1 - p) = pU(g) + (1 - p)U(h)$$

$$= p \sum_{i=1}^{n} U(g_i)p_i + (1 - p) \sum_{j=1}^{m} U(h_j)q_j$$

$$= U[g_1, p_1p; . . . , g_n, p_np; h_1, q_1$$
$$(1 - p); . . . ; h_n, q_n(1 - p)].$$

Thus, according to the EU representation,

$$(g, p; h, 1 - p) \sim [g_1, p_1p; . . . ;g_n, p_n p; h_1, q_1(1 - p); . . . ;$$
$$h_n, q_n(1 - p)]. \qquad (57)$$

This property is known as *reduction of compound lotteries*. Combining consequence monotonicity with the (often implicit) reduction of compound

gambles is known among economists as *independence*.[17] The use of the re-
duction-of-compound-gambles principle is implicit when, for example, one
assumes, as is common in economics, that the lotteries can be modeled as
random variables, in which case Eq. (57) is actually an equality because no
distinction is made among various alternative realizations of a random variable.

For uncertain alternatives, a principle, similar in spirit to the reduction of
compound lotteries, reads as follows: If two alternatives are identical except
for the sequence in which certain events are realized, then the decision
maker treats them as equivalent. These are called *accounting equivalences* (see,
e.g., Luce, 1990b). When all conceivable equivalences hold, we speak of
universal accounting. Consider the following important specific equivalence.
Let $a\bigcirc_E b$ denote that a is the consequence if E occurs and b otherwise. Then
we say *event commutativity* holds if

$$(a\bigcirc_E b)\bigcirc_D b \sim (a\bigcirc_D b)\bigcirc_E b. \tag{58}$$

The left term is interpreted to mean that two independent experiments are
run and a is received only if event D occurs in the first and E in the second.
Otherwise, the consequence is b. The right term is identical except that E
must occur in the first and D in the second.

Consequence monotonicity and the reduction of compound lotteries are
necessary for EU, and they go a long way toward justifying the representation. Similarly, consequence and event monotonicity and universal accounting equivalences are necessary for SEU and they, too, go a long way toward
justifying SEU. For this reason, they have received considerable empirical
attention.

4. Empirical Violations of Necessary Properties

Perhaps the most basic assumption of these decision models is that preferences are *context independent*. It is implicitly assumed whenever we attach a
utility to an alternative without regard to the set of alternatives from which
it might be chosen. To the extent this is wrong, the measurement enterprise, as usually cast, is misguided. MacCrimmon, Stanburg, and Wehrung
(1980) have presented very compelling evidence against context independence. They created two sets of lotteries, each with four binary lotteries plus
a fixed sum, s. The sum s and one lottery, l, were common to both sets.
Medium level executives, at a business school for midcareer training, were
asked (among other things) to rank order each set by preference. A substantial fraction ordered s and l differently in the two sets.

---

[17] The word *independence* has many different but related meanings in these areas, so care is
required to keep straight which one is intended.

The next most basic assumption to the utility approach is transitivity of preference. To the degree failures have been established, they appear to derive from other considerations. Context effects are surely one source. A second is demonstrated by the famed preference reversal phenomena in which lottery *g* is chosen over *h* but, when asked to assign monetary evaluations, the subject assigns less value to *g* than to *h* (Lichenstein & Slovic, 1971; Luce, 1992b, for a list of references; Slovic & Lichenstein, 1983). This intransitivity probably reflects a deep inconsistency between judged and choice certainty equivalents rather than being a genuine intransitivity.

Long before intransitivity or context effects were seriously examined, independence and event monotonicity were cast in serious doubt by, respectively, Allais (1953; see Allais & Hagen, 1979) and Ellsberg (1961), who both formulated thought experiments in which reasonable people violate these conditions. These are described in detail in various sources including Luce and Raiffa (1957/1989) and Fishburn (1970). Subsequent empirical work has repeatedly confirmed these results; see Luce (1992b) and Schoemaker (1982, 1990).

The major consequence for theory arising from the failure of event monotonicity is that Eq. (56) can still hold, but only if S is a weight that is not a probability. In particular, additivity, that is, for disjoint events $D, E,$ $S(D \cup E) = S(D) + S(E)$—although true of probability—cannot hold if event monotonicity is violated. This has led to the development of models leading to the representation of Eq. (56), but with S a nonadditive weight, not a probability.

The failure of independence is less clear-cut in its significance: Is the difficulty with consequence monotonicity, with the reduction of compound gambles, or both? As Luce (1992b) discussed, there has been an unwarranted tendency to attribute it to monotonicity. This has determined the direction most (economist) authors have taken in trying to modify the theory to make it more descriptive.

Data on the issue have now been gathered. Kahneman and Tversky (1979) reported studies, based on fairly hypothetical judgments, of both independence and monotonicity, with the former rejected and the latter sustained. Several studies (Birnbaum, 1992; Birnbaum, Coffey, Mellers, & Weiss, 1992; Mellers, Weiss, & Birnbaum, 1992) involving judgments of certainty equivalents have shown what seem to be systematic violations of monotonicity. Figure 11 illustrates a sample data plot. In an experimental setting, von Winterfeldt, Chung, Luce, and Cho (1997), using both judgments and a choice procedure, questioned that conclusion, especially when choices rather than judgments are involved.[18] They also argued that even

---

[18] This distinction is less clear than it might seem. Many methods exist for which the classification is obscure, but the studies cited used methods that lie at the ends of the continuum.

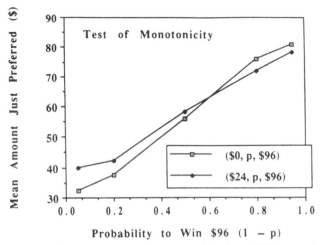

FIGURE 11   Certainty equivalents for binary gambles $(x, p; \$96)$ versus $1 - p$ for two values of x, $0 and $24. Note the nonmonotonicity for the two larger values of $1 - p$. From Figure 1 of "Violations of Monotonicity and Contextual Effects in Choice-Based Certainty Equivalents," by M. H. Birnbaum, 1992, *Psychological Science, 3,* p. 312. Reprinted with the permission of Cambridge University Press.

with judgments, the apparent violations seem to be within the noise level of the data.

Evidence is accumulating that judged and choice-determined CEs of gambles simply are not in general the same (Bostic, Herrnstein, & Luce, 1990; Mellers, Chang, Birnbaum, & Ordóñez, 1992; Tversky, Slovic, & Kahneman, 1990). This difference is found even when the experimenter explains what a choice certainty equivalent is and asks subjects to report them directly. Evidence for the difference is presented in Figure 12. A question of some interest is whether, throughout psychophysics, judged indifferences such as curves of equal brightness, fail to predict accurately comparisons between pairs of stimuli. Surprisingly, we know of no systematic study of these matters; it has simply been taken for granted that they should be the same.

Among decision theorists, the most common view is that, to the degree a difference exists, choices are the more basic, and most theoretical approaches have accepted that. One exception is Luce, Mellers, and Chang (1993) who have shown that the preceding data anomalies, including Figure 12, are readily accounted for by assuming that certainty equivalents are basic and the choices are derived from them somewhat indirectly by establishing a reference level that is determined by the choice context, recoding alternatives as gains and losses relative to the reference level, and then using a sign-dependent utility model of a type discussed in section VI.D.2. Indeed, in that section we take up a variety of generalized utility models.

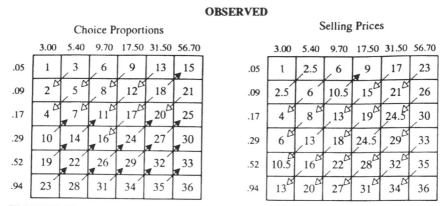

OBSERVED

FIGURE 12   Rank orders of 36 gambles established from choices and from selling prices (a form of certainty equivalent). The stimuli on the negative diagonal are approximately equal in expected value. Note the sharply different patterns. Adapted from Figure 5 of "Is the Choice Correct Primitive? On Using Certainty Equivalents and Reference Levels to Predict Choices among Gambles," by R. D. Luce, B. Mellers, and S. J. Chang, 1992, *Journal of Risk and Uncertainty, 6,* p. 133. Reprinted with permission.

D. Functional Measurement

Anderson (1981, 1982, 1991a, b, c) has provided detailed and comprehensive summaries, along with numerous applications to a wide range of psychological phenomena—including psychophysical, personality, and utility judgments—of a method that he and others using the same approach call *functional measurement,* presumably with the ambiguity intentional. The method begins with a particular experimental procedure and uses, primarily, three types of representations: additive, multiplicative, and averaging. These are described as "psychological laws" relating how the independent variables influence the dependent one.

Stimuli are ordered *n*-tuples of (often discrete) factors, where *n* usually varies within an experiment. This differs from conjoint measurement in which the number of factors, *n,* is fixed. For example, a person may be described along various subsets of several dimensions, such as physical attractiveness, morality, honesty, industry, and so on. Subjects are requested to assign ratings (from a prescribed rating scale) to stimuli that are varied according to some factorial design on the factors. The assigned ratings are viewed as constituting a psychophysical law relating measures of the stimulus to subjective contributions.

Then, assuming that one of the three representations—additive, multiplicative, or averaging—describes the data (usually without any nonlinear transformation of them), Anderson developed computational schemes for estimating the parameters of the representation and for evaluating goodness of fit.

As a simple example, he readily distinguished the additive from averaging representation as follows. Suppose A_1 and A_2 are two stimulus factors and that a_1 and a_2 are both desirable attributes but with a_1 more desirable than a_2. Thus, in an additive representation,

$$\phi_1(a_1) < \phi_1(a_1) + \phi_2(a_2) = \phi(a_1, a_2),$$

whereas in an averaging one

$$\phi_1(a_1) = w\phi_1(a_1) + (1 - w)\phi_1(a_1) > w\phi_1(a_1) + (1 - w)\phi_2(a_2)$$
$$= \phi(a_1, a_2).$$

This observable distinction generalizes to more than two factors.

Much judgmental data in which the number of factors is varied favors the averaging model. For example, data on person perception make clear, as seems plausible, that a person who is described only as "brilliant" is judged more desirable than one who is described as both "brilliant and somewhat friendly." Anderson's books and papers are replete with examples and experimental detail.

VI. SCALE TYPE, NONADDITIVITY, AND INVARIANCE

In the earlier sections we encountered two apparently unrelated, unresolved issues—the possible levels of nonuniqueness, called *scale types,* and the existence of nonadditive structures. We examine these issues now. As we shall see, a close relation exists between them and another topic, invariance, only briefly mentioned thus far.

A. Symmetry and Scale Type

1. Classification of Scale Types

As we have noted, numerical representations of a qualitative structure usually are not unique. The nonuniqueness is characterized in what are called *uniqueness theorems.* We have already encountered three scale types of increasing strength: ordinal, interval, and ratio. The reader may have noted that we said nothing about the uniqueness of threshold structures (section IV.A.3). This is because no concise characterization exists.

S. S. Stevens (1946, 1951), a famed psychophysicist, first commented on the ubiquity of these three types of scales. In a transatlantic debate with members of a commission of the British Association for the Advancement of Science, Stevens argued that what is crucial in measurement is not, as was claimed by the British physicists and philosophers of science, extensive structures as such but rather structures of any type that lead to a numerical representation of either the interval or, better yet,[19] ratio level.

2. The Automorphism Formulation

More than 30 years later, Narens (1981a, b) posed and formulated the following questions in an answerable fashion: Why these scale types? Are there others? The key to approaching the problem is to describe at the qualitative level what gives rise to the nonuniqueness. It is crucial to note that at its source are the structure-preserving transformations of the structure onto itself—the so-called *automorphisms* of the structure.[20] These automorphisms describe the symmetries of the structure in the sense that everything appears to be the same before and after the mapping. The gist of the uniqueness theorems really is to tell us about the symmetries of the structure. Thus, the symmetries in the ratio case form a one-parameter family; in the interval case they form a two-parameter family; and in the ordinal case they form a countable family.

Moreover, Narens observed that these three families of automorphisms are all *homogeneous:* each point of the structure is, structurally, exactly like every other point in the sense that, given any two points, some automorphism maps the one into the other. A second fact of the ratio and interval cases, but not of the ordinal cases, is that when the values of an automorphism are specified at N points (where N is 1 in the ratio case and 2 in the interval one), then it is specified completely. This he called *finite uniqueness.* An ordinal structure is not finitely unique; it requires countably many values to specify a particular automorphism.

Narens attacked following the question: For the class of ordered structures that are finitely unique and homogeneous and that have representations on the real numbers, what automorphism groups can arise?[21] He developed partial answers and Alper (1987) completed the program.[22] Such structures have automorphism groups of either ratio or interval type or something in between the two. Examples of the latter kind are the sets of numerical transformations $x \rightarrow k^n x + s$, where x is any real number, k is a fixed positive number, n varies over all of the integers, positive and

---

[19] Ratio is better in that it admits far more structures than does the interval form. We will see this when we compare Eqs. (59) and (60). Ratio is stronger than interval in having one less degree of freedom, but it is weaker in the sense of admitting more structures.

[20] The term *automorphism* means "self-isomorphism." Put another way, an automorphism is an isomorphic representation of the structure onto itself.

[21] The set of automorphisms forms a mathematical group under the operation * of function composition, which is associative and has an inverse relative to the identity automorphism (see footnote 2).

[22] Alper also gave a (very complex) characterization of the automorphism groups of structures that are finitely unique but not homogeneous.

negative, and s is any real number; these are 1-point homogeneous and 2-point unique.

The key idea in Alper's proof is this. An automorphism is called a *translation* if either it is the identity or no point of the structure stays fixed under the automorphism.[23] For example, all the automorphisms of a ratio-scale structure are translations, but only some are translations in the case of interval scales. The ordering in the structure induces an ordering on the translations: If τ and σ are two translations, define $\tau \gtrsim' \sigma$ if and only if $\tau(a) \gtrsim \sigma(a)$ for all $a \in A$. The difficult parts of the proof are, surprisingly, in showing that the composition of two translations, $\tau * \sigma(a) = \tau[\sigma(a)]$, is also a translation, so * is an operation on the translations, and that this group of translations is itself homogeneous. The ordered group of translations is also shown to be Archimedean, so by Hölder's theorem (section IV.C.3) it can be represented isomorphically in $\langle \mathbb{R}_+, \gtrsim, \cdot \rangle$. Moreover, using the homogeneity of the translations one can map the structure itself isomorphically into the translations and thus into $\langle \mathbb{R}_+, \gtrsim, \cdot \rangle$. This is a numerical representation in which the translations appear as multiplication by positive constants. In that representation, any other automorphism is proved to be a power transformation $x \rightarrow sx^r$, $r > 0$, $s > 0$.

The upshot of the Narens-Alper development is that as long as one deals with homogeneous structures that are finitely unique and have a representation onto the real numbers,[24] *none* lie between the interval and the ordinal-like cases. Between the ratio and interval cases are other possibilities. We know of mathematical examples of these intermediate cases that exhibit certain periodic features (Luce & Narens, 1985), but so far they seem to have played no role in science. When it comes to nonhomogeneous structures, little that is useful can be said in general, but some that are nearly homogeneous are quite important (see section VI.D).

B. Nonadditivity and Scale Type

1. Nonadditive Unit Concatenation Structures

The preceding results about scale type are not only of interest in understanding the possibilities of measurement, but they lead to a far more complete understanding of specific systems. For example, suppose $\mathcal{A} = \langle A, \gtrsim, \bigcirc \rangle$ is a homogeneous and finitely unique concatenation structure (section

---

[23] Structures with singular points that are fixed under all automorphisms—minimum, maximum, or zero points—are excluded in Alper's work. They are taken up in section VI.C.

[24] Luce and Alper (in preparation) have shown that the following conditions are necessary and sufficient for such a real representation: The structure is homogeneous, any pair of automorphisms cross back and forth only finitely many times, the set of translations is Archimedean, and the remaining automorphisms are Archimedean relative to all automorphisms.

IV.C.2) that is isomorphic to a real concatenation structure $\mathfrak{R} = \langle \mathbb{R}_+, \geq, \oplus \rangle$. By the Narens-Alper theorem, we may assume that $\mathfrak{R}$ has been chosen so that the translations are multiplication by positive constants. From that, Luce and Narens (1985), following more specific results in Cohen and Narens (1979), showed, among other things, that $\oplus$ has a simple numerical form, namely, there is a strictly increasing function $f:\mathbb{R} \to \mathbb{R}$ that also has two properties: $f(x)/x$ is a strictly decreasing function of x and

$$x \oplus y = yf(x/y). \tag{59}$$

Such structures are referred to as *unit concatenation structures*. The familiar extensive case is $f(z) = z + 1$, that is, $x \oplus y = x + y$. Equation (59) shows that unit concatenation structures have a very simple structure and that if one is confronted with data that appear to be nonadditive, one should attempt to estimate f.

The function f can be constructed as follows. For each natural number n, define $\theta(a, n) = \theta(a, n - 1)\text{o}a$ and $\theta(a,1) = a$. This is an inductive definition of one sense of what it means to make n copies of the element a of the structure.[25] These are called n-copy operators, and it can be shown that they are in fact translations of the structure. In essence, they act like the equally spaced markers on a ruler, and the isomorphism ϕ into the multiplicative reals can be constructed from them exactly as in extensive measurement. Once ϕ is constructed, one constructs f as follows: For any positive number z, find elements a and b such that $z = \phi(a)/\phi(b)$; then

$$f(z) = \phi(a \bigcirc b)/\phi(b).$$

Note that an empirical check is implicit in this, namely that

$$\frac{\phi(a)}{\phi(b)} = \frac{\phi(c)}{\phi(d)} \quad \text{implies} \quad \frac{\phi(a \bigcirc b)}{\phi(b)} = \frac{\phi(c \bigcirc d)}{\phi(d)}.$$

Because a structural property satisfied by any element of a homogeneous structure is also satisfied by all other elements of the structure, such structures must necessarily satisfy, for all $a \in A$, one of the following: (*positive*) $a \bigcirc a > a$; (*negative*) $a \bigcirc a < a$; or (*idempotent*) $a \bigcirc a \sim a$. It turns out that only the latter can be an interval scale case, and its representation on $\mathbb{R}$ (not $\mathbb{R}_+$) has the following simple rank-dependent form: For some constants $c, d \in (0, 1)$ and all $x, y \in \mathbb{R}$,

$$x \oplus y = \begin{cases} cx + (1 - c)y, & \text{if } x \geq y \\ dx + (1 - d)y, & \text{if } x < y. \end{cases} \tag{60}$$

[25] Recall that the structure is not associative, so a binary operation can be grouped in a large number of ways to form n copies of a single element. We have simply selected one of these, a so-called right-branching one.

This was the form mentioned in section V.C.4. It was first suggested in a psychological application by Birnbaum, Parducci, and Gifford (1971) and used in later papers (Birnbaum, 1974; Birnbaum & Stegner, 1979). As we shall see, it subsequently was rediscovered independently by economists and has been fairly widely applied in utility theory (see Quiggin, 1993, and Wakker, 1989).

2. Homogeneous Conjoint Structures

Without going into much detail, the construction outlined in section IV.C.1 for going from a conjoint to a concatenation structure did not depend on double cancellation being satisfied, so one can use that definition for more general conjoint structures. Moreover, the concept of homogeneity is easily formulated for the general case, and it forces homogeneity to hold in the induced concatenation structure. This reduction makes possible the use of the representation Eq. (59) to find a somewhat similar one for these nonadditive conjoint structures. The details are presented in Luce et al. (1990). Therefore, once again we have a whole shelf of nonadditive representations of ratio and interval types. Of these, only the rank-dependent cases have thus far found applications, but we anticipate their more widespread use once psychologists become aware of these comparatively simple possibilities.

3. Combining Concatenation and Conjoint Structures

Recall that we discussed additive conjoint structures with extensive structures on the components as a model of many simple physical laws and as the basis of the units of physics (section IV.C.7). This result has been generalized to unit concatenation structures, Eq. (59). Suppose a (not necessarily additive) conjoint structure has unit concatenation structures on its components and that the distribution property, Eq. (38), holds. Then one can show that the conjoint structure must in fact be additive and that the representation is that of Eq. (39). Indeed, if the components are endowed with ratio scale structures of any type, not necessarily concatenation structures, then a suitable generalization of distribution is known so that Eq. (39) continues to hold (Luce, 1987).

The upshot of these findings is that it is possible, in principle, to extend the structure of physical quantities to incorporate all sorts of measurements in addition to extensive ones without disturbing the pattern of units being products of powers of base units. Such an extension has yet to be carried out, but we now know that it is not precluded just because an attribute fails to be additive. For additional detail, see Luce et al. (1990, pp. 124–126).

C. Structures with Discrete Singular Points

1. Singular Points

As was remarked earlier, the class of nonhomogeneous structures is very diverse and ill understood.[26] However, one class is quite fully understood, and it plays a significant role in measurement. We discuss that class next.

A point of a structure is called *singular* if it stays fixed under every automorphism of the structure. The many familiar examples include any minimum point, such as zero length or zero mass; any maximum point, such as the velocity of light; and certain interior points, such as the status quo in utility measurement. Still another example arises in a class of preference models proposed by Coombs and summarized in his 1964 book (see also Coombs, 1975). He postulated that an individual's preferences arise from a comparison of the relative "distances" between each alternative and that individual's *ideal point* on the attribute for which preference is being expressed. Clearly, such an ideal point plays a distinctive role, namely, it is the zero point of dis-preference for that person. Coombs developed algorithms that use the data from a number of subjects to infer simultaneously the location of objects and ideal points in the space of preferences. However, the mathematical theory was never very fully developed. In contrast, the role of the status quo in utility theory is better analyzed.

2. Homogeneity Between Discrete Singular Points

Singular points have properties that render them unlike any other point in the structure; indeed, they keep the structure from being homogeneous. However, if a finite number of singular points exist, as is true in the applications just mentioned, the structure can be homogeneous between adjacent points. That is, if a and b are two points of the structure not separated by a singular point, then some automorphism of the structure takes a into b. Furthermore, if the structure has a generalized monotonic operation,[27] and if it is finitely unique, it can be shown (Luce, 1992a) that there are at most three singular points: a minimum, a maximum, and an interior one. Moreover they exhibit systematic properties. One then uses the results on unit structures to derive a numerical representation of this class of structures. Results about such structures underlie some of the developments in the next subsection.

---

[26] As a rough analogy, homogeneous and nonhomogeneous stand in the same relation as do linear and nonlinear equations: The former is highly special, and the latter highly diverse.

[27] This is a function of two or more variables that is monotonic in each. One must be quite careful in formulating the exact meaning of monotonicity at minima and maxima.

3. Generalized Linear Utility Models

A growing literature is focused on exploring ways to modify the EU and SEU models (sections V.C.1 and 2) so as to accommodate some of the anomalies described in section V.C.3.[28] One class of models, which includes Kahneman and Tversky's (1979; Tversky & Kahneman, 1992) widely cited representation called prospect theory, draws on generalized concatenation structures with singular points, identifying the status quo as a singular point. The resulting representation modifies SEU, Eq. (56), to the extent of making $S(E_i)$ depend on one or both of two things beside the event E_i, namely, the sign of the corresponding consequence g_i—that is, whether it is a gain or loss relative to the status quo—and also the rank-order position of g_i among all of the consequences, $g_1, \ldots g_n$, that might arise from the gamble g. These models go under several names, including rank- and sign-dependent utility (RSDU) and cumulative prospect theory. In the binary case, such models imply event commutativity Eq. (58), but *none* of the more complex accounting equivalences that hold for SEU (Luce & von Winterfeldt, 1994).

Measurement axiomatizations of the most general RSDU are given by Luce and Fishburn (1991, 1995) and Wakker and Tversky (1993). The former is unusual in this literature because it introduces a primitive beyond the preference ordering among gambles, namely, the idea of the joint receipt of two things. Therefore, if g and h are gambles, such as two tickets in different state lotteries or stock certificates in two corporations, a person may receive (e.g., as a gift) both of them, which is denoted $g \oplus h$. This operation plays two useful features in the theory. One, which Tversky and Kahneman (1986) called *segregation* and invoked in pre-editing gambles, states that if g is a gamble and s is a certain outcome with the consequences being either all gains or all losses, $g \oplus s$ is treated as the same as the gamble g', which is obtained by replacing each g_i by $g_i \oplus s$. This appears to be completely rational. The second feature, called *decomposition,* formulates the single nonrationality of the theory: Let g be a gamble having both gains and losses, let g^+ denote the gamble resulting from g by replacing all of the losses by the status quo, and g^- that by replacing the gains by the status quo. Then,

$$g \sim g^+ \oplus g^-, \tag{61}$$

where the two gambles on the right are realized independently. This is, in reality, a formal assertion of what is involved in many cost-benefit analyses, the two components of which are often carried out by independent groups of analysts and their results are combined to give an overall evaluation of the

[28] Most of the current generalizations exhibit neither context effects, as such, nor intransitivities.

situation. In fact, Slovic and Lichtenstein (1968), in a study with other goals, tested decomposition in a laboratory setting and found it sustained. More recently Cho, Luce, and von Winterfeldt (1994) carried out a somewhat more focused study, again finding good support for the segregation and decomposition assumptions.

Within the domain of lotteries,[29] economists have considered other quite different representations. For example, Chew and Epstein (1989) and Chew, Epstein, and Segal (1991) have explored a class of representations called *quadratic utility* that takes the form

$$U(g) = \sum_{i=1}^{n} \sum_{j=1}^{n} \phi(g_i, g_j) p_i p_j. \tag{62}$$

A weakened form of independence is key to this representation. It is called *mixture symmetry* and is stated as follows: If $g \sim h$, then for each $\alpha \in (0, \frac{1}{2})$, there exists $\beta \in (\frac{1}{2}, 1)$ such that

$$(g, \alpha; h, 1 - \alpha) \sim (h, \beta; g, 1 - \beta). \tag{63}$$

Equation (63) and consequence monotonicity together with assumptions about the richness and continuity of the set of lotteries imply that $\beta = 1 - \alpha$ and that Eq. (62) is order preserving. We are unaware of any attempts to study this structure empirically.

D. Invariance and Homogeneity

1. The General Idea

A very general scientific meta-principle asserts that when formulating scientific propositions one should be very careful to specify the domain within which the proposition is alleged to hold. The proposition must then be formulated in terms of the primitives and defining properties of that domain. When the domain is rich in automorphisms, as in homogeneous cases or in the special singular cases just discussed, this means that the proposition must remain invariant with respect to the automorphisms, just as is true—by definition—of the primitives of the domain.

2. An Example: Bisection

Let $\mathscr{A} = \langle A, \succsim, \bigcirc \rangle$ be an extensive structure such as the physical intensity of monochromatic lights. It has a representation ϕ that maps it into $\mathscr{R} = \langle \mathbb{R}_+, \geq, + \rangle$ and the automorphisms (= translations) become multiplication by positive constants. Now, suppose a bisection experiment is performed such that when stimuli $x = \phi(a)$ and $y = \phi(b)$ are presented, the subject reports

[29] Money gambles with known probabilities for the consequences.

the stimulus $z = \phi(c)$ to be the bisection point of x and y. We may think of this as an operation defined in $\mathcal{R}$, namely, $z = x \oplus y$. If this operation is expressible within the structure $\mathcal{A}$, then invariance requires that for real $r > 0$,

$$r(x \oplus y) = rx \oplus ry. \tag{64}$$

A numerical equation of this type is said to be *homogeneous of degree 1*, which is a classical concept of homogeneity.[30] It is clearly very closely related to the idea of the structure being homogeneous. In section VII we will see how equations of homogeneity of degree different from 1 also arise.

Plateau (1872) conducted a bisection experiment using gray patches, and his data supported the idea that there is a "subjective" transformation U of physical brightness that maps the bisection operation into a simple average, that is,

$$U(x \oplus y) = \frac{U(x) + U(y)}{2}. \tag{65}$$

If we put Eqs. (64) and (65) together, we obtain the following constraint on the function U: For all $x, y, z \in \mathbb{R}_+$,

$$U\left[rU^{-1}\left[\frac{U(x) + U(y)}{2}\right]\right] = \frac{U(rx) + U(ry)}{2}. \tag{66}$$

An equation of this type in which a function is constrained by its values at several different points is called a *functional equation* (Aczél, 1966, 1987). Applying the invariance principle to numerical representations quite typically leads to functional equations.

In this case, under the assumption that U is strictly increasing, it can be shown to have one of two forms:

$$U(x) = k\log x + c \text{ or} \tag{67a}$$

$$U(x) = cx^k + d. \tag{67b}$$

These are of interest because they correspond to two of the major proposals for the form of subjective intensity as a function of physical intensity. The former was first strongly argued for by Fechner, and the latter, by Stevens.

Falmagne (1985, chap. 12) summarized other, somewhat similar, invariance arguments that lead to functional equations. We discuss related, but conceptually quite distinct, arguments in section VII.

3. Invariance in Geometry and Physics.

In 1872, the German mathematician F. Klein, in his famous Erlangen address, argued that within an axiomatic formulation of geometry, the only entities that should be called "geometric" are those that are invariant under

---

[30] The degree of the homogeneity refers to the exponent of the left-hand r, which as written is 1.

the automorphisms of the geometry (for a recent appraisal, see Narens, 1988). Klein used this to good effect; however, a number of geometries subsequently arose that were not homogeneous and, indeed, in which the only automorphism was the trivial one, the identity. Invariance in such cases establishes no restrictions whatsoever. This illustrates an important point—namely, that invariance under automorphisms is a necessary condition for a concept to be formulated in terms of the primitives of a system, but it is by no means a sufficient condition.

During the 19th century, physicists used, informally at first, invariance arguments (in the form of dimensional consistency) to ensure that proposed laws were consistent with the variables involved. Eventually this came to be formulated as the method of dimensional analysis in which numerical laws are required to be dimensionally homogeneous of degree 1 (dimensional invariance). Subsequently, this method was given a formal axiomatic analysis (Krantz et al., 1971, chap. 10; Luce et al., 1990, chap. 22), which showed that dimensional invariance is, in fact, just automorphism invariance. Again, it is only a necessary condition on a physical law, but in practice it is often a very restrictive one. Dzhafarov (1995) presented an alternative view that is, perhaps, closer to traditional physical presentations. Nontrivial examples of dimensional analysis can be found in Palacios (1964), Sedov (1959), and Schepartz (1980). For ways to weaken the condition, see section VII.

4. Invariance in Measurement Theory and Psychology

In attempting to deal with general structures of the type previously discussed, measurement theorists became very interested in questions of invariance, for which they invented a new term. A proposition formulated in terms of the primitives of a system is called *meaningful* only if it is invariant under the automorphisms of the structure. Being meaningful says nothing, one way or the other, about the truth of the proposition in question, although meaningfulness can be recast in terms of truth as follows: A proposition is meaningful if it is either true in every representation (within the scale type) of the structure or false in every one. Being meaningless (not meaningful) is not an absolute concept; it is entirely relative to the system in question, and something that is meaningless in one system may become meaningful in a more complete one. As noted earlier, the concept has bite only when there are nontrivial automorphisms. Indeed, in a very deep and thorough analysis of the concept of meaningfulness, Narens (in preparation) has shown that it is equivalent to invariance only for homogeneous structures.

In addition to meaningfulness arguments leading to various psychophysical equations, such as Eqs. (65) through (67), some psychologists, beginning with Stevens (1951), have been involved in a contentious controversy about applying invariance principles to statistical propositions. We do not attempt to recapitulate the details. Suffice it to say that when a statistical proposition is cast in terms of the primitives of a system, it seems reasonable to require that it be true (for false) in every representation of the system. Thus, in the ordinal case it is meaningless to say (without further specification of the representation) that the mean of one group of subjects is less than the mean of another because the truth is not invariant under strictly increasing mappings of the values. In contrast, comparison of the medians is invariant. A list of relevant references can be found in Luce et al. (1990). See also Michell (1986) and Townsend and Ashby (1984).

VII. MATCHING AND GENERAL HOMOGENEOUS EQUATIONS

A. In Physics

Many laws of physics do not derive from the laws that relate basic physical measures but are, nonetheless, expressed in terms of these measures. This section describes two such cases, which are handled differently.

1. Physically Similar Systems

Consider a spring. If one holds the ambient conditions fixed and applies different forces to the spring, one finds, within the range of forces that do not destroy the spring, that its change in length, Δl, is proportional to the force, F, applied, $\Delta l = kF$. The is called Hooke's law. Note that such a law, as stated, is not invariant under automorphisms of the underlying measurements. This is obvious because Δl has the dimension of length, whereas force involves mass, length, and time. This law is expressible in terms of the usual physical measures, but it is not derivable from the underlying laws of the measurement structure.

A law of this type can be recast in invariant form by the following device. The constant k, called the spring constant, is thought of as characterizing a property of the spring. It varies with the shape and materials of the spring and has units that make the law dimensionally invariant, namely, $[L][T]^2/[M]$, where $[L]$ denotes the unit of length, $[T]$ of time, and $[M]$ of mass. This is called a *dimensional constant*. Such constants play a significant role in physics and can, in general, be ascertained from the constants in the differential equations characterizing the fundamental physical relations underlying the law when these equations are known. The set of entities characterized in this fashion, such as all springs, are called *physically similar systems*.

2. Noninvariant Laws

In addition to invariant laws or laws that can be made invariant by the inclusion of dimensional constants that are thought to be characteristic of the system involved, there are more complex laws of which the following is an example taken from rheology (material science) called a Nuttig law (Palacios, 1964, p. 45).[31] For solids not satisfying Hooke's law (see the preceding), the form of the relationship is $d = k(F/A)^{\beta}t^{\gamma}$, where $d = \Delta l/l$ is the deformation and F the applied force. New are the area A to which F is applied, the time duration t of the application, and the two exponents β and γ, both of which depend on the particular material in question. Thus, the dimension of k must be $[L]^{\beta}[m]^{-\beta}[T]^{2\beta-\gamma}$, which of course varies depending on the values of β and γ.

To understand the difficulty here, consider the simplest such case, namely $y = kx^{\beta}$, where x and y are both measured as (usually, distinct) ratio scales. Thus, the units of k must be $[y]/[x]^{\beta}$. There is no problem so long as all systems governed by the law have the same exponent β; the situation becomes quite troublesome, however, if not only the numerical value of k depends on the system but, because of changes in the value of β, the units of k also depend on the particular system involved. Such laws, which are homogeneous of degree β, cannot be made homogeneous of degree 1 by introducing a dimensional constant with fixed dimensions. In typical psychology examples, several of which follow, the value of β appears to vary among individuals just as it varies with the substance in rheology. Both Falmagne and Narens (1983) and Dzhafarov (1995) have discussed different approaches to such problems.

There is a sense, however, in which invariance is still nicely maintained. The ratio scale transformation (translation) r on the dimension x is taken into a ratio scale transformation r^{β} on the dimension y. Put another way, the law is *compatible* with the automorphism structures of dimensions x and y even if it is not invariant with respect to the automorphisms (Luce, 1990a). Such homogeneous laws are very useful in psychophysics because they narrow down to a limited number of possibilities the mathematical form of the laws (see Falmagne, 1985, chap. 12).

B. Psychological Identity

Some psychophysical laws formulate conditions under which two stimuli are perceived as the same. We explore two illustrations.

1. Weber-Type Laws

Consider a physical continuum of intensity that can be modeled as an extensive structure $\langle A, \succsim, \bigcirc \rangle$ with the ratio scale (physical) representation ϕ onto $\langle \mathbb{R}_+, \geq, + \rangle$. In addition, suppose there is a psychological ordering $>_{\psi}$[32] on A that arises from a discrimination experiment where, for $a, b \in A$, $b >_{\psi} a$

---

[31] We thank E. N. Dzhafarov (personal communication) for bringing these rheology examples to our attention. See Scott Blair (1969) for a full treatment.

[32] The subscript Ψ is intended as a reminder that this ordering is psychological and quite distinct from $\gtrsim$, which is physical.

means that b is perceived as more intense than a. In practice, one estimates a psychometric function and uses a probability cutoff to define $>_\Psi$; see Eq. (20) of section IV. Not surprisingly, such orderings are usually transitive. However, if we define $b \sim_\Psi a$ to mean neither $b >_\Psi a$ nor $a >_\Psi b$, then in general $\sim_\Psi$ is not transitive: The failure to discriminate a from b and b from c does not necessarily imply that a cannot be discriminated from c, although that may happen. It is usually assumed that $>_\Psi$ satisfies the technical conditions of a semiorder or an interval order (see section IV.A.3), but we do not need to go into those details here.

Narens (1994) proved that one cannot define the structure $\langle A, \gtrsim, O \rangle$ in terms of $\langle A, >_\Psi \rangle$; however, one can formulate the latter in terms of the former in the usual way. One defines $T(a)$ to be the smallest (inf) b such that $b >_\Psi a$. Then T establishes a law that maps A into A, namely, the *upper threshold function*. Typically, this is converted into a statement involving increments. Define $\Delta(a)$ to be the element such that $T(a) = a \, O \, \Delta(a)$. Auditory psychologists (Jesteadt, Wier, & Green, 1977; McGill & Goldberg, 1968) have provided evidence (see Figure 2) that intensity discrimination of pure tones exhibits the property that the psychologically defined $\Delta(a)$ is *compatible* with the physics in the sense that for each translation τ of the physical structure, there is another translation σ_τ, dependent on τ, such that

$$\Delta[\tau(a)] = \sigma_\tau[\Delta(a)]. \tag{68}$$

When recast as an equivalent statement in terms of the representations, Eq. (68) asserts the existence of constants $\alpha > 0$ and $\beta > 0$ such that

$$\phi[\Delta(a)] = \alpha\phi(a)^{1-\beta}, \tag{69}$$

which again is a homogeneous equation of degree $1 - \beta$ (Luce, 1990a).

The latter formulation is called the *near miss to Weber's law* because when ϕ is the usual extensive measure of sound intensity, β is approximately 0.07, which is "close to" $\beta = 0$, the case called *Weber's law* after the 19th-century German physiologist E. H. Weber. Note that Weber's law itself is special because it is dimensionally invariant, that is, in Eq. (68) $\sigma_\tau = \tau$, but the general case of Eq. (68) is not. It is customary to rewrite Weber's law as

$$\frac{\Delta\phi(a)}{\phi(a)} = \frac{\phi[\Delta(a)]}{\phi(a)} = \alpha. \tag{70}$$

This ratio, called the *Weber fraction*, is dimensionless and some have argued that, to the extent Weber's law is valid, the fraction α is a revealing parameter of the organism, and, in particular, that it is meaningful to compare Weber fractions across modalities. This common practice has recently been questioned by measurement theorists, as we now elaborate.

2. Narens-Mausfeld Equivalence Principle

Narens (1994) and Narens and Mausfeld (1992) have argued that one must be careful in interpreting the constants in laws like Eq. (69) and (70). They note that the purely psychological assertion about discriminability has been cast in terms of one particular formulation of the qualitative physical structure, whereas there are an infinity of concatenation operations all of which are equally good in the following sense. Two qualitative formulations $\langle A, \succsim, \bigcirc \rangle$ and $\langle A, \succsim, * \rangle$ are equivalent if each can be defined in terms of the other. This, of course, means that they share a common set of automorphisms: If τ is an automorphism of one, then it is of the other; that is, both $\tau(a \bigcirc b) = \tau(a) \bigcirc \tau(b)$ and $\tau(a * b) = \tau(a) * \tau(b)$ hold. Indeed, Narens (1994) has shown that if the former has the ratio scale representation ϕ, then the latter must have one that is a power function of ϕ. Thus, if the former structure is replaced by the latter, then Eq. (70) is transformed into

$$\frac{\phi^\gamma[\Delta^*(a)]}{\phi^\gamma(a)} = (1 + \alpha)^\gamma - 1, \tag{71}$$

where γ is chosen so ϕ^γ is additive over $*$. Thus, the fact that Weber's law holds is independent of which physical primitives are used to describe the domain, and so within one modality one can compare individuals as to their discriminative power. Across modalities, no such comparison makes sense because the constant $(1 + \alpha)^\gamma - 1$ is not invariant with the choice of the concatenation operation, which alters the numerical value of γ.

If one reformulates the law in terms of $T(a) = a \bigcirc \Delta(a)$, Weber's law becomes

$$\frac{\phi[T(a)]}{\phi(a)} = 1 + \alpha. \tag{72}$$

Note that this formulation does not explicitly invoke a concatenation operation, except that choosing ϕ rather than ϕ^γ does, and so the same strictures of interpretation of the ratios remain.[33]

Carrying out a similar restatement of the near miss, Eq. (69) yields

$$\frac{\phi^\gamma[T(a)]}{\phi^\gamma(a)} = (1 + \alpha\phi^\gamma(a)^{-\beta/\gamma}]^\gamma. \tag{73}$$

Here the choice of a concatenation operation clearly affects what one says about the "near-miss" exponent because the value β/γ can be anything.

The principle being invoked is that psychologically significant propositions can depend on the physical stimuli involved, but they should not depend on the specific way we have chosen to formulate the physical situation.

---

[33] This remark stands in sharp contrast to Narens' (1994) claim that $\alpha + 1$ is meaningful under circumstances when α is not.

We should be able to replace one description of the physics by an equivalent one without disturbing a psychologically significant proposition.

This principle is being subjected to harsh criticism, the most completely formulated of which came from Dzhafarov (1995) who argued that its wholesale invocation will prove far too restrictive not only in psychology but in physics as well. It simply may be impossible to state psychological laws without reference to a specific formulation of the physics, as appears likely to be the case in the next example.

3. Color Matching

A far more complex and interesting situation arises in color vision. The physical description of an aperture color is simply the intensity distribution over the wave lengths of the visible spectrum. A remarkable empirical conclusion is that there are far fewer color percepts than there are intensity distributions: The latter form an infinite dimensional space that, according to much psychological data and theory, human vision collapses into a much lower dimensional one—under some circumstances to three dimensions.[34] The experimental technique used to support this hypothesis is called *metameric matching* in which a circular display is divided into two half-fields, each with a different intensity distribution. When a subject reports no perceived difference whatsoever in the two distributions, which may be strikingly different physically, they are said to *match*.

One possible physical description of the stimuli is based on two easily realized operations. Suppose **a** and **b** denote two intensity distributions over wave length. Then $\mathbf{a} \oplus \mathbf{b}$ denotes their sum, which can be achieved by directing two projectors corresponding to **a** and **b** on the same aperture. For any real $r > 0$, $r\mathbf{a}$ denotes the distribution obtained from **a** by increasing every amplitude by the same factor r, which can be realized by changing the distance of the projector from the aperture. In terms of this physical structure and the psychological matching relation, denoted $\sim$, Krantz (1975a, b; Suppes et al., 1989, chap. 15) has formulated axiomatically testable properties of $\sim$, $\oplus$, $\cdot$, and of their interactions that, if satisfied, result in a three-dimensional vector representation of these matches. Empirical data provide partial, but not full, support for these so-called Grassman laws.

The dimension of the representation is an invariant, but there are infinitely many representations into the vector space of that dimension. A substantial portion of the literature attempts to single out one or another as having special physiological or psychological significance. These issues are described in considerable detail in chapter 15 of Suppes et al. (1989), but as yet they are not fully resolved.

---

[34] It is worth noting that sounds also are infinite dimensional, but no such reduction to a finite dimensional perceptual space has been discovered.

To our knowledge no attempt has been made to analyze these results from the perspective of the Narens-Mausfeld principle. It is unclear to us what freedom exists in providing alternative physical formulations in this case.

C. Psychological Equivalence

1. Matching across Modalities

As was discussed in section IV.B.1, psychologists often ask subjects to characterize stimuli that are equivalent on some subjective dimension even though they are perceptually very distinct. Perhaps the simplest cases are the construction of equal-X curves, where X can be any suitable attribute: brightness, loudness, aversiveness, and so on. Beginning in the 1950s, S. S. Stevens (1975) introduced three new methods that went considerably beyond matching within an attribute: magnitude estimation, magnitude production, and cross-modal matching. Here two distinct attributes—a sensory attribute and a numerical attribute in the first two and two sensory attributes in the third—are compared and a "match" is established by the subject. The main instruction to subjects is to preserve subjective ratios. Therefore if M denotes the matching relation and aMs and $bMt,$ then the instruction is that stimuli a and b from modality A should stand in the same (usually intensity) subjective ratio as do s and t from modality S.

In developing a theory for such matching relations, the heart of the problem is to formulate clearly what it means "to preserve subjective ratios." In addition, of course, one also faces the issue of how to deal with response variability, which is considerable in these methods, but we ignore that here. Basically, there are three measurement-theoretic attempts to provide a theory of subjective ratios.

The first, due to Krantz (1972) and Shepard (1978, 1981), explicitly introduced as a primitive concept the notion of a ratio, formulated plausible axioms, and showed that in terms of standard ratio scale representations of the physical attributes, ϕ_A and ϕ_S, the following is true for some unspecified monotonic function F and constant $\beta > 0$:

$$aMs \text{ and } bMt \quad \text{if and only if} \quad \frac{\phi_A(b)}{\phi_A(a)} = F\left[\left(\frac{\phi_S(t)}{\phi_S(s)}\right)^\beta\right]. \quad (74)$$

Although the power function character is consistent with empirical observations, the existence of the unknown function F pretty much obviates that relationship.

A second attempt, due to Luce (1990a, and presented as an improved formulation of Luce, 1959b), stated that ratios are captured by translations. In particular, he defined a psychological matching law M to be *translation consistent* (with the physical domains A and S) if for each translation τ of the domain A there exists a corresponding translation σ_τ of the domain S such that for all $a \in A$ and $s \in S$,

$$aMs \text{ if and only if } \tau(a)M\sigma_\tau(s). \tag{75}$$

From this it follows that if ϕ_A and ϕ_S are ratio scale representations of the two physical domains, then there are constants $\alpha > 0$ and $\beta > 0$ such that

$$aMs \text{ is equivalent to } \phi_A(a) = \alpha\phi_S(s)^\beta. \tag{76}$$

Observe that Eqs. (68) and (69) are special cases of (75) and (76).

The third attempt, due to Narens (1996), is far deeper and more complex than either of the previous attempts. He carefully formulated a plausible model of the internal representation of the stimuli showing how the subject is (in magnitude estimation) constructing numerals to produce responses. It is too complex to describe briefly, but any serious student of these methods should study it carefully.

2. Ratios and Differences

Much of the modeling shown in section II was based on functions of differences of subjective sensory scales. Similarly, methods such as bisection and fractionation more generally seem to rest on subjects evaluating differences. By contrast, the discussion of cross–modal matching (and of magnitude estimation and production) emphasizes the preservation of ratios. Torgerson (1961) first questioned whether subjects really have, for most dimensions, independent operations corresponding to differences and to ratios, or whether there is a single operation with two different response rules depending on the instructions given. Michael Birnbaum, our editor, has vigorously pursued this matter.

The key observation is that if there really are two operations, response data requiring ratio judgments cannot be monotonically related to those requiring difference judgments. For example, $3 - 2 < 13 - 10$ but $1.5 = 3/2 > 13/10 = 1.3$. On the other hand, if ratio judgments are found to covary with difference judgments in a monotonic fashion, a reasonable conclusion is that both types of judgments are based on a single underlying operation.

A series of studies in a variety of domains ranging from physical manipulable attributes (such as weight and loudness) to highly subjective ones (such as job prestige) has been interpreted as showing no evidence of non-monotonicity and to provide support for the belief that the basic operation is really one of differences. The work is nicely summarized by Hardin and Birnbaum (1990), where one finds copious references to earlier work.

Hardin and Birnbaum conclude that the data support a single operation that involves subtracting values of a subjective real mapping s, and that depending on the task required of the subject, different response functions are employed for the two judgments, namely,

$$\text{Response} = J_D[s(a) - s(b)] \text{ for difference judgments}$$

$$\text{and} \tag{77}$$

$$\text{Response} = J_R[s(a) - s(b)] \text{ for ratio judgments.}$$

Moreover, the evidence suggests that approximately $J_R(x) = \exp J_D(x)$. They do point out that, for a few special modalities, ratios and differences can be distinct. This is true of judgments of length: most people seem to understand reasonably clearly the difference between saying two height ratios are equal and that two differences in length are equal.

The empirical matter of deciding if ratio and difference judgments are or are not monotonically related is not at all an easy one. One is confronted by a data figure such as that reproduced in Figure 13 and told that it represents a single monotonic function. But are the deviations from a smooth monotone curve due to response error, or "noise," or are they small but systematic indications of a failure of monotonicity? It is difficult to be sure in average data such as these. A careful analysis of the data from individual subjects might be more convincing, however; and Birnbaum and Elmasian (1977) carried out such an analysis, concluding that a single operation does give a good account of the data.

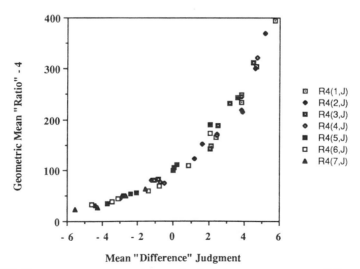

FIGURE 13   Geometric mean estimates of ratio judgments versus mean difference judgments of the same stimulus pairs of occupations. From Figure 1 of "Malleability of 'Ratio' Judgments of Occupational Prestige," by C. Hardin and M. H. Birnbaum, 1990, *American Journal of Psychology, 103,* p. 6. From *American Journal of Psychology.* Copyright 1990 by the Board of Trustees of the University of Illinois. Used with the permission of the University of Illinois Press.

Assuming that the issue of monotonicity has been settled, there remains the question whether the underlying operation is one of differences or ratios. For, as is well known, we can replace the right-hand terms in Eq. (77) by corresponding expressions involving ratios rather than differences, namely

$$J'_D[s'(a)/s'(b)] \text{ and } J'_R[s'(a)/s'(b)],$$
$$\text{where } s'(a) = \exp[s(a)], J'_D(x) = J_D[ln(x)],$$
$$\text{and } J'_R(x) = J_R[ln(x)]. \tag{78}$$

It turns out, however, that in an appropriate four-stimulus task the operation can be identified. For example, Hagerty and Birnbaum (1978) asked subjects to judge (i) "ratios of ratio," (ii) "ratios of differences," (iii) "differences of ratios," and (iv) "differences of differences." They found that the observed judgments for conditions (i), (iii), and (iv) could be explained in terms of a model involving a single scale s, with all comparisons being based on differences of the form

$$[s(a) - s(b)] - [s(c) - s(d)].$$

On the other hand, condition (ii) was accounted for by a model based on subjective ratios of differences of scale values:

$$\frac{s(a) - s(b)}{s(c) - s(d)}.$$

The conclusion is that the scale s is consistent with the subtraction model of Eq. (77) applied to ratio and difference judgments of stimulus pairs.

Thus, although pairs of stimuli seem to be compared by computing differences, subjects can and do compute ratios, particularly when those ratios involve differences of scale values. This latter observation is consistent with the fact, mentioned earlier, that people are well aware of the distinction between ratios of lengths and differences of those same lengths.

VIII. CONCLUDING REMARKS

Our general knowledge about the conditions under which numerical representations can arise from qualitative data—representational measurement—has grown appreciably during the past 40 years. Such measurement theory has so far found its most elaborate applications in the areas of psychophysics and individual decision making. This chapter attempted both to convey some of our new theoretical understanding and to provide, albeit sketchily, examples of how it has been applied. Of course, much of the detail that is actually needed to work out such applications has been omitted, but it is available in the references we have provided.

The chapter first exposited the very successful probability models for simple binary experiments in which subjects exhibit their ability to detect and to discriminate signals that are barely detectable or discriminable. These models and experiments focus on what seem the simplest possible questions, and yet complexity arises because of two subject-controlled trade-offs: that between errors of commission and errors of omission and that between overall error rate and response times. We know a lot about psychometric functions, ROC curves, and speed-accuracy trade-offs, although we continue to be plagued by trial-by-trial sequential effects that make estimating probabilities and distributions very problematic. Generalizing the probability models to more complex situations—for example, general choice, categorization, and absolute identification—has been a major preoccupation beginning in the 1980s, and certainly the advent of ample computer power has made possible rather elaborate calculations. Still, we are always battling the tendency for the number of free parameters to outstrip the complexity of the data.

The second major approach, which focused more on structure than simple order, involved algebraic models that draw in various ways on Hölder's theorem. It shows when an order and operation have an additive representation, and it was used in several ways to construct numerical representations. The line of development began historically with empirical operations that are associative and monotonic, moved on to additive conjoint structures in which an operation induced on one component captures the trade-off between components, and most recently has been extended to the work on homogeneous, finitely unique structures. The latter, which lead to a wide variety of nonadditive representations, are studied by showing that the translations (automorphisms with no fixed points) meet the conditions of Hölder's theorem. In this representation the translations appear as multiplication by positive constants. Further generalizations to conjoint structures with the empirical (not the induced) operations on components and to structures with singular points make possible the treatment of fairly complex problems in individual decision making. The most extensive applications of these results so far have been to generalized theories of subjective expected utility. These new results have not yet been applied in psychophysics except for relations among groups of translations to study various matching experiments. Such models lead to homogeneous equations of degree different from 1.

The apparent similarity of the probability and algebraic models in which both kinds of representations are invariant under either ratio or interval scale transformations is misleading. For the probability models in the ordinal situation this restriction does not reflect in any way the automorphism group of the underlying structure, which after all is ordinal, but rather certain arbitrary conventions about the representation of distributions. In particular, the data are, in principle,, transformed so that the error distributions are Gaussian, in which case only affine transformations retain that parametric form. This last comment is not meant to denigrate what can be done with the probability models, which as we have seen is considerable, especially in binary situations (see section II).

As we have stressed, the field to date has failed to achieve a true melding of randomness with structure. This failure makes empirical testing difficult because we usually are interested in moderately structured situations and invariably our data are somewhat noisy. Exaggerating slightly, we can handle randomness in the ordinal situation—witness sections II and III—and we know a lot about structure in the ratio and interval scale cases provided we ignore the fact that the data are always noisy—witness sections IV through VII, but we cannot treat both together very well.

One result of this bifurcation is notable differences in how we test the two kinds of models. Those formulating randomness explicitly are ideally suited to the response inconsistencies that we observe. But because of their lack of focus on internal structure, they can be evaluated only globally in terms of overall goodness of fit. The algebraic models suffer from having no built-in means of accommodating randomness, but they have the advantage that various individual structural properties—monotonicity, transitivity, event commutativity, and so on—can be studied in some isolation. This allows us to focus rather clearly on the failings of a model, leading to modified theories. One goal of future work must be to meld the two approaches.

Acknowledgments

This work was supported in part by National Science Foundation grants SBR-9308959 and SBR-9540107 to the University of California at Irvine. We thank Michael Birnbaum for his helpful comments and criticisms.

References

Aczél, J. (1966). *Lectures on functional equations and their applications*. New York: Academic Press.

Aczél, J. (1987). *A short course on functional equations*. Dordrecht: D. Reidel.

Allais, M. (1953). Le comportment de l'homme rationnel devant le risque: Critique des postulates et axiomes de l'école americaine. *Econometrica, 21,* 503–546.

Allais, M., &, Hagen, O. (Eds.). (1979). *Expected utility hypothesis and the Allais' paradox*. Dordrecht: Reidel.

Alper, T. M. (1987). A classification of all order-preserving homeomorphism groups of the reals that satisfy finite uniqueness. *Journal of Mathematical Psychology, 31,* 135–154.

Anderson, N. H. (1982). *Methods of information integration theory*. New York: Academic Press.

Anderson, N. H. (Ed.) (1991a, b, c). *Contributions to information integration theory (Vol. 1: Cognition; Vol. 2: Social; Vol. 3: Developmental)*. Hillsdale, NJ: Erlbaum.

Ashby, F. G. (1992a). Multidimensional models of categorization. In F. G. Ashby (Ed.), *Multidimensional models of perception and cognition* (pp. 449–483). Hillsdale, NJ: Erlbaum.

Ashby, F. G. (1992b). Multivariate probability distributions. In F. G. Ashby (Ed.). *Multidimensional Models of Perception and Cognition* (pp. 2–34). Hillsdale, NJ: Erlbaum.

Ashby, F. G., & Perrin, N. A. (1988). Toward a unified theory of similarity and recognition. *Psychological Review, 95,* 124–150.

Ashby, F. G., & Townsend, J. T. (1986). Varieties of perceptual independence. *Psychological Review, 93,* 154–179.

Berg, B. G. (1989). Analysis of weights in multiple observation tasks. *Journal of the Acoustical Society of America, 86,* 1743–1746.

Berg, B. G. (1990). Observer efficiency and weights in a multiple observation task. *Journal of the Acoustical Society of America, 88,* 149–158.

Berg, B. G., & Green, D. M. (1990). Spectral weights in profile listening. *Journal of the Acoustical Society of America, 88,* 758–766.

Berliner, J. E., Durlach, N. I., & Braida, L. D. (1977). Intensity perception. VII. Further data on roving-level discrimination and the resolution and bias edge effects. *Journal of the Acoustical Society of America, 61,* 1577–1585.

Birnbaum, M. H. (1974). The nonadditivity of personality impressions [monograph]. *Journal of Experimental Psychology, 102,* 543–561.

Birnbaum, M. H. (1992). Violations of monotonicity and contextual effects in choice-based certainty equivalents. *Psychological Science, 3,* 310–314.

Birnbaum, M. H., Coffey, G., Mellers, B. A., & Weiss, R. (1992). Utility measurement: Configural-weight theory and the judge's point of view. *Journal of Experimental Psychology: Human Perception and Performance, 18,* 331–346.

Birnbaum, M. H., & Elmasian, R. (1977). Loudness ratios and differences involve the same psychophysical operation. *Perception & Psychophysics, 22,* 383–391.

Birnbaum, M. H., Parducci, A., & Gifford, R. K. (1971). Contextual effects in information integration. *Journal of Experimental Psychology, 88,* 158–170.

Birnbaum, M. H., & Stegner, S. E. (1979). Source credibility: Bias, expertise, and the judge's point of view. *Journal of Personality and Social Psychology, 37,* 48–74.

Block, H. D., & Marschak, J. (1960). Random orderings and stochastic theories of responses. In I. Olkin, S. Ghurye, W. Hoeffding, W. Madow, & H. Mann (Eds.), *Contributions to probability and statistics* (pp. 97–132). Stanford, CA: Stanford University Press.

Böckenholt, U. (1992). Multivariate models of preference and choice. In F. G. Ashby (Ed.), *Multidimensional models of perception and cognition* (pp. 89–114). Hillsdale, NJ: Erlbaum.

Bostic, R., Herrnstein, R. J., & Luce, R. D. (1990). The effect on the preference-reversal phenomenon of using choice indifferences. *Journal of Economic Behavior and Organization, 13,* 193–212.

Braida, L. D., & Durlach, N. I. (1972). Intensity perception. II. Resolution in one-interval paradigms. *Journal of the Acoustical Society of America, 51,* 483–502.

Busemeyer, J. R., & Townsend, J. T. (1993). Decision field theory: A dynamic-cognitive approach to decision making in an uncertain environment. *Psychological Review, 100,* 432–459.

Carroll, J. D., & DeSoete, G. (1990). Fitting a quasi-Poisson case of the GSTUN (General Stochastic Tree UNfolding) model and some extensions. In M. Schader & W. Gaul (Eds.), *Knowledge, data and computer-assisted decisions* (pp. 93–102). Berlin: Springer-Verlag.

Chew, S. H., & Epstein, L. G. (1989). Axiomatic rank-dependent means. *Annals of Operations Research, 19,* 299–309.

Chew, S. H., Epstein, L. G., & Segal, U. (1991). Mixture symmetry and quadratic utility. *Econometrica, 59,* 139–163.

Cho, Y., Luce, R. D., & von Winterfeldt, D. (1994). Tests of assumptions about the joint receipt of gambles in rank- and sign-dependent utility theory. *Journal of Experimental Psychology: Human Perception and Performance, 20,* 931–943.

Cohen, M., & Narens, L. (1979). Fundamental unit structures: A theory of ratio scalability. *Journal of Mathematical Psychology, 20,* 193–232.

Coombs, C. H. (1964). *A theory of data.* New York: John Wiley & Sons.

Coombs, C. H. (1975). Portfolio theory and the measurement of risk. In M. F. Kaplan & S. Schwartz (Eds.), *Human judgment and decision processes* (pp. 63–86). New York: Academic Press.

Davison, M., & McCarthy, D. (1988). *The matching law. A research review.* Hillsdale, NJ: Erlbaum.

Decoene, S., Onghena, P., & Janssen, R. (1995). Representationalism under attack (book review). *Journal of Mathematical Psychology, 39,* 234–241.

DeSoete, G., & Carroll, J. D. (1986). Probabilitic multidimensional choice models for representing paired comparisons data. In E. Diday, Y. Escoufier, L. Lebart, J. Pagès, Y. Schektman, & R. Tommasone (Eds.), *Data analysis and informatics* (Vol. 4, pp. 485–497). Amsterdam: North-Holland.

DeSoete, G., & Carroll, J.D. (1992). Probabilistic multidimensional models of pairwise choice data. In F. G. Ashby (Ed.), *Multidimensional models of perception and cognition* (pp. 61–88). Hillsdale, NJ: Erlbaum.

Durlach, N. I., & Braida, L. D. (1969). Intensity perception. I. Preliminary theory of intensity resolution. *Journal of the Acoustical Society of America, 46,* 372–383.

Dzhafarov, E. N. (1995). Empirical meaningfulness, measurement-dependent constants, and dimensional analysis. In R. D. Luce, M. D'Zmura, D. D. Hoffman, G. Iverson, and K. Romney (Eds.), *Geometric representations of perceptual phenomena: Papers in honor of Tarow Indow on his 70th birthday* (pp. 113–134). Hillsdale, NJ: Erlbaum.

Ellis, B. (1966). *Basic concepts of measurement.* London: Cambridge University Press.

Ellsberg, D. (1961). Risk, ambiguity, and the Savage axioms. *Quarterly Journal of Economics, 75,* 643–669.

Falmagne, J.-C. (1976). Random conjoint measurement and loudness summation. *Psychological Review, 83,* 65–79.

Falmagne, J.-C. (1978). A representation theorem for finite random scale systems. *Journal of Mathematical Psychology, 18,* 52–72.

Falmagne, J.-C. (1980). A probabilistic theory of extensive measurement. *Philosophy of Science, 47,* 277–296.

Falmagne, J.-C. (1985). *Elements of psychophysical theory.* New York: Oxford University Press.

Falmagne, J.-C., & Iverson, G. (1979). Conjoint Weber laws and additivity. *Journal of Mathematical Psychology, 86,* 25–43.

Falmagne, J.-C., Iverson, G., & Marcovici, S. (1979). Binaural "loudness" summation: Probabilistic theory and data. *Psychological Review, 86,* 25–43.

Falmagne, J.-C. & Narens, L. (1983). Scales and meaningfulness of qualitative laws. *Synthese, 55,* 287–325.

Fechner, G. T. (1860/1966). *Elemente der psychophysik.* Leipzig: Breitkopf and Hartel. Translation of Vol. 1 by H. E. Adler. E. G. Boring & D. H. Howes, (Eds.) *Elements of psychophysics* (Vol. 1). New York: Holt, Rinehart & Winston.

Fishburn, P. C. (1970). *Utility theory for decision making.* New York: John Wiley & Sons.

Fishburn, P. C. (1982). *The foundations of expected utility.* Dordrecht: Reidel.

Fishburn, P. C. (1985). *Interval orders and interval graphs: A study of partially ordered sets.* New York: John Wiley & Sons.

Fishburn, P.C. (1988). *Nonlinear preference and utility theory.* Baltimore, MD: Johns Hopkins Press.

Galambos, J. (1978/1987). *The asymptotic theory of extreme order statistics.* New York: John Wiley & Sons; 2nd ed., Malabar, FL: Robert E. Krieger.

Garner, W. R. (1974). *The processing of information and structure.* New York: John Wiley & Sons.

Gescheider, G. A. (1976). *Psychophysics: Method and theory*. Hillsdale, NJ: Erlbaum.

Gescheider, G. A., Wright, J. H., & Polak, J. W. (1971). Detection of vibrotactile signals differing in probability of occurrence. *The Journal of Psychology, 78*, 253–260.

Gigerenzer, G., & Strube, G. (1983). Are there limits to binaural additivity of loudness? *Journal of Experimental Psychology: Human Perception and Performance, 9*, 126–136.

Gravetter, F., & Lockhead, G. R. (1973). Criterial range as a frame of reference for stimulus judgments. *Psychological Review, 80*, 203–216.

Green, D. M., & Luce, R. D. (1973). Speed-accuracy trade off in auditory detection. In S. Kornblum (Ed.), *Attention and performance* (Vol. IV, pp. 547–569). New York: Academic Press.

Green, D. M., & Swets, J. A. (1966/1974/1988). *Signal detection theory and psychophysics*. New York: John Wiley & Sons. Reprinted, Huntington, NY: Robert E. Krieger. Reprinted, Palo Alto, CA: Peninsula Press.

Hagerty, M., & Birnbaum, M. H. (1978). Nonparametric tests of ratio vs. subtractive theories of stimulus comparison. *Perception & Psychophysics, 24*, 121–129.

Hardin, C., & Birnbaum, M. H. (1990). Malleability of "ratio" judgments of occupational prestige. *American Journal of Psychology, 103*, 1–20.

Hölder, O. (1901). Die Axiome der Quantität und die Lehre vom Mass. *Berichte über die Verhandlungen der Königlich Sächsischen Gesellschaft der Wissenschaften zu Leipzig, Mathematisch-Physische Klasse, 53*, 1–64. Translation of Part I by J. Michell & C. Ernst (1996). The axioms of quantity and the theory of measurement. *Journal of Mathematical Psychology, 40*, 235–252.

Holland, M. K., & Lockhead, G. R. (1968). Sequential effects in absolute judgments of loudness. *Perception & Psychophysics, 3*, 409–414.

Iverson, G. J., Bamber, D. (1997). The generalized area theorem in signal detection theory. In A. A. J. Marley (Ed.), *Choice, decision and measurement: Papers in honor of R. Duncan Luce's 70th birthday* (pp. 301–318). Mahwah, NJ: Erlbaum.

Iverson, G.J., & Falmagne, J.-C. (1985). Statistical issues in measurement. *Mathematical Social Sciences, 14*, 131–153.

Iverson, G. J., and Sheu, C.-F. (1992). Characterizing random variables in the context of signal detection theory. *Mathematical Social Sciences, 23*, 151–174.

Jesteadt, W., Wier, C. C., & Green, D. M. (1977). Intensity discrimination as a function of frequency and sensation level. *Journal of the Acoustical Society of America, 61*, 169–177.

Kadlec, H., & Townsend, J. T. (1992). Signal detection analyses of dimensional interactions. In Ashby, F. G. (Ed.), *Multidimensional models of perception and cognition* (pp. 181–227). Hillsdale, NJ: Erlbaum.

Kahneman, D., & Tversky, A. (1979). Prospect theory: An analysis of decision under risk. *Econometrica, 47*, 263–291.

Keren, G., & Baggen, S. (1981). Recognition models of alphanumeric characters. *Perception & Psychophysics, 29*, 234–246.

Klein, F. (1872/1893). A comparative review of recent researches in geometry. *Bulletin of the New York Mathematical Society, 2*, 215–249. (The 1872 Erlangen address was transcribed and translated into English and published in 1893.)

Krantz, D. H. (1972). A theory of magnitude estimation and cross-modality matching. *Journal of Mathematical Psychology, 9*, 168–199.

Krantz, D. H. (1975a, b). Color measurement and color theory. I. Representation theorem for Grassman structures. II. Opponent-colors theory. *Journal of Mathematical Psychology, 12*, 283–303, 304–327.

Krantz, D. H., Luce, R. D., Suppes, P., & Tversky, A. (1971). *Foundations of measurement* (Vol. I.) New York: Academic Press.

Krumhansl, C. L. (1978). Concerning the applicability of geometric models to similarity data:

The interrelationship between similarity and spatial density. *Psychological Review, 85,* 445–463.

Kuczma, M. (1968). *Functional equations in a single variable.* Monografie Mat. 46. Warsaw: Polish Scientific.

Lacouture, &., & Marley, A. A. J. (1995). A mapping model of bow effects in absolute identification. *Journal of Mathematical Psychology, 39,* 383–395.

Levelt, W. J. M., Riemersma, J. B., & Bunt, A. A. (1972). Binaural additivity in loudness. *British Journal of Mathematical and Statistical Psychology, 25,* 1–68.

Levine, M. V. (1971). Transformations that render curves parallel. *Journal of Mathematical Psychology, 7,* 410–441.

Levine, M. V. (1972). Transforming curves into curves with the same shape. *Journal of Mathematical Psychology, 9,* 1–16.

Lichtenstein, S., & Slovic, P. (1971). Reversals of preference between bids and choices in gambling decisions, *Journal of Experimental Psychology, 89,* 46–55.

Link, S. W. (1992). *The wave theory of difference and similarity.* Hillsdale, NJ: Erlbaum.

Lockhead, G. R. (1966). Effects of dimensional redundancy on visual discrimination. *Journal of Experimental Psychology, 72,* 94–104.

Lowen, S. B., & Teich, M. C. (1992). Auditory-nerve action potentials form a nonrenewal point process over short as well as long time scales. *Journals of the Acoustical Society of America, 92,* 803–806.

Lowenstein, G., & Elster, J. (1992). *Choice over time.* New York: Russell Sage Foundation.

Luce, R. D. (1959a). *Individual choice behavior: A theoretical analysis.* New York: John Wiley & Sons.

Luce, R. D. (1959b). On the possible psychophysical laws. *Psychological Review, 66,* 81–95.

Luce, R. D. (1963). Detection and recognition. In R. D. Luce, R. R. Bush, & E. Galanter (Eds.), *Handbook of mathematical psychology* (Vol. 1, pp. 103–189). New York: John Wiley & Sons.

Luce, R. D. (1977). A note on sums of power functions. *Journal of Mathematical Psychology, 16,* 91–93.

Luce, R. D. (1986). *Response times. Their role in inferring elementary mental organization.* New York: Oxford University Press.

Luce, R. D. (1987). Measurement structures with Archimedean ordered translation groups. *Order, 4,* 391–415.

Luce, R. D. (1990a). "On the possible psychophysical laws" revisited: Remarks on cross-modal matching. *Psychological Review, 97,* 66–77.

Luce, R. D. (1990b). Rational versus plausible accounting equivalences in preference judgments. *Psychological Science, 1,* 225–234. Reprinted (with minor modifications) in W. Edwards (Ed.), (1992), *Utility theories: Measurements and applications* (pp. 187–206). Boston: Kluwer Academic.

Luce, R. D. (1992a). Singular points in generalized concatenation structures that otherwise are homogeneous. *Mathematical Social Sciences, 24,* 79–103.

Luce, R. D. (1992b). Where does subjective-expected utility fail descriptively? *Journal of Risk and Uncertainty, 5,* 5–27.

Luce, R. D. (1993). *Sound and hearing. A conceptual introduction.* Hillsdale, NJ: Erlbaum.

Luce, R. D., & Alper, T. M. (in preparation). *Conditions equivalent to unit representations of ordered relational structures.* Manuscript.

Luce, R. D., & Edwards, W. (1958). The derivation of subjective scales from just-noticeable differences. *Psychological Review, 65,* 227–237.

Luce, R. D., & Fishburn, P. C. (1991). Rank- and sign-dependent linear utility models for finite first-order gambles. *Journal of Risk and Uncertainty, 4,* 29–59.

Luce, R. D., & Fishburn, P. C. (1995). A note on deriving rank-dependent utility using additive joint receipts. *Journal of Risk and Uncertainty, 11,* 5–16.

Luce, R. D., & Galanter, E. (1963). Discrimination. In R. D. Luce, R. R. Bush, & E. Galanter (Eds.), *Handbook of mathematical psychology* (Vol. I, pp. 191–243). New York: John Wiley & Sons.

Luce, R. D., Green, D. M., & Weber, D. L. (1976). Attention bands in absolute identification. *Perception & Psychophysics, 20,* 49–54.

Luce, R. D., Krantz, D. H., Suppes, P., & Tversky, A. (1990). *Foundations of Measurement* (Vol. 3). San Diego: Academic Press.

Luce, R. D., Mellers, B. A., & Chang, S.-J. (1993). Is choice the correct primitive? On using certainty equivalents and reference levels to predict choices among gambles. *Journal of Risk and Uncertainty, 6,* 115–143.

Luce, R. D., & Narens, L. (1985). Classification of concatenation measurement structures according to scale type. *Journal of Mathematical Psychology, 29,* 1–72.

Luce, R. D., & Nosofsky, R. M. (1984). Sensitivity and criterion effects in absolute identification. In S. Kornblum & J. Requin (Eds.), *Preparatory states and processes* (pp. 3–35). Hillsdale, NJ: Erlbaum.

Luce, R. D., Nosofsky, R. M., Green, D. M., & Smith, A. F. (1982). The bow and sequential effects in absolute identification. *Perception & Psychophysics, 32,* 397–408.

Luce, R. D., & Raiffa, H. (1957/1989). *Games and Decisions. Introduction and Critical Survey.* New York: John Wiley & Sons. Reprinted New York: Dover Publications.

Luce, R. D., & Suppes, P. (1965). Preference, utility, and subjective probability. In R. D. Luce, R. R. Bush, & E. Galanter (Eds.), *Handbook of Mathematical Psychology,* (Vol. III, pp. 249–410). New York: Wiley.

Luce, R. D., & von Winterfeld, D. (1994). What common ground exists for descriptive, prescriptive, and normative utility theories? *Management Science, 40,* 263–279.

MacCrimmon, K. R., Stanburg, W. T., & Wehrung, D. A. (1980). Real money lotteries: A study of ideal risk, context effects, and simple processes. In T. S. Wallsten (Ed.), *Cognitive process in choice and decision behavior* (pp. 155–177). Hillsdale, NJ: Erlbaum.

Macmillan, N. A., & Creelman, C. D. (1991). *Detection theory: A user's guide.* New York: Cambridge University Press.

Maddox, W. T. (1992). Perceptual and Decisional Separability. In Ashby, F. G. (Ed.), *Multidimensional models of perception and cognition* (pp. 147–180). Hillsdale, NJ: Erlbaum.

Marley, A. A. J. (1990). A historical and contemporary perspective on random scale representations of choice probabilities and reaction times in the context of Cohen and Falmagne's (1990, *Journal of Mathematical Psychology, 34*) results. *Journal of Mathematical Psychology, 34,* 81–87.

Marley, A. A. J., & Cook, V. T. (1984). A fixed rehearsal capacity interpretation of limits on absolute identification performance. *British Journal of Mathematical and Statistical Psychology, 30,* 136–151.

Marley, A. A. J., & Cook, V. T. (1986). A limited capacity rehearsal model for psychophysical judgments applied to magnitude estimation. *Journal of Mathematical Psychology, 37,* 339–390.

Marschak, J. (1960). Binary-choice constraints and random utility indicators. In K. J. Arrow, S. Karlin, & P. Suppes (Eds.), *Proceedings of the fist Stanford symposium on mathematical methods in the social sciences, 1959* (pp. 312–329). Stanford, CA: Stanford University Press.

McGill, W. J., & Goldberg, J. P. (1968). A study of the near-miss involving Weber's law and pure-tone intensity discrimination. *Perception & Psychophysics, 4,* 105–109.

Medin, D. L., & Schaffer, M. M. (1978). Context theory of classification learning. *Psychological Review, 85,* 207–238.

Mellers, B. A., Chang, S., Birnbaum, M. H., & Ordóñez, L. D. (1992). Preferences, prices, and ratings in risky decision making. *Journal of Experimental Psychology: Human Perception and Performance, 18,* 347–361.

Mellers, B. A., Weiss, R., & Birnbaum, M. H. (1992). Violations of dominance in pricing judgments. *Journal of Risk and Uncertainty, 5,* 73–90.

Michell, J. (1986). Measurement scales and statistics: A clash of paradigms. *Psychological Bulletin, 100,* 398–407.

Michell, J. (1990). *An introduction to the logic of psychological measurement.* Hillsdale, NJ: Erlbaum.

Michell, J. (1995). Further thoughts on realism, representationalism, and the foundations of measurement theory [A book review reply]. *Journal of Mathematical Psychology, 39,* 243–247.

Miller, G. A. (1956). The magical number seven plus or minus two: Some limits on our capacity for processing information. *Psychological Review, 63,* 81–97.

Narens, L. (1981a). A general theory of ratio scalability with remarks about the measurement-theoretic concept of meaningfulness. *Theory and Decision, 13,* 1–70.

Narens, L. (1981b). On the scales of measurement. *Journal of Mathematical Psychology, 24,* 249–275.

Narens, L. (1985). *Abstract measurement theory.* Cambridge, MA: MIT Press.

Narens, L. (1988). Meaningfulness and the Erlanger program of Felix Klein. *Mathématiques Informatique et Sciences Humaines, 101,* 61–72.

Narens, L. (1994). The measurement theory of dense threshold structures. *Journal of Mathematical Psychology, 38,* 301–321.

Narens, L. (1996). A theory of ratio magnitude estimation. *Journal of Mathematical Psychology, 40,* 109–129.

Narens, L. (in preparation). *Theories of meaningfulness.* Manuscript.

Narens, L., & Mausfeld, R. (1992). On the relationship of the psychological and the physical in psychophysics. *Psychological Review, 99,* 467–479.

Niederée, R. (1992). What do numbers measure? A new approach to fundamental measurement. *Mathematical Social Sciences, 24,* 237–276.

Niederée, R. (1994). There is more to measurement than just measurement: Measurement theory, symmetry, and substantive theorizing. A discussion of basic issues in the theory of measurement. A review with special focus on *Foundations of Measurement. Vol. 3: Representation, Axiomatization, and Invariance* by R. Duncan Luce, David H. Krantz, Patrick Suppes, and Amos Tversky. *Journal of Mathematical Psychological, 38,* 527–594.

Noreen, D. L. (1981). Optimal decision rules for some common psychophysical paradigms. *SIAM-AMS Proceedings, 13,* 237–279.

Nosofsky, R. M. (1983). Information integration and the identification of stimulus noise and critical noise in absolute judgment. *Journal of Experimental Psychology: Human Perception and Performance, 9,* 299–309.

Nosofsky, R. M. (1984). Choice, similarity, and the context theory of classification. *Journal of Experimental Psychology: Learning, Memory and Cognition, 10,* 104–114.

Nosofsky, R. M. (1986). Attention, similarity, and the identification-categorization relationship. *Journal of Experimental Psychology: General, 115,* 39–57.

Nosofsky, R. M. (1987). Attention and learning processes in the identification and categorization of integral stimuli. *Journal of Experimental Psychology: Learning, Memory and Cognition, 13,* 87–109.

Nosofsky, R. M. (1989). Further test of an exemplar-similarity approach to relating identification and categorization. *Perception & Psychophysics, 45,* 279–290.

Nosofsky, R. M. (1991). Tests of an exemplar model for relating perceptual classification and recognition memory. *Journal of Experimental Psychology: Human Perception and Performance, 9,* 299–309.

Palacios, J. (1964). *Dimensional Analysis.* London: Macmillan & Co.

Pelli, D. G. (1985). Uncertainty explains many aspects of visual contrast detection and discrimination. *Journal of the Optical Society of America A, 2,* 1508–1531.

Perrin, N. A. (1986). *The GRT of preference: A new theory of choice.* Unpublished doctoral dissertation, Ohio State University.

Perrin, N. A. (1992). Uniting identification, similarity and preference: General recognition theory. In F. G. Ashby (Ed.), *Multidimensional models of perception and cognition* (pp. 123–146). Hillsdale, NJ: Erlbaum.

Pfanzagl, J. (1971). *Theory of measurement.* Würzburg: Phusica-Verlag.

Plateau, J. A. F. (1872). Sur las measure des sensations physiques, et sur loi qui lie l'intensité de ces sensation à l'intensité de la cause excitante. *Bulletin de l'Academie Royale de Belgique, 33,* 376–388.

Pruzansky, S., Tversky, A., & Carroll, J. D. (1982). Spatial versus tree representations of proximity data. *Psychometrika, 47,* 3–24.

Quiggin, J. (1993). *Generalized expected utility theory: The rank-dependent model.* Boston: Kluwer Academic Publishers.

Regenwetter, M. (1996). Random utility representation of finite *n*-ary relations. *Journal of Mathematical Psychology, 40,* 219–234.

Roberts, F. S. (1979). *Measurement theory.* Reading, MA: Addison-Wesley.

Savage, C. W., & Ehrlich, P. (Eds.). (1992). *Philosophical and foundational issues in measurement theory.* Hillsdale, NJ: Erlbaum.

Savage, L.J. (1954). *The foundations of statistics.* New York: John Wiley & Sons.

Schepartz, B. (1980). *Dimensional analysis in the biomedical sciences.* Springfield, IL: Charles C. Thomas.

Schoemaker, P. J. H. (1982). The expected utility model: Its variants, purposes, evidence and limitations. *Journal of Economic Literature, 20,* 529–563.

Schoemaker, P. J. H. (1990). Are risk-attitudes related across domain and response modes? *Management Science, 36,* 1451–1463.

Scott Blair, G. W. (1969). *Elementary rheology.* New York: Academic Press.

Sedov, L. I. (1959). *Similarity and dimensional methods in mechanics.* New York: Academic Press. (Translation from the Russian by M. Holt and M. Friedman)

Shepard, R. N. (1957). Stimulus and response generalization: A stochastic model relating generalization to distance in psychological space. *Psychometrica, 22,* 325–345.

Shepard, R. N. (1978). On the status of 'direct' psychophysical measurement. In C. W. Savage (Ed.), *Minnesota studies in the philosophy of science* (Vol. IX, pp. 441–490). Minneapolis: University of Minnesota Press.

Shepard, R. N. (1981). Psychological relations and psychophysical scales: On the status of "direct" psychophysical measurement. *Journal of Mathematical Psychology, 24,* 21–57.

Shepard, R. N. (1987). Toward a universal law of generalization for psychological science. *Science, 237,* 1317–1323.

Sjöberg, L. (1980). Similarity and correlation. In E. D. Lanterman & H. Feger (Eds.), *Similarity and choice* (pp. 70–87). Bern: Huber.

Slater, P. (1960). The analysis of personal preferences. *British Journal of Statistical Psychology, 13,* 119–135.

Slovic, P., & Lichtenstein, S. (1968). Importance of variance preferences in gambling decisions. *Journal of Experimental Psychology, 78,* 646–654.

Slovic, P., & Lichtenstein, S. (1983). Preference reversals: A broader perspective. *American Economic Review, 73,* 596–605.

Stevens, S. S. (1946). On the theory of scales of measurement. *Science, 103,* 677–680.

Stevens, S. S. (1951). Mathematics, measurement and psychophysics. In S. S. Stevens (Ed.), *Handbook of experimental psychology* (pp. 1–49). New York: John Wiley & Sons.

Stevens, S. S. (1975). *Psychophysics.* New York: John Wiley & Sons.

Suppes, P., Krantz, D. H., Luce, R. D., & Tversky, A. (1989). *Foundations of measurement* (Vol. 3). San Diego, CA: Academic Press.

Thompson, W. J., & Singh, J. (1967). The use of limit theorems in paired comparison model-building.*Psychometrica, 32,* 255–264.

Thurstone, L. L. (1927a). A law of comparative judgment. *Psychological Review, 34,* 273–286.

Thurstone, L. L. (1927b). Psychophysical analysis. *American Journal of Psychology, 38,* 68–89.

Thurstone, L. L. (1927c). Three psychophysical laws. *Psychological Review, 34,* 424–432.

Torgerson, W. S. (1961). Distances and ratios in psychological scaling. *Acta Psychologica, 19,* 201–205.

Townsend, J. T., & Ashby, F. G. (1984). Measurement scales and statistics: The misconception misconceived. *Psychological Bulletin, 96,* 394–401.

Treisman, M. (1985). The magical number seven and some other features of category scaling: Properties of a model for absolute judgment. *Journal of Mathematical Psychology, 29,* 175–230.

Treisman, M., & Williams, T. C. (1984). A theory of criterion setting with an application to sequential dependencies. *Psychological Review, 84,* 68–111.

Tucker, L. R. (1960). Intra-individual and inter-individual multidimensionality. In H. Gulliksen & S. Messick (Eds.), *Psychological scaling: Theory and applicatons.* New York: Wiley.

Tversky, A. (1972a). Choice by elimination. *Journal of Mathematical Psychology, 9,* 341–367.

Tversky, A. (1972b). Elimination by aspects: A theory of choice. *Psychological Review, 79,* 281–299.

Tversky, A. (1997). Features of similarity. *Psychological Review, 84,* 327–352.

Tversky, A., & Kahneman, D. (1986). Rational Choice and the Framing of Decisions. *Journal of Business, 59,* S251–S278. Reprinted in R. M. Hogarth and M. W. Reder (Eds.), (1986), *Rational choice: The contrast between economics and psychology* (pp. 67–94). Chicago: University of Chicago Press.

Tversky, A., & Kahneman, D. (1992). Advances in prospect theory: Cumulative representation of uncertainty. *Journal of Risk and Uncertainty, 5,* 204–217.

Tversky, A., & Sattath, S. (1979). Preference trees. *Psychological Review, 86,* 542–573.

Tversky, A., Slovic, P., & Kahneman, D. (1990). The causes of preference reversal. *The American Economic Review, 80,* 204–217.

Ulehla, Z. J., Halpern, J., & Cerf, A. (1968). Integration of information in a visual discrimination task. *Perception & Psychophysics, 4* 1–4.

van Acker, P. (1990). Transitivity revisited. *Annals of Operations Research, 23,* 1–25.

von Winterfeldt, D., Chung, N.-K., Luce, R. D., & Cho, Y. (1997). Tests of consequene monotonicity in decision making under uncertainty. *Journal of Experimental Psychology: Learning, Memory, and Cognition,* in press.

Wakker, P. P. (1989). *Additive representations of preferences: A new foundation of decision analysis.* Dordrecht: Kluwer Academic Publishers.

Wakker, P. P., & Tversky, A. (1993). An axiomatization of cumulative prospect theory. *Journal of Risk and Uncertainty, 7,* 147–176.

Wandell, B., & Luce, R. D. (1978). Pooling peripheral information: Averages versus extreme values. *Journal of Mathematical Psychology, 17,* 220–235.

Ward, L. M., & Lockhead, G. R. (1970). Sequential effects and memory in category judgments. *Journal of Experimental Psychology, 84,* 27–34.

Ward, L. M., & Lockhead, G. R. (1971). Response system processes in absolute judgment. *Perception & Psychophysics, 9,* 73–78.

Weber, D. L., Green, D. M., & Luce, R. D. (1977). Effects of practice and distribution of auditory signals on absolute identification. *Perception & Psychophysics, 22,* 223–231.

Wickelgren, W. A. (1968). Unidimensional strength theory and component analysis of noise in absolute and comparative judgments. *Journal of Mathematical Psychology, 5,* 102–122.

Yellott, J. I. (1977). The relationship between Luce's choice axiom, Thurstone's theory of comparative judgment, and the double exponential distribution. *Journal of Mathematical Psychology, 15,* 109–144.

CHAPTER 2

Psychophysical Scaling

Lawrence E. Marks
Daniel Algom

I. INTRODUCTION

Consider the following three biblical scenes. In the aftermath of the fight with Goliath, a victorious David is respected more than Saul the king, and the celebrating women sing: "Saul hath slain his thousands, and David his ten thousands" (I Samuel 18:7). Or take Amos 5:2, where the threat facing the people is phrased: "The city that went out by a thousand shall leave an hundred, and that which went forth by an hundred shall have ten." Finally, examine the advice given to Moses to mitigate the burden of judging the people—that he should appoint "rulers of thousands, and rulers of hundreds, and rulers of fifties, and rulers of tens," so that "every great matter they shall bring unto thee, but every small matter they shall judge" (Exodus 18:21–22).

Three points are noteworthy. First, all three verses deal with matters "psycho-physical": Feelings of reverence, magnitude of threat, and gravity of offenses are all projected onto objective continua that can be described numerically. Second, the use of numbers to depict sensations appears in the Bible, as well as in other works of literature, both classical and modern. Most remarkable, however, is the way that the respective sensations are mapped onto numbers. In each case, changes or increments in sensation are associated with a geometric series of numeric, physical values. If we take

Measurement, Judgment, and Decision Making

these sensations to increase in equal steps—and exegesis makes such an assumption plausible—we have an *arithmetic* series of psychological values covarying with the respective *geometric* series of physical values. This relation, so familiar now with students of psychophysics, defines a logarithmic function.

One should not construe this foray into biblical psychophysics as a mere exercise in the history of metaphoric allusion. In fact, the aforementioned texts may have played a direct role in establishing the science of psychophysics. For it was our last example that captured the attention of Daniel Bernoulli, who gave the preceding interpretation when he derived his famous logarithmic function for utility some quarter millennium ago. And, according to his own testimony, the founder of psychophysics, Gustav Fechner, was influenced in turn by Bernoulli's discourse in developing his own logarithmic law—the first explicit, quantitative, psychophysical statement relating sensations to stimuli.

Psychophysics is the branch of science that studies the relation between sensory responses and the antecedent physical stimuli. Born in the 19th century, psychophysics can claim parentage in two important scientific traditions: the analysis of sensory-perceptual processes, brilliantly realized at the time in the work of H. L. F. von Helmholtz, and the mathematical account of mental phenomena, associated then with the work of J. F. Herbart. A main theme is the quantification of sensory responses, or, more generally, the measurement of sensations. Although it falls properly in the general domain of experimental and theoretical psychology, the very name *psychophysics* points to a corresponding set of issues in philosophy concerning the relation of the mental and the physical. From its inception in the work of Fechner, attempts to measure sensation have been controversial, as psychophysicists have merged empirical operations with theoretical frameworks in order to mold a discipline that is at once philosophically sound and scientifically satisfying.

We start by reviewing issues and criticisms that marked the first program to measure sensations. Because many of these topics remain pertinent today, this section provides perspectives to evaluate the virtues and vulnerabilities of the scaling methods and theories, both classical and modern. The main body of the chapter reviews a wide array of relevant data and theories. The two notions of sensory *distance* and sensory *magnitude* serve as our main categories of classification.

In places, we allude to a distinction between what have been called "old psychophysics" and "new psychophysics," a distinction that in some ways remains useful. Classical, or old, psychophysics rests on the conviction that scales of sensation comprise objective, scientific constructs. By this view, *magnitude of sensation* is a derived concept, based on certain theoretical assumptions augmented by mathematical analysis, and hence is largely independent of any subjective feeling of magnitude. Empirically, one of the hallmarks of classical psychophysics is the explicit comparison of two stimuli. The resulting responses then serve to define a unit for the unseen mental events, measurement of which entails marking off distances or differences along the psychological continuum. Consequently, the notion of *sensory distance* or *difference* has been widely used as the basis for scaling sensation.

By way of contrast, the new psychophysics tries to define sensation magnitude by quantifying a person's verbal responses. The approach is, therefore, largely operational, and it frequently claims to assess sensations "directly." A popular contemporary technique within this tradition is magnitude estimation, which asks people to estimate numerically the strength of the sensation aroused by a given stimulus (usually in relation to the strength of other stimuli). Magnitude estimation, category rating, and related methods have greatly diversified the stock of modern psychophysics, helping to create a large database for students of decision processes and judgments as well as students of sensory processes.

To be sure, the terms *old* and *new* psychophysics are misnomers, because many new approaches rest on basic tenets of the old. So are the terms *indirect* and *direct* measurement, often used to characterize the two classes of scaling. Regardless of the particular theoretical stance, the measurement of sensation always entails assumptions or definitions. As a result, it is not wholly appropriate to characterize methods by their *directness:* If we take sensation magnitude to be an intervening variable, a common view (cf. Gescheider, 1988), then clearly sensation can be measured only indirectly.

The last point is notable, for it indicates the need for adequate theoretical frameworks to underpin scales derived from magnitude estimation and from various numeric or graphic rating procedures, as well as from discrimination tasks. Consequently, after comparing the approaches through "distance" and "magnitude," we proceed by examining recent multidimensional models of scaling and the theoretical frameworks that underlie the models. By relating measurement to the underlying psychological theory, we seek not only to identify various factors that affect scaling but to illustrate the processes. Foremost among those are the effects of context, which are discussed in a separate section. We conclude by noting the need to integrate scaling data with all other data and theories that are relevant to the psychological representation of magnitude.

II. PSYCHOPHYSICAL SCALING AND PSYCHOPHYSICAL THEORY

Allow us one final bit of biblical exegesis. In Genesis (37:3), we learn that the patriarch Jacob "loved Joseph more than all of his children." This terse statement marks the unfolding of a momentous chain of events known as the story of Joseph and his brothers. Jacob's partiality, intimates the biblical narrative, had far-reaching ramifications. It set the stage for the slavery of the Hebrews in Egypt, their exodus, and, eventually, the founding of the nation of Israel in the Sinai. These fateful consequences notwithstanding, at its base, claimed the philosopher Isaiah Leibowitz (1987), the verse contains only loose, qualitative information. Despite using the same adjective, *more*, the biblical statement differs in a fundamental sense from the formally similar sentence, "The red urn contains more marbles than the blue one." Whereas the latter relation is truly quantitative, measurable, and hence describable numerically, the former is not. There is no answer to the question, "How much more did Jacob love Joseph than, say, Reuben?" simply because sensations are inherently qualitative. Quantitative definition of sensation is meaningless, averred Leibowitz, and thus sensation—indeed, psychology as a whole—is immune to scientific inquiry.

Leibowitz's (1987) objection is no stranger to psychophysics. At least a century old, it restates what has been called the "quantity objection" (e.g., Boring, 1921)—that sensations do not have magnitudes. William James (1892), a major proponent of this view, wrote, "Surely, our feeling of scarlet is not a feeling of pink with a lot more pink added; it is something quite other than pink. Similarly with our sensations of an electric arc-light: it does not contain that many smoky tallow candles in itself" (pp. 23–24). And, in Boring's (1921) rendition of Külpe (1895), "This sensation of gray is not two or three of that other sensation of gray" (p. 45). By this view, what the verse in Genesis really conveys is the sense that Jacob's love for Joseph differed from the love he felt toward his other sons, a difference vividly revealed in the exclusive gift of the "coat of many colors." Quite apart from the quantity objection, Leibowitz implied that mere rank ordering of sensations—even if possible—would not amount to measurement either. This contention too has a long history. Nominal, ordinal, and, in some instances, interval scales were not considered measurement at all, according to a prevailing view held until the late 1940s (Heidelberger, 1993).

Another objection challenges the very existence of a dimension of "sensation magnitude" or "sensation strength." In the context of scaling, the view that we judge stimuli, not sensations, was espoused by Fullerton and Cattell (1892) and by Ebbinghaus (1902). In Cattell's (1893) words, "The question here is whether we do in fact judge differences in the intensity of sensations, or whether we merely judge differences in the stimuli determined by association with their known objective relations. I am inclined to think that the latter is the case. . . . I believe that my adjustment is always determined by association with the known quantitative relations of the physical world. With lights and sounds, association might lead us to consider relative differences as equal differences, and the data would be obtained from which the logarithmic relation between stimulus and sensation has been deduced" (p. 293).

Cattell's position mirrors, almost verbatim, a more recent approach called the "physical correlate theory" (Warren, 1958, 1969, 1981). Perhaps reflecting the Zeitgeist in psychophysics, Warren's rendition replaces Fechner's logarithmic function with a power function. For attributes such as loudness or brightness, the theory assumes that the physical correlate to which the subject responds is distance. Accordingly, to judge the loudness of one sound as half that of another is to say that the former appears to come from a source twice as far away. Because sound energy varies as the inverse square of the distance from its source, the physical correlate theory predicts a square-root relation between loudness and sound energy. The same notion informs the later work of J. J. Gibson (1966, 1979), whose "direct perception" or "ecological approach" is akin to Warren's. Gibson's theory can be construed as an attempt "to state a functional correlate for all aspects of perception" (Baird, 1981, p. 190). Apart from eschewing the notions of subjective magnitude and representation, Gibson and Warren share a pragmatic approach grounded in environmental affordances that help the organism to survive. The similarity is apparent even at the level of the specific environmental cues utilized: "Both say that the perception of size and distance is veridical, and both ignore data to the contrary" (Baird, 1981, p. 191). In our view, the hypothesis that psychophysical scales reflect an amalgamation of sensory and cognitive processes yields a rich network of predictable phenomena. Warren's attack offers no alternative mechanism for generating those data, including, incidentally, the way people judge the physical correlates themselves.

A. What Is Measured?

The quest to stand sensory measurement on a firm basis has sustained several efforts at general formulation. For example, Zwislocki (1991) proposed defining measurement as "matching common attributes of things or events" (p. 20). Matching takes place on an ordinal scale, and it needs neither instruments nor numbers. It can be accomplished internally (i.e., subjectively) and, in fact, is ubiquitous in nature (whence the term *natural measurement*). Only with the introduction of physical variables can the results be expressed quantitatively, but this technicality does not alter the mental origin or nature of measurement. In Zwislocki's scheme, formal physical measurement is only a late derivative of psychophysical or natural measurement.

Another attempt to tie psychophysical and physical measurement in a common conceptual package comes from the physicist and philosopher

Herbert Dingle (e.g., 1960). Dingle challenged us to consider the first sentence of an influential volume on measurement (Churchman & Ratoosh, 1959): "Measurement presupposes something to be measured, and unless we know what that something is, no measurement can have any significance." Self-evident truth? Tautology? No, claimed Dingle—just plainly wrong! Actually, he claimed, in physics as well as in psychology, "far from starting with a something and then [trying] to measure it, we start with a measure and then try to find something to which we can attach it" (Dingle, 1960, p. 189).

Dingle made a compelling case that physical measurement does not uncover something "out there," but rather is a self-contained process that implies nothing beyond the meaning that we choose to confer on the result. Measurement, he stated, contains a manual and a mental part. It is what Stevens (1975, p. 47) called a "schemapiric enterprise." But a system of measurements is a theoretical construct impregnated with meaning only by its designer. In psychology, for instance, "the importance of Intelligence Quotient is not that it measures 'intelligence,' whatever that may be, but that it stands in simple relations to other measurements" (Dingle, 1960, p. 192). Like Stevens, Dingle disposed with the distinction between "fundamental" and "derived" measurement; in his scheme, fundamental measures are also derived. Dingle's approach is strictly operational, as Stevens's sometimes is. But unlike Stevens, Dingle stressed the indispensability of substantive theory. Sensations are difficult to measure not because they are mental, subjective, or inaccessible, but simply for want of good psychophysical theory.

B. Infrastructures and Suprastructures

Dingle would ground psychophysical scales in what we term here theoretical *suprastructures*, that is, in those frameworks that connect the particular property being measured with other properties or processes within the psychological domain. In physics, one example of a suprastructure is found in the principles underlying the *ideal gas law*. As Norwich (1993) has pointed out, it is possible to derive the law from principles of conservation of mass and energy, though the law is also consistent with properties of the forces between gas molecules. The law itself can be written

$$P \cdot V = M \cdot N_a \cdot T, \tag{1}$$

where P is the gas's pressure, V its volume, T its absolute temperature, M the number of moles, and N_a is Avogadro's constant. Note that the multiplicative form of the gas law constrains the scales of pressure, velocity, and temperature with respect to one another. If M is taken to be an absolute measure, with no permissible transformation, then the constraint on scales of P, V, and T is considerable. If M is not absolute, the constraint is smaller. For example, redefining all of the terms (N_a as well as P, V, T, and M) by power transformations—for instance, taking square roots—would produce a new set of scales equally consistent with Eq. (1). On the other hand, additional constraint is provided by other gas laws, for example, the *van der Waals equation*

$$[P + c_1/(M \cdot V)^2] \cdot [M \cdot V - c_2] = N_a \cdot T, \qquad (2)$$

where c_1 and c_2 are constants. In general, power transformations of all of the variables in Eq. (2) do not leave its form invariant.

Unfortunately, there have been relatively few suprastructural theories in psychophysics (cf. Luce, 1972). Two important ones are the theories of Link (1992) and Norwich (1993), described later; here, we simply note that Norwich used the example of the ideal gas law in discussing his approach to psychophysical theory. Suprastructural theories are substantive: They incorporate sensory scales within frameworks that seek to account for a set of empirical phenomena, often with no reference to any particular empirical operations for measurement.

Many, probably most, psychophysical theories are *infrastructural*. That is, these theories seek to provide frameworks that relate a set of empirical operations to a particular psychological scale or property. Often, they are formulated in the language of measurement theory. The most comprehensive and rigorous treatment of measurement theory appears in the foundational approach (e.g., Krantz, Luce, Suppes, & Tversky, 1971; Luce, Krantz, Suppes, & Tversky, 1990; Luce & Narens, 1987; Suppes & Zinnes, 1963). This treatment is axiomatic, resulting in representation theorems that state the existence of functions mapping certain empirical procedures or objects into sets of numbers. Uniqueness theorems then list the ways in which the numbers can be changed without altering the empirical information represented. The foundational approach is informed by the branch of mathematics that deals with ordered algebraic systems (cf. Luce & Krumhansl, 1988). In *conjoint measurement* (Luce & Tukey, 1964), for example, several stimulus factors are varied jointly in a factorial design. Possible behavioral laws referring to the form of their combination (including independence) are then axiomatically tested. Conjoint measurement is at once simple and powerful. Given only an ordering of pairs of stimuli, certain combinatorial patterns possess enough structure to constrain the possible representations, which transcend those of ordinal scales. Although the foundational approach has been criticized as promising more than it has delivered (Cliff, 1992), Narens and Luce (1992) indicated several important contributions to psychology; notable is the role of axiomatic theory in the development of modern decision theory.

Largely infrastructural but potentially suprastructural is the framework of Anderson's (e.g., 1970, 1992) integration psychophysics, or, more generally, the approach called *functional measurement*. Like conjoint measurement, functional measurement treats multivariate phenomena. Primary interest lies in specifying the quantitative rules stating how separate sensations combine in a unitary perception; hence, the conceptual basis of integrational psychophysics is cognitive, lying within the mental realm. Often, these rules comprise algebraic laws of addition, multiplication, or averaging (*cognitive algebra*): If the data conform to the rule, Anderson claimed, then they support not only the rule but the validity of the response scale (e.g., ratings, magnitude estimates) as well (but see Birnbaum, 1982; Gescheider, 1997). In this way, "measurement exists only within the framework of substantive empirical laws" (Anderson, 1974, p. 288). In essence, functional-measurement theory specifies various tests for algebraic models and response scales, and to this extent the theory provides an infrastructural framework to psychophysical judgments. Insofar as one can derive the algebraic models from broader theoretical considerations of perception and cognition, functional measurement—and conjoint measurement—may also provide suprastructure to psychophysical scales.

III. SCALING BY DISTANCE

A. Fechner's Conception: Scaling and the Psychophysical Law

Gustav Fechner's greatness lay in his unprecedented prowess at applying scientific methods to the measurement of sensations. If measurement means more than giving verbal labels to stimuli—if it entails using appropriate units in a process of comparison—then how do we create units for attributes such as loudness, heaviness, or pain? We do not have fundamental units for sensation readily available, a "centimeter" of loudness or a "gram" of pain. And supposing we had such units, how would one perform the necessary comparison? Even granting sensations to have magnitudes, these are bound to remain private and inaccessible, as are all contents of mind. "No instruments," wrote Leahey (1997, p. 181), "can be applied to conscious experiences."

What did Fechner do that eluded his predecessors? Fechner realized that reports by subjects of the magnitude of an experimental stimulus do not measure the resulting sensations any more than do metaphoric descriptions found in literary works, but he was not ready to forswear the notion of sensation strength, an idea with compelling appeal. Consequently, he suggested that sensations could be isolated, then measured, by manipulating the stimuli to which the subject is exposed. Though private, conscious experiences can be controlled by the judicious variation of the appropriate physical stimuli. By varying systematically the values of stimuli, one can elicit a unique conscious experience: success or failure at distinguishing a pair of stimuli. The physical relation between such pairs of stimuli, augmented by a postulate about the concomitant subjective experiences, then can serve to quantify sensation.

Measurement presupposes a process of abstraction, isolating that aspect of the object that one wishes to measure. The sensory error in failing to distinguish a pair of stimuli, or misjudging the weaker of two stimuli to be stronger, served Fechner to isolate a subjective experience in an otherwise inaccessible private realm. He thereby anchored mental measurement in units of the appropriate physical stimuli. To Link (1992),

> Measuring the size of this invisible sensory error in units of the visible physical stimuli was one of the outstanding scientific achievements in the 19th century. . . . In this way Fechner, and his Psychophysics, exposed to scientific scrutiny differences between sensations that were previously hidden from public view and observed only by personal awareness. (p. 7)

Note that Link referred to differences between sensations. Fechner believed that measures of discrimination most directly scale "difference sensations" (Murray, 1993)—though scales of difference sensations may entail sensory magnitudes as well.

Ernst Weber (1834) preceded Fechner in measuring difference thresholds or just noticeable differences (JNDs). And Fechner used Weber's relativity principle, namely that JNDs are proportional to stimulus intensity, in deriving (actually, in justifying) his psychophysical law. Weber's law implies that successive JNDs form a geometric series. If, with Fechner, we assume that JNDs mark off equal units in subjective magnitude along the continuum of intensity, thereby distinguishing *sensation JNDs* from *stimulus JNDs,* then it follows that subjective magnitudes map onto physical ones by a logarithmic function—Fechner's law. Weber did not refer to a quantitative concept of sensation strength or difference. In fact, the sole psychological component in Weber's law is the subject's indication when two stimuli are discriminably different. To be discriminable, Weber learned, the intensities of two stimuli must differ by an amount that is proportional to their absolute level. Yet Weber's law is silent on a crucial question: What sensation is felt at a given JND? Fechner complemented Weber's empirical relation by submitting that JNDs form a subjectively equal series of units, thereby conceiving a truly "psycho-physical" relation.

Fechner assumed the validity of Weber's law, namely, that ΔI, the *stimulus JND,* is proportional to stimulus intensity, I, or,

$$\Delta I/I = c_a, \qquad (3)$$

where c_a is a positive constant, the Weber fraction. Weber's law characterizes thresholds of discrimination along the physical continuum, I. Along the parallel subjective continuum, S, implies Fechner's model, every JND has the same magnitude, so for every ΔI

$$\Delta S = c_b. \tag{4}$$

Thus the *subjective JND*, ΔS, can serve as a unit of sensation. In Fechner's conjecture, the ratios, I_2/I_1, I_3/I_2, . . . , I_j/I_{j-1}, of just noticeably different stimuli—equal according to Weber's law—correspond to equal *increments* in sensation. As a result, a geometrically spaced series of values on the physical continuum gives rise to an arithmetically spaced series of values on the psychological continuum. This relation defines the logarithmic function, Fechner's *Massformel,* or measurement formula,

$$S = c \ln(I/I_o), \tag{5}$$

where $c = c_b/c_a$ is the constant of proportionality, and I_o is the absolute threshold. The stimulus is measured as multiples of the absolute threshold, at which value sensation is zero. Actual scaling, Fechner realized, requires determining ΔI and I_o in the laboratory, and he devised various methods for estimating them. The hallmark of these methods is that the subject merely orders stimuli on a continuum by responses such as "greater," "smaller," or "equal." Such responses avoid many of the pitfalls associated with numerical responses (e.g., Attneave, 1962). First, because the measurement situation is familiar and well defined, the subject presumably knows what she or he means by saying "longer" or "more intense." Therefore, the validity of the responses is warranted, a presupposition of psychophysics in general. Second, ordinal relations are invariant across all positive monotonic transformations. Therefore, assuming only that the psychophysical function is monotonic, the order of the subjective values reproduces the physical order of stimuli.

Fechner derived the logarithmic law using his *mathematical auxiliary principle,* which asserts that the properties characterizing differences as small as JNDs also characterize smaller differences. Thus, dividing Eq. (4) by Eq. (3), rearranging the terms, and rewriting the result as a differential equation gives

$$\delta S = c \, \delta I/I, \tag{6}$$

or the *fundamental formula.* Fechner then integrated Eq. (6) between I_o and I to arrive at the standard logarithmic solution given in Eq. (5) and depicted in Figure 1.

Figure 1 shows how sensation magnitude should increase as stimulus intensity increases, given Fechner's hypothesis. The panel on the top plots both sensation and stimulus in linear coordinates, making clear the rule of diminishing returns. Augmenting stimulus intensity from the 1 stimulus unit (by definition, the absolute threshold) to 1001 stimulus units increases

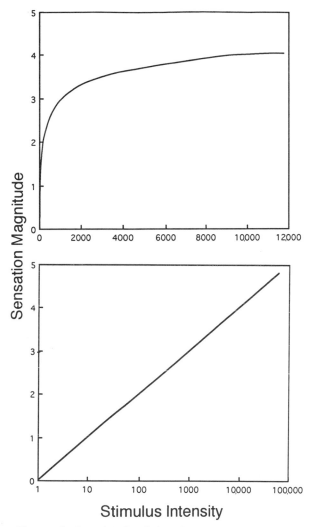

FIGURE 1 Characterization of Fechner's law. Sensation magnitude increases as a negatively accelerated (marginally decreasing) function of stimulus intensity, as shown in the top panel. When stimulus intensity is plotted logarithmically, as in the bottom panel, the function appears as a straight line.

the perceptual experience from zero to about 3 sensation units, but augmenting the stimulus by another 1000 units, to 2001, increases the sensation by only a fraction of unit. The panel on the bottom plots the same psychophysical relation, but now the stimulus levels are spaced logarithmically, turning the concave-downward curve on the top into a straight line, consistent with the form of Eq. (5).

1. Fechner's Conjectures and Weber Functions

Both of the premises underlying the derivation of Fechner's law face difficulties, and plausible alternatives have been offered for both. Following a suggestion made by Brentano (1874), for example, a rule like Weber's law might also hold for sensation, challenging the assumption on the constancy of subjective JNDs. If so, then Fechnerian integration gives a psychophysical power law, where the exponent plays a role analogous to the slope constant c in Fechner's law, Eq. (5). On the stimulus side, the validity of Weber's law itself has long been debated. Often, the Weber ratio $\Delta I/I$ is not constant, particularly at low levels of stimulus intensity, though such deviations frequently can be corrected by a "linear generalization" (Fechner, 1860; Miller, 1947; see also Gescheider, 1997; Marks, 1974b), where ΔI is proportional to I plus a constant rather than proportional to I. Figure 2 shows some characteristic Weber functions for visual brightness, odor intensity, and vibratory touch intensity. Plotted in each case is the difference threshold (ΔI) against stimulus intensity (I), both variables expressed in logarithmic coordinates. Two points are noteworthy. First, these three modalities tend to be characterized by different Weber ratios (ratios of $\Delta I/I$), with intensity discrimination best (Weber ratio smallest) in vision and poorest in touch. Second, the relations in all three cases deviate, at low intensity levels, from the simple form of Weber's law but can be corrected by the inclusion of an additive constant within the linear equation relating ΔI to I.

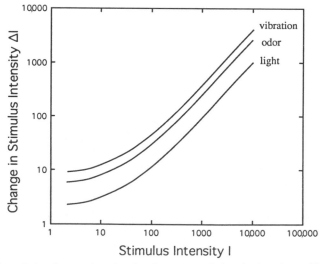

FIGURE 2   Idealized examples of Weber functions, relating the just-detectable change in stimulus intensity, ΔI, plotted on a logarithmic axis as a function of intensity, I, also plotted on a logarithmic axis, for three perceptual modalities: visual brightness, odor, and vibratory touch.

On the other hand, the relation between ΔI and I may be nonlinear. Guilford (1932) proposed that ΔI is proportional to I raised to the power n,

$$\Delta I = c_a I^n, \tag{7}$$

of which both Weber's law and Fullerton and Cattell's (1892) square-root law are special cases. Being rather general, Eq. (7) fits many sets of data, notably discriminations of sound intensity (e.g., Harris, 1963; Jesteadt, Wier, & Green, 1977; Luce & Green, 1974; McGill & Goldberg, 1968), where n is approximately 0.8–0.9. Were Weber's law to hold exactly, n would equal 1.0; the small discrepancy has been dubbed the "near miss to Weber's law" (McGill & Goldberg, 1968).

As indicated, Guilford's law reduces to Weber's law when $n = 1$ and to Fullerton and Cattell's law when $n = 0.5$. One may construe a stimulus to represent the sum of many smaller components, whose variances contribute to the observed variability (ΔI, or the stimulus JND) of the global stimulus. This conjecture was explored by Woodworth (1914; see also Cattell, 1893; Solomons, 1900), who analyzed the correlations between the errors of the components. If these correlations are zero, the Fullerton-Cattell law follows; if they are $+1$, Weber's law follows. The notion that perceived magnitude is the end result of such elemental processes has proven powerful in current models of psychophysics.

Given the violations of Fechner's assumptions and the available alternatives, a fruitful approach would retain only the general routine for determining psychophysical functions, allowing alternative *Weber functions* and *Fechner functions*. By this generalization, any relation between ΔI and I is a Weber function, and any relation between cumulated sensation JNDs and cumulated stimulus JNDs is a Fechner function (e.g., Baird & Noma, 1978). Such an approach is acceptable when S is determined by summing the finite values of JNDs (e.g., by graphical addition) but may be erroneous when each difference, ΔI, is transformed to an infinitesimal and then integrated mathematically. Integration leads to mathematically acceptable results with only a limited number of Weber functions (including Weber's law and its linearizations, but not other values of n in Guilford's law: Luce & Edwards, 1958; see also Baird & Noma, 1978; Falmagne, 1971, 1974, 1985; but see Krantz, 1971). Though infrequently applied to psychophysical data, solutions derived through functional equations (Aczél, 1966) can be used instead to derive legitimate Fechner functions (Luce & Edwards, 1958).

The lesson taught by Luce and Edwards (1958) is that Fechner's "mathematical auxiliary principle" is not universally appropriate. Graphically summated JND scales are appropriate to all forms of the Weber function. Nevertheless, graphically summated JND scales may fail other tests of consistency. For example, because JNDs are defined statistically, the exact values depend on the criterion (e.g., 75% correct identification of the stronger stimulus, 85%, or whatever). For the scales to be invariant in form over changes in criterion, the psychometric functions relating percent correct to stimulus intensity I must be homogenous, for instance, of the same shape when plotted against log I.

Furthermore, graphically summated JND scales often fail tests of consistency across multidimensional variation in stimulation (e.g., Nachmias & Steinman, 1965; Newman, 1933; Piéron, 1934; Zwislocki & Jordan, 1986), though they sometimes pass them (Heinemann, 1961). One test of consistency takes two stimuli (for instance, lights differing in color), first matches them for subjective intensity, then asks whether the stimuli continue to match after both are augmented by the same number of JNDs. A strong version of Fechner's conjecture says that the two stimuli should still match in subjective intensity, but results do not always support the prediction. For example, Durup and Piéron (1933) equated blue and red lights for brightness at various levels but found that different numbers of JND steps separated the matching intensity levels of the two colors. For overviews, see Piéron (1952), Marks (1974b), and Krueger (1989).

An alternative test of consistency measures JNDs at a given intensity under two stimulus conditions in which sensation magnitude S is the same, but the rate of growth with intensity differs; in this case, according to Fechner's conjecture, the JNDs should be inversely proportional to rate of growth: the greater the rate of growth, the smaller the stimulus JND. Hellman, Scharf, Teghtsoonian, and Teghtsoonian (1987) measured Weber fractions for discriminating the intensity of 1000-Hz tones embedded within narrowband and wideband noises, conditions that produce markedly different loudness functions as determined by direct matching. Despite the difference in the slopes of the loudness functions, the Weber fractions at equal loudness were nearly identical, implying that, at equal values of S, JNDs may correspond to markedly different changes in subjective magnitude (ΔS) (and hence also to markedly different values of the ratio $\Delta S/S$; see also Stillman, Zwislocki, Zhang, & Cefaratti, 1993).

Finally, an alternate formulation, first suggested by Riesz (1933) and later elaborated by Lim, Rabinowitz, Braida, and Durlach (1977), relaxes the strong version of the Fechnerian assumption. Assuming that stimuli A and B have identical dynamic ranges (for instance, from threshold to some maximal or quasi-maximal value), it follows from the strong assumption that the number of JNDs from threshold of stimulus A to maximum is equal to the number of JNDs from the threshold of B to maximum. Both Riesz and Lim et al. hypothesized that the number of JNDs from threshold to maximum need not be constant, but that a constant *proportion* of JNDs will mark off constant increments in subjective magnitude at both A and B. If, for example, maximum perceived magnitude lay 50 JNDs above the threshold at A, but 100 JNDs above the threshold at B, then a stimulus 5

JNDs above A's threshold would match a stimulus 10 JNDs above B's threshold, a stimulus 10 JNDs above A's threshold would match one 20 JNDs above B's threshold, and so forth. Although some evidence supports the *proportional-JND* hypothesis (e.g., Rankovic, Viemeister, Fantini, Cheesman, & Uchiyama, 1988; Schlauch, 1994), not all does (e.g., Schlauch, 1994).

Methodologically, Fechner made extensive use of statistical tools, employing the Gaussian model for the treatment of error and variance in order to derive the distance or difference between two sensations (see Link, 1992). The "difference sensations" then could be used to estimate sensation magnitudes. It is noteworthy that sensory distance itself is inferred by statistical reasoning, not by asking the subject to estimate distance. The methods of bisection (Delboeuf, 1873; Plateau, 1872) and equal-appearing intervals (e.g., Guilford, 1954), later espoused by Fechner, do call for subjects to mark off a psychological interval defined by two stimuli into two or more equal-appearing distances. So do other partition methods, such as rating or ranking by categories. Easily overlooked, however, is the fact that none of these methods asks subjects to estimate quantitatively the size of the differences or distances; subjects merely match them, an operation that is at once natural and simple (Zwislocki, 1991) and that obviates the use of numbers. Fechnerian scaling eschews complex numerical estimates of individual stimuli; instead, the scaling derives sensory differences (or magnitudes) from a theoretically guided, mathematical analysis of data that is largely independent of the subject's judgment or report about magnitude.

Three principles largely define Fechnerian scaling. First, the subjects' tasks are simple, requiring ordinal comparison or matching. Second, the mental operation is treated as one of differencing or subtracting. Third, the lack of numerical responses notwithstanding, interval-level and even ratio-level scales of sensation may be constructed through formal derivations that rely on basic theoretical assumptions.

Fechnerian methods, and the underlying conceptions, continue to offer much to contemporary psychophysics. Eisler (1963; Montgomery & Eisler, 1974) has argued that Fechnerian scales are compatible with "pure" interval scales, obtained from "unbiased" rating procedures. Moreover, measuring sense distances through rating procedures has received major impetus from multicomponential models, particularly Anderson's (1981, 1982) functional measurement. Subtractive processing is supported by the work of Birnbaum (e.g., 1978, 1980, 1982, 1990; see also, Birnbaum & Elmasian, 1977) and, with qualification, by that of Poulton (1989). The logarithmic law itself is compatible with fundamental theories of psychophysics (cf. Ward, 1992). Finally, the notion that sensation magnitude is the end result of hidden processes—that sensation is cognitively impenetrable—enjoys growing acceptance in current psychophysical theories.

2. Critiques of Fechner's Psychophysics

Fechner's enterprise saw several major objections. These criticisms carry more than historical significance, as they foreshadow important developments in psychophysical scaling. We already mentioned the "quantity objection," namely, the claim that sensations do not have magnitudes. This position seems to preclude any possibility of mental measurement, simply because there are no magnitudes "out there" to gauge. However plausible at first look, the conclusion is unwarranted. Thurstone (1927), whose "law of comparative judgment" relies on Fechnerian logic, provided one clue:

> I shall not assume that sensations . . . are magnitudes. It is not even necessary . . . to assume that sensations have intensity. They may be as qualitative as you like, without intensity or magnitude, but I shall assume that sensations differ. In other words, the identifying process for red is assumed to be different from that by which we identify or discriminate blue. (p. 368)

So one might agree that, phenomenally, sensations do not possess magnitude but nevertheless erect a scale of sensation. All that is necessary is to assume, first, that sensations differ and, second, that they are subject to error. These minimal assumptions underlie both Fechner's and Thurstone's endeavors. If we apply the assumptions to quantal processes operating at the level of the receptor, then they also underlie such recent formulations as Norwich's (1993) entropy theory of perception and Link's (1992) wave theory of discrimination and similarity.

Interpreting Fechner's enterprise (indeed, psychophysical scaling in general) as a process of indirect measurement, based on primitive theoretical assumptions, immunizes it against many of the criticisms—for example, against a variant of the quantity objection that denies that sensations are composed of (smaller) units. As Titchener (1905) put it, "We can say by ear that the roar of a cannon is louder, very much louder, than the crack of a pistol. But the cannon, as heard, is not a multiple of the pistol crack, does not contain so and so many pistol cracks within it" (p. xxiv); and James (1890) quoted Stumpf: "One sensation cannot be a multiple of another. If it could, we ought to be able to subtract the one from the other, and feel the remainder by itself. Every sensation presents itself as an indivisible unit" (p. 547). As Thurstone recognized, introspection may be a poor guide for measurement.

The weightiest, and perhaps most tenacious, criticism of Fechner's endeavor says that sensations cannot be measured in the way that physical length, time, or mass can. Von Kries (1882) argued that sensations lack objective, agreed-upon units, which in turn precludes defining invariances like equality or commutativity—and, in general, precludes operations commensurate with the "axioms of additivity." By this view, such operations are fundamental to establishing any measurement device or scale. One cannot ostensibly lay unit sensations alongside a given percept the way one can lay meter-long sticks along a rod. Therefore, claimed von Kries, the numbers assigned to sensations, whether directly or indirectly, are not quantities. The numbers are labels on an ordinal scale (substitutes for terms like *dazzling* or *noisy*) and consequently are not really scalable. In fact, the use of numbers may be misleading in that it provides a sense of quantitative measurement and precision where there is none (cf. Hornstein, 1993).

As Murray (1993) noted, Fechner recognized that von Kries's argument is "an attack on the very heart of psychophysics" (p. 126). For von Kries's objections apply not only to Fechner's conception but to any future psychophysics that might come forth. In particular, the very same criticism applies to Stevens's (1975) "new psychophysics." For this reason, we defer considering further the implications of von Kries's arguments to the section on scaling by magnitude.

B. Two Fundamental Psychophysical Theories

Following Ward (1992), we denote as *fundamental psychophysics* those attempts to find "a core of concepts and relations from which all the rest of psychophysics can be derived" (p. 190). Fundamental psychophysical theory may focus on conservational or mechanistic concepts (Ward, 1992). In physics, thermodynamics and quantum electrodynamics, respectively, are examples, themselves linked by the more basic concepts of motion and energy. In psychophysics, Ward observed, conservational theories may treat laws of information exchange, whereas mechanistic ones seek to characterize basic sensory processes. We describe two recent attempts at formulating fundamental theories, one primarily conservational (Norwich, 1993), the other primarily mechanistic (Link, 1992).

1. Norwich's Entropy Theory of Perception

The basic premise of Norwich's (1993) theory is that perception entails the reduction of entropy with respect to stimulus intensity, captured by the organism as information. In general, to state the theory in words, more intense stimuli have greater information content (greater entropy) than do weaker ones, and sensation provides a measure of (is proportional to) this entropy. Norwich's approach replaces the account offered by traditional psychophysics in terms of energy with one that uses terms of information (see also Baird, 1970a, 1970b, 1984).

In mathematical terms,

$$S = kH, \tag{8}$$

where k is a positive constant, H is the stimulus information available for sensory transmission and processing, and S is a perceptual variable taken here as sensation magnitude. Following Shannon (1948; see Garner, 1962, and Garner & Hake, 1951, for psychophysical applications), H is calculated by

$$H = -\Sigma p_i \ln p_i, \tag{9}$$

where p_i is the probability of occurrence of each steady-state stimulus i that is given for categorical judgment, classification, or identification.

The association between the logarithmic character of Fechner's law and the logarithmic character of Shannon's formula for information has been noted in the past (e.g., Moles, 1958/1966). Baird (1970a, 1970b) sought to derive Fechner's law explicitly from concepts in information theory (but see MacRae, 1970, 1972, 1982). An immediate problem, of course, is that the fixed stimuli used in psychophysics (usually applied suddenly, in the form of a step function) entail no uncertainty with respect to their macroscopic magnitude. Norwich's theory, however, treats the quantal structure of sensory signals impinging at the level of receptors. Because receptors operate at a microscopic level, they experience moment-by-moment fluctuations in, say, the density of molecules of a solute (with a macroscopically constant taste stimulus) or density of photons (with a macroscopically constant light). Thus sensory receptors may be regarded as sampling molecules or photons at discrete instants of time. Receptors operate to reduce uncertainty about the mean intensity of the steady stimulus after m individual samples of the stimulus.

To calculate sensory information from receptor uncertainty, one must manage probability densities, not discrete probabilities. To pass from the discrete to the continuous case, however, one cannot simply proceed from summation, as in Eq. (9), to integration. Instead, one must calculate the difference between two differential entropies. Norwich showed that, regardless of the probability density function that characterizes a given sensory signal (e.g., photon density), as a consequence of the central limit theorem, the *mean* sensory signal density will approximate the normal distribution. If the variance of the original signal is σ^2, the variance of the means of the samples of size m will be σ^2/m. If m samplings of the stimulus are made in time t, then the absolute entropy H is given by

$$H = (\tfrac{1}{2}) \cdot \ln[1 + (\beta'/\sigma^2)/t], \tag{10}$$

where β' is a constant of proportionality. H is measured here in natural logarithmic units ($H/\ln 2$ gives uncertainty in bits). Equation (10) still expresses its argument in terms of variance, not in terms of magnitude or intensity. Norwich suggested taking the variance as proportional to the mean intensity of the stimulus raised to a power, namely,

$$\sigma^2 = \kappa I^n, \tag{11}$$

where κ and n are constants. The exponent n is characteristic of the species of particle, and should, in principle, be determined by physical and physiological considerations. Basically, Eq. (11) expresses the fact that larger quantities are associated with greater errors of measurement or fluctuations. If we take σ^2 to reflect ΔI or the stimulus JND, then Eq. (11) is mathematically identical to Guilford's law, and contains the Fullerton-Cattell law as a special case where $n = 1$.

Having evaluated H, we can substitute Eq. (10) and (11) in Eq. (8) to obtain Norwich's psychophysical law,

$$S = kH = (k/2) \cdot \ln[1 + (\gamma I^n)], \tag{12}$$

where the proportionality constant $\gamma = \beta'/(\kappa \cdot t)$ for constant duration t. Equation (12) says that perceived magnitude S is proportional to the amount of uncertainty experienced by the subject about the mean intensity or macroscopic magnitude of the stimulus I. Significantly, Norwich's function still retains the logarithmic nature of Fechner's law. Given constant stimulus duration, with high-intensity stimuli, or more precisely when $\gamma I^n \gg 1$, Eq. (12) approximates Fechner's law. At lower levels, or more generally where γI^n is $\ll 1$, Eq. (12), or the first-order term of its Taylor expansion, approximates a power function with exponent n, that is, Stevens's law.

Equation (12) enables Norwich to derive a rich network of psychophysical relations, including measures of sensory adaptation over time, information per stimulus and maximum information transfer (channel capacity), response time (RT), and relations among stimulus range, power-function exponent, Weber fractions, and the total number of JNDs spanned by the plateau of the Weber function. Full mathematical derivations are given in a book and in several articles (e.g., Norwich, 1984, 1987, 1991, 1993). Here, we conclude with a note on Weber's law. Norwich derived Weber's fraction by differentiating the psychophysical entropy function with respect to I. Rearranging terms gives

$$\Delta I/I = (2\Delta H/n) \cdot (1 + [1/\gamma I^n]). \tag{13}$$

For large values of I, the Weber fraction tends to fall to a plateau, because $1/\gamma I^n$ approaches zero. In this region, given Fechner's assumption that ΔS (corresponding to ΔH) is constant, we can write

$$\Delta I/I = (2/n) \cdot \Delta S = \text{constant}, \tag{14}$$

which, when integrated, yields Fechner's logarithmic law. Incidentally, differentiating the simple power function does not yield an empirically acceptable Weber function, because it would predict $\Delta I/I$ to approach zero when I is large.

2. Link's Wave Theory of Sensation

Link's (1992) theory postulates a process by which a given stimulus is sampled continuously over time in a given trial; the result of this sampling is the envelope of a time-amplitude waveform. A value sampled from the stimulus wave is compared, by subtraction, to a value sampled from a referent wave in order to create a comparative wave. The differences created through a trial cumulate over time until their sum exceeds a subject-controlled threshold, A. The latter measures the subject's resistance to respond; its reciprocal, $1/A$, gives the subject's responsiveness. Another parameter, θ^*, characterizes discriminability or response probability. As the difference between two stimuli (or between a stimulus and an internal reference) increases, so does θ^*, and hence the probability of reaching the upper response threshold.

The perception of an external stimulus originates at the body surface by the quantized action of sensory receptors or transceivers. The situation is modeled by a Poisson process,

$$\Pr(k) = e^{-\alpha}\alpha^k/k!, \tag{15}$$

where $\Pr(k)$ is the probability of k elements responding out of a large population, and α is the mean, indicating stimulus intensity. Signals are then transmitted as a sequence of electrical events onto new locations for subsequent (central) processing. Significantly, the Poisson model depicts those temporal processes—the number of electrical pulses emitted during a unit of time—as easily as it does the spatial processes at the sensory surface. Thus, the model "offers a unique method of digitally recording external events and digitally transmitting their characteristics through a chain of Poisson processes that maintain the integrity of the original event" (Link, 1992, p. 189). Equally important, the combination of several Poisson processes is a new Poisson process that preserves values of the original parameters that sum to produce the global output. Thus, Link showed that the overall Poisson intensity is a similarity transformation of the number of transceivers. The latter, it is well known, mirrors stimulus intensity because the greater the stimulus intensity, the larger the number of areas (and receptors) affected. Therefore, the output of the Poisson process is a similarity transformation of the intensity of the stimulus.

Fechner's law is a consequence of Poisson comparisons. A standard stimulus with intensity I_a and a just noticeably different stimulus with intensity I_b produce two Poisson waves. Because Poisson means are similarity transformations of the physical stimuli, the waves have amplitudes $L\alpha$ (activating L independent Poisson variables at mean intensity α) and $M\beta$ (activating M variables at mean intensity β), respectively. Their comparison generates a wave difference, θ^*, where

$$\theta* = \ln[(L\alpha)/(M\beta)]. \tag{16}$$

Because multiplying stimulus intensities by a constant value leaves $\theta*$ unchanged, Eq. (16) characterizes Weber's law. Moreover, rewriting Eq. (16) in terms of I_a and I_b, and taking I_b to be I_o, the absolute threshold, gives

$$\theta* = \ln(I_a/I_o). \tag{17}$$

In wave theory, the subject senses the stimulus when the value of A is first reached. Sensation thus depends on both $\theta*$ and A; the former derives from the physical features of the stimuli and the sensory apparatus, whereas the latter is subjectively controlled. To satisfy Fechner's requirement that sensation be zero at the absolute threshold, Link suggested that sensation is equal to discriminability multiplied by the resistance to respond, A,

$$S = \theta*A. \tag{18}$$

Combining Eqs. (17) and (18) yields Fechner's law,

$$S = A \cdot \ln(I_a/I_b). \tag{19}$$

Thus, discriminability depends on the amplitude parameters of the threshold and comparison stimulus waves. But sensation magnitude depends on both the discriminability and the subject's resistance to respond.

Like other logarithmic formulations, Link's theory predicts a linear relation between the logarithms of the stimuli equated for sensation in cross-modality matching (CMM)—a result often obtained. However, in Link's theory, the slopes of the CMM functions represent the ratio of the respective response thresholds, A, and power-function exponents are interpreted as resistances to respond, which can be gauged by the size of the Weber fraction. Cross-modality matches, therefore, are byproducts of the Poisson processes that generate Weber's law and Fechner's law, not of power functions for sensation. Thus wave theory provides a theoretical underpinning to the mathematical argument, made decades earlier (e.g., MacKay, 1963; Treisman, 1964; cf. Ekman, 1964), that CMMs are equally compatible with logarithmic and with power functions relating sensation to stimulus. Note, however, that slopes of CMM functions can often be predicted from the exponents of power functions derived from methods such as magnitude estimations; for logarithmic functions to provide comparable predictive power, they must provide constant ratios of their slope parameter, comparable to the parameter A in Eq. (19).

3. Fundamental Theories and Fechnerian Scaling

As different as they are, the theories offered by Norwich and Link share several features, including the ability to account for Fechner's law. First, both theories take as their point of departure quantal responses at the sensory surface. Second, both theories treat sensation magnitude as a derived concept, constructed from hidden, nonconscious elemental processes. Third, both models also rely on measures of variance but do not treat variance as error; instead, variance inheres in the stimulus. Fourth, both theories consider the stimulus at the microscopic level, eschewing definition of stimulus magnitude in terms of steady-state intensity but considering global stimulus magnitude itself to be a derived concept. Fifth, both theories take comparisons as the basic mental act: Differencing or subtraction is an explicit premise of wave theory; subtraction is implicit in entropy theory, in that absolute entropy, Eq. (10), reflects the difference between two differential entropies. At a more basic level, both theories support the relativity of sensation and judgment. Judgments always are made relative to a referent (wave theory) or to the alternative stimuli expected by the perceiver (entropy theory). As Garner (1974) observed, "Information is a function not of what the stimulus is, but rather of what it might have been, of its alternatives" (p. 194). Sixth, as already noted, both theories support Fechner's law, deriving it from basic principles. Yet both formulations also leave room for Stevens's power function (Norwich applied it to "weak" stimuli, where $\gamma I^n \ll 1$; Link applied it to the realm called "feeling"). Finally, both theories treat Weber's law as a consequence of psychophysical processing—not as a starting point for deriving the psychophysical law.

C. Thurstonian Scaling

That variability in sensory responding might form the basis for uncovering sensation difference was first pursued in detail by Solomons (1900). Consider, for example, his rendition of Weber's law (cf. Gigerenzer & Murray, 1987). Relative variability may be expressed as a constant proportion p of stimulus intensity I (i.e., p is independent of I). Therefore, variability $I \cdot p$ increases linearly with I, which is Weber's law. Fechner himself speculated that relative variability might be constant, and he devised methods to gauge it. And both Helmholtz (1856/1962) and Delboeuf (1873) considered how variability might affect measures of sense distance. But it was Thurstone (1927, 1959) who capitalized on the Fechnerian ideas of differencing and variability to develop a general model of scaling (for recent assessments, see Dawes, 1994; Luce, 1994).

Thurstone postulated an internal continuum onto which the representations of stimuli are projected. A stimulus is identified by a "discriminal process," marking a value along the psychological continuum. Given momentary fluctuations in brain activity, repeated exposures to a given stimulus result in a distribution of such values, the standard deviation of which is called *discriminal dispersion*. Because many factors contribute to the internal noise, the psychological representations are assumed to be random variables with normal distributions. The psychological scale value associated with a stimulus is given by the mean of the distribution of its internal values. The standard deviation of this distribution provides the unit of measurement used to quantify distances along the hypothetical subjective continuum. When two stimuli are presented for comparative judgment, the separation between the means expressed in terms of the respective discriminal dispersions measures their psychological distance. To calculate scale values for the stimuli, one therefore needs to know the means, the standard deviations, and the correlations between discriminal processes. Unfortunately, under most conditions, we cannot directly determine these parameters. They must be recovered instead from the matrix of observed choice probabilities.

Scale values are determined by the following assumptions and procedures. Given two stimuli, j and k, presented for comparative judgment, each generates a discriminal process, the difference between them being a "discriminal difference." Repeated presentation produces a distribution of these discriminal differences. Because the discriminal processes are assumed to be Gaussian distributed, so are the discriminal differences. The mean of the distribution of the differences is equal to the difference between the means of the two discriminal processes; the standard deviation of the difference, s_{j-k}, is given by

$$s_{j-k} = (s_j^2 + s_k^2 - 2r_{jk}s_js_k)^{\frac{1}{2}}, \tag{20}$$

where s_j and s_k stand for the discriminal dispersions and r is the correlation between the momentary values of the discriminal processes.

With each presentation of a given pair of stimuli, the subject selects the stronger stimulus when the momentary discriminal difference is positive; otherwise she or he (erroneously) selects the weaker one. The respective proportions of choices can be represented as complementary areas under a normal curve that describes the entire distribution of the discriminal differences. These areas can be converted into standard scores, z, which mark off distances on the psychological continuum in standard deviation units. Therefore, Thurstone's *law of comparative judgment* is

$$u_j - u_k = z_{jk} (s_j^2 + s_k^2 - 2r_{jk}s_js_k)^{\frac{1}{2}}, \tag{21}$$

where u_j and u_k correspond to the means of the discriminal processes. Because of the difficulties in estimating the parameters, Thurstone's complete law has rarely been used. Thurstone outlined five cases containing simplifying assumptions. The most useful is his Case V, where the discriminal dispersions are assumed to be equal and uncorrelated. The common discriminal dispersion then serves as the unit of measurement, and the law simplifies to

$$u_j - u_k = \sqrt{2}(s \cdot z_{jk}), \tag{22}$$

in which the means (the scale values) are derived by averaging over the z-scores arising from the matrix of probabilities $p(j,k)$ (cf. Baird & Noma, 1978). Using the empirical probabilities, Case V can be written as

$$p_{jk} = \phi(u_j - u_k), \tag{23}$$

where p_{jk} is the probability of choosing stimulus j over stimulus k, ϕ is the standard normal distribution function, and u_j and u_k are the scale values.

Measuring physical stimuli like tones or weights by Thurstone's Case V generates results consistent with Fechner's law as long as Weber's law holds. Actually, the assumption of constant variability in Case V amounts to the Fechnerian assumption that the sensation JND, ΔS, is constant. It is, of course, an assumption, or a postulate, that equally often noted differences are equal psychologically. Should one conceive of a Case VI, with discriminal dispersions increasing in proportion to sensation (Stevens, 1959d, 1975), one might arrive at a power function relating sensation to intensity.

Unlike Fechnerian scaling, which relies on well-defined and quantified physical stimuli, Thurstonian scaling needs no physical measure. Stimuli may be tones, lights, or weights—but they may just as well be preferences for nationalities or flavors of ice cream. As Thurstone said, "psychophysical experimentation is no longer limited to those stimuli whose physical magnitudes can be objectively measured" (1959, p. 228). Even without measurable stimuli, scales that are unique to affine transformations can result from the elaboration of a few elemental postulates. Given a minimal number of simple assumptions, equal-interval scales of sensation are routinely derived. And by adding some strong (yet reasonable) assumptions (cf. Thurstone, 1959), one may arrive at ratio-level scales as well.

1. Related Developments

Given relatively modest assumptions, Thurstone's method readily generalizes to all kinds of probabilistic data in contexts far removed from those typical of psychophysics. In particular, Thurstone's model has been used to scale dominance probabilities in the realm of decision and choice. The general problem then becomes one of explaining the process of choice between objects that, as a rule, lack a physical metric. In decision making, the usual terminology is one borrowed from economics, with utility—the subjective value of a commodity or money—replacing sensation magnitude as the psychological variable of interest. Thus, when applying Thurstone's Case V to choice data, the scale values u_j and u_k in Eq. (22) are relabeled as utilities. Because it assumes a random distribution of internal values for each stimulus, Thurstone's model is sometimes called a *random utility* model. However, alternative views of stimulus representation and the subsequent comparison and decision processes are possible and have been pursued.

Statistical analysis of paired-comparison data suggested by Bradley and Terry (1952) was later extended and given an axiomatic basis by Luce (1959). In this *constant utility* model, each alternative has a single internal representation or strength, and the variability inheres in the process of choice itself. For binary choices, the Bradley-Terry-Luce (BTL) model is usually stated as

$$p_{jk} = v_j/(v_j + v_k), \qquad (24)$$

where p_{jk} is the probability of preference as in Eq. (23), and v_j and v_k are the internal values or utilities for alternatives j and k. If we define $u_i = \log (v_i)$, Eq. (24) can be written

$$p_{jk} = \Lambda(u_j - u_k), \qquad (25)$$

where Λ stands for the standard logistic distribution. Given that the logistic distribution differs only subtly from the normal, it is clear from comparing Eqs. (23) and (25) that Thurstone's model and the BTL model are very similar. Different conceptions of the decision process notwithstanding, common computational routines are used to determine the scale values.

Both the Thurstone and the BTL models may be construed as special cases of an inclusive class called *general Fechnerian scales,* or GFS (cf. Baird & Noma, 1978; see Luce, 1977a, 1977b; Luce & Krumhansl, 1988; Yellott, 1971, 1977). GFS models share Fechner's idea of treating variability as an authentic part of the scaling enterprise, and they use Fechner's assumptions of random variability and subtractive comparison in order to derive scale values on an internal continuum. Because they require only nominal definition of stimuli, GFS models have wide applicability.

GFS models handle well many choice situations but fail conspicuously in others. The reason for the shortcomings is easily pinpointed, and, in our opinion, it may well signal the boundary condition dissociating the scaling of sensation from processes of decision and choice between complex entities. In the BTL model and in Thurstone's Case V, the only variable affecting stimulus comparison is the difference in utility between the stimuli. This assumption is realistic enough in the realm of psychophysical measurement, in which we scale the subjective magnitudes of physical stimuli. It also serves well to describe the pattern of choice behavior when the choice set is fairly heterogeneous. However, data obtained in realistic choice situations often violate the predictions of these strong utility models (e.g., De Soete & Carroll, 1992; Krantz, 1967; Rumelhart & Greeno, 1971; Tversky, 1969). People tend to be influenced by the similarity structure among the choice alternatives, not merely by the set of the respective utilities. This tendency is especially pronounced when the objects are similar, or when a heterogeneous choice set contains highly homogeneous subsets. Many real-life situations entail just such sets, resulting in discrepancies between the observed preferences and those predicted on the basis of strong utility models such as GFS.

To handle the choices made in realistic settings, one should model the effect of similarity as well as that of utility. The explicit inclusion of the similarity structure in the theory also means relaxing the condition of strong stochastic transitivity. Following Halff (1976) and Sjöberg (1980), a family of *moderate utility* models that captures the empirical influence of similarity can be written

$$p_{jk} = G([u_j - u_k]/D_{jk}),$$ (26)

where D_{jk} quantifies the dissimilarity between the objects (cf. De Soete & Carroll, 1992). Many popular models of choice, including the set-theoretic models developed by Restle (1961; Restle & Greeno, 1970; Rumelhart & Greeno, 1971) and Tversky (1972; Tversky & Sattath, 1979), and the multidimensional probabilistic models developed by De Soete and Carroll (1992; see references therein) can be shown to reduce to the basic form of Eq. (26), namely, to a differencing process scaled in terms of a dissimilarity parameter. Actually, the latter measure derives directly from Thurstone's discriminability parameter, s_{j-k}, the standard deviation of the distribution of the discriminal differences. In fact, s_{j-k} itself satisfies the metric axioms of an index of distance (Halff, 1976) and may validly be interpreted as one (Sjöberg, 1980; cf. Bockenholt, 1992). This maneuver also relaxes the often unrealistic condition of strong transitivity. Empirical data are consistent with the more permissive requirements of the moderate utility model.

Many issues await resolution. The multidimensional models of De Soete and Carroll exemplify a class called *generalized Thurstonian* models, which allow for multidimensional scaling of the choice objects (see also Ramsay, 1969). They contrast with the discrete (e.g., Tversky & Sattath's 1979, treelike) representations also aimed at elucidating human choice behavior. Do we have grounds to prefer one kind of representation over the other? Pruzansky, Tversky, and Carroll (1982) suggested that spatial models may apply to "perceptual" stimuli, whereas discrete models may describe better the similarity structure of "conceptual" stimuli. In several of the models mentioned (e.g., those of Restle and Tversky), a stimulus is associated with more than one number. This feature is easily handled by certain multivariate models, but it poses a problem for the axiomatic approach to psychophysical measurement (cf. Luce & Krumhansl, 1988). Finally, and most important for the present concerns, many of the models apply primarily in the broader realm of decision and choice. It is not entirely clear how the same models apply in measuring sensation (although, as Melara, 1992, showed, these multidimensional methods are directly traceable to Fechnerian psychophysics). What features are primarily "cognitive" as opposed to "sensory?" Earlier, we hinted at a possible distinction, but a more sustained attack is needed to disentangle the principles that apply to scaling sensation and those that apply to choice and decision. Link's (1992) analysis of sensation and feeling provides one avenue to distinguish the measurement of stimuli with and without a physical metric.

2. Violations of Transitivity

Thurstone's model requires that dominance data show transitivity: If, on most occasions, *A* is preferred to *B,* and if *B* is preferred to *C,* then *A* is preferred to *C.* But, as mentioned earlier, many studies show systematic failures of transitivity. A theory developed by Coombs (1950, 1964) explains failures of transitivity without having to resort to multidimensional representations, either spatial or discrete (note, incidentally, that Coombs's theory has been extended to the multidimensional case; see Bennet & Hays, 1960; Carroll, 1980). Following Thurstone, Coombs's model assumes that the objects vary along a single psychological dimension. Failures of transitivity occur because the subject prefers a certain value along the psychological continuum—an ideal point—whose location need not coincide with the scale extremes (i.e., the ideal point need not inhere in the representation of the strongest or weakest stimulus). In paired comparisons, the subject chooses the stimulus that is closer to her or his ideal value. The scale is folded, so to speak, around each subject's ideal point. Subjects are represented by their unique ideal points, which lie on a common continuum with the stimuli. Representations of the stimuli are said to be invariant across subjects. Given this assumption and the joint distribution of subjects and stimuli, values on the psychological dimension are recovered by using the preference data of the various subjects to unfold it. Coombs's *unfolding model* has informed psychophysical theory and scaling, although applications have been relatively sparse.

3. Theory of Signal Detectability

Although the *theory of signal detectability (TSD),* imported by Tanner and Swets (1954) from engineering and statistical-decision theory to psychology, treats issues of detection and discrimination, it bears a close affinity to Thurstonian scaling. According to TSD, a subject faced with a task of detection (or discrimination) must decide whether a noise background contains a signal (or whether two noisy signals differ). The decision is informed by the rules of statistical hypothesis testing to the extent that "the mind makes the decision like a Neyman and Pearson statistician" (Gigerenzer & Murray, 1987, p. 45). However, neither this interpretation nor the accepted nomenclature is consequential. Formally, TSD is equivalent to Thurstone's random variable model. Like Thurstone's model, TSD assumes that, over repetitions, both the signal + noise and the noise (or the two noisy signals) generate overlapping Gaussian distributions.

The measure known as d' represents the distance between the means of the noise and the signal + noise distributions in units of standard deviation. TSD also introduces a decisional variable that determines the subject's response criterion; the theory allows the subject to move the criterion in response to various nonsensory features of the experiment. Indeed, the ability to set apart sensory and cognitive factors is a signature of TSD. TSD then is Thurstone's random variable model with added emphasis on the process of decision. Actually, Thurstone too had a decision rule: "Respond that stimulus A is greater than B if the discriminal difference is positive, otherwise respond that B is greater than A." Why Thurstone did not develop TSD is a fascinating question discussed by Luce (1977b) and more recently by Gigerenzer and Murray (1987). Whatever the reason, d' can be construed as a Thurstonian unit of sensory distance.

Several authors (e.g., Braida & Durlach, 1972; Durlach & Braida, 1969; Luce, Green, & Weber, 1976; see also Macmillan & Creelman, 1991) have used a total d' or a summed d' (between adjacent pairs of stimuli) to measure supraliminal sensitivity. These measures usually derive from identification or classification data, showing the robustness of d'. Braida and Durlach have applied Thurstone's model by estimating the parameters of the discriminal processes from such data. For a fixed range of stimuli, assuming normal distributions for the discriminal processes, results are consistent with Fechner's law. Importantly, from a theoretical vantage, scaling by TSD, like scaling by other random-variable models, "reflects the belief that differences between sensations can be detected, but that their absolute magnitudes are less well apprehended" (Luce & Krumhansl, 1988, p. 39).

According to Durlach and Braida (1969), classification of stimuli depends on both sensory and context resolution. Both factors contribute to the variance of the internal distributions. Context variance is a function of stimulus range: the greater the range the greater the variance due to the added memory load. Memory variance thus dominates at larger ranges, where the discrepancy between classification and discrimination is notable (see also Gravetter & Lockhead, 1973; Marley & Cook, 1984). Luce and Green (1974; see also Luce, Green, & Weber, 1976) offered a different explanation. In their theory, the representation of the stimulus is unaffected by the range of stimuli. Performance is hampered instead by limitations on central information processing. The authors postulate an "attention band," 10 to 20 decibels (dB) wide for sound intensity, that roves over the stimulus continuum. Only stimuli that happen to fall within the band are fully processed. Stimuli falling outside the band are inadequately sampled, increasing the variance of their neural samplings. The greater the stimulus range, the smaller the probability that a given stimulus will fall within the roving band and consequently the greater neural variance and poorer identification. Any adequate theory must account for effects of stimulus range, as well as robust effects of stimulus sequence and stimulus position, which also characterize identification and estimation (for which Luce & Green, 1978, and Treisman, 1984, provided alternative models; and Lacouture & Marley, 1991, sought to develop a model for choice and response times within the framework of a connectionist architecture). For a review of the attention-band model, see Luce, Baird, Green, and Smith (1980).

D. Discrimination Scales, Partition Scales, and Rating Scales

1. Discrimination Scales

Discrimination methods seek to erect scales of sensation from a subject's discriminative or comparative responses (cf. Gescheider, 1997). So these methods espouse Fechner's dictum of scaling by differencing. A straightforward approach within this tradition is to obtain stimulus JNDs experimentally (not calculate them by Weber's law), then cumulate them as a function of stimulus intensity, treating each JND as a constant sensory unit. The *dol scale* for pain (Hardy, Wolff, & Goodell, 1947) provides one well-known example, Troland's (1930) scale of "brilliance" or visual brightness another. Thurstonian scales and summated-d' scales are variations on this approach. The latter scales make use of more information available from the comparative judgments than do summated-JND scales based on a preselected, arbitrary, and presumably constant cutoff level of discrimination (Marks, 1974b). Nevertheless, the famous dictum, "equally often noticed differences are equal," that epitomizes Thurstone's Case V parallels the Fechnerian assumption that JNDs have equal subjective magnitudes.

The validity of summated-JND scales rests on the psychological constancy of JNDs. One approach is to make the subjective equality of JNDs a postulate rather than an hypothesis (Luce & Galanter, 1963; see Falmagne, 1971, 1974, 1985). Attempts to test the consistency of summated-JND scales by cross-modal and intramodal matches have met with mixed success (see Marks, 1974b, and Krueger, 1989, for summaries and references). However, those tests assume the commensurability of qualitatively different sensory events. Often, integrated-JND scales are logarithmically related to stimulus intensity and approximately logarithmically related to corresponding scales generated by procedures such as magnitude estimation. This nonlinear relation has often been taken to reflect negatively on the validity of JND scales (e.g., Stevens, 1960, 1961), but it can be just as well interpreted to challenge the validity of Stevens's magnitude scales (e.g., Garner, 1958).

2. Partition Scales

In partition scaling, subjects are asked to divide the psychological continuum into equal intervals. In one of the earliest examples, Plateau (1872) asked eight artists to paint a gray that appeared midway between a white and a black. For all its seeming simplicity, however, the method of *bisection* is affected by many contextual factors, for example, the tendency, termed *hysteresis* (Stevens, 1957), for bisection points to fall higher when stimuli are presented in ascending order rather than descending order. Although the method of bisection has also served to test the psychophysical laws developed by Fechner and Stevens, these efforts have produced no conclusive evidence in favor of either (see Marks, 1974b). Later, Anderson and his collaborators (e.g., Anderson, 1976, 1977; Carterette & Anderson, 1979; Weiss, 1975) tested bisection by functional measurement. The bisection model was supported in the continua of grayness and loudness, but not in length.

In a modification of the method, called *equisection,* subjects are asked to set values of several stimuli so as to mark off equidistant sensations on the judged continuum. Two procedures may be used to extract those equal-appearing intervals (see Gescheider, 1997). In the simultaneous version of equisection, the subject is presented with the two end points and asked to set stimuli to create a series of equal sensory intervals. In the progressive version, the subject repeatedly bisects sense distances until the desired number of intervals is reached. Commutativity and transitivity—the need for which is particularly apparent in the sequential procedure—are not always satisfied by such bisections (e.g., Gage, 1934a, 1934b; Pfanzagl, 1959).

Stevens and Volkmann's (1940) *mel* scale for pitch (see also Torgerson, 1958) and Garner's (1954) *lambda* scale for loudness are examples of equisection scales of considerable importance in psychophysics. Garner's approach is notable for using converging operations: Subjects were asked to set both equal intervals (equisection) and ratios (fractionation); assuming that the equisections constitute psychologically equal differences and that fractionations define equal but unknown ratios, the two sets of data were combined to a single scale, which Garner called lambda. The lambda scale is nearly a logarithmic function of the stimulus and can be characterized as about a 0.3 power of sound pressure (smaller than the values usually obtained by magnitude estimation, described later).

3. Thurstonian Category Scales

In category scaling or rating, the subject's task is to assign categories (often integer numbers or adjectives) to stimuli so that succeeding categories mark off constant steps in sensation. The number of categories is usually smaller than the number of stimuli, often between 3 and 20. The variability of the categorical assignments for a given stimulus can be treated in a manner analogous to the way Thurstone treated comparative judgments of pairs of stimuli. In this approach, both category widths and scale values are estimated from the ratings and their variability, the analysis augmented by certain simplifying assumptions (e.g., that the distribution of judgments for each stimulus is normal or that the category boundaries remain constant from moment to moment). Several authors have described variants of this method (e.g., Attneave, 1949; Garner & Hake, 1951; Saffir, 1937; see also Adams & Messick, 1958). Thurstone himself, in an unpublished procedure, called it the "method of successive intervals." Guilford (1954) described the computational procedures under the rubric of the "method of successive categories." The most general application, called the *law of categorical judgment* (Torgerson, 1954), betrays its close affinity to Thurstonian analysis. Much of the more recent work by Durlach and Braida (e.g., 1969; see also Braida, Lim, Berliner, Durlach, Rabinowitz, & Purks, 1984) is informed by similar ideas, and may be construed as extending the analyses entailed by the method of successive categories.

Successive-interval scales, like summated-JND scales, can be logarithmic functions of stimulus intensity and nonlinearly related to "direct" magnitude scales (Galanter & Messick, 1961; see also Indow, 1966). Garner (1952) derived an equal-discriminability scale for loudness from categorical judgments that was an approximately logarithmic function of sound pressure and that was linearly related to a scale of summated JNDs obtained by Riesz (1928).

4. Mean Rating Scales

A popular form of category scaling simply takes as scale values the averages (means or medians) of the ratings. Implicit in this procedure is the view that each consecutive category reflects a constant unit change along the psychological continuum. The method of successive categories, it should be recalled, allows unequal category widths to be estimated from the respective variabilities. In typical category scaling, a psychophysical function is produced by plotting the mean (or median) rating against stimulus intensity. Category ratings, C, are often nearly linear functions of log stimulus intensity, as Fechner's law dictates, though more often, curvilinearly related (positively accelerated), in which case power functions may provide better descriptions:

$$C = cI^{\alpha} + c' \tag{27}$$

In Eq. (27), α is the exponent of the category scale, and c and c' are constants. Figure 3 gives some examples of rating scales obtained when subjects made categorical judgments of brightness under various experimental

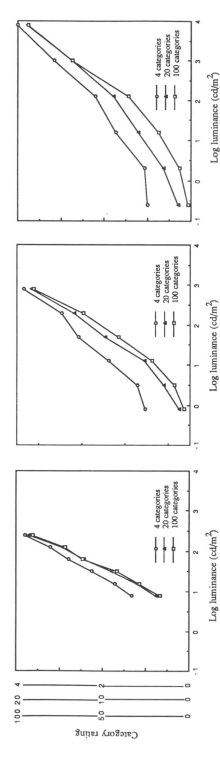

FIGURE 3 Examples of mean category ratings of brightness, each plotted as a function of log luminance, for three different stimulus ranges (31:1, 100:1, and 313:1) and three different numbers of categories (4, 20, and 100). Based on data of Marks (1968).

conditions, the experimenter systematically varying both the range of luminance levels and the number of categories on the rating scale (Marks, 1968). When the luminance range is small, the ratings are nearly linear functions of log luminance, consistent with Fechner's law; but with larger stimulus ranges, the functions are clearly upwardly concave.

Given that magnitude estimates often follow a power function (as described later), category scales relate to corresponding magnitude-estimation scales either as approximately logarithmic functions (e.g., Baird, 1970a, 1970b; Eisler, 1963; Torgerson, 1961) or as power functions. When a power function is fitted to the relation between mean ratings and magnitude estimates, the exponent may be smaller than unity (e.g., Marks, 1968; Stevens, 1971; Stevens & Galanter, 1957; see also Ward, 1972), or it may be equal to unity if c' in Eq. (27) is taken as zero (Foley, Cross, Foley, & Reeder, 1983; Gibson & Tomko, 1972). A good test of the relation between category ratings and magnitude estimates comes from a straightforward linear, graphic plot of one versus the other. It is difficult to make firm generalizations about these relations, however, because both mean ratings and magnitude estimates are sensitive to stimulus context (e.g., Foley et al., 1983; Marks, 1968; Parducci, 1965), a matter considered later.

Stevens (e.g., 1971, 1975) argued that category ratings do not generally provide adequate scales of sensation because, at best, they measure relative stimulus discriminability or variability, not sensation magnitude, and because, as just noted, rating scales are particularly susceptible to the influence of such contextual variables as range and distribution of stimuli, so they may not even measure resolution well. These arguments are not compelling. First, it may be possible to use iterative methods to minimize contextual distortions of scales (e.g., Pollack, 1965a, 1965b). Second, Anderson (e.g., 1981, 1982) has claimed that appropriately determined rating scales do provide valid measures, using as a criterion the equivalence of scales obtained in different tasks. As these authors and others (see Curtis, 1970) also noted, average judgment functions inferred from category scaling (see section V.A) are often nearly linear, more so than those inferred from magnitude estimates. In general, when tasks require subjects to integrate multidimensional stimulus information, results suggest that ratings more closely reflect the underlying sensations than do magnitude estimates. In an alternative formulation, suggested by Marks (1979b), both magnitude scales and rating scales are power functions of the stimulus but are governed by different exponents. In this theory, each scale measures its own psychological property, the former measuring sensation magnitude, the latter sensation difference or dissimilarity (see also Algom & Marks, 1984; Parker & Schneider, 1980; Popper, Parker, & Galanter, 1986; Schneider, 1980, 1988).

If the number of categories equals the number of stimuli, then the subject's task reduces to one of stimulus coding, or identification. The ability of a subject to classify stimuli often is expressed by the statistical measure *transmitted information,* developed within the framework of *information theory* (Shannon, 1948). The sensitivity measure of TSD, d', provides another index of performance. Equation (9) defines the information or entropy of a unidimensional array of stimuli. Transmitted information is defined as the difference between the stimulus entropy and stimulus equivocation, where equivocation is a function of errors in identification (for details of the techniques for calculating the information transmitted and other measures of information, see Attneave, 1959, or Garner, 1962).

Stimulus entropy is governed by the number of stimuli (usually equal to the number of categories). When the number of stimuli is small, say 4 or 6, the subject's task becomes one of stimulus coding, and the subject may identify the stimuli infallibly. In the language of information theory, the equivocation would then be zero, transmitted information would equal stimulus entropy, and we can talk of perfect communication. As the number of stimuli (and categories) increases, however, errors of identification mount considerably, and transmitted information falls short of stimulus entropy. Miller's (1956) celebrated paper puts the number of perfectly identifiable stimuli, varying in just one dimension, at 7 +/− 2, a limit called *channel capacity.* Although this limit seems extremely low, recognize that it applies to stimuli varying along a single dimension. With multidimensional stimuli like those experienced in the everyday environment, channel capacity can be substantially greater (see Garner, 1962, for review and references).

Miller suggests that channel capacity is roughly constant for unidimensionally varying stimuli regardless of modality. Baird (e.g., Baird & Noma, 1978) has challenged Miller's conclusion and argues for a general negative relationship between channel capacity and the Weber fraction: the greater the channel capacity, the smaller the Weber fraction. In Baird's scheme, both measures are indices of relative sensitivity or resolution.

E. Estimation of Sensory Differences

Spacing stimuli in unit psychological differences or intervals may constitute the most natural form of measurement (Zwislocki, 1991). The procedure need not involve numbers: Subjects may adjust the distance between stimuli to match a standard. Or subjects may give numerical estimates of sensory intervals or differences. The use of such direct estimates violates, of course, the spirit of Fechnerian psychophysics. The violation seems less serious, however, when the judgments are construed to give only rank-order information; thus greater or smaller numerical responses can be taken as mere indicants of larger or smaller sensory intervals. Nonmetric data often contain sufficient information to constrain metric (interval-scale) properties (cf. Kruskal, 1964; Shepard, 1962a, 1962b, 1966). If there is an interval-scale representation of stimuli, ordered $I_1, I_2, I_3, \ldots I_n$, then differences among pairs must show weak transitive ordering, that is,

$$\text{if } (I_1, I_2) \geq (I_2, I_3) \text{ and } (I_2, I_3) \geq (I_3, I_4) \text{ then } (I_1, I_2) \geq (I_3, I_4), \quad (28a)$$

and monotonicity,

$$\text{if } (I_1, I_2) \geq (I_4, I_5) \text{ and } (I_2, I_3) \geq (I_5, I_6) \text{ then } (I_1, I_3) \geq (I_4, I_6) \quad (28b)$$

see Krantz et al., 1971). Given a sufficiently dense array of stimuli (≥ 10), a complete rank ordering of differences suffices to retrieve the representations, unique to affine (interval-scale) transformations (Shepard, 1966), that is, transformations that permit addition of a constant or multiplication by a positive constant. The same principle underlies methods to retrieve interval-scale representations in more than one dimension, but this extension falls within the domain of multidimensional scaling (see Chapter 3, "Multidimensional Scaling," by Carroll & Arabie).

Importantly, numerical estimates can be taken to provide a kind of matching: All stimuli (here, pairs of them) assigned the same number are treated as equal on the judged attribute (sensory interval, difference, or dissimilarity). Thus Beck and Shaw (1967) reported that subjects, when asked to estimate loudness intervals, gave equivalent responses to various pairs of tones defined by constant differences on Garner's (1954) lambda scale. Basing measurement on differencing or dissimilarity is, of course, compatible with the Fechnerian tradition.

Since Beck and Shaw (1967), several papers have reported loudness scales derived from estimates of loudness intervals (e.g., Algom & Marks, 1984; Dawson, 1971; Parker & Schneider, 1974; Popper et al., 1986; Schneider, Parker, Valenti, Farrell, & Kanow, 1978). In many of these studies, only the rank-order of the differences is used to uncover the scale, as described earlier. Because only the ordinal properties of the differences are of concern, other studies omit numerical estimates entirely, for instance, by obtaining direct comparisons of loudness differences (Schneider, 1980; Schneider, Parker, & Stein, 1974). Results using all of these paradigms agree: The scale of loudness difference is a power function with a relatively small exponent, roughly 0.3 when calculated as a function of sound pressure. Consistent with Fechner's conjecture, this scale of loudness difference appears to correspond well with a scale of JNDs for sound intensity, despite (better, because of) the near miss to Weber's law (Parker & Schneider, 1980; Schneider & Parker, 1987). Moreover, there is evidence of substantial variation among the functions obtained from individuals (Schneider, 1980; see also Schneider, 1988). Nonmetric analysis also produced relatively small exponents (less than unity) in functions derived from quantitative judgments of differences in line length (Parker, Schneider, & Kanow, 1975).

In general, results obtained by direct comparison or judgments of differences conflict with results obtained by such methods as magnitude estimation, as described later. We consider the issue again later, after considering scaling of magnitudes.

F. Response Times for Comparative Judgment

In a typical experiment, subjects are shown a pair of stimuli, such as two lines or two circles; then the subjects must decide, while timed, which stimulus is larger or smaller. The three central findings in this paradigm are termed the *distance effect,* the *semantic congruity effect,* and the *serial position effect.* The distance effect refers to the functional dependence of response time (RT) on stimulus difference: the larger the difference between the two items being compared, the shorter the RT. The contingency was documented by Cattell as early as 1902. The reciprocal relation between RT and stimulus difference (for even perfectly discriminable stimuli) remains a cornerstone of research and theory into response times (e.g., Curtis, Paulos, & Rule, 1973; Link, 1975; Link & Heath, 1975; Welford, 1960). The semantic congruity effect refers to an interaction between the direction of the comparison, dictated by the instructions, and the size of the compared items on the relevant continuum. Two relatively large items are compared faster in terms of which is larger, but two relatively small items are compared faster in terms of which is smaller (e.g., Banks, Clark, & Lucy, 1975). Finally, subjects respond faster to stimuli located near the ends of the stimulus series than to stimuli from the middle of the range—the serial position effect or end effect.

Link's (1992) wave theory, like his earlier relative judgment theory, seeks a coherent account of the various effects. Response times are affected by discriminability (hence the distance effect), but are also highly sensitive to subjective control. Bias, due to instructions and other features of the experimental context, and resistance to respond are two variables under the direct control of the subject. They explain the congruity effect and end effects. Applying the principle of scale convergence, Birnbaum and Jou (1990) recently proposed a theory, consistent with a random walk model, that assumes that the same scale values underlie comparative RTs and direct estimation of intervals. However, it is not clear how the theories of Link and of Birnbaum and Jou treat differences between comparative judgments for perceptual and symbolic stimuli (e.g., Algom & Pansky, 1993; Banks, 1977; Marschark & Paivio, 1981; see also, Petrusic, 1992).

IV. SCALING BY MAGNITUDE

Although the scaling of magnitudes had fitful starts in the late 19th century—for example, in Merkel's (1888) *Methode der doppelten Reize* and

Münsterberg's (1890) early attempt at cross-modality matching—it gained impetus in the 1930s, stimulated by acoustic engineers who were concerned with the measurement of loudness. Given Fechner's logarithmic law, the loudness of an auditory signal should be proportional to the number of decibels it lies above its absolute threshold; yet there is some sense in which the decibel scale—in common use by the early decades of the 20th century—fails to capture adequately the phenomenal experience of loudness. Consequently, the 1930s saw a spate of studies on scaling loudness (e.g., Geiger & Firestone, 1933; Ham & Parkinson, 1932; Rschevkin & Rabinovich, 1936). The beginning of this endeavor was a seminal paper by Richardson and Ross (1930), who may be considered the originators of the method of magnitude estimation. In this study, subjects were presented a standard tone, to be represented by the numeric response "1," and were asked to give other numbers, in proportion, to various test tones differing from the standard in intensity and frequency. Richardson and Ross fitted a power function to the results: The judgments of loudness were proportional to the voltage across the headphones (essentially, to the resulting sound pressure) raised to the 0.44 power or, equivalently, proportional to acoustic energy flow raised to the 0.22 power. Other studies cited previously, using methods of ratio setting, gave results that more or less agreed.

At about the same time, Fletcher and Munson (1933) approached the quantification of loudness magnitudes from a different tack. They began with the assumption that signals processed in separate auditory channels (that is, in channels with distinct sets of receptors and peripheral neural pathways, like those in the two ears) should combine in a simple, linearly additive manner. If so, Fletcher and Munson reasoned, then equally loud signals presented through two such channels (e.g., binaural stimuli) should produce a sensation twice as great as that produced through either channel alone (monaural stimuli). From this conjecture, plus measurements of loudness matches between monaural and binaural signals and between single and multicomponent tones, Fletcher and Munson constructed a loudness scale for pure tones that can be very closely approximated by a 0.6 power of sound pressure (0.3 power of energy) at relative high signal levels (>40 dB sound pressure level, or SPL) and by the square of pressure (1.0 power of energy) at low signal levels. The exponent of 0.6 follows directly from the empirical finding that combining loudness over two channels (e.g., across the two ears), and thus doubling loudness, is equivalent to increasing the intensity in either one channel alone by 10 dB—because a 0.6-power function means that loudness doubles with every 10 dB increase in stimulation. Figure 4 shows Fletcher and Munson's loudness scale, plotted on a logarithmic axis against SPL in dB. At high SPLs, the function is nearly linear, consistent with a power function.

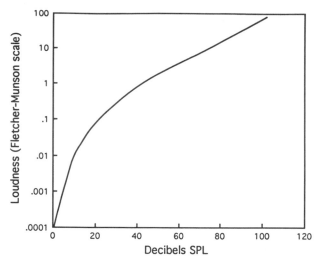

FIGURE 4   The loudness scale derived by Fletcher and Munson (1933), plotted against decibels sound pressure level.

A. Magnitude Estimation

In the 1950s and 1960s, S. S. Stevens (e.g., 1955, 1957, 1960) and others (e.g., Ekman, Eisler, & Künnapas, 1960; Engen & McBurney, 1964; Hellman & Zwislocki, 1961; J. C. Stevens, 1957) amassed an enormous array of empirical evidence showing how people behave when asked to assign numbers to the magnitudes of their sensory experiences—the method known as magnitude estimation (and, to some extent, by the inverse procedure of magnitude production). Following the work of the 1930s, much of this later research went into formulating a prototypical scale of loudness, which, Stevens (1955, 1956) proposed, grows as a power function of sound pressure. In particular, Stevens offered a modern version of the "sone scale": A 1000-Hz tone heard binaurally at 40 dB has unit loudness (1 sone); above 40 dB, loudness doubles with every 10-dB increase in the acoustic signal. In fact, the International Organization for Standarization has taken the sone scale to be *the* measure of loudness.

With many perceptual dimensions, and under many stimulus conditions, the relation between these numeric responses R and various measures of stimulus intensity I could be reasonably well fitted by power functions, with exponent β and constant k,

$$R = kI^{\beta}, \tag{29}$$

leading Stevens (1957, 1975) to propose such a function as *the* psychophysical law, a law to replace Fechner's logarithmic formulation. This proposal was buttressed in various publications by tables and graphs displaying the power functions obtained in various modalities (vision, hearing, touch, taste, and smell) and for various dimensions (brightness, length, and area in vision; vibration intensity, warmth, and cold in somesthesis). According to Stevens, exponents can take on values that vary from much smaller than unity (e.g., 0.33 for the brightness of 1-s flash of light delivered to a dark-adapted eye) through near unity (e.g., 1.0 for perceived length) to much greater than unity (e.g., 3.5 for the perceived intensity of alternating electric current delivered to the fingers). Rosenblith (1959) and Teghtsoonian (1971) suggested that intermodal variations in exponent may reflect the ways that different sensorineural systems map different stimulus ranges into a constant range of perceptual magnitudes: "The various receptor systems can be regarded as performing the necessary expansions or compressions required to map the widely varying dynamic ranges into this constant range of subjective magnitudes" (Teghtsoonian, 1971, p. 74).

Teghtsoonian (1971) also sought to relate the parameters of these power functions to other psychophysical measures. Thus, in modifying Fechner's conjecture, and reappropriating Brentano's in its stead, Teghtsoonian inferred that JNDs correspond not to constant units in sensation magnitude, ΔS, but constant relative changes in sensation, $\Delta S/S$. Moreover, claimed Teghtsoonian, $\Delta S/S$ is more or less uniform across sensory modalities (roughly 3%), making the exponents of power functions directly related to the size of the Weber ratio, $\Delta I/I$. Like Fechner's conjecture, Teghtsoonian's too is vulnerable to evidence, reviewed earlier, indicating that equivalent changes in sensation magnitude (which may be defined as either ΔS or $\Delta S/S$) do not always mark off equal numbers of JNDs.

By implication, the experimental findings of Stevens and his colleagues, and occasionally Stevens's own words, have led to an erroneous, and indeed misleading, view that every modality, or at least every sensory or perceptual dimension in a given modality, has its own characteristic exponent. Even in his last, posthumously published work, Stevens would still write, for example, that "the value of the exponent . . . serves as a kind of signature that may differ from one sensory continuum to another. As a matter of fact, one of the important features of a sensory continuum lies in the value of its exponent" (1975, p. 13). But as Stevens well knew, the notion that each continuum has a single "value of the exponent" is a myth of scientific rhetoric.

If anything is clear from the plethora of psychophysical studies reported over nearly 40 years, it is that magnitude-estimation functions—and especially the exponents of these functions—depend both systematically and sometimes unsystematically on a variety of factors, including the exact methodology used (for instance, the presence or absence of a standard stimulus), the conditions of stimulation (for instance, the duration of flashes of light), the subjects (individual differences abound), and the choice of stimulus context (for instance, the range of stimulus levels) (see Baird, 1997; Marks, 1974a, 1974b; Lockhead, 1992). A brief review of these factors (save the last, which we treat separately at the end of the chapter) is illuminating, for it tells us a good deal about human behavior in the framework of scaling tasks: not just about sensory and perceptual processes, but also about mechanisms of decision and judgment.

B. Methods of Magnitude Scaling

1. Magnitude Estimation and Magnitude Production

First, there are methodological matters—the particular task set before the subject. Many of the studies of loudness in the 1930s used variants of the method of *fractionation,* where the subjects were presented a standard stimulus of fixed intensity and asked to adjust the intensity of a test stimulus to make the sensation some fraction (typically, one-half) that of the standard. Or one could ask the subjects to make the test stimulus appear to be a multiple of (say, double) the standard. As Stevens (1955) noted, halving and doubling give slightly different outcomes (analogous, perhaps, to the order effects seen in bisection). In the 1950s and 1960s, studies using *magnitude estimation* were often complemented by the inverse procedure, *magnitude production,* where subjects were presented numbers and asked to set stimuli to the appropriate levels (e.g., Meiselman, Bose, & Nykvist, 1972; Reynolds & Stevens, 1960; Stevens & Greenbaum, 1966). Again, the outcomes systematically differ. In general, psychophysical functions obtained with magnitude estimation have shallower slopes (when plotted in log–log coordinates) than functions obtained with magnitude production (Figure 5 gives examples of scaling functions for loudness of noise, measured in two individual subjects by Stevens & Greenbaum, 1966). When fitted by power functions, exponents are usually smaller in estimation (unless the stimulus range is small; see Teghtsoonian & Teghtsoonian, 1978). Stevens and Greenbaum (1966) noted that this "regression effect," as they called it, exemplifies a general principle: that subjects tend to constrict the range of whatever response variable is under their control. Thus, relatively speaking, subjects constrict the range of numbers in magnitude estimation and constrict the range of stimuli in magnitude production (but see also Kowal, 1993). Although Stevens and Greenbaum suggested that the "best" estimate of an exponent falls between the values obtained with the two procedures, there is no a priori reason why this should be so.

2. Role of Procedure

Results can vary even when a single procedure, such as magnitude estimation or magnitude production, is used. Although some of these variations could be treated under the heading of "contextual effects," discussed later,

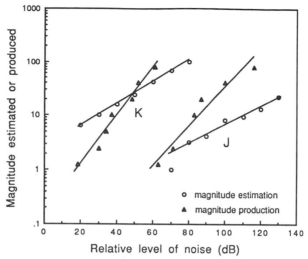

FIGURE 5 Examples of the "regression effect" in the psychophysical judgment of loudness. The slope (power-function exponent) is smaller when subjects give numbers to match stimulus levels (magnitude estimation) than when subjects adjust stimulus levels to match numbers (magnitude production). Results of two individual subjects from Figure 10 of "Regression Effects in Psychophysical Judgment," by S. S. Stevens and H. B. Greenbaum, 1966, *Perception & Psychophysics, 1,* pp. 439–446. Reprinted with permission of The Psychonomic Society and the author.

they are appropriately considered here. In one version of magnitude estimation, subjects are given a standard stimulus (which may appear at the start of a test session only, prior to each test stimulus, or whenever the subject requests it) to which a fixed number is assigned, the modulus. In another version, no standard or modulus is designated, so every subject is free to choose whatever sizes of numbers seem appropriate. The virtue of using a fixed standard and modulus is clear: Their use reduces the variability associated with idiosyncratic choice of numbers. But the choices of standard and modulus can exert consistent effects on the resulting judgments. For example, when a standard stimulus is chosen from the top or bottom of the stimulus range, subjects typically give smaller response ranges (lower exponents) than they do when the standard comes from the middle of the range (e.g., Engen & Lindström, 1963; Engen & Ross, 1966; Hellman & Zwislocki, 1961; J. C. Stevens & Tulving, 1957)—though the results probably depend jointly on the choice of standard stimulus and the numerical modulus assigned to it (Hellman & Zwislocki, 1961).

3. Role of Instructions

It is common, when a standard and modulus are given, to instruct subjects to assign their numbers such that the ratio of numerical responses corresponds to the ratio of the perceptual magnitudes. The method of *ratio magnitude estimation* (RME) emphasizes these relations by instructing subjects to make the ratios of successive numbers equal to the ratio of the sensations (e.g., Luce & Green, 1974). Careful analysis shows, however, that numerical responses depart regularly from a model that holds that subjects respond in this fashion on a trial-to-trial basis.

Evidence that subjects often fail to give consistent judgments of perceptual ratios led to the development of *absolute magnitude estimation* (e.g., Zwislocki, 1983; Zwislocki & Goodman, 1980), or AME, which instructs subjects to assign a number to each stimulus so that the number's subjective magnitude "matches" the magnitude of the sensation. This approach rests on the view that perceptual experiences may be represented as magnitudes per se and not necessarily through ratios (see Levine, 1974). Indeed, a tenet of AME is the careful instruction to subjects that avoids reference to ratio relations, emphasizing instead a direct matching of perceptual magnitudes. Proponents of AME suggest that children at an early age develop notions of magnitude per se; Collins and Gescheider (1989) pointed to evidence that young children may learn cardinal properties of number before learning ordinal properties. Although AME may reduce contextual effects compared to RME (e.g., Gescheider & Hughson, 1991; Zwislocki, 1983), AME probably does not wholly eliminate them (e.g., Gescheider & Hughson, 1991; Ward, 1987).

Borg (e.g., 1972, 1982) has made a related argument with respect to the use of particular kinds of verbal labels or categories. Many of his studies are concerned with the exertion that people perceive during physical work. In this framework, Borg has hypothesized that, when working at their own physical maxima, which can vary greatly from person to person, people experience more or less the same level of exertion and that each person's maximal experience is linked physiologically to her or his maximal level of heart rate. Assuming that a single power function relates perceived exertion to the physical stimulus when this is defined as a proportion of maximum, and assuming further that people can relate other verbal categories to the category denoting "maximal," Borg was able to develop various scales to measure exertion that proved notably successful in making possible direct comparisons among individuals and groups of individuals. In one interesting version, termed a *category-ratio* scale, the subjects' responses provide both categorical labels, such as "very weak," "medium," and "maximal" and numerical values whose properties approximate those of magnitude estimates (Borg, 1982; see also Green, Shaffer, & Gilmore, 1993; Marks, Borg, & Ljunggren, 1983; yet another approach to scaling within the framework of "natural" categories can be found in Heller, 1985).

Regardless of which variant of the method is used, it is clear that magnitude estimates are sensitive to precise instructions. In fact, when instructions refer to large rather than small numeric ratios, subjects tend to give larger rather than smaller response ranges and hence greater-sized exponents (Robinson, 1976).

The upshot is clear: Magnitude estimates reflect more than the ways that sensory-perceptual systems transduce stimulus energies (i.e., more than the internal representations of perceptual magnitudes); they also reflect the results of not-yet-well-specified decisional and judgmental processes. One consequence, discussed later, has been a series of efforts aimed at disentangling sensory-perceptual transformations from judgment functions. Although it seems undoubtedly true that any given magnitude-estimation function might in principle be decomposed into two (or more) concatenated functions, such a deterministic approach may provide only limited theoretical insight into the ways that people go about making judgments. It may be more fruitful instead to try to identify the decision processes themselves, models of which could potentially account for the mapping of perceptual experiences to numeric responses. Models of this sort will almost certainly be probabilistic rather than deterministic—exemplified by Luce and Green's (1978) theory of neural attention, Treisman's (1984) theory of criterion setting, and Baird's (1997) complementarity theory, all of which seek to account for sequential contingencies in response.

4. Interindividual Variation

Individual differences abound in magnitude scaling. As a rule of thumb, if power functions are fitted to a set of magnitude estimates obtained from a dozen or so subjects, one may expect the range of largest to smallest exponents to be about 2:1 or even 3:1 (e.g., Algom & Marks, 1984; Hellman, 1981; Ramsay, 1979; J. C. Stevens & Guirao, 1964; cf. Logue, 1976). Put another way, the standard deviation of the exponents obtained from a group of subjects is typically on the order of 30% of the value of the mean (Künnapas, Hallsten, & Söderberg, 1973; Logue, 1976; J. C. Stevens & Guirao, 1964), or even greater (Collins & Gescheider, 1989; Teghtsoonian & Teghtsoonian, 1983). Sometimes, if many stimulus levels are presented, and each stimulus is given many times per subject, the mean judgments can depart systematically or idiosyncratically from power functions (e.g., Luce & Mo, 1965). It is difficult to determine whether such departures characterize the psychophysical relation between the stimulus and the underlying sensation, the mapping of sensations onto numeric responses, or both. It is likely that decisional processes (response mapping) play an important role (e.g., Poulton, 1989), even if they do not account for all individual variation. Baird (1975) and colleagues (Baird & Noma, 1975; Noma & Baird, 1975; Weissmann, Hollingsworth, & Baird, 1975) have sought to develop models for subjects' numeric response preferences (e.g., for whole numbers, for multiples of "5" and "10," and so forth).

It has long been known that subjects who give large or small ranges of numeric responses in one scaling task tend to give large or small ranges in other tasks, as evidenced by substantial correlations between exponents measured on different stimulus dimensions or modalities (e.g., Foley et al., 1983; Jones & Woskow, 1962; Teghtsoonian, 1973; Teghtsoonian & Teghtsoonian, 1971). Although such correlations could conceivably represent individual differences in sensory responsiveness that transcend modalities (Ekman, Hosman, Lindman, Ljungberg, & Åkesson, 1968), they more likely represent individual differences in the ways people map sensations into numbers, for instance, in what Stevens (1960, 1961) called the "conception of a subjective ratio." Several studies report that individual differences are repeatable over time (e.g., Barbenza, Bryan, & Tempest, 1972; Engeland & Dawson, 1974; Logue, 1976). But other findings suggest that this consistency is transient (Teghtsoonian & Teghtsoonian, 1971) unless the experimental conditions are similar enough (for instance, by using the same numerical modulus in magnitude estimation) to allow the subjects to rely on memory (Teghtsoonian & Teghtsoonian, 1983). Similar conclusions were reached by Rule and Markley (1971) and Marks (1991). Finally, none of this should be taken to deny the presence of real sensory differences in psychophysical functions, such as those observed in various pathological conditions (for example, sensorineural hearing loss) (Hellman, 1981).

C. Magnitude Scaling and Sensory-Perceptual Processing

Beyond its many implications for the quantification of perceptual experiences, magnitude scaling has proven particularly versatile and valuable to the study of sensory processes when applied to research aimed at understanding the mechanisms by which people see, hear, taste, smell, and feel. Indeed, some disciplines, such as chemosensation, have been invigorated in recent decades by the widespread application of scaling methods. Methods such as magnitude estimation are especially well suited to assess the ways that perceptual responses depend on multidimensional variations in stimuli. For instance, a researcher may be interested in determining how brightness depends jointly on stimulus intensity and the state of adaptation of the eye at the time of stimulation, or how loudness depends jointly on stimulus intensity and duration. Holding constant such factors as the instructions (and of course the subjects themselves), subjects typically are called on to judge a set of stimuli that vary multidimensionally within a given test session. Regardless of whether a subject's numerical responses follow a particular psychophysical relation—maybe the loudness judgments double with every 10-dB (10:1) increase in signal intensity, maybe not—the finding that loudness judgments increase to the same extent with a 10-dB increase in intensity and with a 10:1 increase in duration specifies an underlying rule of time-intensity reciprocity: Loudness depends on the product of intensity and time (see Algom & Babkoff, 1984, for review).

Roughly speaking, we may consider procedures of magnitude scaling as analogous to procedures in which "absolute thresholds" are measured over some stimulus dimension (such as sound frequency). As long as the subjects maintain a constant criterion, measures of threshold should provide accurate (inverse) measures of relative sensitivity. By analogy, regardless of the particular decision rules used by subjects when, say, they give magnitude estimates, as long as the subjects apply the same rules to all stimuli presented in the series, the judgments generally can be taken to represent relative suprathreshold responsiveness (for a thorough, though somewhat dated, review of magnitude estimation's role as a kind of "null method," see Marks, 1974b). In particular, it is commonly assumed that if two different stimuli (say, a 70-dB tone presented for 5 ms and a 60-dB tone presented for 50 ms) have the same loudness, then on average they will elicit the same numerical judgment. If so, then magnitude estimation provides for a kind of indirect matching, a set of magnitude estimates containing much the same information as that found in a set of direct intensity matches.

In a classic study, J. C. Stevens and S. S. Stevens (1963) found, with the two eyes differentially light-adapted, that interocular matches and magnitude estimates provide equivalent information about the way adaptation affects relative brightness of flashes of light ranging from threshold levels, where the effects are substantial, to high luminances, where the effects are much smaller. Their results are shown in Figure 6, which replots their data showing brightness against luminance level on log-log axes. Clearly, the greater the level of light adaptation, the higher the absolute threshold (indicated by the way brightness steeply approaches zero at the low end of each function), the smaller the brightness produced by a given, suprathreshold luminance level (indicated by the displacement of the functions), and the greater the exponent of the brightness function (indicated by the slope of the function's linear portion).

To account for these findings, Stevens and Stevens used one of several possible modifications of the simple power Eq. (29) (see the next section) in order to account for a commonly observed departure at low stimulus levels:

$$R = k(I - I_o)^\beta, \tag{30}$$

where the parameter I_o relates to absolute threshold (one of several formulations proposed). It is important to note that all three parameters of this equation—the multiplicative constant k and the threshold parameter I_o, as well as the exponent β—vary systematically with level of adaptation. Hood and Finkelstein (1979) used a model in which responses "saturate" (approach an asymptotic maximum) at high intensities, as is often observed

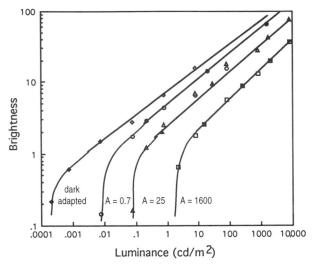

FIGURE 6   How the level of prior light adaptation affects the relation between the brightness of short flashes of light and the luminance of the test flash. Both variables are plotted on logarithmic axes. Each function represents a different luminance of the adapting stimulus. Modified from Figure 4 of "Brightness Function: Effect of Adaptation," by J. C. Stevens and S. S. Stevens, 1963, *Journal of the Optical Society of America, 53*, pp. 375–385. Reprinted with permission.

neurally, in order to relate magnitude estimates to increment thresholds measured under different states of light adaptation.

Through its application to multivariate cases, magnitude scaling has provided numerous opportunities to develop theoretical accounts of sensory processing. At the same time, the development of these theories has frequently revealed deep indeterminacies about the sensory representations that the scales imply. We provide two further examples, one from hearing and the other from vision.

1. Partial Masking of Auditory Loudness

As is well known, a background band of noise of fixed SPL can both raise the threshold of weak acoustic signals (for example, the threshold of a tone whose frequency falls within the noise band) and reduce the loudness of more intense signals. As in the case of brightness after light adaptation, the degree of masking depends on the relative levels of the masker and signal. At least four different models have been proposed to account for the results. One is Stevens's (1966; Stevens & Guirao, 1967) power-transformation model. According to this model, mainly when the SPL of a test signal falls below the SPL of the masking noise is the signal's loudness reduced. Consequently, masked-loudness functions are bisegmented: The upper segment follows the same loudness function obtained in the quiet; noise leaves loud signals unaffected. But the lower segment follows a steeper-than-quiet function (greater exponent), intersecting the upper segments at the point where the SPLs of the tone and masker meet; the more the intensity of the noise exceeds that of the signal, the greater the degree of masking, that is, the larger the exponent. The power transformation of loudness, L, can be written

$$L = k'P_s\beta^*, \quad \beta^* \text{ increasing with } P_m \text{ when } P_m > P_s;$$
$$\text{otherwise } \beta^* = \beta. \tag{31}$$

Here, P_s and P_m are the sound pressures of signal and noise, respectively, and β is the exponent governing the loudness function in quiet. The top panel of Figure 7 shows that the model is able to fit matching data reported by Stevens and Guirao, who had subjects equate the loudness of a tone heard in the quiet and the loudness of a tone heard in wideband noise.

Alternatively, instead of inducing a power transformation of unmasked loudness, noise may subtract loudness. In the simplest version (Lochner & Burger, 1961), a masker of fixed intensity causes a constant number of loudness units to be lost from the signal-in-quiet, the amount of masking being proportional to the masker's loudness. Hence the subtractive model can be expressed

$$L = k(P_s\beta - w_m P_m\beta), \tag{32}$$

where the value of w_m represents the fractional masking. (Note also that Eq. (32) provides one of the formulations that try to account for near-threshold departures from a simple power equation in the quiet.) Like the model of power transformation, the subtractive model predicts that a fixed-level masker produces a *proportionally* greater decrement in loudness when the signal's SPL is low rather than high. But this happens, says the model, by subtracting a constant number of loudness units from different starting (unmasked) levels. The middle panel of Figure 7 shows how this model can be used to fit the loudness-matching data of Stevens and Guirao (1967).

Two variants of subtractive models have also sought to account for partial masking. Garner (1959) too assumes that a masker subtracts a constant number, c, of loudness units, from the signal, but in his model the units are defined by the lambda scale. Thus loudness is given in terms of a scale that, as indicated earlier, is determined through measures of sensory difference rather than magnitude. Garner's model can be written

$$\lambda = k_\lambda(P_s\beta_\lambda - cP_m\beta_\lambda). \tag{33}$$

Because the exponent governing the lambda function, β_λ, is roughly half that of the β governing the sone function (see Marks, 1974a, 1979b), it follows that if L is given in sones, Garner's model can be rewritten

$$L = k(P_s\beta^{/2} - cP_m\beta^{/2})^2. \tag{34}$$

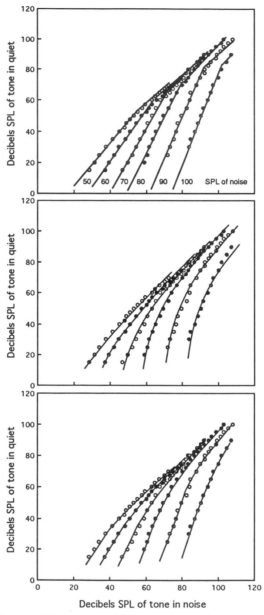

FIGURE 7   Three models to account for the way that masking noise affects the loudness of a tone; shown is the fit of each model to loudness matches between tones heard in the quiet and tones embedded in noise (data of Stevens & Guirao, 1967). The model of power transformation (Stevens, 1966; Stevens & Guirao, 1967), shown in the upper panel, proposes that a masker primarily affects test tones with lower SPLs, increasing the exponent of the power function. The model of subtraction (Lochner & Burger, 1961), shown in the middle panel, proposes that the masker subtracts a constant amount of loudness from the tone, proportional

Zwislocki (1965; see also Humes & Jesteadt, 1989) provided a more elaborate subtractive model (a third formula that aims to account for near-threshold departures from a power function). Zwislocki's model assumes, first, that the physical intensities of the signal and masker summate (sum of squares of sound pressure) within critical bands; second, that the summed signal-plus-noise has an overall loudness; and third, that the loudness of the signal consists of the difference between the overall loudness of the signal-plus-noise and the loudness of the masking noise:

$$L = k[(P_s^2 + P_m^2)^{\beta/2} - (P_m^2)^{\beta/2}]. \tag{35}$$

The final model was developed by Pavel and Iverson (1981; see also Iverson & Pavel, 1981). They postulated that loudness functions measured in the presence of masking noise display "shift invariance." That is, loudness functions in noise and in quiet can all be represented as segments of a single psychophysical function. Although the subtractive model of Lochner and Burger (1961) displays shift invariance, Pavel and Iverson showed that masked loudness is better described through a more complex model, one that assumes that maskers affect a "gain control" in the auditory system, as represented by the loudness-matching equation

$$P' = k[P_s^{\beta_a}/(P_s^{\beta_b} + cP_m^{\beta_b/\theta})]^{1/(\beta_a - \beta_b)}, \tag{36}$$

where P' is the level of a tone heard in quiet whose loudness matches P_s, and θ is a constant governing the degree of masking-induced shift. Note that this model does not treat psychophysical functions per se, but loudness matches—although the model makes it possible to compute exponents β_a and β_b governing the transformations of acoustic signals. By way of contrast, Stevens's and Lochner and Burger's models do rely on the loudness functions themselves; these models assume that masking can be calculated directly on the magnitude functions for loudness, either through subtraction or power transformation. As the bottom panel of Figure 7 shows, Pavel and Iverson's model also does an excellent job of fitting Stevens and Guirao's (1967) data.

2. Time-Intensity Relations in Visual Brightness

The brightness of a flash of light depends on both its duration and luminance, so to be adequate any model of brightness vision must account for

---

to the masker's own loudness. The model of shift invariance (Pavel & Iverson, 1981), shown in the bottom panel, proposes that all matches between tone in quiet and tone in noise of fixed SPL can be represented as displaced segments of a single, complex loudness-matching function. The upper panel was adapted from Figure 8 of "Loudness Functions under Inhibitions," by S. S. Stevens and M. Guirao, 1967, *Perception & Psychophysics, 2*, pp. 459–465. Reprinted with permission of The Psychonomic Society and the author. The bottom panel was adapted from Figure 6 of "Invariant Characteristics of Partial Masking: Implications for Mathematical Models," by M. Pavel and G. J. Iverson, 1981, *Journal of the Acoustical Society of America, 69*, pp. 1126–1131. Reprinted with permission.

three main generalizations. First, just as brightness increases with luminance given a constant flash duration, so too does brightness increase with duration (up to a point) given a constant luminance; this follows from the generalized Bloch's law (originally applied to threshold), which states that over short durations, up to a critical duration τ brightness B depends on the product of luminance I and time t, $B = F(I \cdot t)$. Second, the value of τ is not constant, but decreases as I increases. Third, at any given value of I, there is a duration τ_p at which brightness is greatest (the Broca–Sulzer maximum); brightness is smaller when flash duration is either shorter or longer than τ_p. A wide range of magnitude scaling data and direct brightness matches affirm these principles (Aiba & Stevens, 1964; Broca & Sulzer, 1902a, 1902b; Nachmias & Steinman, 1965; Raab, 1962; J. C. Stevens & Hall, 1966).

One way to account for this array of phenomena, and in particular for the power functions often found to describe magnitude judgments, is to postulate nonlinear feedback in the visual system that influences both the system's gain and its time constant (Mansfield, 1970; Marks, 1972). In a system containing n stages, the output of each stage, i, is B_i, governed by a differential equation of the form

$$\delta B_i/\delta t = a_i B_{i-1} - b_i B_{i-1} (1 + c_i B_n), \tag{37}$$

where a_i, b_i, and c_i are weighting constants. Such a model, first proposed in order to account for nonlinearities in neural responses of the horseshoe crab *Limulus* (Fuortes & Hodgkin, 1964), can also help to account for human flicker discrimination (Sperling & Sondhi, 1968), and, in expanded form, for spatial summation and distribution of responsiveness over the retinal surface (Marks, 1972).

It is especially noteworthy that, in order to account quantitatively for the temporal properties of brightness vision, the feedback filter used in Mansfield's (1970) and Marks's (1972) models needs to contain exactly two stages ($n = 2$). For it turns out that a two-stage filter has another important property: Its input–output characteristic, in the steady state, approximates a power function with exponent of $\frac{1}{3}$—precisely the value that Stevens (e.g., 1975) claimed to govern the magnitude scale for brightness of long flash durations under conditions of dark adaptation. Thus a theory formulated to account for temporal processing in vision has the additional virtue that it can predict the form of the magnitude-scaling function for brightness—an example where substantive theory goes hand in hand with psychophysical scaling.

D. Cross-Modality Matching

In the method of cross-modality matching (CMM), subjects attempt to set stimulus levels so that the perceived magnitude of a signal in one modality equals the perceived magnitude in another. Although CMM studies appeared intermittently from the 19th century on, most of these focused on judgments in which the same stimulus can be perceived through different senses (for example, when subjects compare the lengths of objects perceived haptically and visually: Jastrow, 1886; Mme. Piéron [sic], 1922). Often, however, the stimuli presented to different senses have no clear environmental communality, so their equality may be considered more abstract or even metaphorical. An example is the matching of brightness and loudness. Modern CMM appears to have evolved from J. C. Stevens's (1957) attempts to have subjects equate the ratios of perceived magnitudes in different modalities—a method of cross-modal ratio matching. Whether subjects always perform cross-modality matching by operating on ratios (e.g., Krantz, 1972) or by directly equating magnitudes themselves (Collins & Gescheider, 1989; Levine, 1974; Zwislocki, 1983) remains controversial.

Results garnered by CMM were taken by S. S. Stevens (e.g., 1959a; J. C. Stevens, Mack, & Stevens, 1960) as support for the power law. Consider two modalities, a and b, that are governed by power functions with exponents β_a and β_b, so that $R_a = k_a I_a^{\beta_a}$ and $R_b = k_b I_b^{\beta_b}$. If the responses R_a and R_b represent sensations, and subjects equate sensations on the two modalities, so $R_a = R_b$, then a plot of values of one stimulus against the matching values of the other should conform to a power function whose exponent equals the ratio of the values of β_b and β_a,

$$I_a = (k_b/k_a)^{(1/\beta_a)} I_b^{(\beta_b/\beta_a)}. \tag{38}$$

To the extent that this result obtains (S. S. Stevens, 1959a; J. C. Stevens, Mack, & Stevens, 1960; J. C. Stevens & Marks, 1965), CMMs and magnitude judgments form a coherent, transitive system (although some have argued that the system is not transitive, e.g., Mashhour & Hosman, 1968). Unfortunately, it is possible to transform magnitude scales (that is, transform all scales of R) by an infinitude of continuous increasing transformations and leave the predicted CMMs unchanged; thus CMMs can be as consistent with Fechner's logarithmic function as with Stevens's power function (e.g., Ekman, 1964; MacKay, 1963; Treisman, 1964; Shepard, 1978; Zinnes, 1969; see also Link, 1992), at least as long as the multiplicative scale parameters of the several logarithmic functions, such as c in Eq. (5), are quantitatively related to the same extent as are the corresponding exponents of power functions.

As we already indicated, results obtained by CMM may reflect underlying comparisons of ratios or comparisons of magnitudes. The emphasis on predicting exponents has had the unfortunate consequence of drawing attention away from the issue of magnitude proper. When we ask subjects to match, say, loudness to brightness, do the results tell us that a particular luminance's brightness equals a particular SPL's loudness? Or that, in relation to some other light's luminance and some other sound's SPL, the brightness ratio equals the loudness ratio? Equation (38) would seem to make explicit predictions about stimulus levels and not just their ratios (see also Collins & Gescheider, 1989).

J. C. Stevens and Marks (1980) proposed that subjects can make absolute comparisons of magnitude across different modalities, and they developed a method, magnitude matching, that makes it possible to derive cross-modal matches from magnitude estimates given to sets of stimuli presented in different modalities. The goal in doing this was primarily practical rather than theoretical—to develop a method by which responses given to stimuli on one modality could be used to "calibrate" different individuals or different groups—and in this magnitude matching has seen several successes (e.g., Gent & Bartoshuk, 1983; Murphy & Gilmore, 1989; J. C. Stevens & Cain, 1985). Berglund's (1991) method of "master scaling" relies on a similar principle, but uses as a means for calibration a standardized set of stimuli presented to the same modality. For example, one may start by having subjects estimate the loudness of a series of pink noises (emphasis on low-frequency energy); then, the subjects' judgments of various other stimuli (e.g., environmental noises) can be standardized through the loudness function obtained for pink noise.

E. Critiques of Stevens's Psychophysics

In advocating the methods and results of magnitude scaling, Stevens (e.g., 1961) explicitly attacked Fechnerian scaling. This attack deserves special attention because it also had its constructive side. In criticizing Fechner and proposing to "repeal his law," Stevens offered novel ways to measure sensation—although his own methods are vulnerable on several grounds. Before examining those vulnerabilities, however, let us examine Stevens's arguments over Fechner's conception of psychophysical measurement.

Stevens challenged Fechner's choice of the JND as a unit of sensation strength, objecting to the use of an index of variability, error, or "resolving power" as a unit of measurement. Moreover, Stevens argued that the subjective size of the JND does not remain constant. On a pragmatic level, Stevens objected to "indirect" methods of constructing scales of measurement and suggested alternatives. To the contention that psychophysical measurement is not like physical measurement (the former not being measurement at all), he retorted by proposing a broader conception of measurement for the physical sciences as well (Stevens, 1946, 1951).

A dominant approach to measurement, anticipated by von Kries (1882), grew out of the work of scholars like N. R. Campbell (1920) and crystallized in a "classical view of measurement" (Stevens, 1959b). Essentially, in this view, "fundamental" measurement requires manipulations that are isomorphic with the "axioms of additivity." Fundamental measurement is possible with properties like length or mass. Measurement of other physical properties, such as density or potential energy, is called "derived" and is defined by relations based on fundamental magnitudes. The classical view, followed to its logical conclusion, precludes the possibility of mental measurement. Obviously, "sensations cannot be separated into component parts, or laid end to end like measurement sticks" (Stevens, 1959c, p. 608), so no fundamental measurement of sensation is possible. By implication, however, sensations cannot be gauged by "derived" measurement either. Thus they cannot be measured at all. This pessimistic conclusion was shared by many members of a British committee of scientists appointed in 1932 to consider the possibility of "quantitative estimates of sensory events."

To bypass these difficulties, particularly in creating a unit to measure sensation, Stevens (1946, 1975) sought to broaden the definition of measurement. In his theory, measurement is simply the assignment of numbers to objects according to a rule. Different rules or procedures yield numbers that represent different empirical relations. Stevens then sought to isolate those transformations, or mathematical group structures, that leave the original empirical information invariant. His famous system of scales of measurement anticipated the derivation of the so-called uniqueness theorems within the framework of axiomatic measurement (e.g., Krantz et al., 1971; Luce et al., 1990). Stevens thus first called attention to the importance of determining how unique an array of numerical representations is, then showed how the permissible mappings between equivalent representations can serve to classify scales of measurement.

Psychophysical scaling is concerned, however, with the possibility of mapping stimuli onto numbers, not with the mapping of one representation onto another. Scaling deals with the foundational operations of ordering and matching, whereby it precedes the question of uniqueness chronologically as well as logically. Luce and Krumhansl (1988), for example, discussed Stevens's classification of scales under the rubric of axiomatic measurement (where it properly belongs), not under the rubric of scaling.

If the "scales of measurement" do not deal with scaling, how did Stevens address the issue of scaling? As we have seen, he did this by suggesting that one can measure the strength of sensation "directly," by matching numbers to stimuli. Numerical "introspections," so to speak, are said to measure sensation in the same way that a thermometer measures temperature. Subjects may be asked to give numbers to stimuli such that the numbers are proportional to the subjective magnitudes aroused. These responses are treated quantitatively, often as if they have properties of "ratio scales." Nevertheless, deep theoretical questions plague Stevens's approach.

In his description of the psychophysical law, Stevens used the term ψ, not the more neutral R, to stand for the subjective variable (cf. McKenna, 1985).

The practice has caused a great deal of confusion. If ψ is *hypothesized* to stand for sensation, then how do we ascertain that the overt numerical responses faithfully reflect the underlying sensations? The very designation ψ may have impeded recognition of the crucial role played by decisional processes and hence with the consequent judgment function relating overt responses to the unobservable sensations. Once this role is appreciated, it becomes apparent that, without additional information, the psychophysical function is indeterminate. Alternatively, one may consider ψ a measure of sensation simply by operational definition. This may have well been Stevens's position; however, he did not suggest converging operations to support the premise (McKenna, 1985).

Several investigators (e.g., Garner, 1954; Graham & Ratoosh, 1962; McGill, 1974; Shepard, 1978) have questioned "the procedure of treating numerical estimates as if they were numerical data . . . the quantified outcome of a measuring operation" (Graham, 1958, p. 68). Asserted McGill (1974), "Whatever else they are, the responses are *not* numbers" (p. 295). By this view, one may average the stimuli for a given response, but not, as Stevens did, average the responses for a given stimulus. The method of cross-modality matching (Stevens, 1975) eschews the use of numbers. But the results yielded by that method are consistent with a whole array of possible psychophysical functions, including the logarithmic function of Fechner as well as the power function proposed by Stevens.

Even granting that overt responses are numbers, there remains an inherent arbitrariness about the choice of numbers to measure sensations. It is the same problem that has plagued physicists over the temperature scale, where the choice of thermometric substance is arbitrary. There are two ways to escape the difficulty (actually, the first is a special case of the second). One way "is to ground scales in (metric) properties of *natural kinds*. . . . In this sense, Fechner's intuition of searching for natural units of sensation is better than that of Stevens" (Van Brakel, 1993, p. 164). More fundamentally, however, the usefulness of any scale depends on the available theoretical structure. For the physical property of temperature, "the interval or ratio properties of the thermodynamic scale of temperature can be fully justified only by reference to physical theory" (Shepard, 1978, p. 444). The same applies to psychophysical scaling by the so-called direct methods, for, "Without a theory, . . . how can we assume that the numbers proffered by a subject—any more than the numbers indicated on the arbitrary scale of the thermoscope—are proportional to any underlying quantity?" (Shepard, 1978, p. 453).

The critical ingredient, then, is a comprehensive theoretical structure that includes the particular scale as its natural component. Fechner's approach, with JNDs as "natural units," offers one avenue to develop such a structure, although, as yet, it lacks the rich interconnections characterizing physical measurement (Luce, 1972; Shepard, 1978). Efforts to develop a theory for magnitude estimation (Krantz, 1972; Shepard, 1978, 1981) suggest that Stevens's conception that subjects judge sensations of individual stimuli ("mapping theory") may be untenable, though this remains controversial. Levine (1974) offered a geometric model in which subjects do map numbers onto individual sensations. And Zwislocki (1983; Zwislocki & Goodman, 1980) has argued that people develop individual scales of magnitude, which can be tapped through the method he calls absolute magnitude estimation. In Zwislocki's view, subjects can be instructed to assign numbers to stimuli so that the psychological magnitudes of the numbers match, in a direct fashion, the psychological magnitudes of the stimuli.

On the other hand, it may be that in many, most, or even all circumstances, subjects judge *relations* between stimuli ("relation theory"; see Krantz, 1972). But without strong assumptions, relation theory shows psychophysical functions derived from magnitude scaling to be underdetermined; in particular, there is no empirical or theoretical basis to decide between equally consistent sets of logarithmic and power functions. Only by integrating scaling within some kind of substantive psychophysical theory can we attain valid and useful measurement. To do so, we "have to move outside the circumscribed system of relationships provided by these 'direct' psychophysical operations" (Shepard, 1978, p. 484).

Most attacks on Stevens's psychophysics have been aimed at the implications that he drew from his data, not so much at the reliability of those data themselves (but see McKenna, 1985, and references therein). So-called direct procedures resulted in a psychophysical law incompatible with the one developed by Fechner. Stevens found that magnitude estimates, taken as numerical quantities, are a power function of physical magnitude. But any attempt to form a general psychophysical theory must reckon with the fact that different procedures can lead to different scales (Birnbaum, 1990).

V. MULTISTAGE MODELS: MAGNITUDES, RATIOS, DIFFERENCES

A. Judgments of Magnitude and Scales of Magnitude

Shepard (1978, 1981), Anderson (1970, 1981, 1982), and Birnbaum (1982, 1990) have shown the inadequacy of Stevens's (1956, 1957, 1975) contention that the numbers given by subjects are necessarily proportional to sensation magnitudes. Earlier, Garner (1954), Graham (1958), Attneave (1962), Mackay (1963), and Treisman (1964) made much the same point. The weakness of merely assuming that "direct" scales measure sensation is easily demonstrated (e.g., Gescheider, 1988; Gescheider & Bolanowski, 1991). Denote by S the unobservable sensation, by R the numerical response, and by I the stimulus intensity. Then the psychophysical transformation, F_1, is given by

$$S = F_1(I). \tag{39}$$

The judgment function, F_2, relating sensation magnitude S to the observable response R, can be written

$$R = F_2(S). \tag{40}$$

Combining Eqs. (39) and (40) gives

$$R = F_2[F_1(I)], \tag{41}$$

which is the experimentally observed relation between R and I, usually expressed directly by

$$R = F(I), \tag{42}$$

which conflates the component functions F_1 and F_2. The underlying psychophysical function F_1 must be inferred from the empirically observed function F. But unless one knows the judgment function F_2, it is impossible to determine F_1. Stevens's assertion that the psychophysical law is a power function depends on the strong assumption that R is proportional to S (or to S raised to a power). Stevens provided no justification for this assumption. Attempts at decomposing F_1 and F_2 within two-stage models suggest, in some instances, that F_2 is nonlinear, a matter considered in the next section.

The previous discussion assumes that subjects are able to assign numbers to stimuli in a consistent manner, such that R can be treated as numerical. This assumption too is controversial. As we mentioned earlier, it is not clear whether a verbal response really possesses quantitative magnitude (e.g., Graham, 1958; McGill, 1974; Shepard, 1978). If not, then it is illegitimate to treat the response as numbers, let alone calculate from them statistical quantities such as mean or variance. Such concerns do not apply to Fechnerian methods.

1. Curtis and Rule's Two-Stage Model

Several investigators have sought to disentangle psychophysical functions (relating stimulus to sensation) and judgment functions (relating sensation to overt response). In particular, judgment functions may be nonlinear—if, for example, the psychological magnitudes of numbers are not proportional to numbers themselves, but a power function with exponent different from unity, as suggested by Attneave (1962).

This suggestion was elaborated into a model by Curtis, Rule, and their associates (e.g., Curtis, 1970; Curtis, Attneave, & Harrington, 1968; Curtis & Rule, 1972; Rule & Curtis, 1977, 1978). To decompose an overt magnitude scaling function F into its components, a psychophysical function F_1

and a judgment function F_2, or into what these researchers called "input" and "output" functions, subjects were asked to judge pairs of stimuli— typically, with regard to their perceived difference. The model assumes that the function F_1 applies separately to each stimulus in the pair; after F_1 is applied, a difference is computed between the sensations; and finally this sensory difference is subjected to response transformation F_2. Thus the model can be written

$$R = k(I_i^{\beta_1} - I_j^{\beta_1})^{\beta_2}, \tag{43}$$

where I_i and I_j denote the stimulus intensities of stimuli i and j, β_1 and β_2 are the respective exponents of the power functions governing F_1 (the sensory process) and F_2 (the nonlinear use of numbers), and k absorbs multiplicative constants from both F_1 and F_2. An analogous equation applies to conditions in which the sensory effects of the two components sum, simply by changing the sign of the operation from subtraction to addition.

In this *two-stage model,* the size of the observed exponent β, routinely derived from magnitude estimation, should equal the product of β_1 and β_2. We do not describe the empirical results in detail, but instead list four conclusions important to the present discussion. First, when judgments are obtained by magnitude estimation, the values of β_2 are usually greater than 1.0, implying a nonlinear judgment function in magnitude estimation. Second, various attempts to scale the psychological magnitude of numbers suggest that numeric representations may sometimes be nonlinearly related to numbers (e.g., Banks & Coleman, 1981; Rule & Curtis, 1973; Shepard, Kilpatric, & Cunningham, 1975), though sometimes the relation appears linear (Banks & Coleman, 1981). Third, the value of β_1 usually varies much less over individuals than does β_2, consistent with the notion that there is less interindividual variation in sensory processing than in response mapping. Fourth, when judgments are obtained on rating scales rather than magnitude-estimation scales, the values of β_2 are generally closer to 1.0, consistent with the view that rating scales can provide linear judgment functions (see also Anderson, 1981).

Results obtained by applying the two-stage model to judgments of pairs of stimuli suggest that in one respect, at least, Stevens was correct: The function F_1 governing the transformation from stimulus to sensation is often well described with a power function. But the exponents of F_1 are generally smaller than those obtained with magnitude estimation. Earlier, Garner (1954) came to a similar conclusion, based on the equisections of loudness that he used to construct the lambda scale. In general, judgments of loudness intervals agree better with the lambda scale than with the sone scale (Beck & Shaw, 1967; Dawson, 1971; Marks, 1974a, 1979b). So do scales derived from nonmetric analysis, that is, from the rank order of loudness differences determined over all possible pairs of stimuli (Parker &

Schneider, 1974; Popper et al., 1986; Schneider, 1980; Schneider et al., 1974, 1978). Loudness in lambda units is roughly proportional to the square root of loudness in sones. In sum, research conduced under the rubric of two-stage models, especially in the judgment of sensory differences, has produced a vast array of findings, largely consistent with the view that magnitude estimates are "biased" by strongly nonlinear judgment functions (though a plausible alternative interpretation is given in the next section).

2. Conjoint Measurement

The conclusion of the last section, that magnitude estimates are strongly "biased" by a nonlinear judgment function, rests on the assumption that the same processes underlie judgments of magnitude (where subjects assign numbers to represent the apparent strength of individual stimuli) and judgments of difference (where subjects assign numbers to represent the size of a difference). That this assumption itself deserves careful scrutiny is suggested by studies seeking to disentangle sensory and judgment functions within experimental paradigms in which subjects judge magnitudes rather than differences. These studies are rooted in the classic paper by Fletcher and Munson (1933), who erected a scale of loudness by relying on a hypothesis of linear sensory summation: When pure tones are presented through independent channels (to the two ears, or to the same ear but at very different signal frequencies), the loudnesses of the components add. If this is so, then it follows, for instance, that a tone heard by two ears is exactly twice as loud as the same tone heard by one ear (assuming the ears are equally sensitive). Consequently, to construct a loudness scale, it is sufficient to obtain matches between monaurally presented and binaurally presented signals. If a signal intensity of I_1 presented binaurally has a loudness, $L_b(I_1)$, equal to that of intensity I_2 presented monaurally, so $L_b(I_1) = L_m(I_2)$, and if loudnesses sum across the two ears at any intensity I, so, for example, $L_b(I_1) = 2 \cdot L_m(I_1)$, then it follows that

$$L_m(I_2) = 2 \cdot L_m(I_1). \tag{44}$$

That is, given a model of linear loudness summation, and given that a signal of intensity I_2 presented monaurally matches I_1 presented binaurally, then under monaural (or binaural) presentations, I_2 will be twice as loud as I_1. Unfortunately, Fletcher and Munson had no procedure to test the adequacy of their model of linear summation.

Such tests awaited the development of *conjoint measurement theory* (Luce & Tukey, 1964), which provided an axiomatic grounding for additive measurement of intensive quantities. This approach returns us to the long-revered notion of basing fundamental measurement—be it physical or psychological—in the addition of quantities. But Luce and Tukey showed that additivity is possible even when we cannot mimic empirically the additive operations of extensive physical measurement. Thus conjoint measurement can apply to those very situations, like the measurement of sensation, to which variants of the "quantity objection" have been raised—such as a cannon shot, which "does not contain so and so many pistol cracks within it." In Luce and Tukey's theory, values of two stimulus components can be shown to add even when we have only ordinal information about the relative effects of the conjoined values. Assume a set of stimuli comprising two components, with component A taking on values a_i, and B taking on values b_j. Additivity requires that two main principles hold (e.g., Krantz et al., 1971). One is transitivity:

$$\text{If } a_1,b_1 \geq a_2,b_2 \text{ and } a_2,b_2 \geq a_3,b_3, \text{ then } a_1,b_1 \geq a_3,b_3. \tag{45}$$

The second is cancellation:

$$\text{If } a_2,b_3 \geq a_3,b_2 \text{ and } a_1,b_2 \geq a_2,b_1, \text{ then } a_1,b_3 \geq a_3,b_1. \tag{46}$$

Cancellation is the critical axiom: It entails the commensurability of a given change in one of the variables with a given change in another. If additivity and cancellation hold, then there exist interval-scale representations for dimensions A and B whose values are linearly additive. In demonstrating that fundamental (additive) measurement is not limited to the extensive quantities of physical sciences, conjoint measurement theory provides a deep analysis of additive structures (cf. Luce & Krumhansl, 1988).

Levelt, Riemersma, and Bunt (1972) obtained judgments of relative loudness of tones presented at unequal intensities to the two ears and found the results were consistent with a model of additivity. The loudness scales derived by Levelt et al. could be described by power functions of sound pressure, with exponent averaging about 0.5, closer to the prototypical value 0.6 of Stevens's sone scale than to the 0.3 of Garner's lambda scale. Similar results were reported using conjoint scaling (Marks, 1978c) and a functional-measurement approach, the latter applied both to binaural loudness additivity and to the additivity of loudnesses of tones far separated in sound frequency (Marks, 1978a, 1978b, 1979b). In all cases, the loudness scales had exponents near 0.6 in terms of sound pressure. In touch, the perceived intensity of vibrotactile stimuli comprising multiple sinusoids was also linearly additive on the magnitude-estimation scale (Marks, 1979a).

Schneider (1988) performed a thorough and elegant study of additivity of 2000-Hz and 5000-Hz tones (separated by several critical bandwidths). Applying a conjoint-scaling method to direct comparisons of loudness, Schneider reported that the data of individual subjects satisfied the constraints of additivity, permitting him to derive loudness scales that at each frequency were consistent with power functions; exponents ranged over individuals from 0.5 to 0.7 (re sound pressure). In a related vein, Zwislocki (1983) used a conjoint-scaling approach to confirm the loudness scales that he derived using absolute magnitude estimation. We note, however, some evidence for deviations from additivity in both the case of binaural combinations (Gigerenzer & Strube, 1983) and multifrequency combinations (Hübner & Ellermeier, 1993), tested through a probabilistic generalization called *random conjoint measurement* (Falmagne, 1976).

Last, in this regard, Parker, Schneider, Stein, Popper, Darte, and Needel (1981) and Parker and Schneider (1988) used conjoint scaling to measure the utility of money and other commodities. The results are consistent with the hypothesis that the utility of a bundle of commodities equals the sum of the utilities of the components. The utility of money is a negatively accelerated function of money itself, consistent with power functions with exponents smaller than unity, and roughly similar to those derived from numerical scaling (e.g., Galanter, 1962; Galanter & Pliner, 1974). As an aside, we note that, much like Thurstonian scaling, conjoint scaling, and indeed magnitude scaling in general, makes it possible to quantify psychological responses even to stimuli that lack a clear physical metric. So, for example, a series of studies by Ekman and Künnapas (1962, 1963a, 1963b), used a variant of magnitude scaling—ratio estimation—to quantify such domains as the esthetic value of samples of handwriting, the political importance of Swedish monarchs, and the degree of social-political conservatism of verbal statements.

When they are consistent with linear additivity, results obtained by applying conjoint-measurement theory to numerical judgments, as with other findings discussed earlier, can be characterized in terms of (or shown to be consistent with) a two-stage model. If again we characterize F_1 and F_2 as power functions, the model becomes

$$R = k(I_1^{\beta_1} + I_2^{\beta_1})^{\beta_2}. \tag{47}$$

But now, with magnitude estimation, the average judgment function is typically linear ($\beta_2 = 1$), and the value of β_1 agree much better with magnitude estimates than with difference judgments (e.g., Marks, 1978c, 1979b). These findings suggest that it may be premature to reject magnitude estimation out of hand in favor of measures derived from sensory differences. It is possible that the sensory representations underlying judgments of magnitude simply differ from those underlying judgments of difference but are no less valid (Marks, 1979b).

3. Judgments of Magnitude, Differences, and Ratios

Torgerson (1961) raised the possibility that subjects perceive a single relation between stimuli regardless of whether they are instructed to judge "ratios" or "differences." When ratio and difference judgments are compared directly, the two sets typically have the same rank order (e.g., Birnbaum, 1978, 1982; Mellers, Davis, & Birnbaum, 1984). Were the subjects to follow the respective instructions appropriately, the two sets of judgments would not be identically ordered. So Torgerson's conjecture seems plausible. But because the responses may be affected by nonlinear judgment functions, it is more difficult to ascertain whether it is differences or ratios that subjects report. Asking the subjects to compare stimulus relations (e.g., "ratios of differences," or "differences of differences") may help decide. Convergence of scale values—assuming that equivalent values operate in the two tasks—provides another constraint. Combining results makes it possible to test Torgerson's hypothesis and uncover the nature of the underlying operation—an avenue pursued by Birnbaum.

In Birnbaum's theory, subjects use subtraction regardless of whether they are instructed to judge ratios or differences. Subjectively, the stimuli form an interval scale like positions of cities on a map. On such a scale, differences are meaningful but ratios are not. Because a difference has a well-defined origin or zero, judgments of ratios of differences should obey a ratio model, whereas judgments of differences of differences should obey a difference model; evidence supports these predictions (e.g., Birnbaum, 1978, 1982; Birnbaum, C. Anderson, & Hynan, 1989). The subtractive theory provides a coherent account of several phenomena, including context effects, judgments of inverse attributes, and relations between ratings and magnitude estimates (see Birnbaum, 1990, for summary).

Whatever the subjects judge (differences or ratios) and however they make their judgments (by category rating or magnitude estimation), according to Birnbaum's theory the sensations, S, remain the same. Only the judgment function, F_2, differs. Judgment functions are readily affected by such factors as distribution of stimulus levels, choice of standard, and wording of the instructions. The relation between judgments of ratios and judgments of differences, or between magnitude estimates and fixed-scale ratings, can be systematically manipulated. This granted, in many cases F_2 obtained with judgments of ratios is exponentially related to F_2 obtained with judgments of differences. Consequently, judgments of ratios may appear at first glance to fit a ratio model, and judgments of differences may appear to fit a subtractive, or differencing, model. But in fact both sets of judgments rely on a single, subtractive process operating at the level of the underlying sensory scale values; it is the judgment functions that differ. Furthermore, if subjects try to judge ratios when they give magnitude estimates but try to judge differences when they give category ratings, then the magnitude estimates should likewise be an exponential function of corresponding category ratings—consistent with the common finding that magnitude estimates and category ratings are nonlinearly related.

This said, it is necessary to qualify some of these conclusions. When asked to judge "ratios" and "differences," subjects sometimes do produce different rank orders, as if they were in fact using different mental operations, not just different judgment functions. Although the use of different rank orders is undoubtedly the exception in judgments of continua like loudness, it seems to be the rule in the particular case of length of lines. Judgments of ratios of line lengths are consistent with a ratio model in which subjective values are a power function of physical length (exponent not determinate), whereas judgments of differences in line length are consistent with a subtractive model in which subjective values are proportional to the square root of physical length (Parker et al., 1975). Perhaps subjects can use ratio models when stimuli have well-learned physical units (cf. Poulton, 1989) or when they have extensive rather than intensive properties, and thus, conceivably, better-defined zero points (cf. Hagerty & Birnbaum, 1978).

Another set of problems appears when we try to extend the findings on judgments of ratios and differences to explicate magnitude estimation and category rating. Let us assume, first, that judgments of ratios and differences rely on the single operation of differencing and, second, that an exponential judgment function underlies ratios but a linear judgment function underlies differences. If magnitude estimates and category ratings reflect judgments of ratios and differences, respectively, then it follows that category ratings should be logarithmically related to corresponding magnitude estimates. Further, if magnitude estimates follow a power function of stimulus intensity, the category ratings (or other scales of difference) should follow a logarithmic function of intensity. But category ratings are only infrequently logarithmically related to the corresponding magnitude estimates, or to stimulus intensity. Often, the nonlinearity is less extreme, consistent with a power function with an exponent somewhat smaller than unity (Marks, 1968, 1974a; Stevens, 1971; Ward, 1972). Indeed, sometimes category ratings and magnitude estimates are similar functions of stimulus intensity (Foley et al., 1983; Gibson & Tomko, 1972).

Perhaps one or more of the assumptions is incorrect. It is possible, for example, that subjects do not use implicit ratios in magnitude estimation. But given the sensitivity of judgment functions to stimulus context (for example, the form of rating scales depends systematically on stimulus range and number of available categories: e.g., Marks, 1968; Parducci, 1982; Parducci & Wedell, 1986; Stevens & Galanter, 1957), this evidence is not wholly conclusive. In this matter, see Birnbaum (1980).

More significant in this regard are the various scales derived from judgments of intervals or differences in which nonlinearities in judgment functions have been eliminated or circumvented—either by applying explicit two-stage power-function models or by subjecting the judgments to nonmetric scaling analyses. In virtually all of these cases, the scales of sensory difference turn out to be power functions, not logarithmic functions, of stimulus intensity (e.g., Curtis et al., 1968; Rule & Curtis, 1976; Parker & Schneider, 1974; Schneider, 1980; Schneider et al., 1974). If magnitude estimates were exponentially related to these scale values, the resulting relation should deviate from a power function. The judgment functions obtained from, say, magnitude estimates of sensory differences typically are not as extreme as an exponential rule dictates but can be described by power functions: Eq. (43) with exponents, β_2, generally ranging between about 1.5 and 2.0 (Curtis et al., 1968; Rule & Curtis, 1977; Rule, Curtis, & Markley, 1970).

One possible resolution comes by dissociating judgments of magnitudes from judgments of ratios. This is the position taken by Zwislocki (e.g., 1983), and it traces back to observations made more than 30 years ago (e.g., Hellman & Zwislocki, 1961). By this token, judgments of magnitude rely on, or can rely on, assessments of individual sensory experiences and need not be based on putative ratio relations (cf. Marks, 1979b).

4. Functional Measurement

Norman Anderson's functional measurement originated in work on person perception some three decades ago. That work showed the value of studying the algebraic structures that underlie processes of information integration, with tasks involving adjectival ascriptions of personality (Asch, 1946). Subsequently, the conceptual framework extended to virtually every arena of experimental psychology. These developments and the experimental results are summarized in two volumes (Anderson, 1981, 1982). Several works recount psychophysical data and theory (e.g., Anderson, 1970, 1974, 1992).

Figure 8 depicts a hypothetical chain of transformations from observable stimuli, I_j, to observable response, R. These stimuli are first transformed into sensations, S_j, by appropriate psychophysical functions, the input functions defined by the psychophysical law. The values of S_j then combine to produce an overall sensation, S, the combination governed by a corresponding integration rule, or psychological law. Finally, a judgment or output function, or psychomotor law, maps the outcome of the integration process, S, onto observable response R.

Note that, for a single physical continuum, the functions implied by Figure 8 translate to the two-stage model of magnitude estimation discussed earlier and characterized by Eqs. (43) and (47), where the psychophysical transformation from stimulus to sensation is followed by a judgment transformation mapping the sensation to response. With unidimensionally varying stimuli, however, the model itself does not provide a means to separate the two transformations and uncover the psychophysical function.

The key to functional measurement lies in the use of several physical

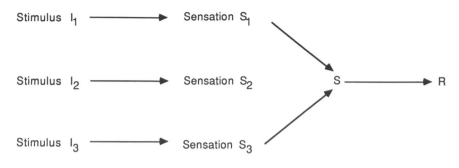

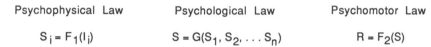

FIGURE 8   The model of functional measurement offered by Anderson (e.g., 1977), in which stimulus values, I_j, are transformed to psychological values, S_j, by a psychophysical law; the psychological values of S_j are integrated by an appropriate psychological law; and the resulting percepts, S, are mapped to response, R, by a psychomotor law. From Figure 1.1 of *Foundations of Information Integration Theory*, by N. H. Anderson, New York: Academic Press, 1977. Reprinted with permission of the author and publisher.

continua, whose values vary according to an appropriate factorial design. The motivation for prescribing a multidimensional design is not just procedural. Rather it provides a framework for theoretical analysis, particularly if it is possible to derive the rule of information integration from a suprastructural, theoretical framework. Primary emphasis is placed, therefore, on stimulus integration.

Often, integration is found to obey simple algebraic rules such as addition or averaging. Collectively, such rules have been called *cognitive algebra*. In Anderson's scheme, the process of information integration involves unobserved sensations, S_j. If, however, the overt response, R, is linearly related to the integrated response, R', then the data can be taken as joint evidence for both the integration rule and the validity of the response scale; analysis of variance and visual examination of the factorial plots provide ways to assess the adequacy of the model. Finally, one can relate S (through R) to the stimulus in order to derive psychophysical functions.

A study of the integration of pain (Algom, Raphaeli, & Cohen-Raz, 1986) illustrates the approach. The authors covaried the values of two separate noxious variables in a factorial design, combining 6 levels of electric current applied to the wrist with 6 levels of uncomfortably loud tones, making 36 tone-shock compounds in all. Subjects gave magnitude estimates

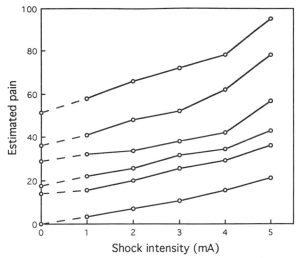

FIGURE 9   An example of functional measurement applied to the perception and judgment of pain induced by systematically combining levels of noxious acoustic and electrical stimulation. Plotted are judgments of pain as a function of shock intensity, each curve representing a different level of constant SPL delivered to the two ears. After Algom, Raphaeli, and Cohen-Raz (1986). Copyright 1986 by the American Psychological Association. Reprinted with permission of the author.

of the painfulness of these concurrent-presented stimuli. Figure 9 reproduces the main results, showing how the judgments of pain increased with increasing shock current. Each curve represents the results for a fixed intensity of the tone; the greater the tone intensity, the greater the pain.

The most salient characteristic of the factorial plot is the roughly equal spacing of the family of curves in the vertical dimension, although a slight trend toward divergence in the upper right is evident (more on this later). Parallel spacing implies linear additivity of the numerical responses. By implication, the aversiveness of an electric shock and a strong tone presented simultaneously at various intensities approximates the linear sum of the individual painful components. Note, too, that the shock-only trials (bottom curve) have the same slope as do the compounds of shock plus tone. This feature supports an additive composition rule over an averaging rule, for in such cases an averaging rule predicts a crossover of the adjacent functions.

Observed parallelism is consistent with three features of the functional-measurement model: First, pain shows additivity; in this particular test, the data corroborate Algom's (1992a) functional theory of pain. Second, the judgment function appears linear. So, third, by implication, the psychophysical functions are valid. Accordingly, Algom et al. derived psychophysical functions separately for shock-induced pain and for acoustically induced pain. Both relations could be approximated by power functions, with exponents of about 1.1 for shock and 0.9 for sound. Note that the function for auditory pain differs appreciably from the functions for loudness that are routinely derived for acoustic sounds.

The use of magnitude estimates for a response measure is an exception within the school of functional measurement. Anderson (1970, 1974) has found interval or category scales superior because, in most cases, ratings but not magnitude estimates reveal directly the anticipated rules of integration. Indeed, Algom et al. (1986) had to apply a nonlinear transformation to their data in order to exhibit full parallelism. That maneuver—monotonically transforming the data to fit the selected model—is routinely followed when the original data fail to support the tested rule. In general, no need for such rescaling arises when ratings are used. This result is interpreted to support the validity of rating scales. Moreover, the criterion of scale convergence across different tasks is satisfied when ratings are used, seldom when magnitude estimates are. Neither argument, however, is conclusive. The data may fail to produce the selected model simply because it is false, not because magnitude estimates are biased. Further, the criterion of scale convergence may not always be appropriate. Though not parsimonious, it is possible that the sensations aroused by the same stimuli actually change over different tasks (e.g., Eisler, 1963; Luce & Edwards, 1958; Marks, 1974a, 1979b; cf. Wasserman, 1991).

The assertion that an observed pattern of responses jointly supports the model and the linearity of the judgment scale is controversial (e.g., Birnbaum, 1982). As Gescheider (1997) and Gigerenzer and Murray (1987) have shown, any number of models can account for a given pattern of data, permitting an appropriately chosen judgment function. And, within functional measurement, there may be no reason to prefer one model over another unless there is an appropriate theory. In this sense, functional measurement provides an infrastructure rather than a theoretically more powerful suprastructure. The trade-off between integration rule and judgment function poses a serious theoretical quandary. It is possible, of course, simply to assume that a particular model is appropriate or that a particular judgment function is linear, but then the approach provides little leverage beyond that of unidimensional designs. Anderson has devised several methods (e.g., two-operation designs) to enable one to reject some alternatives; but thus far no general solution appears.

B. Response Times and Sensory Magnitudes

More than 80 years ago, Piéron (1914) suggested that simple response times—the time from the onset of a stimulus to the initiation of a response indicating that the stimulus was perceived—might provide a measure of sensation magnitude. He proceeded to measure RT versus intensity functions in several modalities, the outcome of this endeavor being an equation that came to be known as Piéron's law:

$$RT = hI^{-\upsilon} + T_o. \tag{48}$$

Equation (48) is an inverse power function, with RT declining linearly with stimulus intensity I raised to the υ power. The asymptotic limit, T_o, represents an irreducible minimum in RT. Modern studies, using more sophisticated equipment and experimental designs, have produced comparable findings, for example, in vision (Mansfield, 1973; Vaughn, Costa, & Gilden, 1966), hearing (Chocholle, 1940; Kohfeld, Santee, & Wallace, 1981a, 1981b; Luce & Green, 1972; McGill, 1961), and warmth (Banks, 1973).

Unlike measures of comparative response, where subjects must choose between two possible stimuli or must respond to some relation between stimuli, measures of simple RT merely require the subject to respond as quickly as possible to the detection or perception of a stimulus. A seemingly straightforward model might postulate that the subject initiates a response only when the amount of information surpasses some criterion (see, e.g., Grice, 1968). Perhaps this is most easily conceived in neurophysiological terms, where the criterion might correspond to a fixed number of neural impulses (though it could instead correspond to a measure of interpulse arrival times; see Luce & Green, 1972). Given that neural firing rates increase with stimulus intensity, the time to reach criterion will be inversely proportional to the firing rate (assuming the criterion stays constant over time; for review, see Luce, 1986). Moreover, if the criterial level of information (or neural response) corresponded to sensory magnitude, then we might expect the exponent υ of Eq. (48) to correspond in some direct or regular manner to exponents of psychophysical functions derived from scales of either differences or magnitudes.

Unfortunately, there does not seem to be any simple or uniform connection between RT and scales of magnitude. For example, studies of simple visual RT (e.g., Mansfield, 1973; Vaughn et al., 1966) show an exponent υ of about 0.33, like the value of β obtained for magnitude scales of brightness under comparable conditions (J. C. Stevens & Stevens, 1963), whereas most comparable studies of auditory RT (e.g., Chocholle, 1940; McGill, 1961) are consistent with an exponent υ, computed in terms of sound pressure, of about 0.3 (corresponding to Garner's lambda scale of loudness difference) instead of 0.6 (Stevens's sone scale of loudness).

Again, it is instructive to examine the extension of response-time measures to stimuli that vary multidimensionally, for such measures provide one way to assess the consistency of any putative relation between RT and sensory magnitude. Thus, we may ask whether different stimuli that match in perceived magnitude produce equivalent RTs. Chocholle (1940) examined such relations in some detail, noting that equal-RT curves, obtained from responses to tones varying in both sound frequency and SPL, closely resemble equal-loudness curves; similarly, embedding a tone within a masking noise reduces the tone's loudness, and similarly increases the RT. But while close, the correspondence between loudness and RT is not perfect, either across sound frequency (Kohfeld et al., 1981a, 1981b), or when tones are partially masked by noise (Chocholle & Greenbaum, 1966). That is, equally loud tones do not always give exactly equal RT. In fact, under certain circumstances, RT and sensation magnitudes can diverge markedly and in important ways: Thus, while both the brightness of flashes of light and RT depend approximately on the total luminous energy (Bloch's law), the critical duration τ for energy integration varies inversely with luminance in measures of brightness (as discussed earlier) but is independent of luminance in measures of RT. And only brightness, not RT, shows a Broca-Sulzer maximum (Raab & Fehrer, 1962; Mansfield, 1973).

VI. CONTEXTUAL EFFECTS

Perception, like so many other psychological processes, is quintessentially contextual: The response given to a nominally constant stimulus can depend on a whole host of factors, including the other stimuli recently presented or available in the ensemble (stimulus-set context), the responses made to recent stimuli relative to the available set of responses (response and response-set context), the presence of other stimuli in the environment, the existing frame of reference, and so forth. Moreover, to advocate "stage theories" of psychophysical processing, like those of Anderson (1981, 1982), Curtis et al. (1968), Marks (1979b), and many others, is to acknowledge the possibility, at least, that context can affect processes occurring at every stage: in early sensory transduction, in later perceptual encoding, in possible cognitive recoding, and in decision/response (see also Baird, 1997). Thus there is perhaps a sense in which a full and viable theory of context would be a "theory of everything" (Algom & Marks, 1990).

A. Effects of Stimulus Context

Psychophysical judgments are especially sensitive to stimulus context, in particular to the levels, spacing, and probability of occurrence of the possible stimuli within the set (cf. Garner, 1962). Judgments are also sensitive to other stimuli in the experimental environment—for example, to stimuli given as "anchors" to identify the end points of rating scales, or to stimuli used as "standards" in magnitude estimation. Such effects are widespread, found using all kinds of stimuli regardless of the perceptual modality, and consequently seem to represent the outcome of very general mechanisms that subserve perceptual encoding and judgment.

1. Helson's Adaptation-Level Theory

Perhaps the most extensive and wide-reaching account of contextual effects appears in Helson's (e.g., 1948, 1959, 1964) theory of adaptation level or AL. According to Helson, every stimulus is perceived and judged homeostatically, within a frame of reference, or relative to the momentary value of the equilibrium value, the AL. The AL itself depends on the recent stimulus history, the presence of any perceptual "anchors," stimuli in the ambient environment, and so forth, and it determines the level of stimulation that is perceived as "medium." To the extent that stimulation exceeds or lags the AL, the stimulus is perceived as relatively strong or weak. Helson's model can be written, in one version, as

$$R_i = F_i(I_i) - AL_i, \tag{49}$$

where R_i is the response given with respect to perceptual dimension i, F_i is the psychophysical function operating on the stimulus I_i, and AL_i is the adaptation level of dimension i.

Clearly, the model is geared to account readily for *contrast effects*: Given three stimuli, ordered in magnitude so that $A < B < C$, contrast is said to describe the tendency to judge B to be larger when it appears in the context of A than when it appears in the context of C. For example, subjects may rate an object as "large" when it falls near the top of the stimulus range (of tiny things) but "small" when it falls near the bottom of the range (of bigger ones). Having learned that a grape is a small fruit and a watermelon a large one (that is, learning to "anchor the scale" by these examples), we may judge a grapefruit to be the prototype of "mid-sized." And similarly learning that a mouse is a small mammal and an elephant a large one, our prototype for a mammal judged midsized may be a human or a horse. But making such judgments does not mean that we infer the size of either Don Quixote or Rosinante to equal that of citrus fruit.

In one popular version, the AL is defined as the weighted geometric average of the prevailing stimuli. This account follows from two principles: first, that the AL represents an average of the psychological values and, second, that these psychological values are logarithmically related to stimulus levels, as dictated by Fechner's law (see, e.g., Helson, 1959; Michels & Helson, 1949). In a general way, then, Helson's AL theory accounts for the pattern of responses obtained when people use rating scales to judge different sets of objects.

Helson's model as given does not speak directly to the mechanism underlying changes in AL (but see Wedell, 1995). Even if the model were to provide an adequate quantitative account of psychophysical judgments, we may ask whether it serves a useful purpose to group what are surely different processes that act to modify judgments. Stevens (1958), for instance, criticized Helson for conflating changes in AL, which may represent shifts in semantic labeling (see also Anderson, 1975), with changes induced by sensory adaptation, the latter conceived to be akin to physiological fatigue, perhaps in peripheral receptor processes. This may, of course, oversimplify the account of adaptation, which itself can represent effects of central as well as peripheral neural processes, and which can entail shifts in response criteria as well as changes in perceptual sensitivity or representation.

2. Parducci's Range-Frequency Theory

Parducci (1965, 1974) proposed a model that relates responses made on category-ratings scales directly to the characteristics of the stimulus set: Range-frequency (RF) theory says that subjects distribute their responses so as to mediate two rules: (1) subjects divide the stimulus *range* into uniform intervals over which the response categories are distributed; and (2) subjects use the categories equally often, thereby distributing their responses in proportion to the relative *frequency* with which the various stimuli are presented. A simple version of the RF principle can be written

$$C_i = wE_i + (1 - w)P_i, \tag{50}$$

where C_i is the average category rating of stimulus i, E_i is its range value (the value that C_i would have in the absence of effects of presentation frequency), P_i is its frequency value (the value that C_i would have if the subject simply made ordinal responses, using response categories equally often), and w ($0 \leq w \leq 1$) is the weighting coefficient of the range component. When stimuli are presented equally often, responses to stimulus i depend on E_i. But if the distribution of stimulus presentations is skewed, so that either weak or strong stimuli are presented more often, values of C_i change, with a corresponding change in the relation of C_i to stimulus magnitude.

Consider the example in Figure 10, showing results reported by Parducci, Knobel, and Thomas (1976), who had subjects rate the size of squares in three conditions that varied the relative frequency with which stimuli were presented. All three conditions used the same set of stimuli, but in one condition the stimuli were presented equally often (the rectangular skewing, indicated by the crosses), whereas in the other two conditions either the weak ones were presented more often than the strong ones (positive skewing, indicated by the open circles) or the strong ones were presented more often than the weak ones (negative skewing, indicated by the filled circles). Given the rectangular distribution, the subjects tend to use the response categories equally often, leading these categories to be distributed uniformly over the set of stimuli and thus to a psychophysical function that depends on the spacing of the stimuli (Parducci & Perrett, 1971; J. C. Stevens, 1958) and to some extent on the number of available response categories (Foley et al.,

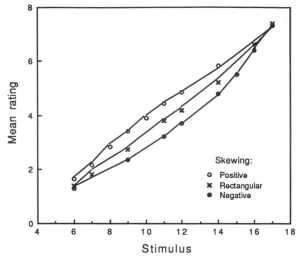

FIGURE 10   Effects of the distribution of stimulus values on category ratings of size of squares. The distributions of stimulus presentations were skewed positively (open circles), rectangular (crosses), and skewed negatively (filled circles). Note that each successive stimulus value corresponds to a proportional increase in the width of the square by a factor of 1.16; thus the spacing of the stimulus magnitudes is logarithmic. Adapted from Figure 5 of "Independent Contexts for Category Ratings: A Range-Frequency Analysis," by A. Parducci, S. Knobel, and C. Thomas, 1976, *Perception & Psychophysics, 1,* pp. 439–446. Reprinted with permission of The Psychonomic Society and the author.

1983; Marks, 1968; Parducci & Wedell, 1986). With positive or negative skewing, the same tendency to use categories equally often causes the subjects to assign relatively larger ratings, on average, to the frequently presented weak stimuli (positive skew) or to the strong stimuli (negative skew).

It may be possible, of course, to explain results like these by principles other than range and frequency. For example, Haubensak (1992) has suggested that distribution effects arise because, first, subjects tend to form their response scale in the first few trials, maintaining the scale throughout a test session, and, second, the most frequently presented stimuli are most likely to be presented early in an experimental session. AL theory can make similar predictions about the effects of stimulus distribution, though RF theory appears to be superior in predicting the effects quantitatively. Moreover, analyses performed in terms of functional measurement support the general features of RF (Anderson, 1975, 1992).

B. Effects of Stimulus Sequence

Within a given test session, as in life outside the laboratory, the immediate, local, or short-term stimulus context is always shifting, for our world

changes with the appearance of every new stimulus—a "blooming and buzzing" world if not one marked by "confusion." Context is never absent, and the only environmental setting that remains contextually constant is one that never changes. A typical experimental session faces the subject with a Heraclitean context, ever ebbing and flowing: a set of signals presented in some order, usually random, perhaps in several replicates. That the same stimulus typically receives different responses over the course of a session is well known (one of the best-known and longest-studied phenomena in psychophysics is the so-called time-order error, where the second of two consecutively presented, identical stimuli is judged to differ from the first and, typically, to appear greater in magnitude; see, e.g., Hellström, 1985, for review). Careful analysis of the trial-by-trial responding shows that much of this variation cannot be attributed either to "psychological noise" (in Thurstone's sense) or intrinsic stimulus variation (in Link's sense). Some of the variation consists of systematic change due to the fluctuating microenvironment—to the stimuli and responses given on recent trials (e.g., Cross, 1973; Jesteadt, Luce, & Green, 1977; Luce & Green, 1974; Ward, 1973; Ward & Lockhead, 1970). Although usually modest in size, trial-by-trial or sequential effects sometimes can be substantial, with magnitude estimates varying by a factor of 2:1 depending on the previous few stimuli (Lockhead & King, 1983; Marks, 1993). Understanding the source of these sequential effects may provide a key to unlock the mechanisms by which stimuli are encoded and decisions made (see Baird, 1997).

Sequential effects are evident in virtually all psychophysical tasks, including magnitude estimation, category rating, and absolute stimulus identification. Here we summarize a few main findings. First and foremost, sequential effects tend to be largely assimilative. That is, the response to a given stimulus on the current trial tends to be greater when the stimulus (or response) on the previous trial was greater than the current one, smaller when the stimulus (response) on the previous trial was smaller. This is true both when no feedback is given (e.g., Cross, 1973; Jesteadt, Luce, & Green, 1977), as is typical in magnitude estimation, and when feedback is given (e.g., Ward & Lockhead, 1971), as is typical in absolute identification (for possible models, see Wagner & Baird, 1981).

Note that the pervasiveness of assimilation runs counter to expectations of contrast based on AL theory. It is still controversial whether, or when, short-term sequential effects may contain a component of contrast. Staddon, King, and Lockhead (1980) inferred the presence of contrast that depended on stimuli two or more trials earlier, but they used an absolute identification task, that is, a task that provided the subjects with feedback. King and Lockhead (1981) came to a similar conclusion with respect to magnitude estimations obtained with feedback. Ward (1979, 1985, 1990) applied a linear-regression model to both magnitude estimation and

ry rating; his model contains an assimilative component, which depends on the magnitude of the responses given on several previous trials (independent of the stimulus, even when the stimuli are presented to different modalities), and a contrastive component, which depends on the intensity of the stimuli on previous trials (but only if the stimuli are qualitatively similar). On the other hand, DeCarlo (1992), using an autocorrelation model that relates responses to the current and previous stimuli, and not to previous responses, inferred that just assimilation takes place, not contrast. As DeCarlo argued, whether one infers the presence of a particular phenomenon—in this case, contrast—can depend on the particular quantitative model used to evaluate the data (see also DeCarlo, 1994).

Jesteadt, Luce, and Green (1977) noted that a simple regression analysis relating responses on successive trials can obscure one interesting aspect of the results: The correlation between successive responses depends on the size of the stimulus difference. Successive judgments of loudness are strongly correlated when the signal levels are identical or nearly so; the correlation drops to near zero when the decibel difference between successive signals reaches about 10 dB (see also Green, Luce, & Duncan, 1977; Ward, 1979). This means that when successive stimuli are near in intensity, the ratio of the responses tends to be constant, consistent with a response-ratio model of magnitude estimation (Luce & Green, 1974). But the response-ratio hypothesis fails when stimuli lie farther apart. Perhaps related is the finding that the coefficient of variation of the ratio of successive magnitude estimates follows a similar pattern, being small when the ratio of successive stimuli is large (Baird, Green, & Luce, 1980; Green & Luce, 1974; Green et al., 1977). That both the correlation and the variability of successive responses depend on the proximity of the stimulus levels led to the hypothesis, mentioned earlier, of a band of neural attention, about 10 dB to 20 dB wide, governing judgments (Green & Luce, 1974; Luce & Green, 1978; see Luce et al., 1980). The frequency and intensity on the previous trial become the center of attention of an adjustable band; if the current signal falls within the band, the signal's representation is presumably more precise. Treisman (1984) has offered an alternative model, in the spirit of Thurstonian theory. In place of attention bands and response ratios, Treisman hypothesized a set of adjustable response criteria, into which the logarithmically transformed stimuli map.

Treisman's (1984) model, like one offered by Braida and Durlach (1972), treats magnitude estimates much like a set of response categories, with boundaries corresponding to locations on a decision axis. As Braida and Durlach pointed out, their model "is a special case of Thurstone's 'law of Categorical Judgement'" (p. 484). These models are probabilistic, unlike the deterministic ones, such as functional measurement and two-state models that are often applied to magnitude judgments. The stochastic properties of magnitude judgments may provide a valuable entrée to understanding the processes of sensory transformation and psychophysical judgment. If, for example, the neural system represents sensory stimuli in terms of a set of independent Poisson processes (cf. Link's, 1992, wave theory), then the distribution of sensory responses, and thus to some extent the distribution of magnitude estimates, should depend on the underlying mechanism: following approximately a Gaussian distribution if the sensory system counts impulses, but approximately a gamma distribution if the system measures the inverse of the time between pulses (Luce & Green, 1972). Perhaps subjects can use both mechanisms (Green & Luce, 1973). As already noted, of course, choosing a counting mechanism or a timing mechanism for a model is by itself not enough to explain the various results, as the distributions of underlying count-based or time-based responses (mental or neural) are modified by whatever mechanisms produce sequential dependencies.

C. Effects of Stimulus Range and Stimulus Level

Within the domain of stimulus-set context are effects of stimulus range and stimulus level. Stimulus range (SR) is generally taken to refer to the ratio of the largest to smallest stimulus in the series; in the case of logarithmically transformed stimulus levels, SR is exponentially related to the (log) difference between largest and smallest levels. A series of tones varying from $0.002 \ N/m^2$ to $0.02 \ N/m^2$ (equivalently, from 40 dB to 60 dB SPL) has a range of sound pressures of 10:1 (20 dB), whereas a series varying from 0.0002 to $0.2 \ N/m^2$ (20 dB to 80 dB) has a range of 100:1 (60 dB). Stimulus levels refer to the absolute values of the stimuli, often characterized by the mean level, independent of range. For example, a series of tones varying from 40 dB to 60 dB and another series varying from 70 dB to 90 dB have the same 20-dB range but different absolute and mean levels. Considerable attention has been directed toward understanding effects of range, less to effects of level (but see Kowal, 1993). The difference probably reflects the partiality of most psychophysicists to the view that judgments depend largely on relations between stimuli, not on absolute levels; this bias can probably stand correction.

1. Stimulus Range

Range effects appear in virtually every kind of psychophysical judgment: not only in magnitude estimates, where they have been studied extensively, but in category ratings and even in measures of discrimination. When responses are made on rating scales, the end points of the response scale are generally fixed. Consequently, the range of responses is effectively forced to remain constant. Nevertheless, SR appears to exert a systematic effect on the degree of curvature of the function relating mean category rating to log stimulus intensity. When such relations are linear, they conform directly to Fechner's logarithmic law. Often, however, the relations are slightly accelerated, in which case they often conform well to a power function, whose exponent tends to increase in size as SR increases (Marks, 1968; but see also Foley et al., 1983, for a different model and interpretation). Finally, the range of stimuli can affect discriminability. This occurs even when one measures discriminability between a fixed pair of stimuli, embedded within different stimulus sets or ranges (Berliner & Durlach, 1973; Lockhead & Hinson, 1986; see also Ward, Armstrong, & Golestani, 1996). Such variations may reflect a limited capacity to attend to signals that vary over a wide range, consistent with notions like that of an attention band for intensity (Luce & Green, 1978).

Stimulus range has long been known to exert systematic effects on magnitude estimation (ME), as if subjects tend to use a constant range of numbers regardless of the range of stimuli. If a power function fits the relation between ME and stimulus intensity, and if the range of ME is constant, independent of SR, the observed exponent β would be inversely proportional to log SR. Typically, MEs are not affected by stimulus range to so great an extent as this hypothesis suggests; instead, exponents change less than predicted by the model of constant number-range (Teghtsoonian, 1971). Moreover, the change in exponent with change in SR is most evident when the SR is small—in loudness, exponents vary when range is smaller than about 30 dB. Increasing stimulus range beyond this point has little effect.

Range effects operate in an analogous fashion when the method is magnitude production (MP), except that the roles of stimuli and numbers reverse. In MP, were the subject to set a constant SR in the face of different ratio ranges of numbers presented, the exponent (calculated from the dependency of log number on log stimulus intensity) would be directly proportional to the number range. Again, though, actual behavior is not so extreme as this, although observed exponents do increase slightly as number range increases (Teghtsoonian & Teghtsoonian, 1983).

Tempting as it may be to attribute effects of stimulus range in ME and MP solely to decisional processes, that is, to processes that encourage subjects to emit a constant set of responses, evidence gleaned from a couple of experimental paradigms suggests that changes in SR may actually induce changes in the representations of sensory magnitude. Algom and Marks (1990) examined range effects within the framework of various intensity-summation paradigms, asking their subjects to judge the loudness of both one-component and two-component tones—e.g., monaural and binaural signals, respectively, in a binaural-summation paradigm. The data were inconsistent with the hypothesis that a given acoustic signal always produces the same internal representation of loudness, and that changes in exponent represent nothing but different mappings of internal representation into numbers. Instead, results obtained in three paradigms (binaural summation of loudness, summation of loudness of multiple frequency components, and temporal integration of loudness) implied that changing SR affects the sensory representations themselves, perhaps by modifying the relative size of the power-function exponents. Further, the changes in the rules of intensity summation, which Algom and Marks took as evidence of changes in the underlying scale, were absent when subjects simply learned different mappings of stimuli to numbers, suggesting that range per se is crucial (Marks, Galanter, & Baird, 1995).

Schneider and Parker (1990) and Parker and Schneider (1994) arrived at a similar conclusion. They had their subjects make paired-comparison judgments of differences in loudness (e.g., whether pair i, j differed less or more in loudness than pair k, l), then derived scales for loudness by means of nonmetric analysis of the rank orders of differences. For example, in different experimental sessions, subjects heard different ranges of SPL of the 500-Hz and 2500-Hz tones, and this resulted in different loudness scales (power functions with different exponents), implying changes in the internal representations. It was notable that the changes in exponent (steepening with small SR) took place only when the absolute levels of the signals were relatively weak, implying that level as well as range of stimuli matters.

2. Stimulus Level

Variation in stimulus level is fundamental, of course, to many of the contrast effects that adaptation-level and range-frequency theories seek to address. Given identical stimulus ranges, but different mean levels, subjects may adapt their categorical ratings to the stimulus set, thereby giving substantially different mean ratings to the same stimulus presented in different contexts. This is hardly surprising, given the constraints intrinsic to the task. In this regard, it is perhaps more interesting to ask about effects of stimulus level within magnitude estimation, where the response scale has fewer constraints. This question takes on special interest in conditions where the stimulus set shifts within a session. Although contrast-type effects have sometimes been reported in ME (Melamed & Thurlow, 1971; Ross & DiLollo, 1971), changes in mean signal level often lead to the opposite behavior, namely, a change in response that suggest assimilation. That is, if all of the stimuli in a set shift upward in constant proportion, the average response to a signal common to different sets is actually greater when the signal appears in the high set and is smaller when the signal appears in the low set (Marks, 1993). This outcome may reflect the outcome of whatever process is responsible for short-term sequential assimilation, described earlier. In this regard, see Baird (1997).

3. Differential Effects of Context

Changes in the average signal levels can have surprisingly strong and unexpected effects on judgments of intensity when signals vary multidimensionally. When subjects judge the loudness of low-frequency and high-frequency signals of various SPL, the rank-order properties of the resulting magnitude estimates depend systematically and *differentially* on the mean SPLs at the two frequencies (Marks, 1988, 1992b, 1993; Marks & Warner, 1991; Schneider & Parker, 1990). Figure 11 gives typical results, in which data from one contextual condition are plotted as circles (SPLs corresponding to the left-hand abscissa) and data from another contextual condition are plotted as squares (SPLs corresponding to the right-hand abscissa). In this example, taken from Marks (1988), the circles refer to data obtained when the ensemble of stimuli contained mostly soft 500-Hz tones and mostly loud 2500-Hz tones and the squares to data obtained when the distribution was reversed, so the ensemble contained mostly loud 500-Hz tones and mostly soft 2500-Hz tones. The change in distribution had a great effect on the judgments: In the first condition, the subjects judged the loudness of a 500-Hz tone of 70 dB to be as loud as a 2500-Hz tone of 73 dB (that is, they gave the same magnitude estimate to both), but in the second condition the subjects judged the same 500-Hz tone at 70 dB to be as loud as a 2500-Hz tone at 58 dB. Such changes in *relative loudness,* observed with multidimensionally varying stimuli, are widespread, evident not only in loudness

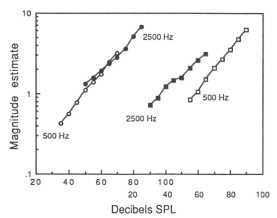

FIGURE 11 Differential effects of context in the perception and judgment of loudness of tones varying in sound frequency and intensity. The circles, at the left, show results obtained when the SPLs presented at 500 Hz were relatively low and those at 2500 Hz were high; the squares, on the right, show results obtained when the SPLs presented at 500 Hz were relatively high and those at 2500 Hz were low. Data of Marks (1988).

perception but also in the perception of taste intensity (Rankin & Marks, 1991), visual length (Armstrong & Marks, 1997; Potts, 1991), and haptic length (Marks & Armstrong, 1996).

Differential context effects appear to be widespread characteristics of perception and judgment of magnitude. They entail change in the rank-order properties of a series of judgments: in one context stimulus i being judged greater than stimulus j, but in another stimulus j being judged greater than stimulus i. So differential effects cannot be explained in terms of changes in, say, a single judgment function. It is conceivable that they might reflect changes in two such functions, one for each kind of stimulus, or in some other decisional process that depends on the multidimensional properties of the stimuli. Several pieces of evidence speak against this interpretation.

First of all, differential context effects are not universal: Although differential effects are evident in judgments of length of lines oriented vertically and horizontally (Armstrong & Marks, 1997; Potts, 1991), they are absent from judgments of length of lines presented in different colors (Marks, 1992b); differential effects are also absent from magnitude estimates of pitch of tones contextually varying in intensity and from magnitude estimates of duration of tones varying in frequency (Marks, 1992b). So the effects are probably not the result of some general process of criterial adjustment, like that proposed by Treisman (1984), extended to multidimensionally varying stimuli (for an analysis of decision rules in categorizing multidimensional stimuli, see, e.g., Ashby & Gott, 1988). Second, similar changes appear in results using obtained in paradigms that omit the use of numerical judgments (Armstrong & Marks, 1997; Marks, 1992a, 1994; Marks & Armstrong, 1996; Schneider & Parker, 1990; Parker & Schneider, 1994), including paradigms in which subjects merely listen to a series of "adapting signals" prior to testing (Marks, 1993). Thus differential contextual effects may well have a sensory-perceptual rather than, or as well as, a decisional basis; in particular, they may reflect the outcome of a stimulus–specific process that resembles adaptation.

VII. PRAGMATICS AND EPISTEMICS OF PSYCHOPHYSICAL SCALING

Psychophysical scaling, indeed psychophysics in general, straddles several borders—between the mental and physical, and between the applied or pragmatic and the more theoretical or epistemic. Psychophysical scaling serves both as a means to various ends, providing a set of procedures that nourish the elaboration and evaluation of sensory and perceptual mechanisms, and as an end in and of itself, providing a quantitative account of the mind's activity.

A. Scaling Is Pragmatic

When all is said and done, regardless of psychophysical scaling's ever-changing theoretical status, it is important neither to forget nor to deprecate the utility of various scaling methods—especially magnitude estimation and category scaling. So many experimental studies of sensory processes bear witness to the value of these methods that it is not possible to summarize the evidence or even to provide an overview. A few examples have popped up in the chapter: for instance, J. C. Stevens and Stevens's (1963) study of how light adaptation affects visual brightness and Algom et al.'s (1986) study, using functional measurement, of multimodal integration of pain. Much of the relevant literature from the 1950s to the early 1970s is reviewed elsewhere (Marks, 1974b).

To a great extent, the success, utility, and indeed the continued widespread use of scaling methods such as magnitude estimation and category rating come from their capacity to provide relatively convenient and rapid means to assess how several different stimulus characteristics—intensity, duration, areal extent, state of adaptation, maskers—jointly influence perceptual experience. Many of the inferences drawn from these studies do not rely in any substantial way on the presumed metric properties of the responses, but rest instead on the much more modest assumption that the response scale (or judgment function) preserves weak ordering among the underlying perceptual experiences.

One consequence is that these scaling methods thereby serve as "null procedures," or indirect methods to obtain stimulus matches: Signals that produce the same average response (numerical estimate or rating) are treated as perceptually equal. Such measures make it possible to determine stimulus-stimulus relations (what Marks, 1974b, called sensory-physical laws), such as the parameters of Bloch's law of temporal summation or the durations at which a flash of light reaches its (Broca-Sulzer) maximum. On the other side of this coin, measures of multidimensionally determined responses, as realized through intensity matches, oftentimes constrain the *relative* properties of psychophysical functions themselves (cf. Marks, 1977). Thus the change in critical duration, determined from brightness matches, implies that brightness grows more quickly with luminance when the duration of a test flash is very brief (< 10 ms) than when duration is relatively long (> 1 s)—even if we cannot decide with certainty whether the difference in rate of growth resides in the value of the exponent of a power function or in the slope constant of a logarithmic function.

Finally, in this regard, it is of course the goal of sensory-perceptual science not only to describe but also to explain. Here, in our view, the data obtained with methods of psychophysical scaling will continue to prove invaluable, for research directed toward evaluating the combined effects of multiple stimulus properties is central to the development of adequate theories both of scaling behavior and of the psychological and biological processes underlying sensation and perception.

B. Scaling Is Epistemic

Beyond the practical, psychophysics also speaks to a goal that is more theoretical—to that aspiration, pervasive in the history of Western thought, to understand and especially to quantify mental life, to give numeric expression to those processes and properties of thought and behavior that lend themselves to enumeration and rationalization. Contemporary applications of psychophysical theory in the domains of utility and psychological value find their roots, for example, in the quantification and implicit metric equations discussed more than two centuries ago by the founder of utilitarianism, Jeremy Bentham (1789), who suggested that certain decisions could be made rationally by totaling up the positive and negative psychological utilities; thus Bentham couched his analysis of economic benefits and costs in terms that may readily be translated into those of functional-measurement or conjoint-measurement theory.

A century earlier, Blaise Pascal (1670) proposed his famous "wager," whose bottom line comprised a payoff matrix together with a rule by which a rational person could calculate an optimal decision: whether to "bet on" (believe in) the existence of God. In a nutshell, Pascal noted that there are two possible psychological stances, belief or disbelief in God's existence, and two existential states, existence or nonexistence (albeit with unknown a priori probabilities). Pascal argued that, given even a small nonzero probability that God exists, the gain associated with averring God's existence and the cost associated with denying it together make belief in God the rational choice: "If you gain, you gain all; if you lose, you lose nothing. Wager, then, without hesitation that He is" (*Pensée* No. 233). Basically, Pascal implied a formal, normative model for decision making—in which a person quantitatively evaluates a set of expected utilities—which he applied to a particular decision that is rarely considered in psychophysical research.

Plato's attempt, in the *Republic,* to compute the happiness of a just king versus that of a tyrant (the former 729 times the latter), Pascal's wager, Bentham's utilitarian metric, Fechner's scales of sensation difference, and Stevens's scales of sensation magnitude—all of these speak to a common quest to quantify. And the quest to quantify is part and parcel of the scientific enterprise. If, as Dingle (1960) suggested, to measure is to define, if measurements are construed as theories, and if theories are construed as models or metaphors, then this quest to quantify may well represent the expression of a deep and abiding scientific impulse—one component of what has been called a metaphorical imperative (Marks, 1978d).

Such a metaphorical imperative, satisfied by the pragmatics of scaling, bears directly on its epistemics, for it could lead to a more mature evaluation of the very edifice of psychophysics. All too often, psychophysics has been viewed, and even practiced, in a rather parochial fashion, exploring the route from sensation to cognition unidirectionally, working from the periphery to the center (cf. Anderson, 1992), and thus depicting an organism whose behavior seems essentially reactive (cf. Galanter, 1992). Studies on information integration and contextual effects, as reviewed in the last few sections of this chapter, document instead the possible roles of potent "top-down" processes in perception and consequently in psychophysical scaling. In a similar vein, many contributors to a recent volume (Algom, 1992b) explore the merger of sensation and cognition in psychophysical scaling, as captured in the notion of a "cognitive psychophysics" (cf. Baird, 1970a, 1970b; Marks, 1992c). Finally, in this regard, in a book that was just published and can be only briefly mentioned, Baird (1997) has proposed an elaborate "complementarity theory," which rests on the assumption that sensori-neural and cognitive explanations provide mutually compatible and even jointly necessary components to a full psychophysical theory; central to Baird's position is the notion that psychophysical responses are variable, and that variability may be associated with either sensory processes, which Baird treats within his Sensory Aggregate Model, or cognitive-judgmental processes, which he treats within his Judgment Option Model. If the metaphorical imperative includes a deep human quest for quantification, then full recognition of its role in scaling may accordingly help shift the conceptual base of psychophysical measurement to one that is driven by psychological theory and that emanates from the person.

Acknowledgments

Preparation of this article was supported in part by grants DC00271 and DC00818 from the U.S. National Institute of Health to Lawrence E. Marks and by grant 89-447 from the U.S.-Israel Binational Science Foundation to Daniel Algom. We gratefully thank John C. Baird, Kenneth H. Norwich, and Joseph C. Stevens for their valuable and thoughtful comments.

References

Aczél, J. (1966). *Lectures on functional equations and their applications*. New York: Academic Press.
Adams, E., & Messick, S. (1958). An axiomatic formulation and generalization of successive intervals scaling. *Psychometrika, 23,* 355–368.
Aiba, T. S., & Stevens, S. S. (1964). Relation of brightness to duration and luminance under light- and dark-adaptation. *Vision Research, 4,* 391–401.

Algom, D. (1992a). Psychophysical analysis of pain: A functional perspective. In H.-G. Geissler, S. W. Link, & J. T. Townsend (Eds.), *Cognition, information processing, and psychophysics* (pp. 267–291). Hillsdale, NJ: Erlbaum.

Algom, D. (Ed.). (1992b). *Psychophysical approaches to cognition.* Amsterdam: North-Holland Elsevier.

Algom, D., & Babkoff, H. (1984). Auditory temporal integration at threshold: Theories and some implications of current research. In W. D. Neff (Ed.), *Contributions to sensory physiology* (Vol. 8, pp. 131–159). New York: Academic Press.

Algom, D., & Marks, L. E. (1984). Individual differences in loudness processing and loudness scales. *Journal of Experimental Psychology: General, 113,* 571–593.

Algom, D., & Marks, L. E. (1990). Range and regression, loudness processing and loudness scales: Toward a context-bound psychophysics. *Journal of Experimental Psychology: Human Perception and Performance, 16,* 706–727.

Algom, D., & Pansky, A. (1993). Perceptual and memory-based comparisons of area. In A. Garriga-Trillo, P. R. Minon, C. Garcia-Gallego, C. Lubin, J. M. Merino, & A. Villarino (Eds.), *Fechner Day 93. Proceedings of the Ninth Annual Meeting of the International Society for Psychophysics* (pp. 7–12). Palma de Mallorca: International Society for Psychophysics.

Algom, D., Raphaeli, N., & Cohen-Raz, L. (1986). Integration of noxious stimulation across separate somatosensory communications systems: A functional theory of pain. *Journal of Experimental Psychology: Human Perception and Performance, 12,* 92–102.

Anderson, N. H. (1970). Functional measurement and psychophysical judgment. *Psychological Review, 77,* 153–170.

Anderson, N. H. (1974). Algebraic models in perception. In E. C. Carterette & M. P. Friedman (Eds.), *Handbook of perception: Vol. 2. Psychophysical judgment and measurement* (pp. 215–298). New York: Academic Press.

Anderson, N. H. (1975). On the role of context effects in psychophysical judgment. *Psychological Review, 82,* 462–482.

Anderson, N. H. (1976). Integration theory, functional measurement, and the psychophysical law. In H.-G. Geissler & Yu. Zabrodin (Eds.), *Advances in psychophysics* (pp. 93–129). Berlin: VEB Deutscher Verlag der Wissenschaften.

Anderson, N. H. (1977). Failure of additivity in bisection of length. *Perception & Psychophysics, 22,* 213–222.

Anderson, N. H. (1981). *Foundations of information integration theory.* New York: Academic Press.

Anderson, N. H. (1982). *Methods of information integration theory.* New York: Academic Press.

Anderson, N. H. (1992). Integration psychophysics and cognition. In D. Algom (Ed.), *Psychophysical approaches to cognition* (pp. 13–113). Amsterdam: North-Holland Elsevier.

Armstrong, L., & Marks, L. E. (1997). Stimulus context, perceived length, and the vertical-horizontal illusion. *Perception & Psychophysics,* in press.

Asch, S. (1946). Forming impressions on personality. *Journal of Abnormal and Social Psychology, 41,* 258–290.

Ashby, F. G., & Gott, R. E. (1988). Decision rules in the perception and categorization of multidimensional stimuli. *Journal of Experimental Psychology: Learning, Memory, and Cognition, 14,* 33–53.

Attneave, F. (1949). A method of graded dichotomies for the scaling of judgments. *Psychological Review, 56,* 334–340.

Attneave, F. (1959). *Applications of information theory to psychology.* New York: Holt, Rinehart, & Winston.

Attneave, F. (1962). Perception and related areas. In S. Koch (Ed.), *Psychology: A study of a science* (Vol. 4, pp. 619–659). New York: McGraw-Hill.

Baird, J. C. (1970a). A cognitive theory of psychophysics. I. *Scandinavian Journal of Psychology, 11*, 35–46.

Baird, J. C. (1970b). A cognitive theory of psychophysics. II. *Scandinavian Journal of Psychology, 11*, 89–103.

Baird, J. C. (1975). Psychophysical study of numbers: Generalized preferred state theory. *Psychological Research, 38*, 175–187.

Baird, J. C. (1981). Psychophysical theory: On the avoidance of contradiction. *The Behavioral and Brain Sciences, 4*, 190.

Baird, J. C. (1984). Information theory and information processing. *Information Processing & Management, 20*, 373–381.

Baird, J. C. (1997). *Sensation and judgment: Complementarity theory of psychophysics.* Mahwah, NJ: Erlbaum.

Baird, J. C., Green, D. M., & Luce, R. D. (1980). Variability and sequential effects in cross-modality matching of area and loudness. *Journal of Experimental Psychology: Human Perception and Performance, 6*, 277–289.

Baird, J. C., & Noma, E. (1975). Psychological studies of numbers. I. Generation of numerical responses. *Psychological Research, 37*, 291–297.

Baird, J. C., & Noma, E. (1978). *Fundamentals of scaling and psychophysics.* New York: Wiley.

Banks, W. P. (1973). Reaction time as a measure of summation of warmth. *Perception & Psychophysics, 13*, 321–327.

Banks, W. P. (1977). Encoding and processing of symbolic information in comparative judgments. In G. H. Bower (Ed.), *The psychology of learning and motivation* (Vol. 11, pp. 101–159). New York: Academic Press.

Banks, W. P., Clark, H. H., & Lucy, P. (1975). The locus of semantic congruity effect in comparative judgments. *Journal of Experimental Psychology: Human Perception and Performance, 104*, 35–47.

Banks, W. P., & Coleman, M. J. (1981). Two subjective scales of number. *Perception & Psychophysics, 29*, 95–105.

Barbenza, C. M. de, Bryan, M. E., & Tempest, W. (1972). Individual loudness functions. *Journal of Sound and Vibration, 11*, 399–410.

Beck, J., & Shaw, W. A. (1967). Ratio-estimations of loudness-intervals. *American Journal of Psychology, 80*, 59–65.

Bennet, J. H., & Hays, W. L. (1960). Multidimensional unfolding determining the dissimilarity of ranked preference data. *Psychometrika, 25*, 27–43.

Bentham, J. (1948). *An introduction to the principles of morals and legislation.* New York: Hafner (originally published, 1789).

Berglund, B. (1991). Quality assurance in environmental psychophysics. In S. J. Bolanowski, Jr., & G. A. Gescheider (Eds.), *Ratio scaling of psychological magnitude* (pp. 140–162). Hillsdale, NJ: Erlbaum.

Berliner, J. E., & Durlach, N. I. (1973). Intensity perception: IV. Resolution in roving-level discrimination. *Journal of the Acoustical Society of America, 53*, 1270–1287.

Birnbaum, M. H. (1978). Differences and ratios in psychological measurement. In N. J. Castellan & F. Restle (Eds.), *Cognitive theory* (Vol. 3, pp. 33–74). Hillsdale, NJ: Erlbaum.

Birnbaum, M. H. (1980). A comparison of two theories of "ratio" and "difference" judgments. *Journal of Experimental Psychology: General, 3*, 304–319.

Birnbaum, M. H. (1982). Controversies in psychological measurement. In B. Wegener (Ed.), *Social attitudes and psychophysical measurement* (pp. 401–485). Hillsdale, NJ: Erlbaum.

Birnbaum, M. H. (1990). Scale convergence and psychophysical laws. In H.-G. Geissler (Ed.), *Psychophysical exploration of mental structures* (pp. 49–57). Toronto: Hogrefe and Huber.

Birnbaum, M. H., Anderson, C. J., & Hynan, L. G. (1989). Two operations for "ratios" and "differences" of distances on the mental map. *Journal of Experimental Psychology: Human Perception and Performance, 15,* 785–796.

Birnbaum, M. H., & Elmasian, R. (1977). Loudness "ratios" and "differences" involve the same psychophysical operation. *Perception & Psychophysics, 22,* 383–391.

Birnbaum, M. H., & Jou, W., Jr. (1990). A theory of comparative response times and "difference" judgments. *Cognitive Psychology, 22,* 184–210.

Bockenholt, U. (1992). Thurstonian representation for partial ranking data. *British Journal of Mathematical and Statistical Psychology, 45,* 31–49.

Borg, G. (1972). A ratio scaling method for interindividual comparisons. *Reports from the Institute of Applied Psychology,* The University of Stockholm, No. 27.

Borg, G. (1982). A category scale with ratio properties for intermodal and interindividual comparisons. In H.-G. Geissler & P. Petzold (Eds.), *Psychophysical judgment and the process of perception* (pp. 25–34). Berlin: Deutscher Verlag der Wissenschaften.

Boring, E. G. (1921). The stimulus-error. *American Journal of Psychology, 32,* 449–471.

Bradley, R. A., & Terry, M. E. (1952). The rank analysis of incomplete block designs. I. The method of paired comparisons. *Biometrika, 39,* 324–345.

Braida, L. D., & Durlach, N. I. (1972). Intensity perception. II. Resolution in one-interval paradigms. *Journal of the Acoustical Society of America, 51,* 483–502.

Braida, L. D., Lim, J. S., Berliner, J. E., Durlach, N. I., Rabinowitz, W. M., & Purks, S. R. (1984). Intensity perception. XIII. Perceptual anchor model of context-coding. *Journal of the Acoustical Society of America, 76,* 722–731.

Brentano, F. (1874). *Psychologie vom empirischen Standpunkte.* Leipzig: Duncker und Humblot.

Broca, A., & Sulzer, D. (1902a). La sensation lumineuse en fonction du temps. *Comptes Rendus de l'Académie des Sciences (Paris), 134,* 831–834.

Broca, A., & Sulzer, D. (1902b). La sensation lumineuse en fonction du temps. *Comptes Rendus de l'Académie des Sciences (Paris), 137,* 944–946, 977–979, 1046–1049.

Campbell, N. R. (1920). *Physics: The elements.* Cambridge, England: Cambridge University Press.

Carroll, J. D. (1980). Models and methods for multidimensional analysis of preferential choice (or other dominance) data. In E. D. Lantermann & H. Feger (Eds.), *Similarity and choice* (pp. 234–289). Bern: Huber.

Carterette, E. C., & Anderson, N. H. (1979). Bisection of loudness. *Perception & Psychophysics, 26,* 265–280.

Cattell, J. McK. (1893). On errors of observations. *American Journal of Psychology, 5,* 285–293.

Cattell, J. McK. (1902). The time of perception as a measure of differences in intensity. *Philosophische Studien, 19,* 63–68.

Chocholle, R. (1940). Variation des temps de réactions auditifs end fonction de l'intensité à diverses fréquences. *L'Année Psychologique, 41,* 65–124.

Chocholle, R., & Greenbaum, H. B. (1966). La sonie de sons purs partiallement masqués. Étude comparative par une méthode d'égalisation et par la méthode des temps de réaction. *Journal de Psychologie Normale et Pathologique, 63,* 387–414.

Churchman, C. W., & Ratoosh, P. (Eds.) (1959). *Measurement: Definition and theories.* New York: Wiley.

Cliff, N. (1992). Abstract measurement theory and the revolution that never happened. *Psychological Science, 3,* 186–190.

Collins, A. A., & Gescheider, G. A. (1989). The measurement of loudness in individual children and adults by absolute magnitude estimation and cross-modality matching. *Journal of the Acoustical Society of America, 85,* 2012–2021.

Coombs, C. H. (1950). Psychological scaling without a unit of measurement. *Psychological Review, 57,* 145–158.

Coombs, C. H. (1964). *A theory of data.* New York: Wiley.

Cross, D. V. (1973). Sequential dependencies and regression in psychophysical judgments. *Perception & Psychophysics, 14,* 547–552.

Curtis, D. W. (1970). Magnitude estimations and category judgments of brightness and brightness intervals: A two-stage interpretation. *Journal of Experimental Psychology, 83,* 201–208.

Curtis, D. W., Attneave, F., & Harrington, T. L. (1968). A test of a two-stage model for magnitude estimation. *Perception & Psychophysics, 3,* 25–31.

Curtis, D. W., Paulos, M. A., & Rule, S. J. (1973). Relation between disjunctive reaction time and stimulus difference. *Journal of Experimental Psychology, 99,* 167–173.

Curtis, D. W., & Rule, S. J. (1972). Magnitude judgments of brightness and brightness difference as a function of background reflectance. *Journal of Experimental Psychology, 95,* 215–222.

Dawes, R. M. (1994). Psychological measurement. *Psychological Review, 101,* 278–281.

Dawson, W. E. (1971). Magnitude estimation of apparent sums and differences. *Perception & Psychophysics, 9,* 368–374.

DeCarlo, L. T. (1992). Intertrial interval and sequential effects in magnitude scaling. *Journal of Experimental Psychology: Human Perception and Performance, 18,* 1080–1088.

DeCarlo, L. T. (1994). A dynamic theory of proportional judgment: Context and judgment of length, heaviness, and roughness. *Journal of Experimental Psychology: Human Perception and Performance, 20,* 372–381.

De Soete, G., & Carroll, J. D. (1992). Probabilistic multidimensional models of pairwise choice data. In F. G. Ashby (Ed.), *Multidimensional models of perception and cognition* (pp. 61–88). Hillsdale, NJ: Erlbaum.

Delboeuf, J. R. L. (1873). Étude psychophysique: Recherches théoretiques et expérimentales sur la mesure des sensations, et spécialement des sensations de lumiére et de fatigue. *Mémoires de l'Académie Royale de Belgique, 23* (5).

Dingle, H. (1960). A symposium on the basic problem of measurement. *Scientific American, 202* (6), 189–192.

Durlach, N. I., & Braida, L. D. (1969). Intensity perception: I. A theory of intensity resolution. *Journal of the Acoustical Society of America, 46,* 372–383.

Durup, G., & Piéron, H. (1933). Recherches au sujet de l'interpretation du phénomème de Purkinje par des différences dans les courbes de sensation des recepteurs chromatiques. *L'Année Psychologique, 33,* 57–83.

Ebbinghaus, H. (1902). *Gundzüge der Psychologie.* Leipzig: Verlag von Veit.

Eisler, H. (1963). Magnitude scales, category scales, and Fechnerian integration. *Psychological Review, 70,* 243–253.

Ekman, G. (1964). Is the power law a special case of Fechner's law? *Perceptual and Motor Skills, 19,* 730.

Ekman, G., Eisler, H., & Künnapas, T. (1960). Brightness of monochromatic light as measured by the method of magnitude production. *Acta Psychologica, 17,* 392–397.

Ekman, G., Hosman, J., Lindman, R., Ljungberg, L., & Åkesson, C. A. (1968). Interindividual differences in scaling performance. *Perceptual and Motor Skills, 26,* 815–823.

Ekman, G., & Künnapas, T. (1962). Measurement of aesthetic value by "direct" and "indirect" methods. *Scandinavian Journal of Psychology, 3,* 33–39.

Ekman, G., & Künnapas, T. (1963a). A further study of direct and indirect scaling methods. *Scandinavian Journal of Psychology, 4,* 77–80.

Ekman, G., & Künnapas, T. (1963b). Scales of conservatism. *Perceptual and Motor Skills, 16,* 329–334.

Engeland, W., & Dawson, W. E. (1974). Individual differences in power functions for a 1-week intersession interval. *Perception & Psychophysics, 15,* 349–352.

Engen, T., & Lindström, C.-O. (1963). Psychophysical scales of the odor intensity of amyl acetate. *Scandinavian Journal of Psychology, 4*, 23–28.

Engen, T., & McBurney, D. H. (1964). Magnitude and category scales of the pleasantness of odors. *Journal of Experimental Psychology, 68*, 435–440.

Engen, T., & Ross, B. M. (1966). Effect of reference number on magnitude estimation. *Perception & Psychophysics, 1*, 74–76.

Falmagne, J.-C. (1971). The generalized Fechner problem and discrimination. *Journal of Mathematical Psychology, 8*, 22–43.

Falmagne, J.-C. (1974). Foundations of Fechnerian psychophysics. In D. H. Krantz, R. C. Atkinson, R. D. Luce, & P. Suppes (Eds.), *Contemporary developments in mathematical psychology. Vol. 2. Measurement, psychophysics, and neural information processing* (pp. 129–159). San Francisco: Freeman.

Falmagne, J.-C. (1976). Random conjoint measurement and loudness summation. *Psychological Review, 83*, 65–79.

Falmagne, J.-C. (1985). *Elements of psychophysical theory*. Oxford: Oxford University Press.

Fechner, G. T. (1860). *Elemente der Psychophysik*. Leipzig: Breitkopf und Härtel.

Fletcher, H., & Munson, W. A. (1933). Loudness, its measurement and calculation. *Journal of the Acoustical Society of America, 5*, 82–108.

Foley, H. J., Cross, D. V., Foley, M. A., & Reeder, R. (1983). Stimulus range, number of categories, and the 'virtual' exponent. *Perception & Psychophysics, 34*, 505–512.

Fullerton, G. S., & Cattell, J. McK. (1892). *On the perception of small differences*. Philadelphia: University of Pennsylvania Press.

Fuortes, M. G. F., & Hodgkin, A. L. (1964). Changes in time scale and sensitivity in the ommatidia of Limulus. *Journal of Physiology, 172*, 239–263.

Gage, F. H. (1934a). An experimental investigation of the measurability of auditory sensation. *Proceedings of the Royal Society (London), 116B*, 103–122.

Gage, F. H. (1934b). An experimental investigation of the measurability of visual sensation. *Proceedings of the Royal Society (London), 116B*, 123–138.

Galanter, E. H. (1962). Contemporary psychophysics. In R. Brown, E. H. Galanter, E. H. Hess, & G. Mandler (Eds.), *New directions in psychology* (pp. 89–156). New York: Holt, Rinehart and Winston.

Galanter, E. H. (1992). Intentionalism—An expressive theory. In D. Algom (Ed.), *Psychophysical approaches to cognition* (pp. 251–302). Amsterdam: North-Holland Elsevier.

Galanter, E., & Messick, S. (1961). The relation between category and magnitude scales of loudness. *Psychological Review, 68*, 363–372.

Galanter, E., & Pliner, P. (1974). Cross-modality matching of money against other continua. In H. R. Moskowitz, B. Scharf, & J. C. Stevens (Eds.), *Sensation and measurement: Papers in honor of S. S. Stevens* (pp. 65–76). Dordrecht: Holland, Reidel.

Garner, W. R. (1952). An equal discriminability scale for loudness judgments. *Journal of Experimental Psychology, 43*, 232–238.

Garner, W. R. (1954). Context effects and the validity of loudness scales. *Journal of Experimental Psychology, 48*, 218–224.

Garner, W. R. (1958). Advantages of the discriminability criterion for a loudness scale. *Journal of the Acoustical Society of America, 30*, 1005–1012.

Garner, W. R. (1959). On the lambda loudness function, masking, and the loudness of multicomponent tones. *Journal of the Acoustical Society of America, 31*, 602–607.

Garner, W. R. (1962). *Uncertainty and structure as psychological concepts*. New York: Wiley.

Garner, W. R. (1974). *The processing of information and structure*. Potomac, MD: Erlbaum.

Garner, W. R., & Hake, H. W. (1951). The amount of information in absolute judgments. *Psychological Review, 58*, 446–459.

Geiger, P. H., & Firestone, F. A. (1933). The estimation of fractional loudness. *Journal of the Acoustical Society of America, 5*, 25–30.

Gent, J. F., & Bartoshuk, L. M. (1983). Sweetness of sucrose, neohesperidin dihydrochalcone, and saccharin is related to genetic ability to taste the bitter substance 6-*n*-propylthiouracil. *Chemical Senses, 7,* 265–272.

Gescheider, G. A. (1988). Psychophysical scaling. *Annual Review of Psychology, 39,* 169–200.

Gescheider, G. A. (1997). *Psychophysics: The fundamentals* (3rd ed.). Mahwah, NJ: Erlbaum.

Gescheider, G. A., & Bolanowski, S. J., Jr. (1991). Final comments on ratio scaling of psychological magnitudes. In S. J. Bolanowski, Jr., & G. A. Gescheider (Eds.), *Ratio scaling of psychological magnitude* (pp. 295–311). Hillsdale, NJ: Erlbaum.

Gescheider, G. A., & Hughson, B. A. (1991). Stimulus context and absolute magnitude estimation: A study of individual differences. *Perception & Psychophysics, 50,* 45–57.

Gibson, J. J. (1966). *The senses considered as perceptual systems.* Boston: Houghton Mifflin.

Gibson, J. J. (1979). *The ecological approach to visual perception.* Boston: Houghton Mifflin.

Gibson, R. H., & Tomko, D. L. (1972). The relation between category and magnitude estimates of tactile intensity. *Perceptions & Psychophysics, 12,* 135–138.

Gigerenzer, G., & Murray, D. J. (1987). *Cognition as intuitive statistics.* Hillsdale, NJ: Erlbaum.

Gigerenzer, G., & Strube, G. (1983). Are there limits to binaural additivity of loudness? *Journal of Experimental Psychology: Human Perception and Performance, 9,* 126–136.

Graham, C. H. (1958). Sensation and perception in an objective psychology. *Psychological Review, 65,* 65–76.

Graham, C. H., & Ratoosh, P. (1962). Notes on some interrelations of sensory psychology, perception, and behavior. In S. Koch (Ed.), *Psychology: A study of a science* (Vol. 4, pp. 483–514). New York: McGraw-Hill.

Gravetter, F., & Lockhead, G. R. (1973). Criterial range as a frame of reference for stimulus judgment. *Psychological Review, 80,* 203–216.

Green, B. G., Shaffer, G. S., & Gilmore, M. M. (1993). Derivation and evaluation of a semantic scale of oral sensation magnitude with apparent ratio properties. *Chemical Senses, 18,* 683–702.

Green, D. M., & Luce, R. D. (1973). Speed-accuracy tradeoff in auditory detection. In S. Kornblum (Ed.), *Attention and performance* (Vol. 4, pp. 547–569). New York: Academic Press.

Green, D. M., & Luce, R. D. (1974). Variability of magnitude estimates: A timing theory analysis. *Perception & Psychophysics, 15,* 291–300.

Green, D. M., Luce, R. D., & Duncan, J. E. (1977). Variability and sequential effects in magnitude production and estimation of auditory intensity. *Perception & Psychophysics, 22,* 450–456.

Grice, G. R. (1968). Stimulus intensity and response evocation. *Psychological Review, 75,* 359–373.

Guilford, J. P. (1932). A generalized psychological law. *Psychological Review, 39,* 73–85.

Guilford, J. P. (1954). *Psychometric methods* (2nd ed.). New York: MaGraw-Hill.

Hagerty, M., & Birnbaum, M. H. (1978). Nonmetric tests of ratio vs. subtractive theories of stimulus comparisons. *Perception & Psychophysics, 24,* 121–129.

Halff, H. M. (1976). Choice theories for differentially comparable alternatives. *Journal of Mathematical Psychology, 14,* 244–246.

Ham, L. B., & Parkinson, J. S. (1932). Loudness and intensity relations. *Journal of the Acoustical Society of America, 3,* 511–534.

Hardy, J. D., Wolff, H. G., & Goodell, H. (1947). Studies on pain: Discrimination of differences in pain as a basis of a scale of pain intensity. *Journal of Clinical Investigation, 19,* 1152–1158.

Harris, J. D. (1963). Loudness and discrimination. *Journal of Speech and Hearing Disorders* (Monograph Supplement 11).

Haubensak, G. (1992). The consistency model: A process model for absolute judgments. *Journal of Experimental Psychology: Human Perception and Performance, 18,* 303–309.

Heidelberger, M. (1993). Fechner's impact for measurement theory. *The Behavioral and Brain Sciences, 16,* 146–148.

Heinemann, E. G. (1961). The relation of apparent brightness to the threshold for differences in luminance. *Journal of Experimental Psychology, 61,* 389–399.

Heller, O. (1985). Hörfeldaudiometrie mit dem Verfahren der Kategorienunterteilung (KU). *Psychologische Beiträge, 27,* 478–493.

Hellman, R. P. (1981). Stability of individual loudness functions obtained by magnitude estimation and production. *Perception & Psychophysics, 29,* 63–70.

Hellman, R., Scharf, B., Teghtsoonian, M., & Teghtsoonian, R. (1987). On the relation between the growth of loudness and the discrimination of intensity for pure tones. *Journal of the Acoustical Society of America, 82,* 448–453.

Hellman, R. P., & Zwislocki, J. J. (1961). Some factors affecting the estimation of loudness. *Journal of the Acoustical Society of America, 33,* 687–694.

Hellström, Å. (1985). The time-order error and its relatives: Mirrors of cognitive processes in comparing. *Psychological Bulletin, 97,* 35–61.

Helmholtz, H. L. F. von (1962). *Treatise on physiological optics.* New York: Dover (originally published, 1856).

Helson, H. (1948). Adaptation level as a basis for a quantitative theory of frames of reference. *Psychological Review, 55,* 297–313.

Helson, H. (1959). Adaptation level theory. In S. Koch (Ed.), *Psychology: A study of a science* (Vol. 1, pp. 565–621). New York: McGraw-Hill.

Helson, H. (1964). *Adaptation level theory: An experimental and systematic approach to behavior.* New York: Harper and Row.

Hood, D. C., & Finkelstein, M. A. (1979). A comparison of changes in sensitivity and sensation: Implications for the response-intensity function of the human photopic system. *Journal of Experimental Psychology: Human Perception and Performance, 5,* 391–405.

Hornstein, G. A. (1993). The chimera of psychophysical measurement. *The Behavioral and Brain Sciences, 16,* 148–149.

Hübner, R., & Ellermeier, W. (1993). Additivity of loudness across critical bands: A critical test. *Perception & Psychophysics, 54,* 185–189.

Humes, L. E., & Jesteadt, W. (1989). Models of additivity of masking. *Journal of the Acoustical Society of America, 85,* 1285–1294.

Indow, T. (1966). A general equi-distance scale of the four qualities of taste. *Japanese Psychological Research, 8,* 136–150.

Iverson, G. J., & Pavel, M. (1981). On the functional form of partial masking functions in psychoacoustics. *Journal of Mathematical Psychology, 24,* 1–20.

James, W. (1890). *The principles of psychology.* New York: Henry Holt.

James, W. (1892). *Psychology: Briefer course.* New York: Henry Holt.

Jastrow, J. (1886). The perception of space by disparate senses. *Mind, 11,* 539–544.

Jesteadt, W., Luce, R. D., & Green, D. M. (1977). Sequential effects in judgments of loudness. *Journal of Experimental Psychology: Human Perception and Performance, 3,* 92–104.

Jesteadt, W., Wier, C. C., & Green, D. M. (1977). Intensity discrimination as a function of frequency and sensation level. *Journal of the Acoustical Society of America, 61,* 169–177.

Jones, F. N., & Woskow, M. H. (1962). On the relationship between estimates of loudness and pitch. *American Journal of Psychology, 75,* 669–671.

King, M. C., & Lockhead, G. R. (1981). Response scales and sequential effects in judgment. *Perception & Psychophysics, 30,* 599–603.

Kohfeld, D. L., Santee, J. L., & Wallace, N. D. (1981a). Loudness and reaction time: I. *Perception & Psychophysics, 29,* 535–549.

Kohfeld, D. L., Santee, J. L., & Wallace, N. D. (1981b). Loudness and reaction time: II. Identification of detection components at different intensities and frequencies. *Perception & Psychophysics, 29,* 550–562.

Kowal, K. H. (1993). The range effect as a function of stimulus set, presence of a standard, and modulus. *Perception & Psychophysics, 54,* 555–561.

Krantz, D. H. (1967). Rational distance functions for multidimensional scaling. *Journal of Mathematical Psychology, 4,* 226–245.

Krantz, D. H. (1971). Integration of just-noticeable differences. *Journal of Mathematical Psychology, 8,* 591–599.

Krantz, D. H. (1972). A theory of magnitude estimation and cross-modality matching. *Journal of Mathematical Psychology, 9,* 168–199.

Krantz, D. H., Luce, R. D., Suppes, P., & Tversky, A. (1971). *Foundations of measurement. Vol. 1: Additive and polynomial representations.* New York: Academic Press.

Krueger, L. E. (1989). Reconciling Fechner and Stevens: Toward a unified psychophysical law. *The Behavioral and Brain Sciences, 12,* 251–320.

Kruskal, J. B. (1964). Nonmetric multidimensional scaling: A numerical method. *Psychometrika, 29,* 115–129.

Külpe, O. (1895). *Outlines of psychology: Based upon the results of experimental investigations.* New York: Macmillan.

Künnapas, T., Hallsten, L., & Söderberg, G. (1973). Interindividual differences in homomodal and heteromodal scaling. *Acta Psychologica, 37,* 31–42.

Lacouture, Y., & Marley, A. A. J. (1991). A connectionist model of choice and reaction time in absolute identification. *Connection Science, 3,* 401–433.

Leahey, T. H. (1997). *A history of psychology: Main currents in psychological thought* (4th ed.) Englewood Cliffs, NJ: Prentice-Hall.

Leibowitz, I. (1987). *Bein Mada Uphilosophia* [Between science and philosophy]. Academon: Jerusalem (Hebrew).

Levelt, W. D. M., Riemersma, J. B., & Bunt, A. A. (1972). Binaural additivity of loudness. *British Journal of Mathematical and Statistical Psychology, 25,* 51–68.

Levine, M. V. (1974). Geometric interpretations of some psychophysical results. In D. H. Krantz, R. C. Atkinson, R. D. Luce, & P. Suppes (Eds.), *Contemporary developments in mathematical psychology* (Vol. 2, pp. 200–235). San Francisco: Freeman.

Lim, L. S., Rabinowitz, W. M., Braida, L. D., & Durlach, N. I. (1977). Intensity perception: VIII. Loudness comparisons between different types of stimuli. *Journal of the Acoustical Society of America, 62,* 1256–1267.

Link, S. W. (1975). The relative judgment theory of two choice response time. *Journal of Mathematical Psychology, 12,* 114–135.

Link, S. W. (1992). *The wave theory of difference and similarity.* Hillsdale, NJ: Erlbaum.

Link, S. W., & Heath, R. A. (1975). A sequential theory of psychological discrimination. *Psychometrika, 40,* 77–105.

Lochner, J. P. A., & Burger, J. F. (1961). Form of the loudness function in the presence of masking noise. *Journal of the Acoustical Society of America, 33,* 1705–1707.

Lockhead, G. R. (1992). Psychophysical scaling: Judgments of attributes or objects? *The Behavioral and Brain Sciences, 15,* 543–601.

Lockhead, G. R., & Hinson, J. (1986). Range and sequence effects in judgment. *Perception & Psychophysics, 40,* 53–61.

Lockhead, G. R., & King, M. C. (1983). A memory model for sequential scaling tasks. *Journal of Experimental Psychology: Human Perception and Performance, 9,* 461–473.

Logue, A. W. (1976). Individual differences in magnitude estimation of loudness. *Perception & Psychophysics, 19,* 279–280.

Luce, R. D. (1959). On the possible psychophysical laws. *Psychological Review, 66,* 81–95.

Luce, R. D. (1972). What sort of measurement is psychophysical measurement? *American Psychologist, 27,* 96–106.

Luce, R. D. (1977a). The choice axiom after twenty years. *Journal of Mathematical Psychology, 15,* 215–233.

Luce, R. D. (1977b). Thurstone discriminal processes fifty years later. *Psychometrika, 42,* 461–498.

Luce, R. D. (1986). *Response times: Their role in inferring elementary mental organization.* New York: Oxford University Press.

Luce, R. D. (1994). Thurstone and sensory scaling: Then and now. *Psychological Review, 101,* 271–277.

Luce, R. D., Baird, J. C., Green, D. M., & Smith, A. F. (1980). Two classes of models for magnitude estimation. *Journal of Mathematical Psychology, 22,* 121–148.

Luce, R. D., & Edwards, W. (1958). The derivation of subjective scales from just noticeable differences. *Psychological Review, 65,* 222–237.

Luce, R. D., & Galanter, E. (1963). Discrimination. In R. D. Luce, R. R. Bush, & E. Galanter (Eds.), *Handbook of mathematical psychology* (Vol. 1, pp. 191–243). New York: Wiley.

Luce, R. D., & Green, D. M. (1972). A neural timing theory for response times and the psychophysics of intensity. *Psychological Review, 79,* 14–57.

Luce, R. D., & Green, D. M. (1974). The response ratio hypothesis for magnitude estimation. *Journal of Mathematical Psychology, 11,* 1–14.

Luce, R. D., & Green, D. M. (1978). Two tests of a neural attention hypothesis for auditory psychophysics. *Perception & Psychophysics, 23,* 363–371.

Luce, R. D., Green, D. M., & Weber, D. L. (1976). Attention bands in absolute identification. *Perception & Psychophysics, 20,* 49–54.

Luce, R. D., Krantz, D. H., Suppes, P., & Tversky, A. (1990). *Foundations of measurement. Vol. 3: Representation, axiomatization, and invariance.* San Diego: Academic Press.

Luce, R. D., & Krumhansl, C. L. (1988). Measurement, scaling, and psychophysics. In R. C. Atkinson, R. J. Herrnstein, G. Lindzay, & R. D. Luce (Eds.), *Stevens' handbook of experimental psychology* (2nd ed.) (Vol. 1, pp. 3–74). New York: Wiley.

Luce, R. D., & Mo, S. S. (1965). Magnitude estimation of heaviness and loudness by individual subjects. A test of a probabilistic response theory. *British Journal of Mathematical and Statistical Psychology, 18,* 159–174.

Luce, R. D., & Narens, L. (1987). Measurement scales on the continuum. *Science, 236,* 1527–1532.

Luce, R. D., & Tukey, J. (1964). Simultaneous conjoint measurement: A new type of fundamental measurement. *Journal of Mathematical Psychology, 1,* 1–27.

MacKay, D. M. (1963). Psychophysics of perceived intensity: A theoretical basis for Fechner's and Stevens's laws. *Science, 139,* 1213–1216.

Macmillan, N. A., & Creelman, C. D. (1991). *Detection theory: A user's guide.* Cambridge, England: Cambridge University Press.

MacRae, A. W. (1970). Channel capacity in absolute judgment tasks: An artifact of information bias? *Psychological Bulletin, 73,* 112–121.

MacRae, A. W. (1972). Information transmission, partitioning and Weber's law: Some comments on Baird's cognitive theory of psychophysics. *Scandinavian Journal of Psychology, 13,* 73–80.

MacRae, A. W. (1982). The magical number fourteen: Making a very great deal of non-sense. *Perception & Psychophysics, 31,* 591–593.

Mansfield, R. J. W. (1970). *Intensity relations in vision: Analysis and synthesis in a non-linear sensory system.* Doctoral dissertation, Harvard University.

Mansfield, R. J. W. (1973). Latency functions in human vision. *Vision Research, 13,* 2219–2234.

Marks, L. E. (1968). Stimulus-range, number of categories, and form of the category-scale. *American Journal of Psychology, 81,* 467–479.

Marks, L. E. (1972). Visual brightness: Some applications of a model. *Vision Research, 12,* 1409–1423.

Marks, L. E. (1974a). On scales of sensation: Prolegomena to any future psychophysics that will be able to come forth as science. *Perception & Psychophysics, 16,* 358–376.

Marks, L. E. (1974b). *Sensory processes: The new psychophysics.* New York: Academic Press.

Marks, L. E. (1977). Relative sensitivity and possible psychophysical functions. *Sensory Processes, 1,* 301–315.

Marks, L. E. (1978a). Binaural summation of the loudness of pure tones. *Journal of the Acoustical Society of America, 64,* 107–113.

Marks, L. E. (1978b). Mental measurement and the psychophysics of sensory processes. *Annals of the New York Academy of Sciences, 309,* 3–17.

Marks, L. E. (1978c). Phonion: Translation and annotations concerning loudness scales and the processing of auditory intensity. In N. J. Castellan & F. Restle (Eds.), *Cognitive theory* (Vol. 3, pp. 7–31). Hillsdale, NJ: Erlbaum.

Marks, L. E. (1978d). *The unity of the senses: Interrelations among the modalities.* New York: Academic Press.

Marks, L. E. (1979a). Summation of vibrotactile intensity: An analogue to auditory critical bands? *Sensory Processes, 3,* 188–203.

Marks, L. E. (1979b). A theory of loudness and loudness judgments. *Psychological Review, 86,* 256–285.

Marks, L. E. (1988). Magnitude estimation and sensory matching. *Perception & Psychophysics, 43,* 511–525.

Marks, L. E. (1991). Reliability of magnitude matching. *Perception & Psychophysics, 49,* 31–37.

Marks, L. E. (1992a). The contingency of perceptual processing: Context modifies equal-loudness relations. *Psychological Science, 3,* 187–198.

Marks, L. E. (1992b). The slippery context effect in psychophysics: Intensive, extensive, and qualitative continua. *Perception & Psychophysics, 51,* 187–198.

Marks, L. E. (1992c). "What thin partitions sense from thought divide": Toward a new cognitive psychophysics. In D. Algom (Ed.), *Psychophysical approaches to cognition* (pp. 115–186). Amsterdam: North-Holland Elsevier.

Marks, L. E. (1993). Contextual processing of multidimensional and unidimensional auditory stimuli. *Journal of Experimental Psychology: Human Perception and Performance, 19,* 227–249.

Marks, L. E. (1994). "Recalibrating" the auditory system: The perception of loudness. *Journal of Experimental Psychology: Human Perception and Performance, 20,* 382–396.

Marks, L. E., & Armstrong, L. (1996). Haptic and visual representations of space. In T. Inui & J. L. McClelland (Eds.), *Attention and Performance XVI* (pp. 263–287). Cambridge, MA: MIT Press.

Marks, L. E., Borg, G., & Ljunggren, G. (1983). Individual differences in perceived exertion assessed by two new methods. *Perception & Psychophysics, 34,* 280–288.

Marks, L. E., Galanter, E., & Baird, J. C. (1995). Binaural summation after learning psychophysical functions for loudness. *Perception & Psychophysics, 57,* 1209–1216.

Marks, L. E., & Warner, E. (1991). Slippery context effect and critical bands. *Journal of Experimental Psychology: Human Perception and Performance, 17,* 986–996.

Marley, A. A., & Cook, V. T. (1984). A fixed rehearsal capacity interpretation of limits on absolute identification performance. *British Journal of Mathematical and Statistical Psychology, 37,* 136–151.

Marschark, M., & Paivio, A. (1981). Congruity and the perceptual comparison task. *Journal of Experimental Psychology: Human Perception and Performance, 7,* 290–308.

Mashhour, M., & Hosman, J. (1968). On the new "psychophysical law": A validation study. *Perception & Psychophysics, 3,* 367–375.

McGill, W. J. (1961). Loudness and reaction time: A guided tour of the listener's private world. *Acta Psychologica, 19,* 193–199.

McGill, W. J. (1974). The slope of the loudness function: A puzzle. In H. R. Moskowitz, B. Scharf, & J. C. Stevens (Eds.), *Sensation and measurement: Papers in honor of S. S. Stevens* (pp. 295–314). Dordrecht, Holland: Reidel.

McGill, W. J., & Goldberg, J. P. (1968). Pure-tone intensity discrimination and energy detection. *Journal of the Acoustical Society of America, 44,* 576–581.

McKenna, F. P. (1985). Another look at the "new psychophysics." *British Journal of Psychology, 76,* 97–109.

Meiselman, H. L., Bose, H. E., & Nykvist, W. F. (1972). Magnitude production and magnitude estimation of taste intensity. *Perception & Psychophysics, 12,* 249–252.

Melamed, L. E., & Thurlow, W. R. (1971). Analysis of contrast effects in loudness judgments. *Journal of Experimental Psychology, 90,* 268–274.

Melara, R. D. (1992). The concept of perceptual similarity: From psychophysics to cognitive psychology. In D. Algom (Ed.), *Psychophysical approaches to cognition* (pp. 303–388). Amsterdam: North-Holland Elsevier.

Mellers, B. A., Davis, D. M., & Birnbaum, M. H. (1984). Weight of evidence supports one operation for "ratios" and "differences" of heaviness. *Journal of Experimental Psychology: Human Perception and Performance, 10,* 216–230.

Merkel, J. (1888). Die Abhängigkeit zwischen Reiz und Empfindung. *Philosophische Studien, 4,* 541–594.

Michels, W. C., & Helson, H. (1949). A reformation of the Fechner law in terms of adaptation-level applied to rating-scale data. *American Journal of Psychology, 62,* 355–368.

Miller, G. A. (1947). Sensitivity to changes in the intensity of white noise and its relation to loudness and masking. *Journal of the Acoustical Society of America, 19,* 609–619.

Miller, G. A. (1956). The magical number seven, plus or minus two: Some limits on our capacity for processing information. *Psychological Review, 63,* 81–97.

Moles, A. (1966). *Information theory and esthetic perception.* Urbana, IL: University of Illinois Press (originally published, 1958).

Montgomery, H., & Eisler, H. (1974). Is an equal interval scale an equal discriminability scale? *Perception & Psychophysics, 15,* 441–448.

Münsterberg, H. (1890). *Beiträge zur experimentellen Psychologie,* Band III. Freiburg: Mohr.

Murphy, C., & Gilmore, M. M. (1989). Quality-specific effects of aging on the human taste system. *Perception & Psychophysics, 45,* 121–128.

Murray, D. J. (1993). A perspective for viewing the history of psychology. *The Behavioral and Brain Sciences, 16,* 115–186.

Nachmias, J., & Steinman, R. M. (1965). Brightness and discriminability of light flashes. *Vision Research, 5,* 545–557.

Narens, L., & Luce, R. D. (1992). Further comments on the "nonrevolution" arising from axiomatic measurement theory. *Psychological Science, 4,* 127–130.

Newman, E. B. (1933). The validity of the just noticeable difference as a unit of psychological magnitude. *Transactions of the Kansas Academy of Science, 36,* 172–175.

Noma, E., & Baird, J. C. (1975). Psychophysical study of numbers: II. Theoretical models of number generation. *Psychological Research, 38,* 81–95.

Norwich, K. H. (1984). The psychophysics of taste from the entropy of the stimulus. *Perception & Psychophysics, 35,* 269–278.

Norwich, K. H. (1987). On the theory of Weber fractions. *Perception & Psychophysics, 42,* 286–298.

Norwich, K. H. (1991). Toward the unification of the laws of sensation: Some food for thought. In H. Lawless & B. Klein (Eds.), *Sensory science: Theory and applications in food* (pp. 151–184). New York: Dekker.

Norwich, K. H. (1993). *Information, sensation, and perception.* Orlando, FL: Academic Press.

Parducci, A. (1965). Category judgment: A range-frequency model. *Psychological Review, 75,* 407–418.

Parducci, A. (1974). Contextual effects: A range-frequency analysis. In E. C. Carterette & M. P. Friedman (Eds.), *Handbook of perception. Vol. 2. Psychophysical judgment and measurement* (pp. 127–141). New York: Academic Press.

Parducci, A. (1982). Category ratings: Still more contextual effects! In B. Wegener (Ed.), *Social attitudes and psychophysical measurement* (pp. 89–105). Hillsdale, NJ: Erlbaum.

Parducci, A., Knobel, S., & Thomas, C. (1976). Independent contexts for category ratings: A range-frequency analysis. *Perception & Psychophysics, 20,* 360–366.

Parducci, A., & Perrett, L. F. (1971). Category rating scales: Effects of relative spacing and frequency of stimulus values. *Journal of Experimental Psychology Monographs, 89,* 427–452.

Parducci, A., & Wedell, D. H. (1986). The category effect with rating scales: Number of categories, number of stimuli, and method of presentation. *Journal of Experimental Psychology: Human Perception and Performance, 12,* 496–516.

Parker, S., & Schneider, B. (1974). Non-metric scaling of loudness and pitch using similarity and difference estimates. *Perception & Psychophysics, 15,* 238–242.

Parker, S., & Schneider, B. (1980). Loudness and loudness discrimination. *Perception & Psychophysics, 28,* 398–406.

Parker, S., & Schneider, B. (1988). Conjoint scaling of the utility of money using paired comparisons. *Social Science Research, 17,* 277–286.

Parker, S., & Schneider, B. (1994). The stimulus range effect: Evidence for top-down control of sensory intensity in audition. *Perception & Psychophysics, 56,* 1–11.

Parker, S., Schneider, B., & Kanow, G. (1975). Ratio scale measurement of the perceived length of lines. *Journal of Experimental Psychology: Human Perception and Performance, 104,* 195–204.

Parker, S., Schneider, B., Stein, D., Popper, R., Darte, E., & Needel, S. (1981). Utility function for money determined using conjoint measurement. *American Journal of Psychology, 94,* 563–573.

Pascal, B. (1958). *Pensées.* New York: Dutton (originally published, 1670).

Pavel, M., & Iverson, G. J. (1981). Invariant characteristics of partial masking: Implications for mathematical models. *Journal of the Acoustical Society of America, 69,* 1126–1131.

Petrusic, W. M. (1992). Semantic congruity effects and theories of the comparison process. *Journal of Experimental Psychology: Human Perception and Performance, 18,* 962–986.

Pfanzagl, J. (1959). A general theory of measurement: Applications to utility. *Naval Research Logistics Quarterly, 6,* 283–294.

Piéron, H. (1914). Recherches sur les lois de variation des temps de latence sensorielle en fonction des intensités excitatrices. *L'Année Psychologique, 20,* 2–96.

Piéron, H. (1934). Le problème du mechanisme physiologique impliqué par l'échelon différentiel de sensation. *L'Année Psychologique, 34,* 217–236.

Piéron, H. (1952). *The sensations: Their functions, processes and mechanisms.* New Haven, CT: Yale University Press.

Piéron, Mme. H. (1922). Contribution expérimentale à l'étude des phénomènes de transfert sensoriel: La vision et la kinésthesie dans la perception des longueurs. *L'Année Psychologique, 23,* 76–124.

Plateau, J. A. F. (1872). Sur la mesure des sensations physiques, et sur la loi qui lie l'intensité de ces sensations à l'intensité de la cause excitante. *Bulletins de l'Académie Royale des Sciences, de Lettres, et des Beaux-Arts de Belgique, 33,* 376–388.

Pollack, I. (1965a). Iterative techniques for unbiased rating scales. *Quarterly Journal of Experimental Psychology, 17,* 139–148.

Pollack, I. (1965b). Neutralization of stimulus bias in the rating of grays. *Journal of Experimental Psychology, 69,* 564–578.

Popper, R. D., Parker, S., & Galanter, E. (1986). Dual loudness scales in individual subjects. *Journal of Experimental Psychology: Human Perception and Performance, 12,* 61–69.

Potts, B. C. (1991). *The horizontal-vertical illusion: A confluence of configural, contextual, and framing factors.* Doctoral dissertation, Yale University.

Poulton, E. C. (1989). *Bias in quantifying judgments.* Hove, England: Erlbaum.

Pruzansky, S., Tversky, A., & Carroll, J. D. (1982). Spatial versus tree representations of proximity data. *Psychometrika, 47,* 3–24.

Raab, D. H. (1962). Magnitude estimation of the brightness of brief foveal stimuli. *Science, 135,* 42–44.

Raab, D. H., & Fehrer, E. (1962). Supplementary report: The effect of stimulus duration and luminance on visual reaction time. *Journal of Experimental Psychology, 64,* 326–327.

Ramsay, J. O. (1969). Some statistical considerations in multidimensional scaling. *Psychometrika, 34,* 167–182.

Ramsay, J. O. (1979). Intra- and interindividual variation in the power law exponent for area summation. *Perception & Psychophysics, 26,* 495–500.

Rankin, K. R., & Marks, L. E. (1991). Differential context effects in taste perception. *Chemical Senses, 16,* 617–629.

Rankovic, C. M., Viemeister, N. F., Fantini, D. A., Cheesman, M. F., & Uchiyama, C. L. (1988). The relation between loudness and intensity difference limens for tones in quiet and noise backgrounds. *Journal of the Acoustical Society of America, 84,* 150– 155.

Restle, F. (1961). *Psychology of judgment and choice: A theoretical essay.* New York: Wiley.

Restle, F., & Greeno, J. G. (1970). *Introduction to mathematical psychology.* Reading, MA: Addison-Wesley.

Reynolds, G. S., & Stevens, S. S. (1960). Binaural summation of loudness. *Journal of the Acoustical Society of America, 32,* 1337–1344.

Richardson, L. F., & Ross, J. S. (1930). Loudness and telephone current. *Journal of General Psychology, 3,* 288–306.

Riesz, R. R. (1928). Differential intensity sensitivity of the ear for pure tones. *Physical Review, 31,* 867–875.

Reisz, R. R. (1933). The relationship between loudness and the minimum perceptible increment of intensity. *Journal of the Acoustical Society of America, 5,* 211–216.

Robinson, G. H. (1976). Biasing power law exponents by magnitude estimation instructions. *Perception & Psychophysics, 19,* 80–84.

Rosenblith, W. A. (1959). Some quantifiable aspects of the electrical activity of the nervous system (with emphasis upon responses to sensory systems). *Reviews of Modern Physics, 31,* 532–545.

Ross, J., & DiLollo, V. (1971). Judgment and response in magnitude estimation. *Psychological Review, 78,* 515–527.

Rschevkin, S. N., & Rabinovich, A. V. (1936). Sur le problème de l'estimation quantitative de la force d'un son. *Revue d'Acoustique, 5,* 183–200.

Rule, S. J., & Curtis, D. W. (1973). Conjoint scaling of subjective number and weight. *Journal of Experimental Psychology, 97,* 305–309.

Rule, S. J., & Curtis, D. W. (1976). Converging power functions as a description of the size-weight illusion. *Bulletin of the Psychonomic Society, 8,* 16–18.

Rule, S. J., & Curtis, D. W. (1977). Subject differences in input and output transformations from magnitude estimation of differences. *Acta Psychologica, 41,* 61–65.

Rule, S. J., & Curtis, D. W. (1978). Levels for sensory and judgmental processing: Strategies for the evaluation of a model. In B. Wegener (Ed.), *Social attitudes and psychophysical measurement* (pp. 107–122). Hillsdale, NJ: Erlbaum.

Rule, S. J., Curtis, D. W., & Markley, R. P. (1970). Input and output transformations from magnitude estimation. *Journal of Experimental Psychology, 86,* 343–349.

Rule, S. J., & Markley, R. P. (1971). Subject differences in cross-modality matching. *Perception & Psychophysics, 9,* 115–117.

Rumelhart, D. L., & Greeno, J. G. (1971). Similarity between stimuli: An experimental test of the Luce and Restle choice models. *Journal of Mathematical Psychology, 8,* 370–381.

Saffir, M. A. (1937). A comparative study of scales constructed by three psychophysical methods. *Psychometrika, 2,* 179–198.

Schlauch, R. S. (1994). Intensity resolution and loudness in high-pass noise. *Journal of the Acoustical Society of America, 95,* 2171–2179.

Schneider, B. (1980). Individual loudness functions determined from direct comparisons of loudness intervals. *Perception & Psychophysics, 27,* 493–503.

Schneider, B. (1988). The additivity of loudness across critical bands. *Perception & Psychophysics, 43,* 211–222.

Schneider, B., & Parker, S. (1987). Intensity discrimination and loudness for tones in notched noise. *Perception & Psychophysics, 41,* 253–261.

Schneider, B., & Parker, S. (1990). Does stimulus context affect loudness or only loudness judgment? *Perception & Psychophysics, 48,* 409–418.

Schneider, B., Parker, S., & Stein, D. (1974). The measurement of loudness using direct comparisons of sensory intervals. *Journal of Mathematical Psychology, 11,* 259–273.

Schneider, B., Parker, S., Valenti, M., Farrell, G., & Kanow, G. (1978). Response bias in category and magnitude estimation of difference and similarity for loudness and pitch. *Journal of Experimental Psychology: Human Perception and Performance, 4,* 483–496.

Shannon, C. E. (1948). A mathematical theory of communication. *Bell System Technical Journal, 27,* 379–423, 623–656.

Shepard, R. N. (1962a). Analysis of proximities: Multidimensional scaling with an unknown distance function. I. *Psychometrika, 27,* 125–140.

Shepard, R. N. (1962b). Analysis of proximities: Multidimensional scaling with an unknown distance function. II. *Psychometrika, 27,* 219–246.

Shepard, R. (1966). Metric structures in ordinal data. *Journal of Mathematical Psychology, 3,* 287–315.

Shepard, R. N. (1978). On the status of "direct" psychological measurement. In C. W. Savage (Ed.), *Minnesota studies in the philosophy of science* (Vol. 9, pp. 441–490). Minneapolis: University of Minnesota Press.

Shepard, R. N. (1981). Psychological relations and psychological scales: On the status of "direct" psychophysical measurement. *Journal of Mathematical Psychology, 24,* 21–57.

Shepard, R. N., Kilpatric, D. W., & Cunningham, J. P. (1975). The internal representation of numbers. *Cognitive Psychology, 7,* 82–138.

Sjöberg, L. (1980). Similarity and correlation. In E. D. Lantermann & H. Feger (Eds.), *Similarity and choice* (pp. 70–78). Bern: Huber.

Solomons, L. M. (1900). A new explanation of Weber's law. *Psychological Review, 7,* 234–240.

Sperling, G., & Sondhi, M. M. (1968). Model for visual luminance discrimination and flicker detection. *Journal of the Optical Society of America, 58,* 1133–1145.

Staddon, J. E., King, M., & Lockhead, G. R. (1980). On sequential effects in absolute judgment experiments. *Journal of Experimental Psychology: Human Perception and Performance, 6,* 290–301.

Stevens, J. C. (1957). *A comparison of ratio scales for the loudness of white noise and the brightness of white light.* Doctoral dissertation, Harvard University.

Stevens, J. C. (1958). Stimulus spacing and the judgment of loudness. *Journal of Experimental Psychology, 56,* 246–250.

Stevens, J. C., & Cain, W. S. (1985). Age-related deficiency in perceived strength of odorants. *Chemical Senses, 10,* 517–529.

Stevens, J. C., & Guirao, M. (1964). Individual loudness functions. *Journal of the Acoustical Society of America, 36,* 2210–2213.

Stevens, J. C., & Hall, J. W. (1966). Brightness and loudness as functions of stimulus duration. *Perception & Psychophysics, 1,* 319–327.

Stevens, J. C., Mack, J. D., & Stevens, S. S. (1960). Growth of sensation on seven continua as measured by force of handgrip. *Journal of Experimental Psychology, 59,* 60–67.

Stevens, J. C., & Marks, L. E. (1965). Cross-modality matching of brightness and loudness. *Proceedings of the National Academy of Sciences, 54,* 407–411.

Stevens, J. C., & Marks, L. E. (1980). Cross-modality matching functions generated by magnitude estimation. *Perception & Psychophysics, 27,* 379–389.

Stevens, J. C., & Stevens, S. S. (1963). Brightness function: Effects of adaptation. *Journal of the Optical Society of America, 53,* 375–385.

Stevens, J. C., & Tulving, E. (1957). Estimations of loudness by a group of untrained observers. *American Journal of Psychology, 70,* 600–605.

Stevens, S. S. (1946). On the theory of scales of measurement. *Science, 103,* 677–680.

Stevens, S. S. (1951). Mathematics, measurement, and psychophysics. In S. S. Stevens (Ed.), *Handbook of experimental psychology* (pp. 1–49). New York: Wiley.

Stevens, S. S. (1955). The measurement of loudness. *Journal of the Acoustical Society of America, 27,* 815–829.

Stevens, S. S. (1956). The direct estimation of sensory magnitude—loudness. *American Journal of Psychology, 69,* 1–15.

Stevens, S. S. (1957). On the psychophysical law. *Psychological Review, 64,* 153–181.

Stevens, S. S. (1958). Adaptation-level vs. the relativity of judgment. *American Journal of Psychology, 71,* 633–646.

Stevens, S. S. (1959a). Cross-modality validation of subjective scales for loudness, vibration, and electric shock. *Journal of Experimental Psychology, 57,* 201–209.

Stevens, S. S. (1959b). Measurement, psychophysics, and utility. In C. W. Churchman & P. Ratoosh (Eds.), *Measurement: Definitions and theories* (pp. 18–63). New York: Wiley.

Stevens, S. S. (1959c). The quantification of sensation. *Daedalus, 88,* 606–621.

Stevens, S. S. (1959d). Review: L. L. Thurstone's *The measurement of values. Contemporary Psychology, 4,* 388–389.

Stevens, S. S. (1960). Ratio scales, partition scales and confusion scales. In H. Gulliksen & S. Messick (Eds.), *Psychological scaling: Theory and applications* (pp. 49–66b). New York: Wiley.

Stevens, S. S. (1961). The psychophysics of sensory function. In W. A. Rosenblith (Ed.), *Sensory Communication* (pp. 1–33). New York: Wiley.

Stevens, S. S. (1966). Power-group transformations under glare, masking, and recruitment. *Journal of the Acoustical Society of America, 39,* 725–735.

Stevens, S. S. (1971). Issues in psychophysical measurement. *Psychological Review, 78,* 426–450.

Stevens, S. S. (1975). *Psychophysics: An introduction to its perceptual, neural, and social prospects.* New York: Wiley.

Stevens, S. S., & Galanter, E. (1957). Ratio scales and category scales for a dozen perceptual continua. *Journal of Experimental Psychology, 54,* 377–411.

Stevens, S. S., & Greenbaum, H. B. (1966). Regression effect in psychophysical judgment. *Perception & Psychophysics, 1,* 439–446.

Stevens, S. S., & Guirao, M. (1967). Loudness functions under inhibition. *Perception & Psychophysics, 2,* 459–465.

Stevens, S. S., & Volkmann, J. (1940). The relation of pitch to frequency: A revised scale. *American Journal of Psychology, 53,* 329–353.

Stillman, J. A., Zwislocki, J. J., Zhang, M., & Cefaratti, L. K. (1993). Intensity just-noticeable differences at equal-loudness levels in normal and pathological ears. *Journal of the Acoustical Society of America, 93,* 425–434.

Suppes, P., & Zinnes, J. L. (1963). Basic measurement theory. In R. D. Luce, R. R. Bush, & E. Galanter (Eds.), *Handbook of mathematical psychology* (Vol. 1, pp. 1–76). New York: Wiley.

Tanner, W. P., Jr., & Swets, J. A. (1954). A decision-making theory of visual detection. *Psychological Review, 61,* 401–409.

Teghtsoonian, M., & Teghtsoonian, R. (1971). How repeatable are Stevens's power law exponents for individual subjects? *Perception & Psychophysics, 10,* 147–149.

Teghtsoonian, M., & Teghtsoonian, R. (1983). Consistency of individual exponents in cross-modal matching. *Perception & Psychophysics, 33,* 203–214.

Teghtsoonian, R. (1971). On the exponents of Stevens's law and the constant in Ekman's law. *Psychological Review, 78*, 71–80.

Teghtsoonian, R. (1973). Range effects in psychophysical scaling and a revision of Stevens's law. *American Journal Psychology, 86*, 3–27.

Teghtsoonian, R., & Teghtsoonian, M. (1978). Range and regression effects in magnitude scaling. *Perception & Psychophysics, 24*, 305–314.

Thurstone, L. L. (1927). A law of comparative judgment. *Psychological Review, 34*, 273–286.

Thurstone, L. L. (1959). *The measurement of values.* Chicago: University of Chicago Press.

Titchener, E. B. (1905). *Experimental psychology: A manual of laboratory practice. Vol. II. Quantitative. 2. Instructor's Manual.* New York: Macmillan.

Torgerson, W. S. (1954). A law of categorical judgment. In L. H. Clark (Ed.), *Consumer behavior* (pp. 92–93). New York: New York University Press.

Torgerson, W. S. (1958). *Theory and methods of scaling.* New York: Wiley.

Torgerson, W. S. (1961). Distances and ratios in psychological scaling. *Acta Psychologica, 19*, 201–205.

Treisman, M. (1964). Sensory scaling and the psychophysical law. *Quarterly Journal of Experimental Psychology, 16*, 11–22.

Treisman, M. (1984). A theory of criterion setting: An alternative to the attention band and response ratio hypotheses in magnitude estimation and cross-modality matching. *Journal of Experimental Psychology: General, 113*, 443–463.

Troland, L. T. (1930). *Principles of psychophysiology. Vol. 2. Sensation.* Princeton, NJ: Van Nostrand.

Tversky, A. (1969). Intransitivity of preferences. *Psychological Review, 76*, 31–48.

Tversky, A. (1972). Elimination by aspects: A theory of choice. *Psychological Review, 79*, 281–299.

Tversky, A., & Sattath, S. (1979). Preference trees, *Psychological Review, 86*, 542–573.

Van Brakel, J. (1993). The analysis of sensations as the foundation of all sciences. *The Behavioral and Brain Sciences, 16*, 163–164.

Vaughn, H. G., Jr., Costa, L. D., & Gilden, L. (1966). The functional relation of visual evoked response and reaction time to stimulus intensity. *Vision Research, 6*, 645–656.

Von Kries, J. (1882). Über die Messung intensiver Grössen und über das sogenannte psychophysische Gesetz. *Vierteljahrsschrift für Wissenschaftliche Philosophie, 6*, 257–294.

Wagner, M., & Baird, J. C. (1981). A quantitative analysis of sequential effects with numeric stimuli. *Perception & Psychophysics, 29*, 359–364.

Ward, L. M. (1972). Category judgments of loudness in the absence of an experimenter-induced identification function: Sequential effects and power-function fit. *Journal of Experimental Psychology, 94*, 179–184.

Ward, L. M. (1973). Repeated magnitude estimation with a variable standard: Sequential effects and other properties. *Perception & Psychophysics, 13*, 193–200.

Ward, L. M. (1979). Stimulus information and sequential dependencies in magnitude estimation and cross-modality matching. *Journal of Experimental Psychology: Human Perception and Performance, 5*, 444–459.

Ward, L. M. (1985). Mixed-modality psychophysical scaling: Inter- and intramodality sequential dependencies as a function of lag. *Perception & Psychophysics, 38*, 512–522.

Ward, L. M. (1987). Remembrance of sounds past: Memory and psychophysical scaling. *Journal of Experimental Psychology: Human Perception and Performance, 13*, 216–227.

Ward, L. M. (1990). Critical bands and mixed-frequency scaling: Sequential dependencies, equal-loudness contours, and power function exponents. *Perception & Psychophysics, 47*, 551–562.

Ward, L. M. (1992). Mind in psychophysics. In D. Algom (Ed.), *Psychophysical approaches to cognition* (pp. 187–249). Amsterdam: North-Holland Elsevier.

Ward, L. M., Armstrong, J., & Golestani, N. (1996). Intensity resolution and subjective magnitude in psychophysical scaling. *Perception & Psychophysics, 58*, 793–801.

Ward, L. M., & Lockhead, G. R. (1970). Sequential effects and memory in category judgments. *Journal of Experimental Psychology, 84*, 27–34.

Ward, L. M., & Lockhead, G. R. (1971). Response system processes in absolute judgment. *Perception & Psychophysics, 9*, 73–78.

Warren, R. M. (1958). A basis for judgments of sensory intensity. *American Journal of Psychology, 71*, 675–687.

Warren, R. M. (1969). Visual intensity judgments: An empirical rule and a theory. *Psychological Review, 76*, 16–30.

Warren, R. M. (1981). Measurement of sensory intensity. *The Behavioral and Brain Sciences, 4*, 175–223.

Wasserman, G. S. (1991). Neural and behavioral assessments of sensory quality. *The Behavioral and Brain Sciences, 14*, 192–193.

Weber, E. H. (1834). *De pulsu, resorptione, auditu et tactu: Annotationes anatomicae et physiologicae.* Leipzig: Köhler.

Wedell, D. H. (1995). Contrast effects in paired comparisons: Evidence for both stimulus-based and response-based processes. *Journal of Experimental Psychology: Human Perception and Performance, 21*, 1158–1173.

Weiss, D. J. (1975). Quantifying private events: A functional measurement analysis of equisection. *Perception & Psychophysics, 17*, 351–357.

Weissmann, S. M., Hollingsworth, S. R., & Baird, J. C. (1975). Psychophysical study of numbers: III. Methodological applications. *Psychological Research, 38*, 97–115.

Welford, A. T. (1960). The measurement of sensory-motor performance: Survey and reappraisal of twelve years' progress. *Ergonomics, 3*, 189–230.

Woodworth, R. S. (1914). Professor Cattell's psychophysical contributions. *Archives of Psychology, 30*, 60–74.

Yellott, J. I. (1971). Correction for fast guessing and the speed-accuracy tradeoff in choice reaction time. *Journal of Mathematical Psychology, 8*, 159–199.

Yellott, J. I. (1977). The relationship between Luce's Choice Axiom, Thurstone's Theory of Comparative Judgment, and the double exponential distribution. *Journal of Mathematical Psychology, 15*, 109–144.

Zinnes, J. L. (1969). Scaling. *Annual Review of Psychology, 20*, 447–478.

Zwislocki, J. J. (1965). Analysis of some auditory characteristics. In R. D. Luce, R. R. Bush, & E. Galanter (Eds.), *Handbook of mathematical psychology* (Vol. 3, pp. 3–97). New York: Wiley.

Zwislocki, J. J. (1983). Group and individual relations between sensation magnitudes and their numerical estimates. *Perception & Psychophysics, 33*, 460–468.

Zwislocki, J. J. (1991). Natural measurement. In S. J. Bolanowski, Jr., & G. A. Gescheider (Eds.), *Ratio scaling of psychological magnitude* (pp. 18–26). Hillsdale, NJ: Erlbaum.

Zwislocki, J. J., & Goodman, D. A. (1980). Absolute scaling of sensory magnitudes: A validation. *Perception & Psychophysics, 28*, 28–38.

Zwislocki, J. J., & Jordan, H. N. (1986). On the relations of intensity jnd's to loudness and neural noise. *Journal of the Acoustical Society of America, 79*, 772–780.

CHAPTER 3

Multidimensional Scaling

J. Douglas Carroll
Phipps Arabie

I. INTRODUCTION

This technique comprises a family of geometric models for representation of data in one or, more frequently, two or more dimensions and a corresponding set of methods for fitting such models to actual data. A much narrower definition would limit the term to spatial distance models for similarities, dissimilarities, or other *proximity data*. The usage we espouse includes nonspatial (e.g., such discrete geometric models as tree structures) and nondistance (e.g., scalar product or projection) models that apply to nonproximity (e.g., preference or other dominance) data as well as to proximities. As this chapter demonstrates, a large class of these nonspatial models can still be characterized as dimensional models—but with discrete rather than continuously valued dimensions.

The successful development of any multivariate technique and its incorporation in widely available statistical software inevitably lead to substantive applications over an increasingly wide range both within and among disciplines. Multidimensional scaling (MDS) is no exception, and within psychology and closely related areas we could catalog an immense variety of different applications (not all of them cause for celebration, however); several thousand are given in the annual bibliographic survey *SERVICE* (Murtagh, 1997) published by the Classification Society of North America.

Further evidence of the vitality of developments in MDS can be found in the numbers of recent (1) books and edited volumes and (2) review chapters and articles on the topic. In the former category, we note Arce (1993); Ashby (1992); Cox and Cox (1994); de Leeuw, Heiser, Meulman, and Critchley (1986); De Soete, Feger, and Klauer (1989); Gower and Hand (1996); Green, Carmone, and Smith (1989); Okada and Imaizumi (1994); and Van Cutsem (1994). The conference proceedings volumes are too numerous even to cite, and the monograph series of DSWO Press at the University of Leiden has many noteworthy contributions. Concerning review chapters and articles, the subareas of psychology recently targeted include counseling (Fitzgerald & Hubert, 1987), developmental (Miller, 1987), educational (Weinberg & Carroll, 1992), experimental (L. E. Jones & Koehly, 1993; Luce & Krumhansl, 1988), and cognitive (Nosofsky, 1992; Shoben & Ross, 1987). Multivariate statistical textbooks also continue to pay due attention to MDS (e.g., Krzanowski & Marriott, 1994, chap. 5). Iverson and Luce's chapter in this volume focuses on a complementary aspect of measurement in psychology and the behavioral sciences, measurement (primarily, but not exclusively, unidimensional) based on subjects' orderings of stimuli, whereas we are concerned with measurement (primarily, but not exclusively, multidimensional, or multiattribute) based on proximity data on pairs of stimuli or other entities.

In this chapter we focus almost exclusively on that substantive area where we see the strongest bonds to MDS and its underpinnings and that seems most likely to spur new methodological developments in MDS, namely that answering fundamental questions about the psychological representation of structure underlying perception and judgment, especially in terms of similarities and dissimilarities. From its inception (Shepard, 1962a, 1962b), nonmetric MDS has been used to provide visualizable depictions of such structure, but current research focuses on much more incisive queries. Question 1 is whether any particular stimulus domain is better fitted by a discrete than by a continuous (usually) spatial model. The latter possibility gives rise to Question 2, which concerns the nature of the metric of the multidimensional stimulus space (often assumed to be either Euclidean or city-block, as defined later).

Question 1, of course, is at the heart of such controversies in experimental psychology as categorical perception (Tartter, in press, chap. 7) and neural quantum theory (Stevens, 1972). With the advent of increasingly general models (discussed later) for discrete structure and associated algorithms for fitting them, it has become possible in some cases to run empirical comparisons of selected discrete versus spatial models for given data sets (cf. Carroll, 1976; De Soete & Carroll, 1996). Pruzansky, Tversky, and Carroll (1982) compared data from several stimulus domains and concluded that: "In general, colors, sounds and factorial structures were better represented by a plane [i.e., a two-dimensional MDS solution], whereas conceptual stimuli from various semantic fields were better modelled by a[n] additive] tree" (p. 17).

Within the literature of experimental psychology, Question 2 effectively begins with Attneave's (1950, p. 521) reflections on "the exceedingly precarious assumption that psychological space is Euclidean" (1950, p. 521). He instead argued: "The psychological implication is that there is a unique coordinate system in psychological space, upon which 'distances' between stimuli are strictly dependent [as opposed to rotation invariant]; and thus our choice of axes is to be dictated, not by linguistic expediency, but by psychological fact." Moreover, Attneave (1950, p. 555) began the tradition of distinguishing between integral and analyzable stimulus domains with his sharp contrast between Euclidean and city-block metrics: "Perhaps the most significant psychological difference between these two hypotheses is that the former assumes one frame of reference to be as good as any other, whereas the latter implies a unique set of psychological axes." For the development of theoretical positions on this distinction between integral and analyzable stimuli, see Shepard's (1991) and other chapters in Lockhead and Pomerantz's (1991) Festschrift for W. R. Garner. For a review of theoretical and algorithmic approaches to city-block spaces, see Arabie (1991).

Since the mid-1980s, the most innovative and significant results pertaining to Question 2 have come from Nosofsky (e.g., 1992) and from Shepard (1987, 1988). In the latter papers, Shepard returned to his earlier interest in stimulus generalization to formulate and derive a universal law of generalization based on the distinctions between analyzable and integral stimuli and between the Euclidean and city-block metrics.

Reviewing recent work on "models for predicting a variety of performances, including generalization, identification, categorization, recognition, same–different accuracy and reaction time, and similarity judgment," Nosofsky (1992, p. 40) noted that "The MDS-based similarity representation is a fundamental component of these models." Additionally (Nosofsky, 1992, p. 34), "*The role of MDS in developing these theoretical relations is critical* [italics added]." The literature on Question 2 has become quite extensive; for example, see chapters in Ashby (1992) and work by Ennis and his collaborators (e.g., Ennis, Palen, & Mullen, 1988).

To explain how MDS can be used to address Questions 1 and 2, we must immediately make some distinctions among types of data matrices, and we do so by summarizing a lengthier taxonomy found in Carroll and Arabie (1980, pp. 610–611). Consider two matrices: one with n rows and the same number of columns (with entries depicting direct judgments of pairwise similarities for all distinct pairs of the n stimuli) and the other matrix with n rows of stimuli and K columns of attributes of the stimuli. Although both matrices have two *ways* (namely, rows and columns), the former is said to have one mode because both its ways correspond to the same set of entities (i.e., the n stimuli). But the matrix of stimuli by their attributes has two disjoint sets (and thus two *modes;* Tucker, 1964) of entities corresponding to the ways. For a one-mode two-way matrix, an additional consideration is whether conjugate off-diagonal entries are always equal, in which case the matrix is symmetric; otherwise it is nonsymmetric.

Another important distinction concerns whether the data are conditional (i.e., noncomparable) between rows/columns or among matrices. Row conditional data arise most commonly when a subject is presented with each of n stimuli in turn and asked to rank the remaining $n - 1$ according to their similarity to the standard. If the ranks are entered as a row/column for each successive standard stimulus in a two-way one-mode matrix, the entries are comparable within but not between rows/columns, and such data are therefore called row/column conditional (Coombs, 1964). If the data are a collection of I one-mode, two-way matrices, all $n \times n$ for the same set of n stimuli, a more general question is whether numerical entries are comparable among the matrices. If not, such three-way data are said to be matrix conditional (Takane, Young, & de Leeuw, 1977).

It is not our intention to dwell on traditional methods of collecting data for multidimensional scaling, given the excellent summaries already available (e.g., Kruskal & Wish, 1978; Coxon, 1982, chap. 2; Rosenberg, 1982, for the method of sorting; L. E. Jones & Koehly, 1993, pp. 104–108). An important distinction offered by Shepard (1972) is whether the input data are the result of direct judgments (e.g., from subjects' judging all distinct pairs of stimuli—say, on a 9-point scale of similarity/dissimilarity—or confusions data) or of indirect or profile data, as result when the data at hand are two-mode, but the model to be fitted requires one-mode data. In such cases, the user typically preprocesses the data by computing an indirect measure of proximity (e.g., squared Euclidean distances) between all pairs of rows or columns to obtain a one-mode matrix of pairwise similarities/dissimilarities. Although Shepard's (1962a, 1962b) original development of nonmetric MDS greatly emphasized applications to one-mode two-way direct similarities, applications of various MDS models to indirect or profile data are quite common.

A noteworthy development of recent years is that of models and associated algorithms for the direct analysis of types of data not previously amenable to MDS without preprocessing: free recall sequences (Shiina, 1986); row conditional rank-order data (Takane & Carroll, 1982): similarity/dissimilarity judgments based on triples (Daws, 1993, 1996; Joly & Le Calvé, 1995; Pan & Harris, 1991) or even n-tuples of stimuli (T. F. Cox, M. A. A. Cox, & Branco, 1991); triadic comparisons (Takane, 1982); and sorting data (Takane, 1981, 1982).

Carroll and Arabie (1980) organized their *Annual Review* chapter on

MDS around the typology of ways and modes for data and for corresponding algorithms. Although these distinctions remain crucial in considering
types of data, the typology is now less clear-cut for algorithms. As we
predicted in that chapter (p. 638), there has been intensive development of
three-way algorithms, and the two-way special cases are often by-products.
Thus, in our present coverage, the two-way algorithms and models are
mentioned only as they are subsumed in the more general three-way approaches.

II. ONE-MODE TWO-WAY DATA

The inventor of the modern approach to nonmetric MDS (Shepard, 1962a,
1962b) began by considering a single one-mode two-way matrix, typically
some form of similarity, dissimilarity, or other proximity data (sometimes
also referred to as "relational" data). Another type of ostensibly dyadic data
is so-called paired comparisons data depicting preferences or other forms of
dominance relations on members of pairs of stimuli. However, such data are
seldom utilized in multidimensional (as opposed to unidimensional) scaling.
We do not cover paired comparisons data in this chapter because we view
such data *not* as dyadic but as replicated monadic data (having $n - 2$ missing
data values within each replication); see Carroll (1980) for an overview.

III. SPATIAL DISTANCE MODELS (FOR ONE-MODE TWO-WAY DATA)

The most widely used MDS procedures are based on geometric *spatial
distance* models in which the data are assumed to relate in a simple and well-
defined manner to recovered *distances* in an underlying *spatial* representation.
If the data are interval scale, the function relating the data to distances is
generally assumed to be inhomogeneously linear—that is, linear with an
additive constant as well as a slope coefficient. Data of interval or stronger
(ratio, positive ratio, or absolute) scale are called *metric,* and the corresponding models and analyses are collectively called *metric MDS.* In the case of
ordinal data, the functional relationship is generally assumed to be monotonic—either monotonic nonincreasing (in the case of similarities) or monotonic nondecreasing (for dissimilarities). Ordinal data are often called *nonmetric* data, and the corresponding MDS models and analyses are also
referred to as *nonmetric MDS.* The distinction between metric and nonmetric approaches is based on the presence or absence of metric properties
in the data (not in the solution, which almost always has metric properties;
Holman, 1978, is an exception).

Following Kruskal's (1964b, 1965) innovative work in monotone regression (as the basic engine for fitting any of the ordinal models considered in

this review), first devised by Ayer, Brunk, Ewing, Reid, and Silverman (1955), there has been much activity in this area of statistics. In addition to Shepard's (1962a, 1962b) early approach and Guttman's (1968) later approach based on the rank image principle, alternative and related methods have been proposed by R. M. Johnson (1975), Ramsay (1977a), Srinivasan (1975), de Leeuw (1977b), de Leeuw and Heiser (1977, 1980, in developing their SMACOF algorithm, considered later), and Heiser (1988, 1991). McDonald (1976) provided a provocative comparison between the approaches of Kruskal (1964b) and Guttman (1968), and the two methods are subsumed as special cases of Young's (1975) general formulation. More recently, Winsberg and Ramsay (1980, 1983), Ramsay (1988), Winsberg and Carroll (1989a, 1989b), and Carroll and Winsberg (1986, 1995) have introduced the use of monotone splines as an alternative to the totally general monotone functions introduced by Kruskal, while other authors (e.g., Heiser, 1989b) have proposed using other not completely general monotonic functions, which, like monotone splines, can be constrained to be continuous and to have continuous derivatives, if desired. (Carroll and Winsberg, 1986, 1995, and Winsberg and Carroll, 1989a, 1989b, have used monotone splines in a somewhat unique manner—predicting data as monotone function(s) of distances, rather than vice versa as is typically the case in fully nonmetric approaches. As discussed later, these authors argue that this quasi-nonmetric approach avoids degeneracies that occur with fully nonmetric approaches.)

A. Unconstrained Symmetric Distance Models (for One-Mode Two-Way Data)

Although one of the more intensely developed areas in recent years has been the treatment of nonsymmetric data (discussed in detail later), most of the extant data relevant to MDS are symmetric, owing in part to the previous lack of models allowing for nonsymmetric data and the ongoing absence of readily available software for fitting such models. Therefore, we first consider recent developments in the scaling of symmetric data, that is, where the proximity of j to k is assumed identical to that obtained when the stimuli are considered in the reverse order.

The most widely assumed metric in MDS is the Euclidean, in which the distance between two points j and k is defined as

$$d_{jk} = \left[\sum_{r=1}^{R} (x_{jr} - x_{kr})^2 \right]^{1/2},$$

where x_{jr} and x_{kr} are the rth coordinates of points j and k, respectively, in an R-dimensional spatial representation. Virtually all two-way MDS procedures use either the Euclidean metric or the Minkowski ρ (or L_ρ) metric, which defines distances as

$$d_{jk} = \left[\sum_{r=1}^{R} |x_{jr} - x_{kr}|^\rho \right]^{1/\rho} \qquad (\rho \geq 1) \qquad (1)$$

and so includes Euclidean distance as a special case in which $\rho = 2$. (Because a variable that later will appear extensively in this chapter will be labeled "p," we are using the nontraditional ρ for Minkowski's exponent.)

B. Applications and Theoretical Investigations of the Euclidean and Minkowski ρ Metrics (for One-Mode Two-Way Symmetric Data)

1. Seriation

A psychologist who harbors proximity data suspected of being *uni*dimensional is caught between a Scylla of substantive tradition and a Charybdis of deficient software. Concretely, the custom in experimental psychology has been to discount unidimensionality and seek only higher-dimensional solutions. For example, Levelt, van de Geer, and Plomp (1966) developed an elaborate two-dimensional substantive interpretation of data later shown to be unidimensional by Shepard (1974) and Hubert and Arabie (1989, pp. 308–310). Similarly, Rodieck (1977) undermined a multidimensional theory of color vision proposed by Tansley and Boynton (1976, 1977).

But a data analyst willing to counter the tradition of overfitting immediately encountered a suspicion that gradient-based algorithms for nonmetric MDS could not reliably yield solutions faithful to an underlying unidimensional structure in a proximities matrix (cf. Shepard, 1974). De Leeuw and Heiser (1977) pointed out that this is in fact a *discrete* problem of analysis masquerading as a continuous one. Hubert and Arabie (1986, 1988) demonstrated analytically why gradient methods fail in the unidimensional case and then provided an alternative algorithm based on dynamic programming, guaranteed to find the globally optimal unidimensional solution. Pliner (1996) has provided a different algorithm that can handle much larger analyses. Also see related work by Hubert and Arabie (1994, 1995a); Hubert, Arabie, and Meulman (1997); Mirkin (1996); and Mirkin and Muchnik (1996, p. 319).

2. Algorithms

Kruskal's (1964a, 1964b) option to allow the user to specify $\rho \neq 2.0$ in Eq. (1) ostensibly made it much easier for experimenters to decide which Minkowski metric was most suitable for their data. But evidence (Arabie, 1973) and hearsay soon accumulated that, at least in the city-block case (where $\rho = 1$), the algorithm found suboptimal solutions, and there was a suspicion (e.g., Shepard, 1974) that the same conclusion was true for unidimensional solutions (no matter what value of ρ was used, because all are mathematically equivalent in the case of one dimension).

As noted earlier, de Leeuw and Heiser (1977) made the crucial observation that the unidimensional case of gradient-based two-way MDS is in fact a discrete problem, and Hubert and Arabie (1986) provided an appropriately discrete algorithm to solve it. Hubert and Arabie (1988) then analytically demonstrated that the same discreteness underlies the problem of city-block scaling in two dimensions and conjectured that the result is actually much more general. Hubert, Arabie, and Hesson-Mcinnis (1992) provided a combinatorial nonmetric algorithm for city-block scaling in two and three dimensions (for the two-way case) and demonstrated the highly inferior fits typically obtained when traditional gradient methods were used instead on the same data sets. Nonetheless, such misguided and clearly suboptimal analyses continue to appear in the experimental psychology literature (e.g, Ashby, Maddox, & Lee, 1994). Using a majorization technique, Heiser (1989a) provided a metric three-way city-block MDS algorithm. Neither the approach of Hubert and colleagues (1992) nor that of Heiser can guarantee a global optimum, but they generally do much better than their gradient counterparts.

In MDS the city-block metric has received more attention during the past two decades than any other non–Euclidean Minkowski metric (see Arabie, 1991, for a review), but more general algorithmic approaches are also available. For example, Okada and Imaizumi (1980b) provided a three-way nonmetric generalization of the INDSCAL model, as in Eq. (5) (where a monotone function is fitted to the right side of that equation). Groenen (1993; also see Groenen, Mathar, & Heiser, 1995) has extended the majorization approach for $1 \leq \rho \leq 2$ in Eq. (1). His impressive results have usually been limited to two-way metric MDS but appear to have considerably greater generality. There have been some attempts at fitting even more general non–Euclidean metrics such as Riemannian metrics (see the review in Carroll & Arabie, 1980, pp. 618–619), but none have demonstrated any lasting impact on the field. Although Indow (1983, pp. 234–235) demonstrated, with great difficulty, that a Riemannian metric with constant curvature fits certain visual data slightly better than a Euclidean metric, Indow concluded that the increase in goodness of fit was not sufficient to justify the effort involved and that, in practice, Euclidean representations accounted exceedingly well for the data he and his colleagues were considering. In later work, however, Indow (1995; see also Suppes, Krantz, Luce, & Tversky, 1989, pp. 131–153, for discussion) has shown that careful scrutiny of the geometric structure of these visual stimuli within different planes of a three-dimensional representation reveals that the curvature is dependent on the specific plane being considered. This discovery suggests that a more general Riemannian metric with nonconstant curvature may provide an even more appropriate representation of the geometry of visual space.

3. Algebraic and Geometric Foundations of MDS in Non-Euclidean Spaces

Confronted with the counterintuitive nature of non-Euclidean and/or high-dimensional spaces, psychologists have regularly culled (and occasionally contributed to) the vast mathematical literature on the topic, seeking results relevant to data analyses in such spaces (see, for example, Carroll & Wish, 1974a; Critchley & Fichet, 1994; de Leeuw & Heiser, 1982; Suppes et al., 1989, chaps. 12–14). Linkages to that literature are impeded by its typical and unrealistic assumptions of (1) a large or even infinite number of stimuli, (2) error-free data, and (3) indifference toward substantively insupportable high dimensionalities. The axiomatic literature in psychology does not always treat these problems satisfactorily, because it postulates systems requiring errorless measurement structures that in turn entail an infinite number of (actual or potential) stimuli. For example, testing of the axiom of segmental additivity for geometric representations of stimuli would be exceedingly difficult in a practical situation in which only a finite number of stimuli are available, and the proximity data are subject to measurement or other error of various types, because, in principle, one has to demonstrate that an intermediate stimulus exists precisely *between* each pair of stimuli so that the distances sum along the implicit line connecting the three. (As a further complication, these distances may be only monotonically related to the true proximities, whereas observed proximities are, at best, measured subject to measurement or experimental error.) Given a finite sample of "noisy" stimuli, it is highly unlikely that, even under the best of circumstances (e.g., errorless data entailing distances measured on a ratio scale), one would find a requisite third stimulus lying precisely, or even approximately, between each pair of stimuli. This instance is but one extreme case illustrating the general difficulty of testing scientific models, whether geometric or otherwise, with finite samples of data subject to measurement or experimental error. For example, it would be equally difficult, in principle, to test the hypothesis that noisy proximity data on a finite sample of stimuli are appropriately modeled via a Euclidean (or city-block, or other metric) spatial model in a specified number of dimensions. In practice, we are often forced to rely on the principle of parsimony (or "Occam's razor"), that is, to choose, among a large set of plausible models for such a set of data, the most parsimonious model, which appears to account adequately for a major portion of the variance (or other measure of variation) in the empirical proximity data. This approach hardly qualifies as a rigorous scientific test of such a geometric model; rather it is more appropriately characterized as a practical statistical rule of thumb for choosing the best among a large family of plausible models. The axiomatic approach, as exemplified by Suppes and colleagues (1989), focuses more on the precise testing of a very specific scientific model and constitutes an ideal toward which researchers in multi-dimensional scaling and other measurement models for the analysis of proximity data can, at the moment, only aspire. We hope that a stronger nexus can be formed between the axiomatic and the empirical camps in future work on such measurement models, effecting a compromise that allows development of practical measurement models for real-world data analysis in the psychological and other behavioral sciences while, at the same time, approaching more closely the ideal of testing such models with a sufficiently well-defined rigor.

IV. MODELS AND METHODS FOR PROXIMITY DATA: REPRESENTING INDIVIDUAL DIFFERENCES IN PERCEPTION AND COGNITION

The kind of differential attention to, or differential salience of, dimensions observed by Shepard (1964) illustrates a very important and pervasive source not only of intraindividual variation but also of interindividual differences in perception. Although people seem to perceive the world using nearly the same dimensions or perceptual variables, they evidently differ enormously with respect to the relative importance (perceptually, cognitively, or behaviorally) of these dimensions.

These differences in sensitivity or attention presumably result in part from genetic differences (for example, differences between color-blind and color-normal individuals) and in part from the individual's particular developmental history (witness the well-known but possibly exaggerated example of the Eskimos' presumably supersensitive perception of varieties, textures, and colors of snow and ice). Although some attentional shifts might result simply from instructional or contextual factors, studies by Cliff, Pennell, and Young (1966) have indicated that it is not so easy to manipulate saliences of dimensions. If a more behavioral measure of proximity were used, for example, one based on confusions in identification learning, the differential weighting could result at least in part from purely behavioral (as opposed to sensory or central) processes, such as differential gradients of response generalization. Nosofsky (1992) and Shepard (1987) have posited mechanisms underlying such individual differences.

A. Differential Attention or Salience of Dimensions: The INDSCAL Model

The INDSCAL (for *IN*dividual *D*ifferences *SCAL*ing) model (Carroll & Chang, 1970; Carroll, 1972; Carroll & Wish, 1974a, 1974b; Wish & Carroll,

1974; Arabie, Carroll, & DeSarbo, 1987) explicitly incorporates this notion of individual differences in the weights, or perceptual importances, of dimensions. The central assumption of the model is the definition of distances for different individuals. As with ordinary, or *two*-way, scaling, these recovered distances are assumed to relate in some simple way—for example, linearly or monotonically—to the input similarities or other proximities. INDSCAL, however, assumes a different set of distances for each subject. The distance between stimuli j and k for subject i, $d_{jk}^{(i)}$, is related to the dimensions of a group (or common) *stimulus* space by the equation

$$ d_{jk}^{(i)} = \left[\sum_{r=1}^{R} w_{ir}(x_{jr} - x_{kr})^2 \right]^{1/2}, \tag{2} $$

where R is the dimensionality of the stimulus space, x_{jr} is the coordinate of stimulus j on the rth dimension of the group stimulus space, and w_{ir} is the weight (indicating salience or perceptual importance) of the rth dimension for the ith subject. This equation is simply a weighted generalization of the Euclidean distance formula.

Another way of expressing the same model is provided by the following equations. We first define coordinates of what might be called a "private perceptual space" for subject i by the equation

$$ y_{jr}^{(i)} \equiv (w_{ir}^{1/2})x_{jr} \tag{3} $$

and then calculate ordinary Euclidean distances according to these idiosyncratic or private spaces, as defined in

$$ d_{jk}^{(i)} \equiv \left[\sum_{r=1}^{R} (y_{jr}^{(i)} - y_{kr}^{(i)})^2 \right]^{1/2} = \left[\sum_{r=1}^{R} w_{ir}(x_{jr} - x_{kr})^2 \right]^{1/2}. \tag{4} $$

[The expression on the right was derived by substituting the definition of $y_{jr}^{(i)}$ in Eq. (3) into the middle expression in Eq. (4), defining $d_{jk}^{(i)}$.] Thus the weighted distance formulation is equivalent to one in which each dimension is simply *rescaled* by the square root of the corresponding weight. This rescaling can be regarded as equivalent to turning the "gain" up or down, thus relatively increasing or decreasing the sensitivity of the total system to changes along the various dimensions.[1]

[1] Tucker and Messick's (1963) "points of view" model, which assumes that subjects form several subgroups, each of which has its own private space, or point of view, can be incorporated within the scope of INDSCAL. At the extreme, the group stimulus space includes the union of all dimensions represented in any of the points of view, and an individual would have positive weights for all dimensions corresponding to the point of view with which he or she is identified and zero weights on all dimensions from each of the other points of view. For an updated treatment of points of view, see Meulman and Verboon (1993).

The input data for INDSCAL, as with other methods of three-way MDS, constitute a matrix of proximity (or antiproximity) data, the general entry of which is $\delta_{jk}^{(i)}$, the dissimilarity (antiproximity) of stimuli j and k for subject i. If there are n stimuli and I subjects, this three-way matrix will be $n \times n \times I$. The ith two-way "slice" through the third way of the matrix results in an ordinary two-way $n \times n$ matrix of dissimilarities for the ith subject. The output in the case of INDSCAL (although not necessarily for other three-way scaling methods) consists of two matrices. The first is an $n \times R$ matrix, $\mathbf{X} \equiv (x_{jr})$ of stimulus coordinates, the second an $I \times R$ matrix $\mathbf{W} \equiv (w_{ir})$ of subject weights. The input and output arrays for INDSCAL are illustrated in Figure 1. The coordinates described in the two matrices $\mathbf{X}$ and $\mathbf{W}$ can be plotted to produce two disjoint spaces, both with dimensionality R, and which we have called, respectively, the group stimulus space and the subject space. These are illustrated in Figure 2 for a purely hypothetical data set, as are two of these subjects' idiosyncratic or private perceptual spaces. Geometrically they are derived by stretching or shrinking each dimension by applying a rescaling factor to the rth dimension, proportional to $(w_{ir})^{1/2}$. The rth weight, w_{ir}, for subject i can be derived from the subject space by simply projecting subject i's point onto the rth coordinate axis.

Quite different patterns of similarity/dissimilarity judgments are predicted in Figure 2 for Subjects 2, 3, and 4. Subject 3 (who weights the dimensions equally and so would have a private space that looks just like the group stimulus space) presumably judges Stimulus A to be equally similar to B and D, because these two distances are equal in that subject's private space. In contrast, Subject 2 would judge Stimulus A to be more similar to D than to B (because A is closer to D), and Subject 4 would judge Stimulus A to be more similar to B than to D. There would, of course, be many other differences in the judgments of these three subjects, even though all three are basing their judgments on exactly the same dimensions.

Subjects 1 and 5, who are both one-dimensional, represent two extreme cases in the sense that each gives nonzero weight to only one of the two dimensions. Geometrically it is as though (if these were the only dimensions and the model fitted the data perfectly) Subject 1 has simply projected the stimulus points onto the Dimension 1 axis so that Stimuli A, D, and G, for example, project into the same point and so are seen by this subject as identical. Subject 5 exhibits the opposite pattern and presumably attends only to Dimension 2; this subject would see Stimuli A, B, and C as identical. Thus, as a special case, some subjects can have private perceptual spaces of lower dimensionality than that of the group stimulus space.

Distance from the origin is also meaningful in this subject space. Subjects who are on the same ray issuing from the origin but at different distances from it would have the same pattern of distances and therefore of *predicted* similarities/dissimilarities. They would have the same private space, in fact,

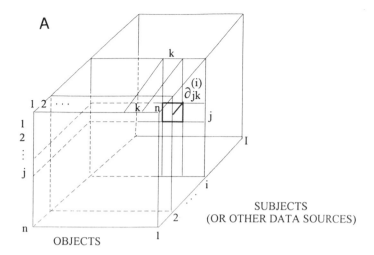

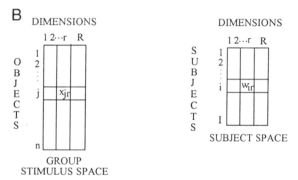

FIGURE 1   A schematic representation of input for (A) and output from (B) INDSCAL. Input consists of $I(\geq2)$ $n \times n$ square symmetric data matrices (or half-matrices) one for each of I subjects (or other data sources), $d_{jk}^{(i)}$ is the dissimilarity of stimuli (or other objects) j and k for subject (or other data source) i. This set of I square matrices can be thought of as defining the rectangular solid, or three-way array, of data depicted at top in the figure. (This is the form of the input for other three-way scaling methods also.) The output from INDSCAL consists of two matrices, an $n \times R$ matrix of coordinates of the n stimuli (objects) on R coordinate axes (or dimensions) and an $I \times R$ matrix of weights of I subjects for the R dimensions. These matrices define coordinates of the *group stimulus space* and the *subject space,* respectively. Both of them can be plotted graphically, as in Figure 2, and a private space for each subject can be constructed, as shown there, by applying the square roots of the subject weights to the stimulus dimensions, as in Equation 3. Note: "Objects" need not be "stimuli." "Subjects" may come from other data sources.

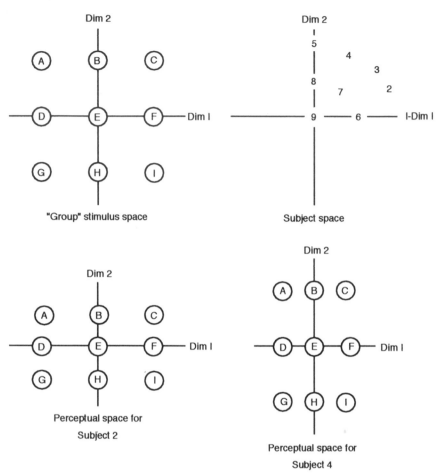

FIGURE 2   Illustration of the Carroll-Chang INDSCAL model for individual differences in multidimensional scaling. Weights (plotted in subject space) are applied to group stimulus space to produce individual perceptual spaces for Subjects 2 and 4, shown at the bottom of the figure. (For purposes of illustration, the dimensions are multiplied by the weights themselves, rather than by their square roots as is more technically correct.)

except for an overall scale factor. The main difference between such subjects is that this same private space and pattern of predicted judgments account for less of the variance in the (scalar products computed from the) data for subjects who are closer to the origin. Thus, although Subjects 3 and 7 in Figure 2 would have the same private space (the one corresponding to the group stimulus space), these two dimensions would account for more variance in the (hypothetical) matrix of Subject 3 than of Subject 7. Subject 9, being precisely at the origin (indicating zero weight on both dimensions), would be completely out of this space; that is, none of that subject's data could be accounted for by these two dimensions. The residual variance may be accounted for by other dimensions not extracted in the present analysis or simply by unreliability, or error variance, in the particular subject's responses.

The square of the distance from the origin is closely analogous to the concept of communality in factor analysis. In fact, the square of that distance is approximately proportional to variance accounted for. Although only an approximation, it is generally a good one and is perfect if the coordinate values on dimensions are uncorrelated. The cosine of the angle between subject points (treated as vectors issuing from the origin) approximately equals the correlation between distances (or, more properly, between scalar products) in their private perceptual spaces. Distances between these points are also meaningful—they approximate profile distances between reconstructed distances (or, again more properly, scalar products) from the respective private perceptual spaces in which the overall scale *is* included. We therefore reject arguments made by Takane et al. (1977), MacCallum (1977), and others that lengths (or distances from the origin) of these subject weight vectors are not meaningful. We believe the lengths (as well as directions) of these subject vectors *are* meaningful and interpretable, *even when the data are matrix conditional rather than unconditional;* in the latter case, Takane et al. (1977), MacCallum (1977), and others have argued these lengths have *no* meaning; thus those authors normalize subject weight vectors to *unit* lengths, contrary to the practice in the INDSCAL/SINDSCAL method of fitting the INDSCAL model. The lengths, in fact, often contain information that is quite critical in distinguishing among well-defined groups of subjects. Wish and Carroll (1974) presented one very good example, entailing perception of the rhythm and accent of English words or phrases by various groups of subjects. Most compelling, in this respect, is the fact that native and nonnative speakers of English were distinguished most clearly by the subject vectors—those for the former group having systematically greater length (terminating farther from the origin) than those for the latter group—implying that *all* dimensions characterizing the rhythm and accent (or stress patterns) of English words were much more salient to native than to nonnative speakers of English.[2]

---

[2] In statistical terms, the small set of "common" dimensions in the group space accounted for more variance in scalar products computed from the data of the native English speakers—the square of the length of the subject vector approximating the proportion of variance accounted for—whereas the nonnative English speakers apparently were largely accounted for by other variables not emerging from this analysis, such as unique linguistic dimensions (which might emerge if higher dimensional solutions were sought) more appropriate to their individual native languages or greater systematic or random errors stemming from an imperfect assimilation of English stress patterns.

One of the more important aspects of INDSCAL is the fact that its dimensions are unique, that is, not subject to the rotational indeterminacy characteristic of most two-way MDS procedures involving the Euclidean metric. INDSCAL recovered dimensions are generally defined uniquely up to what is called an "extended permutation," defined later. In the psychological model, the dimensions are supposed to correspond to fundamental perceptual or other processes whose strengths, sensitivities, or importances vary among individuals. Mathematically, the family of transformations induced by allowing differential weighting (which corresponds geometrically to stretching or compressing the space in directions parallel to coordinate axes) will differ for the various orientations of coordinate axes—that is, the family of admissible transformations is *not* rotationally invariant, as can be seen graphically by considering what kinds of private spaces might be generated in the case illustrated in Figure 2 if one imagines that the coordinate system of the group stimulus space were rotated, say, 45°. Instead of the square lattice transforming into various rectangular lattices, it would transform into various rhombuses, or diamond-shaped lattices. Rotating the coordinate system by something other than 45° would generate other families of parallelograms, generally a unique family for each different angle of rotation. These families are genuinely different, because they allow different admissible *sets* of distances among the objects or stimuli. Statistically speaking, a rotation (not corresponding to a reflection, permutation, or extended permutation) of the axes generally degrades the solution in the sense that the variance accounted for in fitting the model decreases after such a rotation, even if optimal weights are recomputed for the rotated coordinate system.

This dimensional uniqueness property is important because it obviates the need, in most cases, to rotate the coordinate system to find an interpretable solution. If one adopts the psychological model underlying INDSCAL, then these statistically unique dimensions should be psychologically unique as well. Indeed, practical experience has shown that the dimensions obtained directly from INDSCAL are usually interpretable without rotation (even when there is little reason to believe the underlying model's assumptions). Kruskal (1976) has provided a formal proof of this uniqueness property of INDSCAL (and of a wider class of three-way models of which it is a special case). Technically, the INDSCAL stimulus space is identified, under very general conditions, up to a permutation and reflection of coordinate axes, followed by a rescaling of all dimensions via a diagonal scaling matrix (with scale factors that may be either positive or negative). The rescaling transformation is generally resolved via the usual INDSCAL normalization convention, in which stimulus dimensions are scaled so as to have unit sum of squared (and zero mean) coordinate values; this way only the *signs* of the scale factors are nonidentified. In practice INDSCAL dimensions are identified up to a permutation and possible reflection of axes—what we call an *extended permutation*. In fact, even the permutation indeterminacy generally is resolved by ordering axes based on a variance accounted for (averaged over all subjects) criterion.

Space limitations preclude us from giving substantive illustrations of fitting the INDSCAL model (or any of the others covered in this chapter). Two protracted analyses are given in Arabie et al. (1987, pp. 12–16, 25–33).

Because of the particular normalization conventions used in the "standard" formulation described earlier, distances in the group stimulus space are not immediately interpretable but must instead be compared to the interstimulus distances of a hypothetical (or real) subject who weights all dimensions equally.

As is so often the case, the (weighted) Euclidean metric in Eq. (4) was chosen for mathematical tractability, conceptual simplicity, and historical precedence. In many stimulus domains (typically with nonanalyzable or unitary perceptual stimuli, or even with more conceptual analyzable stimuli when dimensionality becomes large) the Euclidean metric seems to fit quite well (Shepard, 1964). Furthermore, there is considerable evidence that methods based on it are robust, so that even if the basic metric is non-Euclidean, multidimensional scaling in a Euclidean space may recover the configuration adequately. We regard this particular choice of basic metric, then, as primarily heuristic and pragmatic, although on many grounds it does seem to be the best single choice we could have made. It is, however, within the spirit of the INDSCAL model to assume a much wider class of weighted metrics, and Okada and Imaizumi (1980) have provided such a generalization, along with gradient-based software to fit the model. Also, as argued in the discussion of two-way MDS models, among certain non-Euclidean metrics, the L_1 or *city-block* metric in particular appears to be more appropriate for the more cognitive or conceptual stimulus domains involving analyzable stimuli in which the dimensions are psychologically separable. For this reason we consider an obvious generalization entailing a weighted Minkowski ρ or power metric of the form

$$d_{jk}^{(i)} = \left[\sum_{r=1}^{R} w_{ir} |x_{jr} - x_{kr}|^{\rho} \right]^{1/\rho} \qquad \rho \geq 1 . \tag{5}$$

According to the rescaling of dimensions, the private space for this generalized L_{ρ} model would be defined as

$$y_{jr}^{(i)} = w_{ir}^{1/\rho} x_{jr} . \tag{6}$$

It is evident that computing ordinary Minkowski ρ metric in this rescaled space, now involving the ρth root of the weights, is equivalent to the weighted Minkowski ρ metric in Eq. (5). See Carroll and Wish (1974b, pp. 412–428) for a technical discussion concerning metrics in MDS.

B. The IDIOSCAL Model and Some Special Cases

The most general in this Euclidean class of models for MDS is what has been called the IDIOSCAL model, standing for *I*ndividual *D*ifferences *i*n *O*rientation *SCAL*ing (Carroll & Chang, 1970, 1972; Carroll & Wish, 1974a). The intuitive appeal of the IDIOSCAL model is demonstrated by the number of times it, or special cases of it, have been invented or reinvented (e.g., "PARAFAC-2" by Harshman, 1972a, 1972b; "Three-Mode Scaling," by Tucker, 1972, and other procedures proposed by Bloxom, 1978, and by Ramsay, 1981, incorporating this general Euclidean metric or some variant of it); indeed, sometimes it has been simultaneously reinvented *and* renamed (e.g., "the General Euclidean Model" by Young, 1984a). In the IDIOSCAL model, the recovered distance $d_{jk}^{(i)}$ between objects j and k for the ith source of data is given by

$$ d_{jk}^{(i)} = \sqrt{\sum_r^R \sum_{r'}^R (x_{jr} - x_{kr})c_{rr'}^{(i)}(x_{jr'} - x_{kr'})}, \qquad (7) $$

where r and r' are indices of the R dimensions in the object space and (separately) the source space. This model differs from the INDSCAL model in Eq. (2) by the inclusion of matrix $\mathbf{C}^{(i)} \equiv (c_{rr'}^{(i)})$, which is an $R \times R$ symmetric positive definite or semidefinite matrix, instead of matrix $\mathbf{W}_i$, which is diagonal, with the weights w_{ir} on the diagonals. If each $\mathbf{C}_i$ is constrained to be such a diagonal matrix[3] $\mathbf{W}_i$ with nonnegative entries, then the diagonal entries in the $\mathbf{C}_i$ matrices are interpretable as source weights in the INDSCAL formulation of distance, and the INDSCAL model follows as a special case. This result can be seen by noting that if in Eq. (7), $c_{rr'}^{(i)} = w_{ir}$ when $r = r'$, and 0 when $r \neq r'$, then the terms $(x_{jr} - x_{kr})c_{rr'}^{(i)}(x_{jr'} - x_{kr'})$ drop out if $r \neq r'$ and become $w_{ir}(x_{jr} - x_{kr})^2$ for $r = r'$, thus producing the INDSCAL model of Equation (2). In the general IDIOSCAL model, C_i provides a rotation of the object space to a new (or IDIOsyncratic) coordinate system for source i, followed by differential weighting of the dimensions of this rotated coordinate system. In the Carroll and Chang (1970, pp. 305–310; 1972) approach to interpreting the model, this rotation will be orthogonal. The alternative approach suggested independently by Tucker (1972) and by Harshman (1972a, 1972b) entails no such rotation but assumes differing correlations (or, more geometrically, cosines of angles) between the same dimensions of the object space over different sources. (Further details on the two interpretations of the C_i matrices are given by Carroll and Wish, 1974a, and in the source articles; also see de Leeuw and Heiser, 1982.)

---

[3] We note here that the matrix $\mathbf{W}_i$ is an $R \times R$ diagonal matrix for the ith subject whereas, previously, the symbol $\mathbf{W}$ has been used to demote the $I \times R$ matrix of weights for the I subjects on the R dimensions (so that the ith row of $\mathbf{W}$ contains the diagonal entries of $\mathbf{W}_i$).

In vector and matrix form, this model can be written as

$$d_{jk}^{(i)} \equiv [(\mathbf{x}_j - \mathbf{x}_k)\mathbf{C}_i(\mathbf{x}_j - \mathbf{x}_k)']^{\frac{1}{2}}, \tag{8}$$

where $\mathbf{C}_i \equiv (c_{rr'}^{(i)})$ is an $R \times R$ matrix. The matrix $\mathbf{C}_i$ is generally assumed to be *symmetric and positive definite or semidefinite*. This metric is exactly what we would obtain if we defined a private perceptual space for individual i by a general linear transformation defined as

$$y_{jr}^{(i)} = \sum_{s=1}^{R} x_{js} q_{sr}^{(i)}, \tag{9}$$

which in vector-matrix notation is

$$\mathbf{y}_j^{(i)} = \mathbf{x}_j \mathbf{Q}_i, \tag{10}$$

and we then computed ordinary Euclidean distances in these private spaces. Matrix $\mathbf{C}_i$ in Eq. (8) will, in this case, simply be

$$\mathbf{C}_i = \mathbf{Q}_i \mathbf{Q}_i', \tag{11}$$

because

$$[d_{jk}^{(i)}]^2 \equiv (\gamma_j^{(i)} - \gamma_k^{(i)})(\gamma_j^{(i)} - \gamma_k^{(i)})'$$

$$= (\mathbf{x}_j - \mathbf{x}_k)\mathbf{Q}_i\mathbf{Q}_i'(\mathbf{x}_j - \mathbf{x}_k)', \tag{12}$$

which is equivalent to Eq. (8) with $\mathbf{C}_i$ as defined in Eq. (11).

Another closely related interpretation is provided by decomposing the (symmetric, positive definite) matrix $\mathbf{C}_i$ into a product of the form

$$\mathbf{C}_i = \mathbf{T}_i\boldsymbol{\beta}_i\mathbf{T}_i', \tag{13}$$

with $\mathbf{T}_i$ orthogonal and $\boldsymbol{\beta}_i$ diagonal. (This decomposition, based on the singular value decomposition and closely related to principal components analysis, can always be effected. If the $\mathbf{C}_i$'s are positive definite or semi-definite, the diagonal entries of $\boldsymbol{\beta}_i$ will be nonnegative.)

Then we can define

$$\boldsymbol{\Phi}_i = \mathbf{T}_i\boldsymbol{\beta}_i^{\frac{1}{2}}, \tag{14}$$

and clearly

$$\mathbf{C}_i = \boldsymbol{\Phi}_i\boldsymbol{\Phi}_i'. \tag{15}$$

Actually, $\boldsymbol{\Phi}_i$ provides just one possible definition of the matrix $\mathbf{Q}_i$ in Eq. (10). Given any *orthogonal* matrix $\boldsymbol{\Gamma}$, we may define

$$\mathbf{Q}_i = \boldsymbol{\Phi}_i\boldsymbol{\Gamma}, \tag{16}$$

and it will turn out that

$$\mathbf{Q}_i\mathbf{Q}_i' = \mathbf{\Phi}_i\mathbf{\Gamma}\mathbf{\Gamma}'\mathbf{\Phi}_i' = \mathbf{\Phi}_i\mathbf{\Phi}_i' = \mathbf{C}_i. \qquad (17)$$

Any $\mathbf{Q}_i$ satisfying Eq. (11) can be shown to be of the form stipulated in Eq. (16), but the decomposition of $\mathbf{C}_i$ defined in Eqs. (13)–(14) or (15) (with Γ as the identity matrix) leads to a particularly convenient geometric interpretation. $\mathbf{T}_i$ can be viewed as defining an orthogonal rotation of the reference frame, and thus of the Individual Differences In Orientation (of the reference system) referred to earlier. The diagonal entries of β_i can be interpreted as weights analogous to the w_{ir}'s in the INDSCAL model that are now applied to this IDIOsyncratic reference frame. The considerable intuitive appeal of the IDIOSCAL model notwithstanding, it has empirically yielded disappointing results in general. A major practical drawback of using the IDIOSCAL model is the potential need to provide a separate figure (or set of them) for the spatial representation of each source.

Young's (1984a) approach to fitting what he called the "General Euclidean Model," specifically in the form of his "Principal Directions Scaling," can be viewed as a special case of IDIOSCAL in which the $\mathbf{C}_i$ matrix for each subject is positive semidefinite, with rank R_i less than R (generally $R_i =$ 2). Young assumes each subject projects the IDIOSCAL-type stimulus space defined by $\mathbf{X}$ into an R_i-dimensional subspace so that in this model $\mathbf{Y}_i = \mathbf{X}\mathbf{\Phi}_i$ where $\mathbf{\Phi}_i$ is an $R \times R_i$ projection matrix (so $\mathbf{\Phi}_i'\mathbf{\Phi}_i = \mathbf{I}_R$; that is $\mathbf{\Phi}_i$ is an *orthonormal section* projecting orthogonally from $\mathbf{X}$ into an R_i-dimensional subspace, $\mathbf{Y}_i$). In this case $\mathbf{C}_i = \mathbf{\Phi}_i\mathbf{\Phi}_i'$ will be positive semidefinite and is of rank R_i. The main advantage of this particular special case of IDIOSCAL appears to be that it enables the graphic representation of each subject's private perceptual space in (usually the same) smaller dimensionality—typically two. It is not clear, however, that this model has a convincing rationale *beyond* this practical graphical advantage (see Easterling, 1987, for a successful analysis).

Other models closely related to IDIOSCAL are discussed at length in Arabie et al. (1987, pp. 44–53), but one final three-way model for proximities that bears mentioning generalizes the IDIOSCAL model by adding additional parameters associated with the stimuli (or other objects): the PINDIS (Procrustean INdividual DIfferences Scaling) model and method of Lingoes and Borg (1978). PINDIS adds to the parameters of the IDIOSCAL model a set of *weights* for stimuli, so the model for an individual, in the scalar product domain, is of the form

$$\mathbf{B}_i \cong \mathbf{A}_i\mathbf{X}\mathbf{C}_i\mathbf{X}'\mathbf{A}_i,$$

where $\mathbf{B}_i$ is an $n \times n$ matrix of *scalar products* among the n stimuli for subject/source i, whereas $\mathbf{A}_i$ is an $n \times n$ diagonal matrix of rescaling weights for stimuli. (Although we shall not demonstrate the result here, the IDIOSCAL model in the scalar product domain is of this form, but with $\mathbf{A}_i \equiv \mathbf{I}$ for all i, so that, in effect, the pre- and postmultiplication by $\mathbf{A}_i$ is omitted.) The interpretation of these additional parameters is difficult to justify on psychological grounds. Even more parameters defining different translations of the coordinates of each individual or other source of data, i, are allowed in the general formulation of PINDIS in its scalar product form. Geometrically, the rescaling parameters for stimuli have the effect of moving each stimulus closer to or farther from the centroid in the stimulus space; they do this by multiplying the coordinates by the weight associated with that object. It is hard to envision a psychological mechanism to account for such nonuniform dilations. Moreover, Commandeur (1991, p. 8–9) provides a trenchant and compelling algorithmic critique of PINDIS. Thus, we pursue this model and method no further.

C. Available Software for Two- and Three-Way MDS

1. The Two-Way Case

KYST2A (Kruskal, Young, & Seery, 1973) is the dominant software for two-way MDS. The acronym stands for "Kruskal, Young, Shepard, and Torgerson," and the software synthesizes some of the best parts of various approaches to nonmetric (two-way) MDS that these four contributors have proposed. These algorithms are described in great detail in the previously cited references, so they will not be further described here. The important distinctions are the following:

    1. KYST2A minimizes a criterion Kruskal calls STRESS. The standard version of STRESS, often called STRESSFORM1, is defined as

$$\text{STRESSFORM1} = \left(\frac{\Sigma_{jk}(\hat{d}_{jk} - d_{jk})^2}{\Sigma_{jk}d_{jk}^2} \right)^{1/2},$$

$$\text{where } d_{jk} = \left[\sum_{r=1}^{R} (x_{jr} - x_{kr})^2 \right]^{1/2}$$

(i.e., the Euclidean distance in the recovered configuration has coordiantes x_{jr}, for $j = 1, 2 \ldots n$, $r = 1, 2 = R$) and $\hat{d}_{jk}$ is, depending on the user's specification, a linear, monotonic, or other function of the input similarity, s_{jk}, or dissimilarity, δ_{jk}, of j and k (a decreasing or nonincreasing function in the former case and an increasing or nondecreasing function in the latter). STRESSFORM2 differs only in the normalization factor in the denominator, which is $\Sigma_{jk}(d_{jk} - \bar{d})^2$, where $\bar{d}$ is the mean of the d_{jk}'s. All sums (and the mean if STRESSFORM2 is used) are over only the values of j and k for which data are given. Generally, the diagonals (s_{jj} or δ_{jj}) or self-similarities/dissimilarities are undefined and therefore are treated as missing data (so that sums and means *exclude* those diagonal values as well).

2. KYST2A allows both metric and nonmetric fitting (and, in fact, includes options for other than either linear or general monotonic functions transforming data into estimated distances; the most important special case allows polynomial functions up to the fourth degree—but such generalized linear functionals are *not* necessarily monotonic). KYST2A allows still other options (see Kruskal et al., 1977, for details) for analyzing three-way data, but fitting only two-way or nonindividual differences models to all subjects or other sources, as well as for performing what Coombs (1964) and others call "multidimensional unfolding" (to be discussed later).

3. KYST2A allows fitting of metrics other than Euclidean—specifically the "Minkowski ρ," or L_ρ, metric of the form given in Eq. (1). In practice, the only two values of ρ that are used at all frequently are $\rho = 2$, the Euclidean case, and, quite inappropriately, $\rho = 1$, the city-block or Manhattan metric case (see Arabie, 1991, for a review). As noted earlier, however, Hubert and Arabie (1988; Hubert, Arabie, & Hesson-Mcinnis, 1992) demonstrated that the problem of fitting an L_1 or city-block metric is more appropriately approached via combinatorial optimization.[4]

Another available algorithm for two-way nonmetric MDS is Heiser and de Leeuw's (1979) SMACOF (*S*caling by *MA*jorizing a *CO*mplicated *F*unction) procedure, based on a *majorization* algorithm, (see de Leeuw and Heiser, 1980, for details), which we will not discuss here except to say that SMACOF optimizes a fit measure essentially equivalent to Kruskal's STRESS. Majorization is an important algorithmic approach deserving much more coverage than space allows. Important references include de Leeuw (1988), Groenen (1993), Groenen, Mathar, and Heiser (1995), Heiser (1991, 1995), Kiers (1990), Kiers and ten Berge (1992), and Meulman (1992).

Wilkinson's (1994) SYSTAT allows many options and considerable flexibility for two-way MDS.

Two other valuable algorithmic developments in two-way (*and* three-way) MDS are the ALSCAL (Takane et al., 1977) procedure and Ramsay's (1978) MULTISCALE. ALSCAL (for *A*lternating *L*east squares *SCAL*ing) differs from previous two-way MDS algorithms in such ways as (1) its loss function, (2) the numerical technique of alternating least squares (ALS) used earlier by Carroll and Chang (1970) and originally devised by Wold (1966; also see de Leeuw 1977a, and de Leeuw & Heiser 1977), and (3) its allowance

---

[4] For other combinatorial approaches to MDS, see Hubert and Schultz (1976), Poole (1990), and Waller, Lykken, and Tellegen (1995).

for nominal scale (or categorical) as well as interval and ordinal scale data. ALSCAL and MULTISCALE are also applicable to two-mode three-way data, and a three-way version of SMACOF is under development. All three programs will be considered again under spatial distance models for such data.

MULTISCALE (*MULTI*dimensional *SCAL[E]*ing), Ramsay's (1977b, 1978a, 1978b, 1980, 1981, 1982a, 1983) maximum-likelihood-based procedure, although strictly a metric approach, has statistical properties that make it potentially much more powerful as both an exploratory and (particularly) a confirmatory data analytic tool. MULTISCALE, as required by the maximum likelihood approach, makes very explicit assumptions regarding distribution of errors and the relationship of the parameters of this distribution to the parameters defining the underlying spatial representation. One such assumption is that the dissimilarity values δ_{jk} are log normally distributed over replications, but alternative distributional assumptions are also allowed.

The major dividend from Ramsay's (1978) strong assumptions is that the approach enables statistical tests of significance that include, for example, assessment of the correct dimensionality appropriate to the data (via an asymptotically valid chi square test of significance for three-way data treated as *replications*) while fitting a two-way *model*. Another advantage is the resulting confidence regions for gauging the relative precision of stimulus coordinates in the spatial representation. The chief disadvantage is the very strong assumptions entailed for the asymptotic chi squares or confidence regions to be valid. Not least of these is the frequent assumption of ratio scale dissimilarity judgments. In addition, there is the assumption of a specific distribution (log normal, normal, or others with specified parameters) and of statistical independence of the dissimilarity judgments.

2. The Three-Way Case

The most widely used approach to fitting the three-way INDSCAL model is the method implemented in the computer program SINDSCAL (for Symmetric *INDSCAL,* written and documented by Pruzansky, 1975), which updated the older INDSCAL program of Chang and Carroll (1969a, 1989).

SINDSCAL begins with some simple preprocessing stages, initially derived by Torgerson and his colleagues (Torgerson, 1952, 1958) for the two-way case (also see Gower, 1966, and Keller, 1962). The first step, based on the assumption that the initial data are defined on at most an *interval* scale (so that the origin of the scale is arbitrary, leading to the similarities/dissimilarities being related to distances by an inhomogeneous linear function), involves solving the so-called additive constant problem. Then a further transformation of the resulting one-mode two-way matrix of estimated distances to one of estimated *scalar products* is effected. (See Torgerson, 1952, 1958, or Arabie et al., 1987, pp. 71–77, for further details on these pre-processing steps.)

In the two-way classical metric MDS, as described by Torgerson (1952, 1958) and others, the derived (estimated) scalar product matrix is thus simply subjected to a singular value decomposition (SVD), which is mathematically equivalent to a principal components analysis of a correlation or covariance matrix, to obtain an estimate of the $n \times R$ matrix $\mathbf{X}$ of coordinates of the n stimuli in R dimensions, $\hat{\mathbf{X}}$, by minimizing what has been called the STRAIN criterion:

$$\text{STRAIN} = \|\mathbf{B} - \hat{\mathbf{X}}\hat{\mathbf{X}}'\|^2 = \sum_{j}^{n} \sum_{k}^{n} (b_{jk} - \hat{b}_{jk})^2, \text{ where } \hat{b}_{jk} = \sum_{r=1}^{R} \hat{x}_{jr}\hat{x}_{kr}.$$

This approach yields a least-squares measure of fit between derived scalar products $\mathbf{B} = (b_{jk})$ and estimated scalar products $\hat{\mathbf{B}} = (\hat{b}_{jk})$. (In some cases, e.g., when fitting nonmetrically, it might be necessary to normalize STRAIN by, say, dividing by the sum of squared entries in the $\mathbf{B}$ matrix; but for the current metric case, and with the preprocessing described earlier, we may use this raw unnormalized form without loss of generality.)

In the three-way case, preprocessing entails these same steps for each similarity or dissimilarity matrix, $\mathbf{S}_i$ or Δ_i, respectively, converting an initial three-way array $\mathbf{S}$ (of similarities) or Δ (of dissimilarities) into a three-way array $\mathbf{B}$ of derived scalar products, where each two-way slice, $\mathbf{B}_i$, is a symmetric matrix of derived (estimated) scalar products for the ith subject or other source of data. CANDECOMP, as applied in this case, optimizes a three-way generalization of the STRAIN criterion discussed earlier, namely,

$$\text{STRAIN} = \sum_{i} \sum_{j} \sum_{k} (b_{jk}^{(i)} - \hat{b}_{jk}^{(i)})^2 = \sum_{i} \text{STRAIN}_i,$$

where STRAIN$_i$ is STRAIN defined for the ith subject or source and where, if the usual matrix normalization option is used, the constraint is imposed that

$$\sum_{i} \sum_{i} (b_{jk}^{(i)})^2 = 1.0, \quad \text{for all } i,$$

$$\hat{b}_{jk}^{(i)} = \sum_{r=1}^{R} \hat{w}_{ij}\hat{x}_{jr}\hat{x}_{kr} \tag{18}$$

is a generalized (weighted) scalar product, and parameters $\hat{w}_{ij}$ and $\hat{x}_{jr}$ are (estimates of) the same parameters (without the "hats") as those entering the weighted Euclidean distance defined for INDSCAL in Eq. (2), as demonstrated in Carroll and Chang (1970) and elsewhere (e.g., Appendix B, Arabie et al., 1987). The INDSCAL/SINDSCAL approach to metric three-way MDS then applies a three-way generalization of the SVD, called (three-way) CANDECOMP (for *CAN*onical *DECOMP*osition of *N*-way arrays) to array **B,** to produce estimates (minimizing the least-squares STRAIN criterion) $\hat{\mathbf{X}}$ and $\hat{\mathbf{W}},$ respectively, of the group stimulus space and the subject weight space. For details of this CANDECOMP procedure and its application to the estimation of parameters of the INDSCAL model, see Carroll and Chang (1970) or Arabie et al. (1987).

Probably the most widely used approach for *nonmetric* fitting of the INDSCAL model is ALSCAL (Takane et al., 1977), which fits the model by optimizing a criterion called SSTRESS, analogous to Kruskal's STRESS, except that it is a normalized least-squares criterion of fit between *squared* distances (in the fitted configuration) and monotonically transformed data (called "disparities" by Takane et al.).

For each subject or data source, SSTRESS is defined analogously to Kruskal's STRESSFORM1, except that, again, *squared* Euclidean distances replace first-power distances. Another difference, irrelevant to the solutions obtained but definitely important vis-à-vis interpretation of values of SSTRESS, is that the square root of the normalized least-squares loss function defines STRESS, whereas SSTRESS is the *untransformed* normalized least-squares criterion of fit. Thus, to the extent that SSTRESS is comparable to STRESS(FORM1) at all, SSTRESS should be compared with squared STRESS. In the three-way case, overall SSTRESS is essentially a (possibly weighted) sum of $SSTRESS_i$, where $SSTRESS_i$ is the contribution to the SSTRESS measure from subject/source i. As in the case of KYST2A, ALSCAL allows either monotonic or linear transformations of the data, in nonmetric or metric versions, respectively. See Young and Lewyckyj (1981) for a description of the most recent version of the ALSCAL program.

In a recently published Monte Carlo study, Weinberg and Menil (1993) compared recovery of structure of SINDSCAL to that by ALSCAL, under conditions in which both metric and nonmetric analyses were appropriate. Because SINDSCAL allows only metric analyses, even if only ordinal scale data are given, one would expect ALSCAL to be superior in recovering configurations under such ordinal scale conditions because ALSCAL allows a more appropriate nonmetric analysis whereas SINDSCAL necessarily treats the data (inappropriately) as interval scale. It is not clear which of the two should yield better recovery of configurations in the case of interval scale data, because both can allow (appropriate) metric analyses in this case.

Surprisingly, the Weinberg and Menil (1993) Monte Carlo study found that SINDSCAL was superior in recovery both of the stimulus configuration and of subject weights, in the case both of interval and of ordinal scale data (with some fairly severely nonlinear monotonic transformations of the data). The Weinberg and Menil findings may confirm some preliminary results reported by Hahn, Widaman, and MacCallum (1978), at least in the case of mildly nonlinear ordinal data. The explanation of this apparent anomaly appears to rest in the SSTRESS loss function optimized by AL-SCAL, probably because SSTRESS measures the fit of transformed data to squared rather than first power distances; the squaring evidently tends to put too much weight on the large distances. A STRESS-based three-way approach might do better in this respect, but unfortunately no such methodology exists at present. Willem Heiser (personal communication) has indicated that he and his colleagues expect eventually to have a three-way version of SMACOF available, which should fill this void.

Version 6 of SYSTAT (Wilkinson, 1994) included, for the first time, software for nonmetric fitting of the INDSCAL model. It is too early to evaluate SYSTAT's performance in this particular domain, but we note that the example given in the documentation (Wilkinson, 1994, p. 140) erroneously suggests that both the subjects and the stimuli are positioned in the same space, rather than in disjoint spaces having a common dimensionality.

Another widely available program for both two- and three-way MDS is Ramsay's (1978, 1982a) MULTISCALE, briefly discussed earlier, which generally assumes *ratio* scale data, and fits via a maximum likelihood criterion, assuming either additive normal error or a lognormal error process. Although a power transformation is allowed, Ramsay's approach generally entails only metric options and in fact makes even stronger metric assumptions than other metric approaches in that it generally requires ratio scale, not the weaker form of interval scale proximity data generally assumed in metric MDS. The main advantage of Ramsay's approach is that it does utilize a maximum likelihood criterion of fit and thereby allows many of the inferential statistics associated with that approach, notably the asymptotic chi square tests that can be used to assess the statistical significance of various effects. (This advantage is undermined somewhat by the fact that the additional parameters associated with subjects or other sources of data in the three-way case can be regarded as *nuisance parameters,* whose number increases with the number of subjects/sources, thus violating one of the key assumptions on which the asymptotic behavior of the asymptotic chi square is based. Ramsay, 1980, however, provided some Monte Carlo results that led to adjustments in the degrees of freedom for the associated statistical tests that correct, at least in part, for this problem.)

Ramsay (1982b) and Winsberg and Ramsay (1984) also introduced a quasi-nonmetric option in MULTISCALE, in which the proximity data are transformed via a monotone spline function or functions in the case of matrix conditional three-way data, which, incidentally, can include an inhomogeneous *linear* function as a special case (thus allowing for more general metric fitting). But this option is not available in most versions of MUL-TISCALE. It is important, however, to note that this quasi-nonmetric option in MULTISCALE is quite different from the one introduced by Winsberg and Carroll (1989a, 1989b) and Carroll and Winsberg (1986, 1995) in their extended Euclidean two-way MDS. It also differs from the extended INDSCAL (or EXSCAL) approach, described next.

D. The Extended Euclidean Model and Extended INDSCAL

Winsberg and Carroll (1989a, 1989b) and Carroll and Winsberg (1986, 1995) proposed an extension of the simple Euclidean model for two-way proximities and of the INDSCAL model for three-way proximities for which the continuous dimensions of common space are supplemented by a set of specific dimensions, also continuous, but relevant only to individual stimuli or other objects. Here we state the extended model for distances for the three-way, extended INDSCAL case because the two-way extended model is a special case,

$$ d_{jk}^{(i)} = \left[\sum_{r=1}^{R} w_{ir}(x_{jr} - x_{kr})^2 + \sigma_{ij} + \sigma_{ik} \right]^{1/2}, \tag{19} $$

where σ_{ij}, called the "specificity" of stimulus j for subject i, is the sum of squares of coordinates of specific dimensions for subject i on stimulus j. Note that we cannot tell in this model how many specific dimensions pertain to a given subject-stimulus combination, only their total effect on (squared) distances in the form of this specificity.

Winsberg and Carroll have adduced both theoretical and strong empirical evidence for the validity of this extended (ordinary or weighted) Euclidean model. They discussed the topic in a series of papers on maximum likelihood methods for either metric or quasi-nonmetric fitting of both the two- and three-way versions of this extended model. As noted in considerable detail in Carroll and Winsberg (1995), there are theoretical reasons why the now classical approach to nonmetric analysis pioneered by Kruskal (1964a, 1964b)—in which a totally general monotonic function (or functions in the three-way case) of the data is sought optimizing either of two forms of Kruskal's STRESS measure (or a large class of other STRESS-like fit measures)—cannot be used for nonmetric fitting of these extended models. The basis of this assertion is the existence of theoretical degeneracies or quasi-degeneracies (solutions yielding apparent perfect or near-perfect fit, but retaining essentially none or very little of the information in the original data) that can always be obtained via such a fully nonmetric fitting. Instead, Winsberg and Carroll (1989a, 1989b) and Carroll and Winsberg (1986, 1995) use a form of quasi-nonmetric fitting in which very (though not totally) general monotonic functions constrained to be continuous and to have continuous first and possibly second derivatives are applied to the distances derived from the model, rather than to the data. Winsberg and Carroll use monotone splines, which can be constrained to have any desired degree of continuity of function and derivatives—although other classes of functions possessing these desiderata could also be utilized. For complete details, see Carroll and Winsberg (1995). Also, see the discussion of the primordial model presented later in this chapter.

Carroll (1988, 1992) has also demonstrated that similar degeneracies would affect attempts at fully nonmetric fitting of discrete models (e.g., ADCLUS/INDCLUS, or tree structures), to be discussed later, and that such quasi-nonmetric fitting would be appropriate here as well. In fact, we argue that even in more well-behaved cases, such as fitting the ordinary two-way Euclidean or three-way INDSCAL model, quasi-degeneracies tend to occur in the case of fully nonmetric fitting, so that such quasi-nonmetric fitting may be more appropriate even in standard MDS. The essence of such quasi-nonmetric fitting is twofold: (1) the monotone function is applied on the model side (as seems more appropriate statistically, in any case), not to the data, and (2) a less than totally general class of monotone functions, such as monotone splines, is utilized so that continuity of the function and at least some of its derivatives can be guaranteed.

Concerning the extended simple and weighted Euclidean models assumed in this work, such extensions, entailing assumptions of dimensions specific to particular stimuli in addition to common dimensions, can be made for such other generalized Euclidean models as IDIOSCAL, three-mode scaling, and PARAFAC-2, or even to non-Euclidean models such as those based on city-block or other L_p metrics.

E. Discrete and Hybrid Models for Proximities

In addition to the continuous spatial models so closely associated with traditional MDS, nonspatial models (which are still geometric in the generic sense of being distance models) entailing discrete, rather than continuous, parameters can also be used profitably for representing proximity data (see, e.g., Gordon, 1996, and other chapters in Arabie, Hubert, and De Soete, 1996; S. C. Johnson, 1967, Hartigan, 1967; Kruskal and Carroll, 1969; Carroll and Chang, 1973; Carroll, 1976; Carroll and Pruzansky, 1975, 1980, 1983, 1986; De Soete & Carroll, 1996; Shepard and Arabie, 1979; Carroll and Arabie, 1980; Arabie et al., 1987). As already argued, such discrete (or "feature") representations may be more appropriate than continuous spatial models for conceptual or cognitive stimuli.

A large number of these discrete models are special cases of a model originally formulated by Shepard and Arabie (1979; see also Shepard, 1974) called ADCLUS, for *AD*ditive *CLUS*tering, and generalized to the three-way, individual differences case by Carroll and Arabie (1983) in the form of the INDCLUS (*IN*dividual *Differences CLUS*tering) model. We can state both models in the single equation

$$s_{jk}^{(i)} \cong \hat{s}_{jk}^{(i)} = \sum_{r=1}^{R} w_{ir} p_{jr} p_{kr} + g_i, \tag{20}$$

where $s_{jk}^{(i)} \equiv$ proximity (similarity or other measure of closeness) of stimuli (or other objects) j and k for subject (or other source of data) i (j, $k = 1, 2 \ldots n$; $i = 1, 2 \ldots I$). Note that $\hat{s}_{jk}^{(i)}$ is the model estimate of $s_{jk}^{(i)}$, and "$\cong$" means "approximately equals" except for error terms that will not be further specified here. In addition, $p_{jr} \equiv$ a binary (0, 1) valued variable defining membership ($p_{jr} = 1$) or nonmembership ($p_{jr} = 0$) of stimulus (or other object) j in class or cluster r ($j = 1, 2 \ldots n$; $r = 1, 2 \ldots R$); $w_{ir} \equiv$ (a continuous nonnegative) importance weight of class or cluster r for proximity judgments (or other measurements) for subject (or other source of data) i; $g_i \equiv$ additive constant for subject (source) i, or, alternatively, that subject's weight for the universal class or cluster of which all the stimuli are members; and $R \equiv$ number of classes or clusters (excluding the universal one).

Equation (20) gives the basic form of the three-way INDCLUS model; ADCLUS is simply the two-way special case in which $I = 1$, so if desired we may drop the "i" subscript.

It might be noted immediately that the ADCLUS/INDCLUS model as stated in Eq. (20) is algebraically of the same form as the scalar product form of the INDSCAL model given in Eq. (18). We simply substitute $b_{jk}^{(i)} = s_{jk}^{(i)}$ and $x_{jr}^{(i)} = p_{jr}^{(i)}$ while we set $g_i = 0$, for all i, and because we are concerned here with models themselves, we may, conceptually, remove the "hats" from Equation (18), of course! In the INDSCAL approach the b's, or (approximate) scalar products, can be interpreted as proximity measures derived from directly judged similarities or dissimilarities.

From the purely algebraic perspective, the ADCLUS/INDCLUS models can be viewed as scalar product models for proximities ($s_{jk}^{(i)}$), but with dimensions' coordinates ($x_{jr} \equiv p_{jr}$) constrained to be binary (0 − 1) rather than continuous. Thus, this particular discrete model for proximities can be viewed simply as a special case of the scalar product form of the continuous, spatial model discussed earlier, and most typically associated with MDS, albeit with the simple and straightforward constraint that the dimensions' coordinates must be discrete (specifically, binary).

An interpretation of the ADCLUS/INDCLUS model was provided by Shepard and Arabie (1979) using what is sometimes called a "common features" model, which can be viewed as a special case of Tversky's (1977) features of similarity model. Each of the R classes or clusters can potentially be identified with what Shepard (1974) called an attribute or what Tversky (1977) later dubbed a feature, which each stimulus or other object either has or does not have—a kind of all-or-none dimension, that is. The similarity (proximity) of two objects is incremented for subject (source) i by an amount defined by the weight (w_{ir}) associated with that particular subject/attribute combination if both objects have the attribute, but it is not incremented if either one fails to possess it. This model defines the similarity of a pair of objects as a *weighted* count of common attributes of those two objects—an intuitively quite compelling model. As with INDSCAL, in the three-way, individual differences case, the subjects or objects are differentiated by the profile of (cluster) weights characterizing the individual subjects.

Arabie and Carroll (1980) devised the MAPCLUS algorithm, the most widely used method for fitting the two-way ADCLUS special case of this model. Published data analyses using MAPCLUS include examples from psychoacoustics (Arabie & Carroll, 1980), marketing (Arabie, Carroll, DeSarbo, & Wind, 1981), and sociometry (Arabie & Carroll, 1989); other references are given in Arabie and Hubert (1996, p. 14).

A more widely used method for the discrete representation of similarity data is hierarchical clustering (Gordon, 1996; Hartigan, 1967; Johnson, 1967; Lance & Williams, 1967), which yields a family of clusters such that either two distinct clusters are disjoint or one includes the other as a proper subset. In the usual representation, the objects being clustered appear as terminal nodes of an inverted tree (known as a *dendrogram*), clusters correspond to internal nodes, and the reconstructed distance between two objects is the height of the internal node constituting their meeting point. The model implies that, given two disjoint clusters, all recovered distances between objects in the same cluster are smaller than distances between objects in the two different clusters, and that for any given pair of clusters these between-cluster distances are equal; all triangles are therefore acute isosceles (isosceles with the two larger distances equal). This property is equivalent to the ultrametric inequality, and the tree representation is called an *ultrametric tree*. The ultrametric inequality (u.i.) states that, for ultrametric distances h,

$$h_{jl} \leq \max(h_{jk}, h_{kl}) \qquad \text{for all } j, k, l. \tag{21}$$

Given a set of distances satisfying the u.i., the associated tree can easily be constructed and numerical height values defined (i.e., the numerical ultrametric values arising during the iterative clustering procedure and traditionally presented in the margins of the dendrogram beside their respective levels). An infinite family of ultrametric distance matrices is associated with the topology of a given rooted tree, but if the height values are specified, the particular ultrametric is correspondingly and uniquely specified. Those values must satisfy a partial order based on the hierarchy defined by the tree; namely, the height of an ancestral node corresponding to a superordinate class or cluster must be greater than or equal to the height of a descendant node representing a subordinate class/cluster (a proper subset of the former). This statement assumes the corresponding one-mode two-way proximity data are keyed as dissimilarities.

As an aside, we note that Holman's (1972) classic result relating (two-way one-mode) ultrametric and (two-way one-mode) Euclidean data engendered a highly productive tradition of formal investigations of the interconnections; see Arabie and Hubert (1996, p. 23–24) for an overview.

Although the two representations just discussed, ADCLUS (as fitted by the MAPCLUS algorithm in this case) and an ultrametric tree structure representation (as fitted by one of the standard hierarchical clustering approaches or other procedures to be discussed later for least-squares tree structure fitting), may at first blush seem to be quite distinct, it turns out that the latter is in fact a special case of the former. First, if we define a dissimilarity measure corresponding to a single linear transformation of $s_{jk}^{(i)}$—namely,

$$\delta_{jk}^{(i)} = t_i - s_{jk}^{(i)} \qquad (j \neq k), \tag{22}$$

where t_i is a large positive constant—the $\delta_{jk}^{(i)}$ can be so defined as to satisfy the triangle inequality, and thus the metric axioms, because the diagonal elements are undefined, and symmetry of $\mathbf{S}_i \equiv (s_{jk}^{(i)})$ is assumed by definition.

If we furthermore assume that the clusters for the ADCLUS representation are hierarchically nested, so that every pair of clusters is either disjoint or one is a proper subset of the other, and define $\hat{\delta}_{jk}^{(i)}$ as $t_i - \hat{s}_{jk}^{(i)}$, where $\hat{s}_{jk}^{(i)}$ is as defined in Eq. (20), then $\hat{\delta}_{jk}^{(i)}$ (for fixed i) will satisfy the ultrametric inequality and correspond to an ultrametric defined on a hierarchical tree. Thus, ultrametric trees, this very important class of discrete geometric models so closely associated with hierarchical clustering, can be viewed as a special case of the ADCLUS/INDCLUS model, after this simple linear transformation from the similarity to this dissimilarity form of the model. As will be evident shortly, a wider class of discrete models can also be viewed as special cases of ADCLUS/INDCLUS. For extended analyses using the INDCLUS model, see Arabie, Carroll, and DeSarbo (1987, chap. 6), as well as references cited there and in Arabie and Hubert (1996, p. 14).

F. Common versus Distinctive Feature Models

As already discussed, ADCLUS and INDCLUS are common feature models, in which similarity is defined by a (weighted) count of features shared by the two objects (a "feature" corresponding to a cluster of which an object is a member). (We can, as previously shown, translate this model into one for dissimilarities by simply subtracting the similarities for a given subject or source from a larger constant.) A different feature model for *dissimilarities* is a *distinctive features model,* which depicts dissimilarities using a weighted count of features *not* found in common; (i.e., distinctive features possessed by one or the other object but not by both). As Sattath and Tversky (1987) have shown, common and distinctive feature models are closely related. We discuss this relation in somewhat different terms from those offered by Sattath and Tversky.

One way to write a distinctive features model for three-way dissimilarities data, $\delta_{jk}^{(i)}$, is

$$\delta_{jk}^{(i)} \cong \hat{\delta}_{jk}^{(i)*} = \sum_{r=1}^{R} w_{ir}^{*} |p_{jr} - p_{kr}|, \tag{23}$$

where w_{ir}^{*} is a weight, and p_{jr} and R are as defined earlier. Therefore, Eq. (23) defines a weighted count of distinctive features. It is also a weighted city-block distance model with binary "dimensions" defined by the p's. Because the p's are binary (0, 1) variables, it might be noted that

$$|p_{jr} - p_{kr}| \equiv (p_{jr} - p_{kr})^2 \tag{24}$$

(in fact, $|p_{jr} - p_{kr}| = |p_{jr} - p_{kr}|^\rho$ for any $\rho > 0$). Therefore it is equally valid to write

$$\hat{\delta}_{jk}^{(i)*} = \sum_{r=1}^{R} w_{ir}^{*}(p_{jr} - p_{kr})^2 \tag{25}$$

[or $\hat{\delta}_{jk}^{(i)} = \sum_{r=1}^{R} w_{ir}^{*} |p_{jr} - p_{kr}|^\rho$, for $\rho > 0$], so that $\hat{\delta}^*$ can with equal validity be viewed as a weighted city-block, or L_1, metric defined on the (discrete) space whose coordinates are defined by $\mathbf{P} = (p_{jr})$ or as a weighted *squared* Euclidean metric defined on the same space (or, indeed, as any weighted L_ρ or Minkowski ρ metric, raised to the ρth power).

We now utilize the definition of $\hat{\delta}^*$ in Eq. (25), as squared Euclidean distances, for mathematical convenience. Expanding

$$\hat{\delta}_{jk}^{(i)*} = \sum_{r} w_{ir}^{*}(p_{jr} - p_{kr})^2,$$

$$= \sum_{r} w_{ir}^{*}(p_{jr}^2 - 2p_{jr}p_{kr} + p_{kr}^2),$$

$$= \sum_r w^*_{ir} p^2_{jr} + \sum_r w^*_{ir} p^2_{kr} - 2 \sum_r w^*_{ir} p_{jr} p_{kr},$$

$$= \sum_r w^*_{ir} p_{jr} + \sum_r w^*_{ir} p_{kr} - 2 \sum_r w^*_{ir} p_{jr} p_{kr},$$

$$= u^*_{ij} + u^*_{ik} - 2 \sum_r w^*_{ir} p_{jr} p_{kr}, \tag{26}$$

(since $p^2 \equiv p$, given p binary), or

$$\hat{\delta}^{(i)*}_{jk} = \hat{\delta}^{(i)}_{jk} + u_{ij} + u_{ik}, \tag{27}$$

where $u_{ij} = u^*_{ij} - (t_i - g_i)/2 = \Sigma_r w^*_{ir} p_{jr} - t^*_i$, $w_{ir} = 2w^*_{ir}$, and $t^*_i = (t_i - g_i)/2$. As stated earlier, $\hat{\delta}^i_{jk} = t_i - \hat{s}^{(i)}_{jk}$, with t_i as defined in Eq. (22), whereas $\hat{s}^{(i)}_{jk}$ and g_i are as defined in Eq. (20).

Thus, the distinctive feature model can be viewed as a common features model supplemented by uniqueness u_{ij} and u_{ik} that have the same mathematical form as the specificities that transform the common space INDSCAL-model into the extended INDSCAL model discussed earlier. It should be stressed that the substantive interpretation of uniqueness in the present case differs greatly from the specificities in the extended Euclidean model/INDSCAL case. In the latter case, specificities are related to dimensions specific to the stimuli j and k, respectively, whereas in the distinctive features model, the uniqueness values pertain to a weighted count of *all* features that the stimulus possesses and can be viewed in the same spirit as Nosofsky's (1991, p. 98) stimulus bias.

As Sattath and Tversky (1987) have shown, the distinctive features model can always be formulated as a special case of the common features model, however, so that the uniquenesses are not (explicitly) necessary. This conversion is accomplished by supplementing the features in the common features model by a set of additional complementary common features—one complementary feature corresponding to each stimulus or other object. A complementary feature for a particular object is a feature possessed by all objects *except* that object, such as a class or cluster containing all $n - 1$ objects *excluding* that one. (Weights for the common features, including these complementary features, and the additive constants, must be adjusted appropriately.)

In the case of hierarchically nested features (classes or cultures), a distinctive features model will lead to the family of path length or additive trees, discussed later. Other discrete structures such as multiple trees (either ultrametric or path length/additive) are also special cases of either common or distinctive features models, whereas distinctive features models are special cases of common features models, as we noted earlier, so that all of a very large class of discrete models to be discussed later are special cases of the ADCLUS/INDCLUS form of common features model.

Although any distinctive features model can be formulated as a common features model with a large set of features (including complementary ones), the more parsimonious form (covering both common and distinctive features models) stated for similarity data is

$$s_{jk}^{(i)} \cong \hat{s}_{jk}^{(i)} = \sum_{r=1}^{R} w_{ir} p_{jr} p_{kr} - u_{ij} - u_{ik}, \tag{28}$$

where for a common features case $u_{ij} = u_{ik} = -g_i/2$ for all i, j, k.

G. The Primordial Model

We can now formulate a general model that includes the INDSCAL model, the two-way (Euclidean) MDS model, and this large class of discrete models, all as special cases. This *primordial model* will be the linchpin for much of the remaining discussion in Section IV and can be written as

$$s_{jk}^{(i)} \cong \hat{s}_{jk}^{(i)} = M_i \left(\sum_{r=1}^{R} w_{ir} x_{jr} x_{kr} - u_{ij} - u_{ik} \right), \tag{29}$$

where M_i is a monotone (nondecreasing) function. In the case of the INDSCAL model $u_{ij} = .5 \sum_{r=1}^{R} w_{ir} x_{jr}^2$, so that the expression in parentheses on the right side of Eq. (29) equals $-.5(d_{jk}^{(i)})^2$, where, as before,

$$d_{jk}^{(i)} = \left[\sum_{r=1}^{R} w_{ir} (x_{jr} - x_{kr})^2 \right]^{1/2}.$$

In the case of the extended INDSCAL (or EXSCAL) model,

$$u_{ij} = 1/2 \left[\sum_{r} w_{ir} x_{jr}^2 + \sigma_{ij} \right] \tag{30}$$

where σ_{ij} denotes the (i, j)th specificity as defined in that model. Here M_i is a linear function only if similarities are assumed to be (inversely) linearly related to squared (weighted) Euclidean distances. (The two-way special cases of both of these should be obvious.) If the M_i's are assumed to be monotonic (but nonlinear), we recommend the quasi-nonmetric approach, for reasons discussed earlier in the case of fitting the extended INDSCAL (i.e., EXSCAL), or the extended Euclidean model in the two-way case.

As we have already shown, if $x_{jr} = p_{jr}$ (i.e., if the coordinates of the R dimensions are constrained to binary $(0, 1)$ values), then the model becomes the common or distinctive features model and thus has all the other discrete models discussed earlier as special cases. Thus, Eq. (29) can be viewed as the primordial model, of which all others are descendants! It might be noted in passing that since, as Joly and Le Calvé (submitted) have shown, a city-block, or L_1, metric can always be written as the square of a Euclidean metric—although in a space, generally, of very high dimensionality—the L_1 metric models—including the three-way (weighted) version discussed earlier—can also, at least in principle, be included as special cases of this primordial scalar product model. In fact, although this primordial model has the form of a scalar product plus some additive constants, it is easy to show that it can in fact be formulated as an overall scalar product model that requires two additional dimensions to accommodate two additional scalar product terms with special constraints. Although most MDS models are based on distances between points, not scalar products among vectors, we have shown here that such distance models can easily be converted to this general scalar product form, at least in the case of Euclidean and city-block-based models. Some have argued, however, that the processes involved in computing, say, Euclidean distances are very "unnatural" (taking differences between coordinates of two stimuli in an internal spatial representation of the stimuli, squaring this difference, and then summing these squares of coordinate differences over all dimensions; this is possibly followed by a final step of taking the square root, at least in the case of ratio scale distance judgments). It is hard to imagine such operations being wired into the human neural apparatus. In contrast, calculating scalar products (simply multiplying the coordinates for the stimulus pair and summing these products) seems much more plausible as an innate neurological/psychological process. In fact, the general semantic model offered by Landauer and Dumais (1997) assumes the representation of words in a high-dimensional semantic space (about 300 dimensions for their data). Those authors argue that such scalar products can be computed by a very simple neural network. (The model assumes that the association of a given word with unordered strings of other words is based on finding the word in this semantic space closest to the centroid of the words in that string, in the sense of maximizing the cosine of the angle between the word and that centroid. The cosine of an angle in multidimensional space is, in turn, a simple function of the scalar products of vectors.)

Now if we just take the one additional evolutionary step of allowing some x's to be continuous and others discrete (binary, in particular), we immediately generate the hybrid models originally discussed by Carroll (1976; De Soete & Carroll, 1996; also see Hubert & Arabie, 1995a) as an even more general family of models in which continuous spatial structure is *combined* with discrete, nonspatial structure. We discuss some of the discrete and hybrid models that emerge as such special cases of the very broad, general model stated in Eq. (29). See Carroll and Chaturvedi (1995) for a general approach, called CANDCLUS, that allows fitting of a large class of discrete and hybrid models, including the (two- and three-way) common features models discussed previously, to many types of data that are two-way, three-way, and higher-way via either least-squares or a *least absolute deviations* (LAD) criterion. Chaturvedi and Carroll (1994) apply this approach to provide a more efficient algorithm, called SINDCLUS, for fitting the ADCLUS/INDCLUS models via an OLS criterion, whereas Chaturvedi and Carroll (1997) have extended this work to fit with a LAD criterion in a procedure called LADCLUS.

A tree with path-length metric (Carroll & Chang, 1973), or simply a path-length tree, is synonymous with what Sattath and Tversky (1977) called an "additive similarity tree." Unlike ultrametric trees, which have a natural root node, a path-length tree has no unique root. It is not necessary to think of it as being vertically organized into a hierarchy. (In fact, such a tree, for n objects, is consistent with $2n - 2$ *different* hierarchies, corresponding to rooting the tree along any one of its $2n - 2$ distinct branches.) Underlying the structure of a path-length tree is the *four-point condition* that must be satisfied by the estimated path-length distances. This condition, which is a relaxation of the ultrametric inequality, is satisfied by a set of distances (π_{jk}) if and only if, for all quadruples of points j, k, l, and m,

$$\pi_{jk} + \pi_{lm} \geq \pi_{jl} + \pi_{km} \geq \pi_{kl} + \pi_{jm} \text{ implies that}$$
$$\pi_{jk} + \pi_{lm} = \pi_{jl} + \pi_{km}. \tag{31}$$

That is, the two largest sums of pairs of distances involving the subscripts j, k, l, and m must be equal. See Carroll (1976), Carroll and Pruzansky (1980), or De Soete and Carroll (1996) for a discussion of the rationale for this four-point condition and its relationship to the u.i.

H. Fitting Least-Squares Trees by Mathematical Programming

1. Fitting a Single Ultrametric Tree

Carroll and Pruzansky (1975, 1980) pioneered a mathematical programming approach to fitting ultrametric trees to proximity data via a least-squares criterion. This strategy basically attempts to find a least-squares fit of a distance matrix constrained to satisfy the u.i. by use of a penalty function, which measures the degree of violation of that inequality, as defined in Eq. (21), to a given matrix of dissimilarities. This approach can be extended easily but indirectly to the fitting of path-length trees satisfying the four-point condition, as described later. A more direct procedure entailing a generalization of the Carroll and Pruzansky penalty function approach was proposed and implemented by De Soete (1983) using a penalty function to enforce the four-point condition.

2. Fitting Multiple Tree Structures Using Mathematical Programming Combined with Alternating Least Squares

Many sets of proximity data are not well represented by either simple or hierarchical clusterings. A general model already discussed is the ADCLUS/INDCLUS model, in which proximity data are assumed to arise from discrete attributes that define overlapping but nonhierarchically organized sets. It may happen, however, that the attributes can be organized into two or more separate hierarchies, each of which could represent an organized family of subordinate and superordinate concepts. For example, in the case of animal names one might imagine one hierarchical conceptual scheme based on the phylogenetic scale and another based on function (or relationship to humankind) involving such categories as domesticated versus wild. The former could be classified as pets, work animals, and animals raised for food; pets could be further broken down into house versus outdoor pets, and so on.

This case requires a method to allow fitting *multiple* tree structures to data—a multidimensional generalization of the single tree structure, as it were. We now describe a procedure for fitting such multiple tree structures to a single two-way data matrix of *dis*similarities.

Consider fitting Δ, the two-way data matrix, with a mixture of hierarchical tree structures (HTSs), each satisfying the u.i. In particular, we want to approximate Δ as a sum

$$\Delta \cong \mathbf{H}_1 + \mathbf{H}_2 + \ldots \mathbf{H}_q, \tag{32}$$

where each $\mathbf{H}$ matrix satisfies the u.i. We use an overall *alternating least-squares* (ALS) strategy to fit the mixture of tree structures. In particular, given current fixed estimates of all $\mathbf{H}$ matrices except $\mathbf{H}_q$, we may define

$$\Delta_q^* = \Delta - \sum_{q' \neq q} \hat{\mathbf{H}}q' \tag{33}$$

and use the mathematical programming procedure discussed earlier to fit a least-squares estimate, $\hat{\mathbf{H}}_q$, of $\mathbf{H}_q$, to Δ_q^*.

3. Fitting a Single Path-Length Tree

J. S. Farris (personal communication), as Hartigan (1975, p. 162) noted, has shown that it is possible to convert a path-length tree into an ultrametric tree by a simple operation, given the distances from the root node to each of the nodes corresponding to objects. Letting π_{jO} represent the distance from the jth object to the root node O and π_{jk} represent the path-length distance from j to k, it can be shown that

$$h_{jk} = \pi_{jk} - \pi_{jO} - \pi_{kO}$$

(34)

satisfies the u.i. The h_{jk} will not, however, necessarily satisfy the positivity condition for distances. But both the u.i. *and* positivity will be satisfied by adding a sufficiently large constant Π by defining h_{jk} as

$$h_{jk} = \pi_{jk} - \pi_{jO} - \pi_{kO} + \Pi \equiv \pi_{jk} - u_j - u_k \quad (j \neq k) \tag{35}$$

where $u_j = \pi_{jO} - \Pi/2$. An equivalent statement is that

$$\left. \begin{array}{l} \pi_{jk} = h_{jk} + u_j + u_k \quad (j \neq k) \\ \text{or } \Pi = H + U \end{array} \right\}, \tag{36}$$

which states that the path-length distance matrix Π is decomposable into a distance matrix H that satisfies the u.i. plus an additive residual (which we shall simply call U) where $u_{jk} = u_j + u_k$ for $j \neq k$, and the diagonals of U are undefined, or zero if defined. The decomposition can be defined so that the u_j's are nonnegative, in which case U is the distance matrix for a very special path-length tree, usually called a "bush" by numerical taxonomists or a "star" by graph theorists, and is a path-length tree with only one nonterminal (or internal) node. (We use the more standard graph-theoretic term *star* henceforth.) The nonnegative constant u_j is, then, just the length of the branch connecting terminal node j to that single internal node, and the distance between any two distinct terminal nodes, j and k, of the star tree equals $u_j + u_k$. Thus we may summarize Eq. (36) verbally as

A path-length tree = An ultrametric tree + A star tree.

It should be noted that this decomposition is not unique. Many different ways exist for decomposing a fixed path-length tree (PLT) into such a sum. In the case of multiple PLTs, because the sum of Q star trees is itself just a single star tree, we have the extended theorem that

$$\sum_q^Q \Pi_q = \sum_q^Q H_q + U \tag{37}$$

or, in words,

A sum of PLTs = A sum of ultrametric trees + One star tree.

It should also be noted that both single and multiple path-length or additive trees are also, by quite straightforward inference, special cases of the primordial model in Eq. (29).

We may thus fit mixtures of path-length trees by simply adding to the ALS strategy defined earlier an additional step in which the constants u_j, defining the single star component, are estimated via least-squares procedures. Details of this and of the procedure implementing estimation of the u_j's can be found in Carroll and Pruzansky (1975, 1980). A more computationally efficient, but heuristic (and therefore more likely to be suboptimal), approach to fitting multiple trees was also devised by Carroll and Pruzansky (1986).

I. Hybrid Models: Fitting Mixtures of Tree and Dimensional Structures

Degerman (1970) proposed the first formal hybrid model combining elements of continuous dimensional structure and of discrete class-like structure, using a rotational scheme for high-dimensional MDS solutions, and seeking subspaces with class-like rather than continuous variation. Since then, much has been said but little done about such mixed or hybrid models.

By further generalizing the multiple tree structure model that Carroll and Pruzansky proposed, it is possible to formulate a hybrid model that would include a continuous spatial component in addition to the tree structure components. To return to our hypothetical animal name example, we might postulate, in addition to the two hierarchical structures already mentioned, continuous dimensions of the type best captured in spatial models. In the case of animals, obvious dimensions might include size, ferocity, or color (which itself is multidimensional).

Carroll and Pruzansky (1975, 1980), in fact, generalized the multiple tree structure model just discussed in precisely this direction. The model can be formally expressed as

$$\Delta \cong D_1 + D_2 + \ldots + D_Q + D^2_{E_R}, \tag{38}$$

where D_1 through D_Q are distance matrices arising from tree structures based on either ultrametric or path-length trees, and $D^2_{E_R}$ is a matrix of squared distances arising from an R-dimensional Euclidean space. (The reason for adding squared rather than first-power Euclidean distances is a technical one largely having to do with mathematical tractability and consistency with the general primordial model in Eq. (29).) In effect, to estimate this additional continuous component, we simply add an extra phase to our alternating least-squares algorithm that derives conditional least-squares estimates of these components. Carroll and Pruzansky (1975, 1980) provided details of this additional step. The same reference also provides an illustrative data analysis with a protracted substantive interpretation. Hubert and Arabie (1995b) and Hubert, Arabie, and Meulman (1997) have provided yet another approach to fitting multiple tree structures.

J. Other Models for Two- and Three-Way Proximities

Another direction, already explored to some extent, involves generalization of the discrete models discussed to the case of nonsymmetric proximity data, such as two-mode matrices of proximities or nonsymmetric one-mode proximities (e.g., confusability measures) between pairs of objects from the same set. More extensive discussions of the analysis of nonsymmetric proximities are found in the next section, but we mention some particularly interesting discrete models and methods here. DeSarbo (1982) has devised a model/method called GENNCLUS, for example, which generalizes the ADCLUS/MAPCLUS approach to nonsymmetric proximity data. Furnas (1980) and De Soete, DeSarbo, Furnas, and Carroll (1984a, 1984b) have done the same for tree structures, in a general approach often called "tree 'unfolding."

Yet another fruitfully explored direction involves three-way extensions of a number of these models, which provide discrete analogues to the INDSCAL generalization (Carroll & Chang, 1970) of two-way multi-dimensional scaling. One such three-way generalization has already been discussed, namely the Carroll and Arabie (1983) INDCLUS generalization of ADCLUS/MAPCLUS to the three-way case—including an application of INDCLUS to some of the Rosenberg and Kim (1975) kinship data (where the third way was defined by those authors' various experimental conditions). In the case of tree structures and multiple tree structures, an obvious direction for individual differences generalization is one in which different individuals are assumed to base their judgments on the same family of trees, but are allowed to have different node heights (in the case of ultrametric trees) or branch lengths (for path-length or additive trees)—that is, single or multiple trees having identical topological structures, but different continuous parameters for each individual or other data source. Carroll, Clark, and DeSarbo (1984) implemented an approach called INDTREES, for fitting just such a model to three-way proximity data. In the hybrid case, a set of continuous stimulus dimensions defining a group stimulus space, together with individual subject weights similar to those assumed in IND-SCAL, could also be introduced.

We emphasize that *all* the models discussed thus far for proximity data (even including IDIOSCAL, PARAFAC-2, Tucker's three-mode scaling model, and DeSarbo's GENNCLUS, if sufficiently high dimensionality is allowed) are special cases of the general primordial scalar products model in Eq. (29), some with continuous dimensions and others with discrete valued coordinates on dimensions constrained to binary values and often called "attributes" or "features." The only model discussed *not* in conformity with this generic framework is Lingoes and Borg's (1978) PINDIS—a model we have argued is substantively implausible and overparametrized, in any case. Thus, a very large class of continuous, discrete, and hybrid models can all be viewed as special cases of the primordial model—relatively simple in algebraic form, as well as in its theoretical assumptions concerning psychological processes underlying perception or cognition. Therefore, all can be viewed as special cases of this generic multidimensional model, with the different models varying only with respect to the class of continuous or discrete constraints imposed on the structure and interrelations of the dimensions assumed.

K. Models and Methods for Nonsymmetric Proximity Data

All the approaches to MDS discussed thus far have involved symmetric models for symmetric proximity data. Several types of proximity data are, however, inherently nonsymmetric; for example, the similarity/dissimilarity of j to k presented in that order is not necessarily equal to that of k to j when presented in the reverse order, so that theoretical problems may arise in modeling these data via distance models—which are inherently symmetric, because one of the metric axioms (which by definition is satisfied by all distance functions) demands that $d_{jk} = d_{kj}$ for all j and k. (We prefer the term *nonsymmetric* to *asymmetric,* which is often used as a synonym of the former, because some definitions of *asymmetric* imply *anti*symmetry—that is, that δ_{jk} is definitely *not* equal to δ_{kj}, or even that $\delta_{jk} = a(\delta_{kj})$, where a is a decreasing monotonic function [e.g., $a(\delta)$ = some constant $-\delta$]).

Examples of inherently nonsymmetric proximities include (1) confusions data, in which the probability of confusing k with j (i.e., responding j when stimulus k is presented) is not necessarily the same as that of confusing j with $k;$ (2) direct judgments of similarity/dissimilarity in which systematic order effects may affect judgments, and the subject judges both (j, k) and (k, j) pairs (perhaps the best example of this involves auditory stimuli, where there may be systematic order effects, so that stimulus η followed by stimulus ζ may appear, and be judged, either more or less similar than ζ followed by η; visual and other psychophysical stimuli may be subject to analogous order and other effects; see Holman, 1979, and Nosofsky 1991, for impressive theoretical and substantive developments in this area); and (3) *brand-switching* data, in which the data comprise estimated probabilities (or observed relative frequencies) of consumers who choose brand η on a first occasion but select brand ζ at some later time (see Cooper & Nakanishi, 1988).

Tversky (1977) argued that even direct judgments of similarity/dissimilarity of conceptual/cognitive stimuli may be systematically nonsymmetric—largely depending (we would argue) on how the similarity or dissimilarity question is phrased—and he provided numerous empirical examples. For instance, if subjects are asked "How similar is Vietnam to China?" the response will be systematically different than if they are asked "How similar is China to Vietnam?" In this particular case Vietnam will generally be judged more similar to China than vice versa. Tversky (1977) argued that this occurs because China has more "features" for most subjects than Vietnam does, and that, in this wording of the similarity question, greater weight is given to "distinctive features" unique to the second stimulus than to those unique to the first. This example will be discussed in more detail later when we consider Tversky's (1977) "features of similarity" theoretical framework. We would argue that a slightly different wording of this question, namely "How similar are η and ζ?" would tend to produce symmetric responses (i.e., that any deviations from symmetry are not systematic but result only from random error). It is, in fact, this latter wording or some variation of it that is most often used when direct judgments of similarities/dissimilarities are elicited from human subjects.

1. The Two-Mode Approach to Modeling Nonsymmetric Proximities

The first of the two approaches to modeling nonsymmetric proximities is the *two-mode* approach, in which the stimuli or other objects being modeled are treated as two sets rather than one—in the two-way case, in effect, the proximity data are treated as two-mode two-way, rather than one-mode two-way, with one mode corresponding to rows of the proximity matrix and the other to columns. In the case of confusions data, for example, the rows correspond to the stimuli treated as *stimuli,* whereas the columns correspond to those same stimuli treated as *responses.* In the case of psychophysical stimuli for which there are or may be systematic order effects, the two modes correspond, respectively, to the first and second presented stimulus. More generally, we have the following important principle: any Θ-mode N-way data nonsymmetric in any *modes* corresponding to two *ways* (say, rows and columns) can be accommodated by a *symmetric* model designed for $(\Theta + 1)$-mode N-way data. The extra mode arises from considering the rows and columns as corresponding to distinct entities, so that each entity will be depicted twice in the representation from the symmetric model. (One could, of course, generalize this approach to data nonsymmetric in more than one mode—perhaps even to generalized nonsymmetries involving more than two-ways for a single mode—but we know of few, if any, actual examples of data of this more general type.)

The two-set distance model approach can be viewed very simply as a special case of Coombs's (1964) *unfolding model,* which is inherently designed for data having two or more modes. (In the two-mode case, with respective cardinalities of the stimulus sets being n_1 and n_2, the two-mode data can also be regarded as being in the "corner" of an augmented $(n_1 + n_2)$ $\times$ $(n_1 + n_2)$ matrix with missing entries for all but the $n_1 \times n_2$ submatrix of observed data—hence the traditional but unhelpful jargon of a "corner matrix.") Because most programs for two-way (and some for three-way) MDS allow for missing data. KYST2A allows the user to provide as input such an $n_1 \times n_2$ matrix. The case with which we are dealing, where $n_1 = n_2$ $= n$, leads directly to a representation in which the stimuli (or other objects) are modeled by $2n$ points—one set of points corresponding to each mode.

Coombs's (1964) distance-based unfolding model assumes preference is inversely monotonically related to distance between the subject's ideal point and a point representing the stimulus in a multidimensional space. Because of the historical association with Coombs's unfolding model, the general problem of analyzing two-mode proximity data (irrespective of whether they are row/column conditional or unconditional and whether ordinal, interval, or ratio scale) is often referred to as the *multidimensional unfolding* problem. From a methodological perspective, there are serious problems with the analysis of two-mode proximities, whether of the type discussed previously or of another type more normally associated with preferential choice (or other dominance) data—which in some cases can lead to data that, as defined earlier, are row or column conditional (e.g., an $I \times n$ matrix of preference ratings for I subjects on n stimuli).

Discussion of the problem of multidimensional unfolding as a special case of MDS, and the associated problems of theoretical degeneracies that make such analyses intractable if great care is not taken, can be found in Kruskal and Carroll (1969) or in Carroll (1972, 1980). To summarize the practical implications for the analyses of two-mode proximities: Either these analyses should be done metrically (i.e., under the assumption of ratio or interval scale data) while assuming row (or column) unconditional off-diagonal data, or they must be done using STRESSFORM2 (or its analogues, in case of other loss functions, such as SSTRESS[5]), whether doing a metric or nonmetric analysis, if row (column) conditional data are entailed. If a fully nonmetric analysis is attempted treating the data as unconditional (whether using STRESSFORM1 or 2), a theoretical degeneracy can be shown always to exist corresponding to perfect (zero) STRESS, although it will account for essentially none of the ordinal information in the data. On the other hand, either a metric or nonmetric analysis assuming (row or column) conditional data, but using STRESSFORM1 instead of STRESSFORM2, will always allow another, even more blatant theoretical degeneracy—as described in Kruskal and Carroll (1969) and Carroll (1972, 1980).

Discrete analogues of the two-set approach to the analysis of nonsymmetric data (or, more generally, rectangular or off-diagonal proximities) are also possible. The tree unfolding approach discussed briefly in the previous section is the most notable example. Note that this analysis was (necessarily) done metrically, assuming row/column unconditional data, for exactly the reasons cited earlier concerning possible degeneracies (which are even more serious in the case of such discrete models as tree structures, where, as discussed earlier, theoretical degeneracies arise in the case of nonmetric analyses—even in the case of symmetric proximities).

---

[5] It should be noted that ALSCAL should *not* be used for unfolding analyses, however, because the appropriate analogue to STRESSFORM2 is not available in any version of the ALSCAL software.

Tree unfolding has been generalized to the three-way case by De Soete and Carroll (1989). Various approaches to generalizing spatial unfolding to the three-way case have been pursued by DeSarbo and Carroll (1981, 1985); all are restricted to the metric case and to unconditional proximity data, for reasons discussed previously.

Although fully nonmetric analyses are inappropriate (except under the conditions mentioned in the case of spatial unfolding models and always in the case of discrete models), the type of quasi-nonmetric analyses described in the case of the extended Euclidean and INDSCAL models should be permissible, though to our knowledge no one has attempted this approach. Heiser (1989b), however, has pursued some different quasi-nonmetric methods as well as other approaches to unfolding by imposing various constraints on the configurations or by using *homogeneity analysis,* which is closely related to correspondence analysis; see Gifi (1990) for a fuller discussion of this approach to multivariate data analysis, or see Greenacre (1984), Greenacre and Blasius (1994), Lebart, Morineau, and Warwick (1984), and Nishisato (1980, 1993, 1996a, 1996b) for discussions of correspondence analysis. For reasons why correspondence analysis should not be considered a routine alternative to either metric or nonmetric MDS, see Carroll, Kumbasar, and Romney (1997) and Hubert and Arabie (1992).

We note tangentially that a large number of multidimensional models used for representing preferential choice data and methods for analyzing these data using these models have been proposed and can be included under the general rubric of multidimensional scaling (broadly defined). If one characterizes preferences, as does Coombs (1964), as measures of proximity between two sets (stimuli and subjects' ideal points), then the models can be classified as MDS models even if we restrict the domain to geometric models/methods for proximity data. In fact, as Carroll (1972, 1980) has pointed out, a large class of models called the *linear quadratic hierarchy* of models, including the so-called vector model for preferences (Tucker, 1960; Chang & Carroll, 1969a) can all be viewed as special cases or generalizations of the Coombsian unfolding or ideal point model.[6] The vector model, frequently fit by use of the popular MDPREF program (Chang & Carroll, 1969b, 1989), can be viewed as a special case of the unfolding model corresponding to ideal points at infinity (a subject vector then simply indicates the direction of that subject's infinitely distant ideal point). Overviews of these and other models/methods for deterministic (i.e., nonstochastic) analyses of preference data are provided by Carroll (1972, 1980), Weisberg (1974), Heiser (1981, 1987), and DeSarbo and Carroll (1985), whereas discussion of some stochastic models and related methods is found in Carroll and De Soete (1991), De Soete and Carroll (1992), and Marley (1992).

---

[6] In an important development, the ideal point model has been extended to the technique of discriminant analysis (Takane, Bozdogan, & Shibayama, 1987; Takane, 1989).

2. The One-Mode Approach to Modeling Nonsymmetric Proximities

The other general approach to analyzing nonsymmetric proximities entails a single set representation that assumes a nonsymmetric model. These models can be viewed as adaptations of either a spatial or a discrete (e.g., feature structure) model, modified to accommodate nonsymmetries.

Many of these models are subsumed as special cases of a *nonsymmetric* modification of what we called the primordial (symmetric) model for proximities in Eq. (29), which, in its most general (three-way) case, can be written for $\delta_{jk}^{(i)}$, the proximity between objects j and k for subject i, as

$$\delta_{jk}^{(i)} \cong M_i(b_{jk}^{(i)} + u_{ij} + v_{ik}),\tag{39}$$

where $b_{jk}^{(i)} = \Sigma_r^R w_{ir} x_{jr} x_{kr}$ (a weighted *symmetric* scalar product between j and k for subject/source i),

x_{jr} = continuous (discrete) value of jth object on rth
   dimension (feature),
w_{ir} = salience weight of rth dimension/feature for
   the ith subject,
u_{ij} = uniqueness of jth object for ith subject in the first (row)
   mode, and
v_{ik} = uniqueness of kth object for ith subject in the second
   (column) mode,

while M_i is a (nonincreasing or nondecreasing) monotonic function for subject i, depending on whether $\delta_{jk}^{(i)}$ is, respectively, a similarity or a dissimilarity measure.

For nonsymmetric proximities, among the special cases of this model are the following.

a. Tversky's Features of Similarity Model

A general statement of this model in set-theoretic terms is (Tversky, 1977)

$$S(j, k) = \theta f(A \cap B) - \alpha f(A - B) - \beta f(B - A)$$
$$\text{for } \theta,\ \alpha,\ \beta \geq 0,\tag{40}$$

where $S(j, k)$ is the similarity of stimuli j and k; A and B are corresponding sets of discrete dimensions/attributes/features (whichever term one prefers); $A \cap B$ is the intersection of sets A and B (or, the set of features common to j and k); $A - B$ is the set difference between A and B or, in words, the set of features possessed by j but not by k (whereas $B - A$ has the opposite meaning); θ, α, and β are numerical weights to be fitted; and f is a finitely additive function, that is,

$$f(\Omega) = \sum_{\Lambda_\Omega \in \Omega} g(\Lambda_\Omega)$$

(where Λ_Ω denotes a feature included in the feature set Ω). An MDS algorithm tailored to fit this model is described by DeSarbo, M. D. Johnson, A. K. Manrai, L. A. Manrai, and Edwards (1992).

When $a = \beta$, this model leads to symmetric proximities S; otherwise it leads to a nonsymmetric model. Tversky (1977) pointed out that the Shepard and Arabie (1979) ADCLUS model corresponds to the special case in which $\alpha = \beta$ (so that the model is symmetric) *and $f(A) = f(B)$*, for all A, B (that is, the weights of the feature sets for stimuli j, k, etc. are all equal). We now demonstrate that the more general model is a special case of the primordial nonsymmetric proximity model expressed in Eq. (39).

First, we rewrite Eq. (40) as

$$
\begin{aligned}
S(j, k) &= \theta f(A \cap B) + (\alpha + \beta)f(A \cap B) - \alpha f(A - B) \\
&\quad - \alpha f(A \cap B) - \beta f(B - A) - \beta f(A \cap B) \\
&= (\theta + \alpha + \beta)f(A \cap B) - \alpha f(A) - \beta f(B),
\end{aligned} \tag{41}
$$

with the last expression resulting from substitutions of the set identity $A \equiv (A \cap B) + (A - B)$.

Rewriting Eq. (41) with the same notation used in formulating the two-way ADCLUS model results in nonsymmetric (similarities) of the form

$$
s_{jk} = \sum_r^R w_r p_{jr} p_{kr} - u_j - v_k, \tag{42}
$$

where

$$
u_j = -\alpha^* \sum_r w_r p_{ir}
$$

and

$$
v_k = -\beta^* \sum_r w_r p_{kr},
$$

while

$$
\alpha^* = \frac{\alpha}{\theta + \alpha + \beta} \quad \text{and} \quad \beta^* = \frac{\beta}{\theta + \alpha + \beta}.
$$

Here $s_{jk} = \frac{1}{\theta + \alpha + \beta} S(j, k)$ (an unimportant scale transformation), and $w_r = \tau(\Lambda_r)$, where Λ_r is the rth "feature" and p_{jr} is a binary indicator variable; $p_{jr} = 1$ iff stimulus j has feature r, and τ is a nonnegative function.

This formulation, of course, is a two-way special case of Eq. (39). Extending this reinterpretation of the features of similarity model to the three-way case, we have

$$s_{jk}^{(i)} \cong \sum_{r=1}^{R} w_{ir} p_{ir} p_{kr} - u_{ij} - v_{ik}, \tag{43}$$

which is a special case of the three-way primordial nonsymmetric scalar product model of Eq. (39), with $x_{jr} \equiv p_{jr}$, that is, with discrete valued dimensions or features (and with $\delta_{jk}^{(i)} \equiv s_{jk}^{(i)}$, with M_i as the identity function). Because Eq. (43) is the three-way generalization of Eq. (39), the u and v terms now have an additional subscript for subject i. Thus, Tversky's (1977) features of similarity model leads to an extended (nonsymmetric) version of the ADCLUS/INDCLUS model—extended by adding the terms u_{ij} and v_{ik}.

Holman (1979) generalized Tversky's features of similarity model to include a monotone transformation of the expression on the right side of Eq. (40), making the model more nearly equivalent to Eq. (39), but only in the two-way case. Holman then formulated a general model for nonsymmetric proximities entailing response biases, a special case of which can be viewed as the two-way case of Eq. (39), with the terms u_j and v_k representing the response biases. Holman defined a general symmetric similarity function as part of his response bias model; our interpretation of Eq. (39) as a special two-way case is dependent on a particular definition of that general similarity function.

Krumhansl (1978) proposed a (continuous) model for nonsymmetric proximities based on what she called a distance-density hypothesis, which leads to an expression for modified distances $\bar{d}$ of the form

$$\bar{d}_{jk} = d_{jk} + \alpha \phi_j + \beta \phi_k, \tag{44}$$

where α, β, and $\bar{d}$, are unrelated to previous usage in this chapter.

The distance-density model has occasioned an impressive algorithmic tradition in two-way MDS. Okada and Imaizumi (1987; Okada, 1990) provide a nonmetric method in which a stimulus is represented as a point and an ellipse (or its generalization) whose center is at that very point in a Euclidean space. Although theirs is a two-way method, it could readily be extended to the three-way case. Distance between the points corresponds to symmetry, and between the radii to skew-symmetry. Bové and Critchley (1989, 1993) devised a metric method for fitting the same model and related their solution to work by Tobler (1979) and Weeks and Bentler (1982). Saito's approach (1991, 1993; Saito & Takeda, 1990) allows the useful option of including unequal diagonal values (i.e., disparate self-similarities) in the analysis. DeSarbo and A. K. Manrai (1992) devised an algorithm that, they maintain, links estimated parameters more closely to Krumhansl's original concept of density.

Krumhansl's original justification for her model, in which ϕ_j and ϕ_k are measures of the spatial density of stimuli in the neighborhoods of j and k, respectively, is actually equally consistent with a formulation using *squared* (Euclidean) distances, namely, modified squared distances $\tilde{d}^2$ defined as

$$\tilde{d}_{jk}^2 = d_{jk}^2 + \alpha\phi_j + \beta\phi_k, \tag{45}$$

which, in the three-way case, is a nonsymmetric generalization of the extended Euclidean model formulated in the symmetric case by Winsberg and Carroll (1989a, 1989b) and extended to the three-way (EXSCAL) case by Carroll and Winsberg (1986, 1995). It should be clear that this slight reinterpretation of Krumhansl's distance-density model also leads, in the most general three-way case, to a model with continuous spatial parameters of the same general form defined in Eq. (39).

b. Drift Models

As a final class of models leading to this same primordial generalized scalar product form, we now consider two frequently discussed models. One entails "drift" in a fixed *direction* (referred to as a slide-vector model in the implementation of Zielman & Heiser, 1993) and the second entails "drift" toward a fixed *point*. (The first can actually be viewed as a special case of the second, with the fixed point at infinity in some direction.)

Before stating the fixed directional form of the drift model in mathematical terms, we consider a stimulus identification task leading to confusions data, in which a stimulus is presented and the subject attempts to identify it by naming or otherwise giving a response associated with the stimulus presented. In the drift model, we assume the presented stimulus is mapped onto a point (in a continuous multidimensional spatial representation) corresponding to the "true" location of that stimulus *plus* a fixed vector entailing a drift in a fixed direction (and for a fixed distance).

Specifically, if $\mathbf{x}_j$ is the vector representing the true position of stimulus j, the effective position of the presented stimulus will be $\mathbf{x}_j + \psi$, where ψ is the fixed drift vector. If we then assume a Euclidean metric space, the perceived distance between j and another (nonpresented) stimulus k will be (in the two–way case)

$$\tilde{d}_{jk} = \left[\sum_{r=1}^{R} (x_{jr} + \psi_r - x_{kr})^2 \right]^{1/2} \tag{46}$$

Now, if we assume that the probability of confusion is a decreasing monotonic function of $\tilde{d}$ then we have

$$s_{jk} \cong \text{Prob}\,(k|j) = M^*(\tilde{d}_{jk})$$

$$= M^{**}\left[\sum_{r} (x_{jr} + \psi_r - x_{kr})^2 \right]$$

$$= M^{**}\left[\sum_r (x_{jr} - x_{kr})^2 + 2\sum_r \psi_r x_{jr}\right.$$

$$\left. - 2\sum_r \psi_r x_{kr} + \sum_r \psi_r^2\right]$$

$$= M^{**}\left[-2\sum_r x_{jr}x_{kr} + \sum_r x_{jr}^2 + \sum_r x_{kr}^2\right.$$

$$\left. + 2\sum_r \psi_r x_{jr} - 2\sum_r \psi_r x_{kr} + \sum_r \psi_r^2\right]$$

$$= M\left[\sum_r x_{jr}x_{kr} - u_j - v_k\right], \tag{47}$$

where M^* is (an arbitrary) monotonic function, and M^{**} and M are also monotonic functions (implied by absorbing first the square root transformation and then the multiplicative factor of -2). (If M^* is monotone decreasing, of course, M will be a monotone *increasing* function.) The important point is that Eq. (47) is of the same form as (the two-way case of) Eq. (39), with $u_j = -.5(\sum_r x_{jr}^2 + 2\sum_r \psi_r x_{jr} + \sum_r \psi_r^2)$ and $v_k = -.5(\sum_r x_{kr}^2 - 2\sum_r \psi_r x_{jr} + \sum_r \psi_r^2)$. Clearly, if we assume a separate drift vector for each subject/source in the three-way case, we get exactly the model form assumed in Eq. (39), with $u_{ij} = -.5(\sum_r w_{ir} x_{jr}^2 + 2\sum_r \psi_{ir} x_{jr} + \sum_r \psi_r^2)$ and $v_{ir} = -.5(\sum_r w_{ir} x_{kr}^2 - 2\sum_r \psi_{ir} x_{kr} + \sum_r \psi_r^2)$.

In the case of the (two-way) model entailing drift toward a fixed point, we assume that the effective position of the presented stimulus, whose true location is $\mathbf{x}_j$, will be $\mathbf{x}_j + \omega(\mathbf{z} - \mathbf{x}_j)$, where $\mathbf{z}$ is the fixed point toward which stimuli drift, while ω is a parameter ($0 \le \omega \le 1$) governing the degree to which $\mathbf{x}_j$ will drift toward $\mathbf{z}$. In this two-way case, the modified Euclidean distance will be

$$\tilde{d}_{jk} = \left[\sum_r^R (x_{jr} + \omega(z_r - x_{jr}) - x_{kr})^2\right]^{1/2}$$

$$= \left[\sum_r ([1 - \omega]x_{jr} + \omega z_r - x_{kr})^2\right]^{1/2}$$

$$= \left[-2(1 - \omega)\sum_r x_{jr}x_{kr} + (1 - \omega)^2\sum_r x_{jr}^2 + \sum_r x_{kr}^2\right.$$

$$+2\omega(1-\omega)\sum_r z_r x_{jr} - 2\omega \sum_r z_r x_{kr} + \omega^2 \sum_r z_r^2 \Big]^{1/2}.$$

Again, if we assume that the probability of confusion, as a measure of proximity, is a monotonic function of $\bar{d}_{jk}$, we have after some simple algebraic manipulations that proximity is of the same form as in Eq. (47) (with M, u_j, and v_k defined appropriately), although, again the three-way generalization (assuming a possibly different fixed point $\mathbf{z}_i$ for each subject) will be of the same primordial form given in Eq. (39). It is important to note that, except for the additive constants u_{ij} and v_{ik}, this generalized (primordial) scalar product model is essentially *symmetric* (for each subject/source i).

To summarize this section, a large number of superficially disparate models for nonsymmetric proximities are of the same general form as the primordial modified three-way scalar product model stated in Eq. (39), although a very large class of discrete, continuous, and hybrid models for symmetric proximities are of that same general form but have the constraint that $u_{ij} = v_{ij}$, leading to the primordial symmetric model stated in Eq. (29).

It thus appears that a large class of seemingly unrelated models (both two- and three-way, symmetric and nonsymmetric) that have been proposed for proximity data of widely varying kinds are special cases of this generic three-way model that we call the primordial scalar product model, expressed in its most general form in Eq. (39).

3. Three-Way Approaches to Nonsymmetric Proximity Data

In a seminal two-way approach to representing structure underlying nonsymmetric one-mode data, Gower (1977) used areas of triangles and collinearities for the graphical representation of the skew-symmetric component of a nonsymmetric matrix. (Each stimulus was represented by two points, one for its row and another for its column.) The degree of nonsymmetry relates to the area (or sum of signed areas) of triangles, defined by pairs of points and the origin, in two-dimensional subspaces corresponding to matched pairs of eigenvalues in an SVD of the skew-symmetric component of the original matrix of proximity data (after a standard decomposition of the matrix into symmetric and skew-symmetric parts); the direction of the nonsymmetry depends on the sign of the area or of the summed signed areas. That approach forms the basis for numerous three-way models.

Bové and Rocci (1993) generalized Escoufier and Grorud's (1980) approach, in which nonsymmetries are represented by areas of triangles, to the three-way case. Kiers and Takane (1994) provided algorithmic advances on earlier work by Chino (1978, 1990). Similarly, Zielman (1993) provided a three-way approach emphasizing directional planes and collinearities for representing the skew-symmetric component of a nonsymmetric three-way matrix.

We have reviewed elsewhere (Arabie et al., 1987, pp. 50–53) other approaches to this problem (e.g., Kroonenberg & de Leeuw, 1980; also see Kroonenberg, 1983; for developments of Tucker's three-mode three-way principal component analysis, see Tucker, 1972) and will not repeat the discussion here. But Kroonenberg and de Leeuw's (1980, p. 83) empirical conclusion after a protracted analysis that "symmetrization does not really violate the structure of the data" they were analyzing is noteworthy. It is our impression that the extensive collective effort to provide MDS algorithms capable of faithfully representing the nonsymmetric psychological structure so emphasized by Tversky (1977) has borne little substantive fruit.[7] Two possible (and nonexclusive) explanations are (1) nonsymmetry is not very important psychologically or is a minor component of most proximity data, and (2) the extant models are failing to capture the implicit structure. Also see remarks by Nosofsky (1992, p. 38) on this topic.

Concerning the former explanation, Hubert and Baker's (1979) inferential test for detecting significant departures from symmetry has been greatly underemployed. Their examples suggest that presence of nonsymmetry in psychological data has been exaggerated. Similarly, Nosofsky's (1991) incisive treatment of the topic suggests that models incorporating terms like those for stimulus uniqueness in Eq. (39) may preclude the need to posit more fundamental nonsymmetries in similarity data. Concerning the appropriateness of extant models, integrative reviews (e.g., Zielman & Heiser, 1994) and comparative analyses (e.g., Takane & Shibayama, 1986; Molenaar, 1986) should afford a better understanding of exactly what is being captured by models for nonsymmetric data.

We now turn to a different class of such models.

4. Nonspatial Models and Methods for Nonsymmetric Proximity Data

The reader who expects to find nonspatial counterparts to the models just discussed will not be disappointed. For the case of one-mode two-way nonsymmetric data, Hutchinson (1981, 1989) provides a *network* model, NETSCAL (for *NET*work *SCAL*ing), in which a reconstructed distance, defined as the minimum path length between vertices corresponding to stimuli, is assumed to be a generalized power function of the input dissimilarities, and the topology of the network is based only on ordinal information in the data. Hutchinson's illustrative data analyses provide impressive support for the usefulness of his approach.

Klauer and Carroll used a mathematical programming approach to fit network models to one-mode two-way symmetric (1989) and nonsymmetric (1991) proximity data. Using a shortest path definition for the reconstructed distances, their metric algorithm, MAPNET (for *MA*thmetical *P*rogramming *NET*work fitting), seeks to provide the connected network

---

[7] Okada and Imaizumi (1997) have provided a noteworthy exception to this statement.

with a least-squares fit using a specified number of arcs. Klauer and Carroll (1991) compared their algorithm to Hutchinson's NETSCAL and found the two yielded comparable results, although MAPNET ran faster and provided better variance accounted for. (MAPNET has also been generalized to the three-way case called INDNET; see Klauer and Carroll, 1995.)

We note that neither Gower's (1977) approach nor these network models are subsumed in the primordial model.

V. CONSTRAINED AND CONFIRMATORY APPROACHES TO MDS

Substantive theory can provide a priori expectations concerning the configuration that MDS algorithms generate in the course of an analysis. Beyond being useful in interpreting the configuration, such expectations can actually be incorporated in the analysis in the form of constraints, if the algorithm and software at hand so allow.

Most of the literature on constrained MDS considers only two-way one-mode analyses, but the extension to the three-way case is usually fairly straightforward; thus, we invoke this distinction here much less than in some of the previous sections (also in contrast to our treatment of the topic in Carroll & Arabie, 1980, pp. 619, 628, 633).

A. Constraining the Coordinates

As Heiser and Meulman (1983a, 1983b) noted, most constrained approaches focus either on the coordinates of the configuration or on the function relating the input data to the corresponding recovered interpoint distances. We now consider the former case. Most of the discussion on this topic in our 1980 review centered on constraining the coordinates, and we will not repeat the coverage here. Important subsequent contributions include de Leeuw and Heiser (1980), Lee and Bentler (1980), Takane and Carroll (1981), Weeks and Bentler (1982), DeSarbo, Carroll, Lehmann, and O'Shaughnessy (1982), Heiser and Meulman (1983a, pp. 153–158; 1983b, pp. 387–390), Takane and Sergent (1983), Carroll, De Soete, and Pruzansky (1988, 1989), and Krijnen (1993).

1. Circular/Spherical Configurations

Shepard (1978) masterfully demonstrated the pervasive relevance of spherical configurations in the study of perception. In response, designers of MDS algorithms have made such configurations a popular form of constrained (two-way) MDS. T. F. Cox and M. A. A. Cox (1991) provided a nonmetric algorithm, and earlier metric approaches were devised by de Leeuw and

Heiser (1980) and Lee and Bentler (1980); also see Hubert and Arabie (1994, 1995a) and Hubert, Arabie, and Meulman (1997).

2. Hybrid Approaches Using Circular Configurations

It is too easy to think only of orthogonal dimensions in a metric space for representing the structure in proximities data via MDS, despite the emphasis earlier in this chapter on trees and related discrete structures. Yet other alternatives to dimensions are circles and the matrix form characterized by permuting input data according to a seriation analysis. That is, instead of a series of axes/dimensions or trees (as in Carroll & Pruzansky's hybrid approach, 1975, 1980, discussed earlier) accounting for implicit structure, a set of circles, for example, could be used to account for successively smaller proportions of variance (or components in some other decomposition of an overall goodness-of-fit measure). Taking this development a step further in the hybrid direction, one could also fit a circle as one component, the seriation form as another component, and yet another structure as a third, all in the same analysis of a one-mode symmetric proximities matrix, using the algorithms devised by Hubert and Arabie (1994) and Hubert, Arabie, and Meulman (1997). Those authors (1995a) subsequently generalized this approach to include two-way two-mode proximity matrices.

B. Constraining the Function Relating the Input Data to the Corresponding Recovered Interpoint Distances

In various programs for nonmetric two-way MDS, the plot of this function is appropriately known as the *Shepard diagram,* to give due credit to Shepard's emphasis on this function, which before the advent of nonmetric MDS was generally assumed be linear between derived measures. (Recall that the subtitle of his two 1962 articles is "Multidimensional scaling with an unknown distance function.") Shepard (1962a, 1962b) and Kruskal (1964a, 1964b) devised algorithms for identifying that function with assumptions no stronger than weak monotonicity. In later developments, Shepard (1972, 1974) pointed to the advantages of imposing such constraints as convexity on the monotone regression function. Heiser (1985, 1989b) extended this approach to multidimensional unfolding.

Work by Winsberg and Ramsay (1980, 1981, 1984) and Ramsay (1982a, 1988) using splines rather than Kruskal's (1964b) unconstrained monotone regression to approximate this function has afforded new approaches to imposing constraints on the monotonic function, such as continuity of the function and its first and possibly second derivatives. As already discussed extensively, these continuity constraints have allowed Winsberg and Carroll (1989a, 1989b) and Carroll and Winsberg (1986, 1995) to reverse the direction of the monotone function—treating the data as a (perturbed) monotone function of the distances in the underlying model rather than vice versa, as is done almost universally elsewhere in nonmetric (or even other approaches to quasi-nonmetric) MDS—in their quasi-nonmetric approach to fitting the Extended Euclidean model or its generalization, the Extended INDSCAL (or EXSCAL) model—which includes the ordinary two-way Euclidean MDS model or the three-way INDSCAL models as special cases. The statistical and other methodological advantages of this strategy have already been discussed. The imposition of some mild constraints on various aspects of MDS models often leads to considerable advantages of greater robustness; it also enables fitting, in many cases, of models that are essentially impossible to fit without such constraints.

C. Confirmatory MDS

As Heiser and Meulman (1983b, p. 394) note, "the possibility of constraining the MDS solution in various ways greatly enhances the options for analyzing data in a confirmatory fashion." Approaches to confirmatory MDS have taken several paths. For example, beginning with a traditional statistical emphasis of looking at the residuals, specifically of a nonmetric two-way analysis, Critchley (1986) proposed representing stimuli as small regions rather than points in the MDS solution. The advantage of this strategy is that the regions allow better goodness of fit to the ordinal proximity data. We noted earlier that Ramsay's maximum likelihood approach to two- and three-way MDS allows computing confidence regions for the stimulus mode.

An alternative strategy, used by Weinberg, Carroll, and Cohen (1984), employs resampling (namely, jackknifing and bootstrapping on the subjects' mode in INDSCAL analyses) to obtain such regions. The latter approach is more computationally laborious but less model-specific than Ramsay's, and the results suggest that Ramsay's estimates based on small samples provide an optimistic view of the actual reliability of MDS solutions. For resampling in the two-way case, de Leeuw and Meulman (1986) provide an approach for jackknifing by deleting one stimulus at a time. This approach also provides guidelines as to the appropriate dimensionality for a two-way solution. Heiser and Meulman (1983a) used bootstrapping to obtain confidence regions and assess the stability of multidimensional unfolding solutions.

Extending earlier results by Hubert (1978, 1979) to allow significance tests for the correspondence (independent of any model of MDS) between two or more input matrices, Hubert and Arabie (1989) provided a confirmatory approach to test a given MDS solution against an a priori, idealized structure codified in matrix form. Hubert's (1987) book is essential reading for this topic of research.

Vocational psychology has recently provided a setting for numerous developments related to confirmatory MDS (Hubert & Arabie, 1987; Rounds, Tracey, & Hubert, 1992; Tracey & Rounds, 1993), including a clever application of the INDSCAL model in such an analysis (Rounds & Tracey, 1993).

VI. VISUAL DISPLAYS AND MDS SOLUTIONS

A. Procrustes Rotations

It is often desirable to compare two or more MDS solutions based on the same set of stimuli. When the interpoint distances in the solution(s) to be rotated to maximal congruity with a target configuration are rotationally invariant (as in two-way MDS solutions in the Euclidean metric), the problem of finding the best-fitting orthogonal rotation and a dilation (or overall scale) factor (and even a possible translation of origin of one of the two to align the centroids of the two configurations, if not already done via normalization) has an analytic least-squares solution. But devising a canonical measure of goodness of fit between a pair of matched configurations has proven to be a more challenging problem (see Krzanowski and Marriott, 1994, pp. 134–141, for a concise history of developments).

Analogous to the shift in emphasis from two- to three-way MDS, advances in rotational strategies have progressed from an emphasis on comparing two MDS solutions to comparing more than two. This problem, one variant of which is known as *generalized Procrustes analysis* (Gower, 1975), has occasioned considerable algorithmic development (e.g., ten Berge, 1977; ten Berge & Knol, 1984; ten Berge, Kiers, & Commandeur, 1993; see Commandeur, 1991, and Gower, 1995a, for overviews) and can be cast in the framework of generalized canonical correlation analysis (Green & Carroll, 1988; ten Berge, 1988). As in the case of generalizing many two-way models and associated methods to the three-way (or higher) case, there are a plethora of different approaches to the multiset (e.g., MDS solutions) case, many (but not all) of which are equivalent in the two-set case. Also, in the case of Procrustes analyses, different techniques are appropriate, depending on the class of transformations to which the user believes, on theoretical or empirical grounds, the two (or more) configurations can justifiably be subjected. For example, Gower's generalized Procrustes analysis assumes that each configuration is defined up to an arbitrary similarity transformation (but that the translation component can generally be ignored because of appropriate normalization—e.g., translation of each so that the origin of the coordinate system is at the centroid of the points in that configuration). The canonical correlation-based approaches, on the other hand, allow more general *affine* transformations of the various configurations.

Yet another approach, first used by Green and Rao (1972, pp. 95–97) as a configuration matching approach (in the case of two as well as of three or more configurations) utilizes INDSCAL, applied to distances computed from each separate configuration, as a form of generalized configuration matching (or an alternative generalized Procrustes approach, implicitly assuming yet another class of permissible transformations too complex to be discussed in detail here). This INDSCAL-based approach to configuration matching has been quite useful in a wide variety of situations and has the advantage, associated with INDSCAL in other applications, of yielding a statistically unique orientation of common coordinates describing all the separate configurations. The general approach of configuration matching has long been used to assess mental maps in environmental psychology (e.g., Gordon, Jupp, & Byrne, 1989) and has also found many applications in food technology (see Dijksterhuis & Gower, 1991/1992) and morphometrics (Rohlf & Slice, 1990). In addition to the earlier applications in marketing by Green, cited earlier, a recent approach utilizing either (1) Gower's generalized Procrustes analyses, (2) INDSCAL-based rotation to congruence, or (3) a canonical correlation or generalized canonical correlation–based technique for configuration matching (Carroll, 1968; Green & Carroll, 1989)—or all three—has been quite successfully applied to provide a highly provocative and quite promising new paradigm for marketing analysis, synthesizing elements of a semantic differential approach in a neo-Kellyian framework with an MDS-type spatial representation (see Steenkamp, van Trijp, & ten Berge, 1994). Although devised in the context of a marketing problem, this novel methodological hybridization could very profitably be used in several areas of applied psychology. Other aspects of MDS that are applied to marketing and that could have useful analogues in psychology are discussed in Carroll and Green (1997).

B. Biplots

As Greenacre (1986) succinctly noted,

> "Biplot" is a generic term for a particular class of techniques which represent the rows and columns of a [two-way two-mode] data matrix Y as points in a low-dimensional Euclidean space. This class is characterized by the property that the display is based on a factorization of the form AB' [notation modified from the original] of a matrix approximation Z of Y. The biplot recovers the approximate elements z_{ij} as scalar products $a_i b_j'$ of the respective i-th and j-th rows of A and B, which represent row i and column j respectively in the display.

(Note: The names of these variables bear no necessary relation to usage elsewhere in this chapter.) Such representations have been available since the advent of MDPREF (Carroll & Chang, 1969), but by emphasizing the graphical presentation and by naming it a "biplot" (after its two modes), Gabriel (1971) contributed to the display's popularity. For advances in the underlying statistical techniques, see Gower (1990, 1992, 1995b), Gower and Harding (1988), Meulman and Heiser (1993), and Gower and Hand (1996).

C. Visualization

Young (1984b, p. 77) predicted that "methods for graphically displaying the results of scaling analyses rather than new scaling methods as such" were the new frontier of MDS developments and emphasized color and interactive graphic hardware. This prophecy has turned out to be highly myopic. Although the graphics capabilities of multivariate statistical packages like SYSTAT's SYSGRAPH (Wilkinson, 1994) are indeed impressive and will no doubt continue to improve, they are in no way specific to MDS analyses. The most dramatic graphics-based advances in our understanding of MDS techniques have come from black-and-white graphics portraying results of highly sophisticated investigations that rely on clever and insightful theoretical analyses and simulations (Furnas, 1989; W. P. Jones & Furnas, 1987; Littman, Swayne, Dean, & Buja, 1992).

VII. STATISTICAL FOUNDATIONS OF MDS

During the 1960s, MDS tended to be ignored in the statistical literature, but in the past 15 years, most comprehensive textbooks on multivariate data analysis have included at least one chapter on MDS (e.g., Krzanowski & Marriott, 1994, chap. 5). But relatively few papers (e.g., Cuadras, Fortiana, & Oliva, 1996; Groenen, de Leeuw, & Mathar, 1996) have looked intently at the problem of estimation in MDS. Focusing on the consistency of the Shepard-Kruskal estimator in two-way nonmetric MDS, Brady (1985) reached several interesting conclusions. For example, in aggregating over sources of data to go from a three-way two-mode matrix to a two-way one-mode matrix (as is typically done when two-way nonmetric MDS is applied), it is better to use medians than the traditional arithmetic mean when the data are continuous (e.g., collected using a rating scale). If the data are not continuous (e.g., aggregated over same-different judgments or overt confusions), then accurate recovery of the monotone function typically displayed as the Shepard diagram is unlikely. Brady also developed the beginnings of an hypothesis test for the appropriate dimensionality of MDS solutions.

Ramsay (1982b) provided a scholarly and comprehensive discussion of the underpinnings of his maximum likelihood–based MULTISCALE algorithms (described earlier).

Using matrix permutation/randomization techniques as the basic engine, Hubert and his collaborators (Hubert, 1985, 1987; Hubert & Arabie, 1989; Hubert & Golledge, 1981; Hubert & Subkoviak, 1979) have provided a variety of confirmatory tests applicable to MDS analyses. This general approach makes considerably weaker distributional assumptions than the other papers cited in this section.

Brady (1990) studied the statistical properties of ALS and maximum likelihood estimators when applied to two-way unfolding (e.g., Greenacre & Browne, 1986) and reached the unsettling conclusion that "even after making some strong stochastic assumptions, the ALS estimator is inconsistent (biased) for any squared Euclidean model with an error term." Further statistically based research that could lead to practical improvements in the everyday use of MDS is sorely needed.

Acknowledgments

We are indebted to Yuko Minowa and Zina Taran for bibliographic assistance and to Kathleen Power for editorial expertise.

References

Arabie, P. (1973). Concerning Monte Carlo evaluations of nonmetric scaling algorithms. *Psychometrika, 38,* 607–608.

Arabie, P. (1991). Was Euclid an unnecessarily sophisticated psychologist? *Psychometrika, 56,* 567–587.

Arabie, P., & Carroll, J. D. (1980). MAPCLUS: A mathematical programming approach to fitting the ADCLUS model. *Psychometrika, 45,* 211–235.

Arabie, P., & Carroll, J. D. (1989). Conceptions of overlap in social structure. In L. Freeman, D. R. White, & A. K. Romney (Eds.), *Research methods of social network analysis* (pp. 367–392). Fairfax, VA: George Mason University Press.

Arabie, P., Carroll, J. D., & DeSarbo, W. S. (1987). *Three-way scaling and clustering.* Newbury Park, CA: Sage. (Translated into Japanese by A. Okada & T. Imaizumi, 1990, Tokyo: Kyoritsu Shuppan)

Arabie, P., Carroll, J. D., DeSarbo, W., & Wind, J. (1981). Overlapping clustering: A new method for product positioning. *Journal of Marketing Research, 18,* 310–317. (Republished in 1989, *Multidimensional scaling,* pp. 235–246, by P. E. Green, F. J. Carmone, Jr., & S. M. Smith, Boston: Allyn and Bacon)

Arabie, P., & Hubert, L. (1996). An overview of combinatorial data analysis. In P. Arabie, L. J. Hubert, & G. De Soete (Eds.), *Clustering and classification* (pp. 5–63). River Edge, NJ: World Scientific.

Arabie, P., Hubert, L. J., & De Soete, G. (Eds.). (1996). *Clustering and classification.* River Edge, NJ: World Scientific.

Arce, C. (1993). *Escalamiento multidimensional* [Multidimensional scaling]. Barcelona: Promociones y Publicaciones Universitarias.

Ashby, F. G. (Ed.). (1992). *Multidimensional models of perception and cognition.* Mahwah, NJ: Erlbaum.

Ashby, F. G., Maddox, W. T., & Lee, W. W. (1994). On the dangers of averaging across subjects when using multidimensional scaling or the similarity-choice model. *Psychological Science, 5,* 144–151.

Attneave, F. (1950). Dimensions of similarity. *American Journal of Psychology, 63,* 516–556.

Ayer, M., Brunk, H. D., Ewing, G. M., Reid, W. T., & Silverman, E. (1955). An empirical distribution function for sampling with incomplete information. *Annals of Mathematical Statistics, 26,* 641–647.

Bloxom, B. (1978). Constrained multidimensional scaling in N spaces. *Psychometrika, 43,* 397–408.

Blumenthal, L. M., & Menger, K. (1970). *Studies in geometry.* New York: W. H. Freeman.

Bové, G., & Critchley, F. (1989). The representation of asymmetric proximities. *Proceedings of the First Meeting of the IFCS Italian Group of the Italian Statistical Society* (pp. 53–68). Palermo: Ila Palma.

Bové, G., & Critchley, F. (1993). Metric multidimensional scaling for asymmetric proximities when the asymmetry is one-dimensional. In R. Steyer, K. F. Wender, & K. F. Widaman (Eds.), *Psychometric methodology: Proceedings of the 7th European Meeting of the Psychometric Society in Trier* (pp. 55–60). Stuttgart: Gustav Fischer Verlag.

Bové, G., & Rocci, R. (1993). An alternating least squares method to analyse asymmetric two-mode three-way data. *Proceedings of the 1993 European Meeting of the Psychometric Society* (p. 58). Barcelona: Universidad Pompeu Fabra.

Brady, H. E. (1985). Statistical consistency and hypothesis testing for nonmetric multidimensional scaling. *Psychometrika, 50,* 509–537.

Brady, H. E. (1990). *Statistical properties of alternating least squares and maximum likelihood estimators for vector and squared Euclidean functional preference models.* Berkeley: University of California, Department of Political Science.

Carroll, J. D. (1968). Generalization of canonical correlation analysis to three or more sets of variables. *Proceedings of the 76th Annual Convention of the American Psychological Association, 3,* 227–228.

Carroll, J. D. (1972). Individual differences and multidimensional scaling. In R. N. Shepard, A. K. Romney, & S. B. Nerlove (Eds.), *Multidimensional scaling: Theory and applications in the behavioral sciences: Vol. 1. Theory* (pp. 105–155). New York: Seminar Press. (Reprinted in Key texts on multidimensional scaling; by P. Davies, & A. P. M. Coxon, Eds., 1984, Portsmouth, NH: Heinemann)

Carroll, J. D. (1976). Spatial, non-spatial and hybrid models for scaling. *Psychometrika, 41,* 439–463.

Carroll, J. D. (1980). Models and methods for multidimensional analysis of preferential choice (or other dominance) data. In E. D. Lantermann & H. Feger (Eds.), *Similarity and choice* (pp. 234–289). Bern: Hans Huber.

Carroll, J. D. (1988). *Degenerate solutions in the nonmetric fitting of a wide class of models for proximity data.* Unpublished manuscript, Rutgers University, Graduate School of Management, Newark, New Jersey.

Carroll, J. D. (1992). Metric, nonmetric, and quasi-nonmetric analysis of psychological data. Presidential Address for Division 5, 1992 American Psychological Association Meeting, Washington, DC. Abstract in October 1992 *Score* (Division 5 Newsletter).

Carroll, J. D., & Arabie, P. (1980). Multidimensional scaling. In M. R. Rosenzweig & L. W. Porter (Eds.), *Annual review of psychology* (Vol. 31, pp. 607–649). Palo Alto, CA: Annual Reviews. (Reprinted in *Multidimensional scaling: Concepts and applications,* pp. 168–204, by P. E. Green, F. J. Carmone, & S. M. Smith, 1989, Needham Heights, MA: Allyn and Bacon)

Carroll, J. D., & Arabie, P. (1983). INDCLUS: An individual differences generalization of the ADCLUS model and the MAPCLUS algorithm. *Psychometrika, 48,* 157–169. (Reprinted in *Research methods for multimode data analysis,* pp. 372–402, by H. G. Law, W. Snyder, J. Hattie, & R. P. McDonald, Eds., 1984, New York: Praeger)

Carroll, J. D., & Chang, J. J. (1969). A new method for dealing with individual differences in multidimensional scaling (Abstract). *Proceedings of the 19th International Congress of Psychology.* London, England.

Carroll, J. D., & Chang, J. J. (1970). Analysis of individual differences in multidimensional scaling via an *N*-way generalization of "Eckart-Young" decomposition. *Psychometrika, 35,* 283–319. (Reprinted in Key texts in multidimensional scaling, by P. Davies & A. P. M. Coxon, Eds., 1984, Portsmouth, NH: Heinemann)

Carroll, J. D., & Chang, J. J. (1972, March). *IDIOSCAL (Individual Differences in Orientation SCALing): A generalization of INDSCAL allowing IDIOsyncratic reference systems as well as an analytic approximation to INDSCAL.* Unpublished manuscript, AT&T Bell Laboratories, Murray Hill, NJ. Presented at a meeting of the Psychometric Society, Princeton, NJ.

Carroll, J. D., & Chang, J. J. (1973). A method for fitting a class of hierarchical tree structure models to dissimilarities data and its application to some "body parts" data of Miller's. *Proceedings of the 81st Annual Convention of the American Psychological Association, 8,* 1097–1098.

Carroll, J. D., & Chaturvedi, A. (1995). A general approach to clustering and multidimensional scaling of two-way, three-way, or higher-way data. In R. D. Luce, M. D'Zmura, D. D. Hoffman, G. Iverson, & A. K. Romney (Eds.), *Geometric representations of perceptual phenomena* (pp. 295–318). Mahwah, NJ: Erlbaum.

Carroll, J. D., Clark, L. A., & DeSarbo, W. S. (1984). The representation of three-way proximities data by single and multiple tree structure models. *Journal of Classification, 1,* 25–74.

Carroll, J. D., & Corter, J. E. (1995). A graph-theoretic method for organizing overlapping clusters into trees and extended trees. *Journal of Classification, 12,* 283–313.

Carroll, J. D., & De Soete, G. (1991). Toward a new paradigm for the study of multiattribute choice behavior. *American Psychologist, 46,* 342–351.

Carroll, J. D., De Soete, G., & Pruzansky, S. (1988). A comparison of three rational initialization methods for INDSCAL. In E. Diday (Ed.), *Data analysis and informatics V* (pp. 131–142). Amsterdam: North Holland.

Carroll, J. D., De Soete, G. & Pruzansky, S. (1989). Fitting of the latent class model via iteratively reweighted least squares CANDECOMP with nonnegativity constraints. In R. Coppi & S. Bolasco (Eds.), *Multiway data analysis* (pp. 463–472). Amsterdam: North Holland.

Carroll, J. D., & Green, P. E. (1997). Psychometric methods in marketing research: Part II, multidimensional scaling [Guest editorial]. *Journal of Marketing Research, 34,* 193–204.

Carroll, J. D., Kumbasar, E., & Romney, A. K. (1997). An equivalence relation between correspondence analysis and classical metric multidimensional scaling for the recovery of Euclidean distances. *British Journal of Mathematical and Statistical Psychology, 50,* 81–92.

Carroll, J. D., & Pruzansky, S. (1975). Fitting of hierarchical tree structure (HTS) models, mixtures of HTS models, and hybrid models, via mathematical programming and alternating least squares. *Proceedings of the U.S.–Japan Seminar on Multidimensional Scaling,* 9–19.

Carroll, J. D., & Pruzansky, S. (1980). Discrete and hybrid scaling models. In E. D. Lantermann & H. Feger (Eds.), *Similarity and choice* (pp. 108–139). Bern, Switzerland: Hans Huber.

Carroll, J. D., & Pruzansky, S. (1983). Representing proximities data by discrete, continuous or "hybrid" models. In J. Felsenstein (Ed.), *Numerical taxonomy* (pp. 229–248). New York: Springer-Verlag.

Carroll, J. D., & Pruzansky, S. (1986). Discrete and hybrid models for proximity data. In W. Gaul & M. Schader (Eds.), *Classification as a tool of research* (pp. 47–59). Amsterdam: North Holland.

Carroll, J. D., & Winsberg, S. (1986). Maximum likelihood procedures for metric and quasi-nonmetric fitting of an extended INDSCAL model assuming both common and specific dimensions. In J. de Leeuw, W. J. Heiser, J. Meulman, & F. Critchley (Eds.), *Multidimensional data analysis* (pp. 240–241). Leiden: DSWO Press.

Carroll, J. D., & Winsberg, S. (1995). Fitting an extended INDSCAL model to three-way proximity data. *Journal of Classification, 12,* 57–71.

Carroll, J. D., & Wish, M. (1974a). Models and methods for three-way multidimensional scaling. In D. H. Krantz, R. C. Atkinson, R. D. Luce, & P. Suppes (Eds.), *Contemporary developments in mathematical psychology* (Vol. 2, pp. 57–105). San Francisco: W. H. Freeman.

Carroll, J. D., & Wish, M. (1974b). Multidimensional perceptual models and measurement methods. In E. C. Carterette & M. P. Friedman (Eds.), *Handbook of perception* (Vol. 2, pp. 391–447). New York: Academic Press. (Reprinted in *Key texts in multidimensional scaling,* by P. Davies & A. P. M. Coxon, Eds., 1984, Portsmouth, NH: Heinemann)

Chandon, J. L., & De Soete, G. (1984). Fitting a least squares ultrametric to dissimilarity data: Approximation versus optimization. In E. Diday, M. Jambu, L. Lebart, J. Pagès, & R. Tomassone (Eds.), *Data analysis and informatics III* (pp. 213–221). Amsterdam: North-Holland.

Chang, J. J., & Carroll, J. D. (1969a). *How to use INDSCAL, a computer program for canonical decomposition of N-way tables and individual differences in multidimensional scaling.* Murray Hill, NJ: AT&T Bell Laboratories.

Chang, J. J., & Carroll, J. D. (1969b). *How to use MDPREF, a computer program for multidimensional analysis of preference data.* Murray Hill, NJ: AT&T Bell Laboratories.

Chang, J. J., & Carroll, J. D. (1989). A short-guide to MDPREF: Multidimensional analysis of preference data. In P. E. Green, F. J. Carmone, & S. M. Smith, *Multidimensional scaling: Concepts and applications* (pp. 279–286). Needham Heights, MA: Allyn and Bacon.

Chaturvedi, A., & Carroll, J. D. (1994). An alternating combinatorial optimization approach to fitting the INDCLUS and generalized INDCLUS models. *Journal of Classification, 11,* 155–170.

Chaturvedi, A., & Carroll, J. D. (1997). An L_1-norm procedure for fitting overlapping clustering models to proximity data. In Y. Dodge (Ed.), *Statistical data analysis based on the L_1-norm and related methods* (IMS Lecture Notes Monograph No. 30, pp. 443–456). Hayward, CA: Institute of Mathematical Statistics.

Chino, N. (1978). A graphical technique for representing the asymmetric relationships between N objects. *Behaviormetrika, 5,* 23–40.

Chino, N. (1990). A generalized inner product model for the analysis of asymmetry. *Behaviormetrika, 27,* 25–46.

Cliff, N., Pennell, R., & Young, F. W. (1966). Multidimensional scaling in the study of set. *American Psychologist, 21,* 707.

Commandeur, J. J. F. (1991). *Matching configurations.* Leiden: DSWO Press.

Coombs, C. H. (1964). *A theory of data.* New York: Wiley.

Cooper, L. G., & Nakanishi, M. (1988). *Market-share analysis.* Boston: Kluwer.

Corter, J., & Tversky, A. (1986). Extended similarity trees. *Psychometrika, 51,* 429–451.

Cox, T. F., & Cox, M. A. A. (1994). *Multidimensional scaling.* London: Chapman & Hall.

Cox, T. F., Cox, M. A. A., & Branco, J. A. (1991). Multidimensional scaling for n-tuples. *British Journal of Mathematical and Statistical Psychology, 44,* 195–206.

Critchley, F. (1986). Analysis of residuals and regional representation in nonmetric multidimensional scaling. In W. Gaul & M. Schader (Eds.), *Classification as a tool of research* (pp. 67–77). Amsterdam: North-Holland.

Critchley, F., & Fichet, B. (1994). The partial order by inclusion of the principal classes of dissimilarity on a finite set, and some of their basic properties. In B. Van Cutsem (Ed.), *Classification and dissimilarity analysis* (pp. 5–66). Heidelberg: Springer-Verlag.

Cuadras, C. M., Fortiana, J., & Oliva, F. (1996). Representation of statistical structures, classification and prediction using multidimensional scaling. In W. Gaul & D. Pfeifer (Eds.), *From data to knowledge* (pp. 20–31). Heidelberg: Springer-Verlag.

Daws, J. T. (1993). *The analysis of free-sorting data: Beyond pairwise cooccurrences.* (Doctoral dissertation, University of Illinois at Urbana-Champaign). (UMI Dissertation NO. 9411601).

Daws, J. T. (1996). The analysis of free-sorting data: Beyond pairwise cooccurrences. *Journal of Classification, 13,* 57–80.

Degerman, R. L. (1970). Multidimensional analysis of complex structure: Mixtures of class and quantitative variation. *Psychometrika, 35,* 475–491.

de Leeuw, J. (1977a). Applications of convex analysis to multidimensional scaling. In J. R. Barra, F. Brodeau, G. Romier, & B. van Cutsem (Eds.), *Recent developments in statistics* (pp. 133–145). Amsterdam: North-Holland.

de Leeuw, J. (1977b). Correctness of Kruskal's algorithms for monotone regression with ties. *Psychometrika, 42,* 141–144.

de Leeuw, J. (1988). Convergence of the majorization method for multidimensional scaling. *Journal of Classification, 5,* 163–180.

de Leeuw, J., & Heiser, W. (1977). Convergence of correction-matrix algorithms for multidimensional scaling. In J. C. Lingoes (Ed.), *Geometric representations of relational data: Readings in multidimensional scaling* (pp. 735–752). Ann Arbor, MI: Mathesis.

de Leeuw, J., & Heiser, W. (1980). Multidimensional scaling with restrictions on the configuration. In P. R. Krishnaiah (Ed.), *Multivariate analysis* (Vol. 5, pp. 501–522). New York: North Holland.

de Leeuw, J., & Heiser, W. (1982). Theory of multidimensional scaling. In P. R. Krishnaiah, & L. N. Kanal (Eds.), *Handbook of statistics Vol. 2: Classification, pattern recognition and reduction of dimensionality* (pp. 285–316). Amsterdam: North-Holland.

de Leeuw, J., Heiser, W., Meulman, J., & Critchley, F. (Eds.). (1986). *Multidimensional data analysis.* Leiden: DSWO Press.

de Leeuw, J., & Meulman, J. (1986). A special jackknife for multidimensional scaling. *Journal of Classification, 3,* 97–112.

DeSarbo, W. S. (1982). GENNCLUS: New models for general nonhierarchical clustering analysis. *Psychometrika, 47,* 446–449.

DeSarbo, W. S., & Carroll, J. D. (1981). Three-way metric unfolding. *Proceedings of the Third ORSA/TIMS Special Interest Conference on Market Measurement and Analysis,* 157–183.

DeSarbo, W. S., & Carroll, J. D. (1985). Three-way metric unfolding via weighted least squares. *Psychometrika, 50,* 275–300.

DeSarbo, W. S., Carroll, J. D., Lehman, D. R., & O'Shaughnessy, J. (1982). Three-way multivariate conjoint analysis. *Marketing Science, 1,* 323–350.

DeSarbo, W. S., Johnson, M. D., Manrai, A. K., Manrai, L. A., & Edwards, E. A. (1992). TSCALE: A new multidimensional scaling procedure based on Tversky's contrast model. *Psychometrika, 57,* 43–69.

DeSarbo, W. S., & Manrai, A. K., (1992). A new multidimensional scaling methodology for the analysis of asymmetric proximity data in marketing research. *Marketing Science,* 11, 1–20.

De Soete, G. (1983). A least squares algorithm for fitting additive trees to proximity data. *Psychometrika, 48,* 621–626.

De Soete, G., & Carroll, J. D. (1989). Ultrametric tree representations of three-way three-mode data. In R. Coppi & S. Bolasco (Eds.), *Analysis of multiway data matrices* (pp. 415–426). Amsterdam: North-Holland.

De Soete, G., & Carroll, J. D. (1992). Probabilistic multidimensional models of pairwise choice data. In F. G. Ashby (Ed.), *Multidimensional models of perception and cognition* (pp. 61–88). Mahwah, NJ: Erlbaum.

De Soete, G., & Carroll, J. D. (1996). Tree and other network models for representing proximity data. In P. Arabie, L. J. Hubert, & G. De Soete (Eds.), *Clustering and classification* (pp. 157–197). River Edge, NJ: World Scientific.

De Soete, G., DeSarbo, W. S., Furnas, G. W., & Carroll, J. D. (1984a). The estimation of ultrametric and path length trees from rectangular proximity data. *Psychometrika, 49,* 289–310.

De Soete, G., DeSarbo, W. S., Furnas, G. W., & Carroll, J. D. (1984b). Tree representations of rectangular proximity matrices. In E. Degreef & J. Van Buggenhaut (Eds.), *Trends in mathematical psychology* (pp. 377–392). Amsterdam: North-Holland.

De Soete, G., Feger, H., & Klauer, K. C. (Eds.) (1989). *New developments in psychological choice modeling.* Amsterdam: North-Holland.

Dijksterhuis, G. B., & Gower, J. C. (1991/1992). The interpretation of generalized Procrustes analysis and allied methods. *Food Quality and Preference, 3,* 67–87.

Easterling, D. V. (1987). Political science: Using the generalized Euclidean model to study ideological shifts in the U.S. Senate. In F. Young & R. M. Hamer (Eds.), *Multidimensional scaling: History, theory, and applications* (pp. 219–256). Mahwah, NJ: Erlbaum.

Ennis, D. M., Palen, J. J., & Mullen, K. (1988). A multidimensional stochastic theory of similarity. *Journal of Mathematical Psychology, 32,* 449–465.

Escoufier, Y., & Grorud, A. (1980). Analyse factorielle des matrices carrees non symetriques. [Factor analysis of square nonsymmetric matrices]. In E. Diday, L. Lebart, J. P. Pagès, & R. Tomassone (Eds.), *Data analysis and informatics* (pp. 263–276). Amsterdam: North-Holland.

Fichet, B. (1994). Dimensionality problems in L_1-norm representations. In B. Van Cutsem (Ed.), *Classification and dissimilarity analysis* (pp. 201–224). Heidelberg: Springer-Verlag.

Fitzgerald, L. F., & Hubert, L. J. (1987). Multidimensional scaling: Some possibilities for counseling psychology. *Journal of Counseling Psychology, 34,* 469–480.

Furnas, G. W. (1980). *Objects and their features: The metric analysis of two-class data.* Unpublished doctoral dissertation, Stanford University, Stanford, CA.

Furnas, G. W. (1989). Metric family portraits. *Journal of Classification, 6,* 7–52.

Gabriel, K. R. (1971). The biplot-graphic display of matrices with application to principal component analysis. *Biometrika, 58,* 453–467.

Gifi, A. (1990). *Nonlinear multivariate analysis.* New York: Wiley.

Glazer, R., & Nakamoto, K. (1991). Cognitive geometry: An analysis of structure underlying representations of similarity. *Marketing Science, 10,* 205–228.

Gordon, A. D. (1996). Hierarchical classification. In P. Arabie, L. J. Hubert, & G. De Soete (Eds.), *Clustering and classification* (pp. 65–121). River Edge, NJ: World Scientific.

Gordon, A. D., Jupp, P. E., & Byrne, R. W. (1989). The construction and assessment of mental maps. *British Journal of Mathematical and Statistical Psychology, 42,* 169–182.

Gower, J. C. (1966). Some distance properties of latent root and vector methods used in multivariate analysis. *Biometrika, 53,* 325–338.

Gower, J. C. (1975). Generalized procrustes analysis. *Psychometrika, 40,* 33–51.

Gower, J. C. (1977). The analysis of asymmetry and orthogonality. In J. Barra, F. Brodeau, G. Romier, & B. van Cutsem (Eds.), *Recent developments in statistics* (pp. 109–123). Amsterdam: North-Holland.

Gower, J. C. (1990). Three-dimensional biplots. *Biometrika, 77,* 773–785.

Gower, J. C. (1995a). Orthogonal and projection Procrustes analysis. In W. J. Krzanowski (Ed.), *Recent advances in descriptive multivariate analysis* (pp. 113–134). Oxford: Clarendon Press.

Gower, J. C. (1995b). A general theory of biplots. In W. J. Krzanowski (Ed.), *Recent advances in descriptive multivariate analysis* (pp. 283–303). Oxford: Clarendon Press.

Gower, J. C., & Greenacre, M. J. (1996). Unfolding a symmetric matrix. *Journal of Classification, 13,* 81–105.

Gower, J. C., & Hand, D. J. (1996). *Biplots.* New York: Chapman & Hall.

Gower, J. C., & Harding, S. A. (1988). Nonlinear biplots. *Biometrika, 75,* 445–455.

Green, P. E., Carmone, F. J., Jr., & Smith, S. M. (1989). *Multidimensional scaling: Concepts and applications.* Boston: Allyn and Bacon.

Green, P. E., & Rao, V. R. (1972). Configural synthesis in multidimensional scaling. *Journal of Marketing Research, 9,* 65–68.

Greenacre, M. J. (1984). *Theory and applications of correspondence analysis.* London: Academic Press.

Greenacre, M. J. (1986). Discussion on paper by Gabriel and Odoroff. In J. de Leeuw, W. Heiser, J. Meulman, & F. Critchley (Eds.), *Multidimensional data analysis* (pp. 113–114). Leiden: DSWO Press.

Greenacre, M. J., & Blasius, J. (Eds.). (1994). *Correspondence analysis: Recent developments and applications.* New York: Academic Press.

Greenacre, M. J., & Browne, M. W. (1986). An efficient alternating least-squares algorithm to perform multidimensional unfolding. *Psychometrika, 51,* 241–250.

Groenen, P. J. F. (1993). *The majorization approach to multidimensional scaling: Some problems and extensions.* Leiden: DSWO Press.

Groenen, P. J. F., de Leeuw, J., & Mathar, R. (1996). Least squares multidimensional scaling with transformed distances. In W. Gaul & D. Pfeifer (Eds.), *From data to knowledge* (pp. 177–185). Heidelberg: Springer-Verlag.

Groenen, P. J. F., Mathar, R., & Heiser, W. J. (1995). The majorization approach to multidimensional scaling for Minkowski distances. *Journal of Classification, 12,* 3–19.

Guttman, L. (1968). A general nonmetric technique for finding the smallest coordinate space for a configuration of points. *Psychometrika, 33,* 465–506.

Hahn, J., Widaman, K. F., & MacCallum, R. (1978). *Robustness of INDSCAL and ALSCAL with respect to violations of metric assumptions.* Paper presented at the Annual Meeting of the Psychometric Society, Hamilton, Ontario, Canada.

Harshman, R. A. (1972a). Determination and proof of minimum uniqueness conditions for PARAFAC1. University of California at Los Angeles, *Working Papers in Phonetics 22.*

Harshman, R. A. (1972b). PARAFAC2: Mathematical and technical notes. University of California at Los Angeles, *Working Papers in Phonetics 22.*

Hartigan, J. A. (1967). Representation of similarity matrices by trees. *Journal of the American Statistical Association, 62,* 1140–1158.

Hartigan, J. A. (1975). *Clustering algorithms.* New York: Wiley (Translated into Japanese by H. Nishida, M. Yoshida, H. Hiramatsu, & K. Tanaka, 1983, Tokyo: Micro Software).

Heiser, W. J. (1981). *Unfolding analysis of proximity data.* Unpublished doctoral dissertation, University of Leiden.

Heiser, W. J. (1985). *Multidimensional scaling by optimizing goodness-of-fit to a smooth hypothesis.* Internal Report RR-85-07. University of Leiden: Department of Data Theory.

Heiser, W. J. (1987). Joint ordination of species and sites: The unfolding technique. In P. Legendre & L. Legendre (Eds.), *Developments in numerical ecology* (pp. 189–221). Heidelberg: Springer-Verlag.

Heiser, W. J. (1988). Multidimensional scaling with least absolute residuals. In H.-H. Bock (Ed.), *Classification and related methods of data analysis* (pp. 455–462). Amsterdam: North-Holland.

Heiser, W. J. (1989a). The city-block model for three-way multidimensional scaling. In R. Coppi & S. Bolasco (Eds.), *Multiway data analysis* (pp. 395–404). Amsterdam: North-Holland.

Heiser, W. J. (1989b). Order invariant unfolding analysis under smoothness restrictions. In G. De Soete, H. Feger, & C. Klauer (Eds.), *New developments in psychological choice modeling* (pp. 3–31). Amsterdam: North-Holland.

Heiser, W. J. (1991). A generalized majorization method for least squares multidimensional scaling of pseudodistances that may be negative. *Psychometrika, 56,* 7–27.

Heiser, W. J. (1995). Convergent computation by iterative majorization: Theory and applications in multidimensional data analysis. In W. Krzanowski (Ed.), *Recent advances in descriptive multivariate analysis* (pp. 149–181). New York: Oxford University Press.

Heiser, W. J., & de Leeuw, J. (1979). *How to use SMACOF-III* (Research Report). Leiden: Department of Data Theory.

Heiser, W. J., & Meulman, J. (1983a). Analyzing rectangular tables by joint and constrained multidimensional scaling. *Journal of Econometrics, 22,* 139–167.

Heiser, W. J., & Meulman, J. (1983b). Constrained multidimensional scaling, including confirmation. *Applied Psychological Measurement, 7,* 381–404.

Holman, E. W. (1972). The relation between hierarchical and Euclidean models for psychological distances. *Psychometrika, 37,* 417–423.

Holman, E. W. (1978). Completely nonmetric multidimensional scaling. *Journal of Mathematical Psychology, 18,* 39–51.

Holman, E. W. (1979). Monotonic models for asymmetric proximities. *Journal of Mathematical Psychology, 20,* 1–15.

Hubert, L. J. (1978). Generalized proximity function comparisons. *British Journal of Mathematical and Statistical Psychology, 31,* 179–192.

Hubert, L. J. (1979). Generalized concordance. *Psychometrika, 44,* 135–142.

Hubert, L. J. (1985). Combinatorial data analysis: Association and partial association. *Psychometrika, 50,* 449–467.

Hubert, L. J. (1987). *Assignment methods in combinatorial data analysis.* New York: Marcel Dekker.

Hubert, L., & Arabie, P. (1986). Unidimensional scaling and combinatorial optimization. In J. de Leeuw, W. Heiser, J. Meulman, & F. Critchley (Eds.), *Multidimensional data analysis* (pp. 181–196). Leiden: DSWO Press.

Hubert, L., & Arabie, P. (1987). Evaluating order hypotheses within matrices. *Psychological Bulletin, 102,* 172–178.

Hubert, L., & Arabie, P. (1988). Relying on necessary conditions for optimization: Unidimensional scaling and some extensions. In H.-H. Bock (Ed.), *Classification and related methods of data analysis* (pp. 463–472). Amsterdam: North-Holland.

Hubert, L., & Arabie, P. (1989). Combinatorial data analysis: Confirmatory comparisons between sets of matrices. *Applied Stochastic Models and Data Analysis, 5,* 273–325.

Hubert, L., & Arabie, P. (1992). Correspondence analysis and optimal structural representations. *Psychometrika, 56,* 119–140.

Hubert, L., & Arabie, P. (1994). The analysis of proximity matrices through sums of matrices having (anti-)Robinson forms. *British Journal of Mathematical and Statistical Psychology, 47,* 1–40.

Hubert, L., & Arabie, P. (1995a). The approximation of two-mode proximity matrices by sums of order-constrained matrices. *Psychometrika, 60,* 573–605.

Hubert, L., & Arabie, P. (1995b). Iterative projection strategies for the least-squares fitting of tree structures to proximity data. *British Journal of Mathematical and Statistical Psychology, 48,* 281–317.

Hubert, L. J., Arabie, P., & Hesson-Mcinnis, M. (1992). Multidimensional scaling in the city-block metric: A combinatorial approach. *Journal of Classification, 9,* 211–236.

Hubert, L. J., Arabie, P., & Meulman, J. (1997). Linear and circular unidimensional scaling for symmetric proximity matrices. *British Journal of Mathematical and Statistical Psychology, 50.*

Hubert, L. J., & Baker, F. B. (1979). Evaluating the symmetry of a proximity matrix. *Quality and Quantity, 13*, 77–84.

Hubert, L. J., & Golledge, R. G. (1981). A heuristic method for the comparison of related structures. *Journal of Mathematical Psychology, 23*, 214–226.

Hubert, L. J., & Schultz, J. R. (1976). Quadratic assignment as a general data analysis strategy. *British Journal of Mathematical and Statistical Psychology, 29*, 190–241.

Hubert, L. J., & Subkoviak, M. J. (1979). Confirmatory inference and geometric models. *Psychological Bulletin, 86*, 361–370.

Hutchinson, J. W. (1981). *Network representations of psychological relations*. Unpublished doctoral dissertation, Stanford University.

Hutchinson, J. W. (1989). NETSCAL: A network scaling algorithm for nonsymmetric proximity data. *Psychometrika, 54*, 25–51.

Indow, T. (1983). An approach to geometry of visual space with no a priori mapping functions: Multidimensional mapping according to Riemannian metrics. *Journal of Mathematical Psychology, 26*, 204–236.

Indow, T. (1995). Psychophysical scaling: Scientific and practical applications. In R. D. Luce, M. D'Zmura, D. D. Hoffman, G. Iverson, & A. K. Romney (Eds.), *Geometric representations of perceptual phenomena* (pp. 1–28). Mahwah, NJ: Erlbaum.

Johnson, R. M. (1975). A simple method for pairwise monotone regression. *Psychometrika, 40*, 163–168.

Johnson, S. C. (1967). Hierarchical clustering schemes. *Psychometrika, 32*, 241–254.

Joly, S., & Le Calvé, G. (submitted). Realisable 0–1 matrices and city block distance.

Joly, S., & Le Calvé, G. (1995). Three-way distances. *Journal of Classification, 12*, 191–205.

Jones, L. E., & Koehly, L. M. (1993). Multidimensional scaling. In G. Keren & C. Lewis (Eds.), *A handbook for data analysis in the behavioral sciences: Methodological issues* (pp. 95–163). Mahwah, NJ: Erlbaum.

Jones, W. P., & Furnas, G. W. (1987). Pictures of relevance: A geometric analysis of similarity measures. *Journal of the American Society for Information Science, 38*, 420–442.

Keller, J. B. (1962). Factorization of matrices by least-squares. *Biometrika, 49*, 239–242.

Kiers, H. A. L. (1990). Majorization as a tool for optimizing a class of matrix functions. *Psychometrika, 55*, 417–428.

Kiers, H. A. L., & Takane, Y. (1994). A generalization of GIPSCAL for the analysis of nonsymmetric data. *Journal of Classification, 11*, 79–99.

Kiers, H. A. L., & ten Berge, J. M. F. (1992). Minimization of a class of matrix trace functions by means of refined majorization. *Psychometrika, 57*, 371–382.

Klauer, K. C., & Carroll, J. D. (1989). A mathematical programming approach to fitting general graphs. *Journal of Classification, 6*, 247–270.

Klauer, K. C., & Carroll, J. D. (1991). A comparison of two approaches to fitting directed graphs to nonsymmetric proximity measures. *Journal of Classification, 8*, 251–268.

Klauer, K. C., & Carroll, J. D. (1995). Network models for scaling proximity data. In R. D. Luce, M. D'Zmura, D. Hoffman, G. J. Iverson & A. K. Romney (Eds.), *Geometric representations of perceptual phenomena* (pp. 319–342). Mahwah, NJ: Erlbaum.

Krijnen, W. P. (1993). *The analysis of three-way arrays by constrained PARAFAC methods*. Leiden: DSWO Press.

Kroonenberg, P. M. (1983). *Three-mode principal component analysis: Theory and applications*. Leiden: DSWO Press.

Kroonenberg, P. M., & de Leeuw, J. (1980). Principal component analysis of three-mode data by means of alternating least squares algorithms. *Psychometrika, 45*, 69–97.

Krumhansl, C. L. (1978). Concerning the applicability of geometric models to similarity data: The interrelationship between similarity and spatial density. *Psychological Review, 85*, 445–463.

Kruskal, J. B. (1964a). Multidimensional scaling by optimizing goodness of fit to a nonmetric hypothesis. *Psychometrika, 29,* 1–27.

Kruskal, J. B. (1964b). Nonmetric multidimensional scaling: A numerical method. *Psychometrika, 29,* 115–129.

Kruskal, J. B. (1965). Analysis of factorial experiments by estimating monotone transformations of the data. *Journal of the Royal Statistical Society, Series B, 27,* 251–263.

Kruskal, J. B. (1976). More factors than subjects, tests and treatments: An interdeterminacy theorem for canonical decomposition and individual differences scaling. *Psychometrika, 41,* 281–293.

Kruskal, J. B., & Carroll, J. D. (1969). Geometrical models and badness-of-fit functions. In P. R. Krishnaiah (Ed.), *Multivariate analysis II* (pp. 639–671). New York: Academic Press.

Kruskal, J. B., & Wish, M. (1978). *Multidimensional scaling.* Newbury Park, CA: Sage.

Kruskal, J. B., Young, F. W., & Seery, J. B. (1973). *How to use KYST, a very flexible program to do multidimensional scaling and unfolding.* Murray Hill, NJ: AT&T Bell Laboratories.

Krzanowski, W. J., & Marriott, F. H. C. (1994). *Multivariate analysis. Part 1: Distributions, ordination and inference.* New York: Wiley.

Lance, G. N., & Williams, W. T. (1967). A general theory of classificatory sorting strategies. I. Hierarchical systems. *Computer Journal, 9,* 373–380.

Landauer, T. K., & Dumais, S. T. (1997). A solution to Plato's problem: The latent semantic analysis theory of acquisition, induction, and representation of knowledge. *Psychological Review, 104,* 211–240.

Lebart, L., Morineau, A., & Warwick, K. M. (1984). *Multivariate descriptive statistical analysis: Correspondence analysis and related techniques for large matrices* (E. M. Berry, Trans.). New York: Wiley. (Original work published 1977).

Lee, S.-K., & Bentler, P. M. (1980). Functional relations in multidimensional scaling. *British Journal of Mathematical and Statistical Psychology, 33,* 142–150.

Levelt, W. J. M., van de Geer, J. P., & Plomp, R. (1966). Triadic comparisons of musical intervals. *British Journal of Mathematical and Statistical Psychology, 19,* 163–179.

Lingoes, J. C., & Borg, I. (1978). A direct approach to individual differences scaling using increasingly complex transformations. *Psychometrika, 43,* 491–519.

Littman, L., Swayne, D. F., Dean, N., & Buja, A. (1992). Visualizing the embedding of objects in Euclidian space. In *Computing science and statistics: Proceedings of the 24th symposium on the interface* (pp. 208–217). Fairfax Station, VA: Interface Foundation of North America.

Lockhead, G. R., & Pomerantz, J. R. (Eds.) (1991). *The perception of structure.* Arlington, VA: American Psychological Association.

Luce, R. D., & Krumhansl, C. L. (1988). Measurement, scaling, and psychophysics. In R. C. Atkinson, R. J. Herrnstein, G. Lindzey, & R. D. Luce (Eds.), *Stevens' handbook of experimental psychology* (pp. 3–74). New York: Wiley.

MacCallum, R. C. (1977). Effects of conditionality on INDSCAL and ALSCAL weights. *Psychometrika, 42,* 297–305.

Marley, A. A. J. (1992). Developing and characterizing multidimensional Thurstone and Luce models for identification and preference. In F. G. Ashby (Ed.), *Multidimensional models of perception and cognition* (pp. 299–333). Mahwah, NJ: Erlbaum.

McDonald, R. P. (1976). A note on monotone polygons fitted to bivariate data. *Psychometrika, 41,* 543–546.

Meulman, J. J. (1992). The integration of multidimensional scaling and multivariate analysis with optimal transformations. *Psychometrika, 57,* 539–565.

Meulman, J. J., & Heiser, W. J. (1993). Nonlinear biplots for nonlinear mappings. In O. Opitz, B. Lausen, & R. Klar (Eds.), *Information and classification* (pp. 201–213). New York: Springer-Verlag.

Meulman, J. J., & Verboon, P. (1993). Points of view analysis revisited: Fitting multidimensional structures to optimal distance components with cluster restrictions on the variables. *Psychometrika, 58,* 7–35.

Miller, K. F. (1987). Geometric methods in developmental research. In J. Bisanz, C. J. Brainerd, & R. Kail (Eds.), *Formal methods in developmental psychology* (pp. 216–262). New York: Springer-Verlag.

Mirkin, B. (1996). *Mathematical classification and clustering.* Dordrecht: Kluwer.

Mirkin, B. G., & Muchnik, I. (1996). Clustering and multidimensional scaling in Russia (1960–1990): A review. In P. Arabie, L. J. Hubert, & G. De Soege (Eds.), *Clustering and classification* (pp. 295–339). River Edge, NJ: World Scientific.

Molenaar, I. W. (1986). Deconfusing confusion matrices. In J. de Leeuw, W. Heiser, J. Meulman, & F. Critchley (Eds.), *Multidimensional data analysis* (pp. 139–145). Leiden: DSWO Press.

Murtagh, F. (Ed.). (1997). *Classification Literature Automated Search Service, 26.*

Nishisato, S. (1980). *Analysis of categorical data: Dual scaling and its applications.* Toronto: University of Toronto Press.

Nishisato, S. (1993). *Elements of dual scaling: An introduction to practical data analysis.* Mahwah, NJ: Erlbaum.

Nishisato, S. (1996a). An overview and recent developments in dual scaling. In W. Gaul & D. Pfeifer (Eds.), *From data to knowledge* (pp. 73–85). Heidelberg: Springer-Verlag.

Nishisato, S. (1996b). Gleaning in the field of dual scaling. *Psychometrika, 61,* 559–599.

Nosofsky, R. M. (1991). Stimulus bias, asymmetric similarity, and classification. *Cognitive Psychology, 23,* 94–140.

Nosofsky, R. M. (1992). Similarity scaling and cognitive process models. *Annual Review of Psychology, 43,* 25–53.

Okada, A. (1990). A generalization of asymmetric multidimensional scaling. In M. Schader & W. Gaul (Eds.), *Knowledge, data and computer-assisted decisions* (pp. 127–138). Heidelberg: Springer-Verlag.

Okada, A., & Imaizumi, T. (1980). Nonmetric method for extended INDSCAL model. *Behaviormetrika, 7,* 13–22.

Okada, A., & Imaizumi, T. (1987). Nonmetric multidimensional scaling of asymmetric proximities. *Behaviormetrika, 21,* 81–96.

Okada, A., & Imaizumi, T. (1994). *pasokon tajigen shakudo kouseihou* [*Multidimensional scaling using a personal computer*]. Tokyo: Kyoritsu Shuppan.

Okada, A., & Imaizumi, T. (1997). Asymmetric multidimensional scaling of two-mode three-way proximities. *Journal of Classification, 14,* 195–224.

Pan, G. C., & Harris, D. P. (1991). A new multidimensional scaling technique based upon association of triple objects-Pijk and its application to the analysis of geochemical data. *Journal of Mathematical Geology, 23,* 861–886.

Pliner, V. (1996). Metric unidimensional scaling and global optimization. *Journal of Classification, 13,* 3–18.

Poole, K. T. (1990). Least squares metric, unidimensional scaling of multivariate linear models. *Psychometrika, 55,* 123–149.

Pruzansky, S. (1975). *How to use SINDSCAL: A computer program for individual differences in multidimensional scaling.* Murray Hill, NJ: AT&T Bell Laboratories.

Pruzansky, S., Tversky, A., & Carroll, J. D. (1982). Spatial versus tree representations of proximity data. *Psychometrika, 47,* 3–24.

Ramsay, J. O. (1977a). Monotonic weighted power transformations to additivity. *Psychometrika, 42,* 83–109.

Ramsay, J. O. (1977b). Maximum likelihood estimation in multidimensional scaling. *Psychometrika, 42,* 241–266.

Ramsay, J. O. (1978a). Confidence regions for multidimensional scaling analysis. *Psychometrika, 43,* 145–160.

Ramsay, J. O. (1978b). *MULTISCALE: Four programs for multidimensional scaling by the method of maximum likelihood.* Chicago: National Educational Resources.

Ramsay, J. O. (1980). Some small sample results for maximum likelihood estimation in multidimensional scaling. *Psychometrika, 45,* 139–144.

Ramsay, J. O. (1981). MULTISCALE. In S. S. Schiffman, M. L. Reynolds, & F. W. Young (Eds.), *Introduction to multidimensional scaling: Theory, method and applications* (pp. 389–405). New York: Academic Press.

Ramsay, J. O. (1982a). *MULTISCALE II manual.* Mooresville, IN: International Educational Services.

Ramsay, J. O. (1982b). Some statistical approaches to multidimensional scaling data [with discussion]. *Journal of the Royal Statistical Society A, 145,* 285–312.

Ramsay, J. O. (1983). MULTISCALE: A multidimensional scaling program. *American Statistician, 37,* 326–327.

Ramsay, J. O. (1988). Monotone splines in action. *Statistical Science, 3,* 425–441.

Rodieck, R. W. (1977). Metric of color borders. *Science, 197,* 1195–1196.

Rohlf, F. J., & Slice, D. (1990). Extensions of the Procrustes method for the optimal superimposition of landmarks. *Systematic Zoology, 39,* 40–59.

Rosenberg, S. (1982). The method of sorting in multivariate research with applications selected from cognitive psychology and person perception. In N. Hirschberg & L. Humphreys (Eds.), *Multivariate applications in the social sciences* (pp. 117–142). Mahwah, NJ: Erlbaum.

Rosenberg, S., & Kim, M. P. (1975). The method of sorting as a data-gathering procedure in multivariate research. *Multivariate Behavioral Research, 10,* 489–502.

Rounds, J., & Tracey, T. J. (1993). Prediger's dimensional representation of Holland's RIASEC circumplex. *Journal of Applied Psychology, 78,* 875–890.

Rounds, J., Tracey, T. J., & Hubert, L. (1992). Methods for evaluating vocational interest structural hypotheses. *Journal of Vocational Behavior, 40,* 239–259.

Saito, T. (1991). Analysis of asymmetric proximity matrix by a model of distance and additive terms. *Behaviormetrika, 29,* 45–60.

Saito, T. (1993). Multidimensional scaling for asymmetric proximity data. In R. Steyer, K. F. Wender, & K. F. Widaman (Eds.), *Psychometric methodology* (pp. 451–456). Stuttgart: Gustav Fischer.

Saito, T., & Takeda, S. (1990). Multidimensional scaling of asymmetric proximity: Model and method. *Behaviormetrika, 28,* 49–80.

Sattath, S., & Tversky, A. (1977). Additive similarity trees. *Psychometrika, 42,* 319–345.

Sattath, S., & Tversky, A. (1987). On the relation between common and distinctive feature models. *Psychological Review, 94,* 16–22.

Shepard, R. N. (1962a). The analysis of proximities: Multidimensional scaling with an unknown distance function. I. *Psychometrika, 27,* 125–140.

Shepard, R. N. (1962b). The analysis of proximities: Multidimensional scaling with an unknown distance function. II. *Psychometrika, 27,* 219–246.

Shepard, R. N. (1964). Attention and the metric structure of the stimulus space. *Journal of Mathematical Psychology, 1,* 54–87.

Shepard, R. N. (1972). A taxonomy of some principal types of data and of multidimensional methods for their analysis. In R. N. Shepard, A. K. Romney, & S. B. Nerlove (Eds.), *Multidimensional scaling: Theory and applications in the behavioral sciences: Vol. I. Theory* (pp. 24–47). New York: Seminar Press.

Shepard, R. N. (1974). Representation of structure in similarity data: Problems and prospects. *Psychometrika, 39,* 373–421.

Shepard, R. N. (1978). The circumplex and related topological manifolds in the study of perception. In S. Shye (Ed.), *Theory construction and data analysis in the behavioral sciences* (pp. 29–80). San Francisco: Jossey-Bass.

Shepard, R. N. (1987). Toward a universal law of generalization. *Science, 237,* 1317–1323.

Shepard, R. N. (1988). Toward a universal law of generalization [Letter to editor]. *Science, 242,* 944.

Shepard, R. N., & Arabie, P. (1979). Additive clustering: Representation of similarities as combinations of discrete overlapping properties. *Psychological Review, 86,* 87–123.

Shiina, K. (1986). A maximum likelihood nonmetric multidimensional scaling procedure for word sequences obtained in free-recall experiments. *Japanese Psychological Research, 28* (2), 53–63.

Shoben, E. J., & Ross, B. H. (1987). Structure and process in cognitive psychology using multidimensional scaling and related techniques. In R. R. Ronning, J. A. Glover, J. C. Conoley, & J. C. Witt (Eds.), *The influence of cognitive psychology on testing* (pp. 229–266). Mahwah, NJ: Erlbaum.

Srinivasan, V. (1975). Linear programming computational procedures for ordinal regression. *Journal of the Association for Computing Machinery, 23,* 475–487.

Steenkamp, J.-B. E. M., van Trijp, H. C. M., & ten Berge, J. M. F. (1994). Perceptual mapping based on idiosyncratic sets of attributes. *Journal of Marketing Research, 31,* 15–27.

Stevens, S. S. (1972). A neural quantum in sensory discrimination. *Science, 177,* 749–762.

Suppes, P., Krantz, D. M., Luce, R. D., & Tversky, A. (1989). *Foundations of measurement: Vol. II. Geometrical, threshold, and probabilistic representations.* New York: Academic Press.

Takane, Y. (1981). MDSORT: A special-purpose multidimensional scaling program for sorting data. *Behavior Research Methods & Instrumentation, 13,* 698.

Takane, Y. (1982). The method of triadic combinations: A new treatment and its application. *Behaviormetrika, 11,* 37–48.

Takane, Y. (1989). Ideal point discriminant analysis and ordered response categories. *Behaviormetrika, 26,* 31–46.

Takane, Y., Bozdogan, H., & Shibayama, T. (1987). Ideal point discriminant analysis. *Psychometrika, 52,* 371–392.

Takane, Y., & Carroll, J. D. (1981). Nonmetric maximum likelihood multidimensional scaling from directional rankings of similarities. *Psychometrika, 46,* 389–405.

Takane, Y., & Sergent, J. (1983). Multidimensional scaling models for reaction times and same-different judgments. *Psychometrika, 48,* 393–423.

Takane, Y., & Shibayama, T. (1986). Comparison of models for stimulus recognition data. In J. de Leeuw, W. Heiser, J. Meulman, & F. Critchley (Eds.), Multidimensional data analysis (pp. 119–138, 147–148). Leiden: DSWO-Press.

Takane, Y., Young, F. W., & de Leeuw, J. (1977). Nonmetric individual differences multidimensional scaling: An alternating least squares method with optimal scaling features. *Psychometrika, 42,* 7–67.

Tansley, B. W., & Boynton, R. M. (1976). A line, not a space, represents visual distinctness of borders formed by different colors. *Science, 191,* 954–957.

Tansley, B. W., & Boynton, R. M. (1977). Letter in reply to R. W. Rodieck. *Science, 197,* 1196.

Tartter, V. C. (in press). *Language processes* (2nd ed.). Newbury Park, CA: Sage.

ten Berge, J. M. F. (1977). Orthogonal procrustes rotation for two or more matrices. *Psychometrika, 42,* 267–276.

ten Berge, J. M. F. (1988). Generalized approaches to the maxbet problem and the maxdiff problem, with applications to canonical correlations. *Psychometrika, 53,* 487–494.

ten Berge, J. M. F., Kiers, H. A. L., & Commandeur, J. J. F. (1993). Orthogonal Procrustes rotation for matrices with missing values. *British Journal of Mathematical and Statistical Psychology, 46,* 119–134.

ten Berge, J. M. F., & Knol, D. L. (1984). Orthogonal rotations to maximal agreement for two or more matrices of different column order. *Psychometrika, 49,* 49–55.

Tobler, W. (1979). Estimation of attractivities from interactions. *Environment and Planning A, 11,* 121–127.

Torgerson, W. S. (1952). Multidimensional scaling: I. Theory and method. *Psychometrika, 17,* 401–419.

Torgerson, W. S. (1958). *Theory and methods of scaling.* New York: Wiley.

Tracey, T. J., & Rounds, J. (1993). Evaluating Holland's and Gati's vocational-interest models: A structural meta-analysis. *Psychological Bulletin, 113,* 229–246.

Tucker, L. R (1960). Intra-individual and inter-individual multidimensionality. In H. Gulliksen & S. Messick (Eds.), *Psychological scaling: Theory and Applications* (pp. 155–167). New York: Wiley.

Tucker, L. .R (1964). The extension of factor analysis to three-dimensional matrices. In N. Frederiksen & H. Gulliksen (Eds.), *Contributions to mathematical psychology* (pp. 109–127). New York: Holt, Rinehart, and Winston.

Tucker, L. R (1972). Relations between multidimensional scaling and three-mode factor analysis. *Psychometrika, 37,* 3–27.

Tucker, L. R, & Messick, S. J. (1963). An individual difference model for multi-dimensional scaling. *Psychometrika, 28,* 333–367.

Tversky, A. (1977). Features of similarity. *Psychological Review, 84,* 327–352.

Van Cutsem, B. (Ed.). (1994). *Classification and dissimilarity analysis.* Heidelberg, Germany: Springer-Verlag.

Waller, N. G., Lykken, D. T., & Tellegen, A. (1995). Occupational interests, leisure time interests, and personality: Three domains or one? Findings from the Minnesota Twin Registry. In D. Lubinski & R. V. Dawis (Eds.), *Assessing individual differences in human behavior: New concepts, methods, and findings* (pp. 232–259). Palo Alto, CA: Consulting Psychologists Press.

Weeks, D. G., & Bentler, P. M. (1982). Restricted multidimensional scaling models for asymmetric proximities. *Psychometrika, 47,* 201–208.

Weinberg, S. L., & Carroll, J. D. (1992). Multidimensional scaling: An overview with applications in educational research. In B. Thompson (Ed.), *Advances in social science methodology* (pp. 99–135). Greenwich, CT: JAI Press.

Weinberg, S. L., Carroll, J. D., & Cohen, H. S. (1984). Confidence regions for INDSCAL using the jackknife and bootstrap techniques. *Psychometrika, 49,* 475–491.

Weinberg, S. L., & Menil, V. C. (1993). The recovery of structure in linear and ordinal data: INDSCAL versus ALSCAL. *Multivariate Behavioral Research, 28,* 215–233.

Weisberg, H. F. (1974). Dimensionland: An excursion into spaces. *American Journal of Political Science, 18,* 743–776.

Wilkinson, L. (1994). SYSTAT for DOS: *Advanced applications, Version 6 edition.* Evanston, IL: Systat.

Winsberg, S., & Carroll, J. D. (1989a). A quasi-nonmetric method for multidimensional scaling of multiway data via an extended INDSCAL model. In R. Coppi & S. Bolasco (Eds.), *Multiway data analysis* (pp. 405–414). Amsterdam: North-Holland.

Winsberg, S. & Carroll, J. D. (1989b). A quasi-nonmetric method of multidimensional scaling via an extended Euclidean model. *Psychometrika, 54,* 217–229.

Winsberg, S., & Ramsay, J. O. (1980). Monotonic transformations to additivity using splines. *Biometrika, 67,* 669–674.

Winsberg, S., & Ramsay, J. O. (1981). Analysis of pairwise preference data using B-splines. *Psychometrika, 46,* 171–186.

Winsberg, S., & Ramsay, J. O. (1983). Monotone spline transformations for dimension reduction. *Psychometrika, 48,* 575–595.

Wish, M., & Carroll, J. D. (1974). Applications of individual differences scaling to studies of human perception and judgment. In E. C. Carterette & M. P. Friedman (Eds.), *Handbook of perception: Psychophysical judgment and measurement* (Vol. 2, pp. 449–491). New York: Academic Press.

Wold, H. (1966). Estimation of principal components and related models by iterative least squares. In P. R. Krishnaiah (Ed.), *Multivariate analysis* (pp. 391–420). New York: Academic Press.

Young, F. W. (1975). Methods for describing ordinal data with cardinal models. *Journal of Mathematical Psychology, 12,* 416–436.

Young, F. W. (1984a). The general Euclidean model. In H. G. Law, C. W. Snyder, Jr., J. A. Hattie, & R. P. McDonald (Eds.), *Research methods for multimode data analysis* (pp. 440–469). New York: Praeger.

Young, F. W. (1984b). Scaling. *Annual Review of Psychology, 35,* 55–81.

Young, F. W., & Lewyckyj, R. (1981). *ALSCAL.4 user's guide.* Unpublished manuscript, L. L. Thurstone Psychometric Laboratory, University of North Carolina, Chapel Hill.

Zielman, B. (1993). Directional analysis of three-way skew-symmetric matrices. In O. Opitz, B. Lausen, & R. Klar (Eds.), *Information and classification* (pp. 156–161). New York: Springer-Verlag.

Zielman, B., & Heiser, W. J. (1993). Analysis of asymmetry by a slide-vector. *Psychometrika, 58,* 101–114.

Zielman, B., & Heiser, W. J. (1994). *Models for asymmetric proximities.* Internal Report RR-94-04. Leiden: Department of Data Theory, University of Leiden.

CHAPTER 4

Stimulus Categorization

F. Gregory Ashby
W. Todd Maddox

The bacterium *E. coli* tumbles randomly in a molecular sea. When it encounters a stream of molecules that it categorizes as a nutrient, it suppresses tumbling and swims upstream to the nutrient source. A recently inseminated female mouse sniffs urine near her nest. If she categorizes it as from an unfamiliar male mouse, implantation and pregnancy are prevented (Bruce, 1959; Parkes & Bruce, 1962). A man views a long sequence of portraits taken from high school yearbooks. Even though he graduated almost 50 years ago, he is remarkably accurate at deciding whether an arbitrary face belongs to the category of his own high school classmates (Bahrick, Bahrick, & Wittlinger, 1975). All organisms divide objects and events in the environment into separate classes or categories. If they did not, they would die and their species would become extinct. Therefore, categorization is among the most important decision tasks performed by organisms (Ashby & Lee, 1993).

Technically, a categorization or classification task is one in which there are more stimuli than responses. As a result, a number of stimuli are assigned the same response. In contrast, an identification task is one in which there is a unique response for every stimulus. For example, many humans are in the category "women" and many objects are in the category "bells," but only one human is identified as "Hillary Clinton" and only one object is

Measurement, Judgment, and Decision Making

identified as "the Liberty Bell." Although the theories and basic phenomena associated with categorization and identification are similar, this chapter focuses on categorization.

A categorization task is one in which the subject assigns a stimulus to one of the relevant categories. Many other tasks require the subject to access stored category information but not to make a categorization judgment. For example, in a typicality rating task the subject sees a category exemplar (i.e., a stimulus belonging to the category) and rates how typical or representative of the category it is. Other experiments might ask the subject to recall all the exemplars of a particular category. Although these related paradigms provide valuable information about category representation, space limitations prevent us from considering them in detail. Instead, we will focus on the standard categorization experiment.

Another important distinction is between categories and concepts. Although these terms are sometimes used interchangeably, we define a category as a collection of objects belonging to the same group and a concept as a collection of related ideas. For example, trees form a category and the many alternative types of love form a concept. When Ann Landers tells a reader that he is in lust rather than in love, she is doing something very similar to categorization. Many of the categorization theories discussed here make definite predictions about the cognitive processes required for such a judgment. Even so, the representations of categories and concepts are probably quite different and a discussion of the two is beyond the scope of this chapter.

I. THE CATEGORIZATION EXPERIMENT

This discussion may leave the impression that the focus of this chapter is narrow. However, the standard categorization experiment has many degrees of freedom, which can result in a huge variety of tasks. Some prominent options available to the researcher designing a categorization task are listed in Table 1. The first choice is the type of stimuli selected. One can choose stimuli that vary continuously along the relevant stimulus dimensions or that only take on some number of discrete values. The most limiting case is binary-valued dimensions. In many such experiments the two levels are "presence" and "absence." Several categorization theories make specific predictions *only* in the special case where the stimulus dimensions are binary valued. This is ironic because in natural settings binary-valued stimulus dimensions are rare, if they exist at all. For example, in one popular experimental paradigm that consistently uses binary-valued dimensions, subjects learn that a patient received a battery of medical tests, that the outcome of each test is either positive or negative, and that a certain pattern of test results is characteristic of a particular disease. The subjects then

TABLE 1   Options in the Design of a Categorization Experiment

Experimental components	Options
Stimulus dimensions	Continuous vs. discrete vs. binary valued
	Separable vs. integral
Category structure	Overlapping vs. nonoverlapping
	Few vs. many exemplars
	Linearly vs. nonlinearly separable
	Normal vs. nonnormal category distributions
Instructions to subjects	Supervised vs. unsupervised vs. free sorting
	Well defined vs. partially defined vs. undefined categories

discover the outcome of a set of tests and make a diagnosis. Is this realistic? How many medical tests give binary-valued results? For example, high blood pressure could indicate heart disease, but blood pressure does not have either a single high value or a single low value. Instead, it is continuous valued. A physician might decide on the basis of some continuous–valued blood pressure level that a patient has high blood pressure, but then it is the decision that is binary valued, not the percept. Even a simple home pregnancy test is not binary valued. For a variety of reasons, the testing material will display a continuum of hues, even if the woman is pregnant.

When selecting stimuli, a second choice is about the interaction between pairs of stimulus dimensions. If the dimensions are *separable* it is easy to attend to one and ignore the other, whereas if they are *integral* it is either difficult or impossible to do so (e.g., Ashby & Maddox, 1994; Ashby & Townsend, 1986; Garner, 1974; Maddox, 1992). Prototypical separable dimensions are hue and shape and prototypical integral dimensions are hue and brightness (e.g., Garner, 1977; Garner & Felfoldy, 1970; Hyman & Well, 1968).

Another set of options concerns the construction of the contrasting categories. For example, they can be *overlapping* or *nonoverlapping*. Overlapping categories have at least one stimulus that is sometimes a member of one category and sometimes a member of another (also called *probabilistic categories*). Thus, whereas perfect performance is possible with nonoverlapping categories, if the categories are overlapping, even the optimal classifier will make errors. Although much of the empirical work in categorization has used nonoverlapping categories, many natural categories are overlapping. For example, a person might look like the prototype of one ethnicity but be a member of another. Overlapping categories are also theoretically important because they provide a strong test of categorization theories. Virtually all theories of categorization can account for the kind of error-free performance that occurs when subjects categorize typewritten characters as *x*'s or

o's (nonoverlapping categories), but only a few (if any) can account for the errors that occur when subjects try to categorize handwritten characters as c's or a's (overlapping categories).

When designing the contrasting categories, the experimenter must also decide how many exemplars to place in each category. This factor may have a crucial effect on the strategy the subject uses to solve the categorization problem. With only a few exemplars in each category the subject literally could memorize the correct response to every stimulus, but if the categories contain many exemplars, the subject might be forced to use a more efficient strategy.

The experimenter must also decide where to place the category exemplars in the stimulus space. Many choices are possible. Often, exemplars are positioned so that a particular decision rule maximizes categorization accuracy. For example, the exemplars might be positioned so that a dimensional rule is optimal (i.e., ignore all stimulus dimensions but one). One important choice, which selects between broad classes of rules, is whether to make a pair of categories *linearly* or *nonlinearly* separable. If the categories are linearly separable, then categorization accuracy is maximized by a rule that compares a linear combination of the stimulus dimensional values to some fixed criterion value. One response is given if the weighted sum exceeds the criterion and the other response is given if it does not. If a pair of categories is nonlinearly separable, then no such linear combination exists. The distinction between linearly and nonlinearly separable categories is important because several theories predict that linearly separable categories should be significantly easier to categorize than nonlinearly separable categories. Another prominent solution to the problem of how to position the exemplars in the stimulus space is to allow their position to be *normally distributed* on each stimulus dimension (Ashby & Gott, 1988; Ashby & Maddox, 1990, 1992; Kubovy & Healy, 1977; Lee, 1963; Lee & Janke, 1964, 1965). With normally distributed exemplars, the categories are always linearly or quadratically separable.

After the stimuli are selected and the categories are constructed, the experimenter must decide what instructions and feedback to give the subject. In a *supervised* task, the subject is told the correct response at the end of each trial. In an *unsupervised* task, no feedback is given after each response, but the subject is told at the beginning of the experiment how many categories are relevant. Finally, in a *free sorting* (or clustering) task, there is no trial-by-trial feedback and the subject is given no information about the number of relevant categories. Instead, the subject is told to form his or her own categories, using as many as seem required.

A task can be supervised only if an objectively correct response can be identified on every trial. In such a case, we say that the categories are *well*

defined.[1] Of course, well-defined categories may also be used in an unsupervised or free sorting task, but sometimes these tasks are run with categories
in which no objectively correct response exists on any trial. Such *undefined
categories* are quite common. For example, suppose a subject is shown color
patches of varying hue and is asked to categorize them according to whether
they make the subject feel happy or sad. Because the subject's affective state
is unobservable, there is no way to decide which response is correct. Thus,
this experiment is an example of unsupervised categorization with undefined categories. (It is not free sorting because the subject was told that the
only possible categories are happy and sad.) Finally, *partially defined categories*
are those for which a correct response is identified on some but not on all
trials. The most common use of partially defined categories is in experiments that use training and transfer conditions. During the training phase,
feedback is given on every trial, but during the transfer phase, no feedback
is given. If a stimulus is presented for the first time during the transfer
phase, it therefore will usually have no objectively correct response.

II. CATEGORIZATION THEORIES

Categorization theories come in many different types and are expressed in
different languages. This makes them difficult to compare. In spite of their
large differences, however, they all make assumptions about (1) representation, (2) category access, and (3) response selection. The representation
assumptions describe the perceptual and cognitive representation of the
stimulus and the exemplars of the contrasting categories. The response
selection assumptions describe how the subject selects a response after the
relevant information has been collected and the requisite computations have
been performed.

The category access assumptions delineate the various categorization theories. These assumptions describe the information that must be collected
from the stored category representations and the computations that must be
performed on this information before a response can be made. At least five
different kinds of theories have been popular. The *classical theory* assumes
that a category can be represented as a set of necessary and sufficient conditions, so categorization is a process of testing whether the stimulus possesses each of these conditions (e.g., Bruner, Goodnow, & Austin, 1956;

[1] Our use of the term *well defined* is different from that of Neisser (1967), who distinguished
between well- and ill-defined categories. According to Neisser, well-defined categories are
structured according to simple logical rules, whereas ill-defined categories are not. These
definitions are somewhat ambiguous because the term *simple* is not rigorously defined. Rules
that are easily verbalized are usually called simple, but, for example, it is unclear whether a rule
that can be verbalized, but not easily, is also simple.

Smith & Medin, 1981). *Prototype theory* assumes that the category representation is dominated by the prototype, or most typical member, and that categorization is a process of comparing the similarity of the stimulus to the prototype of each relevant category (Posner & Keele, 1968, 1970; Reed, 1972; Rosch, 1973, 1977). *Feature-frequency theory* assumes the category representation is a list of the features contained in all exemplars of the category, along with their relative frequency of occurrence (Estes, 1986a; Franks & Bransford, 1971; Reed, 1972). Categorization is a process of analyzing the stimulus into its component features and computing the likelihood that this particular combination of features was generated from each of the relevant categories. *Exemplar theory* assumes the subject computes the similarity of the stimulus to each stored exemplar of all relevant categories and selects a response on the basis of these similarity computations (Brooks, 1978; Estes, 1986a; Hintzman, 1986; Medin & Schaffer, 1978; Nosofsky, 1986). Finally, *decision bound theory* (also called general recognition theory) assumes the subject constructs a decision bound that partitions the perceptual space into response regions (not necessarily contiguous), one for each relevant category. On each trial, the subject determines the region in which the stimulus representation falls, and then emits the associated response (Ashby & Gott, 1988; Ashby & Lee, 1991, 1992; Ashby & Townsend, 1986; Maddox & Ashby, 1993).

Much of the work on testing and comparing these theories has focused on response accuracy. This is a good dependent variable because it has high ecological validity and is easy to estimate. On the other hand, response accuracy is a fairly crude, global measure of performance. In the language of Marr (1982), response accuracy is good at testing between models written at the computational level, but it is poor at discriminating between models written at the algorithmic level. This focus on response accuracy has not yet been a serious problem because the most popular categorization models are computational rather than algorithmic. That is, they specify what is computed, but they do not specify the algorithms that perform those computations.

Currently, however, there is an awakening interest in algorithmic level descriptions of the categorization process. A test between algorithmic level models often requires a dependent variable more sensitive than overall accuracy to the microstructure of the data. In the categorization literature, algorithmic level models are most frequently tested against trial-by-trial learning data, although response times could also be used. The most popular architecture within which to implement the various algorithms that have been proposed has been the connectionist network and virtually all of the current network models instantiate some version of feature-frequency theory (e.g., Gluck & Bower, 1988) or exemplar theory (e.g., Estes, 1993, 1994; Kruschke, 1992). It is important to realize, however, that network versions of classical, prototype, or decision bound theories could also be constructed. Thus, there is no such thing as the connectionist theory of categorization. Rather, connectionist networks should be viewed as an alternative architecture via which any computational theory of categorization can be expressed at the algorithmic level.

The next three sections of this chapter examine the representation, response selection, and category access assumptions in turn. This provides a common language from which to describe and formally compare the various theories. Section VI reviews the empirical tests of the various theories and the last section identifies some important unsolved problems.

III. STIMULUS, EXEMPLAR, AND CATEGORY REPRESENTATION

Figure 1 illustrates the relations between the various theories of stimulus and category representation. The most fundamental distinction is whether the theories assume numeric or nonnumeric representation. Nonnumeric models assume a symbolic or linguistic representation. These models assume that stimuli and category exemplars are described by a generative system of rules, which might be given by a production system or a grammar. Each category is associated with a unique set of rules, so categorization is equivalent to determining which set of rules generated the stimulus. Early proponents of nonnumeric representation in psychology were Allen Newell and Herbert Simon (e.g., Newell & Simon, 1972; see, also, Anderson, 1975; Klahr, Langley, & Neches, 1987).

Numeric representation is of two types. Dimensional theories assume a geometric representation that contains a small number of continuous-valued dimensions. The most widely known examples in psychology are multidimensional scaling (MDS; Kruskal, 1964a, 1964b; Shepard, 1962a, 1962b; Torgerson, 1958; Young & Householder, 1938) and signal detection theory (Ashby & Townsend, 1986; Green & Swets, 1966). Feature theories assume

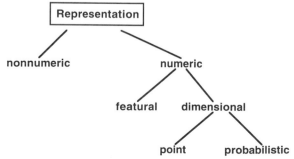

FIGURE 1   Hierarchical relations among theories of stimulus representation.

the stimulus can be represented as a set of features, where a feature is either present or absent and often has a nested relation that is naturally represented in a treelike connected graph. Perhaps the most notable feature models in psychology were developed by Amos Tversky (Corter & Tversky, 1986; Sattath & Tversky, 1977; Tversky, 1972, 1977). Although some argue that feature models are nonnumeric (e.g., Pao, 1989), we classify them as numeric because it is usually possible to depict feature representations geometrically by defining a feature as a binary-valued dimension. In this case, each dimension contributes only one bit of information (i.e., presence or absence), so the resulting perceptual space frequently has many dimensions. With binary-valued dimensions, the natural distance measure is the Hamming metric, defined as the number of features on which the two stimuli disagree. The dissimilarity measure proposed by Tversky (1977) in his feature contrast model, generalizes Hamming distance.

Assumptions about stimulus representation are impossible to test in isolation. At the very least, extra assumptions must be added about how the subject uses the representation. One obvious choice is to assume that representations that are close together are similar or related. A number of attempts to criticize numeric representation, and especially dimensional representation, have been based on this assumption. As we will see, however, a critical point of contention is how one should define "close together."

Most formal theories of categorization assume a numeric representation. In a number of exemplar models, application is restricted to experiments that use binary-valued stimuli, so the stimulus and category representations are featural. This includes the context model (Medin & Schaffer, 1978), the array-similarity model (Estes, 1986a), and several network models (Estes, 1993, 1994; Gluck & Bower, 1988; Hurwitz, 1990). Most other formal models assume a dimensional representation. Most of these use a multidimensional scaling (MDS) representation that assumes (1) the stimuli and category exemplars are represented as points in a multidimensional space and (2) stimulus similarity decreases with the distance between the point representations. Exemplar models based on an MDS representation include the generalized context model (GCM: Nosofsky, 1986) and ALCOVE (Kruschke, 1992), whereas MDS-based prototype models include the fuzzy logical model of perception (FLMP; Massaro & Friedman, 1990) and the comparative distance model (Reed, 1972).

The assumption that similarity decreases with psychological distance is controversial. A distance-based perceptual representation is valid only if the psychological distances satisfy a set of *distance axioms* (Ashby & Perrin, 1988; Tversky, 1977). These include the triangle inequality, symmetry, minimality, and that all self-distances are equal. Unfortunately, there is abundant empirical evidence against these axioms. For example, Tversky (1977) reported that subjects rate the similarity of China to North Korea to be less than the similarity of North Korea to China, an apparent violation of symmetry (see also Krumhansl, 1978). The triangle inequality holds if the psychological distance between stimuli i and j plus the distance between stimuli j and k is greater than or equal to the distance between stimuli i and k. Although the triangle inequality is difficult to test empirically, Tversky and Gati (1982) proposed an empirically testable axiom, called the corner inequality, that captures the spirit of the triangle inequality. Tversky and Gati (1982) tested the corner inequality and found consistent violations for stimuli constructed from separable dimensions.

It is important to note, however, that although these results are problematic for the assumption that similarity decreases with psychological distance, they are not necessarily problematic for the general notion of dimensional representation, or even for the point representation assumption of the MDS model. For example, Krumhansl (1978) argued that similarity depends not only on the distance between point representations in a low dimensional space, but also on the density of representations around each point. Her distance–density model can account for violations of symmetry but not for violations of the triangle inequality. Nosofsky (1991b) argued that many violations of the distance axioms are due to stimulus and response biases and not to violations of the MDS assumptions.

Decision bound theory assumes a dimensional representation, but one that is probabilistic rather than deterministic. A fundamental postulate of the theory is that there is trial-by-trial variability in the perceptual information obtained from every object or event (Ashby & Lee, 1993). Thus, a stimulus is represented as a multivariate probability distribution. The variability is assumed to come from many sources. First, physical stimuli are themselves intrinsically variable. For example, it is well known that the number of photons emitted by a light source of constant intensity and constant duration varies probabilistically from trial to trial (i.e., it has a Poisson distribution; Geisler, 1989; Wyszecki & Stiles, 1967). Second, there is perireceptor noise in all modalities. For example, in vision, the amount of light reflected off the cornea varies probabilistically from trial to trial. Third, there is spontaneous activity at all levels of the central nervous system that introduces more noise (e.g., Barlow, 1956, 1957; Robson, 1975).

One advantage of probabilistic representation is that decision bound theory is not constrained by any of the distance axioms. When stimuli are represented by probability distributions, a natural measure of similarity is distributional overlap (Ashby & Perrin, 1988). The distributional overlap similarity measure contains MDS Euclidean distance measures of similarity as a special case but, unlike the distance measures, is not constrained by the distance axioms (Ashby & Perrin, 1988; Perrin, 1992; Perrin & Ashby, 1991).

In a categorization task, the stimulus is usually available to the subject up to the time that a response is made. Thus, long-term memory has little or no effect on the representation of the stimulus. In contrast, exemplars of the competing categories are not available, so a decision process requiring exemplar information must access the exemplar representations from memory. As a consequence, the representation of category exemplars is affected critically by the workings of memory. Therefore, unlike a theory of stimulus representation, a complete theory of exemplar representation must model the effects of memory. Nevertheless, most categorization theories represent stimuli and exemplars identically. Recently, a few attempts have been made to model the effects of memory on exemplar representation, but these have been mostly limited to simple models of trace-strength decay (e.g., Estes, 1994; Nosofsky, Kruschke, & McKinley, 1992). Clearly, more work is needed in this area.

Another area where more sophisticated modeling is needed is in category representation. In exemplar theory, a category is represented simply as the union or set of representations of all exemplars belonging to that category. Prototype theory assumes the category representation is dominated by the category prototype. Feature-frequency theory assumes the category representation is a list of all features found in the category exemplars. Classical theory assumes a category is represented by a set of necessary and sufficient conditions required for category membership. Thus, there is considerable disagreement among the theories about how much consolidation of the category representation is performed by the memory processes over time. Exemplar theory takes the extreme view that there is little or no consolidation, whereas classical theory posits so much consolidation that exemplar information is no longer available.

Although decision bound theory makes no concrete assumptions about category representation, several applications have tested the hypothesis that subjects assume categories are normally distributed (e.g., Ashby & Gott, 1988; Ashby & Lee, 1991; Ashby & Maddox, 1990, 1992; Maddox & Ashby, 1993). There is good evidence that many natural categories share properties of the normal distribution or at least that subjects assume that they do. First, natural categories generally contain a large number of exemplars (e.g., there are many trees). Second, the dimensions of many natural categories are continuous valued. Third, many natural categories overlap. Finally, there is evidence that people naturally assume category exemplars are unimodally and symmetrically distributed around some prototypical value (Fried & Holyoak, 1984; Flannagan, Fried, & Holyoak, 1986). As early as 1954, Black argued that "if we examine instances of the application of any biological term, we shall find ranges, not classes—specimens (i.e., individuals or species) arranged according to the degree of their variation from certain typical or 'clear' cases" (p. 28). The normal distribution has all these properties. It assumes an unlimited number of exemplars, dimensions that are continuous valued, a small number of atypical exemplars (so it overlaps with other nearby categories), and it is unimodal and symmetric.

According to this interpretation, subjects initially assume the exemplars of an unfamiliar category have a multivariate normal distribution in stimulus space. Gaining experience with a category is a process of estimating the mean exemplar value on each dimension, the variances, and the correlations between dimensions. These estimates allow the subject to compute the likelihood that any stimulus belongs to this category. In fact, subjects need not even assume normality. Suppose they estimate the exemplar means, variances, correlations, and category base rates and then try to infer the correct distribution. If they do not know the appropriate family of distributions, it turns out that the multivariate normal is an excellent choice because it takes maximal advantage of the information available (technically, it is the maximum entropy inference; Myung, 1994). Given estimates of the category means, variances, correlations, and base rates, to infer that the category distribution is anything other than normal requires extra assumptions. In other words, the normal distribution is the appropriate noncommittal choice in such situations. Thus, the multivariate normal distribution is an attractive model of category representation (Ashby, 1992a; Fried & Holyoak, 1984; Flannagan, Fried, & Holyoak, 1986).

IV. RESPONSE SELECTION

There are two types of response selection models. Deterministic models assume that, if on different trials the subject receives the same perceptual information and accesses the same information from memory, then the subject will always select the same response. Probabilistic models assume the subject always guesses, although usually in a sophisticated fashion. In other words, if the evidence supports the hypothesis that the stimulus belongs to category A, then a deterministic model predicts that the subject will respond A with probability 1, whereas a probabilistic model predicts that response A will be given with probability less than 1 (but greater than 0.5).

In many categorization experiments, observable responding is not deterministic. It is not uncommon for a subject to give one response the first time a stimulus is shown and a different response the second time, even if the subject is experienced with the relevant categories (e.g, Estes, 1995). It is important to realize that such data do not necessarily falsify deterministic response selection models. The observable data may be probabilistic because of noise in the subject's perceptual and memory systems. For example, perceptual noise may cause the subject to believe that a different stimulus was presented, a stimulus belonging to the incorrect category. Thus, the distinction between deterministic and probabilistic response selection models does not apply at the observable level of the data but at the unobservable level of the subject's decision processes.

The question of whether response selection is deterministic or probabilistic is not limited to categorization tasks but may be asked about any task requiring an overt response from the subject. In many tasks, the evidence overwhelmingly supports deterministic response selection. For example, if subjects are asked whether individual rectangles are taller than they are wide or wider than they are tall, then, even at the data level, responding is almost perfectly deterministic (Ashby & Gott, 1988). In other tasks, the evidence overwhelmingly supports probabilistic response selection. In a typical probability matching task, a subject sits in front of two response keys. The right key is associated with a red light and the left key is associated with a green light. On each trial, one of these two lights is turned on. The red light is turned on with probability p and the green light is turned on with probability $1 - p$. The subject's task is to predict which light will come on by pressing the appropriate button. Consider the case in which p is considerably greater than one-half. A deterministic rule predicts that the subject will always press the right key. This choice also maximizes the subject's accuracy. However, the data clearly indicate that subjects sometimes press the right key and sometimes the left. In fact, they approximately match the objective stimulus presentation probabilities by pressing the right key on about $100p\%$ of the trials (e.g., Estes, 1976; Herrnstein, 1961, 1970). This behavior is known as *probability matching*. Therefore, the consensus is that humans use deterministic response selection rules in some tasks and probabilistic rules in other tasks. In categorization however, the controversy is still unresolved. It is even possible that subjects use deterministic rules in some categorization tasks and probabilistic rules in others (Estes, 1995).

Virtually all models assuming a probabilistic response selection rule, assume a rule of the same basic type. Consider a categorization task with categories A and B. Let S_{ij} denote the strength of association between stimulus i and category J ($J = A$ or B). The algorithm used to compute this strength will depend on the specific categorization theory. For example, in some prototype models, S_{iA} is the similarity between stimulus i and the category A prototype. In an exemplar model, S_{iA} is the sum of the similarities between the stimulus and all exemplars of category A. In many connectionist models, S_{iA} is the sum of weights along paths between nodes activated by the stimulus and output nodes associated with category A. Virtually all categorization models assuming a probabilistic response selection rule assume the probability of responding A on trials when stimulus i is presented equals

$$P(R_A|i) = \frac{\beta_A S_{iA}}{\beta_A S_{iA} + \beta_B S_{iB}}, \tag{1}$$

where β_J is the response bias toward category J (with $\beta_J \geq 0$). Without loss of generality, one can assume that $\beta_B = 1 - \beta_A$. In many categorization models the response biases are set to $\beta_A = \beta_B = 0.5$.

Equation (1) has various names. It was originally proposed by Shepard (1957) and Luce (1963), so it is often called the Luce-Shepard choice model. But it is also called the similarity-choice model, the biased-choice model, or the relative-goodness rule. If S_{iA} is interpreted as the evidence favoring category A, and if there is no response bias, then Eq. (1) is also equivalent to probability matching.

Deterministic decision rules are also of one basic type. Let $h(i)$ be some function of the stimulus representation with the property that stimulus i is more likely to be a member of category A when $h(i)$ is negative and a member of category B when $h(i)$ is positive. For example, in prototype or exemplar models $h(i)$ might equal $S_{iB} - S_{iA}$. The deterministic decision rule is to

$$\text{respond } A \text{ if } h(i) < \delta + \mathbf{e}_c; \text{ respond } B \text{ if } h(i) > \delta + \mathbf{e}_c. \tag{2}$$

In the unlikely event that $h(i)$ exactly equals $\delta + \mathbf{e}_c$, the subject is assumed to guess. As with the β parameter in the similarity-choice model, δ is a response bias. Response A is favored when $\delta > 0$ and response B is favored when $\delta < 0$. The random variable $\mathbf{e}_c$ represents criterial noise; that is, variability in the subject's memory of the criterion δ. It is assumed to have a mean of 0 and a variance of σ_c^2 and is usually assumed to be normally distributed (e.g., Maddox & Ashby, 1993).

Although the similarity-choice model and the deterministic decision rule of Eq. (2) appear very different, it is well known that the similarity-choice model is mathematically equivalent to a number of different deterministic decision rules (e.g., Marley, 1992; Townsend & Landon, 1982). Ashby and Maddox (1993) established another such equivalence that is especially useful when modeling categorization data. Suppose the subject uses the deterministic response selection rule of Eq. (2) and he or she defines the discriminant function $h(i)$ as $h(i) = \log(S_{iB}) - \log(S_{iA})$. Assume the criterial noise $\mathbf{e}_c$ has a logistic distribution. Ashby and Maddox (1993) showed that under these conditions the probability of responding A on trials when stimulus i is presented is equal to

$$P(R_A|i) = \frac{\beta_A(S_{iA})^\gamma}{\beta_A(S_{iA})^\gamma + \beta_B(S_{iB})^\gamma}, \tag{3}$$

where

$$\gamma = \frac{\pi}{\sqrt{3}\sigma_c} \quad \text{and} \quad \beta_A = \frac{e^{\delta\gamma}}{1 - e^{\delta\gamma}}.$$

In other words, the probability matching behavior of the similarity-choice model, which results when $\gamma = 1$, is indistinguishable from a deterministic decision rule in which $\sigma_c = \pi/\sqrt{3}$. On the other hand, if the subject uses a deterministic decision rule, but $\sigma_c < \pi/\sqrt{3}$, then there is an equivalent probabilistic decision rule of the Eq. (3) type in which $\gamma > 1$. In this case, the observable responding is less variable than predicted by probability matching and the subject is said to be overmatching (Baum, 1974). Similarly, if $\sigma_c > \pi/\sqrt{3}$, then there is an equivalent probabilistic decision rule in which $\gamma < 1$. In this case, the observable responding is more variable than predicted by probability matching and the subject is said to be undermatching (Baum, 1974).

These results indicate that for any deterministic response selection rule there is a probabilistic rule that is mathematically equivalent (and vice versa). Despite this fact, there is some hope for discriminating between these two strategies. This could be done by fitting the Eq. (3) model to categorization data from a wide variety of experiments and comparing the resulting estimates of γ. For example, suppose a subject is using the deterministic rule of Eq. (2). If so, there is no good reason to expect σ_c to turn out to equal $\pi/\sqrt{3}$ exactly (the value equivalent to probability matching). Also, it is reasonable to expect σ_c to vary with the nature of the stimuli and the complexity of the rule that separates the contrasting categories. Therefore, if the estimates of γ are consistently close to 1.0 or even if they are consistently close to any specific value, then a probabilistic rule is more likely than a deterministic rule. On the other hand, if the γ estimates vary across experiments and especially if they are larger in those tasks where less criterial noise is expected, then a deterministic rule is more likely than a probabilistic rule.

Another possibility for testing between deterministic and probabilistic response selection rules is to examine the γ estimates as a function of the subject's experience in the task. With probabilistic rules, γ might change with experience, but there is no reason to expect a consistent increase or decrease with experience. On the other hand, as the subject gains experience in the task, criterial noise should decrease because the strength of the subject's memory trace for the rule that separates the contrasting categories should increase. Thus, deterministic decision rules predict a consistent increase of γ with experience (Koh, 1993).

A number of studies explicitly tried to test whether subjects use deterministic or probabilistic response selection rules in a simple type of categorization experiment called the numerical decision task (Hammerton, 1970; Healy & Kubovy, 1977; Kubovy & Healy, 1977; Kubovy, Rapoport, & Tversky, 1971; Lee & Janke, 1964, 1965; Ward, 1973; Weissmann, Hollingsworth, & Baird, 1975). In these experiments, stimuli are numbers and two categories are created by specifying two different normal distributions. On each trial, a number is sampled from one of the distributions and shown to the subject. The subject's task is to name the category (i.e., the distribution) from which it was drawn. In general, these studies have favored deterministic rules over probabilistic rules. For example, Kubovy et al. (1971) found that a fixed cutoff accounted for the data significantly better than a probability matching model, even when the probability matching model was allowed a response bias parameter.

Maddox and Ashby (1993) fit the Eq. (3) response selection model to data from 12 different categorization experiments. Category similarity S_{ij} was computed from a powerful exemplar model. In several of these experiments the stimuli were rectangles. The category prototypes for two of these experiments are shown in Figure 2. In both cases the contrasting categories were linearly separable. In the first case, the rule that maximized accuracy was as follows:

Respond A if the stimulus rectangle is higher than it is wide.

Respond B if it is wider than it is high.

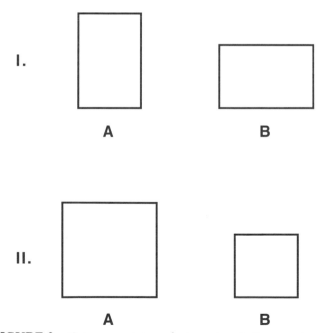

FIGURE 2   Category prototypes for two categorization experiments.

In the second case, the optimal rule was as follows:

Respond A if the height plus the width is greater than some criterion amount.

Respond B if it is less than this criterion amount.

A major difference between these two tasks is that the second task requires the subject to maintain a criterion in memory, whereas the first task does not. Thus, if the subject is using a deterministic response selection rule there should be virtually no criterial noise in the first task but a significant amount in the second, and as a result γ should be much larger in the first task than the second. On the other hand, the Eq. (3) probabilistic rule must predict that γ is the same in the two tasks. The stimuli were the same, the instructions were the same, and optimal accuracy was the same. The categories even had the same amount of variability in the two tasks. As it turned out however, in the first task the median γ estimate was 2.59, whereas in the second task it was 1.00 (the median was taken across subjects). This is compelling evidence that subjects used a deterministic response selection rule in these tasks.

Estes (1995) argued that subjects may have used deterministic response selection rules in these tasks because "when stimuli are defined on only one or two sensory dimensions, subjects can discover a criterion that defines category membership (e.g., all angles greater than 45° belong to Category A) and recode stimuli in terms of their relation to the criterion, whereas with complex, multiattribute stimuli such recoding may be difficult or impossible" (p. 21). Several other data sets fit by Maddox and Ashby (1993) provide at least a partial test of this hypothesis. Six experiments used categories in which the optimal decision rule was highly nonlinear (it was quadratic). In at least four of these cases, there was no straightforward verbal description of this rule, so it would be extremely difficult for subjects to perform the kind of recoding that Estes describes. The subjects in these experiments all completed several experimental sessions and Maddox and Ashby (1993) fit the data of each individual session separately. Across the six experiments, the median γ estimates (computed across subjects) ranged from 1.13 to 4.29 on the first experimental session and from 1.51 to 5.67 on the last session. Thus, even when the subjects were inexperienced, observable responding was less variable than predicted by probability matching. More interesting however, is a comparison of the γ estimates from the first session to the last. In all six experiments, the estimated value of γ increased from the first session to the last. These results favor the deterministic response selection hypothesis. It is true however, that the stimuli in these six experiments varied on only two physical dimensions. Stimuli were rectangles that varied in height and width or circles that varied in size and orientation of a radial line. Thus, the Maddox and Ashby (1993) results do not rule out the possibility that subjects switch to a probabilistic response selection rule when the stimuli vary on many dimensions.

Koh (1993) also examined the effects of experience on the amount of variability in observable responding. Her stimuli were lines that varied in length and orientation and she used categories that were overlapping and linearly separable. As a measure of response variability, she estimated a parameter that is essentially equivalent to γ. For all subjects that were able to learn the task, γ increased with practice and eventually asymptoted at values significantly larger than 1. Perhaps more interesting, however, was that when the model was refit after the data were averaged across subjects, the best fitting value of γ was very close to 1. In other words, although almost all subjects were overmatching, the averaged data satisfied probability matching. This apparent paradox occurred because, although each subject consistently used some decision rule, different subjects settled on different rules. Thus, there was no single rule that described the averaged data.

This discussion indicates that experimental conditions can have a large effect on whether the resulting data seem to support deterministic or probabilistic response selection rules. Some of the more important experimental factors are listed in Table 2. Responding will usually be less variable if the rule that maximizes categorization accuracy has a simple verbal description, if the subjects are highly practiced, and if single subject analyses are performed. Also, any factors that reduce perceptual or criterial noise should make responding less variable. Perceptual noise can be reduced by using high contrast rather than low contrast displays and response terminated rather than tachistoscopic presentation. Criterial noise can be reduced if the task uses an external rather than an internal criterion or referent. On the other hand, responding will usually be more variable if the optimal rule has no straightforward verbal description, subjects are inexperienced in the task, and the data are averaged across subjects.

Although these experimental factors might affect the appearance of the data, there is no reason to believe that they will induce a subject to switch,

TABLE 2   Experimental Conditions Most Likely to Produce Data That Appear to Support Deterministic or Probabilistic Response Selection Rules

Deterministic response selection	Probabilistic response selection
Optimal rule is simple (optimal rule has verbal analogue)	Optimal rule is complex (optimal rule has no verbal analogue)
Optimal rule uses external criterion (limited memory requirement)	Optimal rule uses internal criterion (extensive memory requirement)
Experienced subjects	Inexperienced subjects
Single subject analyses	Averaging across subjects

say, from a deterministic to a probabilistic response selection rule. Until there is good evidence to the contrary, the simplest hypothesis is that subjects use the same type of response selection rule in virtually all categorization tasks. Because of the identifiability problems, deterministic and probabilistic rules are difficult but not impossible to discriminate between. Currently, the best available evidence favors deterministic rules, but the debate is far from resolved.

V. CATEGORY ACCESS

This section reviews five major theories about the type of category information that is accessed and the computations that are performed on that information during categorization. Before beginning however, it is instructive to consider the optimal solution to the category access problem.

The optimal classifier uses the decision rule that maximizes categorization accuracy. Consider a task with two categories A and B. Suppose the stimulus is drawn from category A with probability $P(C_A)$ and from category B with probability $P(C_B)$. Let $f_A(i)$ and $f_B(i)$ be the likelihood that stimulus i is a member of category A or B, respectively. Then on trials when stimulus i is presented, the optimal classifier uses the deterministic rule:

$$
\text{if } \frac{f_A(i)}{f_B(i)} \left.\begin{cases} > \dfrac{P(C_B)}{P(C_A)} & \text{then respond } A \\[2mm] = \dfrac{P(C_B)}{P(C_A)} & \text{then guess} \\[2mm] < \dfrac{P(C_B)}{P(C_A)} & \text{then respond } B \end{cases}\right. .
$$

The set of all stimuli for which $f_A(i)/f_B(i) = P(C_B)/P(C_A)$ is a decision bound because it partitions the perceptual space into response regions. In general, the optimal decision bound can have any shape, but if each category representation is a multivariate normal distribution, then the optimal decision bound is always linear or quadratic.

A subject who would like to respond optimally in a categorization task must solve several problems. First, in a real experiment, the subject will have experience with only a limited sample of exemplars from the two categories. Therefore, even with perfect memory and an error-free perceptual system it is impossible to estimate perfectly the category likelihoods $f_A(i)$ and $f_B(i)$. At best, the subject could compute imperfect estimates of $f_A(i)$ and $f_B(i)$ (and also of the base rates) and use these in the optimal decision rule (Ashby & Alfonso-Reese, 1995). In this case, the subject's decision bound will not agree with the optimal bound. Assuming the subject chooses this path, the next problem is to select an estimator.

In statistics, the likelihoods $f_A(i)$ and $f_B(i)$ are called probability density functions. Density function estimators are either parametric or non-parametric. Parametric estimators assume the unknown density function is of a specific type. In our language, this is equivalent to assuming some a priori category structure. For example, if the subject assumes that the category A distribution is normal, then the best method of estimating $f_A(i)$ is to estimate separately the category mean and variance and insert these estimates into the equation that describes the bell-shaped normal density function (assuming only one relevant dimension). Nonparametric estimators make few a priori assumptions about category structure. The best known example is the familiar relative frequency histogram, but many far superior estimators have been discovered (e.g., Silverman, 1986). We will return to the idea of categorization as probability density function estimation later in this section.

Note that a subject who uses the optimal decision rule with estimates of $f_A(i)$ and $f_B(i)$ need not retrieve *any* exemplar information from memory. No matter what estimators are used, the updating required after each new stimulus could be done between trials. If it is, then when a new stimulus is presented the estimators would be intact and the two relevant likelihoods, that is, the estimates of $f_A(i)$ and $f_B(i)$ could be retrieved directly.

We turn now to an overview of the five major theories and then discuss the many empirical comparisons that have been conducted.

A. Classical Theory

The oldest theory of categorization is classical theory, which dates back to Aristotle, but in psychology was popularized by Hull (1920). Much of the recent work on classical theory has been conducted in psycholinguistics (Fodor, Bever, & Garrett, 1974; Miller & Johnson-Laird, 1976) and psychological studies of concept formation (e.g., Bourne, 1966; Bruner, Goodnow, & Austin, 1956).

Classical theory makes unique assumptions about category representation and about category access. All applications of classical theory have assumed a deterministic response selection rule. First, the theory assumes that every category is represented as a set of singly necessary and jointly sufficient features (Smith & Medin, 1981). A feature is singly necessary if every member of the category contains that feature. For example, "four sides" is a singly necessary feature of the "square" category because every square has four sides. A set of features are jointly sufficient if any entity that contains the set of features is a member of the category. The features (1) four sides, (2) sides of equal length, (3) equal angles, and (4) closed figure are jointly sufficient to describe the "square" category, because every entity with these four attributes is a square.

The category access assumptions follow directly from the representation assumptions. When a stimulus is presented, the subject is assumed to retrieve the set of necessary and sufficient features associated with one of the contrasting categories. The stimulus is then tested to see whether it possesses exactly this set of features. If it does, the subject emits the response associated with that category. If it does not, the process is repeated with a different category.

Although classical theory accurately describes many categorization tasks (e.g., classifying squares versus triangles), the theory is associated with a number of predictions that are known to be false. First, classical theory excludes categories that are defined by disjunctive features, whereas subjects can learn tasks in which the optimal rule is disjunctive, such as the biconditional or exclusive-or problems (e.g., Bourne, 1970; Bruner, Goodnow, & Austin, 1956; Haygood & Bourne, 1965).

Second, it is difficult to list the defining features of many categories. For example, Wittgenstein (1953) argued that no set of necessary and sufficient features exists for the category "game." Some games have a "winner" (e.g., football), but others do not (e.g., ring-around-the-rosie).

The third, and perhaps strongest, evidence against classical theory, is the finding that categories possess graded structure—that is, members of a category vary in how good an example (or how typical) they are of the category. Graded structure has been found in nearly every category (see Barsalou, 1987, for a review). For example, when asked to judge the typicality of different birds, subjects reliably rate the robin as very typical, the pigeon as moderately typical, and the ostrich as atypical (Mervis, Catlin, & Rosch, 1976; Rips, Shoben, & Smith, 1973; Rosch, 1973). In addition, if subjects are asked to verify whether a stimulus belongs to a particular category, response accuracy increases and response time decreases as typicality increases (although only on YES trials; e.g., Ashby, Boynton, & Lee, 1994; Rips et al., 1973; Rosch, 1973). Interesting typicality effects have also been found in the developmental literature. For example, typical category members are learned first by children (Rosch, 1973; Mervis, 1980) and are named first when children are asked to list members of a category (Mervis et al., 1976). Classical theory, on the other hand, predicts that all members of a category are treated equally, because they all share the same set of necessary and sufficient features.

Note that all three of these criticisms are directed at the category representation assumptions of classical theory, not at the category access assumptions. Thus, none of these results rule out the possibility that the category access assumptions of classical theory are basically correct. Especially relevant to this observation is the fact that most of the data on which the criticisms are based were not collected in categorization tasks (but rather, e.g., in typicality rating tasks). The major exception is the fact that subjects can learn categorization tasks in which the optimal rule is disjunctive. The simplest way to handle this is to generalize the classical theory to allow a category to be defined as the union of subcategories,[2] each of which is defined by a set of necessary and sufficient features (e.g., Ashby, 1992a, 1992b; Smith & Medin, 1981; see also, Huttenlocher & Hedges, 1994). For example, the category "games" could be defined as the union of "competitive games" and "noncompetitive games."

A classical theorist could respond to the other criticisms by arguing that an exemplar-based graded category representation exists, and whereas this graded representation is used in recall and typicality rating tasks, it is not accessed on trials of a categorization task. Instead, when categorizing, the subject only needs to retrieve the categorization rule, which according to classical theory is a list of necessary and sufficient features for each relevant category or subcategory. This more sophisticated version of classical theory can only be falsified by data from categorization experiments. As it turns out, such data is not difficult to collect (e.g., Ashby & Gott, 1988; Ashby & Maddox, 1990), but as we will see, the notion that some category related tasks access a graded category representation whereas other such tasks do not is more difficult to disconfirm.

B. Prototype Theory

The abundant evidence that category representations have a graded structure led to the development of prototype theory (e.g., Homa, Sterling, & Trepel, 1981; Posner & Keele, 1968, 1970; Reed, 1972; Rosch, 1973; Rosch, Simpson, & Miller, 1976). Instead of representing a category as a set of necessary and sufficient features, prototype theory assumes that the category representation is dominated by the prototype, which is the most typical or ideal instance of the category. In its most extreme form, the prototype *is* the category representation, but in its weaker forms, the category representation includes information about other exemplars (Busemeyer, Dewey, & Medin, 1984; Homa, Dunbar, & Nohre, 1991; Shin & Nosofsky, 1992). In all versions however, the prototype dominates the category representation.

Much of the early work on prototype theory focused on recall and typicality rating experiments; that is, on tasks other than categorization. Two alternative prototype models have been developed for application to categorization tasks. The first, developed by Reed (1972), assumes a multidimensional scaling (MDS) representation of the stimuli and category prototypes. On each trial, the subject is assumed to compute the psychological distance between the stimulus and the prototype of each relevant category. Reed's

---

[2] More formally, the distribution of exemplars in the superordinate category is a probability mixture of the exemplars in the subordinate categories.

model assumed a deterministic response selection rule (i.e., respond with the category that has the nearest prototype), but versions that assume probabilistic response selection have also been proposed (e.g., Ashby & Maddox, 1993; Nosofsky, 1987; Shin & Nosofsky, 1992). We refer to all of these as MDS-prototype models. The other prominent prototype model is called the fuzzy-logical model of perception (FLMP; Cohen & Massaro, 1992; Massaro & Friedman, 1990). The FLMP assumes a featural, rather than a dimensional, representation of the stimuli and category prototypes. It also assumes that a stimulus is compared to each prototype by computing the fuzzy-truth value (Zadeh, 1965) of the proposition that the two patterns are composed of exactly the same features.[3] Recently, Crowther, Batchelder, and Hu (1995) questioned whether the fuzzy-logical interpretation purportedly offered by the FLMP is warranted. Response selection in the FLMP is probabilistic [the Eq. (1) similarity-choice model with all response biases set equal]. Although the FLMP appears to be quite different from the MDS-prototype model, Cohen and Massaro (1992) showed that the two models make similar predictions.

Although prototype theory was seen as a clear improvement over classical theory, it quickly began to suffer criticisms of its own. If the prototype is the only item stored in memory, then all information about category variability and correlational structure is lost. Yet several lines of research suggested that nonprototypical category exemplars can have a pronounced effect on categorization performance (e.g., Brooks, 1978; Hayes-Roth & Hayes-Roth, 1977; Medin & Schaffer, 1978; Medin & Schwanenflugel, 1981; Neumann, 1974; Reber, 1976; Reber & Allen, 1978; Walker, 1975). In particular, subjects are highly sensitive to the correlational structure of the categories (e.g., Ashby & Gott, 1988; Ashby & Maddox, 1990, 1992; Medin, Altom, Edelson, & Freko, 1982; Medin & Schwanenflugel, 1981; Nosofsky, 1986, 1987, 1989). Note that this criticism is directed at the category access assumptions of prototype theory, not at the category representation assumptions.

Rosch (1975, 1978) understood the importance of the criticisms against prototype theory and in an attempt to strengthen the theory argued that almost all categories contain multiple prototypes. In fact, she argued that "in only some artificial categories is there by definition a literal single prototype" (p. 40). For example, both robin and sparrow seem to be prototypes for the category "bird." In this spirit, Anderson (1990, 1991) proposed a multiple prototype model, called the rational model. The rational model

---

[3] The overall fuzzy-truth value of this proposition is equal to the product of the fuzzy-truth values of the propositions that each specific feature of the stimulus is equal to the analogous feature in the prototype (Massaro & Friedman, 1990). Fuzzy-truth value has many of the properties of similarity, so the FLMP product rule is analogous to the assumption that similarity is multiplicative across dimensions (Nosofsky, 1992b).

assumes that the category representation is a set of clusters of exemplars, each of which is dominated by a prototype. The probability that an exemplar is grouped into a particular cluster is determined by (1) the similarity of the exemplar to the cluster's prototype and (2) a prior probability that is determined by the number of exemplars in each cluster and by the value of a coupling parameter. When presented with a stimulus to be categorized, the subject is assumed to compute the similarity between the stimulus and the prototype of each cluster and to select a response on the basis of these similarity computations. Few empirical tests of this model have been conducted (however, see Ahn & Medin, 1992; Nosofsky, 1991a).

C. Feature-Frequency Theory

Feature-frequency theory (Estes, 1986a; Franks & Bransford, 1971; Reed, 1972) has its roots in feature-analytic models of pattern perception, which assume that a visual stimulus is perceived as the set of its constituent features (Geyer & DeWald, 1973; Gibson, Osser, Schiff, & Smith, 1963; Townsend & Ashby, 1982). A key assumption of feature-analytic models is feature-sampling independence, which states that the probability of perceiving features f_a and f_b equals the probability of perceiving feature f_a times the probability of perceiving feature f_b (Townsend & Ashby, 1982; Townsend, Hu, & Ashby, 1981). In other words, feature-analytic models assume separate features are perceived independently. Townsend and Ashby (1982) found strong evidence against this assumption and, as a consequence, feature-analytic models of pattern perception are no longer popular.

Feature-frequency theories of categorization borrow their stimulus representation assumptions from the feature-analytic models of pattern perception. Suppose stimulus i is constructed from features $f_1, f_2, \ldots, f_n$. Then the strength of association of stimulus i to category J, denoted as before by S_{iJ}, is assumed to equal

$$S_{iJ} = \hat{P}(C_J)\hat{P}(i|C_J) = \hat{P}(C_J) \prod_{k=1}^{n} \hat{P}(f_k|C_J) ,$$

where $\hat{P}(C_J)$ is the subject's estimate of the a priori probability that a random stimulus in the experiment is from category J, $\hat{P}(i|C_J)$ is an estimate of the probability (or likelihood) that the presented stimulus is from category J, and $\hat{P}(f_k|C_J)$ is an estimate of the probability (or likelihood) that feature f_k occurs in an exemplar from category J. The latter equality holds because of the sampling independence assumption. Some feature-frequency models assume the probabilistic response selection rule of Eq. (1) (e.g., Estes, 1986a; Gluck & Bower, 1988), and some assume the deterministic rule of Eq. (2) [with $h(i) = S_{iB} - S_{iA}$, e.g., Reed, 1972].

Feature-frequency theory can take on many forms depending on what assumptions are made about how the subject estimates the feature frequencies, that is, the $\hat{P}(f_k|C_J)$. The original, and perhaps the most natural, interpretation is that the category J representation is a list of the features occurring in all exemplars of category J, along with the relative frequency with which each feature occurred (Franks & Bransford, 1971; Reed, 1972). Another possibility is that the feature frequencies of the presented stimulus are estimated by doing a feature-by-feature comparison of the stimulus to the category prototypes. This type of feature-frequency model is equivalent to a prototype model that assumes feature-sampling independence. A third possibility is that the category J representation is the set of all exemplars that belong to category J. To estimate $\hat{P}(f_k|C_J)$ the subject scans the list of stored category J exemplars and computes the proportion that contain feature f_k. This interpretation leads to a special case of exemplar theory (Estes, 1986a).

Gluck (1991) argued against the feature-frequency model offered by Gluck and Bower (1988; i.e., the adaptive network model) on the basis of its failure to account for the ability of subjects to learn nonlinearly separable categories. It is important to note that not all feature-frequency models are so constrained. For example, suppose all features are continuous–valued and that the subject assumes the values of each feature are normally distributed within each category, with a mean and variance that varies from category to category. To estimate $\hat{P}(f_k|C_J)$, the subject first estimates the mean and variance of the values of feature f_k within category J and then inserts these estimates into the equation for the probability density function of a normal distribution. Then categories A and B are nonlinearly separable and the subject will learn these categories (i.e., respond with a nonlinear decision bound) if the following conditions hold: (1) all feature values are normally distributed, (2) the values of all feature pairs are statistically independent (so that feature sampling independence is valid), (3) the values of at least one feature have different variances in the two categories, and (4) the subject uses the response selection rule of the optimal classifier, i.e., Eq. (4).

Given the strong evidence against the feature-sampling independence assumption (e.g., Townsend & Ashby, 1982) and the fact that so many of the feature-frequency models are special cases of the more widely known categorization models, we will have little else to say about feature-frequency theory.

D. Exemplar Theory

Perhaps the most popular approach to dealing with the criticisms against prototype theory is embodied in exemplar theory (Brooks, 1978; Estes, 1986a, 1994, Hintzman, 1986; Medin & Schaffer, 1978; Nosofsky, 1986). Exemplar theory is based on two key assumptions:

1. *Representation:* a category is represented in memory as the set of representations of all category exemplars that have yet been encountered.[4]
2. *Access:* categorization decisions are based on similarity comparisons between the stimulus and the memory representation of *every* exemplar of each relevant category.

Two aspects of these assumptions are especially controversial. First, the assumption that categorization depends exclusively on exemplar or episodic memory has recently been called into question. A series of neuropsychological studies has shown that amnesic patients, with impaired episodic memory, can perform normally on a number of different category learning tasks (Knowlton, Ramus, & Squire, 1992; Knowlton & Squire, 1993; Kolodny, 1994). Second, the assumption that the similarity computations include *every* exemplar of the relevant categories is often regarded as intuitively unreasonable. For example, Myung (1994) argued that "it is hard to imagine that a 70 year-old fisherman would remember ever instance of fish that he has seen when attempting to categorize an object as a fish" (p. 348). Even if the exemplar representations are not consciously retrieved, a massive amount of activation is assumed by exemplar theory. One possibility that would retain the flavor of the exemplar approach is to assume that some random sample of exemplars are drawn from memory and similarity is only computed between the stimulus and this reduced set. However, one advantage of exemplar theory over prototype theory is that it can account for the observed sensitivity of people to the correlational structure of a category (Medin et al., 1982; Medin & Schaffer, 1978). It displays this sensitivity because the entire category is sampled on every trial. If only a subset of the category exemplars are sampled, the resulting model must necessarily be less sensitive to correlational structure. Ennis and Ashby (1993) showed that if only a single random sample is drawn, then exemplar models are relatively insensitive to correlational structure. To date, no one has investigated the question of how small the random sample can be, before adequate sensitivity to correlation is lost.

Many different exemplar models have been proposed. Figure 3 presents the hierarchical relations among some of these, as well as the relations among other types of categorization models. Models that are higher up in the tree are more general, whereas those below are special cases.

Perhaps the most prominent of the early exemplar models are the context model (Medin & Schaffer, 1978), the array-similarity model (Estes, 1994; also called the basic exemplar-memory model, Estes, 1986a), and the generalized context model (GCM; Nosofsky, 1985, 1986). In addition to the two

---

[4] This assumption does not preclude the possibility of decay in the information with time or that only partial exemplar information is stored.

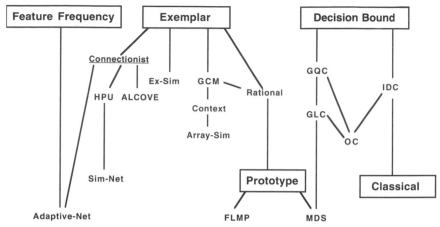

FIGURE 3   Hierarchical relations among models of category access. (Adaptive-Net = Adaptive Network Model, HPU = Hidden Pattern Unit Network Model, Sim-Net = Similarity-Network Model, Ex-Sim = Exemplar-Similarity Model, GCM = Generalized Context Model, Array-Sim = Array-Similarity Model, FLMP = Fuzzy Logical Model of Perception, MDS = MDS Prototype Model, GQC = General Quadratic Classifier, GLC = General Linear Classifier, OC = Optimal Classifier, IDC = Independent Decisions Classifier.)

assumptions listed earlier, these models all assume the probabilistic response selection rule of the similarity-choice model—that is, Eq. (1)—although the context and array-similarity models allow no response bias. These latter two models also assume that all psychological dimensions are binary valued, and that the similarity between a stimulus and a stored exemplar is multiplicative across dimensions.[5] In other words, if there are m dimensions, the similarity between stimulus i and stored exemplar j equals

$$S_{ij} = \prod_{k=1}^{m} s_k(i, j) \, ,$$

where $s_k(i, j)$ is the similarity between the dimension k values of stimulus i and exemplar j. From Assumption (2), all exemplar models assume the overall similarity of stimulus i to category J equals

$$S_{iJ} = \sum_{j \in J} S_{ij} \, .$$

[5] It is possible to define an exemplar model in which similarity is additive. However, as shown by Nosofsky (1992b), an additive similarity exemplar model is equivalent to an additive similarity prototype model.

In the context model, the component similarity function is defined as

$$s_k(i, j) = \begin{cases} 1, & \text{if } i = j \\ q_k, & \text{if } i \neq j \end{cases}$$

The array-similarity model[6] uses the same definition, except the similarity parameter q_k is assumed to be the same on every dimension (i.e., $q = q_1 = q_2 = \ldots = q_m$).

The generalized context model (GCM) assumes continuous-valued dimensions. Similarity is defined flexibly and, as a result, only some versions of the GCM assume similarity is multiplicative across dimensions (Nosofsky, 1984). In all versions, however, the component similarity function, that is, $s_k(i, j)$, decreases symmetrically with distance from the stimulus representation. The model has two types of parameters that can stretch or shrink the psychological space. An overall discriminability parameter, c, expands or contracts the space uniformly in all directions. The attention weight parameters, w_k, selectively stretch or shrink dimension k only. As a subject gains experience with a stimulus set, individual stimuli begin to look more distinct and, as a result, the similarity between a fixed pair of stimuli should decrease with experience. The GCM models this phenomenon by increasing the overall discriminability parameter c with the subject's level of experience (e.g., Nosofsky et al., 1992). Increasing a specific attention weight, say, w_k, stretches dimension k relative to the other psychological dimensions. This selective stretching acts to decrease the dimension k component similarities. The idea is that with more attention allocated to dimension k, the subject is better able to discriminate between stimuli that have different values on that dimension.

Although the context model has no attention weight or overall discriminability parameters, it is able to mimic the effects of these parameters by changing the magnitudes of the component similarity parameters (i.e., the q_k). Decreasing all q_k by the same proportion is equivalent to increasing overall discriminability, and decreasing a single q_k is equivalent to increasing a single attention weight. Under this interpretation, the assumption of the array-similarity model that all q_k are equal is equivalent to assuming that equal amounts of attention are allocated to all stimulus dimensions.

The context and generalized context models have been used to account for asymptotic categorization performance from tasks in which the categories (1) were linearly or nonlinearly separable (Medin & Schwanenflugel, 1981; Nosofsky, 1986, 1987, 1989), (2) differed in baserate (Medin & Edelson, 1988), (3) contained correlated or uncorrelated features (Medin et al.,

---

[6] Hintzman's (1986) MINERVA2 is similar to the context and array-similarity models. All three make identical representation assumptions, although MINERVA2 does not assume a multiplicative similarity rule.

1992), (4) could be distinguished using a simple verbal rule (or a conjunction of simple rules; Nosofsky, Clark, & Shin, 1989), and (5) contained differing exemplar frequencies (Nosofsky, 1988a). The array-similarity model was developed primarily to predict category learning. The model has been applied to learning data in which the categories (1) were defined by independent or correlated features (Estes, 1986b) and (2) differed in base rate (Estes, Campbell, Hatsopoulis, & Hurwitz, 1989). Recently, Estes (1994; see also Nosofsky et al., 1992) elaborated the model to predict a wider range of category learning phenomena.

In experiments where the stimuli are constructed from continuous-valued dimensions, unique parameter estimation problems are encountered. For example, in the GCM, the coordinates in psychological space of every category exemplar are free parameters (as well as the attention weights, overall discriminability, and response biases). Estimation of all these parameters requires many more degrees of freedom than are found in a typical categorization experiment. Nosofsky (1986) discovered an interesting solution to this problem. In a typical application, the coordinates of the stimuli in the psychological space are first estimated from data collected in a similarity judgment or stimulus identification task. Next, a recognition memory, typicality rating, or categorization task is run with the same stimuli. The GCM is then fit to this new data under the assumption that the stimulus coordinates are the same in the two experiments (see Nosofsky, 1992a for a review).

Ashby and Alfonso-Reese (1995) showed that the context model, the array-similarity model, and the GCM are all mathematically equivalent to a process in which the subject estimates the category likelihoods with a powerful nonparametric probability density estimator that is commonly used by statisticians (i.e., a Parzen, 1962, kernel estimator). This means that with a large enough sample size, these models can recover any category distribution, no matter how complex. The only requirements are that the subject does not completely ignore any stimulus dimensions and that overall discriminability slowly increases with sample size (as in Nosofsky et al., 1992). Thus, in most applications, the only suboptimality in these exemplar models that cannot be overcome with training is that they assume a probabilistic decision rule instead of the deterministic rule of the optimal classifier. In other words, the assumptions of exemplar theory, as embodied in the context model, the array-similarity model, or the GCM, are equivalent to assuming that the subject estimates all the relevant category distributions with an extremely powerful probability density estimator. The estimator is so powerful that it is bound to succeed, so these exemplar models predict that subjects should eventually learn any categorization problem, no matter how complex.

Recently, there has been a surge of interest in developing and testing models of category learning. The context, array-similarity, and generalized context models provide adequate descriptions of asymptotic categorization performance, but these models are severely limited in their ability to account for the dynamics of category learning. The models have two main weaknesses. First, they all assume that the memory strength of an item presented early in the learning sequence remains unchanged throughout the course of the experiment. Thus, the influence of early items on performance during the last few trials is just as strong as the influence of items presented late in the learning sequence. Yet recency effects are well established in the memory literature—that is, a recently presented item will have a larger effect on performance than an item presented early in learning. To account for recency effects in category learning, exemplar theorists proposed that the memory strength of an exemplar decreases with the number of trials since it was last presented as a stimulus (Estes, 1993, 1994; Nosofsky et al., 1992).

A second problem with the context, array-similarity, and generalized context models is that they predict categorization response probabilities early in the learning sequence that are more extreme (i.e., closer to 0 and 1) than those observed in the empirical data. To see this, consider a categorization task with two categories, A and B. If the first stimulus in the experiment is from category A, then the models predict that the probability of responding A on the second trial is 1. The empirical data, on the other hand, suggest that early in the learning sequence, response probabilities are close to 0.5. To deal with this weakness, exemplar theorists postulated that subjects enter a category learning task with some information already present in the memory array that they will use for the representation of the contrasting categories. This *background noise* (Estes, 1993, 1994; Nosofsky et al., 1992) is assumed to be constant across categories and remains unchanged throughout the learning sequence. Early in the sequence, exemplar information is minimal and the background noise dominates, so categorization response probabilities are near 0.5. As more exemplars are experienced, the exemplar information in the memory array begins to dominate the background noise in the computation of the category response probabilities. Following Estes (1993, 1994), we will refer to context or array-similarity models that have been augmented with memory decay and background-noise parameters as the *exemplar-similarity* model (Ex-Sim; also called the sequence-sensitive context model by Nosofsky et al., 1992).

Another set of category learning models have been implemented in connectionist networks (e.g., Estes, 1993, 1994; Estes et al., 1989; Gluck & Bower, 1988; Gluck, Bower, & Hee, 1989; Hurwitz, 1990; Kruschke, 1992; Nosofsky et al., 1992). These models assume that a network of nodes and interconnections is formed during learning. The nodes are grouped into layers and information from lower layers feeds forward to the next higher layer. The input layer consists of nodes that correspond to individual features, or collections of features (possibly even complete exemplar patterns). The output layer has a node associated with each of the contrasting categories. The amount of activation of a category (i.e., output) node is taken as the strength of association between the stimulus and that particular category. In most models, response selection is probabilistic. Whereas the exemplar-similarity model learns through a gradual accumulation of exemplar information, the connectionist models learn by modifying the weights between nodes as a function of error-driven feedback.

One of the earliest connectionist models of category learning was Gluck and Bower's (1988) adaptive network model. This is a feature-frequency model instantiated in a two-layer network. Gluck et al. (1989) proposed a configural-cue network model that generalizes the adaptive network model by including input layer nodes that correspond to single features, pairs of features, triples of features, and so on. Several exemplar-based connectionist models have also been developed. Estes (1993, 1994) proposed a two-layer connectionist model, called the similarity-network model (or Sim-Net), in which the input layer consists of exemplar nodes only. The hidden pattern unit model (HPU; Hurwitz, 1990, 1994) and ALCOVE (Kruschke, 1992) are three-layer networks in which the input layer consists of stimulus feature nodes, the second layer consists of exemplar nodes, and the output layer consists of category nodes.

Gluck and Bower (1988) reported data exhibiting a form of base-rate neglect that is predicted by the adaptive network models, but which has proved troublesome for the exemplar-similarity models. Subjects were presented with a list of medical symptoms and were asked to decide whether the hypothetical patient had one of two diseases. One of the diseases occurred in 75% of the hypothetical patients and the other disease occurred in 25% of the patients. After a training session, subjects were asked to estimate the probability that a patient exhibiting a particular symptom had one of the two diseases. On these trials, Gluck and Bower found that subjects neglected to make full use of the base-rate differences between the two diseases (see, also, Estes et al., 1989; Medin & Edelson, 1988; Nosofsky et al., 1992). This result is compatible with several different adaptive network models and incompatible with the exemplar-similarity model. For several years, it was thought that ALCOVE could account for the Gluck and Bower form of base-rate neglect (Kruschke, 1992; Nosofsky et al., 1992), but Lewandowsky (1995) showed that this prediction holds only under a narrow set of artificial circumstances. Thus, it remains a challenge for exemplar-based learning models to account for the results of Gluck and Bower (1988).

Although the exemplar-similarity model and the exemplar-based connectionist models have each had success, neither class has been found to be uniformly superior. In light of this fact, Estes (1994) attempted to identify experimental conditions that favor one family of models over the other by comparing their predictions across a wide variety of experimental situations. Although a review of this extensive work is beyond the scope of this chapter, some of the experimental conditions examined by Estes (1994) include manipulations of category size, training procedure, category confusability, repetition and lag effects, and prototype learning. Estes (1986b; 1994; see also Estes & Maddox, 1995; Maddox & Estes, 1995) also extended the models to the domain of recognition memory.

Figure 3 shows Anderson's (1990, 1991) rational model as a special case of exemplar theory. This is not exactly correct because the rational model does not assume that the subject automatically computes the similarity between the stimulus and all exemplars stored in memory. When the coupling parameter of the rational model is zero, however, each exemplar forms its own cluster (Nosofsky, 1991a) and, under these conditions, the rational model satisfies our definition of an exemplar model. If, in addition, the similarity between the category labels is zero, and the subject bases his or her decision solely on the stored exemplar information, then the rational model is equivalent to the context model (Nosofsky, 1991a). Figure 3 also shows the prototype models to be special cases of the rational model. When the value of the coupling parameter in the rational model is one, and the similarity between the category labels is zero, the rational model reduces to a multiplicative similarity prototype model (Nosofsky, 1991a), such as Massaro's (1987) fuzzy logical model of perception.

E. Decision Bound Theory

The final theoretical perspective that we will discuss is called decision bound theory or sometimes general recognition theory (Ashby, 1992a; Ashby & Gott, 1988; Ashby & Lee, 1991, 1992; Ashby & Maddox, 1990, 1992, 1993; Ashby & Townsend, 1986; Maddox & Ashby, 1993). As described in the representation section, decision bound theory assumes the stimuli can be represented numerically but that there is trial-by-trial variability in the perceptual information associated with each stimulus, so the perceptual effects of a stimulus are most appropriately represented by a multivariate probability distribution (usually a multivariate normal distribution). During categorization, the subject is assumed to learn to assign responses to different regions of the perceptual space. When presented with a stimulus, the subject determines which region the perceptual effect is in and emits the associated response. The *decision bound* is the partition between competing response regions. Thus, decision bound theory assumes no exemplar information is needed to make a categorization response; only a response label is retrieved. Even so, the theory assumes that exemplar information is available. For example, in recall and typicality rating experiments, exemplar information must be accessed on every trial. Even in categorization tasks, the subject might use exemplar information between trials to update the decision bound.

Different versions of decision bound theory can be specified depending on how the subject divides the perceptual space into response regions. The five versions that have been studied are (1) the independent decisions classifier (IDC), (2) the minimum distance classifier (MDC), (3) the optimal classifier (OC), (4) the general linear classifier (GLC), and (5) the general quadratic classifier (GQC). An example of each of these models is presented in Figure 4 for the special case in which the category exemplars vary on two

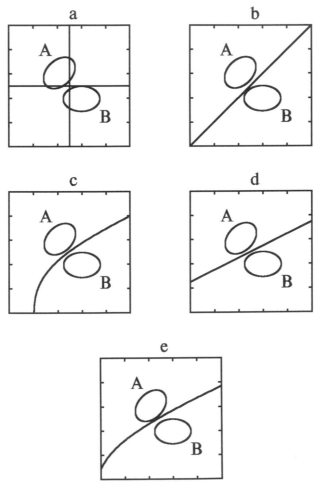

FIGURE 4   Decision bounds from five different decision bound models. (a) independent decisions classifier, (b) minimum distance classifier, (c) optimal decision bound model, (d) general linear classifier, and (e) general quadratic classifier.

perceptual dimensions. Figure 4 also assumes the category representations are bivariate normal distributions, but the models can all be applied to any category representation. The ellipses are contours of equal likelihood for the two categories. Every point on the same ellipse is an equal number of standard deviation units from the mean (i.e., the category prototype) and is equally likely to be selected if an exemplar is randomly sampled from the category. The exemplars of category A have about equal variability on perceptual dimensions x and y but the values on these two dimensions are positively correlated. In category B there is greater variability on dimension x and the x and y values are uncorrelated.

The independent decisions classifier (Figure 4a; Ashby & Gott, 1988; Shaw, 1982) assumes a separate decision is made about the presence or absence of each feature (e.g., the animal flies or does not fly) or about the level of each perceptual dimension (e.g., the stimulus is large or small). A categorization response is selected by examining the pattern of decisions across the different dimensions. For example, if category A was composed of tall, blue rectangles, then the subject would separately decide whether a stimulus rectangle was tall and whether it was blue by appealing to separate criteria on the height and hue dimensions, respectively. If the rectangle was judged to be both tall and blue, then it would be classified as a member of category A. Using a set of dimensional criteria is equivalent to defining a set of linear decision bounds, each of which is parallel to one of the coordinate axes (as in Figure 4a). The decision rule of the independent decisions classifier is similar to the rule postulated by classical theory. In both cases the subject is assumed to make a separate decision about the presence or absence of each stimulus dimension (or feature). Thus, classical theory is a special case of the independent decisions classifier (Ashby, 1992a).

Recently, Nosofsky, Palmeri, and McKinley (1994) proposed a model that assumes subjects use independent decisions bounds but then memorize responses to a few exemplars not accounted for by these bounds (i.e., exceptions to the independent decisions rule). Category learning follows a stochastic process, so different subjects may adopt different independent decisions bounds and may memorize different exceptions. The model was developed for binary-valued dimensions. It is unclear how it could be generalized to continuous-valued dimensions, since there is an abundance of continuous-valued data that is incompatible with virtually all independent decisions strategies, even those that allow the subject to memorize exceptions (e.g., Ashby & Gott, 1988; Ashby & Maddox, 1990, 1992).

The minimum distance classifier (Figure 4b) assumes the subject responds with the category that has the nearest centroid. An A response is given to every stimulus representation that is closer to the category A centroid, and a B response is given to every representation closer to the B centroid. The decision bound is the line that bisects and is orthogonal to the line segment connecting the two category centroids. If the category centroid is interpreted as the prototype and if the similarity between the stimulus and a prototype decreases with distance, then the minimum distance classifier is an MDS prototype model.

The optimal decision bound model (Figure 4c) was proposed as a yardstick against which to compare the other models. It assumes the subject uses the optimal decision rule, that is, Eq. (4), and that the category likelihoods are estimated without error. Suboptimality occurs only because of perceptual and criterial noise.

The most promising decision bound models are the general linear classifier (Figure 4d) and the general quadratic classifier (Figure 4e), which assume that the decision bound is *some* line or quadratic curve, respectively. These models are based on the premise that the subject uses the optimal decision rule and estimates the category density functions (i.e., the stimulus likelihoods) using a parametric estimator that assumes the category distributions are normal. The assumption of normality is made either because experience with natural categories causes subjects to believe that most categories are normally distributed or because subjects estimate category means, variances, correlations, and base rates and infer a category distribution in the optimal fashion (see the representation section). If the estimated category structures are reasonably similar, the resulting decision bound will be linear (hence the general linear classifier), and if the estimated covariance structures are different, the bound will be quadratic (hence the general quadratic classifier). Specialized versions of the general linear classifier also have been developed to investigate the optimality of human performance when category base rates are unequal (Maddox, 1995).

One of the greatest strengths of decision bound theory is that it can be applied in a straightforward fashion to a wide variety of cognitive tasks. For example, different versions of the theory have been developed for application to speeded classification (Ashby & Maddox, 1994; Maddox & Ashby, 1996), identification and similarity judgment (Ashby & Lee, 1991; Ashby & Perrin, 1988), preference (Perrin, 1992), and same-different judgment (Thomas, 1994). In addition, decision bound theory provides a powerful framework within which to study and understand interactions during perceptual processing (Ashby & Maddox, 1994; Ashby & Townsend, 1986; Kadlec & Townsend, 1992). Although the theory allows for changes in the perceptual representation of stimuli across different tasks, it is assumed that the most important difference between, say, categorization and identification is that the two tasks require very different decision bounds. Ashby and Lee (1991, 1992) used this idea successfully to account for categorization data from the results of an identification task that used the same subjects and stimuli.

VI. EMPIRICAL COMPARISONS

This section reviews empirical data collected in traditional categorization tasks that test the validity of the categorization theories described in section V. We will also try to identify general properties of the stimuli, category structure, and training procedures that are most favorable to each theory. These properties are outlined in Table 3. Although it is usually the case that conditions opposite to those described in Table 3 are problematic for the various theories, this is not always true. As a result, the conclusions expressed in Table 3 must be interpreted with care.

A. Classical Theory

Classical theory assumes categorization is a process of testing a stimulus for the set of necessary and sufficient features associated with each relevant category. As described earlier, classical models are a special case of the independent decisions classifier of decision bound theory (Ashby, 1992a, Ashby & Gott, 1988). Ashby and Gott (1988, Experiments 1 and 3) and Ashby and Maddox (1990, Experiments 3 and 4; see, also Ashby & Maddox, 1992) tested the hypothesis that subjects always use independent decisions classification by designing tasks in which another strategy, such as minimum distance classification, yielded higher accuracy than the independent decisions classifier. The results convincingly showed that subjects were

TABLE 3   Experimental Conditions Most Likely to Favor Particular Categorization Theories

Theory	Experimental conditions
Classical	Stimuli constructed from a few separable dimensions Inexperienced subjects Optimal rule is independent decisions Taxonomic or logically defined categories
Prototype	Stimuli constructed from many integral dimensions Inexperienced subjects Optimal rule is complex or minimum distance More than two categories
Exemplar	Experienced subjects Optimal rule is simple Few category exemplars
Decision Bound	Optimal rule is linear or quadratic

not constrained to use the independent decisions classifier. Instead, the best first approximation to the data was the optimal decision bound model.

Although classical theory is easily rejected, it has a certain intuitive attractiveness. For many tasks it seems the correct theory (e.g., categorizing squares versus pentagons). What properties do tasks that seem to favor classical theory possess? First, the task should use stimuli constructed from a few perceptually separable components. A pair of components are perceptually separable if the perceptual effect of one component is unaffected by the level of the other, and they are perceptually integral if the perceptual effect of one component is affected by the level of the other (e.g., Ashby & Maddox, 1994; Ashby & Townsend, 1986; Garner, 1974; Maddox, 1992). Classical theory predicts that a subject's decision about a particular component is unaffected by the level of other components. Thus, the independent decisions postulated by classical theory is a natural decision strategy when the stimulus dimensions are perceptually separable. Ashby and Maddox (1990) showed that experienced subjects are not constrained to use an independent decisions strategy, even when the stimulus dimensions are separable. Independent decisions is rarely optimal, and as subjects gain experience in a task, their performance naturally improves. Thus, a second experimental prerequisite is that the subjects are inexperienced (or unmotivated). One way to prevent a subject from gaining the kind of detailed category representation that comes from experience is to withhold feedback on each trial as to the correct response. Indeed, in unsupervised categorization tasks, subjects almost always use simple dimensional rules of the type assumed by classical theory (Ahn & Medin, 1992; Imai & Garner, 1965; Medin, Wattenmaker, & Hampson, 1987; Wattenmaker, 1992).

Finally, there are a few rare cases in which the independent decisions classifier is nearly optimal. For example, Ashby (1992a, Fig. 16.5, p. 473) proposed a task with normally distributed categories in which independent decisions is optimal. In such cases, we expect the data of experienced, motivated subjects to conform reasonably well to the predictions of the independent decisions classifier (and hence, to classical theory). In most experiments, of course, no effort is made to select categories for which independent decisions is optimal. If categories are selected without regard to this property, then chances are poor that independent decisions will be optimal. The best chances, however, although still poor, occur with categories that are taxonomic (e.g., as are many in the animal kingdom) or logically defined (e.g., as is the category "square"), because such categories are frequently defined by a list of characteristic features.

B. Prototype Theory

Prototype theory assumes the strength of association between the stimulus and a category equals the strength of association between the stimulus and the category prototype. All other exemplars or characteristics of the category are assumed to be irrelevant to the categorization process. Dozens of studies have shown convincingly that subjects are not constrained to use only the category prototypes (e.g., Ashby & Gott, 1988; Ashby & Maddox, 1990, 1992; Maddox & Ashby, 1993; Medin & Schaffer, 1978; Medin & Schwanenflugel, 1981; Nosofsky, 1987, 1992a; Shin & Nosofsky, 1992). Some of these studies compared prototype models with exemplar models, others compared prototype models with decision bound models. In every case, the prototype models were rejected in favor of either an exemplar or decision bound model.

These studies show that prototype theory does not provide a complete description of human categorization performance, but they do not rule out the possibility that the prototype has some special status within the category representation. For example, the prototype is sometimes classified more accurately (e.g., Homa & Cultice, 1984; Homa et al., 1981) and seems less susceptible to memory loss with delay of transfer tests than other category exemplars (e.g., Goldman & Homa, 1977; Homa, Cross, Cornell, Goldman, & Schwartz, 1973; Homa & Vosburgh, 1976). In addition, as described in sections V.A and V.B, large prototype effects are almost always found in recall and typicality rating experiments.

Two recent categorization studies, however, found few, if any, special advantages for the prototype (Ashby et al., 1994; Shin & Nosofsky, 1992). Ashby et al. (1994) examined categorization response time (RT) in five separate experiments that used three different kinds of stimuli. No prototype effects on RT were found in any experiment. Hypotheses that assumed RT was determined by absolute or by relative distance to the two prototypes were both rejected. The prototypes did not elicit the fastest responses and even among stimuli that were just as discriminative as the prototypes with respect to the categorization judgment, the prototypes showed no RT advantage. The best predictor of the data was an assumption that RT decreased with distance from the decision bound. Thus, the fastest responses were to the most discriminative stimuli (which are furthest from the bound).

Shin and Nosofsky (1992) conducted a series of experiments using random dot stimuli that manipulated experimental factors such as category size, time between training and test, and within-category exemplar frequency. Each of these manipulations have been found to affect categorization accuracy for the prototype (e.g., Goldman & Homa, 1977; Homa & Chambliss, 1975; Homa & Cultice, 1984; Homa, Dunbar, & Nohre, 1991; Homa et al., 1973, 1981; Homa & Vosburgh, 1976). Shin and Nosofsky (1992) replicated some prototype effects (e.g., increases in accuracy to the prototype with category size) but not others (e.g., differential forgetting for the prototype). In each experiment, Shin and Nosofsky tested a combined exemplar-prototype model, which contained a mixture parameter that determined the separate contribution of exemplar and prototype submodels to the predicted response probability. The mixture model provided a significant improvement in fit over a pure exemplar model in only one case, suggesting little, if any, contribution of the prototype abstraction process.

How can the results of Ashby et al. (1994) and Shin and Nosofsky (1992) be explained in light of the large empirical literature showing prototype effects? First, the failure to find prototype effects in categorization tasks is not necessarily damaging to prototype theory. Ashby and Maddox (1994) showed that in a categorization task with two categories, the most popular versions of prototype theory predict no prototype effects. Specifically, in most prototype models the predicted probability of responding A on trials when stimulus i is presented increases with S_{iA}/S_{iB}, whereas the response time decreases. Ashby and Maddox (1994) showed that this ratio increases with the distance from stimulus i to the minimum distance bound. Because the prototype is usually *not* the furthest stimulus from the decision bound in two-category tasks, prototype theory predicts that the highest accuracy and the fastest responding will not be to the category prototypes, but to the stimuli that are furthest from the minimum distance bound.

In a task with a single category, in which the subject's task is to decide whether the stimulus is or is not a member of that category, the category prototype is often the furthest exemplar from the decision bound. Thus, prototype enhancement effects found in such tasks may not be due to an over representation of the prototype but instead to the coincidental placement of the prototype with respect to the subject's decision bound. This hypothesis was strongly supported by Ashby et al. (1994). Before deciding that prototype enhancement has occurred in a categorization task, it is vital to rule out the possibility that the superior performance to the prototype was not simply an artifact of the structure of the contrasting categories. Most studies reporting prototype enhancement in categorization tasks have not included analyses of this type, so the magnitude, and perhaps even the existence, of prototype effects in categorization is largely unknown.

In addition to category structure, other experimental conditions may make prototype effects more or less likely. Table 3 lists several properties that might bias an experiment in favor of prototype theory and thus might make prototype effects more likely. The minimum distance classifier, which uses the decision rule of prototype theory, generally requires the subject to integrate information across dimensions (e.g., Ashby & Gott, 1988). Although subjects can integrate information when the stimulus dimensions are either integral or separable (Ashby & Maddox, 1990), integration should be easier when the stimulus dimensions are perceptually integral. Thus, it seems plausible that prototype theory might perform better when the category exemplars vary along perceptually integral dimensions (however, see Nosofsky, 1987).

Minimum distance classification is rarely optimal. Thus, as with independent decisions classification, any experimental conditions that facilitate optimal responding will tend to disconfirm prototype theory. Optimal responding is most likely when subjects are experienced (and motivated), the stimuli are simple, and the optimal rule is simple. Therefore, subjects should be most likely to use a suboptimal rule such as minimum distance classification if they are inexperienced, if the stimuli vary on many dimensions, if the optimal rule is complex, and if there are more than two categories (thus further complicating the optimal rule).

Much of the empirical support for prototype theory is from experiments that used random dot patterns as stimuli (e.g., Goldman & Homa, 1977; Homa et al., 1973, 1981; Homa & Cultice, 1984; Homa & Vosburgh, 1976; Posner & Keele, 1968, 1970). These stimuli vary along many dimensions that are most likely integral. In addition, most of these experiments tested subjects for only a single experimental session, and thus the subjects were relatively inexperienced. Finally, a number of these experiments used more than two categories (e.g., Homa et al., 1973; Homa & Cultice, 1984), so the experimental conditions were favorable for prototype theory.

Exemplar theorists have also questioned whether the existence of prototype effects necessarily implies that the category representation is dominated by the prototype. They argue that prototype effects are the natural consequence of exemplar-based processes of the kind hypothesized by exemplar theory. For example, Shin and Nosofsky (1992) found that the small prototype effects found in their categorization task could be predicted by an exemplar model. In addition, a number of investigators have shown that many of the prototype effects found in typicality rating, recognition, and recall tasks are qualitatively consistent with predictions from exemplar models (e.g., Busemeyer, Dewey, & Medin, 1984; Hintzman, 1986; Hintzman & Ludlam, 1980; Nosofsky, 1988b).

Another hypothesis that explains the failure of Ashby et al. (1994) and Shin and Nosofsky (1992) to find prototype effects is that prototype effects are small or nonexistent in the majority of categorization tasks, but are robust in other types of cognitive and perceptual tasks. For example, the prevalence of prototype effects (or graded structure) in typicality rating tasks is uncontested. Graded structure has been found in a wide range of category types, for example, in taxonomic categories such as fruit (Rips et al., 1973; Rosch, 1973, 1975, 1978; Rosch & Mervis, 1975; Smith, Shoben, & Rips, 1974), logical categories such as odd number (Armstrong, Gleitman,

& Gleitman, 1983), linguistic categories (see Lakoff, 1986 for a review), and many others (Barsalou, 1983, 1985).[7] As discussed earlier, recognition memory (Omohundro, 1981), and recall (Mervis et al., 1976) also show marked prototype effects.

One thing that typicality rating, recognition memory, and recall tasks have in common is that they all require the subject to access exemplar information from memory. It is a matter of debate whether traditional categorization tasks require exemplar information (e.g., Ashby & Lee, 1991, 1992, 1993; Maddox & Ashby, 1993). Thus, one plausible hypothesis is that the prototype dominates the category representation, so any task requiring the subject to access the category representation will show prototype effects. Categorization experiments usually do not show prototype effects because categorization does not require information about individual exemplars. Why is the prototype over represented? One possibility is that the dominance of the prototype within the category representation is a consequence of consolidation processes. During periods of time in which the subject is gaining no new information about the category, the subject's memory for the category consolidates. The prototype begins to dominate the representation. According to this hypothesis, the prototype's prominence should increase with time because the consolidation process would have longer to operate. This prediction is consistent with the result that the few prototype effects that are found in categorization tasks tend to increase with the length of the delay between the training and testing conditions (e.g., Homa & Cultice, 1984). This result is important because it seems inconsistent with the hypothesis that prototype effects are the result of exemplar-based similarity computations.

C. Exemplar and Decision Bound Theory

In virtually every empirical comparison, exemplar models and decision bound models have both outperformed classical models and prototype models. There have been only a few attempts to compare the performance of exemplar and decision bound models, however. When the category distributions were bivariate normal and the data were analyzed separately for each subject, Maddox and Ashby (1993) found that the general linear and general quadratic decision bound models consistently outperformed Nosofsky's (1986) generalized context model. In cases where the optimal decision bound was linear, the advantage of the decision bound model was due entirely to response selection assumptions. A more general form of the generalized context model that used the deterministic Eq. (3) response selec-

---

[7] Although nearly all categories show graded structure, Barsalou (1983, 1985, 1987) showed convincingly that graded structure is unstable and can be greatly influenced by context.

tion rule, rather than the relative goodness rule of Eq. (1), gave fits that were indistinguishable from the general linear classifier. When the optimal decision bound was quadratic, however, the general quadratic classifier outperformed this deterministic version of the generalized context model. McKinley and Nosofsky (1995) added a memory decay parameter to the deterministic version of the generalized context model, and a parameter that generalizes the representation assumptions. In this way, they produced an exemplar model that fit the quadratic bound data as well as the general quadratic classifier of decision bound theory.

Two studies have fit decision bound and exemplar models to data from experiments with nonnormally distributed categories. Maddox and Ashby (1993) fit a number of models to the data from Nosofsky's (1986) criss-cross and interior–exterior conditions. In all cases, there was a substantial advantage for the general quadratic classifier over the best exemplar model (i.e., the deterministic version of the generalized context model). McKinley and Nosofsky (1995) created categories that were each probability mixtures of two bivariate normal distributions (i.e., in each category, an exemplar was sampled either from one bivariate normal distribution or another). The resulting complex optimal bounds could not be approximated by a quadratic equation. The deterministic version of the generalized context model with extra memory decay and representation parameters fit the data better than the general quadratic classifier. In the more complex of the two experiments, however, neither model fit well. In fact, for 8 of the 11 subjects, the data were best fit by a model that assumes subjects used two quadratic decision bounds (instead of the one assumed by the general quadratic classifier).

Although more empirical testing is needed, much is now known about how to design an experiment to give either exemplar or decision bound models the best opportunity to provide excellent fits to the resulting data. With respect to the exemplar models, the key theoretical result is Ashby and Alfonso-Reese's (1995) demonstration that most exemplar models (e.g., the context, array-similarity, and generalized context models) essentially assume the subject is an extremely sophisticated statistician with perfect memory. Exemplar models almost always predict that with enough training, subjects will perform optimally, no matter how complex the task. Thus, exemplar theory will provide a good account of any data in which the subject responds nearly optimally. Optimal responding is most likely when subjects are experienced and the optimal categorization rule is simple. When the optimal rule is complex, the subject might be able to memorize the correct response to individual stimuli if there are only a few exemplars in each category. This would allow nearly optimal responding, even in cases where the subject never learns the optimal rule. These conditions are summarized in Table 3. Presumably, exemplar models performed poorly in

Experiment 2 of McKinley and Nosofsky (1995) because of the many category exemplars and the complex optimal decision rule.

The general quadratic classifier of decision bound theory will give a good account of any data in which the subject uses a linear or quadratic decision bound (because the general linear classifier is a special case). Thus, if the optimal rule is linear or quadratic and the subjects are experienced, the general quadratic classifier should always perform at least as well as the best exemplar models. If the subjects respond optimally in a task where the optimal rule is more complex than any quadratic equation, then the general quadratic classifier will fit poorly (as in the McKinley & Nosofsky, 1995, experiments).

VII. FUTURE DIRECTIONS

Much is now known about the empirical validity of the various categorization theories and about their theoretical relations. As a result, the direction of research on human categorization is likely to change dramatically during the next decade. For example, advances in the neurosciences may make it possible to test directly some of the fundamental assumptions of the theories. In particular, through the use of various neuroimaging techniques and the study of selective brain-damaged populations, it may be possible to test whether subjects access exemplar or episodic memories during categorization, as assumed by exemplar theory, or whether they access some abstracted representation (e.g., a semantic or procedural memory), as assumed by decision bound theory. The early results seem problematic for exemplar theory, but the issue is far from resolved (Kolodny, 1994; Knowlton et al., 1992).

A second major distinction between exemplar theory and, say, the general quadratic classifier of decision bound theory is which a priori assumptions about category structure the subject brings to the categorization task. Exemplar theory assumes the subject makes almost no assumptions. When learning about a new category, exemplar theory assumes the subject ignores all past experience with categories. The general quadratic classifier assumes the subject brings to a new categorization task the expectation that each category has some multivariate normal distribution. Therefore, an extremely important research question is whether subjects make a priori assumptions about category structure, and if they do, exactly what assumptions they make.

A third important research question concerns optimality. Exemplar theory essentially assumes optimality for all categorization tasks, at least if the subjects have enough experience and motivation. The general quadratic classifier assumes optimality is possible only in some tasks (i.e., those in which the optimal bound is linear or quadratic, or possibly piecewise linear or piecewise quadratic). Are there categorization problems that humans cannot learn? If so, how can these problems be characterized?

A fourth important direction of future research should be to explicate the role of memory in the categorization process. Because prototypicality effects seem to depend on the delay between training and test and on category size, it seems likely that memory processes play a key role in the development of the category prototype. A likely candidate is consolidation of the category representation. If so, then it is important to ask whether other observable effects of consolidation exist.

A fifth goal of future research should be to develop process models of the categorization task (i.e., algorithmic level models). The major theories reviewed in this chapter all have multiple process interpretations. A test between the various interpretations requires fitting the microstructure of the data. Simply fitting the overall response proportions is insufficient. For example, a process model should be able to predict trial-by-trial learning data and also categorization response times.

Finally, we believe that theories of human categorization would benefit greatly from the study of categorization in animals, and even in simple organisms. The first living creatures to evolve had to be able to categorize chemicals they encountered as nutritive or aversive. Thus, there was a tremendous evolutionary pressure that favored organisms adept at categorization. Because it is now believed that all organisms on Earth evolved from the same ancestors (e.g., Darnell, Lodish, & Baltimore, 1990), it makes sense that the categorization strategies used by all animals evolved from a common ancestral strategy. If so, then it is plausible that the fundamental nature of categorization is the same for all animals and that the main difference across the phylogenetic scale is in the degree to which this basic strategy has been elaborated (Ashby & Lee, 1993).

Acknowledgments

Preparation of this chapter was supported in part by National Science Foundation Grant DBS92-09411 to F. Gregory Ashby and by a Faculty-Grant-in-Aid from Arizona State University to W. Todd Maddox. We thank Kyunghee Koh and Leola Alfonso-Reese for their helpful comments on an earlier draft of this chapter.

References

Ahn, W. K., & Medin, D. L. (1992). A two-stage model of category construction. *Cognitive Science, 16,* 81–121.

Anderson, J. R. (1975). *Language, memory, and thought.* Hillsdale, NJ: Erlbaum.

Anderson, J. R. (1990). *The adaptive character of thought.* Hillsdale, NJ: Erlbaum.

Anderson, J. R. (1991). The adaptive nature of human categorization. *Psychological Review, 98,* 409–429.

Armstrong, S. L., Gleitman, L. R., & Gleitman, H. (1983). On what some concepts might not be. *Cognition, 13,* 263–308.

Ashby, F. G. (1992a). Multidimensional models of categorization. In F. G. Ashby (Ed.), *Multidimensional models of perception and cognition* (pp. 449–483). Hillsdale, NJ: Erlbaum.

Ashby, F. G. (1992b). Pattern recognition by human and machine. *Journal of Mathematical Psychology, 36,* 146–153.

Ashby, F. G., & Alfonso-Reese, L. A. (1995). Categorization as probability density estimation. *Journal of Mathematical Psychology, 39,* 216–233.

Ashby, F. G., Boynton, G., & Lee, W. W. (1994). Categorization response time with multi-dimensional stimuli. *Perception & Psychophysics, 55,* 11–27.

Ashby, F. G., & Gott, R. (1988). Decision rules in the perception and categorization of multidimensional stimuli. *Journal of Experimental Psychology: Learning, Memory and Cognition, 14,* 33–53.

Ashby, F. G., & Lee, W. W. (1991). Predicting similarity and categorization from identification. *Journal of Experimental Psychology: General, 120,* 150–172.

Ashby, F. G., & Lee, W. W. (1992). On the relationship between identification, similarity, and categorization: Reply to Nosofsky and Smith (1992). *Journal of Experimental Psychology: General, 121,* 385–393.

Ashby, F. G., & Lee, W. W. (1993). Perceptual variability as a fundamental axiom of perceptual science. In S. C. Masin (Ed.), *Foundations of perceptual theory* (pp. 369–399). Amsterdam: North Holland.

Ashby, F. G., & Maddox, W. T. (1990). Integrating information from separable psychological dimensions. *Journal of Experimental Psychology: Human Perception and Performance, 16,* 598–612.

Ashby, F. G., & Maddox, W. T. (1992). Complex decision rules in categorization: Contrasting novice and experienced performance. *Journal of Experimental Psychology: Human Perception and Performance, 18,* 50–71.

Ashby, F. G., & Maddox, W. T. (1993). Relations among prototype, exemplar, and decision bound models of categorization. *Journal of Mathematical Psychology, 37,* 372–400.

Ashby, F. G., & Maddox, W. T. (1994). A response time theory of separability and integrality in speeded classification. *Journal of Mathematical Psychology, 38,* 423–466.

Ashby, F. G., & Perrin, N. A. (1988). Toward a unified theory of similarity and recognition. *Psychological Review, 95,* 124–15.

Ashby, F. G., & Townsend, J. T. (1986). Varieties of perceptual independence. *Psychological Review, 93,* 154–179.

Bahrick, H. P., Bahrick, P. O., & Wittlinger, R. P. (1975). Fifty years of memory for names and faces: A cross-sectional approach. *Journal of Experimental Psychology: General, 104,* 54–75.

Barlow, H. B. (1956). Retinal noise and absolute threshold. *Journal of the Optical Society of America, 46,* 634–639.

Barlow, H. B. (1957). Increment thresholds at low intensities considered as signal/noise discrimination. *Journal of Physiology, 136,* 469–488.

Barsalou, L. W. (1983). Ad hoc categories. *Memory & Cognition, 11,* 211–227.

Barsalou, L. W. (1985). Ideals, central tendency, and frequency of instantiation. *Journal of Experimental Psychology: Learning, Memory, and Cognition, 11,* 629–654.

Barsalou, L. W. (1987). The instability of graded structure: implications for the nature of concepts. In U. Neisser (Ed.), *Concepts and conceptual development: Ecological and intellectual factors in categorization.* Cambridge, England: Cambridge University Press.

Baum, W. M. (1974). On two types of deviation from the matching law: Bias and undermatching. *Journal of the Experimental Analysis of Behavior, 22,* 231–242.

Black, M. (1954). *Problems of analysis (Collected essays).* Ithaca, NY: Cornell University Press.

Bourne, L. E. (1966). *Human conceptual behavior.* Boston: Allyn and Bacon.

Bourne, L. E. (1970). Knowing and using concepts. *Psychological Review, 77,* 546–556.

Brooks, L. (1978). Nonanalytic concept formation and memory for instances. In E. Rosch & B. B. Lloyd (Eds.), *Cognition and categorization.* Hillsdale, NJ: Erlbaum.

Bruce, H. M. (1959). An exteroceptive block to pregnancy in the mouse. *Nature, 184,* 105.

Bruner, J. S., Goodnow, J., & Austin, G. (1956). *A study of thinking.* New York: Wiley.

Busemeyer, J. R., Dewey, G. I., & Medin, D. L. (1984). Evaluation of exemplar-based generalization and the abstraction of categorical information. *Journal of Experimental Psychology: Learning, Memory, and Cognition, 10,* 638–648.

Cohen, M. M., & Massaro, D. W. (1992). On the similarity of categorization models. In F. G. Ashby (Ed.), *Multidimensional models of perception and cognition* (pp. 395–447). Hillsdale, NJ: Erlbaum.

Corter, J. E., & Tversky, A. (1986). Extended similarity trees. *Psychometrika, 51,* 429–451.

Crowther, C. W., Batchelder, W. H., & Hu, X. (1995). A measurement-theoretic analysis of the fuzzy logical model of perception. *Psychological Review, 102,* 396–408.

Darnell, J., Lodish, H., & Baltimore, D. (1990). *Molecular cell biology.* New York: Freeman.

Ennis, D. M., & Ashby, F. G. (1993). The relative sensitivities of same-different and identification judgment models to perceptual dependence. *Psychometrika, 58,* 257–279.

Estes, W. K. (1976). The cognitive side of probability learning. *Psychological Review, 83,* 37–64.

Estes, W. K. (1986a). Array models for category learning. *Cognitive Psychology, 18,* 500–549.

Estes, W. K. (1986b). Memory storage and retrieval processes in category learning. *Journal of Experimental Psychology: General, 115,* 155–174.

Estes, W. K. (1993). Models of categorization and category learning. *Psychology of learning and motivation, Vol. 29.* San Diego: Academic Press.

Estes, W. K. (1994). *Classification and cognition.* Oxford: Oxford University Press.

Estes, W. K. (1995). Response processes in cognitive models. In R. F. Lorch, Jr., & E. J. O'Brien (Eds.), *Sources of coherence in text comprehension.* Hillsdale, NJ: Erlbaum.

Estes, W. K., Campbell, J. A., Hatsopoulos, N., & Hurwitz, J. B. (1989). Base-rate effects in category learning: A comparison of parallel network and memory storage-retrieval models. *Journal of Experimental Psychology: Learning, Memory, and Cognition, 15,* 556–571.

Estes, W. K., & Maddox, W. T. (1995). Interactions of stimulus attributes, base-rate, and feedback in recognition. *Journal of Experimental Psychology: Learning, Memory, and Cognition, 21,* 1075–1095.

Flannagan, M. J., Fried, L. S., & Holyoak, K. J. (1986). Distributional expectations and the induction of category structure. *Journal of Experimental Psychology: Learning, Memory, and Cognition, 12,* 241–256.

Fodor, J. A., Bever, T. G., & Garrett, M. F. (1974). *The psychology of language: An introduction to psycholinguistics and generative grammar.* New York: McGraw-Hill.

Franks, J. J., & Bransford, J. D. (1971). Abstraction of visual patterns. *Journal of Experimental Psychology, 90,* 65–74.

Fried, L. S., & Holyoak, F. J. (1984). Induction of category distributions: A framework for classification learning. *Journal of Experimental Psychology: Learning, Memory, and Cognition, 10,* 234–257.

Garner, W. R. (1974). *The processing of information and structure.* New York: Wiley.

Garner, W. R. (1977). The effect of absolute size on the separability of the dimensions of size and brightness. *Bulletin of the Psychonomics Society, 9,* 380–382.

Garner, W. R., & Felfoldy, G. L. (1970). Integrality of stimulus dimensions in various types of information processing. *Cognitive Psychology, 1,* 225–241.

Geisler, W. S. (1989). Sequential ideal-observer analysis of visual discriminations. *Psychological Review, 96,* 267–314.

Geyer, L. H., & DeWald, C. G. (1973). Feature lists and confusion matrices. *Perception & Psychophysics, 14,* 471–482.

Gibson, E., Osser, H., Schiff, W., & Smith, J. (1963). *An Analysis of Critical Features of Letters, Tested by a Confusion Matrix. A Basic Research Program on Reading.* (Cooperative Research Project No. 639). Washington: U.S. Office of Education.

Gluck, M. A. (1991). Stimulus generalization and representation in adaptive network models of category learning. *Psychological Science, 2,* 50–55.

Gluck, M. A., & Bower, G. H. (1988). From conditioning to category learning: An adaptive network model. *Journal of Experimental Psychology: General, 117,* 225–244.

Gluck, M. A., Bower, G., & Hee, M. R. (August, 1989). *A configural-cue network model of animal and human associative learning.* Paper presented at the Eleventh Annual Conference of the Cognitive Science Society. Ann Arbor, Michigan.

Goldman, D., & Homa, D. (1977). Integrative and metric properties of abstracted information as a function of category discriminability, instance variability, and experience. *Journal of Experimental Psychology: Human Learning and Memory, 3,* 375–385.

Green, D. M., & Swets, J. A. (1966). *Signal detection theory and psychophysics.* New York: Wiley.

Hammerton, M. (1970). An investigation into changes in decision criteria and other details of a decision-making task. *Psychonomic Science, 21,* 203–204.

Hayes-Roth, B., & Hayes-Roth, F. (1977). Concept learning and the recognition and classification of exemplars. *Journal of Verbal Learning and Verbal Behavior, 16,* 119–136.

Haygood, R. C., & Bourne, L. E. (1965). Attribute and rule-learning aspects of conceptual behavior. *Psychological Review, 72,* 175–195.

Healy, A. F., & Kubovy, M. A. (1977). A comparison of recognition memory to numerical decision: How prior probabilities affect cutoff location. *Memory & Cognition, 5,* 3–9.

Herrnstein, R. J. (1961). Relative and absolute strength of response as a function of frequency of reinforcement. *Journal of the Experimental Analysis of Behavior, 4,* 267–272.

Herrnstein, R. J. (1970). On the law of effect. *Journal of the Experimental Analysis of Behavior, 13,* 243–266.

Hintzman, D. L. (1986). "Schema abstraction" in a multiple-trace memory model. *Psychological Review, 93,* 411–428.

Hintzman, D. L., & Ludlam, G. (1980). Differential forgetting of prototypes and old instances: Simulations by an exemplar-based classification model. *Memory & Cognition, 8,* 378–382.

Homa, D., & Chambliss, D. (1975). The relative contributions of common and distinctive information on the abstraction from ill-defined categories. *Journal of Experimental Psychology: Human Learning and Memory, 1,* 351–359.

Homa, D., & Cultice, J. (1984). Role of feedback, category size, and stimulus distortion on the acquisition and utilization of ill-defined categories. *Journal of Experimental Psychology: Learning, Memory, and Cognition, 10,* 83–94.

Homa, D., Cross, J., Cornell, D., Goldman, D., & Schwartz, S. (1973). Prototype abstraction and classification of new instances as a function of number of instances defining the prototype. *Journal of Experimental Psychology, 101,* 116–122.

Homa, D., Dunbar, S., & Nohre, L. (1991). Instance frequency, categorization, and the modulating effect of experience. *Journal of Experimental Psychology: Learning, Memory, and Cognition, 17,* 444–458.

Homa, D., Sterling, S., & Trepel, L. (1981). Limitations of exemplar-based generalization and the abstraction of categorical information. *Journal of Experimental Psychology: Human Learning and Memory, 7,* 418–439.

Homa, D., & Vosburgh, R. (1976). Category breadth and the abstraction of prototypical information. *Journal of Experimental Psychology: Human Learning and Memory, 2,* 322–330.

Hull, C. L. (1920). Quantitative aspects of the evolution of concepts. *Psychological Monographs* (No. 123)

Hurwitz, J. B. (1990). *A hidden-pattern unit network model of category learning.* Unpublished doctoral dissertation, Harvard University, Cambridge, Massachusetts.

Hurwitz, J. B. (1994). Retrieval of exemplar and feature information in category learning. *Journal of Experimental Psychology: Learning, Memory, and Cognition, 20,* 887–903.

Huttenlocher, J., & Hedges, L. V. (1994). Combining graded categories: Membership and typicality. *Psychological Review, 101,* 157–163.

Hyman, R., & Well, A. (1968). Perceptual separability and spatial models. *Perception & Psychophysics, 3,* 161–165.

Imai, S., & Garner, W. R. (1965). Discriminability and preference for attributes in free and constrained classification. *Journal of Experimental Psychology, 69,* 596–608.

Kadlec, H., & Townsend, J. T. (1992). Implications of marginal and conditional detection parameters for the separabilities and independence of perceptual dimensions. *Journal of Mathematical Psychology, 36,* 325–374.

Klahr, D., Langley, P., & Neches, R. (Eds.). (1987). *Production system models of learning and development.* Cambridge, MA: MIT Press.

Knowlton, B. J., Ramus, S. J., & Squire, L. R. (1992). Intact artificial grammar learning in amnesia: Dissociation of classification learning and explicit memory for specific instances. *Psychological Science, 3,* 172–179.

Knowlton, B. J., & Squire, L. R. (1993). The learning of categories: Parallel brain systems for item memory and category level knowledge. *Science, 262,* 1747–1749.

Koh, K. (1993). *Response variability in categorization: Deterministic versus probabilistic decision rules.* University of California at Santa Barbara, unpublished manuscript.

Kolodny, J. A. (1994). Memory processes in classification learning: An investigation of amnesic performance in categorization of dot patterns and artistic styles. *Psychological Science, 5,* 164–169.

Krumhansl, C. L. (1978). Concerning the applicability of geometric models to similarity data: The interrelationship between similarity and spatial density. *Psychological Review, 85,* 445–463.

Kruschke, J. K. (1992). ALCOVE: An exemplar-based connectionist model of category learning. *Psychological Review, 99,* 22–44.

Kruskal, J. B. (1964a). Multidimensional scaling by optimizing goodness of fit to a nonmetric hypothesis. *Psychometrika, 29,* 1–27.

Kruskal, J. B. (1964b). Nonmetric multidimensional scaling: A numerical method. *Psychometrika, 29,* 115–129.

Kubovy, M., & Healy, A. F. (1977). The decision rule in probabilistic categorization: What it is and how it is learned. *Journal of Experimental Psychology: General, 106,* 427–446.

Kubovy, M., Rapoport, A., & Tversky, A. (1971). Deterministic vs. probabilistic strategies in detection. *Perception & Psychophysics, 9,* 427–429.

Lakoff, G. (1986). *Women, fire, and dangerous things.* Chicago: University of Chicago Press.

Lee, W. (1963). Choosing among confusably distributed stimuli with specified likelihood ratios. *Perceptual and Motor Skills, 16,* 445–467.

Lee, W., & Janke, M. (1964). Categorizing externally distributed stimulus samples for three continua. *Journal of Experimental Psychology, 68,* 376–382.

Lee, W., & Janke, M. (1965). Categorizing externally distributed stimulus samples for unequal molar probabilities. *Psychological Reports, 17,* 79–90.

Lewandowsky, S. (1995). Base-rate neglect in ALCOVE: A critical reevaluation. *Psychological Review, 102,* 185–191.

Luce, R. D. (1963). Detection and recognition. In R. D. Luce, R. R. Bush, & E. Galanter (Eds.), *Handbook of mathematical psychology* (pp. 103–189). New York: Wiley.

Maddox, W. T. (1992). Perceptual and decisional separability. F. G. Ashby (Ed.), *Multidimensional models of perception and cognition* (pp. 147–180). Hillsdale, NJ: Erlbaum.

Maddox, W. T. (1995). Base-rate effects in multidimensional perceptual categorization. *Journal of Experimental Psychology: Learning, Memory, and Cognition, 21,* 288–301.

Maddox, W. T., & Ashby, F. G. (1993). Comparing decision bound and exemplar models of categorization. *Perception & Psychophysics, 53,* 49–70.

Maddox, W. T., & Ashby, F. G. (1996). Perceptual separability, decisional separability, and the identification-speeded classification relationship. *Journal of Experimental Psychology: Human Perception and Performance, 22,* 795–817.

Maddox, W. T., & Estes, W. K. (1995). On the role of frequency in "Word-frequency" and mirror effects in recognition. *Journal of Experimental Psychology: General.* Manuscript submitted for publication.

Marley, A. A. J. (1992). Developing and characterizing multidimensional Thurstone and Luce models for identification and preference. In F. G. Ashby (Ed.), *Multidimensional models of perception and cognition* (pp. 299–333). Hillsdale, NJ: Erlbaum.

Marr, D. (1982). *Vision.* New York: W. H. Freeman.

Massaro, D. W. (1987). *Speech perception by ear and eye: A paradigm for psychological inquiry.* Hillsdale, NJ: Lawrence Erlbaum Associates.

Massaro, D. W., & Friedman, D. (1990). Models of integration given multiple sources of information. *Psychological Review, 97,* 225–252.

McKinley, S. C., & Nosofsky, R. M. (1995). Investigations of exemplar and decision bound models in large, ill-defined category structures. *Journal of Experimental Psychology: Human Perception and Performance, 21,* 128–148.

Medin, D. L., Alton, M. W., Edelson, S. M., & Freko, D. (1982). Correlated symptoms and simulated medical classification. *Journal of Experimental Psychology: Learning, Memory, and Cognition, 8,* 37–50.

Medin, D. L., & Edelson, S. M. (1988). Problem structure and the use of base-rate information from experience. *Journal of Experimental Psychology: General, 117,* 68–85.

Medin, D. L., & Schaffer, M. M. (1978). Context theory of classification learning. *Psychological Review, 85,* 207–238.

Medin, D. L., & Schwanenflugel, P. J. (1981). Linear separability in classification learning. *Journal of Experimental Psychology: Human Learning and Memory, 1,* 335–368.

Medin, D. L., Wattenmaker, W. D., & Hampson, S. E. (1987). Family resemblance, conceptual cohesiveness, and category construction. *Cognitive Psychology, 19,* 242–279.

Mervis, C. B. (1980). Category structure and the development of categorization. In R. Spiro, B. C. Bruce, & W. F. Brewer (Eds.), *Theoretical issues in reading comprehension.* Hillsdale, NJ: Lawrence Erlbaum Associates.

Mervis, C. B., Catlin, J., & Rosch, E. (1976). Relationships among goodness-of-example, category norms, and word frequency. *Bulletin of the Psychonomics Society, 7,* 283–284.

Miller, G. A., & Johnson-Laird, P. N. (1976). *Language and perception.* Cambridge, MA: Harvard University Press.

Myung, I. J. (1994). Maximum entropy interpretation of decision bound and context models of categorization. *Journal of Mathematical Psychology, 38* 335–365.

Neisser, U. (1967). *Cognitive Psychology.* New York: Appleton-Century-Crofts.

Neumann, P. G. (1974). An attribute frequency model for the abstraction of prototypes. *Memory & Cognition, 2,* 241–248.

Newell, A., & Simon, H. A. (1972). *Human problem solving.* Englewood Cliffs, NJ: Prentice-Hall.

Nosofsky, R. M. (1984). Choice, similarity, and the context theory of classification. *Journal of Experimental Psychology: Learning, Memory, and Cognition, 10,* 104–114.

Nosofsky, R. M. (1985). Overall similarity and the identification of separable-dimension stimuli: A choice model analysis. *Perception & Psychophysics, 38,* 415–432.

Nosofsky, R. M. (1986). Attention, similarity, and the identification-categorization relationship. *Journal of Experimental Psychology: General, 115,* 39–57.

Nosofsky, R. M. (1987). Attention and learning processes in the identification and categorization of integral stimuli. *Journal of Experimental Psychology: Learning, Memory, and Cognition, 13,* 87–108.

Nosofsky, R. M. (1988a). Exemplar-based accounts of relations between classification, recognition, and typicality. *Journal of Experimental Psychology: Learning, Memory, and Cognition, 14,* 700–708.

Nosofsky, R. M. (1988b). Similarity, frequency, and category representations. *Journal of Experimental Psychology: Learning, Memory, and Cognition, 14,* 54–65.

Nosofsky, R. M. (1991a). Relations between the rational model and the context model of categorization. *Psychological Science, 2,* 416–421.

Nosofsky, R. M. (1991b). Stimulus bias, asymmetric similarity, and classification. *Cognitive Psychology, 23,* 91–140.

Nosofsky, R. M. (1992a). Exemplar-based approach to relating categorization, identification and recognition. In F. G. Ashby (Ed.), *Multidimensional models of perception and cognition* (pp. 363–393). Hilldale, NJ: Erlbaum.

Nosofsky, R. M. (1992b). Exemplars, prototypes, and similarity rules. In A. Healy, S. Kosslyn, & R. Shiffrin (Eds.), *Festschrift for William K. Estes.* Hillsdale, NJ: Erlbaum.

Nosofsky, R. M., Clark, S. E., & Shin, H. J. (1989). Rules and exemplars in categorization, identification, and recognition. *Journal of Experimental Psychology: Learning, Memory, and Cognition, 15,* 282–304.

Nosofsky, R. M., Kruschke, J. K., & McKinley, S. C. (1992). Combining exemplar-based category representations and connectionist learning rules. *Journal of Experimental Psychology: Learning, Memory, and Cognition, 18,* 211–233.

Nosofsky, R. M., Palmeri, T. J., & McKinley, S. C. (1994). Rule-plus-exception model of classification learning. *Psychological Review, 101,* 53–79.

Omohundro, J. (1981). Recognition vs. classification of ill-defined category exemplars. *Memory & Cognition, 9,* 324–331.

Pao, Y. H. (1989). *Adaptive pattern recognition and neural networks.* Reading, MA: Addison-Welsey.

Parkes, A. S., & Bruce, H. M. (1962). Pregnancy-block of female mice placed in boxes soiled by males. *Journal of Reproduction and Fertility, 4,* 303–308.

Parzen, E. (1962). On estimation of a probability density function and mode. *The Annals of Mathematical Statistics, 33,* 1065–1076.

Perrin, N. (1992). Uniting identification, similarity, and preference: General recognition theory. F. G. Ashby (Ed.), *Multidimensional models of perception and cognition* (pp. 123–146). Hillsdale, NJ: Erlbaum.

Perrin, N. A., & Ashby, F. G. (1991). A test of perceptual independence with dissimilarity data. *Applied Psychological Research, 15,* 79–93.

Posner, M. I., & Keele, S. W. (1968). On the genesis of abstract ideas. *Journal of Experimental Psychology, 77,* 353–363.

Posner, M. I., & Keele, S. W. (1970). Retention of abstract ideas. *Journal of Experimental Psychology, 83,* 304–308.

Reber, A. S. (1976). Implicit learning of synthetic languages: The role of instructional set. *Journal of Experimental Psychology: Human Memory and Learning, 2,* 88–94.

Reber, A. S., & Allen, R. (1978). Analogical and abstraction strategies in synthetic grammar learning: A functionalist interpretation. *Cognition, 6,* 189–221.

Reed, S. K. (1972). Pattern recognition and categorization. *Cognitive Psychology, 3,* 382–407.

Rips, L. J., Shoben, E. J., & Smith, E. E. (1973). Semantic distance and the verification of semantic relations. *Journal of Verbal Learning and Verbal Behavior, 12,* 1–20.

Robson, J. G. (1975). Receptive fields: Neural representation of the spatial and intensive attributes of the visual image. *Handbook of Perception, 5,* 81–116.

Rosch, E. (1973). Natural categories. *Cognitive Psychology, 4,* 328–350.

Rosch, E. (1975). Cognitive reference points. *Cognitive Psychology, 7,* 532–547.

Rosch, E. (1977). Human categorization. In N. Warren (Ed.), *Studies in cross-cultural psychology.* London: Academic Press.

Rosch, E. (1978). Principles of categorization. In E. Rosch, & B. B. Lloyd (Eds.), *Cognition and categorization* (pp. 27–48). Hillsdale, NJ: Erlbaum.

Rosch, E., & Mervis, C. (1975). Family resemblances: Studies in the internal structure of categories. *Cognitive Psychology, 7,* 573–605.

Rosch, E., Simpson, & Miller, R. S. (1976). Structural bases of typicality effects. *Journal of Experimental Psychology: Human Perception and Performance, 2,* 491–502.

Sattath, S., & Tversky, A. (1977). Additive similarity trees. *Psychometrika, 42,* 319–345.

Shaw, M. L. (1982). Attending to multiple sources of information. I: The integration of information in decision making. *Cognitive Psychology, 14,* 353–409.

Shepard, R. N. (1957). Stimulus and response generalization: A stochastic model relating generalization to distance in psychological space. *Psychometrika, 22,* 325–345.

Shepard, R. N. (1962a). The analysis of proximities: Multidimensional scaling with an unknown distance function I. *Psychometrika, 27,* 125–140.

Shepard, R. N. (1962b). The analysis of proximities: Multidimensional scaling with an unknown distance function II. *Psychometrika, 27,* 219–246.

Shin, H. J., & Nosofsky, R. M. (1992). Similarity-scaling studies of "dot-pattern" classification and recognition. *Journal of Experimental Psychology: General, 121,* 278–304.

Silverman, B. W. (1986). *Density estimation for statistics and data analysis.* London: Chapman and Hall.

Smith, E. E., & Medin, D. L. (1981). *Categories and concepts.* Cambridge, MA: Harvard University Press.

Smith, E. E., Shoben, E. J., & Rips, L. J. (1974). Structure and process in semantic memory: A featural model for semantic decisions. *Psychological Review, 81,* 214–241.

Thomas, R. (1994, August). *Assessing perceptual properties via same-different judgments.* Paper presented at the Twenty-Seventh Annual Mathematical Psychology Meetings. Seattle, Washington.

Torgerson, W. S. (1958). *Theory and methods of scaling.* New York: Wiley.

Townsend, J. T., & Ashby, F. G. (1982). Experimental tests of contemporary mathematical models of visual letter recognition. *Journal of Experimental Psychology: Human Perception and Performance, 8,* 834–864.

Townsend, J. T., Hu, G. G., & Ashby, F. G. (1981). Perceptual sampling of orthogonal straight line features. *Psychological Research, 43,* 259–275.

Townsend, J. T., & Landon, D. E. (1982). An experimental and theoretical investigation of the constant-ratio rule and other models of visual letter confusion. *Journal of Mathematical Psychology, 25,* 119–162.

Tversky, A. (1972). Elimination by aspects: A theory of choice. *Psychological Review, 79,* 281–299.

Tversky, A. (1977). Features of similarity. *Psychological Review, 84,* 327–352.

Tversky, A., & Gati, I. (1982). Similarity, separability and the triangle inequality. *Psychological Review, 89,* 123–154.

Walker, J. H. (1975). Real-world variability, reasonableness judgments, and memory representations for concepts. *Journal of Verbal Learning and Verbal Behvior, 14,* 241–252.

Ward, L. M. (1973). Use of Markov-encoded sequential information in numerical signal detection. *Perception & Psychophysics, 14,* 337–342.

Wattenmaker, W. D. (1992). Relational properties and memory-based category construction. *Journal of Experimental Psychology: Learning, Memory, and Cognition, 15,* 282–304.

Weissmann, S. M., Hollingsworth, S. R., & Baird, J. C. (1975). Psychophysical study of numbers. III: Methodological applications. *Psychological Research, 38,* 97–115.

Wittgenstein, L. (1953). *Philosophical investigations*. New York: Macmillan.

Wyszecki, G., & Stiles, W. S. (1967). *Color science: Concepts and methods, quantitative data and formulas*. New York: Wiley.

Young, G., & Householder, A. S. (1938). Discussion of a set of points in terms of their mutual distances. *Psychometrika, 3,* 19–21.

Zadeh, L. A. (1965). Fuzzy sets. *Information and Control, 8,* 338–353.

CHAPTER 5

Behavioral Decision Research: An Overview

John W. Payne
James R. Bettman
Mary Frances Luce

I. INTRODUCTION

This chapter concerns an area of inquiry referred to as behavioral decision research (BDR), which has grown rapidly over the past four decades. To illustrate the types of decisions with which BDR is concerned, consider the following examples.

Sue Terry is faced with a decision about where to go to college. She is an excellent swimmer and wishes to attend a school with a good women's athletic program. Sue has received letters from a large number of schools that are interested in giving her an athletic scholarship. She decides to apply to the four schools with the top-ranked women's swimming teams in the country. She is undecided about which school is her first choice. One school's swimming team has dominated women's intercollegiate swimming for several years. However, Sue wonders if she would be among the top swimmers in her event at that school. A second school does not have quite as good a team but has an excellent overall women's athletic program. Sue is certain she can be the top or second best swimmer in her event on this team. A third school has just brought in a new swimming coach who had coached two Olympic medalists in Sue's event. That school also has an excellent academic reputation. Sue cannot decide which of the schools she prefers and finds it very difficult to trade off a school with a better team (which will probably win the national championship) against another school where she is more assured of competing against a third school with the best academics. Sue also wishes she had a better idea about her odds of getting the kind of coaching attention she wants at the school with the best swimming program.

Jim Johnson, an assistant professor in psychology, is concerned about how to invest a modest amount of money he has just received from an uncle as a gift. His stockbroker friend has given him lots of information about the investment options available to him; in fact, Jim thinks that perhaps he has been given too much information. Some stock options seem to offer high returns along with substantial risk. Other options, like money market funds, don't seem to have as much risk; however, the potential return with such funds also seems low. Which option seems best also appears to depend on whether the general state of the economy improves, stays the same, or gets worse. Jim vacillates about which investment option he prefers.

The goals of BDR are to describe and explain judgment and choice behavior and to determine how knowledge of the psychology of decision making can be used to aid and improve decision-making behavior. Although psychological concepts and methods have played a major role in the development of BDR as a field, BDR is intensely interdisciplinary, often using concepts and methods from economics, statistics, and other fields. In addition, BDR is nearly unique among subdisciplines in psychology because it often proceeds by using psychological concepts in general, and perceptual and cognitive mechanisms in particular, to test the descriptive adequacy of normative theories of judgment and choice.

This chapter provides an overview of the field of behavioral decision research. We hope not only to arouse interest in decision making as a research focus, but also to suggest approaches and directions for new research. To keep the scope of the chapter manageable, we focus mostly on the topics of multiattribute preferences (values), the formation of beliefs about uncertain events, and the making of risky decisions. Further, we focus on decision tasks that are relatively well structured in terms of the objectives and alternatives available. Research on the structuring of decision problems is more limited (however, for work on identifying possible options, see Adelman, Gualtieri, & Stanford, 1995; Gettys, Plisker, Manning, & Casey, 1987; Keller & Ho, 1988; and Klein, Wolf, Militello, & Zsambok, 1995; for work on identifying cues for inference, see Klayman, 1988; and for recent work on representing decision problems in various ways, see Coupey, 1994, and Jones & Schkade, 1995). A recurring theme of the chapter is the important role that considerations of information processing limitations and cognitive effort play in explaining decision behavior.

II. DECISION TASKS AND DECISION DIFFICULTY

What makes a decision difficult? The difficulty of a decision seems to depend on a number of cognitive and emotional elements. For example, decisions are often complex, containing many alternatives and several possible outcomes. As we will discuss later, a good deal of research suggests that people respond to cognitively difficult, complex decisions by trying to simplify those decisions in various ways. Decisions can also be difficult because of uncertainties about the possible outcomes. Generally, the more uncertain you are about what will happen if you choose various options, the more difficult the decision. We discuss research focusing on how people deal with decisions characterized by uncertainties about possible outcomes. We also consider research on using cues (e.g., a student's GPA in high school, SAT scores, and letters of recommendation) to make predictions (e.g., a judgment about how well someone will do in college).

Even when we feel we know what we will receive when we choose an option, we may not know how we feel about it. A prestigious Ivy League school may offer a competitive and high-pressure undergraduate program, but we might be uncertain about how we would like that environment. Thus, there can be uncertainty in values as well as uncertainty in outcomes (March, 1978). Related to the uncertainty in values is the fact that decisions often involve conflicting values, where we must decide how much we value one attribute relative to another. In other words, no single option may be best on all our valued objectives. Conflict among values has long been recognized as a major source of decision difficulty (Hogarth, 1987; Shepard, 1964). Consequently, we will also review work on how people make decisions among options with conflicting values.

A variety of other factors affect decision difficulty. One major factor is the emotional content of the decision. For most people, there is an enormous difference between choosing a brand of mayonnaise and buying an automobile for family use. In the former case, the decision is often routine, has relatively few consequences, and is made almost automatically, with little effort. In the latter case, the decision maker may devote a great deal of effort, search for a large amount of information, solicit advice, and agonize over difficult trade-offs in making a choice, such as deciding between additional safety features in a car and an increased price. The decision maker may even try to avoid making trade-offs at all (Baron & Spranca, 1997). Although there is relatively little research on how the emotional content of the decision affects how judgments and choices are made, we discuss that issue and provide a conceptual framework. Finally, although we will not discuss them in order to keep the scope of the chapter reasonable, other factors that influence decision difficulty extend beyond the individual decision maker and the specific task at hand to include such factors as whether the decision maker is accountable to others for the decision that is made (e.g., Tetlock, 1985; Tetlock & Beottger, 1994; Siegel-Jacobs & Yates, 1996). See also Hinz, Tindale, and Vollrath (1997) and Kerr, MacCoun, and Kramer (1996) for recent examples of the extensive literature on group decision making.

We have argued that decisions can become quite difficult for a variety of reasons. How do people cope with such difficulty? To what extent do people solve difficult decisions by obtaining complete information, making trade-offs, and always selecting the alternative that maximizes their values? One approach to decision making, favored by many economists, argues that decision makers are exquisitely rational beings in solving judgment and choice problems. The rational or economic person is assumed to have

> knowledge of the relevant aspects of his environment which, if not absolutely complete, is at least impressively clear and voluminous. He is assumed also to have a well-organized and stable system of preferences and a skill in computation that enables him to calculate, for the alternative courses of action that are available to him, which of these will permit him to reach the highest attainable point on his preference scale. (Simon, 1955, p. 99)

Neoclassical economics argues that models of rational, optimizing behavior also describe actual human behavior: "The same model is used as a normative definition of rational choice and a descriptive predictor of observed choice" (Thaler, 1987, p. 99). Specific models that have been used both as normative definitions of behavior and as descriptive predictors of actual judgments and choices are Bayes' theorem in the area of probabilistic judgment and the expected utility model in the area of risky decision making, described later in this chapter. Another approach to characterizing decision making, which most psychologists feel is more descriptive of actual decision making, is that of bounded rationality.

III. BOUNDED RATIONALITY

> *"Human rational behavior is shaped by a scissors whose two blades are the structure of task environments and the computational capabilities of the actor."*
>
> H. Simon, 1990, p. 7

In one of the most important papers in the history of BDR, Simon (1955) argued that understanding actual decision behavior would require examining how perceptual, learning, and cognitive factors cause human decision behavior to deviate from that predicted by the normative "economic man" model. In contrast to the normative assumptions, Simon argued that the decision maker's limited computational capabilities would interact with the complexity of task environments to produce bounded rationality—that is, decision behavior that reflects information processing limitations. As a result, Simon suggested that actual decision behavior might not even approximate the behavior predicted by normative models of decision tasks (Simon, 1978). For example, Simon (1955) suggested that people often select among options such as those facing Sue Terry and Jim Johnson in the introduction by identifying an option that is "good enough." That is, instead of trying to select the optimal or best option, which may be too daunting a task, people may just try to "satisfice" and select the first option that meets one's minimum requirements to be satisfactory.

The information processing capacity limitations emphasized by Simon may explain results showing that preferences for and beliefs about objects or events are often constructed—not merely revealed—in responding to a judgment or choice task. The concept of constructive preferences and beliefs is that people do not have well-defined values for most objects, questions, and so on. Instead, they may construct such preferences on the spot when needed, such as when they are asked how much they like an option (Bettman, 1979; Slovic, 1995). The notion of constructive preferences does not simply deny that observed preferences result from reference to a master list in memory; it also implies that expressed judgments or choices are not necessarily generated by using some invariant algorithm such as expected utility calculation.

Individuals may construct preferences on the spot because they do not have the cognitive resources to generate well-defined preference orderings. According to March (1978), "Human beings have unstable, inconsistent, incompletely evoked, and imprecise goals at least in part because human abilities limit preference orderliness" (p. 598). The theme of constructive judgments and choices underlies much current behavioral decision research.

The constructive nature of preferences and beliefs also implies, and is implied by, the fact that expressed judgments and choices often appear to be highly contingent upon a variety of task and context factors, such as the order in which options are examined. Task factors are general characteristics of a decision problem (such as response mode, [e.g., judgment or choice], information format, or order of alternative search) that do not depend on particular values of the alternatives. Context factors, such as similarity of alternatives, on the other hand, are associated with the particular values of the alternatives. One of the major findings from behavioral decision research is that the information and strategies used to construct preferences or beliefs are highly contingent on and predictable from a variety of task and context factors. We will review some of this research as we continue.

The effects of bounded rationality are also evident in the observation that people are sometimes relatively insensitive to factors that should matter from a normative perspective. For example, people sometimes ignore normatively relevant information such as base-rates in making probability judgments. People may also be sensitive to factors that should not matter from a normative perspective, for example, equivalent response modes. More generally, task and context factors cause different aspects of the problem to be salient and evoke different processes for combining information. Thus, seemingly unimportant characteristics of the decision problem can at least partially determine the preferences and beliefs we observe. An emphasis on decision behavior as a highly contingent form of information processing is stressed throughout this chapter.

The rest of this chapter is organized as follows. First, we review research on choice with conflicting values and preferences. We consider various strategies used to make decisions among multiobjective (multiattribute) alternatives and discuss research showing how the use of such strategies varies depending on properties of the choice task. We assume in this section that people know what they will get when they choose an option, but the problem is a difficult one because no option best meets all of their objectives. Second, we review research dealing with how people judge the probabilities or likelihoods of uncertain events. Next, we briefly review the extensive literature on how people make risky choices that involve trade-offs between the desirability of consequences and the likelihoods of those consequences (choices among gambles), for example, deciding among investment options. We then describe research methods useful for studying decision behavior. Finally, we explore how concepts such as emotion, affect, and motivation may be combined with the more cognitive notions of bounded rationality to further our understanding of decision behavior.

IV. CONFLICTING VALUES AND PREFERENCES

Conflict among values arises because decisions like the ones illustrated at the beginning of this chapter generally involve a choice among options where no single option best meets all of our objectives. In fact, when one option dominates the others (i.e., is better on all objectives), selection of that option is perhaps the most widely accepted principle of rational choice. As noted earlier, conflict is a major source of decision difficulty. If conflict is present and a rule for resolving the conflict is not readily available in memory, decision making is often characterized by tentativeness and the use of relatively simple methods or heuristic strategies, even in well-defined laboratory tasks.

In this section we briefly describe some of the strategies that people use to make preferential choices. A major observation of behavioral decision research is that people use a wide variety of strategies in making preference judgments, some of which can be thought of as confronting conflict and others as avoiding conflict (Hogarth, 1987). After presenting descriptions of various strategies, we discuss research that demonstrates how the use of such strategies is contingent on the nature and context of the task facing the decision maker.

A. Decision Strategies

1. Weighted Additive Value

A common assumption about decisions among multiattribute alternatives is that individuals confront and resolve conflicts among values by considering the trade-off between more of one valued attribute (e.g., economy) against less of another valued attribute (e.g., safety). The weighted additive value model (WADD) is often used to represent the trading-off process. A measure of the relative importance (weight) of an attribute is multiplied by the attribute's value for a particular alternative and the products are summed over all attributes to obtain an overall value for that alternative, WADD(X); that is,

$$\text{WADD} (X) = \sum_{i=1}^{n} W_i X_i ,$$

where X_i is the value of option X on attribute i, n is the total number of relevant attributes, and W_i is the weight given to attribute i.

Consistent with normative procedures for dealing with multiattribute problems (Keeney & Raiffa, 1976), the WADD model uses all the relevant problem information, explicitly resolves conflicting values by considering trade-offs, and selects the alternative with the highest overall evaluation. Almost 20 years ago, Edwards and Tversky (1967) stated that this notion of additive composition "so completely dominates the literature on riskless choice that it has no competitors" (p. 255). As we shall see, such competitors now exist in abundance.

How do people think of "weights" within the context of the WADD rule? Weights are sometimes interpreted locally; that is, the relative weights reflect the ranges of attribute values over the options in the choice set so that the greater the range, the greater the attribute's importance (Goldstein, 1990). At other times, subjects interpret the weight given to an attribute more globally; for example, safety may be considered much more important than cost, regardless of the local range of values (Beattie & Baron, 1991).

Whether the influence of the weights on preferences reflects an adding or averaging process is also at issue. In an averaging model, the weights are normalized, or constrained to sum to one. Perhaps the key distinction between an adding or averaging process is what happens to a judgment when new information is obtained. For instance, assume you have received two strongly positive pieces of information about an applicant for a job. On the basis of that information you have formed a favorable overall impression of the applicant. Now assume that you receive a third piece of information about the applicant that is positive, but only moderately so. What happens to your overall impression of the applicant? Under a strict adding process, your impression should be even more favorable, because you have received more positive information. Under an averaging process, your overall impression may be less favorable than it was, even though the new information is positive, because you will average two strongly positive pieces of information with a moderately positive piece of information. See Jagacinski (1995) for an example of a study that distinguishes between adding and averaging models in the context of a personnel selection task. Research suggests that the averaging model better describes judgments in many situations (Anderson, 1981).

Variations on the adding and averaging models include versions of each model that allow for an initial impression of an option or versions of each model that allow for configural terms. Configural terms allow for possible interactions among attributes. For example, a worker who is both prompt and works at a high level of efficiency might be given extra credit in a performance evaluation, that is, a positive configural term; see Birnbaum, 1974; Birnbaum, Coffey, Mellers, and Weiss (1992), and Champagne and Stevenson (1994) for discussions of configural strategies for combining information into an evaluation of an alternative.

Three strategies related to the additive rule—the expected value, expected utility, and subjective expected utility (SEU) rules—may be used in making decisions under risk. To calculate expected value, the value X_i (i.e., the consequence or monetary amount) of each possible outcome of a lottery or gamble is by multiplied by its probability of occurrence (P_i), and these value-probability products are summed over all the outcomes to obtain the expected value. Then the lottery or gamble with the highest EV is selected. The expected utility rule is similar, but it substitutes the utility of each outcome, $U(X_i)$, for its monetary value in the calculation. The EU rule thus applies to a broader domain than monetary gambles, but at the cost of additional processing effort. In general, however, the processing characterizing both of these models is very similar. The SEU rule allows for a subjective probability function $S(P_i)$ to be used along with a utility function to represent risky decisions. The subjective expected utility of a risky option X is then given by

$$SEU\ (X) = \sum_{i=1}^{n} S(P_i)\,U(X_i)\,.$$

The EV, EU, and SEU rules, especially the latter two, are considered normative rules for choice, so these rules are often used in the literature as both descriptions of actual behavior and as normative prescriptions for behavior. In fact, a great deal of research on decision making has been motivated by ascertaining the extent to which such normative rules describe actual choice behavior; for example, see Fox, Rogers, and Tversky (1996). As we outline later in the chapter, choice behavior often departs substantially from these normative prescriptions.

2. Probabilistic Models of Choice

Before we review some of the other strategies for choice that have been identified, we briefly discuss the idea that choice behavior can be modeled as a probabilistic process. The idea that the alternative with the highest overall evaluation (perhaps derived from a WADD or EV) rule is always chosen is a deterministic one. That is, if $V(X)$ represents the value of alternative X, it is assumed that A will be chosen from the two options A and B if $V(A) > V(B)$. However, when faced with the same alternatives under seemingly identical conditions, people do not always make the same choice. Thus, some researchers have argued that the deterministic notion of preference should be replaced by a probabilistic one, which focuses on the probability of choosing A from the total set of options—that is, choosing A rather than B, denoted $P(A;\{A,B\})$, if the total set of options is A and B). Such a probability is often viewed as a measure of the degree to which A is preferred to B.

There is extensive literature on probabilistic choice models (see Meyer & Kahn, 1991, for a recent review of that literature). Perhaps the best known probabilistic choice model is the multinominal logit model (McFadden, 1981), in which the probability of choosing an option X_i from the choice set $(X_1 \ldots X_n)$ is given by the equation

$$P(X_i; \{X_1, \ldots, X_n\}) = e^{V(X_i)} \Big/ \sum_j e^{V(X_j)}\,,$$

where $V(X_i) = b_i + \Sigma\, b_k\, X_{ik}$, X_{ik} is the value of option i on attribute k, b_k is a scaling parameter (weight) for attribute k, and b_i is a constant meant to capture those aspects of the attractiveness of option i not captured by the values on the attributes. Note that the $V(X_i)$ function is essentially an additive composition rule similar to the WADD strategy mentioned earlier.

An important implication of the multinominal logit model, and many other probabilistic choice models, is the property called *independence of irrelevant alternatives (IIA)*. The basic idea of the IIA principle is that the relative preference between options does not depend on the presence or absence of other options and is thus independent of the context of choice as defined by the offered choice set. For example, the IIA principle means that the probability of a decision maker's selecting steak over chicken for dinner from a menu is the same for all menus containing both entrees (Coombs, Dawes, & Tversky, 1970). More generally, Tversky and Simonson (1993) have argued that the IIA assumption is essentially equivalent to the idea of "value maximization" and the belief that "the decision maker has a complete preference order of all options, and that—given an offered set—the decision maker always selects the option that is highest in that order" (p. 1179).

Although it is clear that people sometimes make decisions in ways consistent with the WADD, EV, and EU models, and probabilistic versions of those models such as the multinominal logit model, it has also become obvious over the past 20 years that people often make decisions using simpler decision processes (heuristics) more consistent with the idea of bounded rationality. Further, at least partially as a result of the use of those heuristics, people often exhibit choices that are context dependent. That is, principles such as IIA are systemically violated (e.g., see Simonson & Tversky, 1992). Tversky and Simonson (1993) have proposed a componential context model of such effects that specifically considers the relative advantage of each alternative when compared to other options in the set.

We describe some of the more common heuristics next. Each heuristic represents a different method for simplifying decision making by limiting the amount of information processed or by making the processing of that information easier. In addition, these heuristics often avoid conflict by not making trade-offs among attributes. That is, many of the heuristics are noncompensatory, meaning that a good value on one attribute cannot compensate for a bad value on another. Given space limitations, we focus on deterministic versions of these heuristics, although probabilistic forms of some of these strategies exist.

3. Satisficing (SAT)

One of the oldest heuristics in the decision-making literature is the *satisficing* strategy described by Simon (1955) and mentioned earlier. Alternatives are considered one at a time, in the order they occur in the set, and the value of each attribute of the alternative is compared to a predefined cutoff, often viewed as an aspiration level. The alternative is rejected if any attribute value is below the cutoff, and the first option with all values surpassing the cutoffs is selected. If no alternatives pass all the cutoffs, the process can be repeated with lower cutoffs or an option can be selected randomly. A major implication of the satisficing heuristic is that choice depends on the order in which alternatives are considered. No comparison is made of the relative merits of alternatives; rather, if alternative A and alternative B both pass the cutoffs, then whether A or B is chosen depends on whether A or B is evaluated first.

4. The Equal Weight (EQW) Heuristic

The equal weight strategy considers all alternatives and all the attribute values for each alternative but simplifies the decision by ignoring information about the relative importance or probability of each attribute (outcome). Assuming that the attribute values can be expressed on a common scale of value, this heuristic is a special case of the weighted additive rule, which obtains an overall value for each option by summing the values for each attribute for that alternative. Several researchers have argued that the equal weight rule is often a highly accurate simplification of the decision-making process (Dawes, 1979; Einhorn & Hogarth, 1975).

5. The Majority of Confirming Dimensions (MCD) Heuristic

The MCD heuristic chooses between pairs of alternatives by comparing the values for each of the two alternatives on each attribute and retaining the alternative of the pair with a majority of winning (better) attribute values. The retained alternative is then compared in a similar fashion to the next alternative among the set of alternatives and such pairwise comparisons repeat until all alternatives have been processed and the final winning alternative has been identified (Russo & Dosher, 1983).

The MCD heuristic is a simplified version of Tversky's (1969) additive difference (ADDIF) model. Tversky's model takes the difference between the subjective values of the two alternatives on each dimension. A weighting function is applied to each of these differences, and the results are summed over all the dimensions, yielding an overall relative evaluation of the two options. Under certain conditions, the preference orderings produced by the additive difference rule and the WADD rule are identical, even though the two rules differ in their processing details (see Tversky, 1969, for a further discussion of the relationship between the ADDIF and WADD models).

Aschenbrenner, Bockenholt, Albert, and Schmalhofer (1986) have proposed a variation on the additive difference process. In their model, attribute differences are processed sequentially, with the summed differences accumulating until the advantage of one option over the other exceeds some criterion value (this value may reflect the decision maker's desired balance between the effort involved and the quality of the decision process; see Bockenholt, Albert, Aschenbrenner, & Schmalhofer, 1991).

6. The Lexicographic (LEX) Heuristic

The lexicographic heuristic is quite simple: the alternative with the best value on the most important attribute is selected. If two alternatives are tied for the best value, the second most important attribute is considered the tie-breaker, and this process continues until the tie is broken.

Sometimes the notion of a just-noticeable difference (JND) is added to the LEX rule; that is, options are considered to be tied on an attribute if they are within a JND of the best alternative on that attribute (Tversky, 1969). This version of the LEX rule is sometimes called lexicographic-semiorder (LEXSEMI). One implication of using a lexicographic-semiorder decision rule is that a person may exhibit intransitivities in preferences in which $X >$ Y, $Y > Z$, and $Z > X$, as shown in the following example, adapted from Fishburn (1991). Suppose that Professor P is about to change jobs and feels that if two offers are far apart on salary (e.g., more than \$10,000 apart), then she will choose the job with the higher salary. Otherwise, the prestige of the university will be more important to her. Suppose her three offers are as follows:

	Salary	Prestige
X	\$65,000	Low
Y	\$50,000	High
Z	\$58,000	Medium,

In this case she will prefer X to Y on the basis of X's better salary, will prefer Y to Z because they are less than \$10,000 apart in salary and Y has greater prestige, and she will prefer Z to X on the basis of prestige. Overall, therefore, she exhibits an intransitive pattern of preferences. The general assumption is that choice rationality requires transitive preferences, although Fishburn (1991) has presented arguments for the reasonableness of sometimes violating transitivity.

7. The Elimination-by-Aspects (EBA) Heuristic

First suggested by Tversky (1972), an EBA choice strategy first considers the most important attribute, retrieves the cutoff value for that attribute, and eliminates all alternatives with values below the cutoff for that attribute (Tversky actually assumed that attribute selection was probabilistic, with the probability of attribute selection a function of its weight or importance). This process eliminates options that do not possess an aspect, defined as that which meets or exceeds the cutoff level on the selected attribute. The EBA process continues with the second most important attribute, and so on, until one option remains. Although the EBA process violates the normative notion that one should use all relevant information to make a decision, it reflects rationality in using attribute weight or importance to order the attributes. Such "partial" rationality in processing characterizes most choice heuristics.

8. Combined Strategies

Individuals sometimes combine strategies, typically with an initial phase where poor alternatives are eliminated and a second phase where the remaining alternatives are examined in more detail (Payne, 1976). One combined heuristic that is frequently observed in decision behavior is an elimination-by-aspects strategy in the initial phase to reduce the set of alternatives, followed by use of a weighted additive strategy on the reduced set of options. See Russo and Leclerc (1994) for another view of phases in decision processes.

Beach (1990, 1993) has advanced a theory of decision making called image theory that emphasizes the prechoice screening of options. In image theory, prechoice screening of options both prevents the choice of an option that is "too unacceptable" and reduces the workload of the decision maker. According to Beach, screening involves testing the compatibility of a particular option with the decision maker's standards, which reflect morals, goals, values, and beliefs relevant to the decision problem. The degree of fit or compatibility of an option depends on the number of standards that are violated by the option's various features. The compatibility testing process is noncompensatory; nonviolations cannot compensate for violations. Beach (1993) reviewed some of the research in support of image theory. A major implication of those results is that screening may play a more important role in decision making than has been generally accepted.

We have now described many decision-making strategies, but we have not yet specified the conditions leading to the use of one strategy as opposed to another. In the next section, we first review work showing multiple strategy use in how people adapt to the complexity of decisions. Then we consider the extensive research showing that decision behavior is highly contingent on seemingly minor changes in how preferences are expressed and how options are presented.

B. Contingent Decision Behavior

1. Task Complexity

Although many striking examples exist of multiple strategy use and contingent judgment and choice, some of the most compelling and earliest to be demonstrated concern how people adapt their decision processes to deal with decision complexity. The primary hypothesis for this research is that people use simplifying decision heuristics to a greater extent for more complex decision problems. This hypothesis has been supported by a number of studies manipulating decision complexity using the number of alternatives, number of attributes, and time pressure, among other factors.

Perhaps the most well-established task-complexity effect is the impact of changes in the number of alternatives available (Payne, 1976). When faced with two alternatives, people use compensatory decision strategies which involve trading off a better value on one attribute against a poorer value on another (e.g., weighted adding). However, when faced with multialternative decision tasks, people prefer noncompensatory choice strategies (Billings & Marcus, 1983; Johnson, Meyer, & Ghose, 1989; Klayman, 1985; Önken, Hastie, & Revelle, 1985).

Another way to manipulate decision complexity is to vary the amount of attribute information. Several studies, though not all, find that decision quality can decrease as the number of attributes is increased above a certain level of complexity (Keller & Staelin, 1987; Sundstrom, 1987). Such "information overload" studies have been criticized on a variety of methodological grounds (e.g., Meyer & Johnson, 1989), and Grether and Wilde (Grether & Wilde, 1983; Grether, Schwartz, & Wilde, 1986) argue that in "real" tasks people are able to ignore the less-relevant information so that overload is not a serious issue. On the other hand, Gaeth and Shanteau (1984) found that judgments were adversely influenced by irrelevant factors, although training reduced that influence. The crucial question appears to be how people selectively focus on the most important information and avoid getting distracted by irrelevant information.

People also respond to decision problems varying in time pressure using several coping mechanisms, including acceleration of processing, selectivity in processing, and shifts in decision strategies. As time constraints become more severe, the time spent processing an item of information decreases substantially (Ben Zur & Breznitz, 1981), processing focuses on the more important or more negative information about alternatives (Ben Zur & Breznitz, 1981; Payne, Bettman, & Johnson, 1988; Svenson & Edland, 1987; Wallsten & Barton, 1982), and decision strategies may shift (Payne et al., 1988; Payne, Bettman, & Luce, 1996; Zakay, 1985). Finally, there may be a hierarchy among these responses to time pressure. Payne et al. (1988) found that under moderate time pressure subjects accelerated processing and to a lesser extent became more selective. Under more severe time pressure, people accelerated processing, selectively focused on a subset of the available information, and changed processing strategies. Similar effects were found by Payne, Bettman, and Luce (1996) when time stress was manipulated by varying the opportunity cost of delaying decisions and by Pieters, Warlop, and Hartog (1997) in a naturalistic consumer choice domain. See Svenson and Maule (1993) for a collection of papers dealing with time pressure effects on decision making.

Studies of people's contingent responses to complex decisions provide clear examples of constructive decision processes. However, many other striking cases of constructive processes exist, including differential responses to what might seem trivial changes in task or information presentation. We consider several cases of this sort next.

2. Response Mode and Procedure Invariance

One of the most important characteristics of a decision task is the method by which the decision maker is asked to respond. Figure 1 provides examples of different response modes used in decision research. Decision research has generally used two types of response modes: (1) A choice task involves presenting two or more alternatives and asking the subject to select the alternative(s) that is most preferred, most risky, and so forth; (2) A judgment task usually involves successively presenting individual alternatives and requesting that the subject assign a value (e.g., the option's worth or riskiness) to each. A matching task is a variant of a judgment task involving the presentation of two alternatives and requiring the subject to fill in a missing value for one option in the pair so as to make the two options in the pair equal in value.

Procedure invariance is a fundamental principle of rational decision making: Strategically equivalent ways of eliciting a decision maker's preferences should result in the same revealed preferences. However, the use of different response modes can lead to differential weighting of attributes and can change how people combine information, resulting in different preference assessments. Research on the effects of choice versus matching tasks and on preference reversals documents such response mode effects.

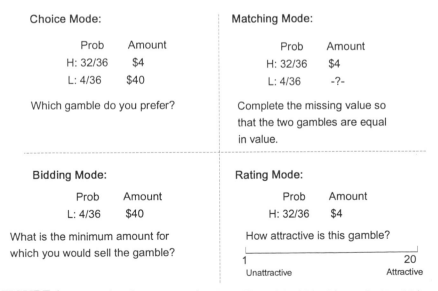

FIGURE 1   Examples of response modes. From Figure 2.1 of *The Adaptive Decision Maker,* by J. W. Payne, J. R. Bettman, and E. J. Johnson, Cambridge: Cambridge University Press, 1993, p. 41. Reprinted with the permission of Cambridge University Press.

a. Choice versus Matching

The so-called prominence effect (Tversky, Sattath, & Slovie, 1988) provides an excellent example of the contingent weighting of attributes as a function of response mode. The prominence effect is the finding that the predominant or more important attribute (e.g., lives saved in comparison to the cost of a safety program) is given even more weight when preferences are assessed using choice than when preferences are assessed using a matching task.

To illustrate the difference between matching and choice tasks, imagine that you must consider two programs for dealing with traffic accidents. The programs are both described to you in terms of their yearly dollar costs and the number of fatalities per year. In a matching task, you are given all of the values but one. For example, suppose that Program A is expected to lead to 570 fatalities and cost $12 million, whereas Program B is expected to lead to 500 fatalities and cost $X. Then for the matching task you would be asked to give a value $X for the cost of program B—presumably an amount greater than $12 million since Program B leads to fewer fatalities—that would equate the overall values of Programs A and B according to your preferences.

In a choice task, on the other hand, you would be given all of the cost and fatality values for both programs (e.g., all the values in the example above plus a cost of $55 million for Program B) and be asked to choose the program you most prefer. For these specific values, most people choose Program B over Program A. This implies that saving 70 lives is more important than saving $43 million. In a matching task, on the other hand, people often provide values for $X that are less than $55 million, implying that a cost difference of less than $43 million is equivalent to 70 fewer fatalities. Therefore, the trade-off between cost and fatalities differs depending on whether it is assessed with a choice task or a matching task.

Tversky et al. (1988) have suggested that the two tasks encourage use of different heuristics or computational schemes. Choice, they argue, involves more qualitative, ordinal, lexicographic reasoning (i.e., one selects the option that is ordinally superior on the most important attribute). Such lexicographic reasoning is easier cognitively than explicit trade-offs, avoids rather than confronts conflict, and is easier to justify to oneself and others. Matching tasks, on the other hand, require a more cardinal, quantitative assessment in which one must consider the size of the differences for both attributes and the relative weights of the attributes.

More generally, Tversky et al. (1988) suggested that there is strategy compatibility between the nature of the required response—ordinal or cardinal—and the types of reasoning employed by a decision maker. They argue that choice, for example, requires an ordinal response and evokes arguments (processes) based on the ordering of the attribute values. Hawkins (1994) provided evidence that processing characteristics do vary systematically across response modes and that these processing variations are predictive of preference reversals.

b. Preference Reversals

Fischer and Hawkins (1993) discuss the notion of scale compatibility, an idea related to, but distinct from, the concept of strategy compatibility. Scale compatibility states that enhanced weight is given to a stimulus attribute to the extent it is compatible with the response scale. The general idea of scale compatibility has played a major role for some time in understanding the classic preference reversal phenomenon (Lichtenstein & Slovic, 1971). In the standard preference-reversal paradigm, individuals evaluate two bets of comparable expected value. One of the bets offers a high probability of winning a small amount of money, whereas the other bet offers a low probability of winning a large amount of money. Most people prefer the bet with the higher probability of winning when asked to choose between the two bets. However, if they are asked to bid for (assign a cash equivalent to) each bet, most people assign a higher value to the low-probability, high-payoff bet. Thus, preferences "reverse" between the two response modes.

Tversky, Slovic, and Kahneman (1990) have shown that a major cause of preference reversals is such overpricing of the low-probability, high-payoff bet, perhaps due to the scale compatibility between the payoff amount and the bid response mode (see also Bostic et al., 1990). Finally, Schkade, and Johnson (1989), using computer-based monitoring of information-acquisition behavior, also support scale compatibility as a factor underlying preference reversals. Delquié (1993) provided strong evidence of scale compatibility effects using both risky and nonrisky decision stimuli.

Although scale compatibility plays a role in preference reversals, other mechanisms may also be contributing factors. For example, Goldstein and Einhorn (1987) have argued that the evaluation process is the same for all response modes and have claimed that reversals are mainly due to expressing the underlying internal evaluation on different response scales. How individuals reframe decisions under certain response modes also may lead to preference reversals (Bell, 1985; Casey, 1991; Hershey & Schoemaker, 1985). Suppose that a person is given one option, which is a sure thing, and a second option, which is a gamble offering either a specific greater amount with probability p or a specific lesser-amount with probability $1 - p$. Suppose further that the person is asked to set (match) the probability p of obtaining the greater amount in order to make the sure-thing option and the gamble equivalent in value. Hershey and Schoemaker (1985), for instance, suggested that this matching task encourages the person to use the amount of the sure thing as a reference point, with the two outcomes of the gamble then coded as a gain and as a loss.

Preference reversals may also be due to changes in evaluation processes across response modes (e.g., Johnson, Payne, & Bettman, 1988; Mellers, Ordóñez, & Birnbaum, 1992; Schkade & Johnson, 1989), as suggested by the strategy-compatibility hypothesis discussed previously. If different strategies are used to generate each type of response, reversals can easily result. Fischer and Hawkins (1993) found in a series of experiments that strategy compatibility effects were stronger than scale compatibility as explanations of procedural variance.

An obvious hypothesis is that the more ambiguity in one's existing preferences, perhaps due to a lack of familiarity with the objects to be valued, the more one's expressed preferences will be subject to task factors such as how you ask the question. There is support for this hypothesis. For example, Coupey, Irwin, and Payne (1998) have reported that the difference between choice and matching responses is greater for unfamiliar consumer products than for more familiar product categories. Further, familiarity exhibits a stronger influence on matching responses than on choice responses. The data suggest that subjects tend to weight attributes more equally, and perhaps depend more on the information presented as part of the task itself rather than on information brought to the task, when constructing preferences using a matching response in an unfamiliar product category.

In summary, either framing, strategy selection, weighting of information, or expression of preferences can explain preference reversals. However, preference reversals may be as prevalent and robust as they are because there are multiple underlying causes, each operative in some situations but not others (e.g., Creyer & Johar, 1995; Goldstein & Einhorn, 1987; Hsee, 1996). Regardless of which particular cause is operative, it is now abundantly clear that the answer to how much you like a decision option can depend greatly on how you are asked the question.

3. Descriptive Invariance

Although the principle of descriptive invariance (i.e., that different representations of the same choice problem should lead to equivalent preferences), seems to be reasonable, research has shown consistently that how problems are presented affects preferences. Not only how you ask the question but also how the options are described affects preferences, even when the descriptions or presentations are normatively equivalent (Tversky & Kahneman, 1986). Two major streams of research that demonstrate descriptive variance are investigations of framing and the effects of information presentation.

a. Framing Effects

Framing affects how the acts, contingencies, and outcomes of a decision are determined. Framing can be influenced by both the presentation of the decision problem and by the decision maker's norms, habits, and expectations (Tversky & Kahneman, 1986). Tversky and Kahneman (1981), for example, showed that simple changes in wording—for example, describing outcomes in terms of lives saved rather than describing them in terms of lives lost—can lead to vastly different preferences (for other demonstrations of such wording effects, see also Huber, Neale, & Northcraft, 1987; Kramer, 1989; Levin & Gaeth, 1988; Paese, 1995; Puto, 1987; Schneider, 1992). There appears to be a crucial distinction between (1) framing that leads to coding outcomes as gains and (2) framing that results in outcomes' being coded as losses, because people clearly treat negative consequences and positive consequences differently. Tversky and Kahneman's (1991) concept of loss aversion (the impact of a difference on a dimension is greater when that difference is seen as a loss than when it is seen as a gain) stresses the importance of this difference.

A theory of framing has proven difficult to formalize, however, although some progress has been made. For instance, Thaler (1985; Thaler & Johnson, 1990) suggested that framing is an active process rather than simply a passive response to the given decision problem, and he examined the hypothesis that people frame outcomes to make them appear the most pleasant or the least unpleasant. In particular, Thaler (1985) argued that people generally prefer to keep gains separate (segregated) and to integrate (package together) all negative outcomes. Thaler and Johnson (1990) called this view *hedonic editing.*

Linville and Fischer (1991) suggested that framing is driven by the need to conserve the limited, but renewable, psychological, cognitive, and social resources available for coping with emotional events. They showed that the original hedonic-editing hypothesis does not fully account for peoples' preferences for temporally separating or combining good and bad news; rather, people prefer to segregate bad news but to combine a positive and negative event on the same day.

Thus, reference points, target levels, or aspiration levels can contribute to framing effects (see Schneider, 1992) and to procedural variance. As noted in our descriptions of heuristics presented earlier, this idea is also of long standing in theories of decision making (Siegel, 1957; Simon, 1955). For instance, Simon suggested that individuals simplify choice problems by coding an outcome as satisfactory if the outcome is above the aspiration level or unsatisfactory if it is below. Such codings play a crucial role in his notion of satisficing. Finally, there is a great deal of evidence that choice depends on the reference level used in coding outcomes (Fischer, Kamlet,

Fienberg, & Schkade, 1986; Highhouse & Johnson, 1996; Payne, Laughhun, & Crum, 1984; Tversky & Kahneman, 1991). One particularly important type of reference-level effect is the status quo bias (Kahneman, Knetsh, & Thaler, 1990; Samuelson & Zeckhauser, 1988), in which the retention of the status quo option is favored over other options.

b. Information Presentation Effects

Information presentation differences also influence decision behavior. Slovic (1972) suggested that decision makers tend to use information in the form it is displayed, without transforming it, as a way to conserve cognitive effort. This "concreteness" principle is the basis for predicting several types of information format effects. For example, Russo (1977) showed in a classic study that the use of unit price information in a supermarket increased when the information was displayed in lists ranking brands by unit price. He argued that standard displays using a shelf tag for each item made items hard to compare. Information must be easily processable as well as available. In other demonstrations of concreteness effects, Aschenbrenner (1978) inferred that subjects used the dimensions of gambles as presented, and Bettman and Kakkar (1977) showed that individuals acquired information in a fashion consistent with the format of the display. Jarvenpaa (1989) extended the Bettman and Kakkar (1977) results by showing that information was processed in a manner consistent with how graphic displays were organized, that is, by alternative or by attribute. MacGregor and Slovic (1986) showed that people will use a less important cue simply because it is more salient in the display. Finally, Schkade and Kleinmuntz (1994) examined the differential influence of the organization and sequence of information on decision processes. Although the finding that information acquisition proceeds in a fashion consistent with display format is perhaps not surprising, it has important implications both for using relatively simple changes in information presentation to aid decision makers and for the design of graphics for computer-based decision support systems.

Other work has examined the effects of different representations of values. For example, Stone and Schkade (1991) found that using words to represent attribute values led to less compensatory processing than numerical representation of the values (see also Schkade & Kleinmuntz, 1994). Wallsten and his colleagues (Budescu, Weinberg, & Wallston, 1988; Erev & Cohen, 1990; Wallsten, 1990) have carried out an important series of experiments testing differences between representing probability information in numerical or verbal form. People prefer to receive information about probabilities in numerical form, but they prefer to use words (e.g., *doubtful, likely*) to express event probabilities to others. González-Vallejo and Wallsten (1992) have shown that preference reversals are also impacted by whether probability information is given a numerical or verbal form; reversals are less with a verbal format.

Another series of experiments has dealt with the completeness of information displays (Dube-Rioux & Russo, 1988; Highhouse & House, 1995; Jagacinski, 1995; Weber, Eisenführ, & von Winterfeldt 1988). Individuals may respond differently to the problem if they do not realize that information is missing, and the apparent completeness of a display can blind a decision maker to the possibility that important information is lacking (a result earlier obtained by Fischhoff, Slovic, & Lichtenstein, 1978). Finally, Russo, Medvec, and Meloy (1996) have shown that preexisting preferences can lead to distortion of the new information in favor of the preferred alternative. This last result suggests dynamic aspects of information use in the construction of preferences.

4. Asymmetric Dominance Effects

Number of alternatives, response mode, and information display are examples of task factors. Contingent decision behavior has also been shown for context factors reflecting the particular values of the alternatives. One striking example of context-dependent preferences is the asymmetric dominance effect. An alternative is asymmetrically dominated if it is dominated by at least one option in the choice set and is also not dominated by at least one other option (e.g., for the case of three options, A, B, and C, if B were dominated by A but not by C, B would be asymmetrically dominated). The striking effect of asymmetric dominance (Heath & Chatterjee, 1995; Huber, Payne, & Puto, 1982; Simonson & Tversky, 1992) is that adding an asymmetrically dominated option to a choice set *increases* the choice share of the dominating option (e.g., A in our example). This violates the principle of regularity, that is, that adding a new option cannot increase the probability of choosing one of the original options. Regularity is a necessary condition for most probabilistic choice models.

Explanations for the asymmetric dominance effect include agenda affects relating to the order of comparison of pairs of options (Huber, Payne, & Puto, 1982), simplifying choice by searching for dominant alternatives (Montgomery, 1983), and problems with simplicity of the stimuli (Ratneshwar, Shocker, & Stewart, 1987; see Wedell, 1991, for evidence inconsistent with this view, however). A recent explanation that has received some support is the notion that the effect arises because people use the relations among options as reasons for justifying their choices; that is, one can justify the choice of the dominating option by saying it is clearly better than the asymmetrically dominated option (Simonson, 1989). Wedell (1991) also reported data consistent with this explanation.

The task and context effects discussed so far have illustrated that decision behavior is contingent upon a variety of factors. As we have also discussed, one explanation for a number of task and context effects is that individuals use different decision strategies in different situations. Why would this be so? One explanation is that an individual's contingent use of multiple strategies is an adaptive response of a limited-capacity information processor to the demands of a complex world (Payne, Bettman, & Johnson, 1993). The basic idea is that using multiple strategies allows a decision maker to adaptively trade off the accuracy or quality of the decision against the cognitive effort needed to reach a judgment or choice. Svenson (1996) outlined another framework for explaining contingent decision behavior; Hammond, Hamm, Grassia, and Pearson (1987), Montgomery (1983), and Tversky and Kahneman (1986) provided other frameworks that do not emphasize cognitive effort to such an extent. The general question of how to account for contingent decision behavior remains an active area of research.

So far in this chapter we have focused on decisions that are difficult due to conflicting objectives (that is, there are multiple objectives and no option is best on all of them). Decisions can also be difficult because of the need to make guesses about the future consequences of current actions. A great deal of research has been concerned with the question of how people judge the likelihoods or probabilities of uncertain events. As we will see, recent work on how, and how well, people assess the probability of an event has adopted many of the same concepts used to explain preferential decisions. In particular, people have available several different strategies for assessing beliefs about uncertain events, and individuals use these different modes of probabilistic reasoning in a highly contingent fashion. People also often construct probability responses (Curley, Browne, Smith, & Benson, 1995). In the following sections, we consider different strategies for probabilistic reasoning and then consider evidence for the contingent use of such strategies.

V. BELIEFS ABOUT UNCERTAIN EVENTS

A focus of much of the early work on probabilistic reasoning was the extent to which intuitive judgements about probabilities matched the normative predictions made by the rules of statistics. For example, many studies have examined the extent to which people revise their opinions about uncertain events in ways consistent with such statistical laws as Bayes' theorem. Bayes' theorem deals with problems of the following type: Imagine that you are a physician trying to make a diagnosis concerning whether or not one of your patients has cancer. Denote the hypothesis that the patient has cancer as H. Before you collect any new information about this patient, you have a prior probability that the patient has cancer. Denote that prior probability as $P(H)$. The prior probability that the patient does not have cancer will then be denoted $1 - P(H)$. This prior will likely be based on whatever you know about the patient up to this point. Now assume that you collect some new evidence about the patient's condition by conducting some diagnostic, but imperfect, test. Thus, there is some probability that the test will be positive if the patient has cancer but there is also some probability that the test will be positive even if the patient does not have cancer. Denote the first probability as $P(D/H)$, or the probability of a test result indicating cancer given that the true condition of the patient is that he or she has cancer. Denote the second probability as $P(D/\text{ not } H)$, or the probability of a test result indicating cancer given that the patient does not have cancer. Given your prior probability $P(H)$ and the probabilities of the two test results, $P(D/H)$ and $P(D/\text{ not } H)$, what is the revised probability that your hypothesis that the patient has cancer is true after the data are observed, that is, $P(H/D)$?

More than 200 years ago, an English clergyman, Reverend Bayes, offered the solution to this type of problem. His solution is given by the following equation:

$$P(H/D) = \frac{P(D/H)\,P(H)}{P(D/H)\,P(H) + P(D/\text{ not } H)(1 - P(H))}$$

Essentially Bayes' theorem is a way of combining what you already believe about an uncertainty with new information that is available to you to yield an updated belief about the likelihood of that uncertainty. See Yates (1990) for a good discussion of Bayes' theorem from the perspective of psychology and decision making.

For more than 30 years, people have been using Bayes' theorem as a standard against which to compare people's actual probability judgments (e.g., Dawes, Mirels, Gold, & Donahue, 1993; Phillips & Edwards, 1966). The general result has been that people's probability judgments deviate substantially from the predictions of Bayes' theorem, with the nature of the deviation dependent on the situation (see Fischhoff & Beyth-Marom, 1983). Although the fact that intuitive judgments often deviate from laws of probability such as Bayes' theorem is now widely accepted, some investigators question both the meaning and relevance of errors in intuitive judgments (see von Winterfeldt & Edwards, 1986, for example). Nevertheless, Bayes' theorem has been, and continues to be, a useful benchmark against which to compare intuitive human judgments.

Another benchmark for intuitive judgment is simply the accuracy of the judgment. That is, does the predicted event (judgment) correspond to the actual event that occurs? A related accuracy question is the ability of a judge to know how likely it is that his or her judgments are correct. The hope is that stated confidence matches expected accuracy, that is, confidence judgments are well "calibrated" (Yates, 1990). See Hammond (1996) for a discussion of alternative standards against which to compare intuitive judgments and Wallsten (1996) for a discussion of methodological issues in analyzing the accuracy of human judgment.

A. Strategies for Probabilistic Reasoning

If people are not reasoning in ways consistent with the laws of probability when making intuitive judgments, how are they thinking about uncertainties? Roughly 20 years ago, Kahneman and Tversky (1973) argued that people use a variety of heuristics to solve probability judgment tasks. The specific heuristics suggested included availability, representativeness, and anchoring and adjustment. The availability heuristic refers to assessing the probability of an event based on how easily instances of that event come to mind. Kahneman and Tversky argued that availability is a useful procedure for assessing probabilities because instances of more frequent events are usually retrieved faster and better; however, availability is affected by factors like vividness and recency that do not impact relative frequency and probability. Consequently, the use of the availability heuristic can lead to predictable errors in judgment.

The representativeness heuristic assesses the probability of an event by judging the degree to which that event corresponds to an appropriate mental model for that class of events, such as a sample and a population, an instance and a category, or an act and an actor. For example, a manager is using representativeness as a heuristic when he or she predicts the success of a new product based on the similarity of that product to past successful and unsuccessful product types. As with the use of the availability heuristic, the representativeness heuristic can be useful in probabilistic judgment. As with availability, however, the representativeness heuristic can lead people to ignore or misuse information that affects actual probabilities.

Finally, anchoring and adjustment is a general judgment process in which an initially generated or given response serves as an anchor; that anchor is adjusted based on other information, but the adjustment is generally insufficient (see Chapman & Johnson, 1994, for an investigation of some of the limits on anchoring). An example of anchoring and adjustment is when a manager uses this year's sales to forecast next year's sales. The notion of insufficient adjustment means that the forecast for next year may not reflect the differences to be expected next year as much as it reflects this year's sales.

The availability heuristic has been investigated for judgments about political events (Levi & Pryor, 1987), perceptions of the risk of consumer products (Folkes, 1988), accountants' hypothesis generation (Libby, 1985), and judgments about others (Shedler & Manis, 1986). The relationship between memory access and judgment has been examined more generally by Lichtenstein and Srull (1985), Hastie and Park (1986), and MacLeod and Campbell (1992).

The representativeness heuristic has been studied in detail by Bar-Hillel (1984), and Camerer (1987) showed in an innovative study that representativeness affects prices in experimental markets, although the effect is smaller for more experienced subjects. Finally, anchoring and adjustment has been investigated in a variety of domains, including accounting (Butler, 1986), marketing (Davis, Hoch, & Ragsdale, 1986; Yadav, 1994), the assessment of real estate values (Northcraft & Neale, 1987), negotiations (White & Sebenius, 1997), and as a general process for updating beliefs (Hogarth & Einhorn, 1992).

B. Contingent Assessments of Uncertainty

As noted earlier, heuristics often ignore potentially relevant problem information. Using heuristics adaptively, even though some information may be neglected, can save substantial cognitive effort and still produce reasonably good solutions to decision problems (Gigerenzer & Goldstein, 1996; Payne, Bettman, & Johnson 1993). It is still the case, however, that people make systematic errors in forming probability judgments in many situations (Kahneman & Tversky, 1996). Much decision research over the past two decades has tried to identify biases (errors) in probabilistic reasoning. Others have argued that there has been an overemphasis on biases in judgment (e.g., Beach, Barnes, & Christensen-Szalanski, 1986). As we illustrate next with reference to two of the most studied "errors" in judgment, the relevant question is not whether biases exist, but under what conditions relevant information will or will not be used when responding to a probability judgment task.

1. The Use/Misuse of Base-Rate Information

More than 20 years ago, Kahneman and Tversky (1973) reported a series of studies in which subjects were presented with a brief personality description of a person along with a list of different categories to which the person might belong, and were asked to indicate to which category the person was most likely to belong. Their findings were clear and striking; subjects essentially ignored the relative sizes of the different categories (i.e., the base rates) and based their judgments almost exclusively on the extent to which the description matched their various stereotypes about the categories (representativeness). Since then, many researchers have investigated the utilization of base-rate information in decision making (see Bar-Hillel, 1990, for an overview of base-rate studies; see Birnbaum, 1983, and Koehler, 1996, for criticisms of some of these studies).

Overall, it appears that base-rate information is sometimes ignored and at times used appropriately. For example, Medin and Edelson (1988) stated that in their studies "participants use base-rate information appropriately, ignore base-rate information, or use base-rate information inappropriately (predict that the rare disease is more likely to be present)" (p. 68). Such variability in the use of base-rate information to assess the probability of an event has led to a contingent processing view of probabilistic reasoning. Gigerenzer, Hell, and Blank (1988) and Ginossar and Trope (1987) provided two examples of contingent-processing approaches to base-rate, both of which show that the use of base-rate information is highly sensitive to a variety of task and context variables. For example, Gigerenzer et al. found greater use of base-rate information when the problem context changed from guessing the profession of a person to predicting the outcome of a soccer game. They argued that "the content of the problem strongly influenced both subjects' performance and their *reported strategies* [emphasis added]" (p. 523).

Ginossar and Trope (1987) proposed that people have a variety of strategies, both statistical and nonstatistical, for making probabilistic judgments. Which heuristic is used for a particular judgment task is contingent upon the recency and frequency of prior activation of the rules, the relationship between the rules and task goals, and the applicability of the rules to the problem givens. They concluded that the appropriate question is not whether people are inherently good or bad statisticians, but what cognitive factors determine when different inferential rules, statistical or nonstatistical, will be applied. The Ginossar and Trope viewpoint is consistent with much of the research on preferences reported earlier in this chapter and is one we share.

2. The Conjunction Fallacy

Research on the conjunction fallacy has also argued that the same person may use a variety of strategies for solving probabilistic reasoning problems. Tversky and Kahneman (1983) distinguished between intuitive (holistic) reasoning about the probabilities of events and extensional (decomposed) reasoning, where events are analyzed into exhaustive lists of possibilities and compound probabilities are evaluated by aggregating elementary ones. One law of probability derived from extensional logic is that the probability of a conjunction of events, $P(A \text{ and } B)$, cannot exceed the probability of any one of its constituent events, $P(A)$ and $P(B)$. Tversky and Kahneman have argued that intuitive reasoning, on the other hand, is based on "natural assessments" such as representativeness and availability, which "are often neither deliberate nor conscious" (1983, p. 295). Tversky and Kahneman demonstrated numerous instances in which people violate the conjunction rule by stating that the probability of A and B is greater than the probability of B, consistent with their hypothesis that probabilistic reasoning is often intuitive. Crandall and Greenfield (1986), Fisk (1996), Thuring and Jungermann (1990), Wells (1985), and Yates and Carlson (1986) have provided additional evidence for violations of the conjunction rule.

Although Tversky and Kahneman argued that violations of the conjunction rule are both systematic and sizable, they note that "availability judgments are not always dominated by nonextensional heuristics . . . [and] judgments of probability vary in the degree to which they follow a decompositional or holistic approach" (1983, p. 310). Thus, it is critical to understand when the decision maker will use one approach or another in solving problems under uncertainty, as was the case for understanding differential strategy use in assessing preferences. Reeves and Lockhart (1993), for instance, have shown that conjunctive fallacies vary as a function of whether probability problems were presented in a frequency versus case-specific form. Examples of frequency and case-specific versions, respectively, are (1) Jimmy will probably get a birthday present from his Uncle Marvin because Uncle Marvin has sent him a present many times in the past, and (2) Jimmy will probably get a birthday present from his Uncle Marvin because Uncle Marvin is conscientious and has often remarked that Jimmy is his favorite nephew (p. 207). Reeves and Lockhart show that violations of the conjunctive rule are generally greater with case-specific versions of problems. Jones, Jones, and Frisch (1995) have extended this important line of reasoning by showing that representiveness affects occur primarily when people are making judgments about single cases, whereas availability effects occur primarily in judgments of relative frequency.

Tversky and Koehler (1994; see also Rottenstreich & Tversky, 1997) have developed a theory of subjective probability judgment that helps explain the conjunction fallacy and other biases. This theory, called "support theory," asserts that subjective probability is attached to descriptions of events, called hypotheses, rather than to events. Judged probability then reflects the strength of evidence or support for the focal relative to the alternative hypothesis. A key implication of support theory is that the judged probability of an event, such as a plane crash, can be increased by "unpacking" the description into disjoint components, such as an accidental plane crash or a nonaccidental plane crash caused by sabotage. Unpacking thus relates to the notion discussed earlier that different descriptions of the same event (i.e., different ways of framing that event) can lead to different preferences.

C. Expertise and Uncertainty Judgments

Although thus far we have emphasized properties of the task as determinants of behavior, the processes used to construct a solution to a decision problem clearly may differ as a function of individual differences as well. One particularly important individual difference factor is the degree of knowledge or expertise an individual possesses.

One question of great interest is the extent to which expertise improves the assessment of uncertainty. Experience does not necessarily improve judgment. Garb (1989), for example, reviewed the effects of training and experience on the validity of clinical judgments in mental health fields and concluded that "the results on validity generally fail to support the value of experience in mental health fields. However, the results do provide limited support for the value of training" (p. 391). Garb did argue that experienced judges know to a greater extent which of their judgments is more likely to be correct; that is, their judgments are better calibrated. Wright, Rowe, Bolger, and Gammack (1994) have shown that self-rated expertise is a good predictor of probability forecasting performance. See also Winkler and Poses (1993) for evidence of good probability assessment by physicians.

Gigerenzer, Hoffrage, and Kleinbolting (1991) have strongly made the related argument that performance on probabilistic reasoning tasks depends on whether the problem refers to a natural environment known to an individual, with performance much better in natural environments. On the other hand, Griffin and Tversky (1992) have argued that when the knowledge of experts is high, and consequently, the predictability of tasks is reasonably high, experts will do better than lay people in terms of calibration. However, when predictability is very low, experts may do worse on some measures of probability assessment. In particular, experts may be overconfident about their ability to predict (see Spence, 1996, for a comparison of expertise differences on problems differing in complexity).

Expertise, however, is not a panacea for making assessments of uncertain events; experts also use heuristics, such as representativeness, and show biases in the use of base-rate information. Cox and Summers (1987), for example, found that experienced retail buyers used representativeness heuristics when making sales forecasts. Why might expertise not lead to better assessments? Because the prediction of future events often depends on learning from and understanding past events, the hindsight bias (Fischhoff, 1975), or the "I knew it all along" phenomenon, may cause people to learn less from experience than they should. Indeed, Hawkins and Hastie (1990) concluded that hindsight issues affect the judgments of experts in "real" tasks. For other reasons why expertise may not lead to better assessments, see Camerer and Johnson (1991). Finally, see Dawes (1994) for a very thought-provoking discussion of the "myth of expertise" in the context of psychotherapy.

Although not directly an expertise issue, a growing topic of interest deals with individual differences in probability judgments due to natural or cultural variations. Examples of this program of research include studies by Whitcomb, Önkal, Curley, and Benson (1995), Wright and Phillips (1980), and Yates, Zhu, Ronis, Wang, Shinotsuka, and Toda (1989).

Next we examine in more detail how people make decisions under risk and uncertainty, which draws on studies of both preferences and judgments about uncertain events.

VI. DECISIONS UNDER RISK AND UNCERTAINTY

How people choose among gambles, which involves tradeoffs between the desirability of consequences and the likelihood of consequences, has been one of the most active areas of decision research. Understanding decision making under risk and uncertainty not only provides insight into basic psychological processes of judgment and choice, but also is directly relevant for improving decisions in a wide range of contexts (e.g., medical care, public policy, business). It is increasingly clear that decisions under risk are sensitive to the same types of influences described earlier for preferences among multiattribute alternatives and for the assessment of uncertainties. In the following sections, we consider generalizations of expected-utility models (how values depend on the specific set of available options and interactions between payoffs and probabilities), responses to repeated-play gambles, and ambiguity and risky choice.

A. Generalizations of Expected-Utility Models

Although their descriptive validity has long been questioned, expected utility (EU) theory (von Neumann & Morgenstern, 1947) and subjective expected utility (SEU) theory have been the standard models for decisions under risk. Mark Machina recently summarized risky-decision research by noting that "choice under uncertainty is a field in flux" (Machina, 1987, p. 121). Evidence of violations of the standard EU and SEU models has accumulated to such an extent that numerous theorists have developed alternatives to the standard models that allow the trade-offs between probabilities and values to reflect contextual factors. For example, one possibility is to allow the value of an outcome of one gamble to depend on the outcome that would have been received if a different gamble had been chosen instead and the same random event had occurred—that is, the notion of regret (Bell, 1982; Loomes & Sugden, 1987).

Many proposed generalizations of EU and SEU also depart from the notion that it is essential to disentangle belief and value (Shafer, 1986). For example, the probabilities (decision weights) of outcomes could be weighted by the rank order of the attractiveness of the outcomes so that the lowest-ranked, least-attractive outcomes could be given relatively greater weight (Quiggin, 1982; Segal, 1989). Because people appear to respond differently to gains and losses, as noted earlier, one could also allow decision weights to differ for gain outcomes and loss outcomes (Einhorn & Hogarth, 1986). Other generalizations of the expected utility model allow the decision weights assigned to the outcomes to vary as a function of both the rank *and* the sign of the payoffs (Luce, 1990; Luce & Fishburn, 1991; Tversky & Kahneman, 1992) or allow configural weights (Weber, Anderson, & Birnbaum, 1992). Such weights can also vary depending on whether the decision maker is evaluating a prospect from the perspective of a buyer or seller (Birnbaum & Beeghley, 1997).

Rank- and sign-dependent models demonstrate impressive predictive power (however, see Wakker, Erev, & Weber 1994). Nonetheless, Tversky and Kahneman have argued that formal models of the valuation of risky options are at best approximate and incomplete, and that

> choice is a constructive and contingent process. When faced with a complex problem, people employ a variety of heuristic procedures in order to simplify the representation and the evaluation of prospects. The heuristics of choice do not readily lend themselves to formal analysis because their application depends on the formulation of the problem, the method of elicitation, and the context of choice. (1992, p. 317)

Should we attempt further generalizations of EU beyond those already proposed, or should we move away from such models in the attempt to understand risky decision behavior (Camerer, 1989)? Fennema and Wakker (1997) have argued that the mathematical form of such generalized utility models as cumulative prospect theory (Tversky & Kahneman, 1992) is well suited for modeling psychological phenomena associated with risky choice. Shafir, Osherson, and Smith (1993) suggested that the absolute approach of expectation models, in which the attractiveness of a gamble is assumed to be independent of other alternatives, should be combined with a comparative approach, in which the attractiveness of a gamble depends on the alternatives to which it is compared. Lopes (1987; Schneider & Lopes, 1986) argued that we should move away from expectation models in favor of models that more directly reflect the multiple and conflicting goals that people may have in making risky decisions (e.g., maximizing security, maximizing potential gain, and maximizing the probability of coming out ahead). This focus on multiple goals is similar in spirit to the early idea of characterizing gambles by risk dimensions rather than moments (Slovic & Lichtenstein, 1968).

1. Repeated-Play Gambles

The notion that multiple goals can underlie risky choice may affect how people respond to gambles involving single play versus repeated-play gambles. People may emphasize different goals depending on how often a gamble will be played (Lopes, 1981) or whether the decision involves a single individual or a group of comparable individuals (Redelmeir & Tversky, 1990). Recent work shows that risky-choice behavior can differ for unique and repeated gambles (Joag, Mowen, & Gentry, 1990; Keren & Wagenaar, 1987; Koehler, Gibbs, & Hogarth, 1994). Wedell and Bockenholt (1990), for example, showed that there are fewer preference reversals under repeated-play conditions. There may be an interesting connection between the repeated play of gambles and when people will reason statistically. Framing an apparently unique risky decision as part of a much larger set of risky choices may lead to behavior more in line with a considered trade-off of beliefs and values (Kahneman & Lovallo, 1992).

2. Ambiguity and Risky Choice

It is generally assumed that in decision making under risk, decision makers have well-specified probabilities representing their uncertainties about events. However, ambiguity often characterizes event probabilities. A decision maker might tell you, for example, that his or her best guess is that the probability of an event is .4, but the estimate is shaky. The standard theory of subjective expected utility states that an expected probability is adequate to represent the individual's uncertainty about an event; however, people respond differently, even when the expectations of the probabilities are the same, if some probabilities are more uncertain than others. In particular, individuals are often averse to ambiguity, at least when the probabilities of the events are moderate (e.g., .5) or larger (Ellsberg, 1961). In fact, Frisch and Baron (1988) argued that it may be reasonable to show such ambiguity aversion. However, ambiguity seeking can occur for lower-probability events (Curley & Yates, 1989), a result Ellsberg also suggested.

Einhorn and Hogarth (1985) modeled how people adjust probabilities under ambiguity to reflect what might be imagined and compared imagination to a mental simulation process. The adjustment is made from an initial estimate of the probability of an event and the size of the adjustment depends on both the amount of ambiguity and the initial probability value. Hogarth and Kunreuther (1985, 1989) used this ambiguity model to try to understand when, and at what prices, insurance coverage will be offered for different uncertainties. Hogarth and Kunreuther (1995) proposed that people deal with situations involving no relevant probability information by generating arguments that allow them to resolve choice conflicts such as potential feelings of regret if an action is not taken.

Concern about others' evaluations of one's decisions may be a partial explanation for ambiguity avoidance. In the standard Ellsberg task, where there is one urn containing 50 red balls and 50 black balls and another urn containing 100 red and black balls in unknown proportions, the preference for a bet based on the known 50:50 urn is enhanced when subjects anticipate that the contents of the unknown urn will be shown to others (Curley, Yates, & Abrams, 1986).

Heath and Tversky (1991) extended the study of ambiguity to situations where the probabilities are based on knowledge rather than chance. They argued that the willingness to bet on an uncertain event depends not only on the estimated likelihood of that event and the precision of that estimate but also on the degree to which one feels knowledgeable or competent in a given context. They found that more knowledgeable subjects in a domain (e.g., politics) were more likely to prefer a bet based on their judged probability than on a matched chance bet, but that the chance bet was preferred over a matched judgmental bet in domains where one felt less competent. Heath and Tversky concluded that the effect of knowledge or competence far outweighs that of ambiguity or vagueness in understanding how beliefs and preferences interact to determine risky decisions. Factors beyond beliefs about values and likelihoods (e.g., personal feelings of competence) may have a major influence on risk-taking behavior.

We have briefly and selectively reviewed the extensive literature on the psychology of decision making. However, an interesting feature of behavioral decision research that we have not yet addressed is the richness of the methods used to investigate judgment and choice behavior. In the next section, we examine some of the methods used to study decision processes.

VII. METHODS FOR STUDYING DECISION MAKING

"The theory of bounded rationality requires close, almost microscopic, study of how people actually behave."

H. A. Simon, 1991, p. 364

There are two basic categories of methods for studying decision making: input-output methods and process-tracing approaches. In this section of the chapter we briefly compare and discuss each approach. For more details on the methods of decision research see Carroll and Johnson (1990). For a theoretical argument regarding different approaches to decision research, see Svenson (1996).

A. Input-Output Approaches

Rather than attempting to directly measure the decision process, input-output approaches postulate an underlying decision process and select factors that should affect the process in certain ways. Then an experiment is carried out to manipulate those factors (the input) and if the effects (the output) are as predicted, the researcher might claim that the experiment supported the hypothesized process. Abelson and Levi (1985) referred to this approach as the "structural" approach, that is, it determines the structure of the relationship between inputs and outputs.

To illustrate an input-output or structural approach to investigating judgment, consider work conducted by Lusk and Hammond (1991). The context of that work was severe weather forecasting, specifically the short-term forecasting (0–30 minutes) of microbursts (brief, localized windstorms that are a potentially fatal hazard to aircraft). As part of the work described by Lusk and Hammond, forecasters were presented with a set of hypothesized precursors to microbursts (cues) and were asked to judge the probability of the occurrence of a microburst based on the set of cue values representing a hypothetical storm. See Figure 2 for an example of a profile of storm cues.

By giving the forecasters a series of such profiles (the inputs) and recording the judged probabilities of microbursts for the various profiles (the outputs), a number of interesting questions about the structure of the judgments could be answered. For example, a common question is whether the judgments can be "captured" by a simple linear model in which the judged probabilities are a weighted function of the cue values. Typically, the observed judgments are related to the input values through the use of statistical techniques such as regression or analysis of variance. Lusk and Hammond (1991) reported that the judgments of their expert forecasters could be adequately represented by a linear model.

Lusk and Hammond's finding that a simple linear combination of cues fit the observed judgments well is quite common. Many studies have shown that judgments can be captured very successfully by a simple linear model based on a weighted combination of cue values (Slovic & Lichtenstein, 1971), even though in many of these studies, as in Lusk and Hammond, the subjects believed that they were in fact employing a more complex non-linear model.

Mellers et al. (1992) provided another good example of an input-output approach to decision research. In that study, subjects were asked to state their preferences for simple gambles using a variety of response modes. In addition to variations in response modes, experiments differed with respect to whether the gambles involved gains or losses and the presence of financial incentives. The gambles were constructed from a 6 × 6 (amount by probability) factorial design. Amounts ranged from $3 to $56.70 and the probabilities ranged from .05 to .94. In the actual task the only data point collected on each experimental trial was the preference expressed using one of the response modes. After the test trials, the subjects were asked to write a paragraph describing what they did. By examining the responses obtained and by fitting alternative models to the data using statistical procedures, Mellers et al. were able to show that the preference reversals they observed seemed to be due to changes in decision strategies as a function of response mode. One feature of the Mellers et al. experiments was that each subject generated approximately 108 judgments of single gambles and 225

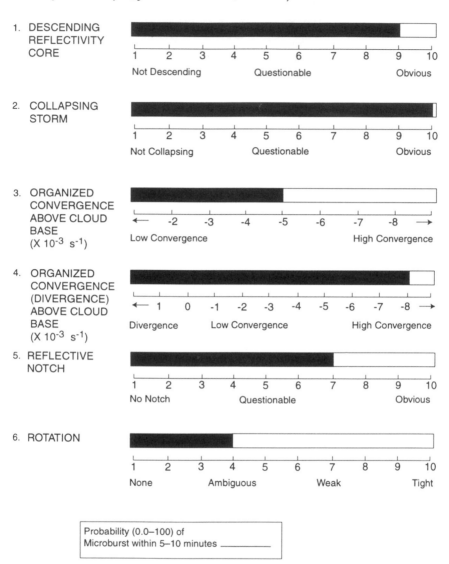

FIGURE 2   Example of microburst profile. From Figure 2 of "Example of a Microburst Profile," by C. A. Lusk and K. R. Hammond, 1991, *Journal of Behavioral Decision Making, 4,* p. 58. Copyright John Wiley & Sons Limited. Reproduced with permission.

comparative judgments of pairs of gambles, thus providing a large amount of data that could be used to relate changes in input (gambles and response modes) to changes in output (expressed preferences).

As noted earlier, there is a large body of research demonstrating that human judgment can be successfully captured by simple relatively linear models. There is a great deal of doubt, however, about whether the linear model, or simple variants like averaging, accurately reflects the underlying decision process (Hoffman, 1960). Dawes and Corrigan (1974), for example, argued that the characteristics of most decision tasks that have been studied almost ensure that the linear model will provide a good fit. It has also been shown that a simple linear model will fit simulated data generated by nonlinear rules reasonably well (Yntema & Torgerson, 1961). This is not to say that input-output analyses cannot be used to investigate how information is being processed in making a judgment or choice. Many studies have contributed greatly to our understanding of the psychology of decision making using input-output or structural approaches. However, a number of researchers have concluded that data reflecting more than just the end product of the decision process are needed. In the words of Pitz (1976), "If a theorist is seriously interested in the processes used by a subject in arriving at a decision, it is essential to devise a technique for exploring the predecisional behavior." A description of some of the techniques used in decision research to investigate process at a detailed level is presented next.

B. Process-Tracing Approaches

In process-tracing approaches, the researcher attempts to measure the ongoing decision process directly. The basic idea is to increase the density of observations about a decision process over the time course of that process. We will consider three major process-tracing methods: verbal protocols, information acquisition approaches, and, to a lesser extent, chronometric methods.

1. Verbal Protocols

Protocol analysis is one approach to gathering detailed process-tracing data on decision making (Adelman, Gualtieri, & Stanford, 1995; Payne, 1994; Payne, Braunstein, & Carroll, 1978; Schkade & Payne, 1994). To use this approach, the subject is asked to think out loud as he or she is actually performing the task of interest, such as choosing among several alternatives. Such a verbal record is called a protocol. Protocols differ from introspection or retrospective reports about decision processes because the subject is asked to verbalize thoughts as they occur in the course of making a decision. The protocol data are then analyzed to attempt to gain insights into the subject's decision processes. For example, Bettman and Park (1980a, 1980b) developed an extensive scheme for coding protocols which was used and expanded on by Biehal and Chakravarti (1982a, 1992b, 1983, 1989). The major advantage of protocol collection and analysis is that a great deal of data on internal events is made available.

The four panels of Figure 3 provide excerpts from the protocols of two subjects (*A* and *D*) faced with tasks characterized by two levels of complexity: (1) choice problems with two alternatives (Panels a and b), and (2) multialternative choice problems (Panels c and d) (Payne, 1976). The verbal

a Additive Utility	b Additive Difference
A24: O.K., the decision is now between the two rent prices A25: in accordance with the other qualities A26: Now apartment A has the advantage A27: because the noise level is low A28: and the kitchen facilities are good A29: even though the rent is $30 higher than B	D238: O.K., we have an A and a B D239: First look at the rent for both of them D240: The rent for A is $170 D241: The rent for B is $140 D242: $170 is a little steep D243: but it might have a low noise level D244: So we'll check A's noise level D245: A's noise level is low D246: We'll go to B's noise level D247: It's high D248: Gee, I can't really study very well with a lot of noise D249: So I'll ask myself the question, is it worth spending that extra $30 a month to be able to study in my apartment?
c Satisficing	d Elimination-by-Aspects
A163: The rent for apartment E is $140 A164: which is a good note A165: The noise level for the is apartment is high A166: That would almost deter me right there A167: Ah, I don't like a lot of noise A168: And, if it's high, it must be pretty bad A169: Which means, you couldn't sleep A170: I would just put that one aside right there. I wouldn't look any further than that A171: Even though, the rent is good	D289: Since we have a whole bunch here, D290: I'm going to go across the top and see which noise levels are high D291: If there are any high ones, I'll reject them immediately ..... D295: Go to D D296: It has a high noise level D297: So, we'll automatically eliminate D ..... D303: So, we have four here D304: that are O.K. in noise level

FIGURE 3   Verbal protocols of choice strategy. From Figure 4.4 of *The Adaptive Decision Maker*, by J. W. Payne, J. R. Bettman, and E. J. Johnson. Cambridge: Cambridge University Press, p. 152. Reprinted with the permission of Cambridge University Press.

protocols illustrate a variety of decision strategies, (e.g., satisficing and elimination by aspects). Further, by comparing Panels a and b to Panels c and d, we see that how people decide how to decide may be a function of the number of alternatives available (i.e., processing appears to be simplified in the case of several alternatives).

Although protocol analysis often allows the researcher to gain important insights into decision making, there are disadvantages. Collecting protocol data in quantity is extremely time-consuming, so small samples of subjects have typically been used. In addition, protocol data may not be entirely reflective of subjects' decision processes. The protocols may reflect subjects' biases or may be censored by subjects while they are being reported. In addition, subjects may be unable to verbalize retrospectively some internal processes (Nisbett & Wilson, 1977). Finally, protocols may not provide insights into all of the processing performed, and there may not be output corresponding to all internal states (Lindsay & Norman, 1972, pp. 517–520). Subjects may select aspects of processing to verbalize based upon what they believe is important and may not verbalize those data most valuable to the researcher (Frijda, 1967). Although such problems with selectivity in verbal reporting may exist, several researchers have argued and have provided convincing evidence that decision makers do have self-insight (e.g., Ericsson & Simon, 1993). For further discussion, see Lynch and Srull (1982); Biehal and Chakravarti (1989); Russo, Johnson, and Stephens (1989); Ericsson and Simon (1993); and Payne (1994).

There is also concern that attempting to observe the details of choice processes may affect those processes. For example, having to use processing capacity to verbalize ongoing thoughts might make subjects simplify their processing. Ericsson and Simon (1993) reported many studies showing no effects of taking protocols on decision processes. In studies of decision making, however, the results have been more mixed. Although Smead, Wilcox, and Wilkes (1981) and Biehal and Chakravarti (1983) reported no significant differences between protocol and no-protocol conditions, Biehal and Chakravarti (1989) found differences in the extent of alternative-based processing and problem framing due to verbal protocols. Therefore, although verbal protocols can provide invaluable data on choice processes, one must be very careful to control for any effects of taking protocols (see Biehal & Chakravarti, 1989, and Russo, Johnson, & Stephens, 1989, for suggestions).

2. Information Acquisition Approaches

Early attempts to monitor the amount and sequence of information acquired during decision making (e.g., Jacoby, 1975; Payne, 1976) used an information display board, often a matrix with brands as rows and attributes as columns. In each cell of the matrix, information cards were placed giving the value for the particular attribute and brand appearing in that row and column (e.g., the price for Brand X). Subjects were asked to examine as many cards as desired, one at a time, and choose a brand. The amount of information acquired and the order in which it was acquired were the major data provided. Therefore, by exerting control over the selection process, a detailed record of the sequence of information examined was obtained. This technique has been updated by using computer displays, (e.g., Brucks, 1988; Dahlstrand & Montgomery, 1984; Jacoby, Mazursky, Troutman, &

Kuss, 1984; Payne, Bettman, & Johnson, 1993; Payne & Braunstein, 1978), which can also be programmed to provide data on the time taken for each piece of information in addition to data on amount and sequences. An example of a computer-based information display used to monitor processing is given in Figure 4.

Information monitoring approaches have several disadvantages as measures of decision processes. First, the monitoring process is relatively obtrusive; subjects may bias or change their information-seeking behavior since it is so obviously under observation. Second, only external responses (namely which information is selected) are examined. Not only is internal processing not studied directly, but only a subset of the internal processing has an explicit trace in the information-seeking sequence. For example, the researcher does not observe any internal memory search that may take place in parallel with the external search through the matrix. However, the amount of time spent on an information acquisition may provide some insights on the amount of internal processing. Third, the normal matrix format for presenting the information makes it equally easy for a decision maker to process by alternative or by attribute, unlike many actual decision tasks in which information is organized by alternative (e.g., brands on supermarket shelves) and processing by alternative is thus relatively more easy than attribute processing. A matrix display also helps structure the decision problem by providing the alternatives and attributes. Brucks (1988) has addressed this problem by not presenting the alternatives and attributes to subjects.

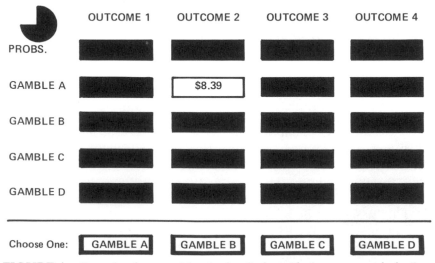

FIGURE 4   Example of a mouselab stimulus display with time pressure clock. From Figure 2 of "Adaptive Strategy Selection in Decision Making," by J. W. Payne, J. R. Bettman, and E. J. Johnson, 1988, *Journal of Experimental Psychology: Learning, Memory, and Cognition, 14,* p. 543. Copyright © 1988 by the American Psychological Association. Reprinted with permission.

Instead, subjects make inquiries about the attributes of the alternatives of interest using their own words, and the requested information is provided by artificial intelligence programs or unobtrusive human intervention.

Another approach for studying information acquisition is the analysis of eye movements (e.g., Pieters et al., 1997; Russo & Dosher, 1983; Russo & Leclerc, 1994; Russo & Rosen, 1975; van Raaij, 1977). Typically, the alternatives are displayed in tabular format on a screen in front of the subject (Russo & Dosher, 1983; Russo & Rosen, 1975) or as separate options (van Raaij, 1977). Specialized equipment records the sequence of eye movements used by the subject to examine the choice objects. The recording process may entail some restrictions to prevent large head movements, and the researcher must prevent subjects from using peripheral vision by providing relatively large separations between items in the visual display.

Eye movement data have several advantages: they provide a very detailed and dense trace of the information search; eye movements may be relatively more difficult for subjects to censor than verbal protocols; and eye movement data may be useful when protocols fail, such as studying processes that occur rapidly or which involve nonverbal representations or automated processes (Ericsson & Simon, 1993).

Eye movement data also pose problems, however. Collecting and analyzing such data is time-consuming, expensive, and usually uses small sample sizes. Also, the apparatus is obtrusive, so subjects are aware that their eye movements are being monitored. The choice stimuli used in eye movement studies have often been simplistic arrays because researchers must localize eye movements. Finally, eye movement data directions reveal only external search, not necessarily internal processes.

We have developed a computer-based information display that employs a mouse to control information acquisition (Payne, Bettman, and Johnson, 1993). Because pointing with the mouse is a relatively effortless response, Payne et al. have argued that it can approximate the detail provided by eye movements with much less cost. This acquisition system measures both the sequence and timing of information gathering in several different types of task environments.

3. Chronometric Analysis

Analysis of response times, or chronometric analysis, has also been used to study choice (e.g., Johnson & Russo, 1978; Sujan, 1985). The times taken to complete a response are the basic data collected, so that in a sense this is a form of input-output analysis where the output is total time. Researchers usually assume that the time taken directly reflects the amount of processing effort used in completing the task. By comparing the mean response times over different experimental conditions, it is hoped that one can learn about the information processing characterizing such tasks. For example, researchers have used such analyses to study the structure of memory (e.g., Johnson & Russo, 1978); to examine the usage of various heuristics for evaluating alternatives (e.g., Sujan, 1985); and to test models of cognitive effort in decision processes (Bettman, Johnson, & Payne, 1990).

This discussion of methods for studying decision making has been quite brief; more detail can be found in Carroll and Johnson (1990) and in Ford, Schmitt, Schechtman, Hults, and Doherty (1989). What is clear from even our brief discussion is that no method is perfect; rather, each has its own biases and disadvantages. Because the various methods have different strengths and weaknesses, using several complementary approaches in the same study seems to hold the greatest promise for separating the effects of the research method from those associated with the phenomenon under study.

Having discussed some basic concepts in behavioral decision research and some of the methods used to study decision making, we conclude with a discussion of an area we believe is particularly promising for future research, namely, how such "hot" psychological concepts as emotion, affect, and motivation may be combined with the more "cold" cognitive notions of bounded rationality to further our understanding of decision behavior.

VIII. EMOTIONAL FACTORS AND DECISION BEHAVIOR

Over the past 40 years, the emerging field of BDR has progressed from the neoclassical economic conceptualization that choice behavior follows normative, utility-maximizing guidelines to a conceptualization of choice behavior as a compromise between task environments and humans' limited information processing abilities. The work reviewed in this chapter demonstrates that these ideas of cognitive limitations, or bounded rationality, have been well integrated into our understanding of choice. However, at least one potentially relevant psychological aspect of decision makers—that they experience emotion, particularly negative emotion—has been less so. Negative emotion experienced by decision makers may influence reactions to decision task environments, and even the very prospect of having to make a decision may arouse negative emotion (e.g., Hogarth, 1987; Janis & Mann, 1977; Kahneman, 1993; Lopes, 1987; Simon, 1987).[1] Emotional or motivational influences on decision behavior have been gaining increasing attention

---

[1] Positive emotions are also relevant to, and may also impact, decision processes. We focus on negative emotion because negative emotion is often proposed to be commonly, or even inherently, associated with all but the most trivial decisions (e.g., Festinger, 1957; Janis & Mann, 1977; Larrick, 1993; Shepard, 1964; Tversky & Shafir, 1992).

(e.g., Beattie & Barlas, 1993; Larrick, 1993; Lopes, 1987; Simonson, 1992), although this work has yet to be well integrated into the majority of behavioral decision research.

Like cognitive limitations or bounded rationality, emotional factors may cause decision behavior to deviate from normative optimality. For instance, decision makers may cope with emotionally difficult decisions by using simplified heuristics, just as they often do with cognitively complex decisions. In fact, it seems that the concept of decision complexity, or any purely cognitive analysis, cannot fully explain the phenomenology of or the typical reactions to truly difficult decisions. For instance, Hogarth (1987) noted that conflict-avoidant heuristic decision rules may be attractive in part because they protect the decision maker from the distressing prospect of explicitly confronting value trade-offs. Some classic works also have noted that the resolution of these conflicts between important goals, which is necessary for the resolution of many decision situations, is inherently unpleasant (Festinger, 1957; Janis & Mann, 1977; Shepard, 1964). Thus, at least one of the variables that has been important in understanding cognitive limitations and decision difficulty, conflict among decision attributes, has also been recognized as potentially encouraging negative emotion. Next we outline the types of affect, including conflict among important goals, that may influence decision behavior. Then, we offer some suggestions regarding how to incorporate an understanding of emotion into theoretical approaches to decision behavior.

A. Sources of Emotion During Decision Making

Following Lazarus (1991), we conceptualize negative emotions as resulting from threats to important or valued goals (see also Frijda, 1988; Oatley & Jenkins, 1992). Thus, we consider how and when goals may be threatened during a decision task in order to define sources of emotion that may potentially influence the decision maker. We identify three such sources. Specifically, goals may become threatened, and hence negative emotion may be elicited (1) through the specific characteristics or consequences of relevant alternatives, (2) through more general characteristics of the decision task, and (3) through background characteristics influencing the decision maker but unrelated to the decision task itself. Each of these sources of decision-related emotion is discussed next.

1. Specific characteristics or aspects of decision alternatives may arouse emotion. These emotion–arousing context factors include the possible outcomes or consequences of considered alternatives, such as when a person investing a sum of money is distressed over the possibility of losing it (Janis & Mann, 1977; Simon, 1987). They also include conflict among goal-relevant

attributes, such as when an automobile purchaser feels she must sacrifice safety in return for monetary savings (Festinger, 1957; Janis & Mann, 1977; Tversky & Shafir, 1992). More generally, emotion-arousing context factors are present when the potential consequences associated with considered alternatives threaten a decision maker's goals.

2. More general characteristics of decision problems, such as time pressure or the amount of information to be considered, may cause negative emotion. By interfering with decision makers' abilities to process decision information, these task factors may threaten goals regarding decision accuracy. Emotional task factors may also indirectly threaten goals related to decision outcomes (e.g., a decision maker may worry about possible decision consequences if task factors seem to be compromising her ability to accurately resolve a decision). Thus, task factors should be particularly distressing when potential decision consequences involve high stakes or goal relevance. Emotion-arousing task factors have been studied under the rubric of "stress" and decision making (e.g., Ben Zur & Breznitz, 1981; Hancock & Warm, 1989; Keinan, 1987). However, it seems this research can be integrated into theory involving decision making under emotion, given recent movements to conceptualize psychological stress as simply a class of negative emotion (Lazarus, 1993).

3. Background or ambient sources of emotion, for instance an uncomfortable room temperature or a lingering negative mood, may influence decision processing. Thus, a decision maker may feel emotional when goals unrelated to the decision itself are threatened, and this emotion may influence her cognitive functioning during the decision task. Much of the literature on stress and decision making actually involves these ambient emotion sources. However, our interest is in emotion that is more directly related to the task itself, so we will now concentrate on the way that emotional task and context factors can be integrated into a theoretical understanding of choice. We believe this is an important new area of inquiry for BDR.

B. Influences of Emotion on Decision Behavior

It seems that emotion aroused by both context variables (e.g., potential decision consequences) and task variables (e.g., time pressure) may influence the process by which a decision is resolved. Explaining this influence of emotion on decision strategy selection will likely necessitate that current theoretical approaches to BDR be broadened. Recent movements in both psychology (e.g., Kruglanski & Webster, 1996; Kunda, 1990; Lazarus, 1991; Zajonc, 1980) and behavioral decision research (e.g., Kahneman, 1993; Larrick, 1993; Lopes, 1987) have encouraged such a broadening of theoretical approaches to encompass the interaction of emotion and cognition in determining behavior. We now discuss two possible approaches to broadening BDR theories to account for the influence of emotional task and context factors.

First, it seems possible that emotion will generally interfere with decision processes, degrading cognitive performance (e.g., Hancock & Warm, 1989). Thus, one could model the effects of negative emotion on decision processing by assuming that any cognitive operation will both take more time and contain more error as negative emotion is increased (see Eysenck, 1986, for the related idea that anxiety reduces short-term storage capacity and attentional control). This viewpoint implies that decision makers adapting to negative emotion will shift to easier-to-implement decision strategies in order to compensate for emotion-induced decreases in cognitive efficiency. Thus, this viewpoint implies that increasing negative emotion will function in a manner similar to increasing task complexity, causing a shift to simpler, easier-to-implement decision strategies.

A second possible theoretical view involves the idea that decision makers may more directly adapt to negative emotion itself, in addition to adapting to the effects of negative emotion on processing efficiency. Specifically, as the potential for negative emotion increases, people may choose decision strategies in the interest of coping with negative emotion, as well as choosing strategies in the interest of satisfying goals such as minimizing expended cognitive effort. This view is consistent with some of the more general literature on emotion and coping (e.g., Folkman & Lazarus, 1988; Lazarus, 1991). A coping approach leads to questions regarding which decision strategies will satisfy a proposed desire to cope and how they will do so. By considering this question, we have derived two more specific predictions regarding how decision strategies may be altered under an increasing potential for negative emotion. Each prediction is discussed next.

One way to cope with negative emotion is to make efforts to solve the environmental problem that is the source of that emotion. For instance, someone worried about the possibility of having cancer may cope with those emotions by making an appointment to see a doctor (i.e., see Folkman and Lazarus's problem-focused coping). Consistent with this coping mechanism, decision makers adapting to negative emotion may devote increased attention and effort to the decision task itself, attempting to ensure that the best possible decision is made. Thus, coping goals aroused by negative emotion may motivate a decision maker to work harder. This effect seems particularly likely when the experienced negative emotion is directly tied to possible decision consequences (i.e., when an emotional context factor is present), as it is when maximizing decision accuracy will potentially guard against undesired outcomes (e.g., Eysenck, 1986).

At the same time that they try to solve environmental problems, indirectly minimizing experienced negative emotions, decision makers may more directly act to mitigate or minimize negative emotion. For example, a person with health concerns may cope with the associated negative emotion by concentrating on a distracting hobby (i.e., see Folkman & Lazarus's emotion-focused coping). Consistent with this coping mechanism, individuals may process such that they avoid the most distressing aspect(s) of decision processing, especially as the emotional potential of the decision increases. Making explicit trade-offs between attributes is often considered to be particularly distressing (e.g., Hogarth, 1987). Thus, it seems that decision makers attempting to protect themselves from negative emotion may shift to simpler, more conflict-avoidant decision strategies. This may actually happen at the same time that the decision maker works harder (perhaps by processing more information or prolonging deliberation time), consistent with Folkman and Lazarus's (1980, 1988) findings that *both* problem-focused and emotion-focused coping strategies tend to be brought to bear on any emotional situation.

In conclusion, the two possible theoretical approaches outlined here yield similar, but not perfectly overlapping, predictions regarding decision behavior in negatively emotional environments. The processing efficiency approach argues that individuals will shift to simpler strategies under emotion, whereas the coping approach argues that decision makers will use strategies that simplify in some respects (e.g., shifting to conflict-avoidant rules) but that are more complex in other respects (e.g., processing information more completely or vigorously). Luce, Bettman, and Payne (1997) tested these predictions in three experiments and found evidence more consistent with the coping approach—decision processing became both more extensive and more conflict-avoidant under negative emotion.

IX. SUMMARY

In this chapter we have provided an overview of the field of behavioral decision research. As an area of active psychological inquiry, BDR is relatively young. The vast proportion of research on the psychology of decision making has occurred in the past two or three decades. Nevertheless, we have achieved a number of important insights into decision behavior. For example, it is clear that the classical economic man model of decision making is seriously flawed as a description of actual decision behavior. On a more positive note, we now understand a number of the strategies used to make judgments and choices and some of the task and context factors that determine when various strategies are used. We have also identified properties of decisions, such as loss aversion and the importance of the gain-versus-loss distinction, that are important for understanding risky choice.

The field of BDR has also developed a rich set of tools for investigating decisions and decision processing. Those tools are being applied to understand both cognitive and emotional influences on decision making. Another exciting trend in BDR is the fact that the results and methods of the field are increasingly being used to inform a wide variety of applied areas of study, including health, business, and public policy. Behavioral decision research holds promise for both a better understanding of how people make decisions and the development of better methods to aid decision making.

Acknowledgments

The research reported in this chapter was supported by a grant from the Decision, Risk, and Management Science Program of the National Science Foundation.

References

Abelson, R. P., & Levi, A. (1985). Decision making and decision theory. In G. Lindzey & E. Aronson (Eds.), *The handbook of social psychology, Vol. 1* (pp. 231–309). New York: Random House.

Adelman, L., Gualtieri, J., & Stanford, S. (1995). Effects of earned focus on the option generation process: An experiment using protocol analysis. *Organizational Behavior and Human Decision Processes, 61,* 54–66.

Anderson, N. H. (1981). *Foundations of information integration theory.* New York: Academic Press.

Aschenbrenner, K. M. (1978). Single-peaked risk preferences and their dependability on the gambles' presentation mode. *Journal of Experimental Psychology: Human Perception and Performance, 4,* 513–520.

Aschenbrenner, K. M., Bockenholt, U., Albert, D., & Schmalhofer, F. (1986). The selection of dimensions when choosing between multiattribute alternatives. In R. W. Scholz (Ed.), *Current issues in West German decision research* (pp. 63–78). Frankfurt: Lang.

Bar-Hillel, M. (1984). Representativeness and fallacies of probability judgment. *Acta Psychologica, 55,* 91–107.

Bar-Hillel, M. (1990). Back to base-rates. In R. M. Hogarth (Ed.), *Insights in decision making: Theory and applications—A tribute to Hillel J. Einhorn* (pp. 200–216). Chicago: University of Chicago Press.

Baron, J., & Spranca, M. (1997). Protected values. *Organizational Behavior and Human Decision Processes,* in press.

Beach, L. R. (1990). *Image theory: Decision making in personal and organizational contexts.* Chichester: John Wiley.

Beach, L. R. (1993). Broadening the definition of decision making: The role of prechoice screening of options. *Psychological Science, 4,* 215–220.

Beach, L. R., Barnes, V. E., & Christensen-Szalanski, J. J. J. (1986). Beyond heuristics and biases: A contingency model of judgmental forecasting. *Journal of Forecasting, 5,* 143–157.

Beattie, J., & Barlas, S. (1993). Predicting perceived differences in tradeoff difficulty. Working paper, University of Sussex, Sussex, England.

Beattie, J., & Baron, J. (1991). Investigating the effect of stimulus range on attribute weight. *Journal of Experimental Psychology: Human Perception and Performance, 17,* 571–585.

Bell, D. E. (1982). Regret in decision making under uncertainty. *Operations Research, 30,* 961–981.

Bell, D. E. (1985). Disappointment in decision making under uncertainty. *Operations Research, 33,* 1–27.

Ben Zur, H., & Breznitz, S. J. (1981). The effects of time pressure on risky choice behavior. *Acta Psychologica, 47*, 89–104.

Bettman, J. R. (1979). *An information processing theory of consumer choice.* Reading, MA: Addison Wesley.

Bettman, J. R., Johnson, E. J., & Payne, J. W. (1990). A componential analysis of cognitive effort in choice. *Organizational Behavior and Human Decision Processes, 45*, 111–139.

Bettman, J. R., & Kakkar, P. (1977). Effects of information presentation format on consumer information acquisition strategies. *Journal of Consumer Research, 3*, 233–240.

Bettman, J. R., & Park, C. W. (1980a). Effects of prior knowledge and experience and phase of the choice process on consumer decision processes: A protocol analysis. *Journal of Consumer Research, 7*, 234–248.

Bettman, J. R., & Park, C. W. (1980b). Implications of a constructive view of choice for analysis of protocol data: A coding scheme for elements of choice processes. In J. C. Olson (Ed.), *Advances in consumer research, Vol. 7* (pp. 148–153). Ann Arbor, MI: Association for Consumer Research.

Biehal, G. J., & Chakravarti, D. (1982a). Experiences with the Bettman-Park verbal protocol coding scheme. *Journal of Consumer Research, 8*, 442–448.

Biehal, G. J., & Chakravarti, D. (1982b). Information presentation format and learning goals as determinants of consumers' memory retrieval and choice processes. *Journal of Consumer Research, 8*, 431–441.

Biehal, G. J., & Chakravarti, D. (1983). Information accessibility as a moderator of consumer choice. *Journal of Consumer Research, 10*, 1–14.

Biehal, G. J., & Chakravarti, D. (1989). The effects of concurrent verbalization on choice processing. *Journal of Marketing Research, 26*, 84–96.

Billings, R. S., & Marcus, S. A. (1983). Measures of compensatory and noncompensatory models of decision behavior: Process tracing versus policy capturing. *Organizational Behavior and Human Performance, 31*, 331–352.

Birnbaum, M. H. (1974). The nonadditivity of personality impressions. *Journal of Experimental Psychology, 102*, 543–561.

Birnbaum, M. H. (1983). Base rates in Bayesian inference: Signal detection analysis of the cab problem. *American Journal of Psychology, 96*, 85–94.

Birnbaum, M. H., & Beeghley, D. (1997). Violations of branch independence in judgments of the value of gambles. *Psychological Science, 8*, 87–94.

Birnbaum, M. H., Coffey, G., Mellers, B. A., & Weiss, R. (1992). Utility measurement: Configural-weight theory and the judge's point of view. *Journal of Experimental Psychology: Human Perception & Performance, 18*, 331–346.

Bockenholt, U., Albert, D., Aschenbrenner, M., & Schmalhofer, F. (1991). The effects of attractiveness, dominance, and attribute differences on information acquisition in multiattribute binary choice. *Organizational Behavior and Human Decision Processes, 49*, 281.

Bostic, R., Herrnstein, R. J., & Luce, R. D. (1990). The effect on the preference reversal phenomenon of using choice indifferences. *Journal of Economic Behavior and Organization, 13*, 193–212.

Brucks, M. (1988). Search monitor: An approach for computer-controlled experimenting consumer information search. *Journal of Consumer Research, 15*, 117–121.

Budescu, D. V., Weinberg, S., & Wallsten, T. S. (1988). Decisions based on numerically and verbally expressed uncertainties. *Journal of Experimental Psychology: Human Performance, 14*, 281–294.

Butler, S. A. (1986). Anchoring in the judgmental evaluation of audit samples. Review, 61, 101–111.

Camerer, C. F. (1987). Do biases in probability judgment matter in markets? Experimental evidence. *American Economic Review, 77*, 981–997.

Camerer, C. F. (1989). An experimental test of several generalized utility theories. *Journal of Risk and Uncertainty, 2,* 61–104.

Camerer, C., & Johnson, E. J. (1991). The process-performance paradox in expert judgment: How can experts know so much and predict so badly? In A. Ericsson and J. Smith (Eds.), *The study of expertise: Prospects and limits* (pp. 195–207). Cambridge: Cambridge University Press.

Carroll, J. S., & Johnson, E. J. (1990). *Decision research: A field guide.* Newbury Park, CA: Sage.

Casey, J. T. (1991). Reversal of the preference reversal phenomenon. *Organizational Behavior and Human Decision Processes, 48,* 224–251.

Champagne, M., & Stevenson, M. K. (1994). Contrasting models of appraisals judgments for positive and negative purposes using policy modeling. *Organizational Behavior and Human Decision Processes, 59,* 93–123.

Chapman, G. B., & Johnson, E. J. (1994). The limits of anchoring. *Journal of Behavioral Decision Making, 7,* 223–242.

Coombs, C. H., Dawes, R. M., & Tversky, A. (1970). *Mathematical psychology: An elementary introduction.* Englewood Cliffs, NJ: Prentice-Hall.

Coupey, E. (1994). Restructuring: Constructive processing of information displays in consumer choice. *Journal of Consumer Research, 21,* 83–99.

Coupey, E., Irwin, J. R., & Payne, J. W. (in press). Product category familiarity and preference construction. *Journal of Consumer Research.*

Cox, A. D., & Summers, J. D. (1987). Heuristics and biases in the intuitive projection of retail sales. *Journal of Marketing Research, 24,* 290–297.

Crandall, C. S., & Greenfield, B. (1986). Understanding the conjunction fallacy: A conjunction of effects? *Social Cognition, 4,* 408–419.

Creyer, E. H., & Johar, G. V. (1995). Response mode bias in the formation of preference: Boundary conditions of the prominence effect. *Organizational Behavior and Human Decision Processes, 62,* 14–22.

Curley, S. P., Browne, G. J., Smith, G. F., & Benson, P. G. (1995). Arguments in the practical reasoning underlying constructed probability responses. *Journal of Behavioral Decision Making, 8,* 1–20.

Curley, S. P., & Yates, J. F. (1989). An empirical evaluation of descriptive models of ambiguity reactions in choice situations. *Journal of Mathematical Psychology, 33,* 397–427.

Curley, S. P., Yates, J. F., & Abrams, R. A. (1986). Psychological sources of ambiguity avoidance. *Organizational Behavior and Human Decision Processes, 38,* 230–256.

Dahlstrand, U., & Montgomery, H. (1984). Information search and evaluative processes in decision making: A computer based process tracing study. *Acta Psychologica, 56,* 113–123.

Davis, H. L., Hoch, S. J., & Ragsdale, E. K. (1986). An anchoring and adjustment model of spousal predictions. *Journal of Consumer Research, 13,* 25–37.

Dawes, R. M. (1979). The robust beauty of improper linear models in decision making. *American Psychologist, 34,* 571–582.

Dawes, R. M. (1994). *House of cards: Psychology and psychotherapy.* New York: The Free Press.

Dawes, R. M., & Corrigan, B. (1974). Linear models in decision making. *Psychological Bulletin, 81,* 95–106.

Dawes, R. M., Mirels, H. L., Gold, E., & Donahue, E. (1993). Equating inverse probabilities in implicit personality judgments. *Psychological Science, 4,* 396–400.

Delquié, P. (1993). Inconsistent trade-offs between attributes: New evidence in preference assessment biases. *Management Science, 39,* 1382–1395.

Dube-Rioux, L., & Russo, J. E. (1988). An availability bias in professional judgment. *Journal of Behavioral Decision Making, 1,* 223–237.

Edwards, W., & Tversky, A. (Eds.) (1967). *Decision making.* Harmondsworth, UK: Penguin.

Einhorn, H. J., & Hogarth, R. M. (1975). Unit weighting schemes for decision making. *Organizational Behavior and Human Performance, 13,* 171–192.

Einhorn, H. J., & Hogarth, R. M. (1985). Ambiguity and uncertainty in probabilistic inference. *Psychological Review, 93,* 433–461.

Einhorn, H. J., & Hogarth, R. M. (1986). Decision making under ambiguity. *Journal of Business, 59,* S225–S250.

Ellsberg, D. (1961). Risk, ambiguity, and the Savage axioms. *Quarterly Journal of Economics, 75,* 643–669.

Erev, I., & Cohen, B. L. (1990). Verbal versus numerical probabilities: Efficiency, biases, and the preference paradox. *Organizational Behavior and Human Decision Processes, 45,* 1–18.

Ericsson, K. A., & Simon, H. A. (1993). *Protocol analysis: Verbal reports as data* (Rev. ed.). Cambridge, MA: MIT Press.

Eysenck, M. W. (1986). *A handbook of cognitive psychology.* London: Erlbaum.

Fennema, H., & Wakker, P. (1997). Original and cumulative prospect theory: A discussion of empirical differences. *Journal of Behavioral Decision Making, 10,* 53–64.

Festinger, L. (1957). *A theory of cognitive dissonance.* Evanston, IL: Row, Peterson.

Fischer, G. W., & Hawkins, S. A. (1993). Strategy compatibility, scale compatibility, and the prominence effect. *Journal of Experimental Psychology: Human Perception and Performance, 19,* 580–597.

Fischer, G. W., Kamlet, M. S., Fienberg, S. E., & Schkade, D. (1986). Risk preferences for gains and losses in multiple objective decision making. *Management Science, 32,* 1065–1086.

Fischhoff, B. (1975). Hindsight ≠ foresight: The effect of outcome knowledge on judgment under uncertainty. *Journal of Experimental Psychology: Human Perception and Performance, 1,* 288–299.

Fischhoff, B., & Beyth-Marom, R. (1983). Hypothesis evaluation from a Bayesian perspective. *Psychological Review, 90,* 239–260.

Fischhoff, B., Slovic, P., & Lichtenstein, S. (1978). Fault trees: Sensitivity of estimated failure probabilities to problem representation. *Journal of Experimental Psychology: Human Perception and Performance, 4,* 330–344.

Fishburn, P. (1991). Nontransitive preferences in decision theory. *Journal of Risk and Uncertainty, 4,* 113–124.

Fisk, J. E. (1996). The conjunction effect: Fallacy or Bayesion inference? *Organizational Behavior and Human Decision Processes, 67,* 76–90.

Folkes, V. S. (1988). The availability heuristic and perceived risk. *Journal of Consumer Research, 15,* 13–23.

Folkman, S., & Lazarus, R. S. (1980). An analysis of coping in a middle-aged community sample. *Journal of Health and Social Behavior, 21,* 219–239.

Folkman, S., & Lazarus, R. S. (1988). Coping as a mediator of emotion. *Journal of Personality and Social Psychology, 54,* 466–475.

Ford, J. K., Schmitt, N., Schechtman, S. L., Hults, B. M., & Doherty, M. L. (1989). Process tracing methods: Contributions, problems, and neglected research questions. *Organizational Behavior and Human Decision Processes, 43,* 75–117.

Fox, C. R., Rogers, B. A., & Tversky, A. (1996). Options traders exhibit subadditive decision weights. *Journal of Risk and Uncertainty, 13,* 5–19.

Frijda, N. H. (1967). Problems of computer simulation. *Behavioral Science, 12,* 59–67.

Frijda, N. H. (1988). *The emotions.* Cambridge, England: Cambridge University Press.

Frisch, D., & Baron, J. (1988). Ambiguity and rationality. *Journal of Behavioral Decision Making, 1,* 149–157.

Gaeth, G. J., & Shanteau, J. (1984). Reducing the influence of irrelevant information on experienced decision makers. *Organizational Behavior and Human Performance, 33,* 263–282.

Garb, H. N. (1989). Clinical judgment, clinical training and professional experience. *Psychological Bulletin, 105,* 387–396.

Gettys, C. F., Pliske, R. M., Manning, C., & Casey, J. T. (1987). An evaluation of human act generation performance. *Organizational Behavior and Human Decision Processes, 39,* 23–51.

Gigerenzer, G., & Goldstein, D. G. (1996). Reasoning the fast and frugal way: Models of bounded rationality. *Psychological Review, 103,* 650–669.

Gigerenzer, G., Hell, W., & Blank, H. (1988). Presentation and content: The use of base rates as a continuous variable. *Journal of Experimental Psychology: Human Perception and Performance, 14,* 513–525.

Gigerenzer, G., Hoffrage, U., & Kleinbolting, H. (1991). Probabilistic mental models: A Brunswikian theory of confidence. *Psychological Review, 98,* 506–528.

Ginossar, Z., & Trope, Y. (1987). Problem solving in judgment under uncertainty. *Journal of Personality and Social Psychology, 52,* 464–474.

Goldstein, W. M. (1990). Judgments of relative importance in decision making: Global vs. local interpretations of subjective weight. *Organizational Behavior and Human Decision Processes, 47,* 313–336.

Goldstein, W. M., & Einhorn, H. J. (1987). Expression theory and the preference reversal phenomena. *Psychological Review, 94,* 236–254.

González-Vallejo, C., & Wallsten, T. S. (1992). Effects of probability mode on preference reversal. *Journal of Experimental Psychology: Learning, Memory, and Cognition, 18,* 855–864.

Grether, D. M., Schwartz, A., & Wilde, L. L. (1986). The irrelevance of information overload: An analysis of search and disclosure. *Southern California Law Review, 59,* 277–303.

Grether, D. M., & Wilde, L. L. (1983). Consumer choice and information: New experimental evidence. *Information Economics and Policy, 1,* 115–144.

Griffin, D., & Tversky, A. (1992). The weighing of evidence and the determinants of confidence. *Cognitive Psychology, 24,* 411–435.

Hammond, K. R. (1996). *Human judgment and social policy.* Oxford: Oxford University Press.

Hammond, K. R., Hamm, R. M., Grassia, J., & Pearson, T. (1987). Direct comparison of the efficacy of intuitive and analytical cognition in expert judgment. *IEEE Transactions on Systems, Man, and Cybernetics, 17,* 753–770.

Hancock, P. A., & Warm, J. S. (1989). A dynamic model of stress and sustained attention. *Human Factors, 31,* 519–537.

Hastie, R., & Park, B. (1986). The relationship between memory and judgment depends on whether the judgment task is memory-based or on-line. *Psychological Review, 93,* 258–268.

Hawkins, S. A. (1994). Information processing strategies in riskless preference reversals: The prominence effect. *Organizational Behavior and Human Decision Processes, 59,* 1–26.

Hawkins, S. A., & Hastie, R. (1990). Hindsight: Biased judgments of past events after the outcomes are known. *Psychological Bulletin, 107,* 311–327.

Heath, C., & Tversky, A. (1991). Preference and belief: Ambiguity and competence in choice under uncertainty. *Journal of Risk and Uncertainty, 4,* 5–28.

Heath, T. B., & Chatterjee, S. (1995). Asymmetric decoy effects on lower-quality versus higher-quality brands: Meta-analytic and experimental evidence. *Journal of Consumer Research, 22,* 268–284.

Hershey, J. C., & Schoemaker, P. J. H. (1985). Probability versus certainty equivalence methods in utility measurement: Are they equivalent? *Management Science, 31,* 1213–1231.

Highhouse, S., & House, E. L. (1995). Missing information in selection. An application of the Einhorn-Hogarth Ambiguity Model. *Journal of Applied Psychology, 80,* 81–93.

Highhouse, S., & Johnson, M. A. (1996). Gain/loss asymmetry and riskless choice: Loss aversion among job finalists. *Organizational Behavior and Human Decision Processes, 68,* 225–233.

Hinz, V. B., Tinsdale, R. S., & Vollrath, D. A. (1997). The emerging conceptualization of groups as information processors. *Psychological Bulletin, 121,* 43–64.

Hoffman, P. J. (1960). The paramorphic representation of clinical judgment. *Psychological Bulletin, 57,* 116–131.

Hogarth, R. M. (1987). *Judgment and choice* (2nd ed.). New York: John Wiley.

Hogarth, R. M., & Einhorn, H. J. (1992). Order effects in belief updating: The belief-adjustment model. *Cognitive Psychology, 24,* 1–55.

Hogarth, R. M., & Kunreuther, H. (1985). Ambiguity and insurance decisions. *American Economic Review, 75,* 386–390.

Hogarth, R. M., & Kunreuther, H. (1989). Risk, ambiguity, and insurance. *Journal of Risk and Uncertainty, 2,* 5–35.

Hogarth, R. M., & Kunreuther, H. (1995). Decision making under ignorance: Arguing with yourself. *Journal of Risk and Uncertainty, 10,* 15–36.

Hsee, C. K. (1996). The evaluability hypothesis: An explanation for preference reversals between joint and separate evaluations of alternatives. *Organizational Behavior and Human Decision Processes, 67,* 247–257.

Huber, J., Payne, J. W., & Puto, C. P. (1982). Adding asymmetrically dominated alternatives. Violations of regularity and the similarity hypothesis. *Journal of Consumer Research, 9,* 90–98.

Huber, V. L., Neale, M. A., & Northcraft, G. B. (1987). Decision bias and personnel selection strategies. *Organizational Behavior and Human Decision Processes, 40,* 136–147.

Jacoby, J. (1975). Perspectives on a consumer information processing research program. *Communication Research, 2,* 203–215.

Jacoby, J., Mazursky, D., Troutman, T., & Kuss, A. (1984). When feedback is ignored: Disutility of outcome feedback. *Journal of Applied Psychology, 69,* 531–545.

Jagacinski, C. M. (1995). Distinguishing adding and averaging models in a personnel selection task: When missing information matters. *Organizational Behavior and Human Decision Processes, 61,* 1–15.

Janis, I. L., & Mann, L. (1977). Decision making. New York: The Free Press.

Jarvenpaa, S. L. (1989). The effect of task demands and graphical format on information processing strategies. *Management Science, 35,* 285–303.

Joag, S. G., Mowen, J. C., & Gentry, J. W. (1990). Risk perception in a simulated industrial purchasing task: The effects of single versus multi-play decisions. *Journal of Behavioral Decision Making, 3,* 91–108.

Johnson, E. J., Meyer, R. M., & Ghose, S. (1989). When choice models fail: Compensatory representations in negatively correlated environments. *Journal of Marketing Research, 26,* 255–270.

Johnson, E. J., Payne, J. W., & Bettman, J. R. (1988). Information displays and preference reversals. *Organizational Behavior and Human Decision Process, 42,* 1–21.

Johnson, E. J., & Russo, J. E. (1978). The organization of product information in memory identified by recall times. In H. K. Hunt (Ed.), *Advances in consumer research, Vol. 5* (pp. 79–86). Chicago: Association for Consumer Research.

Jones, S. K., Jones, K. T., & Frisch, D. (1995). Baises of probability assessment: A comparison of frequency and single-case judgments. *Organizational Behavior and Human Decision Processes, 61,* 109–122.

Jones, D. R., & Schkade, D. A. (1995). Choosing and translating between problem representations. *Organizational Behavior and Human Decision Processes, 61,* 213–223.

Kahneman, D. (1993, November). J/DM President's Address. Paper presented at the meeting of the Judgment/Decision Making Society, Washington, D.C.

Kahneman, D., Knetsch, J. L., & Thaler, R. (1990). Experimental tests of the endowment effect and the Coase theorem. *Journal of Political Economy, 98,* 1325–1348.

Kahneman, D., & Lovallo, D. (1992). Timid decisions and bold forecasts: A cognitive perspective on risk taking. *Management Science, 39,* 17–31.

Kahneman, D., & Tversky, A. (1973). On the psychology of prediction. *Psychological Review,* *80,* 237–251.

Kahneman, D., & Tversky, A. (1996). On the reality of cognitive illusions. *Psychological Review, 103,* 582–591.

Keeney, R. L., & Raiffa, H. (1976). *Decisions with multiple objectives: Preferences and value trade-offs.* New York: Wiley.

Keinan, G. (1987). Decision making under stress: Scanning of alternatives under controllable and uncontrollable threats. *Journal of Personality and Social Psychology, 52,* 639–644.

Keller, K. L., & Staelin, R. (1987). Effects of quality and quantity of information on decision effectiveness. *Journal of Consumer Research, 14,* 200–213.

Keller, L. R., & Ho, J. L. (1988). Decision problem structuring: Generating options. *IEEE Transactions on Systems, Man, and Cybernetics, 18,* 715–728.

Keren, G., & Wagenaar, W. A. (1987). Violation of utility theory in unique and repeated gambles. *Journal of Experimental Psychology: Learning, Memory, and Cognition, 13,* 387–391.

Kerr, N. L., MacCoun, R. J., & Kramer, G. P. (1996). Bias in judgment: Comparing individuals and groups. *Psychological Review, 103,* 687–719.

Klayman, J. (1985). Children's decision strategies and their adaptation to task characteristics. *Organizational Behavior and Human Decision Processes, 35,* 179–201.

Klayman, J. (1988). Cue discovery in probabilistic environments: Uncertainty and experimentation. *Journal of Experimental Psychology: Learning, Memory, and Cognition, 14,* 317–330.

Klein, G., Wolf, S., Militello, L., & Zsambok, C. (1995). Characteristics of skilled option generation in chess. *Organizational Behavior and Human Decision Processes, 62,* 62–69.

Koehler, J. J. (1996). The base rate fallacy reconsidered: Descriptive, normative, and methodological challenges. *Behavioral and Brain Sciences, 19,* 1–53.

Koehler, J. J., Gibbs, B. J., & Hogarth, R. M. (1994). Shattering illusion of control: Multi-shot versus single-shot gambles. *Journal of Behavioral Decision Making, 7,* 183–191.

Kramer, R. M. (1989). Windows of vulnerability or cognitive illusions? Cognitive processes and the nuclear arms race. *Journal of Experimental Social Psychology, 25,* 79–100.

Kruglanski, A. W., & Webster, D. M. (1996). Motivated closing of the mind: "Seizing" and "Freezing." *Psychological Review, 103,* 263–283.

Kunda, Z. (1990). The case for motivated reasoning. *Psychological Bulletin, 108,* 480–498.

Larrick, R. P. (1993). Motivational factors in decision theories: The role of self-protection. *Psychological Bulletin, 113,* 440–450.

Lazarus, R. S. (1991). Progress on a cognitive-motivational-relational theory of emotion. *American Psychologist 46,* 819–834.

Lazarus, R. S. (1993). From psychological stress to the emotions: A history of changing outlooks. *Annual Review of Psychology, 44,* 1–21.

Levi, A. S., & Pryor, J. B. (1987). Use of the availability heuristic in probability estimates of future events: The effects of imaging outcomes versus imagining reasons. *Organizational Behavior and Human Decision Processes, 40,* 219–234.

Levin, I. P., & Gaeth, G. J. (1988). How consumers are affected by the framing of attribute information before and after consuming the product. *Journal of Consumer Research, 15,* 374–378.

Libby, R. (1985). Availability and the generation of hypotheses in analytical review. *Journal of Accounting Research, 23,* 648–667.

Lichtenstein, M., & Srull, T. K. (1985). Conceptual and methodological issues in examining the relationship between consumer memory and judgment. In L. F. Alwitt & A. A. Mitchell (Eds.), *Psychological processes and advertising effects: Theory, research, and application* (pp. 113–128). Hillsdale, NJ: Erlbaum.

Lichtenstein, S., & Slovic, P. (1971). Reversals of preference between bids and choices in gambling decisions. *Journal of Experimental Psychology, 89,* 46–55.

Lindsay, P. H., & Norman, D. A. (1972). *Human information processing.* New York: Academic Press.

Linville, P. W., & Fischer, G. W. (1991). Preferences for separating or combining events. *Journal of Personality and Social Psychology, 59,* 5–21.

Loomes, G., & Sugden, R. (1987). Some implications of a more general form of regret. *Journal of Economic Theory, 92,* 805–824.

Lopes, L. L. (1981). Decision making in the short run. *Journal of Experimental Psychology: Human Learning and Memory, 7,* 377–385.

Lopes, L. L. (1987). Between hope and fear: The psychology of risk. *Advances in Experimental Social Psychology, 20,* 255–295.

Luce, M. F., Bettman, J. R., & Payne, J. W. (1997). Choice processing in emotionally difficult decisions. *Journal of Experimental Psychology: Learning, Memory, and Cognition, 23,* 384–405.

Luce, R. D. (1990). Rational versus plausible accounting equivalences in preference judgments. *Psychological Science, 1,* 225–234.

Luce, R. D., & Fishburn, P. C. (1991). Rank- and sign-dependent linear utility models for finite first-order gambles. *Journal of Risk and Uncertainty, 1,* 29–59.

Lusk, C. M., & Hammond, K. R. (1991). Judgment in a dynamic task: Microburst forecasting. *Journal of Behavioral Decision Making, 4,* 55–73.

Lynch, J. G., & Srull, T. K. (1982). Memory and attentional factors in consumer choice: Concepts and research methods. *Journal of Consumer Research, 9,* 18–37.

MacGregor, D., & Slovic, P. (1986). Graphical representation of judgmental information. *Human-Computer Interaction, 2,* 179–200.

Machina, M. J. (1987). Decision-making in the presence of risk. *Science, 236,* 537–543.

MacLeod, C., & Campbell, L. (1992). Memory accessibility and probability judgments: An experimental evaluation of the availability heuristic. *Journal of Personality and Social Psychology, 63,* 890–902.

McFadden, D. (1981). Econometric models of probabilistic choice. In C. F. Manski & D. McFadden (Eds.), *Structural analysis of discrete data with econometric applications* (pp. 198–272). Cambridge, MA: MIT Press.

March, J. G. (1978). Bounded rationality, ambiguity, and the engineering of choice. *Bell Journal of Economics, 9,* 587–608.

Medin, D. L., & Edelson, S. M. (1988). Problem structure and the use of base-rate information from experience. *Journal of Experimental Psychology: General, 117,* 68–85.

Mellers, B. A., Ordóñez, L. D., & Birnbaum, M. H. (1992). A change of process theory for contextual effects and preference reversals in risky decision making. *Organizational Behavior and Human Decision Processes, 52,* 331–369.

Meyer, R. J., & Johnson, E. J. (1989). Information overload and the nonrobustness of linear models: A comment on Keller and Staelin. *Journal of Consumer Research, 15,* 498–503.

Meyer, R. J., & Kahn, B. (1991). Probabilistic models of consumer choice behavior. In T. S. Robertson & H. H. Kassarjian (Eds.), *Handbook of consumer behavior* (pp. 85–123). Englewood Cliffs, NJ: Prentice-Hall.

Montgomery, H. (1983). Decision rules and the search for a dominance structure: Towards a process model of decision making. In P. C. Humphreys, O. Svenson, & A. Vari (Eds.), *Analyzing and aiding decision processes* (pp. 343–369). North Holland: Amsterdam.

Nisbett, R. E., & Wilson, T. D. (1977). Telling more than we can know: Verbal reports on mental processes. *Psychological Review, 84,* 231–259.

Northcraft, G. B., & Neale, M. A. (1987). Experts, amateurs, and real estate: An anchoring-and-adjustment perspective on property pricing decisions. *Organizational Behavior and Human Decision Processes, 39,* 84–97.

Oatley, K., & Jenkins, J. M. (1992). Human emotions: Function and dysfunction. *Annual Review of Psychology, 43,* 55–85.

Önken, J., Hastie, R., & Revelle, W. (1985). Individual differences in the use of simplification strategies in a complex decision-making task. *Journal of Experimental Psychology: Human Perception and Performance, 11,* 14–27.

Paese, P. W. (1995). Effects of framing on actual time allocation decisions. *Organizational Behavior and Human Decision Processes, 61,* 67–76.

Payne, J. W. (1976). Task complexity and contingent processing in decision making: An information search and protocol analysis. *Organizational Behavior and Human Performance, 16,* 366–387.

Payne, J. W. (1994). Thinking aloud: Insights into information processing. *Psychological Science, 5,* 241, 245–248.

Payne, J. W., Bettman, J. R., & Johnson, E. J. (1988). Adaptive strategy selection in decision making. *Journal of Experimental Psychology: Learning, Memory, and Cognition, 14,* 534–552.

Payne, J. W., Bettman, J. R., & Johnson, E. J. (1993). *The adaptive decision maker.* Cambridge: Cambridge University Press.

Payne, J. W., Bettman, J. R., & Luce, M. F. (1996). When time is money: Decision behavior under opportunity-cost time pressure. *Organizational Behavior and Human Decision Processes, 66,* 131–152.

Payne, J. W., & Braunstein, M. L. (1978). Risky choice: An examination of information acquisition behavior. *Memory & Cognition, 6,* 554–561.

Payne, J. W., Braunstein, M. L., & Carroll, J. S. (1978). Exploring predecisional behavior: An alternative approach to decision research. *Organizational Behavior and Human Performance, 22,* 17–44.

Payne, J. W., Laughhunn, D. J., & Crum, R. (1984). Multiattribute risky choice behavior: The editing of complex prospects. *Management Science, 30,* 1350–1361.

Phillips, L. C., & Edwards, W. (1966). Conservatism in a simple probability inference task. *Journal of Experimental Psychology, 72,* 346–354.

Pieters, R., Warlop, L., & Hartog, M. (1997). The effects of time pressure and task motivation in visual attention to brands. *Advances in Consumer Research, 24,* 281–287.

Pitz, G. F. (1976). Decision making and cognition. In H. Jungermann & G. de Zeeuw (Eds.), *Decision making and change in human affairs* (pp. 403–424). Dordrecht, Netherlands: D. Reidel.

Puto, C. P. (1987). The framing of buying decisions. *Journal of Consumer Research, 14,* 301–315.

Quiggin, J. (1982). A theory of anticipated utility. *Journal of Economic Behavior and Organizations, 3,* 323–343.

Ratneshwar, S., Shocker, A. D., & Stewart, D. W. (1987). Toward understanding the attraction effect: The implications of product stimulus meaningfulness and familiarity. *Journal of Consumer Research, 13,* 520–533.

Redelmeir, D. A., & Tversky, A. (1990). Discrepancy between medical decisions for individual patients and for groups. *New England Journal of Medicine, 322,* 1162–1164.

Reeves, T., & Lockhart, R. S. (1993). Distributional vs. singular approaches to probability and errors in probabilistic reasoning. *Journal of Experimental Psychology: General, 122,* 207–226.

Rottenstreich, Y., & Tversky, A. (1997). Unpacking, repacking, and anchoring: Advances in support theory. *Psychological Review, 104,* 406–415.

Russo, J. E. (1977). The value of unit price information. *Journal of Marketing Research, 14,* 193–201.

Russo, J. E., & Dosher, B. A. (1983). Strategies for multiattribute binary choice. *Journal of Experimental Psychology: Learning, Memory, and Cognition, 9,* 676–696.

Russo, J. E., Johnson, E. J., & Stephens, D. M. (1989). The validity of verbal protocols. *Memory & Cognition, 17,* 759–769.

Russo, J. E., & Leclerc, F. (1994). An eye-fixation analysis of choice processes for consumer nondurables. *Journal of Consumer Research, 21,* 274–290.

Russo, J. E., Medvec, V. H., & Meloy, M. G. (1996). The distortion of information during decisions. *Organizational Behavior and Human Decision Processes, 66,* 102–110.

Russo, J. E., & Rosen, L. D. (1975). An eye fixation analysis of multialternative choice. *Memory and Cognition, 3,* 267–276.

Samuelson, W., & Zeckhauser, R. (1988). Status quo bias in decision making. *Journal of Risk and Uncertainty, 1,* 7–59.

Schkade, D. A., & Johnson, E. J. (1989). Cognitive processes in preference reversals. *Organizational Behavior and Human Decision Processes, 44,* 203–231.

Schkade, D. A., & Kleinmuntz, D. N. (1994). Information displays and choice processes: Differential effects of organization form and sequence. *Organizational Behavior and Human Decision Processes, 57,* 319–337.

Schkade, D. A., & Payne, J. W. (1994). How people respond to contingent valuation questions: A verbal protocol analysis of willingness-to-pay for an environmental regulation. *Journal of Environmental Economics and Management, 26,* 88–109.

Schneider, S. L. (1992). Framing and conflict: Aspiration level contingency, the status quo, and current theories of risky choice. *Journal of Experimental Psychology: Human Learning and Memory, 18,* 1040–1057.

Schneider, S. L., & Lopes, L. L. (1986). Reflection in preferences under risk: Who and when may suggest why. *Journal of Experimental Psychology: Human Perception and Performance, 12,* 535–548.

Segal, U. (1989). Axiomatic representation of expected utility with rank-dependent probabilities. *Annals of Operations Research, 19,* 359–373.

Shafer, G. (1986). Savage revisited. *Statistical Science, 1,* 463–485.

Shafir, E. B., Osherson, D. N., & Smith, E. E. (1993). The advantage model: A comparative theory of evolution and choice under risk. *Organizational Behavior and Human Decision Processes, 55,* 325–378.

Shedler, J., & Manis, M. (1986). Can the availability heuristic explain vividness effects? *Journal of Personality and Social Psychology, 51,* 26–36.

Shepard, R. N. (1964). On subjectively optimum selection among multiattribute alternatives. In M. W. Shelley & G. L. Bryan (Eds.), *Human judgments and optimality* (pp. 257–281). New York: Wiley.

Siegel, S. (1957). Level of aspiration and decision making. *Psychological Review, 64,* 253–262.

Siegel-Jacobs, & Yates, J. F. (1996). Effects of procedural and outcome accountability on judgment quality. *Organizational Behavior and Human Decision Processes, 65,* 1–17.

Simon, H. A. (1955). A behavioral model of rational choice. *Quarterly Journal of Economics, 69,* 99–118.

Simon, H. A. (1978). Rationality as process and as product of thought. *American Economic Review, 68,* 1–16.

Simon, H. A. (1987, February). Making management decisions: The role of intuition and emotion. *Academy of Management Executive,* 57–64.

Simon, H. A. (1990). Invariants of human behavior. *Annual review of psychology, 41,* 1–19.

Simon, H. A. (1991). *Models of my life.* New York: Basic Books.

Simonson, I. (1989). Choice based on reasons: The case of attraction and compromise effects. *Journal of Consumer Research, 16,* 158–174.

Simonson, I. (1992). Influences of anticipating decision errors and regret on purchase timing and choices between brand name and price. *Journal of Consumer Research, 19,* 105–115.

Simonson, I., & Tversky, A. (1992). Choice in context: Tradeoff contrast and extremeness aversion. *Journal of Marketing Research, 29,* 281–295.

Slovic, P. (1972). From Shakespeare to Simon: Speculations—and some evidence—about man's ability to process information. *Oregon Research Institute Bulletin, 12* (3).

Slovic, P. (1995). The construction of preference. *American Psychologist, 50,* 364–371.

Slovic, P., & Lichtenstein, S. (1968). The relative importance of probabilities and payoffs in risk taking. *Journal of Experimental Psychology, 78*, monograph supplement, part 2.

Slovic, P., & Lichtenstein, S. (1971). Comparison of Bayesian and regression approaches to the study of information processing in judgment. *Organizational Behavior and Human Performance, 6*, 649–744.

Smead, R. J., Wilcox, J. B., & Wilkes, R. E. (1981). How valid are product descriptions and protocols in choice experiments? *Journal of Consumer Research, 8*, 37–42.

Spence, M. T. (1996). Problem-problem solver characteristics affecting the calibration of judgments. *Organizational Behavior and Human Decision Processes, 67*, 271–279.

Stone, D. N., & Schkade, D. A. (1991). Numeric and linguistic information representation in multiattribute choice. *Organizational Behavior and Human Decision Processes, 49*, 42–59.

Sujan, M. (1985). Consumer knowledge: Effects on evaluation strategies mediating consumer judgments. *Journal of Consumer Research, 12*, 16–31.

Sundstrom, G. A. (1987). Information search and decision making: The effects of information displays. *Acta Psychologica, 65*, 165–179.

Svenson, O. (1996). Decision making and the search for fundamental psychological regularities: What can be learned from a process perspective? *Organizational Behavior and Human Decision Processes, 65*, 252–267.

Svenson, O., & Edland, A. (1987). Changes of preferences under time pressure: Choices and judgments. *Scandinavian Journal of Psychology, 28*, 322–330.

Svenson, O., & Maule, A. J. (Eds.). (1993). *Time pressure and stress in human judgment and decision making*. New York: Plenum.

Tetlock, P. E. (1985). Accountability: The neglected social context of judgment and choice. *Research in Organizational Behavior, 7*, 297–332.

Tetlock, P. E., & Boettger, R. (1994). Accountability amplifies the status quo effect when change creates victims. *Journal of Behavioral Decision Making, 7*, 1–24.

Thaler, R. H. (1985). Mental accounting and consumer choice. *Marketing Science, 4*, 199–214.

Thaler, R. H. (1987). The psychology of choice and the assumptions of economics. In A. Roth (Ed.), *Laboratory experiments in economics: Six points of view* (pp. 99–130). New York: Cambridge University Press.

Thaler, R. H., & Johnson, E. J. (1990). Gambling with the house money and trying to break even: The effects of prior outcomes on risky choice. *Management Science, 36*, 643–660.

Thuring, M., & Jungermann, H. (1990). The conjunction fallacy: Causality vs. event probability. *Journal of Behavioral Decision Making, 3*, 61–74.

Tversky, A. (1969). Intransitivity of preferences. *Psychological Review, 76*, 31–48.

Tversky, A. (1972). Elimination by aspects: A theory of choice. *Psychological Review, 79*, 281–299.

Tversky, A., & Kahneman, D. (1981). The framing of decisions and the psychology of choice. *Science, 211*, 453–458.

Tversky, A., & Kahneman, D. (1983). Extensional vs. intuitive reasoning: The conjunction fallacy in probability judgment. *Psychological Review, 90*, 293–315.

Tversky, A., & Kahneman, D. (1986). Rational choice and the framing of decisions. *Journal of Business, 59*, S251–S278.

Tversky, A., & Kahneman, D. (1991). Loss aversion in riskless choice: A reference-dependent model. *Quarterly Journal of Economics, 106*, 1039–1062.

Tversky, A., & Kahneman, D. (1992). Advances in prospect theory: Cumulative representation of uncertainty. *Journal of Risk and Uncertainty, 5*, 297–323.

Tversky, A., & Koehler, D. J. (1994). Support theory: A nonextensional representation of subject probability. *Psychological Review, 101*, 547–567.

Tversky, A., Sattath, S., & Slovic, P. (1988). Contingent weighting in judgment and choice. *Psychological Review, 95*, 371–384.

Tversky, A., & Shafir, E. (1992). Choice under conflict: The dynamics of deferred decisions. *Psychological Science, 5,* 305–309.

Tversky, A., & Simonson, I. (1993). Context-dependent preferences. *Management Science, 39,* 1179–1189.

Tversky, A., Slovic, P., & Kahneman, D. (1990). The determinants of preference reversal. *American Economic Review, 80,* 204–217.

Van Raaij, W. F. (1977). *Consumer choice behavior: An information processing approach.* Voorschoten, Netherlands: VAM.

Von Neumann, J., & Morgenstern, O. (1947). *Theory of games and economic behavior* (2nd ed.,). Princeton, NJ: Princeton University Press.

Von Winterfeldt, D., & Edwards, W. (1986). *Decision analysis and behavioral research.* Cambridge: Cambridge University Press.

Wakker, P., Erev, I., & Weber, E. (1994). Comonotonic independence: The critical test between classical and rank dependent utility theories. *Journal of Risk and Uncertainty, 9,* 195–230.

Wallsten, T. S. (1990). The costs and benefits of vague information. In R. M. Hogarth (Ed.), *Insights in Decision Making: A Tribute to Hillel J. Einhorn* (pp. 28–43). Chicago: University of Chicago press.

Wallsten, T. S. (1996). An analysis of judgment research. *Organizational Behavior and Human Decision Processes, 65,* 220–226.

Wallsten, T. S., & Barton, C. (1982). Processing probabilistic multidimensional information for decisions. *Journal of Experimental Psychology: Learning, Memory, and Cognition, 8,* 361–384.

Weber, M., Anderson, C. J., & Birnbaum, M. H. (1992). A theory of perceived risk and attractiveness. *Organizational Behavior and Human Decision Processes, 52,* 492–523.

Weber, M., Eisenführ, F., & von Winterfeldt, D. (1988). The effects of splitting attributes on weights in multiattribute utility measurement. *Management Science, 34,* 431–445.

Wedell, D. H. (1991). Distinguishing among models of contextually induced preference reversals. *Journal of Experimental Psychology: Learning, Memory, and Cognition, 17,* 767–778.

Wedell, D. H., & Bockenholt, U. (1990). Moderation of preference reversals in the long run. *Journal of Experimental Psychology: Human Perception and Performance, 16,* 429–438.

Wells, G. L. (1985). The conjunction error and the representativeness heuristic. *Social Cognition, 3,* 266–279.

Whitcomb, K. M., Önkal, D., Curley, S. P., & Benson, P. G. (1995). Probability judgment accuracy for general knowledge: Cross-national differences and assessment methods. *Journal of Behavioral Decision Making, 8,* 51–67.

Whyte, G., & Sebenius, J. K. (1997). The effect of multiple anchors on anchoring in individual and group judgment. *Organizational Behavior and Human Decision Processes, 69,* 75–85.

Winkler, R. L., & Poses, R. M. (1993). Evaluating and combining physicians' probabilities of survival in an intensive care unit. *Management Science, 39,* 1526–1543.

Wright, G. N., & Phillips, L. D. (1980). Cultural variation in probabilistic thinking: Alternative ways of dealing with uncertainty. *International Journal of Psychology, 15,* 239–257.

Wright, G., Rowe, G., Bolger, F., & Gammack, J. (1994). Coherence, calibration, and expertise in judgmental probability forecasting. *Organizational Behavior and Human Decision Processes, 57,* 1–25.

Yadav, M. S. (1994). How buyers evaluate product bundles: A model of anchoring and adjustment. *Journal of Consumer Research, 21,* 342–353.

Yates, J. F. (1990). *Judgment and decision making.* Englewood Cliffs, NJ: Prentice Hall.

Yates, J. F., & Carlson, B. W. (1986). Conjunction errors: Evidence for multiple judgment procedures, including signed summation? *Organizational Behavior and Human Decision Processes, 37,* 230–253.

Yates, J. F., Zhu, Y., Ronis, D. L., Wang, D. F., Shinotsuka, H., & Toda, M. (1989). Probabilistic judgment accuracy: China, Japan, and the United States. *Organizational Behavior and Human Decision Processes, 43,* 145–171.

Yntema, D. B., & Torgerson, W. S. (1961). Man–computer cooperation in decisions requiring common sense. *IRE Transactions on Human Factors in Electronics, 2,* 20–26.

Zajonc, R. B. (1980). Feeling and thinking: Preferences need no inferences. *American Psychologist, 35,* 75–80.

Zakay, D. (1985). Post-decisional confidence and conflict experienced in a choice process. *Acta Psychologica, 58,* 75–80.

Index

361